ECONOMICS NOW

ANALYZING CURRENT ISSUES

ANGELO BOLOTTA / CHARLES HAWKES / RICK MAHONEY / JOHN PIPER

OXFORD

UNIVERSITY PRESS

OXFORD

UNIVERSITY PRESS

70 Wynford Drive, Don Mills, Ontario M3C 1J9
www.oup.com/ca

Oxford University Press is a department of the University of Oxford

It furthers the University's objective of excellence in research, scholarship,
and education by publishing worldwide in

Oxford New York
Auckland Bangkok Buenos Aires Cape Town
Chennai Dar es Salaam Delhi Hong Kong Istanbul Karachi
Kolkata Kuala Lumpur Madrid Melbourne Mexico City Mumbai Nairobi
São Paulo Shanghai Taipei Tokyo Toronto

Oxford is a registered trade mark of Oxford University Press
in the UK and in certain other countries

Published in Canada
By Oxford University Press

Copyright © Oxford University Press Canada 2002

National Library of Canada Cataloguing in Publication Data

Main entry under title:
Economics now: analyzing current issues / Angelo Bolotta ... [et al.].

Includes index.

ISBN 0-19-541445-4

1. Economics. I. Bolotta, Angelo, 1951-

HB171.5.E366 2002   330   C2002-902643-1

Printed and bound in Canada
This book is printed on permanent (acid-free) paper

3 4 — 05 04 03

Acquisitions editor: Patti Henderson
Developmental editors: Elaine Aboud,
Jenifer Ludbrook, Margaret Hoogeveen
Copy editor: Francine Geraci
Production editor: Heather Kidd
Permissions editor: Ann Checchia
Photo researcher: Paula Joiner
Cartography and text design: VISU Tronx
Technical art: Bookman Typesetting
Cover design: Joan Dempsey

Acknowledgements

The publisher would like to thank Bill Jennings
for his contribution to this project.

The authors wish to extend special thanks to
Elaine Aboud, Margaret Hoogeveen, Jenifer
Ludbrook, and Heather Kidd for their profes-
sionalism and instructive editing.

Statistics Canada information is used with the
permission of the Minister of Industry, as
Minister responsible for Statistics Canada.
Information on the availability of the wide
range of data from Statistics Canada can be
obtained from Statistics Canada's regional
offices, its World Wide Web site at
http://www.statcan.ca, and its toll-free access
number 1-800-263-1136.

Cover Images: globe: Coneyl Jay/Getty Images;
business commuters: Crowther & Carter/
Getty Images; red maple leaf: Chris
McElcheran/Masterfile.

Dedications

To Mara, Alissa, and Alanna for their help and understanding, and to my parents for impressing upon me from an early age the value of economic reasoning.

—Angelo Bolotta

To Pat for her patience and support.

—Charles Hawkes

To my wife Cathie; my children Andrew, Daniel, and Jacob; and my parents for providing me with love, support, and the strength to achieve.

—Rick Mahoney

Table of Contents

Features

Skill Builders: Thinking Like an Economist

A Matter of Opinion

Economics in the News

Primary Source

Case Studies

Foreword

Welcome to *Economics Now!* If you are new to economics, rest assured that this subject is interesting, relevant to your life and future, and not difficult to grasp. Even if you do not go on to study economics in college or university, this course will give you a good understanding of how the Canadian economy works. At the same time, the authors hope that this text, and your class experience, will stimulate you to go on to further study—both to deepen your understanding of economic issues and to possibly prepare you for an economics-related career.

As you flip through the text, you will notice that there are 20 chapters divided into five major units and an epilogue. Each unit begins with a brief overview of the content in the three or four chapters to follow, a list of learning goals you will achieve, and an outline of skills you will master as you complete your study of the unit.

Features

- **Chapter Openers** contain questions relating to a cartoon, a photograph, a game, an activity, or an excerpt, all intended to start you thinking about the content of the chapter that follows.
- **Chapter Goals** tell you what you can expect to learn in the chapter.
- **Case Studies** ask you to examine economic issues and concepts as they apply to real-life situations and to examine how the people and/or organizations involved are impacted.
- **Check Your Understanding** questions (which appear after major sections within each chapter) prompt you to review your knowledge of the chapter's content.
- **Economics in the News** features ask you to reflect on current news articles that profile real examples of issues and topics covered within the chapter.
- **A Matter of Opinion** features ask you to develop your own opinions about the controversies and arguments in which economists engage.
- **Primary Source** features ask you to consider quotes and original material from individuals and organizations discussed in the chapter.

- **Skill Builder: Thinking Like An Economist** features ask you to apply the skills that economists use (such as graphing, calculating, and applying theories) to economic problems or issues.
- **Chapter Summaries** condense the chapter into its major points in order to help you review its content.
- **Key Terms** lists the essential vocabulary defined in each chapter.
- **Activities** at the end of each chapter are divided into three sections.
  - *Thinking/Inquiry* questions ask you to think analytically and to investigate economic issues.
  - *Communication* questions allow you to be creative in presenting economic ideas and issues from the chapter.
  - *Application* questions direct you to apply your knowledge and skills to problems and new situations.
- The **Glossary** at the end of the book helps you recall the key terms that you have come across throughout the text.

Performance Tasks

At the end of each unit, a performance task has been included. Each unit's task puts you in a real-life role that requires you to draw together the content, theories, and skills from the chapters in that unit. Each performance task has a suggested method of evaluation that you and your teacher can use and adapt for your work. The final (or culminating) performance task found at the end of the text gives you an opportunity to creatively demonstrate the knowledge, ideas, and skills you have learned throughout the entire course.

The authors sincerely hope that this text helps make your study of economics stimulating and enjoyable.

UNIT 1

THE NATURE OF ECONOMICS AND THE ECONOMY

A business magazine rolls off the printing press. How have investors addressed the basic economic questions of *what* to produce, *how* to produce, and *for whom* to produce? What strategies have they used to make their enterprise more productive and profitable?

Unit Overview

This unit will help to build a solid foundation for the learning that follows in the rest of this text. First, we'll explore some basic concepts and principles of economic thinking. Then, we'll identify career opportunities for those trained in economics and related fields. Next, we'll turn our attention to the concept of productive resources in order to understand how different types of economic systems attempt to answer basic production questions and set economic goals. Finally, we'll investigate seven "worldly philosophers" whose ideas have greatly advanced the science of economics. With this foundation, we'll be able to make sense of the issues and activities that unfold in the following units.

Learning Goals

In this unit, you will
- apply economic concepts and models that are used to identify and analyze choices, to forecast economic change, and to define a reality, problem, or issue,
- compare the nature of economic inquiry with that of scientific inquiry,
- identify specific examples of economic choices (both individual and collective) that Canadians must make as a result of scarce economic resources,
- examine the issues arising from competing goals and self-interests,
- compare the ways in which different economic systems make choices about how productive resources are owned and used,
- compare different national economies with regard to their ability to produce and share wealth, respect individual economic freedom, and promote responsible decision making and the common good,
- explain the criteria used by different groups of stakeholders and economists to evaluate economic change, issues, and choices, and account for the disagreement among them,
- describe how groups of stakeholders and markets within a free-enterprise economy are interdependent and may be affected simultaneously by a change,
- demonstrate an understanding of the major ideas and theories of prominent economists in the context of the economic issues and challenges of their times,
- conduct research to locate information from a variety of different media, institutions, businesses, interest groups, and other sources,
- communicate economic information and analysis clearly, effectively, and accurately in an appropriate format and style.

Skill Builder
Thinking Like an Economist

In this unit, you can develop some of the skills that economists use. These include
- using graphs to understand relationships,
- valuing productive resources,
- differentiating between production and productivity,
- testing hypotheses.

Unit Performance Task

The activity at the end of this unit provides a focused opportunity for you to
- assume the role of a manager of human resources for a growing Canadian corporation,
- apply economic knowledge and skills in order to recommend the best course of action for the corporation,
- prepare and support a persuasive argument, and
- use a performance task rubric and feedback to produce high-quality work.

CHAPTER 1
BASIC PRINCIPLES OF ECONOMICS

The Economics of Terrorism

On 11 September 2001, terrorists hijacked commercial airliners in the US and turned them into weapons of mass destruction. Two of the airliners were crashed into the World Trade Center in New York City. Of the 50 000 people who worked in the twin towers each day, an estimated 3000 perished in the attack. The world will never be the same—politically, economically, militarily, and socially—as a result of this attack on the world's most powerful nation.

Evidence indicates that the terrorists planned and executed their suicide missions carefully. It appears that their targets were specifically chosen to cause as much pain and suffering as possible, to attack important symbols of American strength and power, and, ultimately, to have maximum negative impact on global economic systems. Stock markets around the world experienced a sharp decline as a result of the attack and its destabilization of investor confidence. The recovery was slow and fragile.

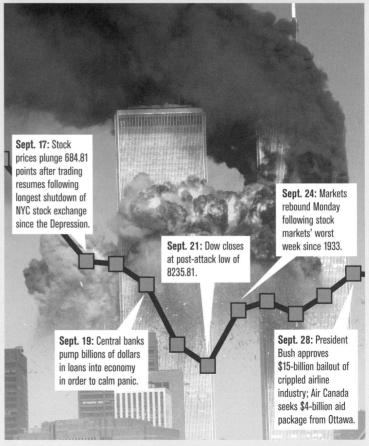

Sept. 17: Stock prices plunge 684.81 points after trading resumes following longest shutdown of NYC stock exchange since the Depression.

Sept. 19: Central banks pump billions of dollars in loans into economy in order to calm panic.

Sept. 21: Dow closes at post-attack low of 8235.81.

Sept. 24: Markets rebound Monday following stock markets' worst week since 1933.

Sept. 28: President Bush approves $15-billion bailout of crippled airline industry; Air Canada seeks $4-billion aid package from Ottawa.

QUESTIONS

1. What was the symbolic significance of a successful terrorist attack on the World Trade Center?
2. Explain the economic significance of the changes in stock market prices illustrated by the graph above.
3. The short-term consequences of the attack appear significant. Do you expect the long-term effects to be as significant? Explain.

Chapter Goals

By the end of this chapter, you will be able to

- realize the importance of economics as a social science,
- understand how an economy works,
- begin thinking like an economist,
- use models to explore basic economic laws and fallacies,
- explore career opportunities in the field of economics.

A Beginner's Perspective on Economics

This chapter introduces you to the most basic concepts and principles of economics—the social science of scarcity and choice. It also presents several examples of disciplined economic reasoning and some of the most common examples of faulty economic thinking. You will encounter a number of opportunities in this first chapter to apply the decision-making and graphing skills that you'll need to complete this course of study successfully and to analyze current economic issues.

Decisions, Decisions, Decisions

- How badly do I need a new winter coat? Should it be leather, wool, or polyester?
- Should we rent or buy a family home?
- Who will use the family car tonight?
- Should I spend my entire paycheque on the weekend, or should I save some money for later?
- Will I go to college next fall or take a full-time job as a sales clerk?
- Will I study for my unit test or go to my friend's birthday party tonight?
- Will I cook dinner, or will the family eat out tonight?

There are, indeed, many decisions each of us has to make on a daily basis. For this reason, and whether or not we realize it, economics is continually at work in our lives. If we use time, energy, money, or materials to do one thing instead of another, we are engaged in economic decision making. If we face questions about what we need, what we want, and what we can afford to do, we are engaged in economic decision making.

We constantly face economic decisions because our needs and wants are virtually unlimited, while our means to satisfy them (what economists call our available resources) are quite limited. For most of us, available resources consist of our income and savings, and since these are limited, we must **economize**, or use these resources wisely. We can define "wise use" as that which most furthers our personal or group goals while consuming the least amount of available resources. Since there is a relative scarcity of these resources, we will always live with the economic dilemma of our wants exceeding our ability to satisfy them.

What Is Economics?

If we look in the dictionary, we'll find economics defined rather dryly as a practical science dealing with the production, distribution, and use of goods, services, resources, and wealth. If we consider the origin of the word, however, we can arrive at a simpler and more concrete idea of what it means in its most basic sense. The word *economics* can be traced back to ancient Greece where it was formed by joining two shorter words together: *oikos*, the word for "house," and *nemo*, the word for "to manage." In its root sense, then, *oikonomia* dealt with matters relating to the wise management of one's own household.

Today, economics is often referred to as "the science of scarcity and choice." As mentioned previously, the fact that human material wants always exceed the available resources means that we live in a condition of constant scarcity. Each person, family, business, society, and government attempts to economize by making decisions that satisfy the largest number of material wants while using the smallest amount of resources possible. In a nutshell, **economics** is the study of the way we make decisions about the use of scarce resources.

Economics as a social science

Economics involves the study of people (either individually or in groups) making decisions about the choices available to them; it therefore falls into the category of a **social science**. Other social sciences include history, geography, sociology, and anthropology. Like economics, each of these sciences attempts to understand an important aspect of the human condition and of the world in which we live. This social aspect of the study gives economics both relevance and complexity.

When we broaden the study to consider the way economic decision making affects society as a whole, we can see how important

Xenophon's *Oeconomicus*

Xenophon was born a free citizen-soldier of Athens around 430 BCE. As a young man, he studied under the philosopher Socrates until he joined a group of mercenary soldiers. Eventually, he rose to the rank of general. After being expelled from Athens around 395 BCE for favouring the enemy forces of Sparta, Xenophon was granted a family estate by the Spartans.

While in exile, his past experiences led him to theorize about private estate management, the division of labour between men and women, and the accumulation of personal wealth. His work, entitled *Oeconomicus* and published around 362 BCE, is recognized as one of the richest primary sources of the social, economic, and intellectual history of classical Athens. *Oikonomia* refers to the science of household or estate management. The ***oikos***, the basic unit of classical Greek society, was a large family estate or household, including land, crops, a house, family members, slaves, animals, and accumulated wealth. The economy of Greece was based on agriculture, and society consisted of two distinct, yet complementary, spheres. The public, or political, sphere was a world where men were dominant. The private, or domestic, sphere was the realm of women.

The following excerpts are taken from Sarah Pomeroy's translation of the original Greek text.

. . . a wife who is a good partner in the estate carries just as much weight as her husband in attaining prosperity. Property generally comes into the house through the exertions of the husband, but it is mostly dispensed through the housekeeping of the wife. If these activities are performed well, estates increase, but if they are managed incompetently, estates diminish.

. . . the man who is going to be a successful farmer must make his labourers eager and disposed to be obedient. . . . Slaves need some good thing to look forward to no less, in fact, even more than free men so that they will be willing to stay. . . . When farming is successful, all other arts prosper, but whenever the earth is forced to lie barren, the other arts, both on earth and sea, are virtually extinguished.

. . . land is not wealth for a man who cultivates it in such a way that by its cultivation he incurs loss. . . . Things [including money] . . . can be wealth for the person who knows how to use . . . them, but not wealth for one who does not know. . . . enemies . . . are wealth to anyone who can benefit from enemies. . . ➜ knowing how to use enemies so as to derive benefit from them is a characteristic of a good estate manager.

Source: Excerpts from *Xenophon, Oeconomicus: A Social and Historical Commentary* by Sarah B. Pomeroy (Oxford: Clarendon Press, 1995). Reprinted by permission of the author.

QUESTIONS

1. Why was a steady supply of cheap labour available to Greek estate owners?
2. According to Xenophon, how should the landowner class view marriage?
3. What relationship existed between agriculture and the arts in Greek society?
4. According to Xenophon, what is the ultimate proof that an estate is properly managed?
5. How can enemies be considered an economic asset?

economic decisions are to the well-being of an entire nation or group of nations. We can also see how complicated economics becomes when we try to balance the needs of one group with those of another. For example,

loggers may seek to harvest a forest, while environmentalists may seek to preserve it.

Human behaviour and value systems greatly complicate studies in the social sciences. This is one difference that separates the social sciences from the "pure" sciences such as physics and chemistry. An apple falling from a tree today behaves exactly as it did for Isaac Newton in 1665. The natural laws of physics remain unchanged, although human understanding of these laws has increased. On the other hand, human behaviour has changed significantly since 1665 and continues to change as society evolves. Refinements in economic theory, changes in social conditions, and evolving political systems (and priorities) all mean that there are considerable differences among economists on any given question. Hence the cynical conclusion, illustrated in Figure 1.1, that the one thing economists know how to do best is disagree!

Predicting human behaviour

Since people for the most part are both rational and social beings, their behaviour can often be explained by reference to the values and belief systems they share with the other members of society. The question of predictability, however, is a difficult one for social scientists. Although people as a group are certainly influenced by the society in which they live, the behaviour of an individual person within that group is not always predictable. To understand this idea better, consider an example. In the summer, more people go to public swimming pools as the temperature rises. We can safely predict that, over the summer, more people will visit a given pool on a day when the temperature is 30°C than on a day when the temperature is 20°C. However, we cannot predict whether an individual person will visit the pool on the day the thermometer hits 30°C. Therefore, the behaviour of the group is often predictable, while the behaviour of the individual person is not. Knowledge of group behaviour and general tendencies can be useful information for decision makers.

Why Study Economics?

Today, students in large numbers make the deliberate decision to study economics, and they do this for a number of reasons. First, it is difficult to read a newspaper or turn on a TV newscast without encountering a multitude of economic issues and interpretations. To make

By permission of Johnny Hart and Creators Syndicate, Inc.

Figure 1.1 Since economics is a social science, its theories and applications are often hotly debated. Can you explain why this is so?

An economy . . .

- is a very complex or intricate system.
- is dynamic or subject to movements and exchanges.
- consists of interdependent people, groups, and institutions, each performing specialized roles.
- involves a series of independent transactions motivated by economic goals.
- involves numerous transactions that create two circular flows (money moves in one direction while goods and services move in the opposite direction).

Figure 1.2 What is an economy? An **economy** can best be described as a self-sustaining system in which many independent transactions (often triggered by self-interest) create distinct flows of money and products.

sense of all this information, you need a practical understanding of economic concepts and principles. You also need to understand the ways in which both the Canadian and the global economies work and the ways people, businesses, and government institutions function within them.

Second, since students have to make daily choices regarding the use of scarce resources (will I spend my entire paycheque or allowance this week, or will I put a part of it in my savings account?), they come to value the skills of economic reasoning. This textbook profiles these skills in features (such as Thinking Like an Economist) and provides many opportunities for you to develop and apply decision-making and problem-solving strategies. These are lifelong skills that will always be useful and marketable.

Third, economic knowledge and skills can lead to more effective civic participation. If students are to vote wisely for the politicians who will make important decisions for them, they should be able to understand the interrelatedness of economic factors such as interest rates, foreign exchange rates, taxes, public debt, and laws protecting competition. Otherwise, how will they know whom to believe?

Economics, Materialism, and Opportunity Cost

Some critics dismiss economics on the grounds that it is preoccupied with studying material things and does not show enough concern for human values. It is true that economics is concerned mostly with such things as resources and products, but at no time does it recognize these things as ends in themselves. Remember that material things can be used for noble purposes, such as saving lives, eliminating poverty and illiteracy, preserving peace, upholding justice, and protecting the environment. Most people will not take great satisfaction in merely building up piles of material goods; they will also use them to achieve other ends—ends that are determined by personal or societal value systems. So economics does not try to establish goals for the people who study it; rather, it gives them the tools they will need to achieve their goals more efficiently, that is, by wasting fewer resources.

In this respect, it is important to realize that the economic perspective distinguishes between the **effective** and the **efficient** use of resources. If we consume a certain amount of resources and, in the end, achieve the desired result then our use of those resources can be called *effective*. However, if we use the bare minimum of resources necessary to achieve the desired end then our use of these resources can also be considered *efficient*. Economic decisions must be both effective and efficient. Efficiency enables us to use the saved resources in achieving other goals—goals that we may not have been able to achieve unless we had economized. We can see, then, that although economics studies the material world, it does not urge us to place undue importance on material things and on maximizing consumption. Given the scarcity of most things in our world, the economic imperative is to conserve and put these things to wise use, that is, to achieve the right goals (effectiveness) in the right way (efficiency).

The idea of efficiency becomes even more important when we realize that any time we use material goods to achieve one end, we have to do without something else. This is what economists call the opportunity cost of our actions. We can define **opportunity cost** as the sum of all that is lost from taking one course of action over another. This is a fundamental concept in economics; in making any economic decision, we must always consider not just what we are gaining but also what we stand to lose (see Figure 1.3).

To make the concept of opportunity cost clearer, let's look at an example. Suppose you find yourself with $2000 that's burning a hole in your pocket. There are three things you would like to do, each of which will cost exactly $2000:

1. Take a two-week winter vacation on the Caribbean island of Cuba.
2. Buy a DVD player and a home-theatre system.
3. Finance yourself to spend a summer working in Africa for a volunteer organization affiliated with the Canadian International Development Agency (CIDA).

Whichever one of these alternatives you choose, you will have to do without the other

Steps	Details and Example(s)
1. Define the problem.	At the heart of every decision is a choice that has to be made—the selection of one alternative over others. State the problem in a clearly focused question. • What should Lani do over the weekend?
2. Clarify goals and priorities.	Identify the most important issues involved in the problem. Establish goals and priorities in response to these issues. • Lani wants to go to university. • She needs to maintain good marks to be accepted at the school of her choice. • She needs to save money to cover tuition and other expenses. • She enjoys spending time with her friends and listening to music.
3. List the possible alternatives.	Identify all choices available to decision makers. • Lani's alternatives include – attending the concert with her friends, – working extra hours to make more money, or – producing a more thorough research paper.
4. Establish the criteria used to judge the alternatives.	Identify three or four standards that can be used to evaluate each alternative. • Lani's weekend can be spent in the pursuit of income, marks, fun, or preparation for post-secondary education. Each alternative includes positive and negative considerations. These considerations represent the criteria to be used in making a sound decision.
5. Weight each criterion based on goals and priorities.	Use *goals and priorities* to determine the relative importance of each criterion. Make value judgements. • Because of the importance of the research paper in determining her final mark and of effective research and writing skills in post-secondary education, Lani gives these two criteria more weight in making her decision. On this particular weekend, she gives income moderate weight and fun with friends a lower priority. Next weekend these values could change.
6. Evaluate each alternative.	Use the weighted criteria to evaluate each alternative. Produce a decision-making matrix to weigh all options relative to established criteria. • In completing the matrix shown in Figure 1.4 (page 10), Lani must consider the positive and negative aspects of each alternative and weight them according to her goals and priorities. She gives important criteria triple weight in the decision, moderate criteria double weight, and lesser criteria single weight. By tabulating the results of this weighted analysis, Lani can determine her best alternative.
7. Make a decision.	Select the best alternative based on the results of the weighted evaluation. • The decision matrix clearly identifies the third alternative as the best. It provides the most benefits (or positive aspects) while limiting the costs or negative aspects. Lani will spend her weekend working on the research paper.
8. Act on the decision.	Implement the selected alternative. • Lani invests extra time at the library and on the computer to acquire additional data, conduct a more thorough analysis of her findings, and produce a more polished written report.
9. Assess effectiveness.	Assess the effectiveness of the action plan and revise it as needed. • Lani is pleased with the mark she receives on the major assignment because it improves her course grade. The concert she missed was described by friends as "the best of the year!"

Figure 1.3 A decision-making model. The issue is, What should Lani do this weekend? Although we apply the model to Lani's problem, it can also serve as a general model for deciding what to do with scarce resources. What scarce resource is Lani dealing with?

Alternatives	Criteria (rank in order of importance—most important first)				
Priority/Weight	Marks	Preparation for Post-Secondary Studies	Income	Fun with Friends	TOTAL WEIGHTED VALUE
	High (3X)	High (3X)	Moderate (2X)	Low (1X)	
1. Attend the concert.	– – –	– – –	– –	+	1+ 8–
2. Work extra hours.	– – –	– – –	+ +	–	2+ 7–
3. Produce a better research paper.	+ + +	+ + +	– –	–	6+ 3–

Figure 1.4 A decision-making matrix like this can help you establish your priorities.

two. The opportunity cost of your vacation in the Caribbean is based on the satisfaction lost from the "next best" alternative use of the money. In other words, the opportunity cost of your vacation is either the satisfaction obtained from the home-theatre system or from helping a less developed community, but not both since you can do only one or the other. The opportunity cost of the vacation also includes any earnings you will lose while you are on vacation.

Any time you have to decide among several possibilities, a well-thought-out decision-making model can make it easier for you to choose. For example, Lani is in her final year of high school. She has to hand in a major research paper on Monday morning. She also has an opportunity to work extended weekend hours at the ice cream parlour and a chance to go with friends to a rock concert featuring her favourite band. What should Lani do? Figures 1.3 and 1.4 illustrate the decision making in this example.

Facts and Values

Traditionally, the science of economics has attempted to explain human behaviour and assist in rational decision making by using both fact- and value-based considerations. Facts and values have been described as the two sides of the economic coin. Let's explore the distinction

between them to get an idea of the way they work together in economic decision making.

Analytical economics

The branch of economics that deals with facts and direct observation of the world around us is called **analytical (or positive) economics**. This branch is concerned with two types of statements: *descriptive* and *conditional*. Descriptive statements portray things as they are in the present or have been in the past. The following is a descriptive statement: "Automobile sales in Canada in this quarter are 7 per cent higher than in the last quarter." This is a statement of fact that can be verified statistically.

Conditional statements, on the other hand, are forecasts based on the careful analysis of economic behaviour. Often these statements take the form "If *x* occurs then *y* will follow." This forecast can be either confirmed or refuted by referring to known facts and by observing the accuracy of the prediction. For example, consider this conditional statement: "If the price of cigarettes decreases, the quantity purchased will increase." This forecast was confirmed in the early 1990s when the federal and provincial governments lowered taxes on cigarettes to combat organized smuggling operations that were bringing large quantities of American cigarettes into Canada. The tax cut lowered the price of Canadian cigarettes, and consumers did indeed purchase more of them as a result.

SKILL BUILDER

Thinking Like an Economist

Using Graphs to Understand Relationships

Given their visual nature, graphs are an effective way to show the relationships that exist between two different variables. By plotting data along two axis lines, we can clearly see the relationship between the two sets of data. Let's look at a specific example to understand how economists use graphs. We'll assume that the data table below (Figure 1.5) reports changes in ice cream sales in your community as the selling price per cone fluctuates between $1 and $3.

While the table does indicate a pattern, we can better understand the relationship between price and ice cream cone sales by graphing the data. Our graph will require an axis for both variables: price and quantity sold. The two axes are plotted to create a 90° angle. The point where the two lines intersect is called the **origin**. The vertical line is called the y-axis, and the horizontal line is the x-axis. Traditionally, in economics, price is plotted along the y-axis, with quantity along the x-axis. Each square along each axis must be assigned a constant value to maintain accuracy.

After examining the graph in Figure 1.6, answer the following questions:
• What is the value of each grid square along the y-axis?
• What is the value of each square along the x-axis?
• What would happen to your graph if you were to use one square to represent 1000 cones along the x-axis?

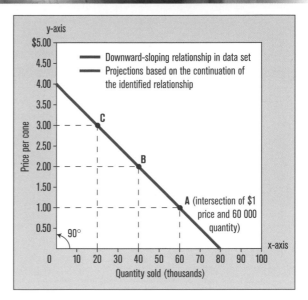

Figure 1.6 Ice cream cone sales relative to price.

Price per Cone	Number of Cones Sold	Point on Graph
$1	60 000	A
$2	40 000	B
$3	20 000	C

Figure 1.5 Ice cream cone sales relative to price.

The data are plotted on the graph consistent with both axis scales. For example, the placement of point A on the graph represents a price of $1 and a quantity of 60 000 cones sold. No other placement on the grid would accurately represent both variables. A line is drawn to connect the three data points. This line illustrates the relationship between the two variables. Since the line moves downward (from left to right), it is said to have a downward slope. This represents an *inverse*, or opposite, relationship between price and sales. As price increases, the quantity sold decreases. The two variables therefore change in opposite directions. Having shown the relationship between price and ice cream sales, the graph can now be used to determine additional information about this relationship:
• If the selling price is $1.50, how many cones will most probably be sold?
• If the price is increased to $2.50, how many cones will most probably be sold?

• If the price is increased to $3.50, how many cones will most probably be sold?
• Why can the price of an ice cream cone never be increased to $5 in this community?

The value of this graph as an economic tool is becoming clear! Now let's consider a case in which the relationship between variables is *direct*, or positive. The table in Figure 1.7 presents data comparing ice cream cone sales to outdoor temperatures. When temperature increases, so do ice cream cone sales, reflecting a direct relationship.

Temperature	Number of Cones Sold	Point on Graph
12°C	20 000	X
24°C	50 000	Y
32°C	70 000	Z

Figure 1.7 Ice cream cone sales relative to temperature.

Draw a graph of the economic relationship between temperature and ice cream sales using the graph in Figure 1.6 as a model. Replace price with temperature on the *y*-axis of your graph, but use the same scale for the sales axis. Decide on an appropriate scale for the temperature axis. Use your new graph to answer the following questions.

1. If the temperature climbs to 38°C, how many ice cream cones will be sold in your community? Mark this as point A on your graph.
2. How many cones will be sold when the temperature drops to 8°C? Mark this as point B on your graph.
3. What temperature would generate sales of 35 000 cones? Mark this as point C on your graph.
4. At what temperature would ice cream sales stop completely in your community? Explain.
5. How does the slope of the curve help explain the kind of relationship that exists between temperature and ice cream sales and between price and sales? Explain.

Normative economics

The other branch of economics is called **normative (or policy) economics**; it deals primarily with statements that contain value judgements. Normative statements express what a particular economist or group of economists thinks should be the case, based on their value judgements. These statements cannot be confirmed or refuted solely by reference to facts. Goals and policy statements of governments, firms, institutions, and interest groups are often based on value judgements and, therefore, are normative statements. The following is an example of a normative statement: "Municipal governments should provide more housing for homeless people." Clearly, this is an expression of opinion reflecting a value judgement. It is not a statement of fact and is therefore open to debate.

As we enter this new millennium and participate more actively in the global economy, we find it more and more necessary to use both facts and values in making wise economic decisions. One reason for this is that, in a global economy, local decisions often have far-reaching consequences. Consider, for example, the financial crisis that rocked South Korea, Indonesia, Japan, and Russia in 1998. Not our problem, you say? Think again: these events contributed to a weaker Canadian dollar, instability on Canadian stock markets, and increased prices for imported goods. In other words, they scored a direct hit on your wallet. Similarly, the terrorist attack of 11 September 2001 hastened the slide toward a global economic downturn.

Value judgements play a major role in some decisions made by the Canadian government on international trade. In 1999, relations between Canada and its long-time trading partner Cuba cooled when the Cuban government jailed four journalists who were protesting against restrictions on free speech in that country. Value judgements concerning human rights were an important enough issue to affect relations between these two trading partners.

Key Steps	Economic Examples
Observation • The noting of an interesting occurrence that triggers human curiosity. • Formulating a question to focus the search for an answer. (Usually, we want to know why something happens or what the relationship is between two things.)	During a recent heat wave, three local stores ran out of your favourite ice cream. This prompted you to inquire "What effect does temperature have on ice cream sales?"
Data Collection • The collection of evidence about what is being observed. • The recording of data. (Verbal information constitutes *qualitative* data, while numerical information constitutes *quantitative* data.)	Interviews with store managers reveal that ice cream orders increase during the summer months. Clerks confirm they have to restock freezers more frequently during heat waves. Customer surveys indicate that ice cream is a preferred summer dessert. Monthly production data from major manufacturers indicate an increase in the quantity of ice cream produced and sold from June to August.
Explanation • The organization of data in a logical way to formulate a possible answer to the original question. • The reaching of a tentative conclusion in order to find a basis for explaining observations and measurements. (The tentative explanation is called a *hypothesis*.)	You organize the collected data by season as well as by source (manufacturer, retailer, consumer) to determine a consistent pattern. Then you formulate the following tentative hypothesis: Ice cream sales appear to increase as outdoor temperatures increase.
Verification • The testing of the hypothesis to account satisfactorily for known facts, to explain new data, and to forecast future events. • The rejecting, modifying, or accepting of the hypothesis as an accurate generalization of reality (a general rule, theory, law, principle, or model that can be validly used as a simplified picture of a more complex reality). Note that an hypothesis cannot be proven true. The best verdict is that we have failed to reject it.	You test your hypothesis by examining new data from other communities. You also use the hypothesis to forecast sales patterns for subsequent summers and winters. Once the hypothesis has been proven accurate through testing, it becomes the General Theory of Ice Cream, which states: "The volume of ice cream sales is directly related to seasonal changes in temperature." (In economics, the words *theory, rule, law,* and *principle* are used interchangeably to identify accurate models of reality. Therefore, our discovery could have just as easily been called the Law of Ice Cream Sales.)

Figure 1.8 Applying the scientific method to a sample economic discovery.

The Scientific Method and Mathematics in Economics

When we defined economics as a social science earlier in this chapter, we looked mainly at its social rather than its scientific aspect. Now, let's consider what it is about economics that makes it a science. A discipline, or field of study, is called a science based not on what it studies but on how it studies it, that is, based not on its subject matter but on its method. Economics, like all other natural and social sciences, uses a common investigative approach called the scientific method. The four basic components of the **scientific method**, as first outlined by the English scientist Francis Bacon (1561–1626), are

• observation,
• data collection,
• explanation, and
• verification.

Even though scientists today use many different processes to make their discoveries, the four steps outlined by Bacon are almost always involved. The table in Figure 1.8 (page 13) explains the scientific method and illustrates each step with an economic example.

By the time you reach the end of this first chapter, you will have noticed that mathematics is often used in the study of economics. Math is used principally to help us recognize and explain number patterns and statistical relationships. Since this is applied (rather than theoretical) mathematics, students who are not math majors have no cause for alarm. In fact, many students welcome the opportunity that economics provides to explore the practical applications of mathematics.

Check Your Understanding

1. Why is scarcity a constant, even in a resource-rich country such as Canada?

2. Explain the difference between a social science and a natural science. Why is economics a social science?

3. Explain the importance of the concept of opportunity cost in economic reasoning.

4. Draw a flow-chart note or complete a summary table to explain the difference between positive and normative economics and to help clarify the different terms used.

5. Use examples to explain the difference between a direct and an inverse economic relationship.

Basic Fallacies, Laws, and Theories of Economics

Earlier, we examined the scientific method and saw that it is used in economics to prove hypotheses or to validate generalizations that attempt to explain economic realities. After they have been validated or proven, these generalizations become economic principles, laws, or theories. First, though, we must examine the three most common economic fallacies. A **fallacy** is a hypothesis that has been proven false but is still accepted by many people because it appears, at first glance, to make sense.

The Fallacy of Composition

In economics, there are several things that may be true from an individual perspective but become false when examined in light of the economy as a whole. For example, an individual farmer may decide to clear more land and plant more corn in an attempt to earn extra income. There is no question that this could be a profitable venture for this particular farmer. However, suppose that every farmer in Canada attempts the same strategy simultaneously. The result would be an overproduction of corn that would drive its market price much lower. If the new price is so low that it does not allow the farmers to recover their operating expenses, many of them may go bankrupt. It would take several years for the Canadian corn market to recover from this type of collapse. We can see, then, that what is good for the individual is not automatically good for society as a whole. This mistaken belief that individual benefit automatically translates into social benefit is called the **fallacy of composition**.

This fallacy can also work the other way—with the idea that what is good for society as a whole must be good for its individual members. Free trade can generally benefit Canadian society by resulting in lower prices for certain manufactured goods. This does not mean that everyone in Canada has benefited from free trade. In fact, some Canadians have lost their jobs because cheaper foreign goods are now available to compete with the more expensive goods produced in Canada.

The Post Hoc Fallacy

The **post hoc fallacy** is derived from the Latin phrase *post hoc ergo propter hoc*, which means, literally, "after this therefore because of this." Sometimes people assume that, because it took place after event A, event B must have been caused by event A. We can use another agricultural example to illustrate this fallacy. A rooster wakes up every morning before dawn and instinctively crows. Moments later the sun rises. Would it not be ridiculous to assume that the rooster's crowing (and not the rotation of the Earth) causes the sun to rise? By the same token, when a newly elected government takes credit for improving the economy, this, too, demonstrates post hoc thinking. Since the economy improved after the election, so the reasoning goes, the election result must have been responsible. Has the new government had time to implement new economic policies? Have the new policies had sufficient time to bring about economic improvement? Unfortunately, many people do not ask these critical questions, preferring instead the apparent logic of the post hoc argument.

This fallacy is also known as the **cause-and-effect fallacy** because of the false assumption that what comes before automatically causes what follows. Some prior events are obviously not connected to later events in any meaningful way. As with our rooster crowing just before dawn, sometimes the relationship between two events is more a matter of coincidence than cause and effect.

The Fallacy of Single Causation

Closely related to the post hoc fallacy, the **fallacy of single causation** is based on the premise that a single factor or person caused a particular event to occur. For example, a historian might argue that the stock market crash of 1929 caused the Great Depression of the 1930s. This, like other examples of the single causation fallacy, is an oversimplification. In reality, the stock market crash was a symptom of economic illness rather than a direct cause of the Great Depression. When the stock market did crash in October 1929, investors' confidence was devastated, which contributed, in turn, to the Great Depression. However, it was by no means the single cause. Reduced gov-

ernment and investment spending, as well as a marked decline in the rate of technological advancements, greatly contributed to the Depression. Had there been no meaningful connection between the crash of 1929 and the Depression of the 1930s, the argument would have been a good example of the post hoc fallacy. Since there was a meaningful connection but other factors were also involved, this oversimplification best illustrates the fallacy of single causation.

Economic Laws Affecting Production Possibilities

In order to improve your ability to think like an economist, let's now look at some of the most important generalizations economists make. Economists use graphs of the **production possibilities curve** to illustrate the fundamental problem of scarcity. Since wants will always exceed available resources, people living in a given economy must make production choices.

Figure 1.9 Unemployed people march during the Great Depression. To claim that the Depression was caused by a single event is an example of the fallacy of single causation.

The production possibilities curve provides a visual model of the production choices faced by people in a simple economy. Before examining a graph of this curve, we must understand the assumptions on which this model is based:

- *Only two products can be produced by this simple economy.*

In an economy capable of producing hundreds of thousands of different products, decision making is extremely complex. In order to reduce economic decision making to its most basic form, the model assumes that only two products can be produced by this economy. This assumption makes the classic economic **trade-off** very clear: the increased production of one good can be achieved only by sacrificing a sufficient quantity of the alternative product.

In our model, we shall assume that the two goods that can be produced are bread and ploughs. Bread represents the production of **consumer goods**—those products and services that directly satisfy human wants. Ploughs, important agricultural tools, represent the production of **capital goods**—those goods used in the production of other goods. For example, ploughs are needed to prepare the soil for planting. The ploughs in operation today contribute to a successful wheat harvest tomorrow and, therefore, to the future production of bread.

- *The economy has fixed technology and resources.*

Since it is examining the economy over a short period of time, the model assumes that no technological innovations will be introduced to improve the rate of production. It also assumes that the amount of productive resources available does not change. Existing resources can be shifted, as desired, between the production of bread and ploughs, but no additional resources can be imported into the economy. For this reason, the only way to make more bread is to produce fewer ploughs, and vice versa.

- *The economy is at full employment.*

The model assumes that all productive resources, including labour, are fully employed and that they are being used effectively and

efficiently to produce the maximum output of goods and services.

What combination of ploughs and bread should our simple economy choose to produce? This question involves the concept of opportunity cost. Since the way we answer it will clearly reflect the values of our society, it is also a question that involves normative, or policy, economics.

The law of increasing relative cost

We can see by examining the production possibilities schedule in Figure 1.10 that the opportunity cost of increasing plough production is clearly reflected in the simultaneous decline in the production of bread. For example, in moving from alternative A to alternative B, the opportunity cost of producing one plough is the 1000 loaves of bread that must be sacrificed. The production managers in the economy have effectively transformed the 1000 loaves of bread into one new plough by shifting their resources out of bread production and into plough production. The economic cost of one plough relative to bread is not given in dollars but in the number of loaves, that is, 1000 loaves. This is referred to as the plough's **relative cost** and is directly proportional to the opportunity costs of increased plough production.

Figure 1.10, then, clearly reflects the existence of an important economic rule, known as the **law of increasing relative cost**. This law comes into play whenever a society, in order to get greater amounts of one product, sacrifices an ever-increasing amount of other products. It is reflected in the graph in Figure 1.11 (page 18) by the bowed-out, or concave, line of the production possibilities curve. If the opportunity cost of each extra plough were constant at 1000 loaves, the production possibilities curve would be a straight line. To confirm this, create a production possibilities schedule that reflects a constant trade-off between bread and ploughs (that is, 1000 loaves of bread for each new plough) and then graph the production possibilities curve.

The law of increasing relative cost causes this concave curvature of the production possibilities curve because, although plough production

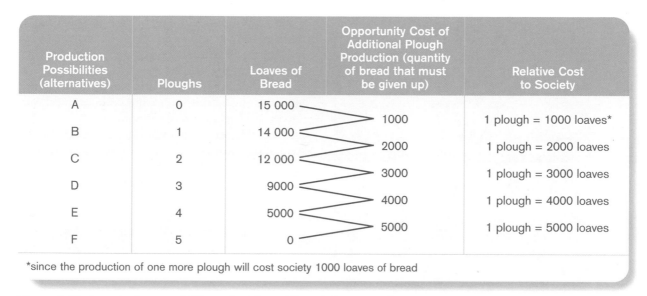

Production Possibilities (alternatives)	Ploughs	Loaves of Bread	Opportunity Cost of Additional Plough Production (quantity of bread that must be given up)	Relative Cost to Society
A	0	15 000		
			1000	1 plough = 1000 loaves*
B	1	14 000		
			2000	1 plough = 2000 loaves
C	2	12 000		
			3000	1 plough = 3000 loaves
D	3	9000		
			4000	1 plough = 4000 loaves
E	4	5000		
			5000	1 plough = 5000 loaves
F	5	0		

*since the production of one more plough will cost society 1000 loaves of bread

Figure 1.10 A production possibilities schedule and the relative costs of producing ploughs and bread.

(the horizontal movement) changes by a constant amount each time, the quantity of bread production (the vertical movement) changes by an increasingly larger amount each time. (Look again at Figure 1.11.) In other words, the slope of the curve becomes steeper as a result of this ever-increasing vertical change.

In order to understand this economic phenomenon, we must take into account the nature of the goods being produced and the difference in the productive resources that each one requires. Our first product, bread, is an agricultural product made primarily from wheat. The principal resource required to grow wheat is fertile land. Labour is also involved but is not as important.

Our second product, the plough, is a farm tool. The principal resource required to manufacture ploughs is human labour. Land, which provides the natural resources required (such as wood and iron), is also necessary but not as important. Therefore, the production of bread and ploughs uses resources in different proportions. As we move from production alternative A to alternatives B and C, those resources more suited to producing ploughs and less suited to producing bread (such as carpenters and blacksmiths) will be shifted from making bread to making ploughs.

As society moves from alternative C to alternatives D, E, and F, however, resources more suited to producing bread are put to use producing additional ploughs. The use of our limited resources has become less efficient and less effective. For instance, some farmland is being converted to woodlots, and some bakers are being retrained as blacksmiths. This inefficient use of resources is evident in the large amount of bread that must be sacrificed in order to produce the last two ploughs.

The production possibilities curve as a frontier

The production possibility schedule contains the *maximum potential output* that can be produced for each of the two products. The resulting curve, therefore, represents the outer limit, or **frontier**, of production possibility. This frontier is attainable only if all productive resources are fully employed. In reality, however, we know that resources are not always fully employed. For example, part of the labour force may be unemployed, some land may be left uncultivated, or some machines and factories may be idle. In addition, as a result of human error, some resources may be used ineffectively.

These realities will cause the economy to perform below the level of maximum potential

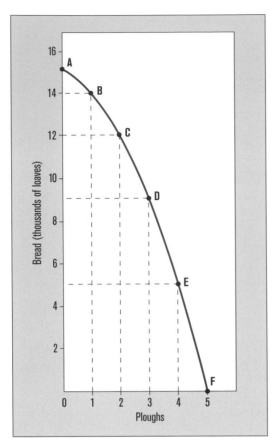

Figure 1.11 The production possibilities curve for ploughs and bread. This graph gives us a clear picture of the way opportunity cost works. Note that at point A, the economy produces no ploughs and 15 000 loaves of bread. At point B, the economy has shifted some of its productive resources to producing ploughs, with the result that only 14 000 loaves are produced. It is easy to see that, from A to B, the opportunity cost of producing one plough is 1000 loaves of bread. From B to F, as the production of ploughs increases, the production of bread falls off at a very rapid rate. The result is that, from E to F, the opportunity cost of one more plough has grown drastically to 5000 loaves of bread.

output. In Figure 1.12, point L (inside and there-fore below the frontier of maximum production) illustrates this situation. Most economies will achieve production levels inside or below the frontier. Nevertheless, each society sets for itself economic goals that aim to reach the production possibility frontier in the short term and to force the frontier to grow outward in the long term.

Point M on our graph is clearly beyond the production possibility frontier and so is unat-tainable at this time. An economy's capacity to produce can be increased over the long term by such changes as population growth (which expands the labour force) and technological advances (such as the development of more effi-cient machinery). This kind of structural change will allow the economy to produce, simultane-ously, more bread and ploughs in the long run, thereby shifting the production possibilities frontier outward as the productive capacity of the whole economy expands. In time, this expansion will make M an attainable point on the expanded production possibilities frontier.

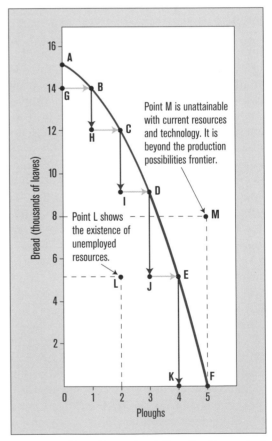

Figure 1.12 The production possibilities curve as a frontier. The curve is concave, or bowed out, because (moving to the right) the opportunity cost of producing one extra plough increases constantly in terms of the quantity of bread that must be sacrificed each time.

Economists use models and graphs . . .

- to simplify and explain complex patterns, relationships, and behaviours.
- to outline and highlight the elements at work in an economic system or process.
- to make supportable generalizations about economic behaviours.
- to apply economic reasoning to issue analysis and decision making.
- to identify general trends and tendencies in order to support forecasts and predictions.

Figure 1.13 Economists use models to simplify complex economic realities and to support forecasts.

The law of diminishing returns

While the law of increasing relative cost deals with the relationship between two **outputs**, or products (in our case, bread and ploughs), the **law of diminishing returns** deals with the relationship between an **input** (a productive resource such as labour) and the resulting output. More specifically, the law of diminishing returns states that outputs will increase when a particular input is increased, but only to a point. After this point has been reached, increasing inputs will not have an appreciable effect on the production of outputs. Another agricultural example will give us a better idea of the way this law operates.

Suppose a farmer is working, without the use of machinery or hired help, a farm that is 10 hectares (ha). There are only two productive resources, or inputs, involved in this enterprise: land and the farmer's own labour. For the sake of our demonstration, we shall assume that no additional land is available to the farmer. Let's further assume that the farmer is able to hire additional workers as needed. Therefore, the operation of this farm requires one input that is variable (labour) and one that is constant (land). Our farmer wants to increase the crop yieldage as a way of making the enterprise more profitable. For seven growing seasons in a row, the farmer experiments by hiring one additional person each year to help work the farm. The workforce therefore expands from one worker (the farmer alone) to seven (the farmer plus six hired hands). Figure 1.14 outlines the results of this experiment.

At first, the additional workers contribute to a sizable increase in yieldage. In later years, however, further increases in the labour force result in less and less extra production. Finally, there is no more increase in what 10 ha of soil can produce, no matter how many workers are added. This is a good illustration of the law of diminishing returns, which states:

For any productive enterprise, when at least one input is held constant [in our example, land] *while other inputs are increased* [in our

Year	Cultivated Land (ha)	Labour Force (workers)	Total Production (bushels of corn)	Increase in Yieldage (extra bushels)
1	10	1	1000	
				1000
2	10	2	2000	
				800
3	10	3	2800	
				600
4	10	4	3400	
				400
5	10	5	3800	
				100
6	10	6	3900	
				0
7	10	7	3900	

Figure 1.14 A farmer's attempt to increase output (Experiment A), which illustrates the law of diminishing returns.

example, labour], *there will be an eventual decline in the rate of extra output or yieldage.*

This decline may not be as immediate as in our example. Often, diminishing returns will appear only after several more increases in the variable resource have occurred.

The law of increasing returns to scale

Examining another economic principle will help us to understand the law of diminishing returns even better. The **law of increasing returns to scale** tells us what happens when all productive resources are increased simultaneously. To see how this works, let's return to our cornfield and conduct a slightly different experiment. This time, as the farmer hires additional workers, additional parcels of land are being cultivated as well. Just as in our last example, we assume that all work is done manually. Figure 1.15 outlines the results of this second experiment.

In this experiment, the outcome is very different from that of the first experiment. Why? Have we refuted the law of diminishing returns? Not at all. In this second experiment, the farmer has increased *all* productive resources at the same time and in the same quantity. Every time a new worker is added, another 10 ha of cultivated land are also added. The farmer has therefore increased the *scale* of operations. An operation that began as a single farmer working on a small parcel of land has

grown into a large farm employing seven full-time workers. The net result of this conversion to larger-scale operations is a steady increase in the rate of extra output.

When the farmer doubled the amount of all productive resources used, total production also doubled. When the farmer doubled resource input again (from year 2 to year 4), output more than doubled (2000 bushels of corn became 4600 bushels). By the end of the experiment, a sevenfold increase in inputs has led to a tenfold increase in production. Clearly, there are increased returns to show for this systematic increase in the amount of productive resources the farmer puts to use. Through effective teamwork and specialization, economies of scale make the farmer's operations more efficient. In the real world, increased returns to scale (also referred to as economies of scale) help to explain why so many of the products we buy are produced by large companies. Even in agriculture, the large corporate enterprise is increasingly replacing the small family farm. In later chapters of this text, we shall explore various applications of the theory of increased returns to scale.

Since in the real world productive resources are limited, it is not always possible for an enterprise to increase all resource inputs indefinitely. Ultimately, therefore, the availability of some productive resources will end, and the law of diminishing returns will once again prevail.

Year	Cultivated Land (ha)	Labour Force (workers)	Total Production (bushels of corn)	Increase in Yieldage (extra bushels)
1	10	1	1000	
				1000
2	20	2	2000	
				1200
3	30	3	3200	
				1400
4	40	4	4600	
				1600
5	50	5	6200	
				1800
6	60	6	8000	
				2000
7	70	7	10 000	

Figure 1.15 A farmer's attempt to increase output (Experiment B), which illustrates the law of increasing returns to scale.

Case Study   Career Opportunities

Throughout this chapter, we have been considering what the study of economics involves, but we haven't yet looked seriously at what economists actually do. Perhaps the most practical way to do this is to research the career opportunities available to people who have a background in economics and in the related fields of accounting, business administration, commerce and finance, computer sciences, marketing, political sciences, and sociology.

Figure 1.16 Stock exchanges are well-known for providing career opportunities related to economics. On the trading floor, a variety of professionals buy and sell stocks using "high-tech" computer links.

Since the study of economics develops problem-solving, analytical, and critical-thinking skills, successful students enjoy a wide variety of potential career paths in business, government, and education. Figure 1.17 (page 22) outlines the range of job opportunities available to people trained in economics and related fields. You may be able to add to these lists of careers by consulting the "Careers" section of different newspapers.

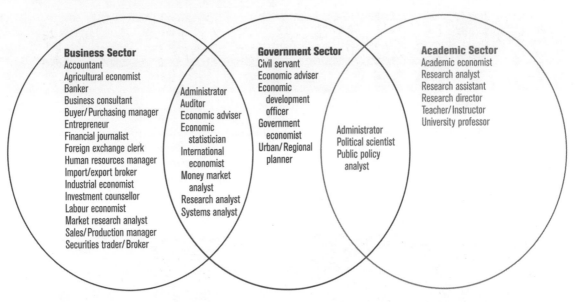

Figure 1.17 Career opportunities related to economics are listed for the business, government, and academic sectors of the economy.

QUESTIONS

1. Using Figure 1.17 as a guide, collect job advertisements from your local newspaper to further your analysis of employment opportunities.

Based on your research, what roles would you say economists play in our society?

2. Create a chart similar to the one below to compare jobs available to people who have trained in economics. What job opportunities related to economics most interest you? Why?

Company	Job Title	Salary	Education Required	Skills Required	Background Required	Nature of Work

Check Your Understanding

1. How does the fallacy of composition help to shed light on the tension that exists between individual self-interest and the common good? Explain one specific application of the fallacy of composition that you have experienced.

2. Develop a strategy that you can use to distinguish between single-causation fallacies and cause-and-effect fallacies. Explain your strategy.

3. What is meant by the relative cost of a product? Explain how increased relative costs are related to opportunity costs and diminishing returns.

4. In order to experience increased returns, what economic conditions must be available to producers? What effect does the relative scarcity of resources eventually have on outputs or returns?

5. Why are so many of the products we buy manufactured by large-scale producers?

CHAPTER SUMMARY

- Economics is the social science of scarcity and choice. Economists attempt to allocate scarce resources wisely in order to satisfy the most wants possible while using up the smallest amount of resources possible.

- Opportunity cost is the sum of all that is lost from taking one course of action over another. In making any economic decision, we must always consider not just what we are gaining but also what we stand to lose in choosing one alternative over another.

- Group behaviour is often predictable, but individual behaviour is harder to predict.

- Economists use models to explain complex patterns, processes, and relationships and to support forecasts and predictions.

- Analytical (or positive) economics deals with the analysis of economic facts and the development of economic theories based on direct observation. It represents the factual side of economics.

- The normative (or policy) side of economics deals with statements that contain value judgements and cannot, therefore, be confirmed or denied solely by reference to facts. This is the controversial side of economics.

- Economists apply a method of inquiry called the scientific method. This investigative approach includes the steps of observation, data collection, explanation, and verification.

- A fallacy is a hypothesis that has been proven false but is still accepted by many people because, at first glance, it appears to make sense.

- The fallacy of composition is based on the faulty premise that what is good for the individual is automatically good for society as a whole.

- The post hoc fallacy is based on the mistaken assumption that what comes before automatically causes what follows.

- The fallacy of single causation is based on the faulty premise that a single factor or person caused a particular event to occur.

- The production possibilities curve is an excellent model to demonstrate how a simple economy can produce additional quantities of a desired product by shifting productive resources out of another industry.

- The concave curvature of the production possibilities curve demonstrates the effect of the law of increasing relative cost. As society attempts to produce increased amounts of one product, increasingly larger amounts of other products must be sacrificed because of the inefficiencies created. Relative cost is directly proportional to changes in opportunity cost.

- For any productive enterprise, when at least one input is held constant while other inputs are increased, there will be an eventual decline in the rate of extra output, or yieldage. This is known as the law of diminishing returns.

- The law of increased returns to scale states that when all productive resources (inputs) are simultaneously increased, there is an even greater increase in yieldage (outputs). This increased yieldage is the outcome of the improved efficiency resulting from specialization and mass production technology. This explains why most of the goods we buy are produced by large enterprises.

- There are many career opportunities for people who have trained in economics.

Key Terms

economize
economics
social science
oikos
economy
effective
efficient
opportunity cost
analytical (or positive) economics
origin
normative (or policy) economics
scientific method
fallacy
fallacy of composition
post hoc fallacy (or cause-and-effect fallacy)
fallacy of single causation
production possibilities curve
trade-off
consumer goods
capital goods
relative cost
law of increasing relative cost
frontier
output
law of diminishing returns
input
law of increasing returns to scale

Activities

Thinking/Inquiry

1. Are all personal goals achievable at the same time? Use the decision-making matrix in Figure 1.4 (page 10) to explain how complicated, conflicting, and less important goals can be addressed in a systematic manner.

2. "In decision-making situations, the key role of economists should not be to dictate values to others. Economists serve best by focusing attention on the opportunity costs of a prospective decision and the potential benefits of each major alternative." Do you agree or disagree with this statement? Use examples to justify your answer.

3. Explain the difference between analytical and normative economics. In a daily newspaper, find three examples of analytical statements and three examples of normative statements.

Communication

4. Assume you are writing an email to a friend about your economics class. In your own words, explain to your friend what economics is and why it is considered a social science.

5. If you were the parent of a teenager, how would you explain to him or her what it means to economize and why it is important?

6. Working in small groups, discuss the following statements. Through group consensus, identify the type of reasoning error each statement contains: the fallacy of composition, the post hoc fallacy, or the fallacy of single causation. In order to keep you on your toes, one statement is fallacy free.

   a) An economic crisis in Japan caused the 1998 decline of the Canadian dollar in international money markets.

   b) What is good for General Motors is good for the Canadian economy.

   c) Victoria, British Columbia, has one of the highest death rates in the country, therefore, it must be unhealthy to live there.

   d) Jasna found the work experience she got through her school's co-operative education program to be of great personal benefit. Co-operative education should be a compulsory requirement for all secondary-school students.

   e) A multi-car accident on the Trans-Canada Highway was caused by bad weather.

   f) If every Canadian worker received a 10 per cent pay increase, the nation as a whole would be better off.

   g) The four components of the scientific method first outlined by Francis Bacon are observation, data collection, explanation, and verification. Although scientists today use many different processes to make their discoveries, they almost always make use of the four steps outlined by Bacon.

h) Former prime minister Brian Mulroney was responsible for the economic recession of 1990.

i) Ali's marks improved after she broke up with Evan. He was not a good influence.

Application

7. After graduation, do you plan to continue your education, get a job, or travel? What are the opportunity costs for each alternative?

8. Give three examples of economic decisions you had to make this week. Explain why each was an economic decision. What was the opportunity cost of each decision?

9. Analyze the sales pitch of a televised infomercial to identify the use of suspect economic reasoning and other strategies intended to sell the viewer on the product. Identify specific examples of analytical and normative statements or claims.

10. Examine Figure 1.18.

Production Possibility	Bicycles	Cheese (kg)	Opportunity Cost of Each Bicycle
A	0	170	
B	1	160	
C	2	140	
D	3	110	
E	4	60	
F	5	0	

Figure 1.18 Production possibilities for country X.

a) Calculate the opportunity cost for each additional bicycle being produced.

b) Use the data in the table to graph a production possibilities curve.

c) Mark a point H on the graph that indicates widespread unemployment in country X.

d) Mark a point J that represents a production level that cannot be reached by X's economy. Explain why this point is unattainable under present conditions. How might this production level be reached in the future?

e) Explain why this production possibility curve has a concave (bowed-out) curvature. What economic law is responsible for this curvature?

11. Figure 1.19 outlines some combinations of corn and beef that can be produced annually from a given parcel of farmland.

Production Possibility	Corn (bushels)	Beef (kg)
A	16 000	0
B	8000	900
C	6000	1200
D	4000	1400
E	2000	1450
F	0	1500

Figure 1.19 Production possibilities for an agricultural enterprise.

a) Draw a production possibilities curve for this agricultural enterprise.

b) Can this farmland produce 6000 bushels of corn and 1500 kg of beef during the same year? Mark this production level as point H on your graph. Explain what must happen in order for this agricultural enterprise to reach this level of production.

c) What is the opportunity cost of expanding beef production from 900 kg to 1200 kg annually?

d) What is the opportunity cost of expanding corn production from Level B to Level A annually?

e) If a decision is made to produce 5000 bushels of corn, how much beef can be produced on this farm at the same time? Mark this production level as point K on your graph.

f) Given this set of production possibilities, should this enterprise specialize (in either corn or beef production) or produce ample quantities of both products? Justify your decision.

CHAPTER 2

PRODUCTIVE RESOURCES AND ECONOMIC SYSTEMS

Make As Much Money As You Can

Welcome to the widget business! Divide the class into six competing companies. Each company of investors will produce identical imaginary products called widgets. Each widget produced will cost your company $2 in raw materials, labour, and equipment. You will be able to sell your widgets based on the following formula: P = $100 − Q. In other words, for each round of production, the market price for widgets will be $100 minus the total quantity of widgets produced by all companies.

Clearly, the market price of widgets is adversely affected by the total quantity produced. During each of the six production rounds, you will meet with your associate investors to decide how many widgets your company will produce. You are not free to consult with competitors in making your production decisions because this kind of consultation can constitute illegal collusion. At the end of round three, you will be permitted to send one representative to meet with rival companies in order to discuss business conditions and to suggest improvements. No other communication with rivals is allowed. Good luck, and may the best business managers win!

QUESTIONS

1. Explain the production strategy that your company used. To what degree were the following skills used effectively: understanding the marketplace, anticipating the actions of others, willingness to take risks, leadership and persuasiveness, and diplomacy (the ability to negotiate and compromise).

2. Which management skills seemed to help the successful companies most?

3. What would be the effect—on both consumers and producers—of a government regulation requiring each company to produce 16 widgets each round? Explain the economic reasons that a government would have for making this decision.

4. What would your company's reaction be to government regulation of the widget industry?

Chapter Goals

By the end of this chapter, you will be able to

- recognize tangible and intangible productive resources as a nation's real wealth,
- classify political economies and compare the different decision-making processes used to set and achieve economic goals,
- identify the principal goals of the Canadian economy and examine the links and trade-offs that exist among them.

Round	Quantity Produced (Q)	Market Price (P) (P = $100 − Q)	Sales Revenue (R) (R = Q × P)	Production Costs (C) (C = Q × $2)	Profit (F) (F = R − C)
1					
6					
				TOTAL PROFIT EARNED	

Figure 2.1 Widget game worksheet. Reproduce it to track the effectiveness of your management decisions.

Decisions About Productive Resources

In Chapter 1, we examined the importance of productive resources in determining an economy's production possibilities frontier. In this chapter, we shall look more closely at the concept of productive resources to better understand the basic production questions that every economic system has to answer. We'll also examine the way different types of economic systems attempt to answer these production questions.

By **productive resources**, economists mean anything that can be used to create or manufacture valuable goods or services. These resources are also known as **factors of production**. Originally, economists recognized only three types of productive resources: land, labour, and capital. Over time, the definitions of these three types have been broadened to include other resources.

The resource of **land** includes not only the fertile soil found on the surface of the Earth but also all natural resources found on or below the surface. Resources such as mineral deposits, groundwater, fossil fuels, and forest reserves are extremely useful in providing the **raw materials** needed to produce the goods and services that people want.

The resource of **labour** now includes not just physical labour provided by the workforce but also mental effort and other elements human beings contribute to the production process. In an Ipsos–Reid national survey of business leaders in 2001, 60 per cent of the 300 chief executive officers interviewed identified attracting high-calibre employees as a major priority, while 80 per cent identified retaining employees as a major priority. Economists now recognize the resources of entrepreneurship and knowledge as important factors of production that allow for the more efficient use of land, raw materials, labour, and capital. Economists also recognize the importance of labour resources, whether they constitute a paid service (such as the work carried out on an automobile assembly line) or a volunteer service (such as the homemaking work done by a stay-at-home parent).

Entrepreneurship refers to the ability to organize economic activity, assume risks, and achieve effective results. This is the contribution that an owner, a manager, or an innovator makes to the production process. The entrepreneur organizes and directs the other factors of production and seeks to develop new products, production processes, and marketing strategies. For example, the accidental development of a low-grade adhesive, the result of a failed experiment to create an inexpensive high-grade adhesive, led to the creation of Post-it® Notes by the 3M Corporation. What seemed, at first glance, to be a useless material was transformed by 3M into a marketable product that grew into one of the greatest success stories in the company's history. Although less tangible than physical labour, entrepreneurship and knowledge are today recognized as important factors of production.

The resource of **capital** refers to the goods that aid in the production of other goods and services, such as factories, warehouses, machin-

Figure 2.2 Should labour that does not directly earn a wage be considered a valuable productive resource? Explain.

ery, and equipment. Since we also use the term *capital* to mean the money available in an enterprise to acquire these necessary goods, we must be more precise in our terminology. For this reason, the facilities, machinery, and equipment are often referred to as **real capital**, while the funds to acquire them are called **money capital**. Real capital is extremely important to a growing economy. An economy's investment in capital goods today will allow it to expand its total production and improve its **productivity** and efficiency in the future. The large amounts of tax dollars spent annually on public education in Canada represent a sizable investment in what is sometimes described as "human capital."

Tangible and Intangible Resources

Figure 2.3 summarizes and classifies productive resources by identifying them as either tangible or intangible resources. **Tangible resources** have physical properties that can be seen and touched and are therefore easily quantified. Examples include a hundred tonnes of nickel, a thousand people in the labour force, or six punch presses on an industrial assembly line.

Intangible resources lack the physical properties that make them easy to quantify. Although economists cannot see or weigh something like entrepreneurship, they know it is important to the economy because of the positive effect that certain risk-taking and organizational activities have on production levels and on a company's ability to operate efficiently. Economists have concluded that, although it is difficult to quantify, entrepreneurship directly affects national productivity and is therefore an important intangible factor of production. Knowledge is becoming an increasingly important resource as well, given Canada's transformation from a manufacturing economy to an information economy. Information that is accurate and timely increases business productivity.

Economists also recognize a third, and even more intangible, factor as important in the production of goods and services—an economy's

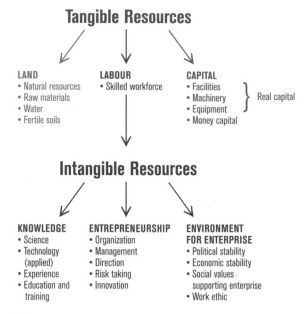

Figure 2.3 A summary of productive resources.

environment for enterprise. This involves examining a country's social and cultural values and its political and economic institutions to see if they are conducive to doing business. For example, a stable government gives people and firms the security they need to make sound planning and production decisions. It also bolsters both investor and consumer confidence, thereby creating a climate favourable to increased economic activity. As Figure 2.3 shows, most intangible resources involve productive human contributions—contributions that go beyond the physical or tangible form of labour.

In the final analysis, tangible and intangible resources work together to form the real source of a nation's wealth and prosperity. The nation's treasury can always print more money, but without goods and services to buy and sell, money means very little. An economy's capacity to produce goods and services in response to the wants and needs of its citizens—in other words, the sum total of its tangible and intangible productive resources—is a clear indicator of economic wealth and the cornerstone of long-term growth and prosperity.

Valuing Productive Resources

Not everything that counts can be counted and not everything that can be counted counts.

—Albert Einstein

Figure 2.4 follows one particular wheat harvest through four production stages. *Market value* represents the dollar value that a product will fetch in the marketplace. **Value added** represents the increase in market value resulting from the additional processing or refinement of the product. Operating expenses represent all costs of processing incurred by a contributor. For example, the operating expenses of the farmer include land rental or property taxes, equipment rental or purchase, the cost of hired help, and the cost of technical expertise to improve soil quality, seed variety, and crop harvest.

Study the data to identify the relationships that exist between market value, value added, and profit.

QUESTIONS

1. Apply Einstein's principle by providing two examples of things you value highly even though their economic benefit to you cannot be measured directly.

2. How can the value of the economic contribution made at each production stage be measured?

3. Why is bread worth more to consumers on the supermarket shelf than on a baker's rack? What is the price of a loaf of bread on the store shelf?

4. Explain the relationship between value added and profit.

Stage	Contributor	Product	Market Value of Product	Value Added by Contributor	Operating Expenses	Profit
1	farmer	tonnes of wheat	$10 000	$10 000	$8000	$2000
2	miller	bags of flour	$14 000	$4000	$2000	$2000
3	baker	loaves of bread (20 000)	$20 000	$6000	$3000	$3000
4	retailer	packaged bread on store shelf (20 000 bags)	$28 000	$8000	$3500	$4500

Figure 2.4 Determining the economic value of different contributors to the production process.

Check Your Understanding

1. Outline the difference between tangible and intangible productive resources, and explain why they are the real source of a nation's wealth.

2. Explain the difference between real capital and money capital.

3. Explain why political stability is an important productive resource for any economy.

4. Although they are difficult to measure directly, how do economists know that entrepreneurship and technology are valuable productive resources?

Economic Systems and Production Questions

Throughout history, economic systems have been established to answer the three fundamental questions of production outlined in Figure 2.6. These questions are:

What to produce?
• What goods and services should our society produce, and in what quantities?
• What is worth producing and what is not?
• What are we giving up in order to produce these goods and services?

How to produce?
• By whom, with what resources, and in what way should goods be produced?
• How can our limited resources be used most efficiently?
• Should products be made in small, privately owned factories or in large, state-owned corporations?
• How much automation should be used? How much manual labour?

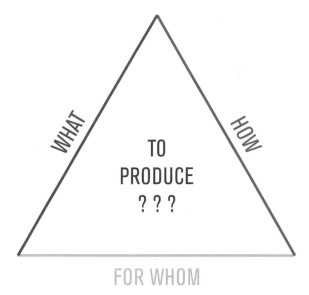

Figure 2.6 The triangle of basic production questions.

For whom to produce?
• How will total output be shared among the different members of society?
• Who will get which goods and services? Will products be shared equally?
• On what basis should decisions concerning distribution be made?

  Although every economy attempts to answer these questions effectively, the way each question is answered will help identify the type of economic system that operates in a specific society or state. Economists define an **economic system** as the set of laws, institutions, and common practices that help a nation determine how to use its scarce resources to satisfy as many of its people's needs and wants as possible. Over time, three distinctly different ways of answering the basic production questions have emerged; that is, the questions can be answered
• by tradition,
• by command, and
• by market forces.
The following sections examine each of these economic systems in its pure, or theoretical, form and explore how each appears in the real world today. Then you'll have the opportunity to compare these three economic systems by reviewing Figure 2.7 (page 33).

Figure 2.5 How has this manufacturer chosen to deal with precision on a tedious assembly line?

The Traditional Economy

In a pure **traditional economy**, the practices of the past determine the answers to the three production questions. The goods and services produced today are the same as those produced in the past, and the manner of production has not changed. Traditional practices and skills are passed on from generation to generation, usually within the same family. The quantity of total output does not vary greatly from year to year. This type of economy is usually found in a relatively static subsistence society in which people engage in little long-term planning and focus primarily on surviving the challenges of each day.

In a traditional economy, each family's economic strategy is to be as self-sufficient as possible; therefore, the question of *what* to produce is determined by the needs of the family, whose members produce goods *for their own use*. Any surplus goods are usually traded to other families for essential items. This trading of goods and services without the use of a monetary system is known as **barter**. In terms of *how* these goods are produced, parents teach their children the necessary skills so that they will be able to assume their parents' roles and responsibilities. As a result, throughout their entire lives, people remain part of the same social class into which they were born.

Centuries ago, this was the most common economic system throughout most of the world. People lived in small rural communities. They had modest needs, most of which could be met by using the natural resources provided by the local environment. They grew much of their own food, built their own homes, and made their own clothing and tools. Over time, population growth, as well as industrial, scientific, and technological advances, have transformed most traditional economies. Those that remain today are found in relatively isolated environments where traditional practices have not been affected by outside contacts. Today, traditional economies (with varying degrees of modification) are found within the societies of
• the Bedouin of the Sahara Desert,
• the Bushmen of the Kalahari Desert,
• the Mongols of the Gobi Desert,
• the Lapps of the Scandinavian tundra,
• the Masai of the African savannah,
• the Waura and Yanomami of the Amazon rain forest,
• the Mbuti of the African rain forest,
• the Senoi and Negrito peoples of Malayasia, and
• other indigenous peoples.

With the arrival of modern communications technology, indigenous peoples have been exposed to more ideas and information, which means their economies are no longer totally isolated. As a result, the pure traditional economy is becoming more difficult to find. For example, the traditional societies of the Inuit and other First Nations of Canada and of the Aboriginal peoples of the Australian outback have been greatly influenced by the technological advances and practices of the people and economic systems with which they have come in contact.

The Command Economy

In a pure **command economy**, all production decisions are made by a small group of political leaders who have the power to enforce their decisions throughout the entire economy. In other words, the pure command economy is centrally planned. The questions of *what* to produce, *how* to produce, and *for whom* to produce are all answered by the central authority based on what is in the best interest of the state. Productive resources are owned by the state and efficiently allocated by the central authority on behalf of the state. The individual person has the obligation of serving the state. In turn, state authorities draw up plans to meet individual needs such as food, housing, medicine, and education.

The central authority rewards people who contribute to the betterment of the state by giving them a share of goods and services and, sometimes, special privileges (such as comfortable living quarters and trips abroad). People who do not contribute are penalized for their lack of productivity, and their special privileges are either denied or taken away. In this way, command economies rely on a system of reward and punishment to promote increased productivity. The central planning authority determines the products and quantities to be produced, who will work where, what machinery will be available to assist production, and how much each worker will be paid. With many of their needs already covered by the state's central plan, workers usually spend their modest wages on consumer goods, such as food, clothing, and shelter. The state plan emphasizes the production of capital goods over consumer goods because capital goods increase the economy's ability to produce more in the future. Consequently, consumer goods are generally in short supply.

Very few pure command economies exist today. Perhaps the two best examples are found in Cuba and China. Until recently, the former Soviet Union and the countries of Eastern Europe operated centrally planned economies under communist rule. Prior to 1991 (the year the Soviet Union was divided into separate countries), one-third of the world's people lived under some version of a command economy.

The Market Economy

In a pure **market economy**, economic activity is co-ordinated by many individuals who make independent decisions in a free marketplace. Since people are acting for themselves, often out of self-interest, this system is also called *free enterprise*; since resources are privately owned, the system is sometimes called **private enterprise**.

The actions of individual buyers and sellers in the marketplace answer the three production questions. *What* will be produced is ultimately determined by consumer demand. Businesses will clear out their unwanted goods at discounted prices and then will no longer produce them. Instead, they will produce "in-demand" goods and services because these will fetch the highest prices and probably generate the highest profits.

The quest for profit also plays a key role in determining *how* goods and services will be produced. Consumers prefer low prices. Producers can maximize their profits by using the least costly and most efficient methods of production. Inefficient producers will not be able to compete in the long run and will be forced to improve their productivity or go out of business.

Distribution in a market economy is determined by the income people receive for their contributions (mostly labour) to the production process. Income levels, therefore, answer the question of *for whom* the economy's goods and services are produced. Since they can afford to pay for it, people with high incomes are entitled to more of the national output than are those with low incomes.

The basic elements of a market economy are private property, freedom of enterprise, profit maximization, and competition. The government's role is only to provide law and order and to assist economic development. Very few pure market economies exist today. Perhaps the closest examples are Hong Kong and the United States. When Hong Kong was under British rule, it was recognized as the most liberal of market economies. In the US, the federal government has expanded its role in the nation's economic life, especially since the Great Depression.

Canada: A Mixed Market Economy

By now, it should be obvious that very few "pure" economic systems exist today. There are two important reasons for this. First, no single type of economic system has achieved perfection. To date, not one of the three types has managed to meet all the needs and wants of its members. In other words, no system holds a monopoly on effectiveness and efficiency. Second, given the free flow of ideas and knowledge in the Information Age, political leaders and economic decision makers will attempt to integrate the best elements of each type of economy into their own system.

The Canadian economy is a classic example of this cross-pollination of economic models. Although, at present, the Canadian economy contains elements of traditional and command economies, it most clearly shows the characteristics of a modified market economy. For this reason, economists classify the Canadian econ-

	Traditional Economy	Command Economy	Market Economy
Economic decision making			
What to produce?	• what is needed now by a family or group	• determined by central authority	• what will sell for the most favourable price
How?	• according to production methods taught by parents/elders	• determined by central authority in the state's best interests	• as efficiently as possible to keep production costs low
For whom?	• for use by immediate family; surpluses are traded	• determined by central authority	• for consumers willing and able to pay a favourable price
Strengths	• minimal change • decisions made as a family unit • little damage to environment • consumption and waste minimized • focus on self-reliance and simplicity	• planning promotes growth (capital goods production favoured over consumer goods) • planning helps reduce waste • equitable distribution of income and wealth • planning provides stability (business cycles eliminated) • individuals serve the state; the state provides for their needs	• maximum freedom of individual choice • variety of goods and services available to consumers • competition helps keep quality high and prices low • profit motive provides incentive to be efficient • flexibility to revise decisions as market conditions change
Limitations	• little opportunity for social improvement • no monetary system (goods are exchanged) • little long-term planning (most decisions day-to-day) • limited quality, quantity, and variety of goods • individualism is discouraged	• bureaucratic and inflexible • limits individual choice, incentive, and initiative • forced to meet production quotas, managers will favour quantity over quality • limited availability of consumer goods • little incentive to innovate	• manipulation of consumer wants by advertising • business cycles of growth and slow-down • income and wealth unevenly distributed • large producers can influence price • over-consumption can cause resources to run out

Figure 2.7 A comparison of economic systems.

omy, like many other complex societies today, as a **mixed economy**. Our country's economy includes both private enterprise and state-owned enterprise. For example, in the television industry, the Canadian Broadcasting Corporation (CBC) is state-owned while the Canadian Television Network (CTV) is privately owned. Although the non-profit, public service mandate of the CBC is somewhat different from that of the commercially motivated CTV, at times these two corporations are in direct competition with each other. A good example of this competition is the bidding wars in which the two networks engage for broadcast rights to the Olympic Games or other major sporting events.

The Canadian system tries to integrate the best features of all three economic types. For instance, in the matter of land ownership, Canada allows for state-owned or **crown land,** which is a feature of command economies. But it also permits private ownership of land, which is a feature of market economies, and has recognized many reserve lands for Aboriginal peoples.

Although there is a great amount of free enterprise in Canada's economy, there are also many government regulations that businesses have to heed. In addition, over the years, the Canadian government has established a "social safety net" for the welfare of its most needy citizens. These social programs, which might be ignored in a pure market economy, include guaranteed income supplements, government-funded medical care, employment insurance for workers, and social security for senior citizens.

Partly because of this elaborate safety net, the United Nations Human Development Report has several times identified Canada as the best country in the world in which to live.

As a final example of the mixed nature of the Canadian economy, we need look no further than the growing practice of bartering one service for another. This return to the traditional exchange of services without the exchange of money is said to be growing rapidly. For example, a cabinetmaker may strike a deal with a bricklayer to exchange services. The bricklayer agrees to repair the cabinetmaker's chimney if, in exchange, the cabinetmaker builds a set of cupboards for the bricklayer. Since these services are being carried on at the personal level and in a reciprocal manner, the quality of work is virtually guaranteed. Furthermore, since no written contract is required and no money actually changes hands, this transaction might not be reported when both parties file their tax returns at the end of the year, providing an additional benefit to both parties. On the other hand, government revenues and, consequently, spending programs are adversely affected when individuals do not pay their legal share of taxes. This is one illustration of what has come to be known as the *underground economy*, or **hidden economy**. Whether the motive may be to avoid taxes (a crime under the Income Tax Act) or to ensure a more personal level of service, the result has been the reintroduction of an element of traditional economic systems to the mainstream of Canadian economic activity.

Check Your Understanding

1. What is an economic system, and what are the three fundamental questions of production that all economic systems must answer?
2. Prepare a summary note to explain the main features of a traditional economy.
3. Explain the importance of central planning in a command economy.
4. Outline the basic elements of a market economy.
5. Explain why the Canadian economy can be accurately identified as a mixed market economy.

Understanding Political Economies

Economic systems rarely exist today outside a government framework, which means that political and economic decision making are closely connected. No study of economic systems would be complete without an investigation of the major political models outlined in Figure 2.8. These models can be broadly classified as either democracies or dictatorships. A **democracy** is a political system characterized by a freely elected government that represents, for a set term of office, the majority of citizens. It is open to many parties or political views. A **dictatorship** is a political system in which a single person or party exercises absolute authority over an entire nation. There are no free elections to allow the people to change their leadership.

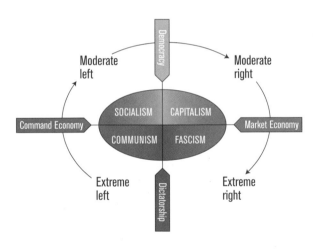

Political Orientation

Figure 2.8 An overview of politico-economic models. At the bottom of this chart is a representation of the political spectrum—the range of political models that proceed from communism on the extreme left to fascism on the extreme right. Fascism and communism are considered "extreme" models because of their tendency to use force to establish authority.

Communism

Communism is a political model based on the theories of Karl Marx, Friedrich Engels, and Vladimir Ilyich Lenin. It calls for government or community ownership of all means of production and wealth. Under communism, private property and free enterprise are abolished. Ideally, individuals produce according to their ability and consume according to their need. The communist ideology calls for a strong central government with complete authority to plan for maximum economic growth. To safeguard the common good, opposing political parties and special-interest groups, such as labour unions, are denied any part in the decision-making process. Since, historically, communists have been willing to use force to achieve their goals, they are seen as occupying the extreme left wing of the political spectrum.

Under communist rule, the Soviet Union developed from a war-shattered society in the early stages of industrialization in 1917 into a military superpower 50 years later. By 1991, however, the Communist Party had lost its absolute power, the Soviet economy had suffered a series of major setbacks, and the Soviet Union itself was dismantled. Today, the Russian economy continues the painful transition to a market economy. Communist systems are still in place in China, Cuba, North Korea, and Vietnam.

Socialism

Socialism, too, is based on public ownership or control of the principal means of production. However, unlike communists, socialists favour democratic and peaceful methods to achieve their goals. Once they've been elected, they do not ban opposition parties. For this reason, they are often called social democrats and are considered to occupy the moderate left position on the political spectrum. Socialists try to allow for fair and equal distribution of available goods and services through a democratic decision-making process. They claim that free enterprise is inefficient, wasteful, and prone to conflicts between workers and capitalists.

Under socialism, co-operation and worker solidarity theoretically replace the capitalistic ideals of self-interest and competition. Experiments in Britain and France in the 1970s and 1980s produced a measurable decline in national productivity. Some critics use such results to question whether human self-interest makes socialism ultimately unworkable.

The politico-economic systems in Scandinavian countries (Norway, Sweden, Denmark, and Finland) are often categorized as "free-enterprise socialism," the most moderate of socialist philosophies. In these countries, the focus is no longer on increasing state ownership (the **nationalization** of enterprise) but rather on private enterprise balanced by socialist government policies that address collective needs. National production levels and living standards in countries like Norway and Sweden continue to grow under free-enterprise socialism. Today, living standards in these countries are among the highest in the world.

Capitalism

When Karl Marx called the free-enterprise system **capitalism**, he meant to criticize its tendency to stress the accumulation of capital resources as a means to greater individual wealth and power. Capitalism requires a democratically elected government to maintain public order and to keep competition free and fair. The private ownership of industry operating under free-market conditions is one of the essentials of capitalism. Producers are motivated to produce by the desire for profit. A business can maximize profits by making products that consumers are willing and able to buy. The opportunity for profit and the threat of loss, therefore, play the same role in capitalism that a dictator's edicts play in a command economy. Adam Smith (1723–1790), often known as the father of capitalism, used the term *natural order* to describe this politico-economic system because he thought it was based on natural laws.

As you can see in Figure 2.8, capitalism occupies the moderate right position on the political spectrum. Capitalist systems operate today in such areas as Hong Kong, Singapore,

the United States, and New Zealand. Since assuming control in 1997, the communist government of China has allowed Hong Kong's healthy free-market system to continue to operate. Countries like Canada, Germany, France, Great Britain, and Italy have primarily capitalist systems blended with some socialist characteristics, such as welfare programs and government-owned enterprises. Economists often categorize these mixed systems as "welfare capitalism."

Fascism

Fascism, occupying the extreme right position on the political spectrum, combines a free-market economy with a non-democratic, or authoritarian, form of government. Fascist governments use force as a means of political and social control. As with the politics of the extreme left, fascist governments do not usually

Figure 2.9 Hong Kong continues to be one of the busiest commercial centres in the world today. How might business investment be affected by the transition from British capitalist to Chinese communist rule?

tolerate political opposition. Citizens are free to own property and businesses as long as they comply with all government dictates. There are clear restrictions on individual freedom. Military dictatorships that allow private ownership and enterprise can be categorized as fascist systems. Italy (1922–1945), Nazi Germany (1933–1945), Spain (1939–1975), and Argentina (1946–1983) are four historical examples of this ideology.

Check Your
Understanding

1. What two factors are used to classify political economies? Explain how they help to differentiate political economies.

2. Explain the difference between an extreme and a moderate political orientation. Why has fascism historically been a bitter rival of communism?

3. a) What is the fundamental difference between free-enterprise socialism and communism?

   b) Where has socialism been most successfully practised to date?

4. Why is the Canadian system often referred to as "welfare capitalism"?

Setting Economic Goals: A Canadian Model

Every politico-economic system attempts to establish economic goals as targets in order to focus the use of productive resources. Some of the goals are *complementary*; that is, reaching one goal makes another goal easier to achieve. For example, in order to reach employment targets, interest rates on business loans are lowered to promote new job creation. In turn, new job creation will automatically help improve income levels in an economy and encourage consumer spending.

Unfortunately, some economic goals are *conflicting*, so that reaching one goal actually makes another goal more difficult to achieve. Strategies to keep prices stable often have an adverse effect on employment rates and national production. Governments can promote price stability by raising interest rates in order to control the amount of money in circulation; as it becomes more expensive to borrow money for investment, businesses hire fewer workers and production levels either remain constant or begin to decline. We can identify increases in employment and production as the opportunity cost of stable prices.

Government policy makers have to recognize this trade-off and decide whether their priority is to achieve price stability or to put more

people to work. They can't count on being able to have both. The setting of economic goals, therefore, is a matter of normative, or policy, economics. In other words, governments must make value judgements before they can set priorities for conflicting goals. On the whole, the economic goals that nations strive for are often similar. However, the way each nation prioritizes its conflicting goals will determine how it distributes its productive resources.

Since the 1960s, a number of goals have emerged as priorities in the Canadian economy. The following sections list and explain each of them. The order of their appearance in the text does not indicate their order of priority. Each successive government has re-examined these goals and set its own priorities. In later chapters, we will examine these goals in greater detail.

Political Stability

A stable government can help long-term planning and investment to flourish. Consistency in policy making promotes investor confidence and provides a climate conducive to economic growth. Each time we approach a sovereignty referendum in Quebec, confidence (both foreign and domestic) is shaken, and the Canadian

SKILL BUILDER
Thinking Like an Economist

Differentiating between Production and Productivity

In order to understand what is meant by productivity, or "maximizing the output from the resources used," let's look at two competing manufacturers of quality shoes: Acme FootWare Company and ComfortMax Shoe Company. Figure 2.10 outlines weekly production figures for both firms.

As we can see in Figure 2.10, the total weekly production of shoes is identical for both firms; therefore, production levels are equal. Now let's consider the production efficiency of each firm. ComfortMax workers are more efficient because they are able to produce 2600 pairs of shoes by employing a workforce of 36 shoemakers. On average, each worker produces 72 pairs of shoes per week. By comparison, each shoemaker at Acme Company produces an average of 52 pairs of shoes each week. If we were to calculate the productivity of capital goods (such as sewing machines), the position of the two competitors would be reversed. Acme Company is able to get more production out of each sewing machine.

Weekly Production Data (based on five 8-h work days)	Acme FootWare Co.	ComfortMax Shoe Co.
Number of shoemakers employed	50	36
Number of sewing machines used	14	20
Number of leather-stamping machines used	7	10
Number of pairs of shoes manufactured	2600	2600

Figure 2.10 Weekly production figures for competing shoe manufacturers.

QUESTIONS

1. In your own words, explain the difference between production and productivity. Why would shoemakers at ComfortMax Shoe be more productive than shoemakers at Acme FootWare?

2. Calculate the average productivity of stamping machines for both firms.

3. These two competitors use the same productive resources (shoemakers and machines), but in different proportions. Calculate the ratio of workers to sewing machines in each firm in order to identify the firm that uses a more *labour-intensive* production process.

4. Which firm uses the most *capital-intensive* production process? Explain your reasoning.

5. Suggest what ComfortMax Shoe might do to use its capital equipment more efficiently.

6. Often, productivity has negative connotations for labour. In order to increase productivity, workers may be forced to work longer hours or for lower wages. Some factories in developing countries are more productive because they are "sweatshops"— their employees must work long hours for little pay. How might labour productivity be increased by Acme FootWare? Suggest three changes that the firm might make to improve worker efficiency without resorting to sweatshop tactics.

economy suffers. Similarly, a political crisis in the White House usually upsets US stock markets. The economic rule of thumb seems to be that political uncertainty has an adverse effect on a country's economy.

Reduced Public Debt

From 1970 to 1996, government spending in Canada increased at a faster rate than the revenues being collected through taxes. This meant that Canada's **public debt** (and the interest payments to service it) grew larger year after year. Just as individuals cannot continue to incur large personal debt without suffering for it economically, governments cannot continue to add to the public debt without adversely affecting the economy. Interest rates inevitably climb higher, as do prices for consumer goods. As well, there is the moral issue involved in running up a debt that future generations of Canadians will someday be forced to pay. Today, Canadians have begun to demand more balanced budgets from their elected governments.

Economic Growth

Economic growth is defined as an increase in the economy's total production of goods and services. Theoretically, it represents an outward shift in the economy's production possibilities frontier. This growth can result from the discovery of new natural resources, an increase in the skilled labour force, technological innovations, and more efficient production processes. As economic production expands, Canadians will have more goods and services at their disposal, thereby increasing the average living standard. As a result of the periods of substantial growth that the Canadian economy has enjoyed since the Second World War, Canadian workers can now command three times as many goods and services as they could in 1945. In addition, as the economy expands, the public debt (if held in check) becomes less significant and easier to manage.

Increased Productivity and Efficiency

Maximizing productivity means that scarce productive resources are put to efficient or wise use in order to get as much as possible out of them. Economic efficiency is often the result of healthy competition. As Canadian firms struggle to be competitive in both local and global markets, they must make their production processes more efficient. The companies with the most efficient practices will maximize profits, prevail in the marketplace, and set new standards for others. Increased productivity will allow these firms to get more out of existing resources.

Equitable Distribution of Income

The equitable, or fair, distribution of income may be the most value-laden of all economic goals; it is certainly the most controversial. When it comes to dividing up total national output, there can be as many interpretations of what makes for a fair division of wealth as there are people. Is it fair that the annual income of a corporate executive in North America is many times higher than that of the average salaried worker in the same company? How much income should be taken away in taxes from someone who earns $10 million a year and redistributed among families whose gross annual income is less than $10 000?

In Canada, the issue of income equity is further complicated by regional differences. As Figure 2.11 (page 40) indicates, average employment incomes for residents of Ontario are statistically higher than for people who live in the Atlantic provinces, a situation that has existed for years. Through **transfer payments** (using revenues from one province to make additional social program payments in another), the federal government attempts to redistribute national wealth.

Socialists advocate a more equal distribution of wealth. Others argue that income equalization will only reward inefficiency and remove the personal incentive to work harder and take risks. As the debate continues, more and more Canadians are forced to use food banks, and this in a country that, between 1992 and 2000, topped the United Nations Human Development Index as the best country in the world in which to live. Canada is not alone in this regard, however; no country, not even the most affluent, has completely solved the problem of poverty.

Province	Unemployment Rate, 2000 (%)	Average Weekly Earnings, 2000
Alberta	5.0	$665.05
New Brunswick	10.0	$584.59
Newfoundland	16.7	$595.07
Nova Scotia	9.1	$559.94
Ontario	5.7	$697.92
Quebec	8.4	$612.91
Canada	6.8	$653.55

Source: Statistics Canada, *Canadian Economic Observer*, Catalogue 11-210-XPB, Vol. 15, 2001.

Figure 2.11 Average weekly earnings and unemployment rates for selected provinces, 2000.

Price Stability

Stable prices generally indicate that an economy is healthy. Fluctuating prices complicate planning and discourage investment. Both **inflation**, a general rise in prices, and **deflation**, a general fall in prices, are symptoms of an unhealthy economy. Periods of price inflation erode the dollar's purchasing power and raise the cost of living for Canadians on fixed incomes. Deflation, though rare in Canada, is commonly associated with periods of great economic crisis, such as the Great Depression of the 1930s. It should come as no surprise, then, that government policy attempts to promote and maintain stable price levels.

Full Employment

In an attempt to reach their optimal production targets, governments try to promote the full employment of the labour force. Unemployed workers result in total output levels well below the national production possibilities curve. An unemployed labour force also represents a waste of human potential and can cause economic hardships for unemployed workers and their families. Sustained periods of high unemployment usually indicate a country in poor economic health. During the Great Depression, Canadian unemployment rates approached 20 per cent, and during economic downturns in the 1980s and 1990s, rates were more than 10 per cent.

"Full employment" is usually defined as between 6 and 7 per cent of the labour force being out of work. As machines continue to replace people on production assembly lines, full employment becomes increasingly difficult to achieve. In the late 1990s, unemployment rates in Canada remained around 8 per cent, despite sustained economic growth.

Viable Balance of Payments and Stable Currency

In a global economy, the international flow of goods and currency in transactions such as importing, exporting, borrowing, and lending has become increasingly more important. The annual dollar value of trade per person is higher in Canada than in any other country in the world. The **balance of payments accounts** summarize all currency transactions between Canadian and foreign economies. If Canadians import significantly more than we export, there will be a negative effect on employment rates in Canada as well as the foreign exchange value of the Canadian dollar. It is important, therefore, that imports and exports roughly balance one another. Similarly, money flows in and out of the country need to

The economic goal of equitable distribution of income conflicts with the goal of reduced public debt. Recent governments have reduced spending on social assistance programs to help balance their operating deficits. Those most affected by these policy decisions are the Canadians least able to care for themselves economically. The rise in food bank use, described in the following article, is one indicator that the gap between wealthy and poor Canadians is widening. The market system does not appear capable of balancing disparities in income without government intervention.

Hunger a Fear for 3 Million Canadians

About 3 million Canadians—one in every ten—live in a household where getting enough food is a constant worry. Almost 2.5 million of them had to compromise what or how much they ate in 1998–99 because of a lack of money, Statistics Canada said in its first report on the problem yesterday. Another 500 000 worried they would not have enough to eat because they were short of cash.

Together, these families have "limited or uncertain access to enough food for a healthy active life," the National Population Health Survey of almost 50 000 Canadians found. About a fifth of them resorted to food banks, soup kitchens or other charitable agencies for emergency supplies. But the survey could be significantly underestimating the number going hungry in Canada because so many poor people don't have phones and would not have been included in the survey, said Sue Cox, executive director of the Daily Bread Food Bank in Toronto. . . .

Close to 1 million Canadians use a food bank at least once a month, according to the food bank, and in some areas they aren't allowed to use it that often. There are many others in need who just won't go to a food bank, Cox said. "For a lot of people, the point when they would go to a food bank would be after going days without food," she said. "It's an act of desperation."

Yesterday morning, Laura, 44, and her 20-year-old daughter Lisa spread their spare change on the kitchen table to see if there was enough to buy bread and milk for the family, which also includes two boys: Matt, 13, and Andrew, 15. They ended up driving in a friend's car to . . . the Daily Bread Food Bank. Since January, it's been a monthly trip. "You don't want to be here but what else can you do?" Laura asked. "It's non-stop; it just keeps getting worse and worse."

Laura—who is diabetic and depressed—was evicted from her $900 a month apartment after 21 years in December. She found a sympathetic landlord and a townhouse on a nearby street for nearly $1200 plus hydro. She can pay the rent through her $700 social assistance cheque and $500 in child support. But she's been neglecting her hydro, and that may be turned off today.

A $300 child tax benefit goes to pay for everything else, while Lisa, who had kidney cancer as a toddler and currently suffers from kidney infections, has moved back home. The foursome is somehow getting by, procuring food from Laura's mother and the food bank. This week it's pasta—no meat—for Laura and her daughter. The boys will get, as usual, the 12 burgers for $3.40 Laura bought at Food Basics . . . .

A total of 420 000 children lived in so-called "food insecure" households, making up the largest proportion of any age group. . . . The fact that 40 per cent of food bank users are kids can lead to "significant health problems," Cox said. . . . Hunger should not be a problem in Canada . . . but the number of food banks continues to grow "and their substantial presence suggests that food insecurity not only exists, but persists."

More than a third of people living in households earning less than $20 000 a year reported some sort of food insecurity in 1998–99 and 30 per cent said they had to compromise their diet. But getting enough food was a problem even for middle-income households, where 14 per cent of residents had problems getting a decent diet, the report said.

That could be because a layoff or job loss at some point in the year left the family vulnerable even though their income for the whole year was higher, it said. That shows "how vulnerable Canadians are in a crisis," said Alan Mirabelli, executive director of the Vanier Institute of the Family. "If you look at how much debt has gone up and savings have gone down, there's probably no margin to draw on in a crisis."

More than half of welfare families didn't have enough food to eat, as did many families relying on other government programs, the report says. A third of all families headed by single mothers were food insecure and 28 per cent had to compromise their diet.

The new president of the Canadian Medical Association says the level of poverty in the country is disgraceful. "About 1.5 million Canadian children go to school with their stomachs empty every morning," Dr. Henry Haddad declared . . . "That's awful and it's not acceptable. Physicians have to be concerned with those who are less well off."

Source: Excerpts from "Hunger a fear for 3 million Canadians" by Elaine Carey, *The Toronto Star*, 16 August 2001. Reprinted with permission—The Toronto Star Syndicate.

Food Bank Facts

- An estimated 3 million Canadians used food banks in 2000—more than twice the number of people who used the service in 1989.
- Close to 1 million Canadians use a food bank at least once a month.
- Some 40 per cent of those being helped are under 18 years of age.
- About 75 per cent of food bank users receive income from social assistance. Only 10 per cent of those using food banks reported earning money from working.
- Food banks operate in 488 Canadian communities, some serving more than one community through branch sites.
- In 2000, food banks in Quebec and Ontario served the largest number of people, but Newfoundland had the highest rate of food bank use as a percentage of provincial population—5.9 per cent.
- Food banks were never meant to be a permanent mechanism for dealing with poverty and hunger.
- Cuts in social assistance programs by government, as well as unemployment, are main causes of increased food bank use.

Source: Surveys conducted by the Canadian Association of Food Banks

---

QUESTIONS

1. The dictionary defines *paradox* as a seemingly absurd though actually well-founded statement. Identify an economic paradox exposed by this news story.

2. Identify the economic goals that are complementary to and those that are conflicting with the goal of reducing hunger and poverty in Canada.

3. Do you agree with the following statements? Present a reasoned economic argument to support your position on each statement.

   a) "If wealth were more evenly distributed, hunger would be eliminated in Canada."

   b) "The existence of food banks takes pressure off government to address poverty and hunger issues through public policy."

   c) "It is not the government's responsibility to help Canadians find well-paying jobs, affordable housing, and affordable daycare."

4. During an election, one political party promises to limit spending on social assistance programs in order to reduce the public debt. A second party advocates increased spending on social assistance programs to fight poverty and hunger. Which party would you support? Explain the economic reasoning involved in your decision.

be balanced in order to foster a stable Canadian dollar in foreign money markets.

Economic Freedom

Economic freedom refers to the freedom of choice available to workers, consumers, and investors in the economy. Canadian workers who want to improve their working conditions and income should be free to find and take another job. In a market economy, consumers should be free not only to purchase the goods and services of their choice but also, through their purchasing decisions, to determine what goods and services are actually produced. This is known as the principle of **consumer sovereignty**. In a market economy, people should be free to choose when and how to consume, save, or invest their money. Canadian public policy generally promotes economic freedom.

Environmental Stewardship

Economic activity must be carried out without significantly harming the natural environment. We have come to realize that the pollution of our air and water, the depletion of our natural resources, the destruction of the ozone layer that protects us from ultraviolet light, and the gradual warming of the global climate are all additional costs of the decisions we make about economic development. If we wish to be more responsible stewards of our planet and protect it for future generations, we have to adjust the way we carry out our economic activities. Even if this means higher prices for consumers and lower profits for producers, we must find a way to reduce the negative effects we are having on the natural environment.

Potential problems can arise if Canada enacts environmental laws that make its products more expensive and its trading partners do not follow suit. This situation can result in making Canadian goods less competitive in world markets. It also raises a moral issue: If Canada trades with a country that has low environmental standards, does this mean that our government is condoning the other country's policy? Clearly, on the normative side of economics, there is more to consider than just price!

Check Your Understanding

1. Explain why each of the following pairs represents either complementary or conflicting goals:
   a) full employment and price stability
   b) increased productivity and stable currency
   c) stable currency and a viable balance of payments
   d) economic growth and reduced public debt
   e) increased productivity and environmental stewardship
   f) reduced public debt and equitable distribution of income
   g) political stability and economic freedom

2. What effect do regional differences have on the equitable distribution of income in Canada?

3. Explain how both inflation and deflation are generally bad news for the Canadian economy.

4. Explain why the principle of consumer sovereignty is important in a market economy.

CHAPTER SUMMARY

- The productive resources (both tangible and intangible) used to manufacture valuable goods and services can be grouped into the general categories of land, labour, and capital.

- All economic systems must address three basic production questions: what to produce, how, and for whom. In traditional economies, families ensure their self-sufficiency by producing their own goods. They trade their surplus goods with other families through barter. In command economies, all productive resources are owned collectively by the state. A central planning authority answers all production questions and allocates resources in the best interests of the state. In market economies, the actions of individual buyers and sellers in the marketplace answer the three production questions. The basic elements are private property, free enterprise, profit maximization, and competition.

- The Canadian economy is often classified as a mixed market economy.

- Political systems range from democratic models, characterized by freely elected governments with set terms of office, to dictatorships, characterized by the exercising of absolute power by a single person or party.

- Democratic systems today range from free-enterprise capitalism as practised in the United States to more socialistic applications found in Scandinavian countries.

- Dictatorships range from fascism, in which the central authority allows private ownership and enterprise, to communism, in which all means of production and wealth are owned collectively by the state. China and the former Soviet Union are two large-scale examples of applied communism. At various times during the 20th century, fascist governments were in power in Italy, Germany, Spain, and Argentina.

- Every political system establishes economic goals. Some goals are complementary because reaching one goal makes another goal easier to achieve. Other goals are conflicting because reaching one goal makes another more difficult to achieve.

- Over the past four decades, the following ten goals have emerged as the economic goals of the Canadian economy: political stability, reduced public debt, economic growth, increased productivity, equitable distribution of income, price stability, full employment, stable currency and balanced foreign trade, economic freedom, and environmental stewardship. Each successive government re-examines these goals and sets its own priorities.

Key Terms

productive resources
factors of production
land
raw materials
labour
entrepreneurship
capital
real capital
money capital
productivity
tangible resources
intangible resources
environment for enterprise
value added
economic system
traditional economy
barter
command economy
market economy
private enterprise
mixed economy
crown land
hidden economy
democracy
dictatorship
communism
socialism
nationalization
capitalism
fascism
public debt
economic growth
transfer payments
inflation
deflation
balance of payments accounts
consumer sovereignty

Activities

Thinking/Inquiry

1. Research one group from the list of indigenous peoples that appears on page 31.

   a) Make a list of important details in the economic system of your chosen group to explain how production decisions are made.

   b) Explain what role the natural environment plays in the economic activities of this group.

   c) List the advantages and disadvantages of the traditional economy used by this group. Maintain objectivity and avoid cultural judgements in your considerations. Make sure to spend as much time reflecting on the advantages as you do on the disadvantages.

   d) As a class, discuss these advantages and disadvantages, and extend your list based on the discussion.

2. Survey working Canadians to identify specific examples of "hidden," or unreported, economic activity in Canada today. Explain why each of these activities developed.

3. Compare and assess the ability of capitalism, socialism, and communism to satisfy needs and achieve economic goals.

4. Research the problems Russia has encountered in the transition from a command economy to a market economy, and prepare a brief report.

5. Using information obtained through an Internet search, prepare a summary of two conflicting viewpoints (one positive and one negative) regarding the effectiveness of democratic socialism as practised in Sweden today. Assess the merits of the two viewpoints. If you wish, select a different Scandinavian country as your case study.

Communication

6. Create a comparison chart to show how different types of political economies make basic production decisions.

7. Complete a summary chart titled "Canada's Mixed Economy" to explain why Canada is considered to be a mixed economy. Use these headings: Market Characteristics, Command Characteristics, Traditional Characteristics.

8. Use the concept of the production possibilities frontier to explain why central planning in command economies traditionally favours the production of capital goods over consumer goods. Draw a graph to illustrate your answer.

Application

9. In a book published in 1958, the economist Kenneth E. Boulding said the four principal objectives of economic policy are:

   • stability,
   • growth,
   • justice, and
   • freedom.

   How do these categories relate to the list of ten goals we are considering over 40 years later? What similarities and differences do you detect?

10. Collect several (five to ten) articles from newspapers and magazines that reflect normative (or policy) decisions that the Canadian government has made. Using the list of ten goals we considered at the end of this chapter, identify the economic goals with which each article deals. A sample article has been included in this chapter starting on page 41.

    a) Arrange the ten economic goals in what you think is their order of importance, 1 being the most important and 10 being the least important. Justify your priorities by referring to the articles you have collected.

    b) In the list of goals, identify those that conflict with each other. For each conflicting goal, identify the opportunity cost involved.

11. Look at the cartoon in Figure 2.12 below and read the caption beneath it.

    a) What strategy is the artist using to draw attention to a serious economic problem?

    b) Why does an unstable dollar create problems for the Canadian economy?

    c) What are the most likely causes of a declining dollar?

    d) What is the best way to achieve the economic goal of stable currency? Justify your decision.

    e) How important a priority is currency stability? Explain your answer.

12. Explain the concept of environmental stewardship as it applies to three economic examples of responsible decision making.

Figure 2.12 This cartoon appeared in the summer of 1998, when the Canadian dollar was hitting an all-time low on world currency markets.

CHAPTER 3
THE EVOLUTION OF ECONOMIC THOUGHT

Thinking About the Free Market

Aside from Xenophon's work in ancient Greece (see page 6), economics as a scholarly discipline is about 225 years old. Economic thinking has evolved greatly and continues to evolve. To better understand contemporary thinking, we need to trace the evolution of economic thought, the subject of this chapter.

As they do with other disciplines, cartoonists sometimes poke fun at the vagaries of economic thinking. The 1999 cartoon shown here lampoons current thinking about free enterprise. Consider its message by answering the following questions.

QUESTIONS

1. In the cartoon, six individuals agree that the system of free-market capitalism works best when free from government interference. However, each person identifies one exception to the rule. What do the exceptions have in common?

2. What point is the cartoonist making about US thinking, at the end of the last millennium, regarding government involvement in the marketplace? Is the cartoon effective? Explain.

3. Survey 12 adults to compare Canadian thinking about government involvement in the marketplace.

Chapter Goals

By the end of this chapter, you will be able to

• understand the major ideas and theories of prominent economists,

• use inquiry research skills and economic concepts to identify historical trade-offs made in response to serious economic problems,

• use primary sources to study the views of individuals who greatly influenced economic thinking.

Changing the World

Ideas that are significant enough to change the world usually emerge during times of serious trouble. Generally speaking, the more radical the idea, the more troubled the society it originates from, if only because it is during times of extreme crisis that people are most willing to listen to radically different ideas. Instead of surveying the 225-year time span of the science of economics, we will focus on seven visionaries whose ideas have greatly advanced economic thought. For each featured economist, or "worldly philosopher," as the economic historian Robert L. Heilbroner calls them, our presentation will include

• a brief biography,
• an account of the historical context in which the ideas developed, and
• an explanation of some of the economist's major ideas and their political and economic impacts.

Adam Smith (1723–1790)

The Scottish philosopher Adam Smith is known today as both the "father of modern economics" and the "founder of capitalism." He was the first thinker to outline in detail the characteristics and benefits of a complete economic system—in his case, the free-market economy. He did this in a two-volume work called *An Inquiry into the Nature and Causes of the Wealth of Nations*. Published in 1776, the same year that the American colonies declared their independence from Great Britain, this work is usually referred to as *The Wealth of Nations* and is now recognized as the foundation of modern economic theory.

Biography

Adam Smith was born into a middle-class family in a fishing village near Edinburgh, Scotland. He entered the University of Glasgow at 14 and, at 17, won a scholarship to Oxford University.

At the age of 27, Smith was offered a position as professor of logic at the University of Glasgow. Shortly afterwards, he earned the more prestigious position of professor of moral philosophy; in 1758, he became dean of the university. With his eccentric personality, the deep-thinking but absent-minded professor became Glasgow's most illustrious citizen.

In 1759, Smith's first book, *The Theory of Moral Sentiments*, made him famous throughout Great Britain. He accepted a lucrative offer in 1764 to become the private tutor of a young English aristocrat. This new position gave him the opportunity to live in France for two years. In Switzerland, he met the French philosopher Voltaire, and back in Paris he became acquainted with a new school of economic thought whose leaders were known as the **physiocrats**.

The physiocrats reasoned that if unchangeable natural laws governed the physical world then natural laws also governed human behaviour and, therefore, the social, economic, and political worlds. They argued that if all human behaviour was controlled by natural laws then all the artificial laws created by humans were unnecessary and ineffective. Since people have a natural tendency to serve their own best interests and to acquire wealth, the pursuit of self-interest would ultimately benefit all individuals if they were left alone to create more wealth. This doctrine of non-interference became known by the French term **laissez-faire**, which means literally "leave to do," or leave things alone so that matters can work out naturally.

While travelling as a tutor, Smith began his most important project, *The Wealth of Nations*, which took him 12 years to complete and have published. Smith was greatly influenced by the American politician and writer Benjamin Franklin, who provided much information about the economic situation in the American colonies. In 1778, Smith was appointed commissioner of customs for Edinburgh, where he lived for the rest of his life.

The Times

Adam Smith was born into a world where **mercantilism** was the prevailing economic system. This system is based on the state's control of economic production and trade, with the goal of exporting as many goods as possible for sale abroad while, at the same time, importing as few foreign goods as possible. When this system is successful, it means that gold and silver from abroad (the money paid for the exported goods) are flowing into the country while very little money is flowing out of it. At the time, gold and silver reserves were thought to constitute the real wealth of any nation.

In order to make mercantilism work, a country's government had to adopt a **protectionist** policy to safeguard its gold and silver reserves by limiting the entry of foreign goods. In order to accomplish this, the authorities imposed stiff taxes, or **tariffs**, on imported goods to make them more expensive than the goods produced in the country. Problems arise, however, as more and more nations adopt this strategy. Trade between nations drops off, and prices of all but the most common domestic products go up. Mercantilism, a product of the Middle Ages, did not sit well with the established merchant class, the growing industrialist class, and the heavily burdened working class. All these classes were feeling increasingly handcuffed by government regulations and taxes.

Laissez-faire philosophy provided a strong argument for replacing state control of the economy with a reliance on natural laws to regulate economic activity. This idea contributed to the political ferment in France that led, in turn, to the French Revolution. Smith learned from Benjamin Franklin that the growing mood of rebellion in the American colonies was a direct reaction to interference by the British government, through various taxes and regulations, in the economic life of the colonists. This interference led to the Declaration of Independence in 1776 and the American Revolution.

Many of Smith's ideas developed in response to the rapid economic changes he observed in Great Britain. The Enclosure Movement broke up the large plots of land that towns had held in common since the Middle Ages and redistributed them in small plots to individual landholders. Owners began to run these farms for profit rather than subsistence. Inventions such as the spinning jenny, the power loom, and the

steam engine made it possible for factory owners to increase both the scale of their operations and the level of their profits. In the new factories that sprang up, workers performed increasingly more specialized tasks and used a variety of machines. This period of technological innovation and new means of production, which started during Adam Smith's lifetime, came to be known as the **Industrial Revolution**.

Ideas That Advanced Economic Thought

Self-interest

Adam Smith believed that human beings are motivated primarily by what he called **self-interest**, or the desire each of us has to better our condition in life. This means that the profit motive provides the major stimulus for economic growth and prosperity. When society requires greater production to satisfy its wants, it does not appeal to the generosity of producers, but rather to the desire of producers to increase their own profits.

The trick is to ensure that this desire for greater profits does not completely overwhelm a producer's sense of obligation to the rest of society. For this reason, in a free market, there is competition between many producers, none of whom can raise their prices too high without losing customers. In this way, self-interest and competition work together to advance the common good. Government regulation is not necessary to control the economy because the forces of market competition will serve, in Smith's famous phrase, as an **invisible hand**, or a natural control. To see how this works, let's consider a hypothetical situation.

Suppose an ambitious farmer decides to charge three times the going rate for a bushel of potatoes. Buyers will naturally do business with one of the many other farmers who sell their potatoes at market prices. The first farmer will have to reduce the price of his potatoes or face the economic consequence of lost sales. Even if all Ontario potato farmers conspire to sell their potatoes for exorbitant prices, entrepreneurs will bring potatoes into Ontario from other markets, such as Prince Edward Island, to realize a profit. At the same time, when local farmers realize that growing potatoes has become more profitable, they will replace some of their other crops with potatoes. This increased supply of potatoes will naturally force the price of potatoes back down again. Smith believed that these natural "laws of the market" are at work in all openly competitive marketplaces.

Ongoing progress and prosperity

After reflecting on the substantial increases in wealth that had occurred in Britain during the previous 100 years, Smith outlined three reasons for the country's continued economic growth and increasing prosperity: the division of labour, the law of accumulation, and the law of population.

For Smith, the **division of labour**, or the specialization of workers in a complex and mechanized production process, led to increases in levels of production. These production increases provided greater profits for investors, more consumer goods for workers, and ultimately greater economic efficiency for society.

The **law of accumulation** worked naturally to fuel further rounds of growth and prosperity. The accumulated profits that industrialists invested in additional capital goods, such as

factories and machinery, permitted increases in total production and efficiency for the economy as a whole. These increases in turn led eventually to greater profits for investor industrialists. The increased profits could then be reinvested in additional capital goods, providing the stimulus for further rounds of economic growth.

According to Smith, the **law of population** also contributed to the maintenance of this steady rate of growth and prosperity. The accumulation of capital naturally increases the demand for labour to operate the additional machinery that the industrialists purchase. In order to attract more workers, competing industrialists must offer higher wages. Wage increases lead to improved living conditions for the workers, which in turn reduce mortality rates. This leads to a natural increase in the population and, therefore, in the labour force. Increases in the labour force mean that workers are competing with one another to find jobs, which tends naturally to keep wages from increasing. Thus, the industrialists continue to make healthy profits.

As a result of the emphasis he placed on the natural laws that regulated the free-market system, Smith became known over time as the "patron saint of laissez-faire capitalism."

Check Your Understanding

1. Do you agree with Adam Smith that self-interest is the main motivator behind our economic actions? Explain.

2. Explain in your own words Adam Smith's concept of the "invisible hand."

3. How might self-interest be controlled in a command economy? in a traditional economy?

4. Using the law of accumulation and the law of population, explain how the division of labour might contribute to the concentration of wealth in the hands of a few.

Thomas Robert Malthus (1766–1834)

Recognized historically as the first professional economist, Thomas Robert Malthus was a mild-mannered clergyman whose shyness was compounded by a severe speech impediment. He challenged Adam Smith's view of a world

governed by natural laws that provided ever-increasing prosperity, and he predicted inevitable poverty and famine for the masses. Malthus first presented his pessimistic views in a book he published in 1798 called *An Essay on the Principle of Population As It Affects the Future Improvement of Society*. He revised and expanded the text five times between 1803 and 1826. Although he softened his views slightly over the years, his pessimistic conclusions did not change. After reading Malthus, the English writer Thomas Carlyle referred to economics as "the dismal science."

Biography

Malthus was born into an English upper-middle-class family in 1766. He was admitted to Jesus College at Cambridge University in 1784, where he studied a wide range of subjects and took prizes in Latin and Greek before earning a Master of Arts degree in 1791. In response to a religious vocation, Malthus took holy orders in the Anglican Church in 1797 and pursued the quiet life of an English country curate.

He was named professor of history and political economy at the East India Company's college at Haileybury, Hertfordshire, in 1805. This was the first time that the term *political economy* was used to designate an academic office, so Malthus can rightly be identified as the first professional economist.

The Times

Malthus's thoughts and writings were greatly influenced by the existing economic conditions in Britain. The nation was in the midst of the Industrial Revolution, a period when great numbers of workers left their farms and crowded into cities, where they hoped to find jobs in factories. They lived in congested and unsanitary quarters, struggling to survive on minimal wages. At the same time, a prolonged, expensive, and bloody war against Napoleon Bonaparte's France added to the misery of the British working class. Poor crop yields and a simultaneous population boom further aggravated the situation. It began to look as if Britain's once-rich farmlands could no longer feed the country's people.

Ideas That Advanced Economic Thought

Population and food production
Malthus based his ideas about population and food production on what he thought were two self-evident premises. The first is that food is necessary to sustain human life. The second premise is that human sexual instinct is constant. Starting with these two premises, Malthus built an argument that the population, if left unchecked, would double every 25 years (about one generation). This doubling effect meant that the population grew in what statisticians call a **geometrical progression**.

Food production, on the other hand, can only grow in an **arithmetical progression**. As more land is required for food production, less-fertile tracts of land will be employed out of necessity, and these less-fertile lands will yield fewer crops. At the same time, as more and more workers cultivate the lands more intensively, the productivity of the added workers also declines. Malthus used the economic principle that we examined in Chapter 1, the law of diminishing returns, to explain why growth in food production would be limited to arithmetical increases from one generation to the next. That is, each generation's food production increases by an amount equal to the original quantity. Figure 3.1 (page 52) illustrates what became known as the "Malthusian dilemma."

Malthus had a very pessimistic outlook. He thought that if wages went up, the workers' improved standard of living would reduce infant mortality rates, which would have the effect of increasing the population at a faster rate than the means of subsistence. Where Adam Smith saw a world of steadily increasing prosperity, Malthus believed that wages and the standard of living should hover around the subsistence level in order to keep the population from growing out of control.

Although Malthus admitted that two types of population control existed, he did not think they would prove strong enough to check the geometric progression of the world's population. **Positive checks**, which increase the death rate, include war, famine, disease, and epidemics. **Preventive checks**, which reduce the birth rate, include moral restraints such as late marriage and sexual abstinence.

In the end, Malthus failed to predict two developments that had major impacts on his theories of population. In the 20th century, a

The Malthusian Dilemma										
Generation	1	2	3	4	5	6	7	8	9	10
Year	1	25	50	75	100	125	150	175	200	225
Population	1	2	4	8	16	32	64	128	256	512
Food	1	2	3	4	5	6	7	8	9	10

Note: Each 25-year period refers to one generation. Each generation, the population doubles itself. Every 25 years, food production increases by an amount equal to the original quantity produced during the first year. To keep this table simple, constant units of population and food production are used instead of actual figures. For example, one unit of population might represent 1 million people, and one unit of food might represent enough wheat to sustain one unit of population from one harvest to the next.

Figure 3.1 In the "Malthusian dilemma," what begins as a balanced economic system (in which one unit of food is available for each unit of population) naturally transforms itself, if left unchecked, into an economically unbalanced situation. After ten generations, or 225 years, 512 population units must subsist on only ten units of food. Unless population growth is controlled, famine awaits the entire human race!

series of technological breakthroughs in the field of agriculture, known collectively as the Green Revolution, increased food production rates beyond anything Malthus might have imagined. Also, continued urbanization has had a negative effect on the birth rate. Whereas additional children in farm families have always been seen as assets to help with the work, this has never been the case in urban families. Average family size in urban industrial nations continues to decline, to the point where several nations in the world today have reached zero population growth. Does this mean Malthus was wrong? Two hundred years after the publication of his ground-shaking text, the debate continues.

Check Your
Understanding

1. Explain the Malthusian dilemma in your own words.

2. How did the law of diminishing returns contribute to Malthus's conclusion that,

eventually, population will outgrow global food production?

3. Explain two global developments that have acted against the Malthusian dilemma.

David Ricardo (1772–1823)

Adam Smith's notion of humankind living in a harmonious world governed by natural laws was most effectively assailed by David Ricardo, the articulate son of a Dutch merchant banker who had immigrated to Britain and made a fortune on the London stock exchange.

Biography

David Ricardo was born into a prosperous family in London in 1772. At 14, he went to work in his father's investment business, but by the time he turned 22, he had established his own business with a capital base of £800. He retired 20 years later with over £1 million.

Recognizing that most investors tend to overreact and exaggerate the importance of events, Ricardo was able to use his knowledge of different kinds of securities to make great profits. For example, in the panic following Napoleon's return to power in France—and with the increased likelihood of war—the market for British government securities declined sharply. Ricardo, however, invested heavily in government securities prior to the Battle of Waterloo. When the Duke of Wellington defeated Napoleon's armies at Waterloo, Ricardo's profits were significant.

When Ricardo retired to the country at the age of 42, he devoted his attention to the new science of political economy. His most famous book, *The Principles of Political Economy and Taxation*, exposed the bitter class conflicts at the heart of any society structured around free-enterprise capitalism. Published in 1817, it challenged the power of the aristocratic landlord class by questioning the contributions of this class to society. The book was hailed by the rising industrialist class and became an influential document of political reform.

Elected to the House of Commons in 1819, Ricardo argued on behalf of free trade and carefully outlined the complex laws of land rent that allowed the idle landlord class to exploit land, labour, and capital. In 1823, he died suddenly at the age of 51, before he could witness first-hand the full impact of his economic ideas.

The Times

Ricardo lived during a period of great social conflict and political unrest in Britain. The British population grew rapidly, putting a strain on food supplies. The Napoleonic Wars and successive years of poor crops further drained food reserves.

Not surprisingly, where Adam Smith saw society as a family making great progress together, Ricardo saw clear divisions into conflicting groups. He identified the three main groups in British society as the working class, who lived on modest wages; the industrialist class, who made healthy profits by operating the factories they owned; and the aristocratic landlord class, who received substantial rent from the land titles they held. One group, Ricardo argued, could prosper only at the expense of the others.

Ricardo reasoned that, given their hold on the land, landlords were best positioned to compete effectively against the other classes. The working class would always struggle to live at or near subsistence levels. The rising industrialists had new-found riches but lacked sufficient representation in Parliament. Therefore, the powerful and entrenched landed aristocracy would always prevail.

To illustrate his case, Ricardo used the example of the landlord-dominated Parliament forcing through legislation known as the **Corn Laws**. These measures imposed stiff taxes on grains imported from other countries. Since there was a shortage of grain in England at the time, this had the effect of driving up the price of grain to levels usually seen only in times of famine. By 1813, a bushel of wheat sold for twice the average worker's weekly wage. This forced the industrialists to pay higher wages (to ensure that their workers would survive), which, in turn, cut into their profits. High grain prices, however, guaranteed the payment of high rents to the landlords. When the industrialists finally succeeded in repealing the Corn Laws in the 1840s, they effectively broke the power of the landed aristocracy and slowly began replacing them as the dominant class in British society.

Ideas That Advanced Economic Thought

The iron law of wages

Ricardo reasoned that, because of the working class's unchecked rate of reproduction, labour's natural wages would always remain at the subsistence level. Higher wages would increase the population by ensuring lower rates of infant mortality but would not raise living standards because the higher wages would have to be distributed among larger families.

Greedy industrialists seized on this economic principle to justify keeping their workers' wages at the lowest level possible, in some cases claiming that they were thereby performing a

PRIMARY SOURCE

On Wages

Labour, like all other things which are purchased and sold, and which may be increased or diminished in quantity, has its natural and its market price. The natural price of labour is that price which is necessary to enable the labourers, one with another, to subsist and to perpetuate their race, without either increase or diminution.

The power of the labourer to support himself, and the family which may be necessary to keep up the number of labourers, does not depend on the quantity of money which he may receive for wages, but on the quality of food, necessaries, and conveniences that become essential to him from habit which that money will purchase. The natural price of labour, therefore, depends on the price of the food, necessaries, and conveniences required for the support of the labourer and his family. With a rise in the price of food and necessaries, the natural price of labour will rise; with the fall in their price, the natural price of labour will fall.

The market price of labour is the price which is really paid for it, from the natural operation of the proportion of the supply to the demand; labour is dear when it is scarce and cheap when it is plentiful. However much the market price of labour may deviate from its natural price, it has, like commodities, a tendency to conform to it.

It is when the market price of labour exceeds its natural price that the condition of the labourer is flourishing and happy, that he has it in his power to command a greater proportion of the necessaries and enjoyments of life, and therefore to rear a healthy and numerous family. When, however, by the encouragement which high wages give to the increase of population, the number of labourers is increased, wages again fall to their natural price, and indeed from a reaction sometimes fall below it.

When the market price of labour is below its natural price, the condition of the labourers is most wretched: then poverty deprives them of those comforts which custom renders absolute necessaries. It is only after their privations have reduced their number, or the demand for labour has increased, that the market price of labour will rise to its natural price, and that the labourer will have the moderate comforts which the natural rate of wages will afford.

David Ricardo

Notwithstanding the tendency of wages to conform to their natural rate, their market rate may, in an improving society, for an indefinite period, be constantly above it; for no sooner may the impulse which an increased capital gives to a new demand for labour be obeyed, than another increase of capital may produce the same effect; and thus, if the increase of capital be gradual and constant, the demand for labour may give a continued stimulus to an increase of people.

Source: David Ricardo, *The Principles of Political Economy and Taxation*, in Howard D. and Natalie J. Marshall, *The History of Economic Thought: A Book of Readings* (New York: Putnam, 1968), 116–117.

QUESTIONS

1. What is the "natural price" of labour? Why might wages depart from this natural price?

2. According to Ricardo, what effects will the demand for labour have on the growth or decline of the population?

3. In what way can industrial capitalists rationalize lower wages for their workers as performing a service to society?

public service. Low wages became the figurative leg irons that shackled the working class to their slums. This was never Ricardo's intent. He always believed that wages should be determined by free-market conditions.

The theory of the comparative advantage of trade

It is a commonly accepted principle that when one community can produce grain more efficiently than another, while the other community can produce wool more efficiently, trade will be of obvious or **absolute advantage** to both communities. Ricardo was the first person able to recognize and explain that even when one community can produce both wheat and wool efficiently, there remains a **comparative advantage** to be shared when both communities trade the products they can each produce most efficiently. (We'll explore both concepts in Chapter 17.)

As a result of his belief in comparative advantage, Ricardo became a strong advocate of free trade at a time when Britain imposed high tariffs on many imports precisely to discourage trade with other countries. While these taxes often protected the earnings of the rich landlords, they hurt the workers and the industrialists. Once again, argued Ricardo, the interests of the landlords ran counter to the interests of the rest of the economy. From Ricardo's perspective, the landlord class grew very rich while others performed all the work and assumed all the risks. Ricardo quickly became the parliamentary champion of the previously unrepresented industrial capitalist.

Check Your
Understanding

1. According to Ricardo, what are the main three classes in any free-enterprise society? How does self-interest result in bitter class conflicts?

2. According to Ricardo, why did the British Parliament pass the Corn Laws during a time of food shortages?

3. Why was Ricardo an advocate of freer trade?

Karl Marx (1818–1883)

By arguing that all of human history is governed by economic laws that perpetuate the conflicts between the different social classes, Karl Marx made clear the importance of economic theory. According to Marx, economics must come before politics, science, art, and religion in importance because it determines the course of human history.

In collaboration with his friend, the wealthy capitalist Friedrich Engels, Marx founded an international workers' movement intended to overthrow the corrupt ruling class of industrial capitalists and aristocratic landlords. These people Marx called the **bourgeoisie**. In 1848, Marx and Engels published the *Communist Manifesto*, in which they incited all exploited workers (whom they called the **proletariat**) to rise up against their oppressors: "Let the ruling classes tremble at a Communistic revolution. The proletariat have nothing to lose but their chains. They have a world to win. Workers of all countries unite!" And so was born the international revolutionary socialist movement of communism. Several rebellions followed in European countries, but none of them succeeded until the Russian Revolution in 1917.

For his radical views, Marx has come to be known as either "the prophet of the proletariat" or "the demonic philosopher." Either way, it is undeniable that he left an indelible mark on the science of economics and on the course of human history.

Biography

Karl Marx was born in the German Rhineland in 1818. An excellent scholar, he attended Bonn University, where he studied philosophy.

Marx became the editor of a small, middle-class liberal newspaper. One of the first editorials to get Marx into trouble with the government denounced a new law that prevented peasants from exercising their traditional right to gather dead wood in the forest. The authorities first censored and then closed down the newspaper. Marx became more and more outspoken as, one by one, the papers he edited were suppressed by the state.

As his views became more radical and even revolutionary, Marx had to flee Germany. He moved first to Paris and then to Brussels, but his troubles with the state followed him until he moved to London in 1849. Marx and his family lived in London in relative poverty for the rest of his life.

His most comprehensive work, *Capital* (*Das Kapital* in the original German text), was published in three volumes in 1867, 1885, and 1894. In this cold and complex critique of economics, Marx explained why capitalism would ultimately destroy itself. The book was completed by Engels after Marx died in 1883.

The Times

Living in the second half of the 19th century, Marx was able to witness first-hand the ill effects of the Industrial Revolution on the working class. By the time of Marx's death, England had been transformed from an agricultural and artisan-based economy to one in which the dominant mode of production was the steam-powered factory.

Workers lived in the slums of crowded cities and worked 18-hour days in unsafe and unclean factories. Since there were no laws against child labour, working-class children had to endure these same hardships. After working long hours, children rarely had the time to acquire the education that might lift them out of such deplorable circumstances.

To Marx, the capitalist system was immoral and the people who exploited it unspeakably evil. He saw a world in which all wealth was achieved on the backs of the workers. Yet, the working class received few of the benefits of their labour. Marx believed capitalism, as an

Figure 3.2 The Matchmakers Procession. This illustration shows an 1871 demonstration in London against factory working conditions. The protest led to reforms but also to charges of police brutality.

On the Program of Revolutionary Socialism

Karl Marx

We have already seen the first step in the working class revolution is the raising of the proletariat to the position of ruling class, the victory of Democracy.

The proletariat will use its political power to wrest by degree all capital from the bourgeoisie, to centralise all instruments of production in the hands of the State, i.e., of the proletariat organised as the ruling class, and to increase as rapidly as possible the total mass of productive forces.

This, naturally, cannot be accomplished at first except by despotic inroads on the rights of property and on the bourgeois conditions of production: by measures, therefore, which appear economically insufficient and untenable, but which in the course of the movement outstrip themselves, and are indispensable as means of revolutionizing the whole mode of production.

These measures will naturally be different, in different countries.

Nevertheless, for the most advanced countries, the following will be pretty generally applicable:

1. Abolition of property in land and confiscation of ground rents to the State.

2. A heavily progressive income tax [that is, taking an increasing percentage in taxes as income increases].

3. Abolition of inheritance.

4. Confiscation of the property of emigrants and rebels.

5. Centralization of credit in the hands of the State, by means of a national bank with State capital and an exclusive monopoly.

6. Centralization of the means of transport in the hands of the State.

7. Extension of national factories and instruments of production, cultivation and improvement of waste lands in accordance with a general social plan.

8. Obligation of all to labour; organization of industrial armies, especially for agriculture.

9. Combination of agricultural and industrial labour, in order to remove the distinction between town and country.

10. Free public education for all children. Abolition of factory labour for children in its present form. Combination of education with material production, etc.

In the place of the old bourgeois society, with its classes and class antagonisms, an association appears in which the free development of each is the condition for the free development of all.

Source: Karl Marx and Friedrich Engels, *The Communist Manifesto*, in Raymond Postgate, *Revolution from 1789–1906* (New York: Harper Torch Books, 1962), 154–155.

QUESTIONS

1. What key characteristics of a command economy can you see in the Marxist program?

2. With which parts of Marx's program do you agree? With which parts do you disagree? Explain why.

3. Critics of Marx argue that the transition to communism inevitably sets the stage for dictatorship. They say that Marx's claim that "despotic inroads" are necessary only in the early stages is politically naive. Once a dictatorship is firmly in place, is a return to democracy really possible? Explain your own views and cite historical examples to illustrate your argument.

economic system, was so morally bankrupt that it would one day destroy itself.

Ideas That Changed Economic Thought

The economic interpretation of history

Marx thought that the laws of economics determine the course of human history. He believed history was a continuing series of class struggles between exploiters and the exploited: free citizens against slaves, patricians against plebeians, lords against serfs, guildmasters against journeymen, and industrial capitalists against workers. Whenever conditions become unbearable, the oppressed rise up in open rebellion against their oppressors. The capitalist system, based on exploitation and self-gratification, has sown the seeds of its own destruction. Capitalist exploitation will continually worsen the living standards of workers. Immersed in misery, workers will eventually unite to overthrow the corrupt ruling class.

The international Communist revolution (revolutionary socialism)

According to Marx, this revolution would begin in the most industrialized countries of Western Europe (where capitalism was strongest and exploited the workers most severely) and then would spread throughout the world. The violent overthrow of capitalism would lead to international socialism based on the common ownership of land and capital. Socialism, once fully evolved, would be transformed into its ideal state of communism: a worker-governed society based on the guiding principle "from each according to ability, and to each according to need."

The labour theory of value

For Marx, the value of any item is the value of all labour used in its production (**labour value**). This includes the direct labour supplied by workers in the manufacturing process as well as the amount of indirect labour, that is, the labour embodied in the machinery and buildings used in the manufacturing process. In a capitalist system, workers receive only a portion of what their labour is worth. The difference, which Marx called **surplus value**, is stolen from the worker in the form of profit for the capitalist.

To better understand this concept, let's use a simple example. Assume that the production of a wool sweater requires $40 worth of labour, $5 worth of materials, and $5 worth of wear and tear on machinery (depreciation). If the industrial capitalist can sell the sweater for $80, then a surplus value of $30 is created in the form of profit for the capitalist. This surplus value arises from the market's determination that the real value of each sweater is $80. Since the value of the indirect labour is $10, the value of the direct labour must be $70. Since workers are only paid $40 for knitting the sweater, $30 represents the amount of worker *exploitation* taking place.

Worker employment in a capitalist system is based on the premise that the worker will always produce more for the employer than the employer will have to pay in the form of wages. Workers are forced to sell their labour to capitalists for less than it is truly worth because there is always what Marx identified as a "reserve army of the unemployed." Capitalists always have the option of hiring desperate unemployed workers at lower wages, which ensures that wages will never rise above the subsistence level.

Check Your Understanding

1. What did Marx predict for the future of capitalism? Outline briefly how he reached this conclusion.

2. Do you agree with Marx that all capitalists exploit workers? Explain your position.

3. Explain the relationship between surplus value and exploitation.

John Maynard Keynes (1883-1946)

In 1936, John Maynard Keynes published *The General Theory of Employment, Interest, and Money*. In it, he defended the "revolutionary" ideas already being applied by governments in Britain, Canada, and the US to deal with the era of massive unemployment known as the Great Depression. He also provided a blueprint that explained how government intervention could save a country from widespread unemployment and the economic stagnation that accompanied it. Keynes's book helped to rescue the capitalist system from self-destruction and the spectre of international communism. The approach we have come to call "Keynesian economics" analyzes relationships among demand, production, and unemployment, and focuses on government's role in sustaining economic activity (also see page 228).

Biography

John Maynard Keynes was born in Cambridge, England, in the same year that Karl Marx died. In addition to teaching economics at Cambridge University, Keynes served as an economic adviser to the British treasury during both World Wars and attended post-war international peace conferences as a representative of the British government. He was also appointed a director of the Bank of England, Britain's central bank. The tireless Keynes served as editor of a major economics journal, chair of an insurance company, and manager of an extremely successful investment trust. Inspired by his mother, Keynes was an early supporter of the movement that eventually won British women the right to vote.

In 1944, Keynes was the chief British representative at the Bretton Woods Conference, which established the International Monetary Fund and the World Bank. His last major public service was the brilliant negotiation in 1945 of a multi-billion-dollar post-war reconstruction loan from the United States to Great Britain.

The Times

Keynes's career spanned the two World Wars and the period of economic upheaval between them known as the Great Depression. At the end of the First World War, the Allies forced Germany to pay more in reparations than its economy could bear. The result was a severe and long-term depression in Germany that Nazi dictator Adolf Hitler exploited to further his own political agenda.

The Great Depression of the 1930s was a difficult time in Europe and North America. At the beginning of the Depression, most capitalist governments believed that skyrocketing unemployment rates were only temporary; they thought economic conditions would improve as their market economies reverted to a more balanced state. They called for unemployed workers to tighten their belts, make do with less, be patient, and ride out this period of badly needed correction. Making no attempts to initiate economic improvements, these governments were clearly part of the problem rather than the solution. In fact, government attempts to cut spending and pay back war debts contributed to a decline in the amount of money in circulation.

Ideas That Advanced Economic Thought

War and sustainable peace

As a representative at the peace conference that followed the First World War, Keynes strongly criticized the Treaty of Versailles, which he predicted would ruin the German economy by forcing the country to pay the victorious Allies more than it could afford. He abruptly resigned from the British government.

While serving as a key economic adviser to the British government during the Second World War, Keynes recommended a daring plan that used "deferred savings" as the principal means of financing the war effort. A portion of every worker's pay would be automatically invested in government war bonds that could not be cashed until after the war. Keynes hypothesized that, during the war, consumer spending would interfere with the war effort; after the war, consumer buying power would help to stimulate investment, permit increased production of consumer goods, and maintain employment levels.

The 1945 peace treaty and post-war reconstruction plan were greatly influenced by

Keynes, who argued that, in order to secure a lasting peace, the defeated enemy should be helped, not punished. As former enemies became business associates, economic co-operation replaced military intervention in Western Europe. With developments such as the European Union, history appears to have proven Keynes correct.

Combating the Great Depression

In *The General Theory*, Keynes advanced an idea considered unconventional at the time: that governments bore a large part of the responsibility for the high unemployment rates (approaching 20 per cent) ushered in by the Great Depression. He believed these rates could be lowered most effectively by government intervention, especially by sponsoring public works projects that would give jobs to idle workers. By taking control of interest rates and increasing public spending, a government could stimulate consumer spending, raise the demand for consumer goods, and bring more people back into the workforce. As these previously unemployed workers spent their wages, the money would be re-spent by those receiving it. In this way, increased employment would trigger additional rounds of consumption, investment, and employment increases, as

the economy continued to put previously idle resources to work. The resulting growth in the economy would have the effect of correcting the problem of high unemployment rates.

Keynes claimed that, since consumers are limited in their spending by the size of their incomes, they are not the source of depressions or any other cyclical business shifts. Business investors and governments are the primary forces behind business cycles. To Keynes, the Great Depression (a major downward cycle) was ultimately a problem of too little investment. If investors were given a reason to invest and favourable interest rates, the economy would necessarily recover, but government intervention was required before this could happen.

Study Figure 3.3 to determine whether Canadian data from the time of the Great Depression support Keynes's theory.

Today, critics of the Keynesian school of economic thought point to his *General Theory* as the leading cause of the high inflation rates and massive public debts that Western nations accumulated over the second half of the 20th century. On the other hand, it is undeniable that national unemployment rates have never yet returned to the levels witnessed during the 1930s.

Year	Gross Investment Spending (millions)	Government Spending (millions)	Estimated Government Revenue from Taxes (millions)
1929	$1948	$1027	$1085
1930	$1608	$1178	
1931	$1143	$1160	
1932	$609	$1041	
1933	$462	$842	$548

Note: All funds are in constant 1949 Canadian dollars. This means that the values have been standardized to 1949 levels as a point of reference. In addition, all data have been rounded to the nearest whole million.

Source: Neil Swan and Henry Kaluza, *Economics: A Canadian Perspective* (Toronto: McGraw-Hill Ryerson, 1973), 74.

Figure 3.3 Investment, government spending, and taxation in Canada during the first five years of the Great Depression.

PRIMARY SOURCE
On Reducing Unemployment

John Maynard Keynes

If the Treasury [government] were to fill old bottles with banknotes [money], bury them at suitable depths in disused coalmines which are then filled up to the surface with town rubbish, and leave it to private enterprise on well-tried principles of laissez-faire to dig the notes up again (the right to do so being obtained, of course, by tendering for leases of the note-bearing territory), there need be no more unemployment and, with the help of the repercussions, the real income of the community, and its capital wealth also, would probably become a good deal greater than it actually is. It would, indeed, be more sensible to build houses and the like; but if there are political and practical difficulties in the way of this, the above would be better than nothing. . . .

Source: John Maynard Keynes, *The General Theory of Employment, Interest, and Money* (New York: Harcourt, Brace and Company, 1964), 129–131.

QUESTIONS

1. What is the most important thing that Keynes is pointing out to political leaders in this excerpt?

2. Keynes proposes the buried treasure project as a last resort. What projects could governments finance that would be more beneficial? Give three specific examples.

3. Explain why government financing is necessary in the example described by Keynes.

Check Your
Understanding

1. Explain how Keynes's "deferred savings" plan would work both during and after the war.

2. According to Figure 3.3, which economic change between 1929 and 1933 most contributed to the Great Depression in Canada?

3. Draw a flow chart to explain how governments can effectively combat high unemployment rates according to Keynes.

John Kenneth Galbraith (born 1908)

The prolific writer and gifted economist John Kenneth Galbraith has been called one of Canada's most notable exports to the United States. When Galbraith published his book *The Affluent Society* in 1958, he coined a term (affluent society) that summed up the remarkable increase in wealth that the United States and Canada had been enjoying since the end of the Second World War. At the same time, the book set out a devastating criticism of government economic policies that did not pay sufficient attention to providing and maintaining public services.

Biography

John Kenneth Galbraith was born in Iona Station, Ontario. After graduating in agricultural economics from the University of Toronto in 1931, he earned a doctorate at the University of California at Berkeley in 1934. He taught economics at Harvard and Princeton Universities until the United States entered the Second World War. During the war, Galbraith worked in the federal Office of Price Administration. After the war, he was appointed director of the US Strategic Bombing Survey, which studied the effects of air raids on Japan and Germany.

Galbraith served as editor of *Fortune* magazine from 1943 to 1948 then returned to Harvard in 1949 to teach economics. He stayed there until his retirement, except for a brief stint as ambassador to India under US President John F. Kennedy. In addition to *The Affluent Society*, his other noted publications include *American Capitalism*, *The New Industrial State*, *Economics and the Public Purpose*, *The Age of Uncertainty*, and *The Nature of Mass Poverty*.

The Times

Galbraith rose to prominence during the period of economic prosperity that followed the Second World War. In spite of the Cold

Figure 3.4 John Kenneth Galbraith castigated US policy makers for emphasizing consumerism and for neglecting the common good. How does this photograph reflect consumerism?

War (which pitted the capitalist US and its allies against the communist USSR and its allies), high levels of employment and consumer spending during this time produced an unparalleled degree of prosperity in Canada and the United States. This affluence, however, did not diminish the amount of poverty in these prosperous societies. At the same time, large international corporations were emerging as a new influence in economic decision making.

Ideas That Advanced Economic Thought

Social balance

In *The Affluent Society*, Galbraith argued that the post-war emphasis on private-sector pro-duction had produced a state of private affluence and public squalor. Although consumer goods, such as automobiles and televisions, were produced in abundance, public goods such as schools, hospitals, and parks were in short supply. Galbraith argued that the real need in society was for the production of public goods serving the common good. He thought national production should be shifted to serve these public priorities.

Galbraith also popularized the view that, in the world of the international corporation, corporate managers (not shareholders or consumers) held the real decision-making power in the economy. He believed that more government involvement and regulation of the economy would help improve society.

Check Your Understanding

1. Describe in your own words Galbraith's theory of social balance.

2. Do you agree with his assessment that far more attention is paid to the private good than is paid to the public good? Give three examples from your own community to support your position.

Milton Friedman (born 1912)

Whereas Galbraith is regarded as a leading proponent of the liberal economic perspective, Milton Friedman is acknowledged as the most articulate champion of the conservative view. He was an influential adviser to Richard Nixon and other US presidents.

Biography

Milton Friedman was born in Brooklyn, New York, in 1912. He enrolled in his first economics course in 1930, a time when the single most important issue facing Western nations was the Great Depression. An accomplished scholar, Friedman studied at Rutgers, Chicago, and Columbia universities before being appointed a government economist during the Second World War. He joined the faculty of the University of Chicago in 1946, where he remained until 1977.

When he received the 1976 Nobel Prize for economics, Friedman was cited for "his achievements in the field of consumption analysis, monetary history and theory, and for his demonstration of the complexity of stabilization policy." Friedman has written many books, the best known of which are *Capitalism and Freedom* and *A Monetary History of the United States, 1867–1960*.

The Times

A contemporary of Galbraith, Friedman was strongly influenced by the amount of unproductive government intervention in the US economy following the end of the Second World War. He believed that government attempts to induce cycles of economic growth

PRIMARY SOURCE

On a Monetary Rule

How can we establish a monetary system that is stable and at the same time free from irresponsible governmental tinkering, a system that will provide the necessary monetary framework for a free enterprise economy yet be incapable of being used as a source of power to threaten economic and political freedom?

The only way that has yet been suggested that offers promise is to try to achieve a government of law instead of men by legislating rules for the conduct of monetary policy that will have the effect of enabling the public to exercise control over monetary policy through its political authorities, while at the same time it will prevent monetary policy from being subject to the day-by-day whim of political authorities. . . .

In the present state of our knowledge, it seems to me desirable to state the rule in terms of the behavior of the stock of money [or money supply]. My choice at the moment would be a legislated rule instructing the monetary authority to achieve a specified rate of growth in the stock of money. For this purpose, I would define the stock of money as including currency outside commercial banks plus all deposits of commercial banks. I would specify that the Reserve System [the central bank] *shall* see to it that the total stock of money so defined rises month by month, and indeed, so far as possible, day by day, at an annual rate of *x* percent, where *x* is some number between three and five. The precise definition of money adopted, or precise rate of growth chosen, makes far less difference than the definite choice of a particular definition and a particular rate of growth. . . .

I should like to emphasize that I do not regard my particular proposal as a be-all and end-all of monetary management, as a rule which is somehow to be written in tablets of stone and enshrined for all future time. It seems to me to be the rule that offers the greatest promise of achieving a reasonable degree of monetary stability in the light of our present knowledge. I would hope that as we operated with it, as we learned more about monetary matters, we might be able to devise still better rules, which would achieve still

better results. Such a rule seems to me the only feasible device currently available for converting monetary policy into a pillar of a free society rather than a threat to its foundations.

Source: From Milton Friedman, *Capitalism and Freedom* (Chicago: University of Chicago Press, 1962), 54–55. Copyright © 1962. Reprinted by permission.

Milton Friedman

QUESTIONS

1. How does Friedman define the money supply, or "stock of money"?

2. Why does Friedman believe it is necessary to have a rule for monetary policy? What is that rule?

3. Does Friedman see this as a permanent rule? Explain.

and full employment (by increasing spending and reducing taxes) resulted in periods of significant inflation and a steady increase in the rate of public debt. In addition, Friedman thought this made both the economy and the individual citizen increasingly more dependent on government assistance and, therefore, weaker.

Ideas That Advanced Economic Thought

Laissez-faire capitalism

According to Friedman, free markets will largely resolve their own economic problems more effectively if they are left alone rather than subjected to government intervention. Friedman sees individual self-sufficiency and the preservation of the work ethic as important pillars of productivity and sustained economic growth. For this reason, he advocates a program of guaranteed income (or negative income tax) over centralized social welfare services and the massive, inefficient bureaucracy they require. The abolition of minimum-wage legislation is another laissez-faire strategy that Friedman recommends to free up the marketplace.

Friedman even advocates the application of the free-market principle to the supply of education. Under his plan, parents would annually receive government vouchers equal in value to the cost of a child's education. They could spend the vouchers at the school of their choice. Schools would then be developed to meet the demands of parents (the people who best know the needs of their children). Excellent schools would have no problem attracting students. Schools that did not attract sufficient numbers would automatically close. The education market could thus take care of itself!

The importance of money supply

Friedman is a leading member of the **monetarist** school of thought. Monetarists believe that the most effective way for governments to influence the economy is by regulating the money supply in circulation. They maintain that business cycles are determined by the money supply and interest rates, not by levels of taxation and government spending. According to Friedman, governments should raise the money supply by a fixed amount each year. This increase should be equal to the long-term growth rate of the economy, that is, between 3 and 5 per cent. Too much money in circulation causes inflation; too little money reduces investment and employment levels.

Check Your Understanding

1. What is Friedman's suggestion for adding more economic freedom to public education? Compile a list of its advantages and disadvantages.

2. Explain the monetarist view of the most effective way for governments to stimulate the economy. How does this compare to the theory presented by Keynes?

The Contemporary Scene

Well, what's wrong with this picture so far? Most readers have probably begun to wonder whether economic problems can ever really be solved. Some problems keep reappearing in cycles, and each reappearance makes them seem more complex and difficult to address.

At the same time, some new problems appear to be the direct results of theories and strategies intended to fix earlier problems. The concept of trade-offs appears to be one of the key concepts in the development of economic theory. We can address one problem, it seems, only at the expense of aggravating something else. Clearly, some of our economic goals are in conflict with one another, and some of our theories need to be rethought in light of changing times.

Midway through this chapter, if not earlier, many readers probably began to wonder if any women have contributed to the development of economic thought. We must remember that the public, or political, world between 1750 and 1950 was essentially a male-dominated one, quite probably to the detriment of the science. As economic principles themselves con-

firm, when the thoughts of half the population are unemployed or underemployed, the production possibilities frontier can never be reached. In Canada today, many leading economists are women, and their contributions to the ongoing advancement of economic thought have been both significant and refreshing. Canadian economists who have made important contributions include Nuala Beck, Dian Cohen, Sherry Cooper, Judith Maxwell, and Sylvia Ostry.

SKILL BUILDER
Thinking Like an Economist

Hypothesis Testing

From time to time, economists are called upon to identify patterns in a set of data and to use this information to gain insight into economic reasoning or to explain and predict human economic behaviour. In this chapter, you have read a great deal about the evolution of economic thought over the past 225 years. What patterns have you noticed?

Use the information in this chapter, and any additional information that you have researched, to defend or refute one of the following hypotheses. A **hypothesis** is a speculative theory

that requires proof or verification. Using your supporting evidence, prepare a reasoned argument to either support or refute the speculative statement.

Hypothesis A: Troubled times create great economists.

Hypothesis B: The advancement of economic thought reinforces the pattern of economic trade-offs. Very often, the solving of one problem creates another.

Hypothesis C: The great economic thinker is more of a reactionary than a visionary.

Check Your
Understanding

1. Explain the concept of a trade-off in your own words. Provide two examples of economic trade-offs that you have had to make. Explain your reasoning for each decision.

2. Explain how, in addressing a specific problem, the ideas and theories of one economist helped create new problems for economists that followed.

CHAPTER SUMMARY

- The science of economics is about 225 years old. Economic ideas that help transform the world often appear during times of serious trouble. The advancement of economic thought reinforces the existence of trade-offs. Very often, the solving of one problem creates another.

- Adam Smith was the first thinker to outline in detail the characteristics and benefits of free-enterprise capitalism. Smith explained how self-interest and competition work together to advance the common good. He said the role of government in a free-market economy should be limited since natural controls (the invisible hand) serve to self-regulate the marketplace.

- Writing in the midst of the Industrial Revolution, Thomas Malthus warned that growth in economic production could not keep pace with population growth. Malthus argued that unless population was held in check by natural means, global famine would be inevitable. This bleak forecast earned economics the name "the dismal science."

- David Ricardo explained the advantages of free trade and challenged the power of the aristocratic landlord class by questioning its contribution to society. His theories exposing class conflicts were hailed by the rising industrialist and merchant classes.

- Witnessing the exploitation of workers that accompanied the Industrial Revolution, Karl Marx founded an international workers' movement intended to overthrow the corrupt ruling class of industrial capitalists and aristocratic landlords.

- John Maynard Keynes recognized the importance of government spending as a stimulant to combat economic downturns like the Great Depression. Keynes explained the importance of investor confidence and investment spending in maintaining high employment levels.

- John Kenneth Galbraith criticized post-1950 US capitalism for neglecting the public good. By arguing in favour of shifting national production to public priorities serving the common good, he helped give capitalism a social conscience. He proposed that, in a world of international corporations, increased government involvement and regulation of the economy would help improve society.

- In contrast to Galbraith, Milton Friedman argued against government intervention in the free-market economy, believing that government intervention resulted in price inflation and increased public debt. Friedman advocated that the most effective way for government to influence the economy is by regulating the supply of money in circulation (monetarism).

- Some economic goals conflict with one another, and some theories need to be rethought in light of changing times.

Key Terms

physiocrat
laissez-faire
mercantilism
protectionist
tariff
Industrial Revolution
self-interest
invisible hand
division of labour
law of accumulation
law of population
geometrical progression
arithmetical progression
positive check
preventive check
Corn Laws
absolute advantage
comparative advantage
bourgeoisie
proletariat
labour value
surplus value
monetarist
hypothesis

Activities

Thinking/Inquiry

1. Keynes once wrote that economic slumps and depressions were the result of "upsetting the delicate balance of spontaneous optimism." Explain the significance of the data presented in Figure 3.3 (page 60) relative to investor, consumer, and government confidence in Canada between 1929 and 1933.

2. Use the Internet to research one of the following contemporary Canadian economists. Outline the specific contributions she has made to the advancement of economic thought.

- Nuala Beck
- Dian Cohen
- Sherry Cooper
- Judith Maxwell
- Sylvia Ostry

Organize your report to resemble one of the profiles in this chapter. Illustrate your report with relevant photos, tables, or graphs.

3. Outline the social and political implications of shifting from Galbraith's model of capitalism to Friedman's model. Which model do you favour? Explain your choice.

4. a) Do you think Marx would have agreed with Smith that self-interest is the major motivator in a capitalist economy? Explain.

   b) What differences are there in the way that Marx and Smith viewed self-interest?

5. Compare Ricardo's "iron law of wages" with the "reserve army of the unemployed" described by Marx. Who did each thinker identify as the principal hero and villain in society?

Communication

6. "Working from within, Galbraith has attempted to give capitalism a social conscience." Prepare a reasoned argument to defend or refute this statement.

7. In order to organize what you have learned about the economic thinkers presented in this chapter, create a study guide in the form of a summary chart.

Application

8. Compare Friedman's view on the best way to stimulate the economy with that of Keynes. Whose views do you think are most correct? Explain why.

9. Use the theories of Malthus to prepare a reasoned argument that supports or challenges additional research into the mass production of genetically modified foods.

Unit 1 Performance Task: Building from a Solid Foundation

For centuries, economists have worked to clarify complex realities, explain human behaviour, and illuminate responsible decision making. Now that you have completed the foundational learning activities in this first unit of study, your challenge is to put the knowledge and skills you have acquired to effective use. This performance task presents you with a realistic challenge, very much like the work presently being carried out by many Canadians with a background in economics or related fields.

Your Task

You are the manager of human resources for Acme Corporation, a young and growing Canadian firm specializing in the manufacture of computer parts. Acme is interested in expanding its successful operations beyond Canada. In order to achieve this goal, its board of directors has set the following performance target.

Performance Target

In order to position itself so that it can compete favourably in the global marketplace, Acme Corporation must generate efficiencies in all departments, leading to a 20 per cent increase in corporate productivity within three years.

The board of directors is divided with regard to the best course of action for achieving this target. The following four options have been identified: (i) requiring all employees to work ten hours longer per week while freezing wages and salaries at current levels; (ii) reinvesting a portion of corporate profits to fund ongoing employee training; (iii) paying employees in ownership shares in the company, instead of money, for all overtime work; (iv) starting a profit-sharing plan to reward all employees for reaching productivity targets and for their direct contribution to higher profits for the firm.

As manager of human resources, you are required to prepare a report to the board of directors that weighs the costs and benefits of each proposed option and makes a specific recommendation regarding the most appropriate course of action. Your report can be either a written report, documenting a thorough analysis and persuasive argument, or an oral report, visually supported by PowerPoint slides.

Task Steps and Requirements

1. Review all the work you have done in this unit to refresh your understanding of related concepts and skills.
2. Select a decision-making process or a model that includes the analysis of costs and benefits in order to make a decision.
3. In preparing your report, be sure to include the economic concepts, principles, and theories most appropriate to your analysis and most useful in supporting your recommendation.
4. Also include the theories of the economic thinkers profiled in Chapter 3 that best support your analysis and recommendation.
5. Strive for high-quality content, thoroughness of detail, and a persuasive argument.

Adapting the Task

Discuss the selection of a format (oral or written) for your report with your teacher. Keep the language appropriate for the intended audience. Share drafts with your teacher, classmates, and parents or guardians in order to obtain useful feedback.

Assessment Criteria

The following criteria will be used to assess your work:
- *Knowledge*—accurately using economic concepts, principles, and theories as well as references to great economic thinkers
- *Thinking and Inquiry*—using sound economic reasoning and thorough analysis; using a decision-making model effectively
- *Communication*—presenting economic information and analysis clearly and accurately, in an appropriate format and style
- *Application*—presenting a persuasive argument to inform decision making

UNIT 2

MICROECONOMICS: UNDERSTANDING THE CANADIAN MARKET ECONOMY

When buying and selling goods and services, consumers and producers act in their own self-interest, yet they are interdependent in terms of the outcome of their decisions. How are the basic economic questions answered in the Canadian economy?

Unit Overview

In Unit 1, we learned how economics is the social science that studies scarcity and how our society is forced to make choices in order to satisfy our wants and needs. We also learned about the three fundamental economic questions that must be answered by an economic system. In Unit 2, we shall explore how these questions are answered in individual markets. How are prices set? How much of a good should a producer make? Should a producer use labour-intensive or capital good–intensive methods?

Some answers seem relatively intuitive. Who hasn't wanted tickets to a popular concert or sporting event and then discovered that the event is sold out? Yet, in spite of this circumstance, why can you still buy tickets from ticket brokers (more commonly known as "scalpers"), but at much higher prices? The shortage of tickets has led to higher prices because some consumers are willing to pay much more than the face value of the ticket. Other answers are much more complex.

We'll explore the factors that influence consumer and producer decisions in individual markets. We'll also identify different types of business organization and learn how these organizations finance their operations. Finally, we'll look at the market for labour and the factors that you, as a student planning to enter the workforce in the next few years, need to consider.

Learning Goals

In this unit, you will
- apply the cost–benefit method of inquiry to current economic issues in order to evaluate choices,
- use the economic model of supply and demand to analyze choices, forecast economic change, and explore economic issues,
- compare the different types of business organization and markets in Canada's economy,
- explain how the self-interest of buyers and sellers in a competitive market guides the use of scarce resources in such a way that both are satisfied,
- describe the factors that influence the labour resource market in Canada,
- evaluate the effectiveness of government legislation designed to enhance the economic security of Canadians,
- explain the nature and importance of productivity and efficiency in the economy and the methods that producers use to finance production and expansion,
- explain, using concepts of marginal analysis, how different stakeholders determine what economic choice is in their own best interest,
- illustrate how the self-interest of one group of stakeholders may conflict with that of another and prevent the achievement of economic goals,
- illustrate the interdependence of buyers and sellers in markets by describing how a change in demand or supply affects price and quantity sold in one market and how that in turn affects the self-interest and decisions of stakeholders in other markets.

Skill Builder

Thinking Like an Economist

In this unit, you can develop some of the skills that economists use. These include
- understanding the cause-and-effect relationship between two factors by assuming that all other factors that might affect this relationship remain constant,
- using the concept of elasticity and supply and demand curve analysis to explain the impact of events on both producers and consumers,
- detecting patterns in data to explain economic relationships,
- calculating the costs of production alternatives,
- maximizing profit in different market structures,
- analyzing a public policy issue.

Unit Performance Task

The activity at the end of this unit provides a focused opportunity for you to
- assume the role of an in-house economist and conduct a cost–benefit analysis on a particular economic decision or proposal,
- research appropriate information related to your topic,
- apply the concepts, principles, and terminology related to microeconomics that are explored in this unit, and
- present your conclusions in a persuasively argued report.

CHAPTER 4

DEMAND AND SUPPLY

The Baseball Market Game

How good a buyer or seller are you? Not only will this game give you a chance to test your bargaining skills, but it will also introduce you to the concepts of demand and supply. The commodity being bought and sold is baseballs.

Divide the class evenly into sellers and buyers. Use name tags to identify each person as a seller or a buyer.

Prepare six separate sets of cards. For each set, mark the cards with a different phrase: seller at $15, seller at $13, seller at $11, buyer at $15, buyer at $13, buyer at $11. (So, for example, all the cards in the first set will read "seller at $15.") Be sure there are extra cards in each set as there are multiple rounds.

Shuffle the cards thoroughly. Randomly distribute the cards marked "seller" among the sellers group and the cards marked "buyer" among the buyers group. Each seller/buyer receives one card.

Each buyer must try to bargain with a seller to buy a baseball for not more than the amount on the "buyer" card; each seller must try to sell a baseball for no less than the amount on the "seller" card. Each round lasts about seven minutes.

When a successful transaction has been made, both buyer and seller must individually record the exchange on a transaction sheet (see Figure 4.1) and report it to the teacher or chosen student recorder. The buyer and seller then each pick up another card.

After several rounds, all buyers and sellers total their own transactions, and the top sellers and buyers are determined.

Transaction	Price on Card	Price Paid	Gains	Losses
Buy	$15	$13	$2	—

Figure 4.1 A sample transaction sheet.

QUESTIONS

1. a) Copy the chart below into your notebook, adding a row for each relevant price level.

Quantity Bought (demanded)	Price	Quantity Sold (supplied)

b) Refer to all the buyers' and sellers' transaction sheets. On your chart, fill in the cumulative quantities bought and sold at each price. For example, if three people bought baseballs at $15 and five people bought them at $13, the three people who paid $15 would willingly pay $13 or less. Thus, the quantity demanded at $13 is 5 + 3 = 8 people. Similarly, if three sellers sold baseballs at $11, and five sellers sold them at $13, the three sellers would willingly sell at $13 or more. Thus, the quantity supplied at $13 is 5 + 3 = 8 people.

c) Does there appear to be one price at which most baseballs are demanded and supplied? If so, what is it?

Chapter Goals

By the end of this chapter, you will be able to

- understand the meaning of demand and supply,
- read and construct your own demand and supply graphs,
- understand how prices are set by the forces of demand and supply,
- predict why prices for particular goods or services might change.

The Market

If we had to choose one aspect of our economic system to identify as its most fundamental and characteristic trait, it would probably be the operation of a market. There is an important distinction to make here between an *economy* on the one hand and a *market* on the other. These terms are often confused in popular thinking. The term **market** has four distinct, but related, meanings, none of which coincide with our definition of an economy:

- A market can be a physical place where a product is bought and sold. A market in this sense can range from your corner convenience store to the Toronto Stock Exchange.
- The term *market* can also be used in a collective sense to refer to all the buyers and sellers of a particular good or service. For example, we talk about the global market for a commodity such as copper.
- A market can be the demand that exists for a particular product or service. For example, a newspaper article may describe the market for used cars as being sluggish.
- The term *market* can also describe the process by which a buyer and seller arrive at a mutually acceptable price and quantity.

A market, then, can be a location, the network of buyers and sellers for a product, the demand for a product, or a price-determination process. As we saw in Chapter 1, an economy includes all these things and more. It is important to be aware of the differences in meaning between each term.

The question that we now have to ask is this: Who determines what the *price* will be for the various goods and services in a market? The answer is that the market itself determines price by matching buyers and sellers of a particular product or service. Buyers, for the most part, want the price to be as low as possible, while sellers want it to be high. Often, they agree on a price that is somewhere in the middle, but there can be wide fluctuations in the price paid for any product or service. What accounts for the rise and fall of prices in a free market? In this chapter, we will answer this question by examining the most important concept in economic theory: demand and supply.

Examining Demand

We can define **demand** as the quantity of a good or service that buyers will purchase at various prices during a given period of time. It is important to understand when it can be said that a person actually has a demand for a certain product—using *demand* in its economic sense.

Picture the following scenario. While walking through a mall, you stop outside the window of a shoe store. Two different pairs of shoes grab your attention. The first is a beautiful pair, made of highly polished leather and showing every sign of craftsmanship. You like these shoes very much but are appalled at the price tag: $300! The second pair of shoes is not as pleasing to the eye as the first. The shoes are made from a lower grade of leather and are not nearly as stylish as the first pair. Nevertheless, they are solidly constructed and comfortable, and the price of $80 is more in line with what you can afford. This is the pair of shoes you actually buy; economists would say you have a "demand" for these shoes.

Whether or not you have a demand for a particular product depends on two factors. One is located in your head or heart, the other in your wallet. In other words, demand exists only for those goods that you both want and can afford to buy. If you have both the desire and the financial resources then it is likely you will make the purchase.

Common sense teaches us another important lesson about demand: The quantity of a product that a consumer will purchase depends on its price. Generally speaking, the higher the price of a product, the less it will be purchased; the lower the price, the more it will be purchased. The trained economist uses more formal language to express the same idea, which is referred to as the **law of demand**:

The quantity demanded varies inversely with price, as long as other things do not change.

But why do consumers buy more of a product when the price falls and less of it when the price rises? There are two reasons to account for this circumstance: the substitution effect and the income effect. First, as the price of a particular good rises, we tend to *substitute* similar goods for it, if possible. If, for example, the price of a name-brand soft drink rises, many consumers will stop buying that brand and buy cheaper no-name brands instead. They will substitute one product for another when the price of the first product rises past a certain point. Conversely, if the price of the name-brand soda falls, consumers will start to substitute the name-brand for the no-name soda, thereby increasing the quantity demanded of the name-brand type.

The second reason involves *income*. Continuing with our example, as the price of the name-brand soda falls, say from $5 to $4 a case,

buyers can buy the same amount of soda for a lower price. The money they save on a case actually represents $1 in extra income. Some buyers will choose to buy another six-pack of soda with that dollar, thus increasing the quantity demanded. Conversely, when the price of the soda rises again, buyers must pay more to receive the same amount. As a result, their real income has declined. Many of them will buy less soda, thereby decreasing the quantity demanded.

A demand schedule

One method of portraying the relationship between price and quantity demanded for a particular product is a **demand schedule**. This is a numerical tabulation, usually organized into a table, of the quantities demanded at selected prices. Figure 4.2 shows a typical

SKILL BUILDER
Thinking Like an Economist

Ceteris Paribus

In our discussion of demand, we want to find out what happens to quantity demanded if price—and only price—changes. We do not take into account other factors, such as the number of buyers, that might affect quantity demanded. When economists want to understand the cause-and-effect relationship between two factors, they must make the assumption that all other factors that might affect this relationship remain constant. This assumption is known as ***ceteris paribus***, a Latin term meaning "other things being equal" or, as we have stated it, "as long as other things do not change."

As an example, let's suppose a retail business discovers that when the price of a certain product increases, people buy more of it, not less. This seems to contradict the law of demand. However, economists would point out that several other factors outside of price are probably responsible for the increase in sales. (It is possible the number of buyers has increased or consumer tastes for

this product have changed.) When economists examine the relationship between the price of the product and the quantity demanded, they hold constant these other external factors. Economists find that, for almost all products, price and quantity demanded are inversely related when "other things remain constant."

QUESTIONS

1. Consider the following comment: "It's easy to see why the bagel store is doing well; it's an attractive place, its prices are competitive, it doesn't have much competition, and there's a new office building nearby."

   a) How many demand factors are cited here to explain the store's success?

   b) Which one(s) would economists want to hold constant? Which one(s) would they vary in order to determine the quantities of bagels the store could sell?

If the price of T-shirts were . . .	The consumer would buy in a given time period (quantity demanded) . . .
$20	4 T-shirts
$24	3 T-shirts
$28	2 T-shirts
$32	1 T-shirt
$36	0 T-shirts

Figure 4.2 An individual consumer's demand schedule for T-shirts over a six-month period.

demand schedule that calculates consumer demand for T-shirts.

Here we should note that there is an important distinction to be made between the terms *demand* and *quantity demanded. Quantity demanded* refers to one relationship that is determined by price. So, if we were to compare the quantities demanded when T-shirts are $24 to when they are $28, we would say that the *quantity demanded* has fallen by one. We do not say that the *demand* has fallen by one because the demand for T-shirts by this consumer is represented by the entire schedule of price–quantity relationships shown in Figure 4.2.

We can see from Figure 4.3 that, on a graph, price is measured on the vertical axis, while quantity demanded is measured on the horizontal axis. (This way of constructing a graph has become a standard practice in economics.) The points are then plotted on the graph and joined together. The resulting line, called a **demand curve** even if it is a straight line, runs downward from top left to bottom right. It runs in this direction for the reason we mentioned earlier: people buy less at higher prices (top left on the graph) and more at lower prices (bottom right). This inverse relationship between price and quantity demanded holds for the majority of goods we buy.

Market demand

Up to this point, we have discussed the demand for T-shirts by an individual consumer. This is not, however, the way the market

demand for goods is decided. It is the buying habits of thousands of consumers that decide the demand for most goods. The sum total of all the consumer demands for a product is called the **market demand schedule**. As an example, let's suppose there are four consumers with different demands for T-shirts. By examining Figure 4.4 (page 76), we can see that the market demand is the total of each of the individual demands of the four buyers at each price level. Figure 4.5 (page 76) illustrates the resulting demand curve for this T-shirt market.

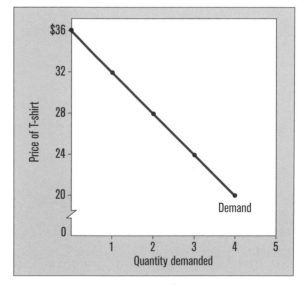

Figure 4.3 One person's demand curve for T-shirts over a six-month period.

Price of T-shirt	Buyer 1	Buyer 2	Buyer 3	Buyer 4	Total Quantity Demanded
$20	4	3	5	4	16
$24	3	2	4	3	12
$28	2	1	3	2	8
$32	1	0	2	1	4
$36	0	0	0	0	0

Figure 4.4 The market demand schedule for T-shirts.

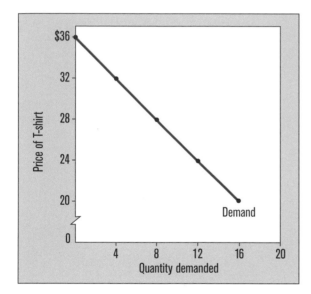

Figure 4.5 The market demand curve for T-shirts.

Examining Supply

Now let's turn our attention away from the consumers' side of the market to the sellers', or suppliers', side. **Supply** is defined as the quantities that sellers will offer for sale at various prices during a given period of time. Like consumers, suppliers react to price changes but in a completely opposite way; that is, as price rises, they want to supply more, while consumers, as we learned, want to purchase less. Why is this so?

Sellers are in business to make a profit. If their costs of doing business remain un-

changed, their profits will increase as the price of their product rises. Consequently, they want to supply more of their product at higher prices because they can make more money this way. If prices slip, sellers prefer to supply less of their product because their profits will fall. Thus, we arrive at the **law of supply**:

> *The quantity supplied will increase if price increases and fall if price falls, as long as other things do not change.*

In contrast to demand, where there is an *inverse* relationship between price and quantity demanded, quantity supplied is *directly* related to price.

A supply schedule

We can get a better idea of the relationship between quantity supplied and price by examining the **supply schedule** for a street vendor of T-shirts displayed in Figure 4.6.

The T-shirt seller's supply schedule has been plotted on the graph in Figure 4.7. By examining this graph, we can see that the same conventions in measuring price and quantity in the demand curve graph (see Figure 4.5) apply here as well. We measure price on the vertical axis and quantity on the horizontal axis. However, the curve is quite different in this case. When the supply figures are plotted on the graph and the points are joined, the supply curve reaches from the bottom left of the graph to the top right. This type of curve illustrates our previous statement that suppliers

If the price of T-shirts were . . .	The seller would like to sell* in a given time period (quantity supplied) . . .
$20	0 T-shirts
$24	4 T-shirts
$28	8 T-shirts
$32	12 T-shirts
$36	16 T-shirts

*The phrase *like to sell* emphasizes the point that "quantity supplied" does not indicate the number of T-shirts the seller will actually sell; rather, it indicates the maximum number the seller is willing to sell at each price. Smaller quantities, but not larger ones, could be sold at any given price.

Figure 4.6 A supply schedule for T-shirts.

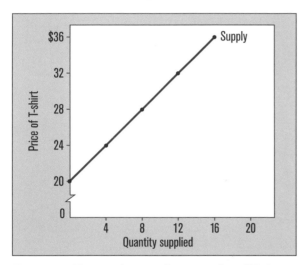

Figure 4.7 The supply curve for one seller of T-shirts.

supply less at lower prices (bottom left) and steadily increase the quantity supplied as prices increase (top right).

Supply and quantity supplied

As with demand and quantity demanded, there is a distinction to be made between the terms *supply* and *quantity supplied*. The word *supply* refers to the whole series of price and quantity relationships, as shown in our T-shirt supply schedule. *Quantity supplied* refers to one relationship that is determined by price. Thus, if we were to compare the quantites supplied when T-shirts are $24 to when they are $28, we would say that *quantity supplied* rose by four T-shirts, not that *supply* increased by four.

Check Your Understanding

1. What is the difference between a *market* and an *economy*?

2. According to the two criteria necessary for demand to exist, determine whether you personally have a demand for the following goods and services:
   - a luxury car
   - a pizza
   - a computer
   - a hammer
   - a post-secondary education

3. a) Suppose the price of milk falls. What will happen to quantity demanded? Which of the two reasons, income or substitution, do you think best explains the change in quantity demanded? Why?

   b) Suppose the price of a brand of orange juice falls. Which of the two reasons, income or substitution, do you think best explains the change in quantity demanded? Why?

4. Explain why a supply curve normally rises from the bottom left to the top right on a graph.

Market Equilibrium

At this point, we have all the tools we need to examine how the actual prices we pay for an item are determined. You have probably guessed by now that, in the real world, the prices that consumers pay and sellers receive are determined by the interaction of demand and supply. If we combine our two schedules for T-shirts, we can see how this occurs.

By examining Figure 4.8, we can see that only at $28 does the quantity demanded equal the quantity supplied. When the price is set lower than $28, the quantity demanded will exceed the quantity supplied, and a shortage will occur. For example, if the price is set at $24, then 12 T-shirts will be demanded, but the seller will supply only four, creating a shortage of eight shirts. In this situation, the seller will then raise the price since the shirts are selling so quickly. The question is this: To what level should the price be raised? Suppose the seller raises the price to $32. The seller wants to sell 12 shirts, but buyers are only willing to purchase four. Now there is a surplus of eight shirts, and the seller will have to lower the price to persuade consumers to buy. The price of $28 is the only price where no shortage or surplus occurs. Economists define this price as the **equilibrium price** because there is no tendency for it to change. It is the only acceptable compromise between consumers who want the lowest prices possible and sellers who want the highest.

A Demand and Supply Graph

We can easily combine both demand and supply figures in one graph by referring to the table in Figure 4.8. In Figure 4.9a, we see that the demand curve crosses the supply curve at exactly $28, which we have identified as our equilibrium price. Suppose we wanted to use this graph to indicate what would happen if the selling price were set above the equilibrium price. In Figure 4.9b, a horizontal dashed line is drawn across the graph from the $32 point on the vertical axis. Then vertical lines are drawn downward from the points at which the horizontal line intersects the demand and supply curves. These vertical lines provide us with a pictorial representation of the information in Figure 4.8: at a price of $32, there will be a demand for four T-shirts and a supply of 12 T-shirts. In other words, a price of $32 will result in a surplus of eight T-shirts.

In Figure 4.9c, we see the opposite situation illustrated, that is, what happens when the selling price is set *below* the equilibrium price. Here, a horizontal dashed line drawn from the $24 point on the vertical axis will intersect the demand and supply curves in such a way as to indicate a shortage of eight T-shirts. By studying these graphs, we can draw the following general conclusion:

Price of T-shirt	Total Quantity Demanded	Quantity Supplied
$20	16	0
$24	12	4
$28	8	8
$32	4	12
$36	0	16

Figure 4.8 The market for T-shirts.

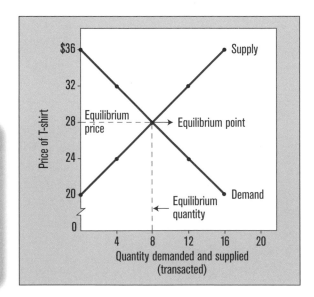

Figure 4.9a Price at equilibrium.

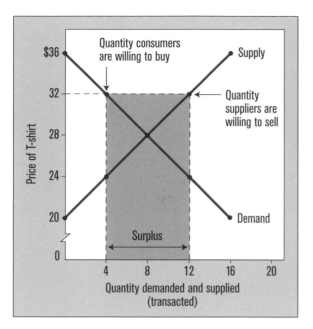

Figure 4.9b Price above equilibrium.

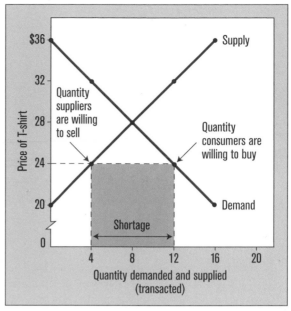

Figure 4.9c Price below equilibrium.

A price above equilibrium will result in a surplus of goods, while a price below equilibrium will result in a shortage of goods, as long as other things do not change.

In our example on pages 75 and 76, we constructed a sample market of four buyers and one seller. It is worth noting that, in the real world, where markets can consist of thousands

P R I M A R Y   S O U R C E

Which Is More Important: Demand or Supply?

Someone once asked the 19th-century British economist Alfred Marshall whether demand or supply was more important in determining price. Can you understand his reply?

We might as reasonably dispute whether it is the upper or the under blade of a pair of scissors that cuts a piece of paper. . . . It is true that when one blade is held still, and the cutting is effected by moving the other, we may say . . . that the cutting is done by the second; but the statement is not strictly accurate, and is to be excused only so long as it claims to be merely a popular and not strictly scientific account of what happens.

Source: A. Marshall, *Principles of Economics* (New York: Macmillan, 1948), 102.

QUESTIONS

1. What do the two blades of the scissors represent?
2. Which of the two blades do you think is more active in each of the following markets?

   a) the market for a particular musical group

   b) the market for oranges

   c) the market for automobiles

or millions of buyers and sellers, the laws of demand and supply operate in the same way as we have seen them operate on a small scale. A price set *below* equilibrium by the sellers will mean that there are many frustrated customers who are unable to purchase the item in question. Some of these customers will start to offer more than the stated price. As they try to outbid each other, they will have the effect of forcing the price to rise. In contrast, a price set *above* equilibrium will result in many unsold goods. In this case, the sellers will try to undercut each other by lowering their price. This process will continue until the quantity demanded equals the quantity supplied, that is, until the market reaches price equilibrium.

Check Your
Understanding

1. a) Copy Figure 4.10 (below) into your notebook and fill in the Surplus/Shortage column. What is the equilibrium price?

   b) Draw a demand and supply graph for this information. Shade in the area that represents a surplus in this market and the area that represents a shortage when market prices of $1.80 and $1.00 are considered.

2. Economists are not generally supportive of governments interfering in markets in order to set prices. Using the example in question 1, explain what undesirable results might occur if the school simply declared a price for cafeteria foods.

Price	Quantity Demanded	Quantity Supplied	Surplus/ Shortage
$2.00	100	190	
$1.80	120	180	
$1.60	140	170	
$1.40	160	160	
$1.20	180	150	
$1.00	200	140	
$0.80	220	130	

Figure 4.10 Demand and supply for hot dogs in a school cafeteria.

Changes in Demand and Supply

Up to this point, we have assumed that "other things do not change" in our discussion of demand and supply. These "other things" are all various **non-price factors** that we have so far held constant in constructing our demand and supply curves. We emphasized that the *quantity demanded* and the *quantity supplied* changed only because price changed. We saw on the graphs in Figures 4.5 and 4.7 (pages 76 and 77) that these changes are represented by movements *along* the curves. Now we shall see that changes in non-price factors cause the *whole curve to shift*, by affecting a product's *demand* or *supply* as opposed to its quantity demanded or quantity supplied. This distinction between movements along a curve and a shift in the

Price of T-shirt	Old Quantity Demanded	New Quantity Demanded	Quantity Supplied
$20	16	20	0
$24	12	16	4
$28	8	12	8
$32	4	8	12
$36	0	4	16

Figure 4.11 An increase in demand for T-shirts.

whole curve is one of the most important distinctions in the entire field of economics. Before proceeding further, it is crucial that we understand this concept and the way it hinges on the distinction between demand and supply on the one hand and quantity demanded and quantity supplied on the other.

Changes in Demand

There are five basic changes that can take place in customer demand for a product. Any one of these changes can have the effect of causing the whole demand curve to shift its position on the graph. Let's consider each of these changes in turn.

Income

Staying with our sample T-shirt market, let's consider what would happen if the incomes of the four potential buyers increased substantially. With more income at their disposal, they might be willing to buy more T-shirts at whatever the prevailing market price is. The schedule in Figure 4.11 shows the result of this increase in buying power, and we can see that quantities demanded increase at all prices. Figure 4.12 shows the new demand curve in relation to the old one. It is easy to see that the increase in demand shifts the whole demand curve upward and to the right. Since the new quantity demanded at the old equilibrium price of $28 now exceeds the quantity supplied (by four), the equilibrium price must shift upward. It moves to $30, where quantity supplied is ten. This increase in income has increased the equilibrium price for T-shirts by $2.

Population

Similar to an increase in incomes, an increase in the number of consumers should translate into an increase in demand, shifting the demand curve to the right with the same increase in equilibrium price. Similarly, a decrease in the number of consumers should have the opposite effect, shifting the demand curve to the left and causing equilibrium prices to fall. Many businesses carefully monitor **demographics**, population statistics that show changes in age, income, and overall numbers. In this way, they hope to determine whether or not the demand for their product is increasing.

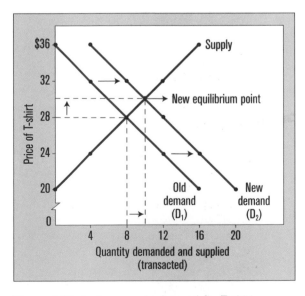

Figure 4.12 An increase in demand for T-shirts.

Case Study   The Boomers

The "baby boomers" are the best-known demographic group in North America. They belong to the generation of people who were born between 1946 to 1966—possibly your parents' generation. Many of these individuals came from families that were considered large by contemporary standards: the average number of children per family during this 20-year period was 3.9.

In 1996, the boomers, numbering 9.8 million, comprised 33 per cent of Canada's population. This number included immigrants of comparable age who came to Canada during that 20-year baby boom. Today, the boomers are middle-aged—moving into their 40s and 50s—and possibly thinking of retirement.

Although the boomers' families are smaller on average, their numbers still produced a mini-baby boom between 1980 and 1995. This generation is known as the "baby boom echo," or the "echo boomers." You might well be one of the echo generation, whose population totalled 6.9 million in 1996.

What impact do the boomers and echo boomers have on the economy? In his book *Boom, Bust, and Echo*, David Foot, a Canadian demographer and economist, explores how demographics can shape attitudes, beliefs, and, most importantly, actions. He sets out the following scenario: In 2000, the first of the echo generation, then aged 20, started to enter the labour market, perhaps moving out of their families' home and setting up their own households. Over the next 20 years, they will want to purchase appliances, furniture, other household items, clothing, and cars. Since money is tight for these young people, retailers must offer low prices and discounts to attract this group of consumers. Many boomers, however, are well established; their homes are furnished, and they may have paid off their mortgages. They are now ready to upgrade their homes and other belongings, and when they go shopping, they are looking for quality and service, not so much for low prices. Boomers are willing to pay more for goods and services that meet their immediate needs.

Foot predicts that those retailers who understand which demographic segment their goods appeal to will do well. Retailers who identify baby boomers as their major customers should emphasize quality and service rather than low prices. In contrast, retailers who want to attract the echo generation will succeed by stressing competitive prices. Foot believes that a business will prosper by choosing one group—not both—on which to focus its marketing strategy.

QUESTIONS

1. If Foot's predictions are correct, which stores and businesses in your area will profit from the echo generation in the future? Explain why.

2. Which of the following goods and services appeal mostly to the boomers? the echo generation? In each case, explain why.
   a) cruise holidays
   b) golf equipment
   c) in-line skates
   d) diet soft drinks
   e) mountain bikes
   f) cell phones
   g) fast food
   h) supplementary vitamins
   i) financial planning

Tastes and preferences

Changes in taste for a product cause increases or decreases in demand for it. Several years ago, several leading T-shirt manufacturers learned through market research that consumers wanted larger-sized T-shirts for a baggier look and more comfortable feel than the snug-fitting shirt that was then the norm. By switching production to baggier T-shirts, these companies were able to increase demand for their product. Companies can also use advertising to increase demand for a product. If they mount a successful advertising campaign, the demand curve will shift to the right.

Similarly, well-publicized medical reports on the dangers of high cholesterol have increased the demand for low-fat foods and decreased the demand for such foods as high-fat milk.

Expectations

If consumers believe that the price of a particular product is going to rise in the future, they may decide to purchase it immediately, thereby increasing the demand for the product. The price of housing is particularly sensitive to changes in **consumer expectations**. In the mid- to late 1980s, housing prices in Toronto and certain other Canadian urban centres rose rapidly. Consumer concern over the rising prices led many people to take on a heavy debt load in order to purchase a house before prices shot up even higher. With so many people rushing to take out mortgages, the supply of houses could not keep up with the demand for them. Prices for even modest homes skyrocketed until, in 1990–1991, the combination of high interest rates and a national recession strangled the housing boom.

Thus, the demand curve for a particular product will shift to the right if consumer expectations lead people to believe that prices will increase in the future. Increased purchases by consumers create a self-fulfilling prophecy: prices start to rise almost immediately, driving the demand curve to the right. Conversely, if consumers expect the price for a product to fall in the future, they may delay purchasing that product, which will drive down the demand for it. In effect, consumers make the lower price of the future a reality in the present.

Prices of substitute goods

Economists include price changes of **substitute goods** under the non-price factors that can cause the whole demand curve to shift. We saw earlier in this chapter that one reason quantity demanded falls for a product as its price rises (a movement along the curve) is that people tend to substitute cheaper goods

Figure 4.13 Digital cameras and the floppy disks used to store the photos are considered complement goods. Unlike substitute goods, a change in the price of a good will inversely affect demand for its complement.

for the more expensive product. Thus, quantity demanded for a name-brand soda falls after a price hike partly because more people are switching to the cheaper no-name brand.

But what would happen if the price of the no-name brand increased for some reason? It is still cheaper than the name-brand soda but not by as wide a margin. Many consumers will reason that the smaller savings are not worth the sacrifice in taste, and they will return to buying the name-brand soda. This will have the effect of increasing demand for the name-brand soda, thereby pushing its demand curve to the right.

Many other goods have substitutes of this sort, and wherever this is the case, the same rule applies. For example, butter and margarine can be substituted for each other. A price change for margarine will affect demand for butter; and a price change for butter will have a corresponding effect on demand for margarine.

Some goods are classified not as substitute goods but as **complement goods**. These are items that are sold together with other goods. Gasoline and automobiles are complements to each other, as are country club memberships and golf equipment. A fall in the price of either complement will increase demand for the other. If car prices fall, car buyers will have more money to spend on gasoline and will tend to drive more often and take longer trips. If the price per litre of gasoline goes down, consumers will reason that owning a car is more affordable, and car sales will then increase.

In summary, a change in the price of one product that can substitute for another will directly increase or decrease the demand for

the competing product, thereby shifting its demand curve one way or the other. A change in the price of a product that complements another will inversely increase or decrease the demand for the product that it complements, also shifting its demand curve.

Changes in Supply

A shift of the whole supply curve can be caused by a number of factors. Here we will focus on the five major factors that can cause such a shift, considering each of them in turn. A change in any of these factors will cause the supply curve to move either to the right (to indicate an increase in supply) or to the left (to indicate a decrease in supply).

Costs

An increase or decrease in production costs will affect the quantities that sellers are willing to supply because a change in costs affects profits. Suppose the cost of cloth for shirt manufacturing falls, and the manufacturer passes on this saving to the retailer, in this case our T-shirt seller. Figure 4.14 shows how such a saving might translate into new quantities supplied at each price level, representing an overall change in supply.

The T-shirt seller's increase in supply is illustrated as a movement from S_1 to S_2 in Figure 4.15. Note that buyers will be happy with this increase in supply because it means that the equilibrium price will drop from $28 to $26 per shirt. On the other hand, note that an increase in manufacturing costs would result in a decrease in supply. This would be

Price of T-shirt	Quantity Demanded	Old Quantity Supplied	New Quantity Supplied
$20	16	0	4
$24	12	4	8
$28	8	8	12
$32	4	12	16
$36	0	16	20

Figure 4.14 An increase in supply of T-shirts.

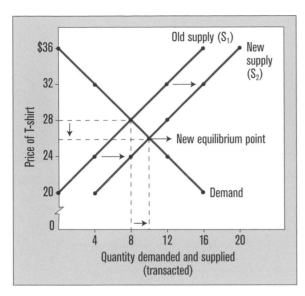

Figure 4.15 An increase in supply of T-shirts.

illustrated by a movement of the curve to the left and a corresponding increase in the equilibrium price.

Number of sellers

The number of sellers may have an effect on the amount of a product that is supplied in a

market. If the number of sellers declines, and if the remaining sellers do not increase their production, then the quantities supplied at any given price in that industry will decrease. This will have the effect of shifting the supply curve to the left. Alternatively, if the number of sellers increases for some reason, the quantity supplied at any given price will increase, shifting the supply curve to the right.

A good example of an increase in supply is the rental market for home videos. When videos first became available for rent in the early 1980s, there were very few suppliers. These suppliers often charged membership fees, and their rental costs were relatively high. Today, the number of rental outlets has increased enormously. In economic terms, what has happened to the supply of home videos and to the supply curve for this particular product?

Technology

An improvement in technology will decrease the cost of production, and this, in turn, will enable manufacturers to supply more of a product at any given price. The economic history of the 20th century is largely a story of

Figure 4.16 Another element that can influence supply is nature and the environment. For example, a farmer displays a handful of potatoes on the dry fields of the family farm near Centreville, Nova Scotia. A five-year drought has forced many farmers in the Atlantic provinces to near bankruptcy.

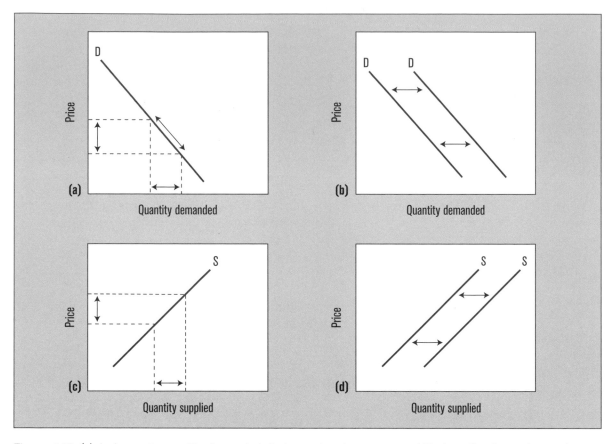

Figure 4.17 (a) A change in quantity demanded. A change in price causes a shift along the demand curve to show a change in the quantity demanded. (b) A change in demand. A non-price change causes the whole curve to shift. (c) A change in quantity supplied. A change in price causes a shift along the supply curve to show a change in the quantity supplied. (d) A change in supply. A non-price change causes the whole curve to shift.

technological progress of such magnitude that the manufacturing costs for almost every product we now buy has fallen. Robots, silicon chips, and improvements to the computerization of industry have all enabled manufacturers to increase the supply of their products, thereby shifting their supply curve to the right.

Nature and the environment

Something as simple as a change in the weather can have an enormous impact on supplies of certain products. Drought, for instance, can dramatically decrease the quantities of crops that farmers can produce. Similarly, an environmental disaster such as the collapse of the Atlantic cod stock has decreased the quantity of cod supplied to fish retailers,

which, in turn, has driven up the price of this particular fish. This decrease in supply has shifted the supply curve for the Atlantic cod to the left.

Prices of related outputs

The production of one item may affect the supply of another related item. Farmers may switch from growing oats to growing barley if the market price of barley rises. This, in turn, will reduce the supply of oats offered at any given price, shifting its supply curve to the left.

Figures 4.17a to 4.17d provide a neat, graphical summary of the way a movement along a demand or supply curve differs from a shift of the whole curve. Study these graphs carefully.

Case Study

The Personal Computer

In 1984, one of the founders of Apple computers, Steve Jobs, predicted that personal computers would soon become as common a household item as toasters and coffee makers. His prediction was derided by the big computer companies, who built only large, expensive computers for business and government. Jobs, however, was proven right; today, around 50 per cent of North American households own a personal computer—a product that is continually evolving to become more powerful, easier to use, and much cheaper to purchase.

Computers have existed for more than half a century, but it was not until the development of the microprocessor chip in the 1960s that it became possible to build a small personal computer. Before the development of this chip, the transistors used in a computer had to be individually wired to each other—a system that was expensive and prone to breakdown. The chip eliminated these problems. It was a single, tiny piece of material (such as silicon) that first contained dozens, then hundreds, and, today, millions, of transistors. The need for expensive wiring was reduced, and, as a result, much smaller computers that operated more reliably were built.

Entrepreneurs immediately understood that the microprocessor chip would allow them to build a small computer for relatively little cost. Scores of small start-up personal computer companies sprang up in the 1970s. Consumers often had a bewildering range of choices in personal computers. The most successful of the new companies was started by Steve Jobs and Steve Wozniak. Calling themselves "two guys in a garage," they designed and marketed a personal computer called the Apple, which grew to dominate the personal computer market until 1981. That year, IBM finally launched its personal computer, along with software designed by a company outsider—Bill Gates, the founder of Microsoft.

The original IBM PC, with 16 KB of memory, was priced at US$2495, similar to the cost of its rival Apple II. Through the 1980s and into the 1990s, the IBM PC and the Apple Macintosh competed vigorously, along with personal computers made by several other companies. Today, one can buy a personal computer for several hundred dollars. Computer technology promises even smaller, cheaper, and more powerful machines in the future.

QUESTIONS

1. In terms of demand and supply for personal computers, in which direction is the supply line moving? Illustrate your answer on a small free-hand graph. In a sentence or two, explain why the shift occurred and what the beneficial results are.

2. a) As personal computers become more important in our daily lives, how is the market affected? Show this effect on the graph you drew for question 1.

   b) In the long run, which of the two curves do you believe will shift more? How will price be affected?

Check Your Understanding

1. What effect will each of the following factors have on the demand for product X? Will demand increase or decrease in each case?

   a) As a result of an imaginative advertising campaign, product X becomes more fashionable.

   b) The people who buy product X find their incomes falling.

   c) A new product Y is invented and is marketed as a cheaper substitute for product X.

   d) Consumers of product X hear that its price will rise over the following month.

2. What effect will each of the following factors have on the supply of product X? Will supply increase or decrease in each case?

   a) Makers of product X introduce a labour-saving technology in their factory.

   b) As the result of a protracted strike, makers of product X find they have to pay higher wages to their workers.

   c) The market price that makers receive for product X rises.

   d) The federal government reduces business taxes.

   e) Several makers of product X go bankrupt, leaving fewer companies to manufacture this product.

3. Which of the four possibilities—a change in quantity demanded, a change in quantity supplied, a shift in demand, or a shift in supply —do each of the following market situations illustrate?

   a) The price of DVDs falls, and consumers buy more of them.

   b) New techniques in steel manufacturing lower the costs of producing steel.

   c) A recession lowers the disposable incomes of North American consumers, affecting consumption of high-end consumer goods.

   d) Gold mining companies try to extract more gold from their mines as world gold prices rise.

The Determination of Price

We are now in a position to analyze the way price is actually determined in a competitive market. By a competitive market, we mean a market that exhibits the following characteristics:

• It has many producers or sellers, with no single one large enough to dominate the market.

• It has many buyers, with no single one large enough to dictate price to sellers.

• Each seller's product is exactly the same as the others so that no seller can increase price based on having a higher-quality product than another seller.

• All sellers and buyers know what the prices and conditions are throughout the entire market, thereby eliminating the possibility of any price differences.

   This kind of market is called **pure (or perfect) competition**. In a modern economy, it is quite rare for all these conditions to be present in a particular market. Nevertheless, pure competition is an ideal or a model that economists use to compare and evaluate actual markets for the products and services bought and sold in Canada and in other countries that have free-market systems.

   For purposes of instruction, let's analyze the coffee market in Canada. This comes as close as any other market to the model, and it shows us how changes in demand and supply, with their shifting curves, cause equilibrium prices to rise and fall.

The Coffee Market in Canada

• *An increase in demand will have the following effect:* Suppose retailers are used to paying a wholesale price of $5 per kilogram for Colombian coffee. Then, in the 1990s, the spread of coffee houses as social meeting places throughout North America increases the demand for Colombian coffee in Canada. In Figure 4.18a, D_1 and S show coffee at the old equilibrium price of $5 per kilogram. Q_1 shows the quantities demanded and supplied at that price. The increase in demand to D_2 causes an excess demand, or shortage, $(Q_2 - Q_1)$ to occur. This excess demand will cause the price to rise to $6 at P_2; quantity demanded and supplied will be equal at Q_3. This new equilibrium price and quantity supplied eliminates the excess demand.

• *A decrease in demand will have the following effect:* Suppose a best-selling book raises health concerns about excessive caffeine intake. As a result, many Canadians cut back on the number of cups of coffee they drink per day and turn to other beverages. This reduces the demand for coffee in Canada. In Figure 4.18b, D_1 and S show coffee at the old equilibrium price of $5 per kilogram. Q_1 indicates the quantities demanded and supplied at that price. The decrease in demand to D_2 causes an excess in supply, or surplus, $(Q_1 - Q_2)$ to

occur. This excess in supply causes the price to fall to $4 at P_2; quantity demanded and supplied will be equal at Q_3. This new equilibrium price and quantity supplied eliminates the excess supply.

• *An increase in supply will have the following effect:* Suppose scientists discover a way to produce a faster-growing coffee plant through genetic manipulation. In Figure 4.18c (page 90), D and S_1 show coffee at the old equilibrium price of $5 per kilogram. Q_1 indicates the quantities demanded and supplied at that price. The increase in supply (S_2) causes an excess supply, or surplus, $(Q_2 - Q_1)$ to occur. This will cause the price to fall to $4 at P_2 and quantity demanded to rise to Q_3. This movement shifts the supply curve to the right. The new equilibrium price and quantity demanded eliminate the excess supply.

• *A decrease in supply will have the following effect:* Suppose a mildew that strikes coffee plants decimates coffee production in the mountains of Colombia. Supplies of Colombian coffee in Canada are at an all-time low. In Figure

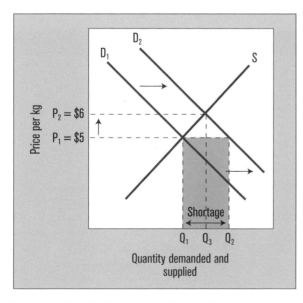

Figure 4.18a An increase in demand in the coffee market.

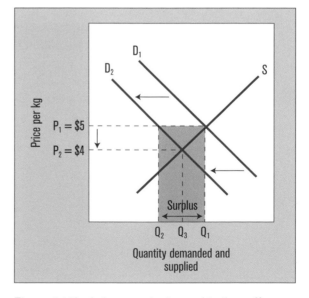

Figure 4.18b A decrease in demand in the coffee market.

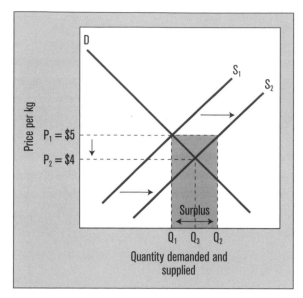

Figure 4.18c An increase in supply in the coffee market.

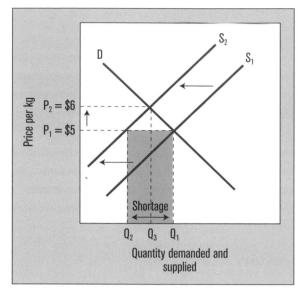

Figure 4.18d A decrease in supply in the coffee market.

4.18d, D and S_1 show coffee at the old equilibrium price of $5 per kilogram; Q_1 shows the quantities demanded and supplied at that price. This decrease in supply to S_2 causes an excess demand, or shortage, ($Q_1 - Q_2$) to occur. This will cause the price to rise to $6 at P_2; quantity demanded and supplied will be equal at Q_3. This new equilibrium price and quantity demanded eliminates the excess demand.

Check Your Understanding

1. Does the equilibrium price for a particular product rise or fall with each of the following changes? Draw small freehand graphs to illustrate your answers.

   a) Demand increases and supply stays the same.

   b) Supply decreases and demand stays the same.

   c) Supply increases and demand stays the same.

   d) Demand decreases and supply stays the same.

   e) Demand increases and supply decreases.

   f) Demand decreases and supply increases.

2. Consider each of the following scenarios in the North American gasoline and oil market. Draw freehand demand and supply graphs to determine the changes in quantities demanded and supplied, and in market prices, in response to these scenarios.

   a) The North American economy is prosperous, and automobile sales, particularly those of fuel-inefficient SUVs and vans, rise.

   b) After 11 September 2001, the North American economy slips into a recession, and automobile sales plummet.

   c) War in the Middle East results in a sharp fall in oil exports to North America.

   d) Automobile manufacturers develop new engines that significantly improve the fuel efficiency of all models.

CHAPTER SUMMARY

- A market can be a place where buyers and sellers meet to exchange goods and services for a price.

- In order to say that a demand for a good exists, a consumer must have both a desire for it and the income necessary to buy it.

- Demand is defined as the quantity of a good or service a buyer will purchase at various prices during a given period of time.

- The law of demand indicates that an inverse relationship exists between price and quantity demanded. The quantity demanded will increase if price decreases and will decrease if price increases, as long as other things do not change. This inverse relationship is represented graphically by a curve that runs from top left to bottom right.

- When the price of a product falls, consumers buy more of it for two reasons. First, their real income increases as the price falls, so they have more money to spend on the product. Second, as the price of a product falls, consumers tend to substitute that product for its more expensive competitors.

- A price change that causes consumers to buy more or less of a product is called a change in quantity demanded. It is represented by a movement along the demand curve.

- A change in demand (as opposed to quantity demanded) can be caused by changes in several non-price factors. These include changes in taste, income, future expectations, and the number of consumers. A change in the price of related or competing goods can also result in a change in demand.

- Changes in demand cause the whole demand curve to shift. It shifts up and to the right for increases in demand, and down and to the left for decreases in demand.

- Supply is defined as the quantities that suppliers sell at various prices during a given period of time.

- The law of supply states that a direct relationship exists between price and quantity supplied. The quantity supplied will increase if the price increases and decrease if the price falls, as long as other things do not change. This direct relationship is represented graphically by a curve that runs from bottom left to top right.

- A price change that causes suppliers to supply more or less is called a change in quantity supplied. It is represented by a movement along the supply curve.

- A change in supply (as opposed to quantity supplied) can be caused by changes in several non-price factors. These include changes in manufacturing costs, technology, the number of suppliers, and nature and the environment. A change in the prices of related or competing goods can also result in a change in supply.

- Changes in supply cause the whole supply curve to shift. It shifts down and to the right for increases in supply, and up and to the left for decreases in supply.

- The point at which the demand curve intersects the supply curve is called the equilibrium point. Only at this point does the quantity demanded equal the quantity supplied. This determines the prevailing market price.

- All prices above equilibrium create excess supply or surpluses because quantity supplied exceeds quantity demanded. All prices below equilibrium create excess demand or shortages because quantity demanded exceeds quantity supplied.

- A change in the equilibrium price is caused by a shift either in demand or supply.

Key Terms

market
demand
law of demand
demand schedule
ceteris paribus
demand curve
market demand schedule
supply
law of supply
supply schedule
equilibrium price
non-price factor
demographics
consumer expectations
substitute goods
complement goods
pure (or perfect) competition

Activities

Thinking/Inquiry

1. Proponents of the market system sometimes defend it on the grounds that consumers are able to "vote" on the goods and services they want.

   a) What tool do consumers use to "vote"?

   b) How do they "register" their votes, and how do producers know how consumers have voted?

2. It's understandable that many of us complain when the price of a product or service rises. What might the price rise indicate about either the demand for or the supply of the product? If price were not allowed to rise, what would be the undesirable result?

3. Suppose a family's income increases. Would its demand for all goods and services rise, or would it rise for some goods and services but fall for others? Explain how a family's demand could change in opposite ways, using two household goods or services as examples.

Communication

4. Draw freehand demand and supply graphs to illustrate each of the following scenarios. Then, in point-form notes, explain how price and quantities change for many consumer goods.

   a) The incomes of people in northern Canada increase significantly as a result of the construction of a new pipeline through their land.

   b) American restrictions on the import of BC lumber cause widespread layoffs in the BC lumber industry.

   c) The widespread use of microprocessors lowers the costs of producing many consumer electronic items.

   d) Restrictions and delays persist in cross-border transportation of goods and supplies between Canada and the United States.

Application

5. Think of an item you would like to purchase but are unable to at the moment because the price is too high. Name two things you would like to see happen

   a) on the demand side to bring the price down,

   b) on the supply side to bring the price down.

6. How can merchants in a competitive market tell if their prices are too low? How can these same merchants tell if their prices are too high?

7. Copy Figure 4.19 in your notebook.

   a) Calculate the surpluses and shortages that would occur depending on the price charged. What price should be charged?

   b) Draw a demand and supply graph and plot these figures.

   c) On the graph, indicate the equilibrium price. Shade in the part of the graph that is the "surplus area," and do the same for the part that is the "shortage area."

8. Refer to the information on the hot dog seller in activity 7. Determine the effect each of the following developments will have on the business. How will demand or supply change in each case? Draw a small freehand graph to

Price	Quantity of Hot Dogs Demanded per Day	Quantity of Hot Dogs Supplied per Day	Surplus/ Shortage
$2.40	100	160	
$2.20	110	140	
$2.00	120	120	
$1.80	130	100	
$1.60	140	80	

Figure 4.19 Demand and supply schedule for a sidewalk hot dog vendor.

illustrate each change, and determine how equilibrium price will be affected.

a) A competing vendor on the next corner goes out of business.

b) The wholesale price of hot dogs falls.

c) The city experiences a tourist boom.

d) A new hamburger outlet opens for business on the same street.

e) The cost of a vendor's licence doubles.

9. Although economists prefer to see prices set automatically by the forces of demand and supply, can you think of goods or services whose prices probably should be controlled by governments? Explain your answer in a paragraph.

10. Review the four conditions that must exist for perfect, or pure, competition to exist.

Then hold three of them constant while you consider the effect of changing one condition. Forecast how prices would be affected, and why. A forecast is included in (a) as an example.

a) The market has many buyers but only one seller. (The seller would have a monopoly and, with no competitors, would be able to charge a higher price.)

b) The market has many sellers but only one buyer.

c) Each seller's product is somewhat different from the other.

d) Buyers are not well informed about the selling prices of the various suppliers of the product.

CHAPTER 5
APPLICATIONS OF DEMAND AND SUPPLY

Going Wireless

The mobile phone is bringing about changes to society as profound as those introduced by the automobile.

—Timo Kopomaa, sociologist, Helsinki University of Technology

Some facts about cellphones as of December 2000:
- One in four Canadians has a cellphone.
- The number of users in Canada is increasing by approximately 4700 per day.
- In Finland, 70 per cent of the population owns a cellphone, in Britain, 60 per cent, and in Japan, 40 per cent.
- By 2003, global sales of cellphones are expected to triple.
- The next generation of cellphones will combine data storage, Internet access, and voice and image communication.

Source: Chris Wood, "The Cell in Your Future," *Maclean's,* 4 December 2000, 34–40; Barry Came, "Wireless Nation," *Maclean's,* 4 December 2000, 41–44.

QUESTIONS

1. Do you own a cellphone? If so, why? If not, do you plan to buy one in the future? Why or why not?
2. How important are cellphones in our lives right now? Do you ever see them becoming a necessity? Explain.
3. If demand for cellphones is increasing so much, why aren't prices? Draw a freehand demand and supply graph to illustrate what you think may be happening in the market.
4. Do you agree with the opinion in the quotation from Timo Kopomaa? Explain.

Chapter Goals

By the end of this chapter, you will be able to

- understand, calculate, and apply a concept known as elasticity to consumers and sellers,
- identify how governments interfere in markets, and explain whether or not it is beneficial,
- understand theories of consumer behaviour such as marginal utility and consumer surplus,
- analyze and debate the issues of rent controls and minimum wages.

Elasticity of Demand

This chapter deals with the practical applications of the demand and supply concepts discussed in Chapter 4. We will see the ways businesses and governments can use these concepts as a guide in making sound economic judgements. We'll begin the chapter by discussing an important concept known as **elasticity**, or the responsiveness of quantities demanded and supplied to changes in price.

In Chapter 4, we learned that consumers buy more of a product when its price falls and less of it when its price rises. What we did not learn is *how much* more they will buy or *how much* less. You may wonder if it is really possible to calculate such numbers with any precision. As a matter of fact, economists have developed a formula to measure the actual change in quantity demanded for a product whose price has changed. This concept is known as the **price elasticity of demand**, and its formula is as follows:

$$\text{coefficient of demand elasticity} = \frac{\%\text{ change in quantity demanded}}{\%\text{ change in price}} \ or \ E_d = \frac{\Delta Q_d}{\Delta P_d}$$

The *effect* of the change is in the numerator of this equation (people buying more or less), while the *cause* is in the denominator (the change in price that affects people's buying decisions). Let's work through an example to see how this concept operates in real life.

Suppose a large gas station sells 10 million litres of gasoline a month at a price of $0.50 per litre. If the station's owners raise their price to $0.54 per litre, the quantity demanded by the station's customers falls to 9.5 million litres. With this information, we can calculate a coefficient that the station owners will find useful in making their pricing decisions.

First, let's calculate the per cent change in price. Between the original price of $0.50 and the new price of $0.54, the change is $0.04. In percentage terms, that is

8% of $0.50 (original price): $\frac{4}{50} \times 100 = 8\%$

or

7.4% of $54 (new price): $\frac{4}{54} \times 100 = 7.4\%$.

Which of these percentages should we use in our calculations? The answer is this: We should compromise by using the average price, which is $0.52. Thus, the per cent change is now

$$\frac{4}{52} \times 100 = 7.69\%.$$

This figure of 7.69 per cent will serve as the denominator of our equation.

Similarly, to determine the per cent change in quantity demanded, we use the average between the original quantity of litres sold and the quantity after the price change. Since the quantity demanded fell from 10 to 9.5 million litres, the average quantity demanded is 9.75 million litres. The change in quantity is −0.5 million litres. Therefore, the per cent change in quantity demanded is

$$\frac{-0.5}{9.75} \times 100 = -5.128\% \ or \ 5.13\%.$$

This figure of 5.13 per cent will serve as the numerator of our equation. (Note that the value of ΔQ_d is negative because the quantity demanded falls. However, we ignore the negative sign because we are interested in the amount of change not in the direction.)

We can now use the general formula to determine the coefficient of demand:

$$\frac{\%\text{ change in quantity demanded}}{\%\text{ change in price}} = \frac{5.13\%}{7.69\%} = 0.667 \ or \ 0.67.$$

Take careful note of the following matter of terminology: any coefficient between zero and one is called an **inelastic coefficient**. This is because a given per cent change in price causes a *smaller* per cent change in quantity demanded (a 7.69 per cent change in price causes a 5.13 per cent change in quantity demanded).

Staying with our gasoline example, however, we find there is a different coefficient for a different set of prices and quantities demanded. This is the case even when the change in price ($0.04) and the change in quantity demanded (0.5 million litres) are the same as in our first example. Refer to Figure 5.1 (page 96) to see how this works. Between $0.66 and $0.70, we find the per cent change in price is 5.88 per cent:

$$\frac{4}{68} \times 100 = 5.88\%.$$

We calculate the per cent change in quantity demanded as 6.45 per cent:

$$\frac{-0.5}{7.75} \times 100 = -6.452\% \; or \; 6.45\%.$$

The coefficient, therefore, is

$$\frac{6.45\%}{5.88\%} = 1.096 \; or \; 1.1.$$

Note here that any coefficient greater than one is called an **elastic coefficient**. This is because a given per cent change in price causes a *greater* per cent change in quantity demanded (a 5.88 per cent change in price causes a 6.45 per cent change in quantity demanded). A coefficient that is equal to one is called a **unitary coefficient** because a given per cent change in price causes an *equal* per cent change in quantity demanded.

The Total Revenue Approach to Elasticity

It is extremely useful for economists and business people to know whether **total revenues** will rise or fall when prices rise or fall. In other words, will a rise in price mean increased rev-

enues for our gas station owner in spite of the fall in quantity demanded? If the elasticity coefficient is inelastic, then the answer is yes. Let's refer again to Figure 5.1, and consider whether total revenues rise when the owners hike the price per litre of gas from $0.50 to $0.54.

At the original price of $0.50 per litre, the owners sell 10 million litres of gas. Total revenue, therefore, is 10 million litres × $0.50 = $5 million. At $0.54, however, revenues are 9.5 million litres × $0.54 = $5.13 million. Thus, this price increase makes sense because, as always happens with an inelastic demand coefficient, when the price of gasoline rises, the quantity demanded falls at a lower rate (5.13 per cent) than the rate at which the price rises (7.69 per cent). In other words, although people buy less gasoline at the higher price, this potential loss of revenue is compensated for by the greater per cent increase in price. Conversely, if the price falls again to $0.50, revenues will fall because even though people buy more gas at the lower price, this potential revenue increase is offset by the greater per cent decrease in price.

This picture changes when the coefficient is elastic. When prices *rise* from $0.66 to $0.70 per litre, revenues *fall* from $5.28 million to $5.25 million. This, too, makes sense because the per cent *rise* in price (5.88 per cent), with its potential to raise revenues, is undercut by an even greater per cent *fall* in quantity demanded (6.45 per cent). When price falls with an elastic coefficient, total revenues will rise. This is because the per cent decrease in price is less than the per cent increase in quantity of gasoline purchased. When the coefficient is unitary, total revenues are not affected by an increase or decrease in price because the per cent increases or decreases in price and quantity demanded are the same. See Figure 5.2 for a summary of what we have learned about demand coefficients and what they can tell us about changes in price and total revenues.

Factors Affecting Demand Elasticity

There are four factors that can have a strong effect on demand elasticity. Let's consider each of these in turn.

Price per Litre of Gasoline	Quantity Demanded (million litres)	Coefficient of Demand
$0.50	10.0	
		0.67
$0.54	9.5	
$0.58	9.0	
$0.62	8.5	
$0.66	8.0	
		1.1
$0.70	7.5	
$0.74	7.0	
$0.78	6.5	
$0.82	6.0	

Figure 5.1 The changing market for gasoline. Copy this table into your notebook, and calculate the remaining coefficients.

- Goods with *inelastic demand coefficients:* When price rises, total revenues rise. When price falls, total revenues fall.
- Goods with *elastic demand coefficients:* When price rises, total revenues fall. When price falls, total revenues rise.
- Goods with *unitary demand coefficients:* When price rises or falls, total revenues stay the same.

Figure 5.2 Demand coefficients and their relation to total revenue.

Availability of substitutes

Goods that have substitutes tend to be more elastic than goods that do not. A single brand of candy, for example, is usually very elastic. Since many other brands of candy are available, consumers will reduce their purchases sharply if the candy manufacturer raises the price. The demand for candy in general is inelastic, however, because there is no close substitute for candy. Consumers will not significantly reduce their expenditures for it if prices rise or significantly increase them if prices fall.

Nature of the item

Goods that are necessities tend to be more inelastic than goods that are considered luxuries. A necessity such as bread is inelastic; price changes do not significantly change the quantities consumers purchase. A luxury such as a vacation cruise, on the other hand, will be quite elastic because if prices rise, people can do without this kind of vacation.

Fraction of income spent on the item

Goods that are expensive and, therefore, take up a large part of the household budget will be elastic. If prices rise for "big-ticket" items such as houses, cars, or furniture, people either do without the item entirely, postpone the purchase, or search for substitutes. By contrast, an item that takes up a smaller percentage of the budget, such as shoelaces, may rise in price without registering a significant decline in the amount purchased. Therefore, such an item is classified as inelastic.

Amount of time available

Over time, some goods may become more elastic because consumers eventually find substitutes for them. In the short run, however, demand for these same goods can be quite inelastic because consumers may not know what substitutes are available immediately after the price rises. Let's look at gasoline as an example. When the price of gasoline rises, car owners initially may reduce the amount of driving they do, but not significantly. However, if gas prices remain high over a long period of time, drivers may switch to smaller cars in order to reduce their gas consumption.

Check Your Understanding

1. For which of the following products would demand be elastic? inelastic? State why in each case.
   a) beef
   b) steak
   c) soft drinks
   d) Coca-Cola
   e) pencils
   f) public transportation
   g) haircuts

2. Suppose the prices of farm products rise. Explain whether farmers' incomes are likely to rise or fall.

3. Determine how each of the following price changes will affect the total revenues received by a seller. In other words, will they rise, fall, or stay the same?

   a) Price falls and demand is elastic.
   b) Price rises and demand is inelastic.
   c) Price rises and demand is elastic.
   d) Price falls and demand is inelastic.
   e) Price rises and demand is unitary.

4. a) An economist estimates that the coefficient of elasticity of demand for a seller's product is 1.5. She advises the seller that he would benefit by lowering his selling price, if possible. Explain why this economist might make such a recommendation.

   b) How would this economist's recommendation change if she estimates that the demand coefficient for the seller's product is 0.9?

Elasticity of Supply

The concept of elasticity also applies to the supply, or sellers', side of the market. You will remember that, generally, as market prices rise, suppliers want to supply more because their profits will increase. Can a supplier increase output as easily as consumers decrease demand, or is it more difficult to increase quantity supplied to take advantage of higher prices? The concept of **elasticity of supply** measures how responsive the quantity supplied by a seller is to a rise or fall in price. The formula to determine the coefficient of supply is as follows:

$$\frac{\text{coefficient of supply elasticity}}{} = \frac{\% \text{ change in quantity supplied}}{\% \text{ change in price}} \quad or \quad E_s = \frac{\Delta Q_s}{\Delta P_s}$$

To see how this formula works, let's take the example of a steel manufacturer. Suppose the market price of steel rises from $120 per tonne to $140. Wishing to take advantage of the higher price, the manufacturer expands production immediately from 1 million tonnes a day to 1.2 million tonnes. What will be the coefficient of supply?

First, we calculate the per cent change in price. Just as with demand elasticities, we have to find the average of the two prices, which, in the case of the steel manufacturer, is

$$\frac{120 + 140}{2} = 130.$$

The change in price is $20, thus the per cent change is

$$\frac{20}{130} \times 100 = 15.38\%.$$

We also must find the average of the two figures for quantity supplied:

$$\frac{1 + 1.2}{2} = 1.1.$$

The change in quantity supplied is 0.2, thus the per cent change is

$$\frac{0.2}{1.1} \times 100 = 18.18\%.$$

Using the supply elasticity formula, we can now calculate the coefficient of supply:

$$\frac{\% \text{ change in quantity supplied}}{\% \text{ change in price}} = \frac{18.18\%}{15.38\%} = 1.18.$$

The same rules apply to supply coefficients as to demand coefficients. Any supply coefficient less than one is classified as *inelastic*, equal to one is *unitary*, and more than one is *elastic*. Thus, the steel manufacturer's ability to increase production supply is *elastic* within this price range. This means that when price increases by a certain percentage (15.38 per cent in this case), the manufacturer is able to increase quantity supplied at an even greater rate (18.18 per cent). A seller with an elastic supply is better positioned to take advantage of an increase in demand for the product. Quantity supplied can easily and quickly be increased to meet demand, resulting in an increase in revenues.

A price range that is supply *inelastic* has a supply coefficient of less than one. This means the seller cannot increase the quantity supplied by a greater percentage than the per cent increase in price. A price range that has a *unitary* supply elasticity has a coefficient equal to one. In this case, the seller is just able to match a price increase by the same percentage increase in quantity supplied.

Factors Affecting Supply Elasticity

There are three factors that can have a strong effect on supply elasticity. Understanding each of these factors will give us a deeper appreciation of the applications of this concept.

Time

The longer the time period a seller has to increase production, the more elastic the supply will be. A classic example is a seller of fresh fruits and vegetables. Suppose the price of tomatoes rises. Growers cannot increase production in one day, or even in one month. Supply, therefore, is inelastic and remains so until more tomatoes can be planted, harvested, and brought to market. In summarizing a situation like this, economists say that in the short term, supply is inelastic, and in the long term, it is elastic.

Ease of storage

When the price of a product drops, sellers have two options. They can either sell the product at the new low price, or they can put some of their inventory into storage and sell it after the price rises again. The steel industry enjoys high supply

Elasticity and the Slope of Demand and Supply Curves

Graphs of demand and supply curves provide us with good visual representations of the different kinds of elasticity we have just considered.

In Figure 5.3, an inelastic demand curve, we see that price changes more when compared with the change in quantity demanded.

In Figure 5.4, an elastic demand curve, price changes less when compared with the change in quantity demanded.

The unitary demand curve in Figure 5.5 illustrates that quantity demanded changes exactly in proportion to the price change.

Figure 5.6, an inelastic supply curve, illustrates that quantity supplied changes less than the change in price.

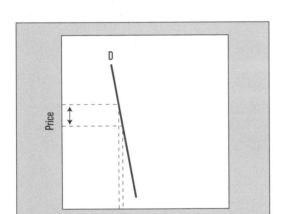

Figure 5.3 An inelastic demand curve.

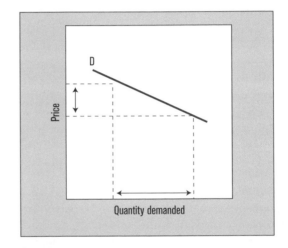

Figure 5.4 An elastic demand curve.

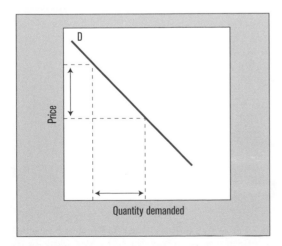

Figure 5.5 A unitary demand curve.

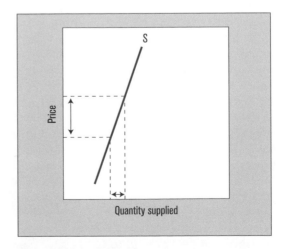

Figure 5.6 An inelastic supply curve.

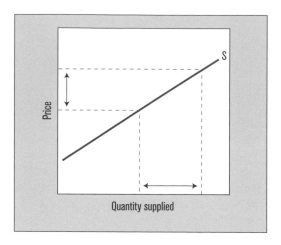

Figure 5.7 An elastic supply curve.

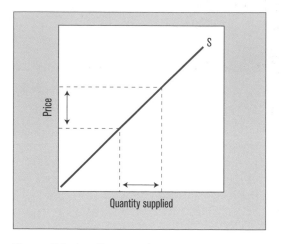

Figure 5.8 A unitary supply curve.

In Figure 5.7, an elastic supply curve, quantity supplied changes more than the change in price.

The unitary supply curve in Figure 5.8 illustrates that quantity supplied changes exactly in proportion to the price change.

These graphs are used by economists to analyze changes in different types of markets, as the following two examples illustrate:

• *The oil and gas market:* In the 1970s, Middle Eastern oil producers cut production, which led to a major energy crisis throughout the world. The producers reasoned correctly that oil has an inelastic demand in the short term. If prices rise when demand is inelastic, revenues increase.

Create a small freehand graph similar to Figure 5.3. Draw a supply line, S_1; above it and to the left, draw another supply line, S_2, to show the cut in production. Mark the equilibrium points at D and S_1 and at D and S_2, then use dashed lines to indicate the price and the quantity demanded and supplied for each point. Examine the increase in price from the point where S_1 crosses the steep demand curve to the point where S_2 crosses it. Examine the fall in quantity demanded caused by the production cut. Can you see that the price rises more than the quantity falls? Your graph will show that when the oil producers cut back production (S_1 to S_2), price rose significantly, but the quantity of oil demanded fell little (Q_1 to Q_2) because con-

sumers and businesses could not cut their usage significantly. The result was a tremendous increase in revenue for Middle Eastern oil producers.

• *The market for automobiles:* In 1908, Henry Ford's Model T sold for $850, far more than most Americans could afford. His company sold only 5986 cars that year. Over the next eight years, Ford introduced assembly-line production in order to cut production costs. By 1916, the Model T was selling for $360, sales had climbed to 577 036, and Henry Ford and his company became very rich indeed.

Create a small freehand graph similar to Figure 5.4. Draw a supply line, S_1; below it and to the right, draw another supply line, S_2, to indicate Ford's cost-cutting production. Mark the equilibrium points at D and S_1 and at D and S_2, then use dashed lines to indicate the price and the quantity demanded and supplied for each point. Examine the decrease in price from the point where S_1 crosses the gradual-sloped demand curve to where S_2 does. Examine the increase in quantity demanded from the point where S_2 crosses the demand line to where S_1 does. Can you see that the quantity demanded increased more than the price fell? A small change in price for a good with an elastic demand causes a greater change in quantity demanded, as your graph will show. The result for Ford was a significant increase in sales and revenues.

QUESTIONS

1. For each of the following market situations, determine the elasticity of the good, and draw a small freehand graph with supply lines to illustrate the change in the market. Determine whether this change will cause sales revenues to rise or fall.

   a) The price of home computers falls for consumers as manufacturers lower production costs.

   b) Restrictions on milk production raise the price of milk for consumers.

   c) Cellphone manufacturers lower production costs; cellphone prices and service charges still fall.

   d) Generic producers of pharmaceutical drugs enter the market and the prices of drugs prescribed for serious diseases fall.

   e) Prices for non-business-class airline seats are cut as new economy-class airlines are allowed into the market.

   f) Advances in agricultural technology have resulted in significant cost cutting in food production.

---

elasticity because it is easy to store steel and, therefore, ride out price changes. Agricultural industries have low price elasticity because it is difficult to store large volumes of their products in a manner that will keep them fresh. This adds to the problems they have in supplying more of a product to the market if prices rise in the short run.

Cost factors

Increasing output (supply) may be costly depending on the industry. Car manufacturers may be able to increase production in the short term by requiring workers to put in more overtime. A permanent increase in production, however, may entail building new factories, which is a far more costly move on the part of the manufacturer. Supply is more elastic in industries that have lower input expenses. CDs, for example, are not costly to manufacture, and their production can be easily expanded if the demand for a particular performer rises.

Check Your Understanding

1. a) Prices for a particular product are rising because of strong consumer demand. An economist estimates that the coefficient of supply for the product is 0.8. Is this good or bad news for the sellers who want to supply and sell more? Explain.

   b) If the coefficient were 1.5 instead, how would the news compare to that in (a)?

2. Figure 5.9 provides data on the supply of ice cream cones. Using the formula for supply elasticity, calculate the coefficients for each price range (from $1 to $2, then from $2 to $3) for both the short-term and longer-term periods.

Price per Cone	Short-Term Supply	Coefficient	Longer-Term Supply	Coefficient
$1	300		1000	
$2	500		5000	
$3	700		10 000	

Figure 5.9 Supply of ice cream cones.

Making Consumption Choices: Utility Theory

In Chapter 4, we saw how a market demand curve is the sum of the many individual demand curves of the consumers who buy a particular product. But what factors determine the demand for the products that each of us buys? Is there a rational way of explaining the decisions we make about buying and consuming? Alfred Marshall, sometimes referred to as "the father of demand and supply," was the first to advance the most widely accepted explanation. His theory is known as the **marginal utility theory of consumer choice**, or **utility theory** for short.

To understand Marshall's theory, let's consider an example. Suppose there is a health-conscious student, Lisa, who has the choice of buying either a veggie burger or frozen yoghurt. What factors might influence Lisa in making her choice?

First, she would probably consider how many veggie burgers she has consumed lately. If she has enjoyed several, she might decide that she would gain little *extra* satisfaction from consuming another. The economic term for "satisfaction" or "usefulness" is *utility*; the term used for "extra" is *marginal*. We would say, then, that the **marginal utility** (extra satisfaction) Lisa would receive from yet another veggie burger is low because she has already consumed several recently. However, if she has bought little frozen yoghurt in the past week, the extra satisfaction she would gain from buying more yoghurt would be higher. Since the marginal utility of

buying more yoghurt is greater for Lisa than the marginal utility of eating another veggie burger, Lisa would most likely buy the yoghurt.

Suppose, however, Lisa wanted both veggie burgers and frozen yoghurt. We assume that, like most consumers, she wants to maximize her satisfaction, or utility, for the income she has available to spend on these items. Suppose that Lisa has $10 to spend this week on these two items. The burgers cost $2 each, and a frozen yoghurt costs $1. How should she determine how much of each she should buy? We can compare Lisa's choices by using the table in Figure 5.10, which arbitrarily assigns numerical values called **utils**, or units of satisfaction, to the burgers and yoghurt.

We see that the utility Lisa receives from consuming one veggie burger or one frozen yoghurt is high. Total utility is ten utils for one burger and 11 utils for frozen yoghurt. For the first unit of the item in question, the marginal utility is always the same as total utility. Lisa is gaining ten utils of extra satisfaction by consuming one veggie burger instead of none and, similarly, 11 utils of extra satisfaction by consuming one frozen yoghurt instead of none. If Lisa buys a second veggie burger or a second frozen yoghurt, the extra satisfaction she experiences drops slightly to eight utils for the second burger and seven for the second frozen yoghurt. Her total satisfaction is now 18 utils for two veggie burgers and is also 18 utils for two frozen yoghurts—a total of 36 utils for the two different items. We see the same pattern through a third and fourth veggie burger or frozen yoghurt: marginal utility steadily falls

Veggie Burgers	Total Utility	Marginal Utility	Frozen Yoghurt	Total Utility	Marginal Utility
1	10	10	1	11	11
2	18	8	2	18	7
3	24	6	3	22	4
4	28	4	4	25	3
5	30	2	5	26	1

Figure 5.10 Lisa's monthly consumption of veggie burgers and frozen yoghurt.

as Lisa consumes one more of either product. Total utility continues to rise as more is consumed, but not as quickly.

Figures 5.11a and 5.11b illustrate how to plot this information on a graph. In Figure 5.11a, *total* utility rises steadily as Lisa consumes more veggie burgers, but in Figure 5.11b, we see that *marginal* utility steadily falls. The same patterns would hold true for her consumption of frozen yoghurt.

If Lisa's budget were unlimited, she could maximize her utility by consuming five veggie burgers and five frozen yoghurts. This would cost her (5 × $2) + (5 × $1) = $15. This combination produces 30 + 26 = 56 utils, which is the highest total utility achievable as measured by Figure 5.10. Since she has limited herself to $10, however, Lisa must find another combination that will yield her the highest satisfaction, or total utility, possible. Which combination of veggie burgers and frozen yoghurt will give her the most satisfaction?

The formula that yields the answer is the utility maximization formula:

$$\frac{MU}{\text{price of product A}} = \frac{MU}{\text{price of product B}}$$

where MU = marginal utility. $\frac{MU}{\text{price}}$ signifies the amount of satisfaction received per dollar.

Figure 5.12 (page 104) shows the calculations we need to perform to determine the $\frac{MU}{\text{price}}$.

We can now determine Lisa's best combination for maximizing her satisfaction. She will do so by purchasing three veggie burgers and four frozen yoghurts because, at these positions, the $\frac{MU}{\text{price}}$ is equal for both items. Since Lisa is receiving the same amount of satisfaction per dollar for each item, she has no reason to buy more of one and less of another. An economist would say she is in a condition of **consumer equilibrium**. She has spent 3 × $2 = $6 on veggie burgers and 4 × $1 = $4 on frozen yoghurt for a total of $10. More importantly, she has maximized her total utility by amassing 49 utils. No other combination will give her more total utils within her $10 budget limit. Using the tables in Figures 5.10 and 5.12, try other combinations to prove this to yourself.

Applications of Utility Theory

Let's look at the application of utility theory as it relates to the demand curve, Adam Smith's paradox, and consumer surplus.

The demand curve

We have seen that the demand curve slopes downward from top left to bottom right

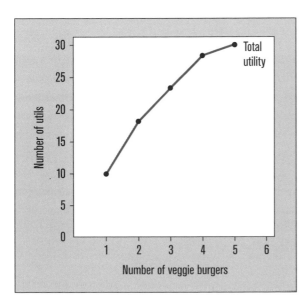

Figure 5.11a Total utility for Lisa's consumption of veggie burgers.

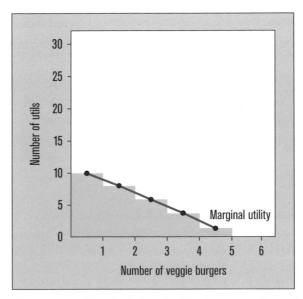

Figure 5.11b Marginal utility for Lisa's consumption of veggie burgers. (The unusual placement of values here is to reflect the fact that marginal utility involves the satisfaction *between* one unit and the next.)

Veggie Burgers	Marginal Utility	$\dfrac{\text{MU}}{\text{Price}}$	Frozen Yoghurt	Marginal Utility	$\dfrac{\text{MU}}{\text{Price}}$
1	10	$\dfrac{10}{\$2} = 5$	1	11	$\dfrac{11}{\$1} = 11$
2	8	$\dfrac{8}{\$2} = 4$	2	7	$\dfrac{7}{\$1} = 7$
3	6	$\dfrac{6}{\$2} = 3$	3	4	$\dfrac{4}{\$1} = 4$
4	4	$\dfrac{4}{\$2} = 2$	4	3	$\dfrac{3}{\$1} = 3$
5	2	$\dfrac{2}{\$2} = 1$	5	1	$\dfrac{1}{\$1} = 1$

Figure 5.12 Lisa's $\dfrac{\text{marginal utility}}{\text{price}}$ for veggie burgers and frozen yoghurt.

because consumers will buy more only if price falls. The theory of marginal utility supports this idea because it tells us that as people consume more, the extra satisfaction they receive declines. If people receive less satisfaction as they consume more of a product, then, obviously, they will want to pay less (not more) for that product the more they buy it.

Adam Smith's paradox

We met the father of capitalism, Adam Smith, in Chapter 3. Smith wrestled with an economic problem he was never able to solve, one he called the **paradox of value**. Why, he wondered, are diamonds more costly than water, when water is essential to human life and diamonds are not? Smith could not understand why the demand for a necessity should not be high enough to assure that its price is as high as the price for luxury items. This paradox remained unsolved until the development of utility theory.

The key to unlocking the paradox lies in the difference between the total and marginal utility for water and diamonds. Clearly, water has infinitely greater total utility (usefulness) than diamonds, which, in comparison, could vanish from the Earth with no harm to the human race. But diamonds are scarce compared to water. Few are bought, thus the satisfaction one receives from a diamond is extremely high. The marginal utility, or extra satisfaction, buyers receive from purchasing a diamond once or twice in a lifetime means they are willing to pay a high price for something that, in reality, has little total utility.

In comparison, the very abundance of water means that most people can consume so much of it that its marginal utility is pushed very low. If a product's marginal utility is low, people are not willing to pay a high price for it, not even for something as vital, and with such great total utility, as water.

Consumer surplus

If we examine the concept of marginal utility closely enough, we shall come to a surprising conclusion: we get a bargain on everything we buy! Economists call this result a **consumer surplus**, which we'll define after working through an example using Lisa's purchases of a different product—her favourite brand of bottled water.

Let's suppose we asked Lisa how many cases of bottled water she would buy at different prices. She provides us with the answers shown in Figure 5.13, which we can identify as Lisa's bottled water demand schedule. This table shows that Lisa would buy only one case of bottled water if the price per case were $9. However, if after consuming this one case the price dropped to $8, she would buy another case, for a total of two cases in one month and a total cost of $17. Lisa would continue to buy one more case of water each time the price fell further, until, by the time the price per case reached $6, she would have bought four cases. The results summarized in Figure 5.13 are a perfect illustration of marginal utility because they demonstrate that Lisa would buy more cases of water only if the price fell.

Price	Number of Cases of Water	Consumer Surplus
$9	1	$9 − $6 = $3
$8	2	$8 − $6 = $2
$7	3	$7 − $6 = $1
$6	4	$6 − $6 = $0

Figure 5.13 Lisa's consumer surplus for bottled water.

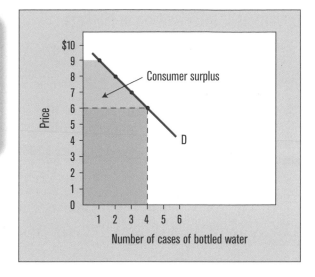

Figure 5.14 Lisa's consumer surplus for bottled water.

In reality, however, the sellers of bottled water do not drop their prices throughout the month to encourage Lisa to buy more of their product. They charge a constant price, say $6 a case. The happy result is that Lisa actually receives a surplus for the first three cases of bottled water she buys. The third column in Figure 5.13 shows that this surplus is calculated by subtracting the amount she *would* have paid for each case of water from the amount she actually paid. Lisa would be willing to pay $30 for the four cases of bottled water she buys each month ($9 + $8 + $7 + $6 = $30). In reality, she pays only $24 ($6 × 4 = $24) for them, achieving a total of $6 for her consumer's surplus. We can best define this concept as the difference between what we are willing to pay for an item and what we actually pay.

Figure 5.14 provides an illustration of this concept. D is Lisa's demand curve for bottled water. Lisa actually pays the blue shaded area for the four cases of bottled water she buys each month. However, the total value to her of the four cases is the entire shaded area (both blue *and* yellow). Thus, the consumer surplus she receives is the yellow area.

Check Your Understanding

1. Explain the difference between total utility and marginal utility using as an example a person drinking cans of soft drinks.

2. Copy Figure 5.15 into your notebook. Fill in the missing values.

3. a) Enrique is willing to go to one movie a month if the price is $10, two if the price drops to $8, and three if the price drops further to $6. If the price of a movie is set at $8, what is Enrique's consumer surplus?

   b) On a graph, draw Enrique's demand curve for movies, and shade in the area of his consumer surplus.

Units Consumed	Total Utility	Marginal Utility
0	0	—
1	6	6
2	—	8
3	24	—
4	34	—
5	—	8
6	48	—

Figure 5.15 Fill in the missing values.

Government Intervention in Markets

Former US President Ronald Reagan once used the phrase "the magic of the market" to explain the buoyant state of the American economy during his term in office (1981–1985, 1985–1989). His brief description of a market economy was accurate in many ways. The market engines of demand and supply automatically produce the vast range of goods and services consumers want and then distribute these goods and services with a minimum of waste or shortages. All this is done without the benefit of any individual or group providing direction for the economy.

Governments do, however, intervene extensively in markets. Why do they do this? Are they threatening the "magic of the market" by intervening? To answer these questions, we'll look at three examples of controversial government actions:

1. If the government believes people are paying too high a price for an item, it will introduce a *ceiling price* as a solution.
2. If the government believes sellers are receiving too low a price for a product, it will introduce a *floor price* as a solution.
3. If the government believes it must intervene in a market for social or environmental reasons, it will introduce a *subsidy* or a *quota* as a solution.

Ceiling Prices

A **ceiling price** is a restriction placed by a government in order to prevent the price of a product from rising above a certain level. If the ceiling price is set below the equilibrium price, a shortage will result. Consider the market for gasoline illustrated in Figure 5.16. Suppose an international crisis has interfered with oil supplies to such an extent that prices start to climb. The government, concerned by the hardship these price increases have caused for motorists, places a price ceiling (PC) on gasoline. The equilibrium price was $0.65 per litre, with 100 million litres per month demanded and supplied. The price ceiling prohibits prices from rising above $0.60 per litre. At this price, 110 million litres (QD$_1$) are demanded, and

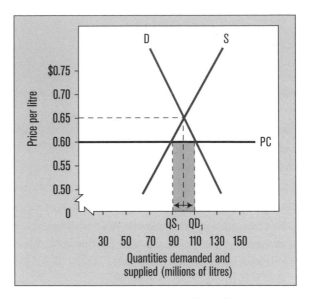

Figure 5.16 The gasoline market. The effect of a ceiling price is a shortage.

90 million litres (QS$_1$) are supplied. This creates a shortage of QD$_1$ – QS$_1$ = 20 million litres.

There are three possible outcomes of price ceilings. First, the shortages can cause long line-ups for the product. This problem occurred in 1974 in the United States when American motorists pressured their government to restrict the rising price of gasoline. This price ceiling led to gasoline shortages and long line-ups that snaked for blocks around gas stations until the ceilings were lifted to allow the price to rise and bring demand and supply into equilibrium.

Second, price ceilings may create a **black market** for certain goods. This happens when a shortage of a product (such as sugar) encourages some people to buy up as much of it as they can at the ceiling price, stockpile it, and then sell it at a higher price to people who can't get enough for their own use. This happened in Canada during the Second World War when the government rationed several basic food items.

Third, price ceilings may cause the quality of a product to suffer if sellers try to reduce their costs in order to make more money. This situation is less likely to occur with natural resource products such as gasoline or foods, but it occurs more frequently when the government places a ceiling on a product such as rental accommodations.

Floor Prices

A **floor price** is a restriction that prevents a price from falling *below* a certain level. If the floor price is set above the equilibrium price, it will cause a surplus. Suppose the government believes that milk producers are making too little profit on milk, priced at $0.50 per litre. The government may set a floor price of $0.60 per litre, below which prices are not allowed to fall. The result can be seen in Figure 5.17.

The line PF is the floor price of $0.60 per litre. At that price, 10 million litres will be supplied—more than the 9 million litres that would have been supplied at the equilibrium price of $0.50 per litre. The higher floor price cuts the quantity demanded to 8 million litres, less than would be demanded at the equilibrium price. The result, $QS_1 - QD_1$, is a surplus of 2 million litres of milk.

Maintaining this floor price causes two problems. First, there is the problem of what to do with the surplus. In order to keep the floor price at $0.60 per litre, the government must buy the surplus of milk (using taxpayers' money) with little chance that the surplus will generate a return. It cannot be sold within the country at prices below the floor price without undercutting the floor price. Sometimes, surpluses can be sold on the world market or donated to less developed countries. Otherwise, since milk is perishable, it must be turned into products that can be stored, such as powdered milk, butter, and cheese.

Second, consumers on the whole pay a higher price for the product and receive less. In Figure 5.17, we can see that consumers in an unregulated market would probably have paid the equilibrium price of $0.50 per litre and would have received 9 million litres of milk. With the floor price set by the government, they pay $0.60 per litre and receive 8 million litres.

Subsidies and Quotas

Both price ceilings and price floors share a common problem: less of the product is actually transacted between sellers and buyers when the price is forced away from its equilibrium price by these policies. (Look again at Figures 5.16 and 5.17 to verify this important point.) In order to avoid this problem, governments sometime enact subsidies. A **subsidy** is a grant of money made to a particular industry by the government.

Let's look at Figure 5.18 to see how the milk market will be affected by a subsidy of

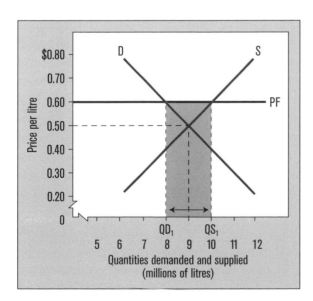

Figure 5.17 The milk market. The effect of a floor price is a surplus.

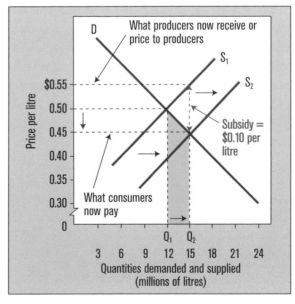

Figure 5.18 The effect of a subsidy is to increase the quantity supplied.

$0.10 per litre. The immediate impact is that the supply line increases by the amount of the subsidy since producers turn out more milk because they are receiving an extra $0.10 per litre. The result is that the new equilibrium price of $0.45 is lower than the old equilibrium price of $0.50, and the quantity sold is increased by 3 million litres (from Q_1 to Q_2).

A subsidy has the advantage of benefiting buyers with lower prices and sellers with extra revenue. It also means that more of the product is exchanged between buyers and sellers. A subsidy has a couple of drawbacks, however; the taxpayer pays for the program, some critics charge that subsidies keep inefficient producers in business, and, in the global economy, subsidies are often seen as a barrier to fair trade.

Quotas are another means of helping producers. A **quota** is a restriction placed on the amount of a product that individual producers are allowed to produce. These restrictions are administered by organizations called **marketing boards**, which are composed of representatives from the government and from the producers. Milk marketing boards operate in every province in Canada.

Figure 5.19 illustrates what happens when a provincial marketing board enforces a reduced quota on all milk producers in the province. S_2 shows the shift of supply to the left. P_2 is the new, higher price, and Q_2 is the new, smaller amount of milk that is actually sold.

Quotas set by marketing boards raise farmers' incomes mainly because food is an inelastic commodity. Remember that when prices rise on an inelastic product, sales revenue also rises because quantity demanded does not fall by much. Farmers were given the authority to establish marketing boards years ago because governments believed that their incomes were, on average, too low. Farmers are producing an essential commodity, and if too many of them go out of business, so the argument goes, Canadians will wind up paying more for their food. Critics reply that marketing boards raise prices above equilibrium, with the result that less of the product is actually produced and exchanged. Whatever the argument, the fact remains that most of the Canadian meat, vegetable, and dairy products we buy in supermarkets are sold to the stores by marketing boards.

Rent controls

A rent-control program is a good example of a price ceiling. Most Canadian provinces and many American states have enacted such programs, and the controversy that surrounds them never seems to end. Let's use the tools of supply and demand to examine the rental market and the effects that controls have on it.

Rent is the price people pay for accommodation and, like any other market price, it is determined by demand and supply. Figure 5.20a shows the rent the market sets for the quantity of apartments demanded and supplied in a particular building. At $500 for a one-bedroom apartment, the owner will supply 50 apartments. We have made the supply line vertical because the owner cannot increase supply immediately (because that would involve building more units). In other words, the supply of apartments is fixed, or *perfectly inelastic,* in the short term.

Suppose an increase in renters occurs, shifting demand upward. This encourages the owner to raise rents to $600 a month. This increase has two effects: those who can afford

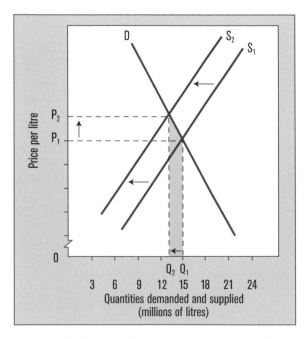

Figure 5.19 The effect of a quota is to increase the income of suppliers by raising the price of a product.

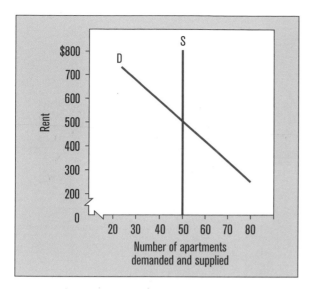

Figure 5.20a How rents are set.

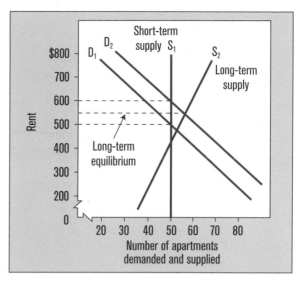

Figure 5.20b What happens when demand increases.

the higher rent will stay and pay while those who cannot will have to find less expensive accommodation elsewhere.

Higher rents mean higher profits for the owner, who is therefore encouraged to build more units. Figure 5.20b illustrates the effect of this long-term decision to construct another apartment building: the supply curve shifts to the right. This long-run supply curve, with greater elasticity, also has beneficial effects for renters, as we can see from the graph. The supply of apartments is increased, and the rental price, at least in theory, falls to $550. This is the way a free rental market tends to work, and it is noteworthy that both renters and apartment owners appear to win in the long run.

Now suppose that in response to the increase in demand that caused rents to rise to $600 in the short term, the government comes under pressure to alleviate the economic hardship renters are experiencing. The government introduces a rent-control program: a law that freezes, reduces, or controls the amount of rent that owners can charge. We'll simplify the discussion at this point, and assume that a freeze on rent for one-bedroom apartments will be fixed at $500. Figure 5.21 shows that if demand continues to rise to D_2, there will be a shortage of supply of ten units.

If this kind of shortage is repeated in buildings all over the city, people will have great difficulty finding essential accommodation. Those who are looking for an apartment will be tempted to offer building owners more money "under the table" in hopes of beating others to a vacancy. Owners, with no incentive to keep their buildings in good repair to attract new tenants, may stop making essential repairs and renovations. With rental prices

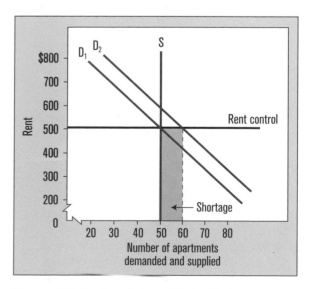

Figure 5.21 Rent controls and their effects.

A Matter of Opinion | The Housing Crisis Grows

" Michelle—a young woman who works for a nonprofit agency in Toronto—was looking for an apartment last year. It was shortly before her marriage, and she was hard-put to find something central that she and her fiancé could afford. They found an ad about a one-bedroom apartment over a store for $1100 per month. It seemed a little steep but it sounded nice.

The landlord set a showing time of 2 p.m. Four couples showed up at about the same time. All were interested. So the landlord held a bidding war and ended up getting $2200 a month.

When Michelle confronted him, saying that the first couple who wanted it should have got it for the advertised price, he shrugged his shoulders. "So what. Now I'm getting double."

Anna fled from the Pinochet regime in Chile 20 years ago and has lived in a co-operative housing unit with her family since then. She talks about immigrants having to pay "finders fees" of up to $5000 to be put on a list for an apartment, and of how some are being asked to pay a full year's rent in advance.

"It used to be nice where I am," she said. "But now everyone is only interested in themselves. They don't care about community and it's just getting worse."

And so it goes when there are no rent controls. There are myriad stories just like Michelle and Anna's; when properties become vacant, owners can raise the price to whatever they can get for it. Doubling the price or more, bidding wars: these are common practices in Toronto since the introduction of the Tenant Protection Act of 1998. [This act eliminated rent controls in Ontario except for premises with existing tenants.] It's the act that also streamlines a landlord's ability to evict people.

. . . In Ontario and Alberta, where rent controls have been eliminated and with minimum wage levels as low as they are in those provinces—$5.50 in Alberta, $6.85 in Ontario—the dilemma of an affordable place

In many communities, organizations such as Habitat for Humanity are working to provide affordable housing for those affected by the elimination of rent controls.

to live is causing the numbers of families with children who populate shelters and subsidized motel rooms to steadily increase, even though the parents may have jobs.

. . . Subsidies for housing have 18-year-long waiting lists in Toronto and even market-rent co-operative units have long waiting lists, some up to ten years. . . . "

Source: Abridged version of "The Housing Crisis Grows" by Margaret Dinsdale from http://www.rabble.ca. Reprinted by permission of the author.

QUESTIONS

1. What are three criticisms of rent controls as explained on pages 109 and 111?

2. What do Anna's and Michelle's stories reveal about the abuses that can occur when rent controls are not in place?

3. "Something as essential as rent should be regulated by the government to prevent abuses. Shelter is too essential to have its price determined solely by the marketplace." Explain why you agree or disagree.

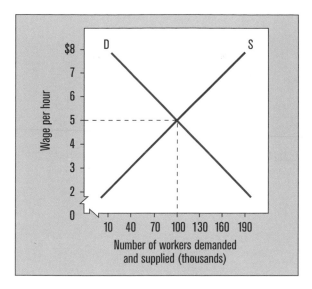

Figure 5.22a The labour market before minimum wage.

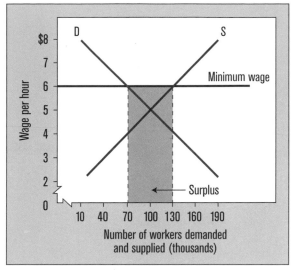

Figure 5.22b The labour market after the government sets a minimum wage.

fixed, they will also be disinclined to build more units. While many people wonder whether rent controls are worth these costs, there is another side to the rent-control issue (as the feature on the facing page illustrates).

Minimum wages

Rent controls are an example of how governments intervene in markets in order to establish a ceiling price when they think the price that sellers are receiving for their product is too high. As we stated before, governments also intervene to establish floor prices when they believe the price sellers are receiving is too low. A **wage** is the price a worker receives for supplying labour to a business with a demand for it. In Figure 5.22a, we see that 100 000 workers are receiving wages of $5 an hour. Suppose the government responds to public pressure to raise the low wages of these workers by setting a **minimum wage**, a wage that is higher than the one set by the forces of demand and supply.

We can see the results of the government's move in Figure 5.22b. The minimum wage is set at $6 an hour. Businesses adjust to this by employing only 70 000 workers, 30 000 fewer than at the old wage rate of $5 an hour. Furthermore, the higher wage rate attracts an additional 30 000 workers into the labour market, for a total of 130 000 workers who are willing to work for $6 an hour. If businesses are willing to hire only 70 000 workers, this means the minimum wage has created an unemployment problem: 60 000 workers who cannot find jobs.

As noted on page 107, floor prices tend to create surpluses. In the case of minimum wages, they create surpluses of potential workers who cannot find jobs. On the other hand, the minimum wage increases the wages of thousands of people at the low end of the wage scale. These people receive a more substantial paycheque than they would have if wages had been set solely by supply and demand. Are the benefits of the minimum wage worth the costs? Read the following feature to understand the contrasting views on this controversial subject.

A Matter of Opinion | Minimum Wages in Canada

The Benefits of Minimum Wage

In September 1999, the Canadian Centre for Policy Alternatives (CCPA) released a major study that profiled minimum-wage workers and discussed the impact that increases to minimum wage have on the labour market. The following are some of the study's findings:

- *Minimum-wage workers are primarily adults and women.*
  A popular misconception is that the majority of minimum-wage workers are teenagers living at home in middle-class families; however, this is not the case. Sixty-one per cent of minimum-wage workers are adults (19 years of age and over) and 64 per cent are women. Minimum-wage work is also an important source of income for many students seeking to finance their post-secondary education. The vast majority of teenage minimum-wage workers, over half of young adult minimum-wage workers, and 12 per cent of adult minimum-wage workers were full-time students at some time during the survey year.
- *Minimum wages disproportionately benefit low-income families.*
  The evidence clearly shows that minimum-wage earners are disproportionately represented among families with low incomes. Thus, increases in the minimum wage will disproportionately benefit low-income families.
- *Increasing the minimum wage has only marginal effects on employment.*
  In-depth analysis clearly disputes the claim that minimum wages are a major "killer of jobs." Over the past two decades, large increases in the minimum wage have been followed by both increases and decreases in employment, demonstrating that other trends in the economy influence employment levels

to a much greater extent than do minimum wages. Studies looking at employment effects of minimum-wage changes typically find very small negative or even positive impacts.
- *Minimum wages should be set at the poverty line.*
  Clear criteria are needed for setting the minimum wage, so that both workers and businesses know the rules and can plan for increases. The minimum wage should be high enough to ensure that individuals working full-time will not find themselves in poverty.

The minimum wage would need to increase to $8 an hour in order for a worker's annual gross income (working a full year at 40 hours per week) to reach Statistics Canada's Low Income Cut Off line (more commonly known as the poverty line) of $16 640.

Source: Adapted from *Raising the Floor: The Social and Economic Benefits of Minimum Wages in Canada* by Michael Goldberg and David Green, Canadian Centre for Policy Alternatives (September 1999). Reprinted by permission.

Minimum Wage: Poverty or Opportunity

" ... Opponents to increasing minimum wage argue that higher minimum wages reduce job opportunities for young and unskilled workers. With each minimum-wage increase, it becomes more difficult for small business employers to be able to afford to hire new employees. This is because they would not only have to raise the salary of their minimum-wage employees, but likely they would have to raise the salaries of higher-paid staff in order to maintain a pay/position hierarchy within the firm. As a result, employers deplete surplus revenue that may otherwise have been used to hire new employees. Opponents also argue that increased levels of minimum wage can lead to higher high school drop-out rates, less on-the-job training and fewer fringe benefits.

... In Canada, about 5 per cent of the workforce, or 545 000 workers, earn minimum wage .... More than half of all minimum-wage workers (58 per cent) are youths between the ages of 15 and 24 and the majority of them are living at home with their parents .... Another one out of four minimum wage earners have an employed partner who is likely earning more than the minimum wage ....

Rather than increasing minimum wage, which may negatively [affect] the majority of current and future minimum-wage workers who are young and/or unskilled, policy needs to be directed at the 18 per cent of minimum-wage earners who are over 25 and are the sole providers of income in their household .... Most 15- to 24-year-olds will likely not remain at minimum wage once they gain work experience and skills. By keeping the wage affordable for employers, more young people can gain the requisite work experience that will eventually earn them higher salaries. Instead, assistance should be targeted at the fewer than one in five minimum-wage earners who may be caught in a poverty trap, unable to earn a decent wage for themselves and their dependents.... **99**

Source: Corinne Pohlmann, "Minimum Wage: Poverty or Opportunity?" from *Behind the Numbers* (Canadian Federation of Independent Business, May 1999), <http://www.cfib.ca/research/reports/minwage.pdf>. Reprinted by permission.

Many young people look for jobs on the job board of their local employment centre. A great number of these positions pay minimum wage.

QUESTIONS

1. How do the two viewpoints differ on the "numbers question"? In other words, who is actually receiving the minimum wage?

2. Compare the two viewpoints in regard to the problem of job losses if the minimum wage is increased.

3. Which viewpoint would most likely be supported by (a) teenagers, (b) people over 25, (c) small-business owners, and (d) anti-poverty activists? In each case, provide one piece of evidence to support your answer.

Check Your Understanding

1. Assume that the demand and supply schedule for wheat in Canada is as indicated in Figure 5.23.

Price per Bushel	Quantity Demanded (million bushels)	Quantity Supplied (million bushels)
$4	11	18
$3	15	15
$2	19	13
$1	23	11

Figure 5.23 A hypothetical demand and supply schedule for wheat in Canada.

a) Suppose the government sets a floor price of $4 a bushel.

i) What will be the effect on the wheat market in terms of quantities demanded and supplied?

ii) Which group, consumers or farmers, is the government trying to help? Explain.

iii) What problem has the government created for itself?

b) Suppose the government sets a ceiling price of $2 a bushel.

i) What will be the effect on the wheat market in terms of quantities demanded and supplied?

ii) Which group, consumers or farmers, is the government trying to help? Explain.

iii) What problem has the government created for itself?

c) If the government believes that the equilibrium price set by the market is too low, what two other methods could it introduce to help farmers?

CHAPTER SUMMARY

- Elasticity measures how responsive demand or supply quantities are to a given change in price.

- The elasticity coefficient of demand is determined by dividing the average of the percentage change between two quantities demanded by the corresponding average of the percentage change in price.

- Coefficients of both demand and supply are classified as inelastic if they are less than one, unitary if equal to one, and elastic if more than one.

- Elasticity of demand can also be determined by calculating the change in sales revenue between two prices. Sales revenue is defined as price times quantity demanded.

- If sales revenue rises when price rises, or falls when price falls, demand is said to be inelastic.

- If sales revenue falls when price rises, or rises when price falls, demand is said to be elastic.

- The elasticity coefficient of supply is determined by dividing the average of the percentage change between two quantities supplied by the corresponding average of the percentage change in price.

- Utility is defined as the usefulness or satisfaction a consumer receives from the consumption of a product or from the use of a service.

- Total utility measures the total satisfaction gained from consuming all the units a consumer purchases. Marginal utility measures the extra satisfaction gained from consuming one more unit of the product.

- Total utility increases as more is consumed, while marginal utility falls.

- Consumer equilibrium is the state of maximum satisfaction a consumer reaches when the marginal utility divided by price is equal for two or more products bought by the consumer.

- Consumer surplus is the difference between what the consumer is willing to pay for a product and what the consumer actually pays.

- Governments intervene in markets by introducing ceiling prices if they believe consumers may have to pay too much in a particular market.

- Governments intervene in markets by introducing floor prices, quotas, and subsidies if they believe sellers are receiving too little in a particular market.

Key Terms

elasticity
price elasticity of demand
inelastic coefficient
elastic coefficient
unitary coefficient
total revenue
elasticity of supply
marginal utility theory of consumer choice (utility theory)
marginal utility
util
consumer equilibrium
paradox of value
consumer surplus
ceiling price
black market
floor price
subsidy
quota
marketing board
rent
wage
minimum wage

Activities

Thinking/Inquiry

1. The elasticity of demand for an urban transit company in winter is estimated to be 0.9. In summer, it rises to 1.4. Suggest reasons why the elasticity of demand for transit service differs depending on the season.

2. A student newspaper has determined that its coefficient of demand is less than one at prices below $1.25 but greater than one at prices above $1.25. Considering the product, why do you think elasticity changes?

3. Sales revenues rise when the price of shoelaces rises 20 per cent. Movie ticket revenues fall at the Movielux theatre when tickets rise by the same percentage. Explain why this difference exists, using three price elasticity factors to compare the two goods.

4. A demand curve normally slopes down from left to right. What does this indicate about consumer behaviour with regard to price and quantity demanded? How does marginal utility help to explain this consumer behaviour and, thus, the direction of the demand curve?

5. Using the example of your favourite soft drink, explain how your demand for it can be derived from the utility you receive from its consumption.

6. Although parking meters in urban centres may yield little revenue because of the costs of installation and the employees who check and maintain them, most cities still regard them as essential for proper traffic flow. Explain why this is so using the concepts of demand, supply, and price.

Communication

7. Work in pairs. One partner draws up a list of ten products believed to have an elastic demand, while the other partner lists products that have an inelastic demand. Then compare lists and justify your choices. Share your findings with the rest of the class, and explain any disagreements or uncertainties.

8. Organize a debate around this issue: "In the interests of fairness and reducing poverty, the minimum wage should be boosted immediately to $8 an hour for all employees, young and old."

Application

9. Copy Figures 5.1 (page 96) and 5.2 (page 97) into your notebook. Using Figure 5.1, calculate the total revenues for gasoline at each price. Label each pair of consecutive prices (there should be eight pairs) either elastic or inelastic according to the sales revenue summary in Figure 5.2.

10. Copy Figure 5.24 into your notebook.

   a) Determine the price elasticity for the computer for each price range.

   b) Give two reasons why this item would have this particular elasticity.

   c) Because of the costs of manufacturing the computer, it is currently priced at $2800. As costs fall, should the manufacturer

Price	Quantity Demanded	Sales Revenue	Elasticity
$3000	8000		
$2800	10 000		
$2600	12 000		
$2400	14 000		
$2200	16 000		

Figure 5.24 A demand schedule for a home computer.

Quantity of Tickets	Price per Ticket	Sales Revenue	Inelastic or Elastic Demand
0	$12		
400	$10		
800	$8		
1200	$6		
1600	$4		
2000	$2		

Figure 5.25 An estimated demand schedule for a theme park's admission tickets.

maintain the same price, raise it, or lower it? Explain your reasoning.

d) Suppose an attachment that most buyers of the computer find useful costs an extra $25. Will this attachment have an inelastic or an elastic demand for the majority of buyers? What would be the best pricing strategy for the seller: to raise, lower, or maintain the price? Why?

11. Copy Figure 5.25 into your notebook, and determine

a) sales revenue at each price,

b) whether demand is elastic or inelastic between each price,

c) the admission price that appears to assure the park of the highest profit.

12. Suppose a certain city has a demand for two-bedroom apartments as shown in Figure 5.26:

a) Plot a demand and supply curve for this schedule assuming there are 3000 apartments. What is the equilibrium rent? Is the supply elastic or perfectly inelastic in the short term?

b) Assume that demand for apartments in the city increases, rising by 1000 at each rental price. What will happen to the equilibrium price?

c) Suppose the city council steps in and freezes rent at the original equilibrium rent. Graph the results of such a rent-control law.

13. Copy Figure 5.27 into your notebook, and calculate the remaining coefficients of supply.

Rent	Quantity Demanded
$1000	1000
$900	2000
$800	3000
$700	4000
$600	5000
$500	6000

Figure 5.26 A demand schedule for two-bedroom apartments.

Price per Tonne	Quantity Supplied (million tonnes)	Coefficient of Supply
$120	1.0	1.19
$140	1.2	
$160	1.4	
$180	1.6	
$200	1.8	
$220	2.0	
$240	2.2	

Figure 5.27 Elasticity of supply for the steel market.

Price	Quantity Supplied (kg)	Coefficient of Supply	Elastic/ Inelastic
$0.60	100		
$0.70	105		
$0.80	115		
$0.90	130		
$1.00	160		

Figure 5.28 A supply schedule for fresh tomatoes.

14. Copy the supply schedule in Figure 5.28 into your notebook.

   a) Determine the coefficients of supply for fresh tomatoes.

   b) Suppose the equilibrium price is $0.60 per kilogram but increased demand pushes the price steadily up to $1 per kilogram. Contrast the elasticity from $0.60 to $0.80 with the elasticity from $0.80 to $1, and give an explanation for the difference.

15. Assume that a province's demand and supply for milk is as indicated in Figure 5.29.

   a) Graph the information in Figure 5.29. In a free market, what would be the price for a litre of milk?

   b) Suppose the government sets a floor price of $1 per litre. How would the market be affected? Show the results on your graph.

   c) Suppose that, instead of a floor price, a marketing board establishes a quota that cuts production by 1 million litres at all possible prices. Graph this restriction on a new graph, and determine what the new price of milk would be.

   d) Suppose the marketing board launches a successful advertising campaign that raises milk consumption by 1 million litres at each price level. On your second graph, indicate what the results would be if this advertising campaign were used along with the quota referred to in part (c), and determine what the price would be.

Price per Litre	Quantity Demanded (million litres)	Quantity Supplied (million litres)
$0.20	10	4
$0.40	9	5
$0.60	8	6
$0.80	7	7
$1.00	6	8
$1.20	5	9
$1.40	4	10

Figure 5.29 A hypothetical demand and supply schedule for milk in a Canadian province.

CHAPTER 6
BUSINESS ORGANIZATION AND FINANCE

Business Enterprise in the Free-Market System

Large multinational corporations (companies with business ventures in various countries) have emerged as one of the most creative and powerful international institutions of the 20th century. In this chapter, we shall investigate corporations and other ways of organizing and financing business enterprises in Canada. Our investigation begins with this political cartoon. Although some critics suggest that multinational corporations use their power and size to secure greater returns on their investments, others claim that their self-interest is no different from the behaviour of most other forms of business enterprise within the free-market system.

QUESTIONS

1. Study the cartoon. What is the cartoonist saying about the ethics of multinational corporations?
2. Why is the US flag seen flying in the background?
3. How are the directors of this corporation portrayed?
4. Do you know of any multinational corporations? In what businesses are they engaged? What do you know about their corporate image?

Chapter Goals

By the end of this chapter, you will be able to

- compare the different forms of business organization and finance (private and public) in Canada,
- investigate the evolution and growth of Canadian industry and the increasing concentration of corporate power in Canada,
- explain the function of securities and commodities markets,
- develop pattern identification/interpretation skills.

Types of Industrial Activity

All human industrial activity can be classified into one of four types, based on the nature of the activity, as demonstrated in Figure 6.1. In order to identify industrial activity that is of a primary nature, we must determine whether natural resources (or raw materials) are being harvested. If the industrial activity goes beyond harvesting and includes the processing of raw materials into final or semi-processed goods, it has become secondary activity, or manufacturing. All five examples of primary activity are listed in Figure 6.1; for all other categories, the examples provided are not intended as a complete listing.

Quaternary activity consists of **high-tech** services provided to people, firms, and institutions. At one time, economists considered this high-tech sector part of the growing tertiary, or service, sector. As high-tech services continued to expand and became more complex and important, a special category was created for them. The importance of the quaternary sector has continued to grow in the contemporary economy. Since industrial activity in this sector is so expensive and highly specialized, its presence, especially in less developed nations, remains limited.

The Historical Development of Canadian Industry

Historically, an economy begins by first developing its natural resources, then its manufacturing activities, then its service sector, and, finally, its high-tech industries. In other words, there is usually a linear progression evident in the development of a nation's economy from the primary through to the quaternary sectors. This is not to say that service industries emerge only after all primary and secondary industries have been fully developed. In fact, some tertiary industries are developed immediately to serve people engaged in primary and secondary industrial activities. Figure 6.2 outlines the growth sequence of some of Canada's main industries.

Primary industries

Canada's economy first emerged and grew in response to the demands of urbanized European communities for Canadian natural resources. During the 16th, 17th, and 18th centuries, fish, fur, and lumber were the export **staples** that gave the new economy the largest part of its income. These abundant resources attracted labour and capital from Great Britain and France. Primary industries were, therefore, the first type of industrial activity to develop in Canada on a significant scale. Since Canadian fish, fur, and lumber could be sold in European markets for gold and silver, the British and French governments carefully controlled the expansion of these industries.

Canadian colonists served as an additional market for European manufactured goods. The early colonists had few manufacturing industries of their own. As settlement in Canada

	Industrial Category	Type of Activity	Specific Examples
Goods-Producing Industries	Primary	Resource extraction	Farming, fishing, forestry, mining, hunting
	Secondary	Manufacturing	Steel mills, paper mills, automobile assembly plants, breweries, furniture and appliance factories
Services-Producing Industries	Tertiary	Provision of services	Wholesale and retail sales outlets, medical clinics, legal offices, schools
	Quaternary	Provision of highly specialized and expensive technology and support services	Research and development laboratories, information technology design, applied nuclear technology

Figure 6.1 The four types of industrial activity.

Industrial Category	1881 (%)	1921 (%)	1955 (%)	1975 (%)	1990 (%)	1999 (%)
Primary (resource extraction)	51.3	36.6	19.8	7.6	5.8	4.7
Secondary (manufacturing)	29.4	26.5	32.5	26.7	23.0	21.4
Services (tertiary through 1975; tertiary and quaternary starting in 1990)	19.3	36.9	47.7	65.7	71.2	73.9

Source: Figures for 1881–1975 from K.W. Osborne, *Canadians at Work* (Toronto: Prentice-Hall Canada: 1984), 39; figures for 1990 and 1999 from Statistics Canada, *Labour Force Historical Review* #71F-0004XCB.

Figure 6.2 Percentage of Canadian labour force employed by different industrial sectors, 1881–1999.

increased and moved westward, first wheat, then iron, nickel, gold, copper, and other metals were added to the growing list of export staples. This attracted more specialized labour and capital into the economy, and Canadians began to manufacture locally some of the expensive consumer goods that had previously been available only from Europe. This local production meant that manufactured goods became cheaper for Canadians to buy.

Secondary industries

The Industrial Revolution that started in Britain around 1780 changed the way manufactured goods were produced; after about 1850, with the development of fast steam-powered trains and ships, it also affected the free trade of goods between countries. As more labour and capital were attracted to secondary industrial activities in Canada, the national infrastructure slowly transformed itself to focus more on manufacturing and distribution than on resource extraction. After Confederation in 1867, the federal government imposed protective taxes called tariffs on Canada's infant industries in order to develop sustained markets for their goods.

The transcontinental railway, the large-scale infrastructure project included in the National Policy of 1879, was built to complement the existing canals and waterways and to help increase the population of western Canada. Around this same time, manufacturers began to build coal-powered steam generators and, later, hydroelectric generators as inexpensive power sources to run the machinery required to make consumer goods in large quantities. This move toward automation in the factories meant that

fewer workers were needed to produce manufactured goods.

Services industries

The resulting surplus of production workers encouraged a shift of labour and capital from export staple production to specialized services such as transportation and warehousing, finance and insurance, retail and wholesale trade, health and education, entertainment, and personal grooming. As primary and secondary industries continued to develop and expand in Canada, the base of staple goods for domestic and foreign markets was strengthened. By the middle of the 20th century, Canada had become an industrial nation and had achieved a more balanced economy with strong primary, secondary, and tertiary sectors. At the same time, Canada's prosperity and growth remained dependent on its ability to find export markets for foodstuffs, raw materials, and manufactured goods. In any economy, the development of a large service, or tertiary, sector is supported by goods-producing industrial sectors that establish a strong export base and a steady flow of money into the economy.

The employment shift toward the service sector intensified during the economic boom that followed the Second World War and continues to the present day. The level of service specialization has increased significantly over the last 25 years as Canada has developed its quaternary industries. Today, Canada is a major exporter of fibre optics technology, nuclear power generation technology, satellite sensing technology, and other high-tech applications.

SKILL BUILDER
Thinking Like an Economist

Detecting Patterns in Data to Explain Economic Relationships

Nation (GDP per capita)	% in primary industry	% in secondary industry	% in service industry
Examples of more developed countries			
United States* ($31 500)	4	23	73
Japan* ($23 100)	7	33	60
France* ($22 600)	7	31	62
Canada ($22 400)	5	21	74
United Kingdom ($21 200)	3	25	72
Examples of less developed countries			
Mexico ($8300)	25	20	55
China ($3600)	65	20	15
Morocco ($3200)	50	21	29
Mozambique ($3200)	46	25	29
Indonesia ($2800)	54	10	36
Nicaragua ($2500)	47	16	37
Cameroon ($2000)	74	5	21
Vietnam ($1770)	66	12	22
India ($1720)	63	11	26
Niger ($970)	85	3	12

*When sector data were not reported for a nation in the 2001 *Almanac*, data from earlier editions were used.

Source: *Canadian Global Almanac 2001* (Toronto: Macmillan, 2000); Statistics Canada, *Labour Force Historical Review* #71F0004XCB.

Figure 6.3 Percentage of labour force in primary, secondary, and service sectors, 1998.

Figure 6.3 shows the percentage of the labour force, in 15 different nations, that is employed in each industrial sector. For most countries, the largest employer of labour in the primary sector is agriculture. **Gross Domestic Product (GDP) per capita** compares the value of all goods and services produced in a year with national population data. It is sometimes referred to as the "standard-of-living" statistic because it reports the value of goods and services available per person living in a nation. The more industrially developed nations achieve a significantly higher GDP per capita rate than is possible for less developed nations. We will examine this important indicator in more detail in Chapter 9.

QUESTIONS

1. Which industrial sector do most less developed nations depend on to employ much of the labour force? How does this compare to the employment patterns reported by more developed countries such as Canada?

2. What relationship exists between GDP per capita and the percentage of the labour force employed in primary industrial activity? Why are the majority of people in poorer nations engaged in agriculture?

3. Applying what you have learned about the development of the Canadian economy, forecast how the labour force will change as less developed nations continue their economic development.

Check Your Understanding

1. Identify the category of industrial activity represented by each of the following examples: barber shop, pig farm, gold mine, steel mill, automobile assembly plant, and nuclear energy research laboratory.

2. Prepare a summary note to explain how Canadian industrial activity evolved over time and why it has become necessary to subdivide the services sector.

3. "Until a nation develops a healthy manufacturing and service sector, it will always be vulnerable to exploitation by other nations." Defend or refute this statement.

Forms of Business Organization

In order to engage in business activities in any sector of the Canadian economy, people organize their funds and abilities into units of ownership called **firms**. Firms are usually designed to achieve maximum profits by providing goods and services for which customers are willing and able to pay. These business ventures can be set up in one of five ways: sole proprietorship, partnership, corporation, co-operative, or government enterprise.

The Sole Proprietorship

As the name suggests, a **sole proprietorship** is a business owned and operated by one person. This is the most uncomplicated way to do business today. Even though proprietors may employ other people, they make all the business decisions. Proprietors are solely responsible for all the firm's debts and solely entitled to all the firm's profits.

Advantages and disadvantages

This usually small-scale form of business organization appeals to those people who prefer to be their own bosses and who prefer to keep their financial affairs, business dealings, and production processes confidential. Most businesses are required to have a municipal licence or a provincial vendor's permit. The name and business particulars of the firm have to be registered with the provincial government only when a name other than the real name of the proprietor is being used.

The biggest disadvantage is the *unlimited personal liability* of the owner. This means that the proprietor's personal assets can be seized to pay off outstanding business debts. In addition, the sole proprietor usually has no one else to rely on to run the business or raise needed funds. Proprietors often find it difficult and expensive to obtain business loans. Since ownership is personal and income tax is **progressive** (the more one earns, the higher the percentage rate of income tax one must pay), the sole proprietor may pay more income tax than under a corporate form of business. In spite of these disadvantages, proprietorship is a very common form of small business organization in Canada today.

The Partnership

A **partnership** is a firm owned by two or more people and bound by the terms of a legal document known as a **partnership agreement**. Although there is no set form for a partnership agreement, this document governs the business conduct of all partners and outlines their rights and obligations. A partnership agreement can establish either a general or a limited partnership. In a general partnership, all partners take part in the management of the firm and have unlimited personal liability for business losses. In a limited partnership, there are limited partners and at least one general partner. Limited partners are not permitted to take part in the management of the business and, in turn, are personally liable for business debts only up to the amount of their original investment. No additional personal assets can be seized to pay off partnership debts.

Advantages and disadvantages

The advantages of the partnership include the pooling of talent and capital, high personal motivation, and relatively few legal expenses and restrictions. Partnerships appeal to people who prefer not to assume by themselves all the risks of business operation. In addition to the pride of ownership and the satisfaction that comes from being self-employed, partners share all after-tax profits according to the distribution formula specified in the partnership agreement.

Since a partnership pools the funds of a number of people, it can attract more **capital** (money or other assets to invest in the business). It is usually easier for a partnership to obtain credit from suppliers or to borrow money from banks because more people are personally responsible for repayment. Since banks consider these loans more secure, they often set a slightly lower interest rate for them than for the loans they make to sole propri-

etors. Partnerships must be registered with the provincial government, and the municipal government may require a business permit. In view of these advantages, professional firms of lawyers, architects, and accountants are often organized as partnerships.

Unfortunately, general partners must all assume unlimited personal liability. Similar to proprietorships, the personal assets of general partners can be seized to pay the balance of business debts once all business assets have been used up. In the case of partnerships, this personal liability is both *joint* and *several*. Under **joint liability**, all general partners are, together, liable for the debts of the partnership. If, however, the other general partners fail to pay their share of the debt, one or more partners may be required to pay all partnership debts under the provisions of **several liability**.

Similar to a sole proprietor, partners have to pay a progressive personal income tax, so the percentage of tax they pay increases as their revenues go up. Another drawback is that it is not easy for a partner to sell his or her share in the firm. Most partnership agreements require that a partner obtain the approval of the other partners before ownership can be transferred to a new partner. The other partners often have the right to buy out the retiring partner rather than allow a new partner into the group. To complicate matters further, partnerships can obtain investment funds only from within the existing partnership. Partners must use personal savings or take out mortgages on personal assets to raise money for the partnership. For this reason, partnerships cannot usually attract large amounts of capital.

Since all the general partners are involved in the daily management of the firm, disputes will inevitably arise from time to time. Personality clashes and disagreements on what is best for the firm cause many partnerships to be terminated. A partnership legally terminates if one of the general partners dies, becomes mentally incapacitated, becomes financially insolvent, or commits a breach of the partnership by acting against the best interests of the firm. Thus, partnerships often do not last for a long period of time.

The Corporation

A **corporation**, or *limited company* as it was once called, is a business firm legally recognized as a separate entity in its own right. Business corporations can be either public or private. The shares of a *private corporation* are privately traded; that is, their transfer or sale must be approved and transacted by the corporation's board of directors. Shares of a *public corporation* can be freely traded, subject to the supervision of the provincial securities commission.

A corporation can be established only through government authorization. A document known as the **articles of incorporation** must be filed with either the federal government (if the corporation intends to conduct business in more than one province) or with the provincial government (if business is to be conducted in one province only).

Corporate assets are divided, with government authorization, into equal parts called **shares**. These ownership shares are made available to prospective buyers and can be quickly re-sold through a stockbroker. The owners of a corporation are known as **shareholders**, and any given corporation can have just a few or thousands of shareholders. In order to run the company on a day-to-day basis, shareholders elect a board of directors at the annual general meeting. Since investors do not personally have to assume responsibility for the day-to-day operation of the firm, more investors and investment dollars are attracted to it.

Generally, corporations can offer two types of ownership shares to investors: *common shares*, which provide a shareholder with voting rights, and *preferred shares*, which give a shareholder a preferential position in regard to profits and assets but do not provide voting rights. Shareholders can vote on decisions at the annual general meeting in person or by **proxy**. A proxy is a document signed by a shareholder appointing another person to vote on behalf of that shareholder.

Advantages and disadvantages

One attractive feature of the corporation is its method of profit distribution. At the end of the fiscal year, the majority of shareholders may vote to reinvest a portion of corporate profits into the firm. This provides an internal source of additional investment capital. Because of their size and scale of operations, many large corporations have become self-financing, no longer requiring bank loans to finance corporate expansion. The promise of even greater profits in the future is usually all the incentive it takes to persuade shareholders to forgo a portion of their current profits. Profits that are not reinvested into the firm are distributed to shareholders in the form of **dividends** and are paid on a per-share basis. Holders of preferred shares collect their guaranteed dividends first, then the remaining profits are divided up among the common shareholders on a per-share basis.

Once a corporation is legally established, it can sue and be sued, enter into contracts, own property, and incur debts and other obligations in the same way as any adult person. Any obligations incurred are generally the legal responsibility of the corporation, but not of the individual owners. Corporate shareholders have the advantage of *limited personal liability*. This means that the risk of the owners is restricted to the amount they have invested in the business. Creditors cannot claim the shareholder's other possessions (such as houses, cars, and personal savings) if the corporation goes bankrupt.

Clearly, the risks of investing in a corporation are substantially less than those of a partnership or proprietorship. Corporations can, therefore, attract a much wider pool of investors and a larger amount of investment capital. As a result, corporations can operate on an extremely large scale. In addition, when a shareholder dies or wishes to leave the firm, the corporation is not dissolved. The shares can be easily transferred to others while the corporation carries on its usual business; longevity is another advantage of firms established as corporations. Finally, corporations generally pay lower rates of income tax than proprietorships and partnerships. Dividends received by shareholders are also taxed at a lower rate.

Nevertheless, corporations do have their disadvantages. First of all, the legal and government fees for establishing a corporation are significantly higher than those for proprietorships and partnerships. Second, corporations are more closely regulated by the government. They must keep a set of books that lists their shareholders, directors, assets, and business dealings. They must also hold annual general meetings, produce an annual financial statement, and file annual corporate tax returns. (Since the corporation is legally recognized as an artificial person, like any other person earning an income, it must file an annual tax return.) Executives of many firms believe that these public disclosures can adversely affect the corporation's level of privacy by providing important information to competitors. However, the government requires the disclosure of this information in order to protect investors.

A final disadvantage is the reduced personal incentive that can be present in large corporations. With professional managers in place, investors are not able to exercise the same hands-on control that proprietors and general partners can exercise. Although they may have great personal ambition and dedication to the business, the incentive and loyalty of a professional manager is rarely as strong as that of an owner. This disadvantage is addressed in some firms by offering managers stock options, profit sharing, and performance bonuses.

The Co-operative Enterprise

A **co-operative** is a business firm owned equally by its various members. Members of a particular co-operative must have a common relationship, goal, or economic purpose. *Retail co-operatives* are formed to provide goods to members at reduced prices. *Marketing co-operatives* are created to sell the produce of members at the best prices possible. *Financial co-operatives* are formed to arrange savings and loans for members at better rates than those available at local banks. *Service co-operatives* exist to provide special services such as housing, medical insurance, and equipment rentals.

Many co-operatives incorporate themselves under their provincial corporations act. This permits them to secure limited personal liability for their members while maintaining all the other privileges of membership.

In any co-operative enterprise, for the purposes of collective decision making, each member (regardless of the amount invested) is entitled to a single vote, and a majority vote is required to carry any decision. To facilitate the day-to-day operation of the co-op, members elect a board of directors annually. Officers generally assume their roles on a voluntary basis. Co-operatives are generally most popular in western Canada and in rural parts of eastern Canada.

Credit unions, known as *caisses populaires* in Quebec, are a well-known example of a co-operative enterprise. Credit unions are financial co-operatives whose members can obtain many of the same services (savings and loans) available from banks but at more favourable interest rates. Unlike banks, credit unions can only accept deposits from and arrange loans and mortgages for members.

Advantages and disadvantages

The one-vote-per-member rule allows each member an equal say in all management decisions. As well, co-operatives are not adversely affected by the death, insolvency, or incapacity of individual members. Members can obtain goods or services through the co-operative or sell their products at better prices than would be otherwise available to them. In addition, members can enjoy limited personal liability for the debts incurred by the co-op. Finally, any profits made by the co-op that are not reinvested into the business are paid out to the members in the form of **patronage** returns. These payments are based on the amount of business transacted by each individual member. In other words, if a member is responsible for buying 1 per cent of the goods sold by a retail co-operative, then that member is entitled to 1 per cent of the profits for the same period.

The disadvantages of co-operative enterprises are linked to management, capital, and transaction issues. First, the decision-making process can be problematic when many equal members have radically different ideas. Second, the voluntary and therefore unpaid nature of the officers' positions may discourage some capable people from offering their management expertise to the group. Third, since co-operatives are able to raise investment funds only from existing members, they have a limited ability to raise capital when needed. Fourth, co-ops are restricted to conducting business with existing members. This limits the number of customers and, ultimately, the volume of business transactions. Co-operatives are designed primarily to serve members rather than to generate substantial profits.

The Government Enterprise

Some businesses in Canada are owned by the federal, provincial, or municipal government. These **government enterprises** generally provide services that the private sector won't offer because the profits generated are low relative to the amount of capital invested. The government may establish an enterprise to provide competition in industries dominated by a single firm or to prevent the total private control of key industries. The government may also set up one of these companies to increase employment or to centralize and standardize services. There is more government enterprise in the Canadian economy than there is in the United States, but western European countries such as Austria, Britain, France, Germany, and Sweden have an even higher degree of state ownership.

In recent years, the federal government and some provinces have actually made a concerted effort to **privatize** all or part of some government enterprises. During the 1980s in Canada, the federal government privatized a number of Crown corporations, including Canadair, de Havilland Aircraft, Teleglobe Canada, and Air Canada. In 1990, the government embarked on a plan to sell Petro-Canada; by 1999, 80 per cent of Petro-Canada shares were privately owned. Provincial governments in Ontario, Quebec, Saskatchewan, Alberta, and British Columbia have also privatized government enterprises. The planned sale of Hydro One, the Crown corporation that owns Ontario's electricity transmission system, was suspended in 2002 pending further study of alternatives that balance private investment and public ownership.

Most businesses owned by the federal government are operated as **Crown corporations**, which, like all other corporations, have the sta-

tus of distinct legal persons. The federal government, rather than private individuals, holds all or most of the ownership shares of these corporations. Examples of Crown corporations include Canada Post, the CBC, Via Rail, and Atomic Energy of Canada.

At the provincial and municipal levels, government enterprises take on various forms:
• Public utilities supply electricity and water.
• Provincial control boards sell liquor.
• Housing corporations provide affordable shelter.
• Transit commissions provide affordable public transportation.

Government enterprises are meant to operate in the best interests of the community rather than to generate profits for shareholders. The government usually covers operating expenses and business losses through grants, subsidies, or annual operating budgets.

Canadians continue to debate the merits of government enterprise relative to private enterprise. Some argue that private enterprise is more efficient and productive. Yet, at some point, all political parties have supported the government takeover of certain firms or industries for the common good. Different provinces have come to different conclusions in regard to certain industries. Private companies in Ontario and Quebec provide telephone communications services, while in Saskatchewan these same services are provided by the provincial Crown corporation Sasktel. Each method seems to work well for the respective provinces. The federal government created Petro-Canada to establish a state watchdog company in a petroleum industry dominated by large foreign corporations. Canadian National and Air Canada were Crown corporations created to provide competition in the transportation industries that would otherwise lack it. Economists often argue that the level of efficiency in a specific industry is determined by the level of competition present.

Certain industries that have a major impact on the public good, such as postal services, power companies, and railways, are state-owned in many countries because they seem to operate best without competition. These enterprises are sometimes referred to as *natural monopolies*. At present, however, the Canadian public seems to favour privatizing government enterprises in order to reduce the size and cost of their government. If, over time, the public concludes that private interests are not serving the common good adequately then it will pressure government to take over these private firms again. In this way, the Canadian mixed-market economy will continue to exhibit simultaneously both capitalistic and socialistic tendencies as it searches for the most effective balance between the two.

Non-Profit and Charitable Organizations

Some organizations are government registered (either federally or provincially) as non-profit charitable organizations. These private institutions are not permitted to generate profits; in return, their activities are income-tax exempt. Many of these institutions raise money to cover operating expenses from donations, grants, and fundraising activities. Examples of private non-profit charitable organizations include the Canadian Cancer Society, the Canadian National Institute for the Blind, and local food banks. District school boards are examples of public non-profit organizations. These enterprises are managed by a board of directors or elected trustees and operate through the work of both hired staff and volunteers. Organizations like the Canadian Save the Children Fund, World Vision, and Development and Peace are actively involved in collecting funds and recruiting volunteers to help people in less developed countries around the world.

Check Your
Understanding

1. Which form of business organization would be most appropriate in each of the following cases? Explain your choice.

   a) a three-person law firm

   b) a corner convenience store owned and operated by a single owner

   c) a savings and loan organization for school-district employees only

   d) a chain of 12 restaurants with 60 owners

   e) an enterprise providing inexpensive public transportation to the residents of a community

2. Explain the difference between each of the following pairs of terms:

   a) a general partner and a limited partner

   b) a public corporation and a private corporation

   c) dividends and patronage

3. Prepare a comparison chart to summarize what you know about the different forms of business. Use the following criteria: ownership, size, decision making, investor liability, profit distribution, and factors attracting investors and capital.

Small and Big Businesses

Small businesses, by virtue of their numbers, constitute the engine that fuels the Canadian economy. Big businesses, each of which employs thousands of Canadians, have a great deal of political influence. Think of them as the wheel that steers the national economy in a given direction. Given the wide range of enterprises in Canada, there is no general definition of a small or large business. The Canadian Federation of Independent Business (CFIB) was formed in 1971 to raise government awareness of the benefits and needs of small business in Canada. Within 20 years, this special-interest, or *lobby*, group exceeded 85 000 members, becoming the most influential group representing small business. The CFIB uses numbers of employees to classify Canadian businesses into the following three categories:

• Small business includes all independently owned firms with fewer than 50 employees.

• Medium-sized business includes all independently owned firms with between 50 and 499 employees.
• Big business includes all independently owned firms employing 500 workers or more.

Small Businesses

Small businesses are generally limited in the size and scope of their operations. In addition, they face intense competition from numerous other small firms. This level of competition keeps small businesses operating efficiently. Many small businesses maintain their competitive advantage by limiting their operations to one specialized field or process. For example, a garage may repair only vintage automobiles. Since they are small and focused on one area of specialization, these firms are usually very sensitive to changes in the niche marketplace.

The most successful small firms are usually those that best anticipate market conditions or that best respond to market changes. Successful small businesses, therefore, tend to be aggressively innovative and tend to maximize profits at the expense of weaker competitors. Over time, the most productive and effectively managed businesses force their weaker rivals out of

business or buy them out. In the process, these successful small firms grow larger.

Big Businesses

Horizontal integration

Smaller firms often grow larger through a process known as **horizontal integration**, which takes place when a firm purchases control of another firm engaged in the production of the same product or in the provision of the same service. This kind of consolidation can generate cost savings if there are economies of scale involved in any of the production processes or if it is possible to eliminate the duplication of effort. For example, if two companies merge and consolidate their **research and development (R&D)** departments, a substantial amount of money in employee salaries will be saved. By increasing the size and efficiency of operations, these larger Canadian firms may compete more effectively on a global scale.

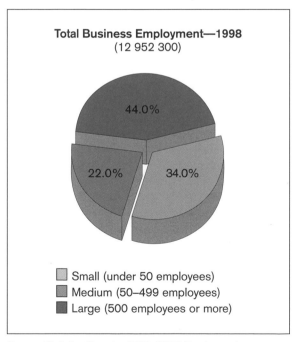

Source: Statistics Canada, *1983–1998 Employment Dynamics* (2001).

Figure 6.4b Private sector employment in Canada. By 1998, small and medium-sized businesses employed six out of every ten working Canadians.

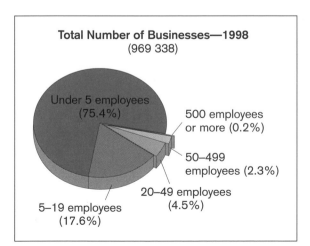

Source: Statistics Canada, *1983–1998 Employment Dynamics* (2001).

Figure 6.4a Business in Canada, 1998. Most Canadian businesses are small.

This sort of **horizontal merger**, or consolidation, can also give the larger enterprise better access to both domestic and foreign markets. For example, in 1998, Chrysler Corporation in the United States merged with Daimler-Benz in Germany to form DaimlerChrysler AG, one of the world's largest automobile manufacturers. This merger opened more European markets for Chrysler vehicles and provided additional marketing opportunities in North America and Asia for Mercedes-Benz products. Billions of dollars were saved by combining purchases, exchanging components, and sharing distribution and technology. Also in 1998, Sobeys Canada Inc. of Stellarton, Nova Scotia (through its corporate parent Empire Co. Ltd.), acquired the Oshawa Group to become one of Canada's largest supermarket chains. These are two examples of friendly mergers, but corporate takeovers can also be hostile if forced by an aggressive buyer.

Vertical integration

When companies involved in successive stages of the production (or consumption) process are combined into a single firm, it is known as **vertical integration**. Examples of vertical integration are when a major publishing house purchases a chain of bookstores or a broadcaster (such as Rogers Communications) buys a sports franchise (such as the Toronto Blue Jays).

Vertical integration can diversify and extend the scope of a firm's operations by helping it to establish ready markets for its products and to secure sources of supplies for the intermediate goods required in the production process. When Rogers bought the Blue Jays, the team provided the company with hours of sports programming for its cable television network. Vertical integration can also enable a firm to assume more control over the quality, quantity, and prices of required goods. In addition, a large and diversified corporation may not be as adversely affected by a decline in one industry. For example, if Acme Corp. manufactures automobiles, computers, and beer, a decline in car sales will not hurt overall profits as much as if the firm produced only cars.

Big businesses benefit from *economies of scale* (see page 148 in Chapter 7) and from the accumulation and concentration of their employees' expertise. Large-scale enterprises can afford to maintain state-of-the-art R&D laboratories to improve products and production processes. Big businesses can acquire the latest technology by purchasing control of smaller companies that have pioneered technological innovations. Large-scale enterprises can assume larger risks and accumulate the investment capital required to initiate expensive and complex undertakings.

Corporate alliances

Firms can also choose to collaborate on specific projects with competitors or suppliers—without precipitating the ownership struggles and investment anxieties that mergers often bring. A growing number of firms, especially in Europe and Asia, are agreeing to collaborate in powerful corporate alliances; some of these alliances bring together such large companies that their combined assets can exceed US$1 trillion.

A **corporate alliance** is a group of companies that form a business network that, in turn, operates as a single company. For example, in 1999, International Business Machines Corp. (IBM), which ranked second in worldwide computer sales at the time, entered into a $16-billion alliance with Dell Computer Corp., which ranked third in worldwide sales. The seven-year agreement calls for the sharing of patented technology between the companies and for joint work on the development of new technologies. IBM will supply component parts and technology to Dell; Dell engineers will integrate and refine IBM technology in future products. This example illustrates how joining forces can be profitable for each ally.

By 1995, some 10 000 corporate alliances were being made annually. Within a decade, the number of alliance agreements was expected to more than double. If present trends continue, the traditional business landscape will be significantly redefined by this volume of corporate collaboration.

Corporate concentration

A large amount of business activity is concentrated in a handful of corporations. Some of these large corporations are, in turn, controlled by a few wealthy individuals. In 1999, the 50 largest corporations in Canada (ranked by sales revenues) controlled close to half of all corporate assets in Canada and accounted for one-third of all business revenues. The 100 largest companies (representing well below 1 per cent of Canada's business enterprises) accounted for 40 per cent of corporate revenues.

Holding companies are enterprises that are not engaged in any form of industrial activity. Instead, the sole purpose of these companies is to acquire large blocks of shares in other companies in order to influence and sometimes control them. Through the systematic acquisition of common stock, holding companies are able to create corporate conglomerates. A **conglomerate** is a group of companies involved in different industries but controlled, to varying degrees, by a central management group, often the directors of the holding company.

Argus Corporation, headed by Conrad Black, is one of the oldest and most recognized holding companies in Canada. Historically, the holdings of Argus Corporation have included Standard Broadcasting, Dominion Stores, Domtar, Noranda Mines, and BC Forest Products. By the end of the 20th century, all of the corporation's investments were in shares of Hollinger Inc., a Canadian company with significant interests in newspapers in Canada, the United States, the United Kingdom, and Israel.

Sometimes enterprises become too big and manipulative. As a result, governments must use existing competition legislation in order to restrict enterprises that seek to manipulate the marketplace for personal gain or to hurt competitors. We will look more closely at the government's role in protecting competition in Chapter 13.

Multinational Corporations in the Global Economy

As part of their natural growth and expansion, many firms sell a portion of their output abroad, license foreign companies to use their manufacturing processes, or even establish their own branch plants, or **subsidiaries**, abroad. Once this involvement abroad has become substantial enough to involve a number of countries, the company's managers begin to base their financial, production, and marketing decisions on global (rather than on domestic or national) concerns. Firms that are large enough to operate from this global perspective are called **multinational corporations (MNCs)**. By capitalizing on the relatively peaceful times that followed the Second World War, MNCs have been able to grow rapidly since the 1950s.

As a result of American managerial ability, technological expertise, and financial resources, many of these multinational corporations are based in the United States. Numerous US multinationals have chosen to operate subsidiaries in Canada because of this country's geographic proximity, political stability, abundance of natural resources, and well-developed markets. The degree of American involvement and control in Canada's economy has been so high at times that Canada has been referred to as having a **branch-plant economy**. At the same time, many Canadian firms operate subsidiaries in other countries, so a good number of MNCs have their home offices in Canada.

One reason corporations prefer to operate as multinationals is to *improve their profitability*. Foreign branch plants provide free access to new markets and the increased revenues these markets represent. In addition, having offices and factories abroad can allow the company direct access to comparatively cheap raw materials and labour, effectively reducing its operating costs. Foreign governments eager to attract industrial activity often provide tax concessions or development grants to firms willing to operate subsidiaries in their country. In turn, the financial stability of an enterprise is greatly enhanced by the *geographic diversification* of having branch plants in a number of countries. Market fluctuations and political upheaval in one country may be effectively offset by stability and growth in others. Today, a substantial portion of international trade is conducted between multinational corporations and their foreign subsidiaries.

Corporate decision making for a multinational enterprise is very complex. Usually, the head office makes decisions about important financial and investment matters, and these decisions are binding on all branch plants. Decisions dealing with marketing and product

Figure 6.5 Canada's Governor General Adrienne Clarkson waves from a streetcar while at a Bombardier branch plant in Bautzen, Germany. Though its home office is in Montreal, Bombardier is a powerful multinational company in the field of aerospace and transportation vehicles. What do you think would be the advantages and disadvantages of operating on such a global scale?

distribution are often made at the branch-plant level. In the important field of research and new product development, decision making is carefully controlled by the parent firm. The bulk of research is usually conducted at the head office and under closely supervised conditions.

Various economists have argued that Canada's R&D industry has been severely limited by the amount of foreign investment in the Canadian economy. Many expert researchers from Canada have been attracted to laboratories in the United States while expert managers have been attracted to head offices both in the US and abroad. It is argued that this drain of expertise (often referred to as the **brain drain**) has had a disruptive effect on Canadian productivity and economic growth.

Large multinational enterprises can generally negotiate favourable terms when dealing with suppliers, governments, and trade unions by playing off one community against another. In terms of raw economic power, some multinationals control corporate assets comparable to (if not greater than) the assets of the governments with which they deal. Since their

activities cross political borders, MNCs can effectively operate beyond the control of national institutions, such as governments. For this reason, they are sometimes referred to as **transnational enterprises**. Their wealth and mobility give MNCs a strong political influence in many of their host countries, which sometimes raises ethical questions. For instance, if an MNC is operating in a country with strict environmental laws, it may react in one of two ways. It may simply shut down its offices in that country and move them to another where the environmental laws are not so strict. It could also influence the politicians in the first country to change their environmental laws or to grant the MNC special exemptions. Either way, critics could charge the MNC with putting concern for its profits ahead of concern for the environment.

One wonders whether it can ever be a level playing field, especially when so many national economies are seeking to increase industry and employment. It may be argued that these large transnational corporate empires are the modern-day equivalent of the exploitative 19th-century colonial empires that grew out of the period of human history known as the Age of Imperialism. From another perspective, the products and profits generated by multinational operations are seen to contribute greatly to

contemporary lifestyles and investment security. The public debate in Canada (and abroad) will heat up from time to time, especially when the behaviour of large multinational enterprises is seen to fall short of good corporate citizenship.

Check Your Understanding

1. Indicate whether each of the following transactions represents an example of vertical integration, horizontal integration, or corporate alliance:

   a) General Motors Ltd. and the Goodyear Rubber Co. collaborate on the design, testing, and marketing of a new line of safety tires.

   b) Ford Motor Co. buys 51 per cent of the common shares of Petro-Canada.

   c) The Steel Co. of Canada is taken over by US Steel.

   d) DaimlerChrysler AG and Mitsubishi Corp. agree jointly to build an automobile assembly plant in Mexico.

   e) Coca-Cola Corp. purchases a plant that manufactures aluminum cans.

2. Prepare a comparison organizer to summarize the advantages and disadvantages of small and big business ventures.

3. List the positive and negative attributes of multinational corporations.

Financing Corporate Expansion

In Canada today, the majority of business enterprises are corporations. For example, in the manufacturing sector alone, more than 95 per cent of the enterprises are corporations. Like proprietorships and partnerships, corporations can obtain the funds needed to finance expansion by borrowing from banks and by reinvesting profits in their growing businesses. In addition, because of their legal status, corporations can also raise investment capital by selling bonds and additional ownership shares.

Different Forms of Securities

Corporate **bonds** represent a fixed debt, which the corporation borrows from a buyer and must pay back at some fixed future date, usually ten, 15, or 20 years after the date of issue. The buyer, or bondholder, will receive periodic interest payments, usually at six-month intervals and for a fixed interest rate. On the maturity date, the holder of the bond will receive the full amount of the original loan, known as the **principal**.

The interest rate the bond pays must be competitive with rates available to investors

elsewhere. As a general rule, the longer the loan period, the higher the interest rate required to persuade investors to tie up their funds for the longer period. The bondholder can resell the bond at whatever price the market will bear. Sometimes bonds are discounted by the seller in order to complete a transaction. A bond with a face value of $100 000 may sell for $90 000 if the seller can't find a buyer willing to pay more. The new buyer assumes all existing conditions of the bond, including the interest rate and date of maturity.

It is important to note that the bondholder is not a part owner of the corporation but merely a creditor entitled to receive payment prior to the shareholders if the corporation is dissolved.

Corporations can also raise investment funds by issuing and selling additional ownership shares. These shares (common or preferred) represent additional part ownership of a corporation's capital. Since the corporation often uses the funds raised to acquire additional assets, the **asset value** of each share may not be adversely affected; the asset value is each share's portion of the corporation's net worth (assets minus liabilities). The **book value** of a share is the value at which it was originally issued. Usually, shares in a publicly traded corporation can be quite easily sold through a stockbroker. There is, however, no guarantee that the stockholder will receive either the asset or book value of the shares. The actual price or value of any share at any particular time is what it will fetch in the stock market. This is known as the **market value** of a share, and it varies significantly over time.

Securities Markets and Trading

Shares in a publicly traded company can be conveniently bought and sold in the **stock market** in which that particular company is listed. The **stock exchange** is the actual building where publicly held shares are traded. The ease with which stocks can be traded through a formal stock exchange encourages individuals and institutions to provide capital for business expansion.

The first stock exchange in Canada opened in Toronto in 1852; the Montreal exchange opened 11 years later. Today, the Canadian cities of Vancouver, Calgary, and Winnipeg also have stock exchanges. The Toronto Stock Exchange (TSX) is the largest exchange in the country, accounting for approximately 95 per cent of total shares traded in the country in 2000, based on the number of transactions and also based (99 per cent) on the dollar value. On a global scale, the largest exchanges (in terms of the value of stocks traded) are in New York, Tokyo, and London.

Since it was founded in 1971, the National Association of Securities Dealers Automated Quotation (**Nasdaq**) has grown to become one of the largest stock markets in the world. By 2001, over 4100 of the world's leading companies were listed on the Nasdaq. Although traditionally the place for smaller and new-technology companies to list their stock, with the rapid expansion of the technology sector, the Nasdaq has quickly grown in importance. Unlike other stock exchanges, Nasdaq has no central location for trading. Instead, brokers acting on behalf of clients place orders with certain Nasdaq brokers, called **market makers**, who concentrate on trading specific stocks. Trades are made directly between brokers and market makers by telephone or through the Internet.

Suppose you decide to invest in a company listed on the Toronto Stock Exchange. First, you have to contact a brokerage firm with a seat on the TSX. A **stockbroker** acts as your agent for all transactions. Trading is done directly by computer through a series of networks linking member brokerage firms to TSX computers. Member brokers of the TSX must pay an annual fee for their trading privileges, which buys them a seat on the exchange. In turn, brokers charge their clients a commission based on the dollar value of all transactions completed on their behalf.

Direct computer links to the TSX allow online brokerage firms to execute trade orders quickly and, sometimes, at discounted rates. As an example, early in 2001, E-Trade Canada (with over 50 000 registered customers) decided to imitate an extremely successful pizza marketing strategy by offering "trades in 60 seconds—or they are free." At the time, E-Trade's standard commission on Internet trade orders was $27 per trade, and 99 per cent of the company's trade orders were completed in less than 60 seconds. As online trading technology continues to advance and as trading rules become more relaxed, major investors may eventually be able to bypass stock exchanges altogether.

The price of a company's stock may fluctuate greatly in response to changes in the *supply* (the amount of shares offered for sale) and the *demand* (the number of shares being sought for purchase). Factors influencing the demand for shares include the current profits and dividend shares of the corporation, the degree of confidence in the corporate management team, trends in the industry to which the firm belongs, and the general economic climate and outlook. Generally speaking, the rule that David Ricardo discovered 200 years ago still applies: investors react to bad news by undervaluing certain stocks and to good news by overvaluing them. Clearly, when investing in the stock market, one must have a calm disposition, a long-term strategy, and a willingness to stay the course.

Mutual funds were developed for people who prefer a more passive investment. They want to own stocks but prefer not to be bothered with the details of buying and selling. For a fee, expert fund managers lump together the investment dollars of many clients, amass a diversified portfolio of investments, and then manage the fund on behalf of their clients.

Commodities Markets

A commodity market is a place or an institution through which **commodities** (standardized raw or semi-processed goods resulting from primary industrial activity) are traded in bulk. Non-standardized commodities such as fish and fresh vegetables, which require physical inspection prior to trading, are often still traded in markets. The Ontario Food Terminal in Toronto, where farmers bring their produce to sell to merchants, restaurateurs, and retailers, is one such example. For standardized commodities (such as gold, heating oil, gasoline, corn, and wheat), the physical marketplace is being replaced by a network of telephone and computer links designed to facilitate instant trading.

Commodities markets include both **spot markets** (where goods are traded for immediate delivery) and **futures markets** (where prices are agreed to in advance, for delivery at various dates in the future). The Ontario Food Terminal is an example of a spot market. In a futures market, speculators invest in crops that are yet to be harvested or minerals that are yet to be mined. If the market price of the commodity changes, the speculators that predicted correctly will realize a profit. In order to facilitate transactions, futures are generally traded through a stock exchange.

Most investors in commodity futures do not intend to receive delivery of the actual product. Futures markets, therefore, deal in the trading of futures contracts, or *options*. These contracts commit both parties to buy and sell commodities at a fixed price and on a set date. A *call option* is a contract giving the holder the right but not the obligation to buy a commodity at a pre-arranged date and price. A *put option* is a contract giving the right but not the obligation to sell a commodity at a pre-arranged date and price. Options are usually purchased for large quantities of a commodity. As a form of security deposit, both parties pay a set percentage of the market value of the contract to the com-

modities market. The difference between the contract price and the market price, on the day the contract matures, is paid by one party to the futures market. The futures market will then transfer this amount into the account of the other party in order to satisfy the contract.

Futures markets are highly speculative and, therefore, full of risk. For example, if you are confident that oil-producing nations are about to cut production in order to improve the market price for crude oil, and if you are confident that the following winter will be cold, you may decide to buy heating oil futures at today's market prices, with the hope of realizing a profit from any increases in market price. As a general rule, if the market price is above the contract price, the futures buyer profits and the futures seller loses money. If the market price is below the contract price, the seller profits and the buyer loses.

Understanding Stock Market Indicators

The **Dow Jones Industrial Average** (often called "the Dow") is the most widely quoted indicator of general stock market trends in the United States. It is calculated daily, based on the closing prices of 30 **blue-chip** (or safe and stable) US corporations traded on the New York Stock Exchange. These companies are carefully chosen to represent all key sectors of the US economy. The Dow is considered a mirror of the stock market as a whole. If it goes up 5 per cent, it is projected that the entire New York Exchange is up, on average, by the same amount. The Dow can be used over a period of time to track patterns in stock price changes on the New York Exchange.

From 1977 to 2002, Canada's leading market indicator was the TSE 300 Composite Index. This indicator was based on 300 stocks divided into 14 groups representing the Canadian economy. Companies were each given a weighting in the index, roughly based on their number of shares. In this way, stock price changes for smaller companies had less impact on the composite index. Changes in the TSE 300 were believed to mirror what was happening in the entire Toronto Stock Exchange. In May 2002, the TSE 300 was replaced by the **S&P/TSX**

Composite Index. Instead of being based on a set number of companies, this new index uses two main criteria for inclusion: company size and trading activity on the TSX. The index incorporates the Standard & Poor's Global Industry Classification Standard, giving investors an accurate comparison of the performance of Canadian indices with those around the world.

The **Nasdaq Composite Index** jumped from 1000 in 1995 to 3000 in 2000 before closing out the year at 2400 because the technology sector had experienced a sharp year-end decline. This decline was fuelled by a decrease in sales and in investor confidence as the US economy started to slow down. These conditions created a **bear market**—a stock market

under the influence of traders who expect prices to fall. Traders may attempt to sell off stock, hoping to buy it back after the price has fallen. When a large number of investors are like-minded, the actions of these traders, known as "bears," tend to be self-fulfilling. The abrupt stock market decline that followed the terrorist attacks of 11 September 2001 is a good example of the bear mentality. Traders who expect stock prices to rise are called "bulls." They will buy stock, speculating that they will profit by owning the stock while it appreciates in value. By increasing the demand for shares, the actions of bulls can also be self-fulfilling. A market influenced by a large number of investors expecting price increases is called a **bull market**.

Figure 6.6 The Bear and the Bull. What point is the cartoonist making about market conditions in September 1998? Would this cartoon be equally appropriate for September 2001? Explain.

Check Your

Understanding

1. Explain the difference between the market value, book value, and asset value of a share of common stock. Which value is the most important? Explain.

2. Explain the difference between the following pairs of terms:

   a) corporate stocks and corporate bonds

   b) bull market and bear market

   c) futures and spot markets

   d) commodities and stock markets

   e) call options and put options

3. Explain how the laws of supply and demand lead to fluctuations in the market value of corporate stock.

CHAPTER SUMMARY

- For many nations, primary industries (natural resource extraction) are the first to develop, then secondary industries (manufacturing), followed by the tertiary sector (service industries) and, finally, the high-tech quaternary sector.

- Fish, furs, and lumber were the original export staples in Canada. In 1867, productive tariffs were imposed by the government in order to protect Canada's infant manufacturing industries. The National Policy of 1879 focused efforts on building a transcontinental railway and on increasing the population of western Canada.

- By the middle of the 20th century, Canada had become an industrialized nation with strong primary, secondary, and tertiary sectors. Today, three out of every four Canadian workers are employed in service industries.

- Most less developed nations depend on primary industries (usually agriculture) to employ the majority of their labour force.

- A sole proprietorship is a business owned and operated by one person. The owner is solely responsible for all debts and solely entitled to all profits. A partnership is a firm owned and operated by two or more people. In a general partnership, all partners are involved in decision making, and each partner is personally liable for the total amount of all business debts. Limited partners are not permitted to take part in decision making and are liable for business debts only up to the amount originally invested.

- In Canada today, the majority of business enterprises are corporations owned by shareholders with limited personal liability. Profits are distributed to shareholders in the form of dividends (on a per-share basis). Professional directors are elected to manage the corporation.

- Co-operatives are firms owned equally by registered members. Decisions are made by allowing each member a single vote. Profits are distributed to members according to patronage.

- Government-owned enterprises are established to provide goods, services, and competition that the private sector is not prepared to provide because profit levels are too low. In recent years, governments in Canada have privatized government enterprises in an effort to reduce the size and cost of government.

- Small and medium-sized businesses (employing under 50 workers) employ six out of ten workers in Canada. Seventy-five per cent of Canada's businesses employ five workers or less. Successful small businesses tend to grow while their less successful counterparts tend to shrink or disappear altogether.

- Through horizontal integration, an enterprise becomes larger by buying out or merging with a competitor. Through vertical integration, an enterprise becomes larger by diversifying its operations or by acquiring suppliers.

- Through a mutually beneficial corporate alliance, firms can collaborate with other independent firms in order to share existing capital, resources, and expertise as well as production and distribution systems.

- Corporations can improve their profitability by operating in several countries. Many of the products we buy and shares we invest in are from these multinational corporations.

- Corporations can raise the capital needed for expansion by selling long-term corporate bonds and/or additional ownership shares (called stocks) to investors. A bondholder is a creditor who is entitled to regular interest payments. By selling additional shares, a corporation takes on additional owners who are entitled to an equal share of dividends. Each additional common share sold entitles the holder to one additional vote in decision making.

- The market value of corporate stock fluctuates regularly as the demand and supply change. Shares in any publicly traded company can be conveniently bought and sold in a stock exchange where that particular company is listed. The Toronto Stock Exchange is the largest stock market in Canada.

Key Terms

high-tech	holding company
staple	conglomerate
Gross Domestic Product (GDP) per capita	subsidiary
firm	multinational corporation (MNC)
sole proprietorship	branch-plant economy
progressive tax	brain drain
partnership	transnational enterprise
partnership agreement	bond
capital	principal
joint liability	asset value
several liability	book value
corporation	market value
articles of incorporation	stock market
share	stock exchange
shareholder	Nasdaq
proxy	market maker
dividend	stockbroker
co-operative	mutual fund
patronage	commodity
government enterprise	spot market
privatize	futures market
Crown corporation	Dow Jones Industrial Average
horizontal integration	blue-chip stock
research and development (R&D)	S&P/TSX Composite Index
horizontal merger	Nasdaq Composite Index
vertical integration	bear market
corporate alliance	bull market

Activities

Thinking/Inquiry

1. Refer to the labour force data in Figure 6.2 (page 121).

   a) Applying the development theory presented in this chapter, what pattern would you expect to exist in the labour force data for 1800? Explain your reasoning.

   b) Use the Internet to obtain the most recent employment-by-industry data compiled by Statistics Canada. Copy Figure 6.2 in your notebook and add one more column to present the data that you found. Graph the data to establish trend curves for each industrial sector. Use a vertical scale of 5 per cent employment per large square and a horizontal scale of five years per large square. After you have determined trend curves for each industrial sector, project what percentage each sector will employ by the year 2025.

2. Research one of Canada's non-profit charitable organizations, and present an oral report on its various activities and how it contributes to Canadian society.

3. Research the activities of two multinational corporations to assess their impact.

4. What constitutes good corporate citizenship in your opinion? Provide specific examples.

5. Over the next month, graph the changes in the S&P/TS Composite Index, the Dow Jones Industrial Average, or the Nasdaq

Composite Index. Account for the changes in the index over this time. Compare the graphs and accounts of your classmates to determine which stock market experienced the most change during the month.

Communication

6. Corporations have different ways of securing the funds they need to finance expansion. Each method has its costs or drawbacks. Create a summary chart to compare these costs.

7. Draw a flow-chart diagram to explain how multinational enterprises contribute to a "brain drain" of skill and expertise in their host countries.

8. Which form of business would you prefer to use if you were starting your own business? Justify your selection in a short speech.

Application

9. Use supply and demand curves to explain how stock prices might fluctuate as a result of one of the following headlines:

   a) Bombardier lands jet plane order for $2.1 billion with US airline—company to consider expanding production facilities

   b) Stelco projected to lose $50 million in fourth quarter as energy costs soar and foreign producers flood the market

   c) New Mitel unit to develop chip that boosts the capacity of fibre optics networks

   d) DaimlerChrysler announces production cuts and temporary plant closings as sales decline and inventories pile up

   e) INCO reports high-grade finds of palladium and platinum in Sudbury, Ontario

10. a) "Profit sharing for corporate executives is a smart application of capitalist principles." Do you agree with this statement? Explain.

    b) In your opinion, does profit sharing make as much sense for all corporate employees, that is, even for those who are not at the executive level? Explain.

11. Will small business become more important or less important in the Canadian economy in the future? Prepare a reasoned economic argument to support your position on this question.

12. Do conglomerates and the concentration of corporate power in Canada pose a threat to Canadian society? Prepare a reasoned economic argument to support your position on this question.

CHAPTER 7
PRODUCTION, FIRMS, AND THE MARKET

By permission of Johnny Hart and Creators Syndicate, Inc.

QUESTIONS

1. What type of economic system does the Kingdom of Id seem to have? Support your conclusion with at least two reasons based on details from the panels of the cartoon.
2. In what ways is this economic system both similar to and different from Canada's?
3. Explain how the King demonstrates an entrepreneurial spirit.
4. Why does the King's business plan seem a safe and sound investment for him?
5. If the King decided to give you the sole authority to produce and sell any one of the five products of your choice, based on the information in the last panel, which product would you choose and why?

Chapter Goals

By the end of this chapter, you will be able to

- determine how much to produce of a product and the best way to do it,
- explain the importance of the role that profit plays in a market,
- understand the nature and importance of productivity and efficiency,
- identify the importance and nature of competition in different markets,
- understand the forms and importance of market regulation,
- analyze proposals to change the way in which goods and services are provided.

How to Produce

The function of any economic system is to provide goods and services to satisfy wants and needs. In Chapter 2, we learned that all economic systems must answer three basic questions to achieve this goal: What will we produce?, How will we produce?, and For whom will we produce?

Our comic kingdom on the previous page illustrates how these questions are answered in a **command economy** (an economy directed by a central governing body). In this case, the central authority is the King, who owns and controls all productive resources. The King, after all, speaks of "my fields" and "my shops," and he can command his workers to do everything from "[die] in my battles" to "take tomorrow off." Although markets exist where goods may be purchased for a price, consumers in the Kingdom of Id have little market power because their choices are limited, and His Majesty sets the prices.

All real systems have elements of this comic kingdom's economy. For example, Canada's governments own productive economic resources (such as crown land), rights to natural resources, and public infrastructure (including most roads and public buildings). The three levels of government provide a wide variety of public goods and services, such as education.

Overall, however, more differences than similarities exist between Canada's and Id's economic systems. Primarily, the Canadian economy is a *market economy*—one largely determined by free competition among businesses. Private companies play a very large role in the production and sale of goods and services in Canada. The Canadian government does take part, though, by providing services funded by taxes. If Canadians decide that the prices (that is, the taxes they pay) are too high, however, they can always elect a new government that promises to lower taxes. No Canadian prime minister has the Idian King's power to determine what people will do, what goods and services are produced, and what price will be paid for them. Nor does the prime minister have the power to make a profit. Canada does have a monarch, but the power she wields is purely symbolic.

Figure 7.1 provides one illustration of the real and relative value of the goods and services provided by Canadian governments. **Real Gross Domestic Product** is a measure of the total value of goods and services produced by the Canadian economy in a year, taking into account the influence of price changes (inflation). This figure includes the goods and services produced by private industry for both national consumption and export. GDP also includes everything that the government produces, which can be measured easily by looking at how much the government spends in a given year, often called *government expenditure*.

The data in Figure 7.1 indicate that government produces nearly 20 per cent of the total value of goods and services produced by the economy. Who provides the rest? The answer, of course, is a wide variety of firms—varying in size, from large to small, and in legal form, from small sole proprietorships to large corporations and co-operatives. These commercial enterprises make up the private sector. Some firms provide goods and services to other companies. Many more provide goods and services to consumers like you. Some produce primarily for export while others sell mostly to Canadians. Occasionally, businesses behave unethically, seeking to primarily benefit their board managers and top executives. Most firms, however,

	1997	1998	1999	2000	2001
1. Real GDP	885 022	919 770	966 362	1 009 182	1 024 196
2. Government expenditure	171 183	174 947	179 555	183 562	187 634

Source: Excerpts from table: "Real gross domestic product, expenditure-based" from <http://www.statcan.ca/english/Pgdb/Economy/Economic/econ05.htm>.

Figure 7.1 Canada's real Gross Domestic Product (in millions of 1997 dollars). Government expenditure shows us how much of the GDP the government "produced" in the form of goods and services provided to Canadians.

seek to make a profit to benefit the shareholders who own them and to stay in business.

In a market economy, it is a multitude of private firms, not a king's court, that answers the basic economic question, How will we produce? Canadians, through their governments, create laws to define, limit, and protect the process of producing. In other words, our society has taken action to give individuals within firms the power to make most of the production decisions. In Canada, private firms largely determine how our scarce economic resources will be developed and used to meet Canadians' needs.

Origins of the Firm

Where did this structure known as the firm come from? After all, at one time, all people hunted, fished, or gathered their food and were self-sufficient. Then humans learned to grow their own food, which eventually led to trading. A necessary ingredient of the firm came with the invention of money, at which point people could hire others for a wage or invest in other people's enterprises. Eventually, firms got bigger and bigger when people figured out the benefits of the division of labour (whereby individual workers specialized in the various tasks required to produce a good) and when they learned to build machinery that made large-scale production possible.

What is the goal of the firm? Its primary goal is to create profit. Its role, however, is to create the goods and services that society needs. You can read one of the earliest analyses of the role of the firm in the feature below.

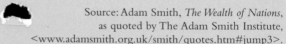

PRIMARY SOURCE

Adam Smith's Wealth of Nations

Adam Smith, whom you first read about in Chapter 3, is considered by many to be the "father" of the discipline of modern economics. He described economics in terms of the pursuit of self-interest restrained by the market. The following excerpts come from his best-known book, *An Inquiry into the Wealth of Nations*, which was published in 1776.

According to the system of natural liberty, the sovereign has only three duties to attend to ... first, the duty of protecting the society from the violence and invasion of other independent societies; secondly, the duty of protecting, so far as possible, every member of the society from the injustice or oppression of every other member of it, or the duty of establishing an exact administration of justice, and thirdly, the duty of erecting and maintaining certain public works and certain public institutions, which it can never be for the interest of any individual, or small number of individuals, to erect and maintain....—Book IV, Chapter IX

It is not from the benevolence of the butcher, the brewer, or the baker, that we expect our dinner, but from their regard to their own interest. We address ourselves, not to their humanity but to their self-love, and never talk to them of our necessities but of their advantages.—Book I, Chapter II

Every individual ... generally, indeed, neither intends to promote the public interest, nor knows how much he is promoting it.... [H]e intends only his own security; and by directing that industry in such a manner as its produce may be of the greatest value, he intends only his own gain, and he is in this, as in many other cases, led by an invisible hand to promote an end which was no part of his intention.—Book IV, Chapter II

Source: Adam Smith, *The Wealth of Nations*, as quoted by The Adam Smith Institute, <www.adamsmith.org.uk/smith/quotes.htm#jump3>.

QUESTIONS

1. What, according to Smith, were the duties of the sovereign (read as "government")?

2. How might Smith react to the data about the Canadian economy contained in Figure 7.1 on page 141? Support your supposition with quotes from the excerpt.

3. In your own words, explain what Smith believes both motivates and does not motivate producers.

4. Explain the metaphor of the "invisible hand." What does it symbolize?

How Firms Think: The Importance and Calculation of Profit

Firms, of course, do not think. Although you read earlier that the goal of a firm is to make a profit, firms cannot have goals. It is the people within firms that make the economic decisions about what and how much to produce as well as about how to do it, all with the principal goal of helping the firm make a profit. In a small firm, one person may make all the decisions. In a large firm, decision making is delegated to a small group of executive managers with specialized training and experience. One manager may handle suppliers, for example, while another oversees the delivery of finished goods. This example illustrates Adam Smith's *division of labour* (see page 50) in the realm of decision making, leading to better decisions and greater productivity.

Firms may make decisions for a wide variety of reasons, but all decisions should take into account what is commonly called "the bottom line." This expression originally referred to the last line of an accounting sheet, which shows whether a firm is taking a loss or earning an accounting profit. **Accounting profit** is what we usually think of and refer to simply as *profit*, that is, the excess of revenues over costs. This is an important concept for decision makers in a firm because it tells them whether they can stay in business. Most firms attempt to maximize profit. All must, ultimately at least, break even; that is, they must cover their costs of production or cease to exist.

Profits are beneficial to a business's success for many reasons. For producers, profits act as an incentive and a reward for the work they do and the risks they take. Further, profits are the producer's least expensive source of money for expanding or improving production. Producers also use profits to evaluate how well their firm is doing by comparing theirs with those of their competitors.

Producers pay close attention to which of their product lines are selling the most and making the most profit. Depending on their assessment, they may shift resources to increase the production of goods and services that clearly meet the most urgent demands.

Consequently, consumer choice improves, as does the company's profitability.

High profits also allow privately owned companies to pay dividends to their shareholders. Many shares in companies are owned by pension funds, insurance companies (which invest premiums for eventual payment on claims), and individuals purchasing stocks or mutual funds through their retirement savings plans. Therefore, when companies make profits, many people within the community benefit because their savings grow.

Theory of the Firm

To understand how firms make decisions, we must analyze the relationship that exists between profits, revenues, and costs—a relationship sometimes referred to as the Theory of the Firm. The **Theory of the Firm** assumes that producers are all profit maximizers. Adam Smith's "invisible hand" of self-interest leads them to increase their revenues and decrease their costs in order to increase their profits.

This theory may seem simple. Fortunately, a good deal of it is just common sense that you already possess and intuitively use. All you have to do to understand the Theory of the Firm is to start thinking like a producer, something you have already done in this chapter. In your answer to question 5 at the beginning of the chapter on page 140, which of the King of Id's five products did you choose to sell? No doubt it was the one that you thought would be most profitable. If so, you're thinking like a producer.

The Theory of the Firm—the economic relationship between total profit, revenues, and costs—can be expressed in the simple equation of accounting profit:

total profit = total revenues − total costs

Total revenue

Total revenue refers to the money a firm receives from its sales. Only two factors influence how much that will be: the price you decide to charge and the quantity you can sell at that price. In other words, if you can sell 20 cookies for a dollar each, you will make a total revenue of $20. In greater detail, then, the economic relationship between profit, revenue, and costs is

$$\frac{\text{total}}{\text{profit}} = (\text{price} \times \text{quantity sold}) - \frac{\text{total}}{\text{costs}}$$

To be profitable, a firm must be able to maximize its revenues. Before launching a new product, a firm's economic decision makers gather information from markets about how many people would probably purchase the potential product and at what price. In other words, they must determine—or estimate as accurately as possible—the demand for the product. At the beach in the Kingdom of Id, it is highly likely that sunburn ointment would be in highest demand.

Total costs

Perhaps you wondered if the higher-priced items for sale in the cartoon panel might generate more income because of their higher prices. The higher prices of products don't necessarily mean greater profit, however. A higher price may simply reflect a higher cost of production. Further, a high price may discourage sales. If you're thinking like a producer, these two observations will support a decision to produce sunburn ointment. To determine profitability, firms must gather information about the necessary costs.

A firm's **total cost** of production refers to the money the firm spends to purchase the productive resources it needs to produce its good or service. This money includes all payments a firm must make to its suppliers, employees, landlords, bankers, and so on.

When economists analyze the production decisions of firms, they divide cost into two basic categories: fixed costs and variable costs. **Fixed costs** are those that remain the same at all levels of output. They must be paid whether or not the firm produces. Examples of fixed costs are rent, property taxes, insurance premiums, and interest on loans. A bakery, for example, has to pay off the loan for a new gas oven no matter how many sales it makes. Fixed costs are difficult to adjust in the short term. They are often referred to as overhead costs.

Variable costs, such as those associated with labour, fuel, raw materials, and power, are relatively flexible. They change with the level of production. As production increases, it becomes necessary to employ more resources, such as labour and raw materials, so these costs tend to rise as production rises. The bakery with the new gas oven will have a higher gas bill as its level of production increases. Variable costs are often targets for "emergency" cutbacks. For example, should sales at the bakery drop suddenly, the baker might think of laying off a part-time counter person. The baker might have to work longer hours on Saturday afternoon, but at least the loan payment for the gas oven is paid. (For more examples of fixed and variable costs, see Figure 7.2.)

Our equation showing the economic relationship between profit, revenue, and costs thus develops as follows:

$$\text{total profit} = (\text{price} \times \text{quantity sold}) - (\text{fixed} + \text{variable costs})$$

After determining both revenue and costs, we can calculate potential profits. As you can see in Figure 7.3, this calculation may sometimes hold surprises and can definitely influence a firm's business decisions.

The short run and the long run

Economists consider two different time periods when assessing the overall costs of a business: the short run and the long run. The costs of some resources, such as labour, fuel, and raw materials, are relatively flexible and can be adjusted very quickly. The **short run** is a period over which the firm's maximum capacity becomes fixed because of a shortage of at least one resource. For example, assume a printing company has purchased enough paper to keep its printing presses running at 80 per cent capacity. Suddenly, it gets a new contract that requires it to expand production immediately. If it is able to quickly acquire the additional paper it needs, the paper is a short-run, or variable, cost and does not limit the firm's ability to expand production.

Some resources cannot be quickly increased. For example, if the new contract was for a huge job, the printing company might have to build an addition to its factory to handle it. This change could not be accomplished quickly, so the company would be unable to accept the order. Its ability to produce is

Fixed Costs	Variable Costs
Fixed costs must be paid and remain the same whether or not production occurs.	Variable costs are those that vary with the level of production; they tend to rise with an increase in production and fall with a decrease in production.
Fixed costs are such items as • lease payments or rent for premises, • loan payments to a bank or lending institution, • property taxes, • payment of insurance premiums, and • cost of security.	Variable costs are such items as • wages or salaries paid to labour; • costs of raw materials or inventory; • cost of electricity used for productive purposes; and • costs of fuel, power, and transportation.

Figure 7.2 Fixed and variable costs. What type(s) of business would have higher fixed costs? Which would have higher variable costs?

limited, or fixed, by the size of its plant. The length of the company's short run would be defined by the length of time it would need to build an extension to its plant so that production could increase.

The **long run** refers to a period when all costs become variable. Over the long run, a firm will be able to adjust not only labour, fuel, raw materials, and so on but also its plant or factory facilities. In a firm's long run, there are no fixed costs of production. All costs become variable, from staffing to location. The long run is considered the planning period when the firm has enough time to enlarge its productive capacity, shift production to generate other goods or services, or, if necessary, shut down completely.

The long-run and short-run periods are not measured in a fixed number of days, months, or years because the periods are different for vari-

ous firms. For example, when executives at the Honda automobile plant in Alliston, Ontario, realized their plant was operating at capacity, they decided to expand. The years that it took to build the new facility, and add new production and assembly lines, constituted Honda's long run. On the other hand, when a small textile firm operating in downtown Vancouver found that it was near plant capacity, it found more space nearby and stocked it with more sewing machines in a matter of weeks. Those weeks constituted the long run for that firm.

Marginal revenue and marginal cost

When considering how to maximize profits, economists spend a lot of energy trying to determine the exact production level that will result in the most profit. These detailed calculations nearly always involve a consideration of the costs and benefits of making small changes

Business	Selling Price	Total Sold	Total Costs of Goods Sold
Leg casts	$50.00	10 units	$300
Rubbing liniment	$12.00	5 units	$5
First aid kits	$28.95	25 units	$400
Resuscitator	$70.00	2 units	$130
Sunburn ointment	$25.00	50 units	$1000

Figure 7.3 Assume you were able to get this information about the five businesses of the King of Id. Calculate the profit made by each of the king's businesses. Why, as it turned out, was the sunburn ointment not the most profitable?

in production. Despite the detailed nature of the work, thinking "at the margin" is very important in a firm's profit calculations and, hence, its business strategy.

If a firm wishes to maximize its profit, it should always produce up to the point at which there is no added benefit (that is, profit) from producing any more. In other words, it should keep producing to the point at which the **marginal cost** (that is, additional cost) of producing one more unit equals the **marginal revenue** (that is, additional revenue) received from the unit's sale. At the point when the marginal cost *exceeds* the marginal revenue that results from producing one more unit, the firm would waste resources and reduce its profit.

Let's consider a dairy that specializes in goat cheese. The dairy is located near a dozen goat farmers, which regularly supply it with the goats' milk it requires to make cheese. Should the dairy decide to increase production, it would have to transport the additional milk from another area, requiring a sharp increase in transportation costs. If the additional revenue to be had from producing more goat cheese did not exceed the additional costs, the dairy would have no incentive to produce more.

A firm will maximize its profit (that is, make the most profit) by producing up to the point at which its marginal revenue equals its marginal cost. The following equation sums up the concept:

Profits are maximized at a production level when marginal revenue = marginal cost

The King of Id's rubbing liniment offers an interesting example of the value of marginal analysis. Figure 7.3 indicated that, at a price of $12, the firm sold five units that cost a total of $5 to produce. That's an impressive $11 profit per unit sold (for a total of $55 profit), but so few units were sold at that price that only the resuscitators produced less total profit ($10), which is what really counts. Perhaps the King forgot the law of demand and set his price too high.

Let's say that the King decides to reassess what he is charging for rubbing liniment. We'll assume that the cost of production remains at $1 per bottle and that the King could sell one more bottle for each dollar reduction in price. What price should he charge, and how many units should he produce to maximize his profit? The King uses marginal analysis. Because he knows his marginal cost will always be $1, he needs only to calculate the marginal revenue he would earn from each additional sale. He can then see at which point his marginal cost would equal his marginal revenue. His calculations would look like those shown in Figure 7.4.

From his marginal analysis, the King can tell he will maximize his profit by reducing his price to $9 and selling eight units. This will allow him to maximize his total profit at $64 rather than the $55 he received when he charged $12. The lower price will also please consumers, who now purchase more. An even lower price would please more consumers, but the King would never sell at this price because

Price	Units of Rubbing Liniment Sold	Total Revenue	Marginal Revenue (revenue for additional unit)
$12	5	$12 × 5 = $60	—
$11	6	$11 × 6 = $66	$66 – $60 = $6
$10	7	$10 × 7 = $70	$70 – $66 = $4
$9	8	$9 × 8 = $72	$72 – $70 = $2
$8	9	$8 × 9 = $72	$72 – $72 = $0

Figure 7.4 The King's marginal analysis. At which price level does the marginal revenue no longer exceed the marginal cost of $1?

Price	Total Cost	Total Profit (revenue − costs)
$12	$1 × 5 = $5	$60 − $5 = $55
$11	$1 × 6 = $6	$66 − $6 = $60
$10	$1 × 7 = $7	$70 − $7 = $63
$9	$1 × 8 = $8	$72 − $8 = $64
$8	$1 × 9 = $9	$72 − $9 = $63

Figure 7.5 Confirming the King's conclusions. Do the data in this table confirm the price level you decided would maximize profits?

his analysis indicates there is no incentive for him to do so. If he charged $8, his total revenues would not increase and he would have to pay an additional dollar in costs to produce the extra unit. His total profits would fall from $64 to $63 (see Figure 7.5).

Making Production Choices

Controlling the costs of production

Many firms have little control over the total revenue they receive in a market. Consumer demand, as we have learned, plays a major role in determining market price and total sales—the two factors that determine total revenue. Competition also contributes to uncertainty.

Instead of attempting to control revenue, firms tend to focus their efforts on controlling the costs of production. The firm that is able to produce the desired product at the lowest pos-

sible cost has the best chance of maximizing profits. This is why *productivity* (maximizing the output from the resources used) and **efficiency** (producing at the lowest possible cost) are of such importance to a firm.

Output per worker is the most common measure of productivity. A great many factors influence productivity. The skills, education, and experience of the workforce are important; so are the quantity and quality of the resources with which labour works. A factory with machinery that is continually breaking down will produce less than a factory with state-of-the-art machinery. How the work is organized is also important. When a firm improves its productivity (and not its costs), it can produce more goods and services for the same cost. Consequently, it can offer its goods or services at a lower price, making the firm more competitive. The same equation applies to an economy. When an economy becomes more productive, it can produce more for the same cost and can, therefore, offer its goods and services to other countries for a lower price. Increased productivity results in increased competitiveness.

Cost per unit produced and unit labour cost are the most common measures of efficiency when applied to either a firm or an economy. **Cost per unit** takes into account all costs entailed in creating a product. **Unit labour cost** measures only the cost of labour involved in producing one unit. (Note that unit labour cost is usually given as a relative measure, not an absolute measure, as you'll see in Figure 7.6.) These measures of efficiency help us

Year	Labour Productivity (%)	Hourly Compensation (%)	Unit Labour Cost (%)
1997	+2.5	+4.7	+2.0
1998	+2.1	+3.9	+1.7
1999	+2.5	+2.0	−0.4
2000	+1.5	+4.2	+2.6

Source: Excerpts from table: "Canada's business sector: Labour productivity and related variables" from <http://www.statcan.ca/Daily/English/011221/d011221b.htm>.

Figure 7.6 Measures of efficiency in Canada's business sector (shown as percentage change from the previous year). When did increases in labour productivity actually outpace increases in labour costs?

gauge competitiveness in the local, national, and global markets. A firm or an economy becomes more efficient when its productivity is increasing faster than its costs of production. The table in Figure 7.6 shows us how labour productivity and hourly compensation affect the unit labour cost, as demonstrated in Canada's business sector.

The data in Figure 7.6 indicate that, while average productivity was increasing each year, average hourly compensation paid to labour increased more rapidly, with the exception of 1999. As a result, unit labour cost, the cost of producing the average unit of output, went up. In other words, efficiency declined in each year except 1999. If the efficiency of a firm decreases—or if the efficiency of its competitors improves—the firm will be at a competitive disadvantage. Many Canadian businesses compete in a global marketplace. If unit labour costs in other countries are decreasing faster than they are in Canada—or at least increasing at a slower rate—then Canada will be less competitive internationally and will lose both sales and profits.

Competitiveness is ultimately determined market by market and company by company. Bombardier, a Canadian aerospace company, is one of the largest producers of transportation vehicles in the world. It would be in trouble if its competitors' production efficiency improved more rapidly than its own. Its international sales and profits would slump if its competitors' unit labour costs decreased more, or increased less, than its own.

Choosing production methods

With the goal of keeping production costs to a minimum, firms will try to produce goods or services in a way that makes the most productive use of available resources. This combination will vary among countries, regions, industries, and individual firms, depending on the available resources. Firms will choose resources and mix them in a way that will result in the most efficient method of production. For example, producers may use parts supplied by another company instead of producing all parts themselves.

Many factors influence the choices made. In the medieval times of Europe, in which the Wizard of Id cartoon is set, most production was carried out in a **labour-intensive** fashion (in which most work is conducted by hand). People worked in small shops or in their homes so this approach was called the **cottage system** of production. The cottage system made economic sense because it was the most efficient way to produce. Labour was plentiful and cheap, the market was usually a small local one, and neither the technology nor large sums of capital existed to do it any other way. Most of the costs of production were variable costs that could be adjusted easily to meet demand. Fixed costs were extremely low.

The Industrial Revolution, which we first explored in Chapter 3, began in the 18th century with the development of new technologies. Entrepreneurs created large pools of investment capital, which they invested in a new form of business called the joint stock company. (These firms are owned jointly by a large number of individuals according to the number of shares of stock they have purchased.) Transportation improved, trade became more certain, and populations and markets grew. Workers flowed from their rural cottages to the rapidly developing urban centres, where work became centralized in large factories with machinery.

Labour-intensive production gave way to the **capital-intensive** production of the factory system. This development made good economic sense because the capital investment in buildings and machinery made the labour force more productive and the production process more efficient. The drawback of switching to capital-intensive production was a sharp increase in fixed costs relative to variable costs. It became difficult to increase production in a boom or to decrease costs in bad times. Financial risks grew, but so did the potential for profit, thanks to economies of scale.

The concept of **economies of scale** refers to the greater efficiency that some firms can achieve when they produce a very large amount of output. While some firms may become less efficient owing to the law of diminishing returns (see Figure 1.14 on page 19), others may see their cost per unit drop sharply as output increases. This is particularly true of firms that produce in a capital-intensive way. This method of production has high fixed costs and lower variable costs. Increasing output allows a firm to spread its fixed costs over the increasing number of units produced, which rapidly reduces cost per unit produced. (For example, consider a firm that produces 200 units per month. If it pays $2000 per month to rent its premises, the rental cost per unit is $10. If the company could increase production to 400 units per month, the rental cost per unit would drop to $5.) Other benefits are derived from the greater specialization of labour that is possible in a large staff. Large firms also have more market power to negotiate better prices from their suppliers. To read about a small company that made big changes to achieve economies of scale, see the Case Study below.

Firms in the private sector largely determine the economic question of "How do we

Case Study Garrison Guitars

Chris Griffiths is the founder and owner of Garrison Guitars, a company that builds acoustic guitars in St. John's, Newfoundland. The guitars, recognized internationally for their quality, are sold in specialty music stores in Canada, the United States, Europe, Australia, Japan, and China.

Griffiths's interest in guitars began when he was 12 years old, taking lessons, playing in groups, and making small repairs to guitars in a St. John's music store. He discovered that customers needing major repairs to their guitars were frustrated by the cost and time involved in sending the guitars to the mainland. Sensing a business opportunity but realizing he needed more knowledge about guitar manufacturing, Griffiths undertook an apprenticeship at a Michigan guitar-repair centre. Armed with this expertise, Griffiths returned to St. John's and began repairing and building guitars on his own. Soon, however, he realized that he needed start-up capital to get his new business on track.

In 1992, Griffiths presented his ideas to Youth Ventures Plan and the Atlantic Opportunities Agency—two government programs that advance capital to promising entrepreneurs. He said that his biggest problem

Figure 7.7 Product production at the Garrison Guitars facilities.

was convincing the lenders that he wasn't "just another 19-year-old kid who wanted to be a rock star." The agencies advanced him sufficient capital to start his first company in St. John's: Griffiths Guitars, a sole proprietorship (that is, a

> *They are beautiful on every front—visually, sonically, and conceptually.*
> —Rob Baker (The Tragically Hip)
>
> *The first time that I picked up a Garrison, I literally flipped out, and it was only a prototype.*
> —Barry Canning (2001 MIANL Winner, Male Artist of the Year)
>
> *Everybody I know in Halifax has seen and played this guitar and Willy, the lead guitarist of SenseAmelia Project, has told a lot of people that it's perhaps the finest guitar in the city.*
> —Amelia Curran (2002 ECMA Nominee, Female Artist of the Year)
>
> *These guitars play and sound like the ones I can't afford to buy!*
> —Paul Lamb (Crush, 2002 ECMA Nominees)

Source: Garrison Guitars, 2002 Garrison Releases.

Figure 7.8 Garrison Guitars has succeeded partially because it produces the high-end instruments desired by musicians at the top of their field. What indications do their endorsements give about why Griffiths has succeeded?

business owned by one individual) specializing in repairing and building acoustic and electronic guitars.

Griffiths wasn't satisfied yet. His years working with guitars inspired him with an idea about a different way to build guitars—and possibly expand his business. The frame that supports the outside sheathing of conventional guitars is made up of several dozen pieces of wood. Griffiths believed that a one-piece frame made from fibreglass would work better, transmitting sound to the top of the guitar and, as a result, improving its overall sound. A second advantage of Griffiths's one-piece design was the lower cost of manufacturing a guitar with fewer pieces.

After building several prototypes—and after six years of experimentation—Griffiths developed the one-piece frame construction, which he unveiled at a trade show in Los Angeles in 2000. The demand for his new guitar was

immediate and a little overwhelming. Griffiths realized he needed to expand his operation to factory size. He managed to raise sufficient capital from venture funds and individuals to open a 1900-m² plant in St. John's. The new plant employs 57 people, for a total investment of $4 million in 2002.

The new company, Garrison Guitars, sells about 5 per cent of its guitars in Canada, 45 per cent to the United States, and the rest in other parts of the world. It advertises on the Internet as well as at trade shows, using endorsements from musicians to create demand for its product. At present, Garrison Guitars is a private corporation (owned by a set of individuals, not traded on public markets); the decision to become a public firm is a future consideration.

QUESTIONS

1. Chris Griffiths began his career by doing guitar repairs in a St. John's music store.

   a) What demand did Griffiths identify in the Newfoundland market?

   b) What did Griffiths need to acquire before he could satisfy that demand?

2. As a sole proprietor, Griffiths saw an opportunity in the form of a new guitar design. What had to happen before Griffiths's company could achieve the economies of scale of a large production facility?

3. Create a chart to compare the company type, size of operation, market, and product or service offered by Griffiths's company when he

   a) repaired guitars,

   b) was a sole proprietorship (Griffiths Guitars), and

   c) was a private corporation (Garrison Guitars).

4. Find out about another company in the business of producing musical instruments by researching Sabian, a cymbal and percussion instrument maker located in a small town on the shores of the Saint John River in New Brunswick. What factors led to this company's success?

produce?" in a market economy. The decision-making process involves the artful acquisition and balancing of economic resources whose prices have been determined by resource markets. Resources must be blended and organized to avoid diminishing returns and maximize productivity at the lowest possible cost. To see how you can compare the costs of various production alternatives, see the Thinking Like an Economist feature below.

Calculating the Costs of Production Alternatives

Economists calculate the costs of various production alternatives so that resources may be used in the most productive, efficient way. Costs must be calculated for various production levels in order to see at which point the benefits of economies of scale apply.

Let's assume that you purchased the King's rubbing liniment business, had done well, and were looking for new opportunities. The day-off-at-the-beach idea had proven so popular that now the King declared one day each week as "beach day." You noted that this caused a substantial increase in the demand for swimsuits, so you acquired a licence to produce swimsuits. Your market research indicates you could sell your suits for $50 each. You now have to decide the best way to produce them. You could stick with the traditional labour-intensive, flexible, cottage industry. Alternatively, you could take the risk of building a factory and stocking it with looms and other equipment run by water power in the hope of increasing productivity and efficiency.

You have carefully researched the costs involved to determine the production data listed in Figure 7.9.

QUESTIONS

1. Produce a chart listing the total costs at all three levels of production for both production methods.
2. Which method of production maximizes profit at each level of production?
3. Calculate efficiency (cost per unit produced) at each level of production for both types of production. Present this information in chart form.
4. Which method of production becomes *more* efficient as output increases? Explain this trend.
5. Which method of production becomes *less* efficient as output increases? Explain this trend.

Level of Production (number of suits)	Labour-Intensive Method		Capital-Intensive Method	
	Total Fixed Costs	Total Variable Costs	Total Fixed Costs	Total Variable Costs
100	1000	2000	15 000	1000
500	1000	15 000	15 000	5000
1000	1000	50 000	15 000	10 000

Figure 7.9 Swimsuit production data.

Firms, Competition, and the Market

Firms in the private sector consider many factors in determining the business strategies that will best serve their self-interest. Financial considerations related to profitability motivate all firms. As we learned earlier in this chapter, however, the ultimate purpose of all economic activity is not the profit of individual firms but the satisfaction of consumer needs. In this larger picture, both firms and profits are means to an end, not ends in themselves.

In Canada, we rely mainly on private firms operating in markets to produce the goods and services we need. A *market* is a group of buyers and sellers of particular goods or services, as we saw in Chapter 4. For example, the energy market consists of all firms that supply energy and all the individuals or companies to whom they sell energy. We rely mainly on competition among producers to create choices for consumers and to keep prices down within markets. *Competition*, then, is the primary mechanism that ensures firms remain accountable to consumers as well as to their managers and shareholders.

Firms compete against one another in many ways. Price is one of the most obvious and significant areas of competition. A lower price will increase the sale of most products. Firms also engage in **non-price competition**—

competition that involves changing anything but price. For example, firms compete on the basis of quality. Which firm offers the best-built good or delivers the most complete and timely service? Which one offers the best warranty, the latest style, the best location, or most convenient care? The competition for customers among firms in the market encourages the supply of good products at low prices. It also encourages firms to use their resources to produce new and better products and to do so more efficiently. Not all markets, however, are the same. In some, there is little competition or choice for consumers.

Market Structure

What factors influence the production decisions of large corporations, such as Nortel Networks, the Royal Bank, and Air Canada? Do the same factors affect the decisions of the small restaurant in rural Ontario? Clearly, a large corporation and a rural restaurant operate within different market structures. In every case, the structure of the industry or market in which a firm operates influences its decisions regarding price and output. The five factors that help to determine market structure are

1. the number (and size) of firms in the market,

2. the degree to which competitors' products are similar,

3. a firm's control over price,
4. the ease with which firms can enter or leave the market, and
5. the amount of non-price competition.

Most markets and industries can be classified into one of four basic market structures: perfect competition, monopolistic competition, oligopoly, and monopoly. Of these, perfect competition and monopoly represent opposite poles of the market spectrum. The other two structures represent benchmarks along this spectrum and characterize the conditions faced by most firms in the Canadian economy. This simple spectrum is illustrated in Figure 7.10. For a summary of the characteristics of these four types of market structures, see the chart in Figure 7.11.

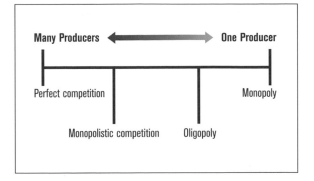

Figure 7.10 Types of market structure.

Perfect competition

Perfect competition is characterized by many producers and a uniform product. Suppliers of agricultural goods, for example, operate within such a market. A perfectly competitive market is distinguished by five main characteristics:

1. There are many buyers and sellers in the market. There are so many sellers that individual firms have no control over total market supply.

2. All the firms sell a standardized product. Imagine a very long country road along which every second farmer has a stand selling the same produce: corn, peaches, and apples.

3. Producers must accept the market equilibrium price for their product. They can sell as much or as little as they choose at that price without changing it. They are price

Characteristics	Perfect Competition	Monopolistic Competition	Oligopoly	Monopoly
1. Number and size of firms in the market	large number of firms; small size	many firms but not large in size	few firms but large in size	one large firm
2. Degree of product similarity in the market	identical	product differentiation (in quality, packaging, marketing, etc.)	some product differentiation	unique
3. A firm's control over price	no control; a price taker	some control; a price influencer	significant control; informal collective pricing	total control; a price maker
4. Ease with which firms can enter or leave the market	no barriers	some barriers	many barriers	almost total exclusion
5. Amount of non-price competition	little (location sometimes)	some (product quality, advertising, packaging)	considerable (packaging, advertising, brand name)	not much (public relations, advertising needed when close substitutes exist)

Figure 7.11 Characteristics of market structures.

takers—they must take the market price—because individually they have no impact on total supply.

4. It is relatively easy to enter and exit the market. That is, the start-up costs or the costs of leaving are not so great as to prevent firms from doing either one.

5. Because all firms sell the same product and each firm can sell as much or as little as it wants at the market price, there is little non-price competition among them.

The success of a firm in a perfectly competitive market depends entirely on how well it manages its costs. Decision making focuses entirely on reducing the costs per unit produced. Because the firm has no influence on price or total quantity sold, profitability depends entirely on making efficient use of the economy's scarce resources. Those firms that are the most efficient (that is, can maintain low costs) will be rewarded with profit. Achieving very low costs can work against a firm, however, because the large profits will attract more producers who, collectively, will increase supply and drive market prices and profits down. Such competitive pressure guarantees the lowest price to consumers with just enough profit for producers to keep them producing.

In reality, the perfectly competitive market does not exist, primarily because there are always some start-up costs and some use of non-price competition. The classic example of a group of producers that comes closest to being perfect competitors are wheat farmers. They produce an identical product, have no influence over the market price, and do not participate in non-price competition. Nonetheless, wheat farmers need huge amounts of capital to start up a new business, so there is a barrier to entering the market.

Monopolistic competition

In most markets, there are some sellers who compete with one another in different ways and with varying degrees of intensity. When the product can be differentiated and there are a substantial number of firms operating in the market, the market structure is called **monopolistic competition**, as opposed to perfect competition.

The major characteristics of the market structure of monopolistic competition are as follows:

1. A substantial number of firms compete in the market.
2. Firms sell a similar but not identical product.
3. Individual firms are large enough to influence total supply, and so they have some influence over price.
4. It is relatively easy for a new firm to start up.
5. Non-price competition is significant.

Monopolistically competitive markets are most prevalent in the service and retail sectors of the Canadian economy. As consumers, we shop in them frequently. Think of your favourite pizza parlour. It competes with several other pizza parlours. The competition might come in the form of a price war if each store attempts to increase its market share by offering lower prices and special deals. Competition might also include non-price factors. For example, each pizza store might try to differentiate itself from the rest by offering different services, such as guaranteed 15-minute delivery, gourmet toppings, thin-crust or deep-dish pizzas, and 24-hour service. It might expand its product line or advertise its goods in various media. The problem with any of these initiatives is that they all have to be factored into the firm's cost of production.

Monopolistically competitive markets are also relatively easy to enter and exit. Generally, the firms are fairly small. The economies of scale and capital requirements are limited. Firms must still distinguish their products from those of their competitors, and this creates some financial barriers.

In monopolistically competitive markets (and in oligopolistic markets, about which you'll read more in the next section), firms seek to distinguish their product or service from those of their competitors in some desirable way. They use a number of techniques to accomplish this **product differentiation**, as you can see in Figure 7.12.

When product differentiation is successful, it leads to something marketers call brand loyalty, a situation in which consumers become attached to a product and will pay more to

Product Differentiation

1. *Product quality:* Firms attempt to create physical or qualitative differences. Examples:
   - tender versus tough meat (at restaurants)
   - high-end computer hardware (in the home computer business)

2. *Services:* Firms offer special follow-up services surrounding the sale of a product. Examples:
   - "Delivery in 15 minutes or your pizza's free!"
   - providing an extended warranty for a new home computer

3. *Location and accessibility:* Firms choose locations convenient to their customers or stay open long hours. Example:
   - 24-hour stores
   - locating a gas station on a highway rather than along a rural route

4. *Promotion and packaging:* Firms attempt to differentiate their products by packaging them in different ways or by advertising them. Examples:
   - glitzy packaging
   - advertising with a celebrity endorsement of one product that is virtually identical to another

Figure 7.12 Firms know that in a competitive market, they must somehow differentiate their goods or services from those of their competitors. What examples of product differentiation have you noticed?

satisfy that preference. Because of brand loyalty, successful firms in a monopolistically competitive market do have some control over price.

Oligopoly

If you made a list of the ten best-known brand-name companies in Canada, you might mention Air Canada, Indigo–Chapters, CIBC, Irving Oil, PetroCan, and Loblaws. All of these are oligopolists. They operate as huge firms in each of their respective markets. CIBC, for example, shares the market for financial services with just a few other major firms. The main characteristics of the market structure know as an **oligopoly** are as follows:

1. It is dominated by a few, very large firms.
2. Competing firms may produce products as similar as steel or as different as automobiles.
3. The firm's freedom to set price varies from slight to substantial.
4. Significant financial and other barriers to entry exist.
5. Non-price competition can be intense.

Many consumers become frustrated as they watch competition play out between firms in an oligopoly. Their frustration comes from a sense of helplessness because oligopolies seem to raise and lower prices at will. Prices do move up or down, but competitors' prices all seem to move in exactly the same way at exactly the same time. Gasoline prices are an excellent example: they all go up about the same time and then go down about the same time. At times, observers suspect that a price conspiracy exists, and they demand that the firms be investigated for illegal activity.

Further suspicion arises because prices for products in an oligopoly tend to stay within a particular range. The service charges on your bank account, for example, will be pretty similar no matter which bank you decide to trust with your savings. Similarly, all banks charge about the same rate of interest on funds borrowed on a credit card. Again, is there a conspiracy going on?

Not necessarily. By shopping around for the lowest price, consumers push firms to compete on the basis of price. In a free-market economy, firms have the right to set prices at any level they see fit. A station that sticks with a slightly higher price will lose a lot of business.

Nonetheless, a common pricing strategy among oligopolists may occur. At the beginning of Chapter 2, for example, you played a game called Make As Much Money As You Can (page 26). At the end of round 3, you had a chance to talk to your competitors. What did

Figure 7.13 Ever noticed that gasoline always seems more expensive just before a long weekend? Is it collusion? Or is it just a consequence of the high demand as people fill up before the long trip to the cottage?

you talk to one another about? Were you tempted to make a deal with your competitors? Did you do so? If so, you participated in a form of **collusion**, which is a secret agreement among firms to set prices, limit output, or reduce or eliminate competition. It is illegal in Canada and the United States for firms to collude. A recent example has occurred in the music and recording industry. In 2000, 28 states launched suits against several recording companies for inflating their production costs for CDs and enforcing minimum prices at which they could be sold in retail stores. The outcome of this case is yet to be decided. You will read more about this in the Production Issues section of this chapter (page 160).

Monopoly

The word *monopoly* comes from the Greek words *monos polein*, which mean "alone to sell." In a **monopoly**, one firm or organization enjoys complete control of the market. The major characteristics of a monopolistic market are as follows:

1. It is a market completely dominated by a single firm. This firm has complete control over total supply.

2. The firm produces a unique product for which there are no close substitutes.
3. The firm is a price maker; that is, by changing supply it can set whatever price will maximize its profits.
4. Major barriers to entry prevent other firms from entering the market.
5. Because it has no direct competitors, a monopoly need not engage in non-price competition.

A firm may establish a monopoly by gaining legal control of its product and the exclusive right to benefit from its sale. *Copyright law* gives writers control of the work they produce. *Patent law* protects the inventors and developers of a new product or technology by giving them the sole right to benefit from its sale for a period of time. Many a private firm owes its birth, growth, and profitability to patent protection.

Government may also create at least a local monopoly by awarding the sole right to provide a product or service to a particular firm. The Canadian Radio–television and Telecommunications Commission (CRTC) awards exclusive rights of service to cable providers in specific areas of Canada. Each provider then holds a monopoly in its area. (For example, Cogeco Cable holds the right to service Kingston, but Rogers Cable holds the right to service Ottawa.) In most cases, the CRTC must approve any price changes.

In a few cases, producers themselves may create a monopoly by selling franchises. Professional sport leagues are an example. Residents in the Hamilton area would probably love to have an NHL team in their city, but NHL team owners in Toronto and Buffalo would oppose such a move.

Are monopolists better at producing goods at lower prices than perfect competitors? Have a look at the Thinking Like an Economist feature on page 157 to learn a way to figure it out for yourself.

We should keep in mind that, like the Kingdom of Id, the example in the Thinking Like an Economist feature is a parody of reality. For one thing, it assumes that the costs of a small perfect competitor are the same as the monopolist's. In fact, monopolists are better able to produce large quantities of output. They have the financial resources to assume the costs and risks of capital-intensive production and can achieve the efficiencies that come from economies of scale.

Some products, particularly those with high fixed costs, are more efficiently produced by a monopoly than by a few or many smaller producers. This type of monopoly is referred to as a **natural monopoly**. It is found most often in the field of public utilities (such as the generation, supply, and delivery of natural gas or electricity; local telephone service; and water and sewer supply) where having more than one supplier would be impractical and wasteful. Many markets that were once considered more efficient as natural monopolies are now being opened up for market competition through a process of deregulation or privatization. **Deregulation** involves opening a market to more competition. This may be accomplished in a variety of ways. **Privatization** refers to one method of deregulation that involves, among other things, the sale of public assets to private firms.

Determining Maximum Number of Goods at Lowest Prices

According to most economists, society is best served when the maximum number of goods is produced at the lowest possible prices. Which type of market structure, perfect competition or monopoly, is most likely to do this? Work it out for yourself.

Maximizing profit in perfect competition

Assume that you are a producer of leg casts back in the days of the Wizard of Id. The King says he will take all you can supply for his injured soldiers and pays you $50 for each. Although this is not a case of perfect competition, in which there would be many competitors, the calculations of your profit would be the same because, as with perfect competition, the price you charge for your product will not change. You can produce as much or little as you choose at that price. The table in Figure 7.14 presents your total costs for producing different numbers of leg casts.

Under these conditions, and assuming you were a profit maximizer, you would probably want to determine how many leg casts you should produce in order to make the most profit. In other words, you would like to determine when the marginal revenue equals the marginal costs, as described on page 146. Remember that in the case of perfect competition the price you charge for the item stays the same, in this case, $50 per leg cast.

Level of Output	Total Costs ($)
0	40
1	70
2	95
3	125
4	160
5	200
6	245
7	300
8	365
9	440
10	520

Figure 7.14 The cost of producing leg casts.

QUESTIONS

1. To determine the level of production that would maximize your profit, create a chart with the following columns:
   - Units Sold (Level of Output in Figure 7.14)
   - Total Revenue (number of units × $50)
   - Marginal Revenue (Total Revenue − Total Revenue of one unit less)
   - Total Costs (column 2 in Figure 7.14)
   - Marginal Costs (Total Cost − Total Cost of one unit less)

   Examine your chart to figure out the final point at which marginal revenue continues to exceed marginal costs. That level of production will provide you with the most profit.

The graph in Figure 7.15 presents the market from the point of view of the perfect competitor. The marginal revenue (MR_1) remains the same as the price regardless of the amount produced (refer back to the Marginal Revenue column from question 1). The marginal revenue line cuts the marginal cost curve (MC) between the sixth and seventh unit of output at point A. This graph clearly demonstrates that the marginal cost of producing the seventh unit would be greater (by $5) than the additional revenue that could be earned. Producing more than Q_1, which is the quantity produced at the production level at point A, will reduce total profit by this amount, so there is no incentive to produce it.

Maximizing profit in monopoly

Now assume that the King gives you the licence to be the sole producer of leg casts in the kingdom, but this time he makes his soldiers pay for them. In this situation, you are a monopoly. The soldiers' ability to pay, rather than the King's ability to pay, will now determine demand. The price you can charge will vary depending on demand. Assume the table in Figure 7.16 represents the soldiers' demand for leg casts.

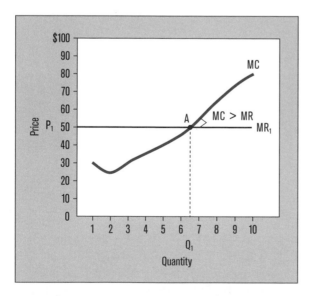

Figure 7.15 The point of profit maximization for a perfect competitor. Under perfect competition, marginal revenue is equal to the market price.

Price Charged ($)	Quantity Demanded
100	1
90	2
80	3
70	4
60	5
50	6
40	7
30	8
20	9
10	10

Figure 7.16 The market demand for leg casts. As you lower the price you charge for leg casts, the quantity you sell increases.

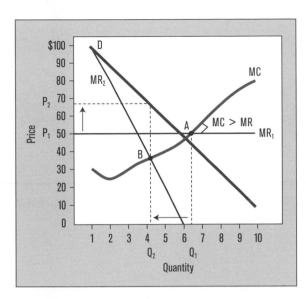

Figure 7.17 The point of profit maximization for a monopoly. Compare Q_1 (determined in Figure 7.15) with Q_2 in this graph. Which encourages higher production levels?

Under these conditions, and assuming your costs of production remain the same and you are a profit maximizer, how many leg casts would you choose to produce?

Assuming you are a profit maximizer, you would probably want to determine how many leg casts you should produce in order to make the most profit, just as you did as a perfect competitor. Remember that in the case of a monopoly the price you charge for the item varies, as you can see in Figure 7.16. Your costs will remain the same as they were for the perfect competitor, as listed in Figure 7.14.

QUESTIONS (cont.)

2. To determine the level of production that would maximize your profit, create a chart with the following columns:
   • Units Sold (Quantity Demanded in Figure 7.16)

   • Price Charged (column 1 in Figure 7.16)
   • Total Revenue (number of units × Price Charged)
   • Marginal Revenue (Total Revenue − Total Revenue of one unit less)
   • Total Costs (column 2 in Figure 7.14)
   • Marginal Costs (Total Cost − Total Cost of one unit less)

Examine your chart to figure out the final point at which marginal revenue continues to exceed marginal costs for a monopoly.

The graph in Figure 7.17 illustrates the difference between production in a perfectly competitive market and production in a monopoly market. The marginal cost curve remains the same, but the new marginal revenue curve, MR_2, slopes downward and cuts the MC curve at a lower production level (at point B) between the fourth and fifth unit of output. Producing more than Q_2, which is the quantity produced at the production level at point B, would mean that marginal costs would exceed marginal revenue, thereby reducing total profit. The demand curve (D) has been added to illustrate how the reduction in quantity supplied will lead to a higher selling price, P_2.

QUESTIONS (cont.)

3. Which market type provided the most goods for the lowest price?
4. Compare the total profit made by the two types of producers.

Our investigations here show that, subject to certain conditions, perfect competition results in the highest efficiency. Intense competition forces firms to produce as much as possible and to offer these goods or services at the lowest possible price. (However, the assumption that both types of producers have identical cost structures is rarely true.)

Check Your Understanding

1. Refer to Figure 7.11 on page 153 (characteristics of market structures). Make a similar chart to give examples of each market structure. Fill it in with the names of firms in your local community or region that compete in each type of market structure.

2. Explain the differences between a firm that is "price taker" and one that is a "price maker."

3. How does the market discourage even a monopolist from charging the highest price possible?

4. Make a list of the ways in which firms engage in non-price competition.

5. Compare and contrast the market structures of (a) monopoly and monopolistic competition, and (b) monopolistic competition and oligopoly.

6. Refer to the list of methods of product differentiation listed in Figure 7.12 on page 155.

   a) For each of the methods, identify examples from your own experience when you have been influenced by this type of product differentiation.

   b) Some economists argue that product differentiation brings both an element of competition and an element of monopoly into a market place. From your experience, evaluate the validity of this claim.

Production Issues

What is the best way to produce goods and services to satisfy our needs? Should we depend on government? Should we rely on firms competing for profit in the market? Are there other options? What matters of public interest can we entrust to the marketplace?

Is Bigger Better?

Adam Smith had reservations about leaving things to competitors in private markets:

People of the same trade seldom meet together, even for merriment and diversion, but the conversation ends in a conspiracy against the public, or in some contrivance to raise prices.

—*The Wealth of Nations*, Book I, Chapter X, Part 2 (1776)

Smith is referring to the temptation of collusion among businesses, which you read about earlier. Smith would have had particular concerns about the production methods of modern industry. Capital-intensive production can be more efficient but also results in fewer, very large producers competing as oligopolists. As the number of competitors in a marketplace drops, Smith's "conspiracy ... to raise prices" is more easily achieved. The benefits of efficient production and the economies of scale are more likely to go to the producer in the form of higher profits than to the consumer in the form of lower prices.

Normal market behaviour may result in less competition, and without the pressure of competition to keep prices down, they can more easily float upward. Successful firms frequently use profits to expand production by purchasing their competitors. Through *mergers* (the combination of two firms into one) and takeovers, firms reduce the risks of competition by controlling it. For example, after taking over a competing firm, the new firm can cease production of any goods or reduce any service that the competing firm supplies, thereby eliminating unwanted competition. In the late 1990s, several of Canada's major banks sought to merge in order to achieve the size they felt was necessary to compete in global markets. Federal regulations blocked the merger because of concerns that it would reduce competition and the availability of banking services in Canada. (For more on this trend, see the Economics in the News feature on page 161.)

Economics in the News

Consumers Beware—Canada Is a Haven for Media Oligopolies

Canada has the dubious honour of being home to one of the planet's most concentrated media and telecommunications markets. A small number of large players control the eyes and ears of an extraordinary number of consumers. Could it become even more concentrated?

The answer is Yes, and the reason is that ownership barriers in the United States are falling, opening the door to concentration of unprecedented levels—the triumph of the oligopoly. Policy fashion, as it is called, is usually set in the United States and history shows that it usually finds its way into Canada. If this happens again, Canada, incredibly, could see another round of media and telecommunications mergers.

The White House and Congress, regardless of which party was in control, was sympathetic to the formation of huge companies during the 1990s. The Depression-era Glass–Steagall Act was dismantled, allowing commercial and investment banks to merge. Diversified financial services monsters such as Citigroup and J.P. Morgan Chase were born. The merger pace in all industries, from defence to publishing, set records year after year. The US courts found that Microsoft violated antitrust laws by illegally maintaining its monopoly. Nonetheless, it was essentially let off the hook under a proposed settlement.

Just as you thought industry behemoths couldn't get any bigger, along came a new court ruling in favour of bigness. Last week, a US federal appeals court ordered the Federal Communications Commission to reconsider rules limiting broadcasters from controlling more than 35 per cent of the TV market. If the rules, as expected, are changed, broadcasters such as NBC, owned by General Electric, and ABC, part of the Walt Disney group, will probably go on an epic buying spree, gobbling up the affiliated TV

stations they don't already own. The appeals court ruling also means that cable companies might be able to buy broadcast networks. In time, three or four companies in the media industry and an equal number in cable will probably control almost the entire market.

Canada itself is no slouch when it comes to ownership concentration. In effect, media ownership rules have all but disappeared. Merger reviews in Canada, unlike the United States, are conducted on a case-by-case basis by the Canadian Radio–television and Telecommunications Commission. Theoretically, a deal can be turned down if it's found not to be in the "public interest." In practice, this rarely happens. Integration … as a result, is tolerated, even encouraged. The Aspers' CanWest Global Communications owns almost every big-city daily newspaper in the land, as well as the No. 2 private broadcasting network. In the Vancouver market, CanWest owns both dailies and two TV stations, a degree of media concentration unparalleled in North America. The reach of the portfolio of rival BCE is equally broad. It controls Bell Canada, satellite broadcaster Bell ExpressVu and Bell Globemedia, owner of CTV, The Globe and Mail and the Sympatico–Lycos Internet portal. BCE is the fusion of content and carriage on a grand scale.

It is unlikely that merger-bound Canadian companies will ever be granted recourse to the courts, as in the United States; the CRTC will remain the judge, jury, and executioner for so long as federal governments continue to prop up the increasingly irrelevant agency. But the fact that American companies no longer seem to face any growth constraints whatsoever will put even more pressure on the CRTC to allow the companies it regulates to do the same. Even though oligopolies can damage competition, raising prices for consumers, the CRTC will likely bend to the argument that Canadian companies can't be pygmies if they want to compete in a land of giants. Better to be big than not to exist at all. The argument is full of holes because Canadian media, cable, or telecom players have yet to use their new-found bulk to attack the US market. Perhaps that may come.

So what shape might the next round of consolidation take in Canada? Star Choice, Shaw Communications' satellite broadcaster, is rumoured to be for sale and the only logical buyer is Bell ExpressVu. The cable companies, like their US counterparts, want to control the landscape from coast to coast. The effort by Rogers Communications to buy Quebec's Vidéotron failed, but the two are natural partners because their networks are contiguous. Down the road, it's not inconceivable that Shaw and Rogers could combine their networks.

Canada is already safe for oligopolies. In the future, it will become even safer for them. Consumers beware.

Source: Eric Reguly, "Consumers beware: Canada is a haven for media oligopolies" from *The Globe and Mail*, 7 March 2002. Reprinted with permission from The Globe and Mail.

QUESTIONS

1. Based on what is stated in the article, what do you think the purpose of the US Glass—Steagall Act was?

2. What evidence does the author use to support his assertion that business concentration and oligopolies are growing in the United States?

3. What is "policy fashion," and how is it relevant to this article?

4. Describe CanWest's media ownership in the Vancouver market. What do you think is the economic advantage to the producer? How might this level of concentration harm consumers?

5. The media are the communicators of information and opinion. Is the concentration of ownership of greater significance because of the type of service provided by this industry?

6. Which do you think is more important—the ability for companies to compete on a more global scale, or the opportunity for consumers to have a greater degree of choice? Be prepared to defend your answer.

Third-Party Costs

Markets have so far flourished under capitalism, but that does not make them perfect. Even a market with many small, privately owned firms will not necessarily ensure that economic resources will be used efficiently. Profit-seeking producers try to reduce their costs of production to a minimum. Markets are not always good at internalizing or passing on all the costs of production to those who consume the product. Pollution is an example. When the wastes of production are released into the water, air, or soil rather than being properly treated as part of the production process, the firm effectively passes on the environmental costs of production to others. These non-monetary costs are called **social costs** or **third-party costs**. The existence of these costs reflects a shortcoming of efficiency as a production objective. Achieving production efficiency by reducing the costs of production can lead to the destruction of scarce resources rather than their efficient use. (For more on this topic, see Chapter 16.)

The Public–Private Balance

The government has also been found wanting as an efficient provider of goods and services. During the three decades after 1960, government expanded its role as a producer, particularly as a provider of essential services such as education and health care. This increased role resulted partly from a growing population. It also stemmed partly from a widespread belief that government was able to satisfy essential needs better than markets and the private sector. By 1990, however, government spending seemed out of control. Annual deficits grew at alarming rates, and our accumulated public debt was threatening the well-being of both the present and future generations.

A Matter of Opinion | On the Business of Delivering Health Care

No public policy issue is currently more important to Canadians than the debate about our health-care system. The most basic regulation concerning the delivery of health care in Canada is the Canada Health Act passed in 1984. It established a health-care system based on the principles of

- public administration: *a non-profit, government-run system,*
- comprehensiveness: *coverage for all identified health services provided by hospitals, medical practitioners, or dentists,*
- universality: *equal coverage and treatment for all citizens,*
- portability: *coverage for all citizens in Canada wherever they live,*
- accessibility: *care within a reasonable time.*

In the past 20 years, both medicine and the needs of the population have changed. Changing the production and delivery of health-care services has been the focus of widespread public debate. The federal government established a commission under the leadership of Roy Romanow, a former premier of Saskatchewan, to investigate and make recommendations. The article below describes the thoughts presented to the commission by various groups and individuals at a one-day meeting held in Vancouver in March 2002.

Private System Crucial, Inquiry Told

❝ VANCOUVER—There's nothing "morally wrong" with Canadians directly spending their own money on medical services, a commission on medicare's future has been told.

Officials with a right-wing think tank and a for-profit hospital in Vancouver yesterday insisted more private-sector involvement is crucial to saving the health-care system.

"We need to follow the trend toward privatization and contesting the supply of all government services," Michael Walker, executive director of the Vancouver-based Fraser Institute, told the federal commission on the future of health care.

"Health care is like any of the other services we need in society, there is no one timeless solution to the problem of its provision," Walker said.

Yesterday's hearing was the third stop of an 18-city tour by the commission, headed by former Saskatchewan premier Roy Romanow.

It has already held meetings in Regina and Winnipeg and travels to Victoria tomorrow.

Not surprisingly, there was no shortage of critics in the polarized debate over the future of medicare and to Walker's call for increased privatization.

Opposition to privatization was led by [former] federal New Democratic Party leader Alexa McDonough and British Columbia's nurses' union.

"Behind the friendly rhetoric of private-sector choice lies the simple reality that for-profit health care offers less care, at a higher cost, than public, not-for-profit care," McDonough told the commission.

"In the public sector, health-care dollars go to health care—not to marketing campaigns, not investor relations, not mergers and acquisitions, and not for profit."

McDonough, who invoked the name of medicare pioneer Tommy Douglas during her presentation, called for an immediate increase in federal government funding on health care to the provinces.

She wants it boosted from the current level of about 14 per cent to one-quarter—and eventually half—of the level at which it sat when the program was created.

McDonough also called for an increased focus on fighting poverty, improving child nutrition, and bettering the conditions of native people as ways to strengthen our health-care system.

"Remodelling, not demolition, should be our watchword," McDonough said to applause.

But Walker said simply putting more public money into the system would not ease waiting lists for procedures ranging from heart surgery to cancer treatment.

Nor would it improve the access Canadians have to high-priced equipment such as CT scans and MRI machines, he added.

Public hospitals should be able to offer services for direct payment from private citizens, and for-profit clinics should be increasingly turned to in order to reduce demand, he said.

Dr. Brian Day of Vancouver's for-profit Cambie Surgery Centre, which has been open since 1996, said such private facilities are better positioned to pay for expensive medical equipment while introducing efficient "business methods" into the health-care system.

"There is nothing morally wrong with a Canadian spending their own, hard-earned, after-tax dollars on health care," said Day, whose hospital sees about 3200 patients per year.

Some of those patients include foreign tourists, out-of-province referrals paying so-called facility fees, workers' compensation claims and children on welfare who receive dental surgery.

"It's actually providing a surgery to people who would otherwise be on waiting lists," Day told reporters later.

Debra McPherson, president of the BC Nurses' Union, called medicare "an integral part of what defines us as Canadian" that must be protected from "profit hunters."

"Private business interests are currently running a massive misinformation campaign aimed at destroying the public's faith in our public health-care system," McPherson said.

Dr. Heidi Oetter, president of the BC Medical Association, agreed that patients' access to care in the public system is "unacceptably poor" and that there's no problem with private providers delivering services.

But, she added, they must be paid for by tax dollars.

"Ideology should no longer prevent Canadians from obtaining care in the most efficient manner," Oetter said.

"I believe there is an important role for the private sector to deliver publicly funded—not privately funded—health-care services."

If Canadians want services, such as pharmacare and home care, to be included in the publicly funded system, they should expect to pay a portion of the cost in the form of user fees, as long as they do not prevent the poor from getting care, she said.

Oetter said it's important that all Canadians, regardless of income, have access to medical services. 99

Source: Daniel Girard, "Private system crucial, inquiry told" from *The Toronto Star*, 13 March 2002. Reprinted with permission—The Toronto Star Syndicate.

QUESTIONS

1. Read the article and create a chart in which you
   a) identify the group or individual expressing an opinion,
   b) describe the problem as the individual sees it,
   c) describe what each proposes, and
   d) analyze both the costs and benefits of each proposal.

2. If you were Mr. Romanow, what suggestions would you accept and why?

3. To what extent does the nature of the service have any bearing on whether it may best be delivered as a private service by competitive firms operating in a market environment or, at the other extreme, as a public service delivered by a government monopoly? Explain your opinion.

During the 1990s, government cut its spending, its payroll, and its services. It downsized, privatized, and deregulated markets. Canada cut its levels of social spending faster than any other developed nation. In their haste, governments made mistakes. Did governments make the right choices? Should we go further, inviting even more participation of private companies in the delivery of social programs such as health care? Should we be wary of transferring cherished social programs into the hands of firms, whose primary goal (as we have learned in this chapter) is profit? Have a look at the Matter of Opinion feature on page 163 to see what other Canadians have to say on this topic.

Is Regulation the Answer?

Markets cannot exist without regulations that define contracts, protect private property and competition, or require certain production standards. Regulations must be effectively enforced. If markets don't work, because of collusion for example, it may be because they are poorly regulated. If we're worried about involving more private business in the delivery of health care, perhaps regulation of the industry would help control the profit motive. If competition isn't working or production is polluting, perhaps it is the regulations that need to be changed, not who is doing the producing. The Competition Act (1986) and other statutes control competition. (To read more about the Competition Act, see Chapter 13.) The Competition Bureau administers and enforces the act. Its role is to promote and maintain fair competition so that Canadians can benefit from lower prices, product choice, and quality services.

In Canada, regulation is a matter of public policy and decided by public debate. That debate should be based on the values we think are most important. Why might we regulate an industry? How best can our governments balance the need to make the business environment attractive—with low taxes, low utility rates, and low safety or environmental standards, for example—against the needs of citizens? We should also ask ourselves if the ways in which we produce goods and services can be better regulated to serve the ultimate needs of society.

Even with the perfect set of regulations, however, we should not expect the market to do more than it can. We want an economy that responds to our needs, but markets can only respond to demands. The difference between a need and a demand is the ability to pay the market's price. Only those who can pay will get a need satisfied by a market. Only money guarantees a choice.

If we don't like the idea that only wealthy people may be able to afford an education or health care—or a comfortable lifestyle—it's not an issue of production. It is an issue of distribution. It's not a question of How do we produce? but rather one of For whom should we produce? Considerations of equity rather than efficiency may be more important. To what extent should production be distributed according to need rather than the ability to pay? Who should get what is provided, whether government or the private sector produces it? Organizing our scarce resources to provide goods and services that are efficiently produced and equitably consumed is a matter of public debate and regulation to which we can all contribute. It is our economic responsibility, as citizens, to address this issue, because we will enjoy the benefits or bear the costs that result.

Check Your Understanding

1. Who benefits from the growing size of firms, and how do they benefit? What are the problems with firms getting larger and larger?

2. Who pays the third-party, or social, costs of production?

3. In your opinion, what are the biggest issues in production in Canada today?

4. "Both production and profit should be seen as means to an end and not ends in themselves." Do you agree with this statement? Explain.

5. In what ways can regulations be used to achieve social goals?

CHAPTER SUMMARY

- Government provides just less than 20 per cent of the total value of goods and services produced by the Canadian economy. The rest comes from the wide variety of firms—of varying legal form and size—that make up the private sector.

- In a market economy, laws define, limit, and protect the process of production, but it is individuals within firms that make most of the production decisions.

- To understand how firms make decisions, we must analyze the relationship that exists between profits, revenues, and costs:

$$\text{total profit} = (\text{price} \times \text{quantity sold}) \\ - (\text{fixed} + \text{variable costs})$$

- Profits are important for many reasons. They act as an incentive and a reward and are also the producer's least expensive source of money for expanding or improving production. Producers use profits to evaluate how well their firm is being run compared to its competitors. Profits help producers identify which needs are greatest so they can shift resources into the production of goods and services that meet the most urgent demands.

- Firms, like economists, often think "at the margin." If a firm wishes to maximize its profit, it should always produce up to the point at which there is no added benefit (that is, profit) from producing any more. In other words, it should keep producing until the potential revenue to be made from producing one more unit would be eliminated by the additional costs:

$$\text{marginal revenue} = \text{marginal cost}$$

- Firms must focus on controlling the total costs of production. The firm that is able to produce the desired product at the lowest possible cost has the best chance of maximizing profits. This is why productivity and efficiency are of such importance to a firm.

- Deciding what and how to produce involves the artful acquisition and balancing of economic resources.

- Markets rely mainly on competition among producers to create choices for consumers and to keep prices down. Competition is a mechanism that ensures firms remain accountable to consumers as well as to their managers and shareholders.

- The structure of the industry or market in which a firm operates influences its decisions regarding price and output.

- Many markets are now being opened up for market competition through a process of deregulation or privatization.

- Market behaviour may result in less competition. Successful firms frequently use profits to expand production by purchasing their competitors.

- Profit-seeking producers try to reduce their costs of production to a minimum. Markets are not always good at internalizing or passing on all the costs of production to those who consume the product. For example, pollution would be a cost not paid directly by the consumer of a product.

- Achieving production efficiency by reducing the costs of production can lead to the destruction rather than the efficient use of scarce resources.

- Markets owe their existence as much to the laws of government as they do to the laws of demand and supply. Markets cannot exist without regulations that define contracts, protect private property and competition, or require certain production standards. Regulations must be effectively enforced.

- If markets don't work, it may be because they are poorly regulated. In Canada, regulation is a matter of public policy and decided by public debate. Organizing our scarce resources to provide goods and services that are efficiently produced and equitably consumed is a matter of public debate to which we can all contribute.

Key Terms

command economy
real Gross Domestic Product
accounting profit
Theory of the Firm
total cost
fixed costs
variable costs
short run
long run
marginal cost
marginal revenue
efficiency
cost per unit
unit labour cost
labour-intensive
cottage system
capital-intensive
economies of scale
non-price competition
perfect competition
monopolistic competition
product differentiation
oligopoly
collusion
monopoly
natural monopoly
deregulation
privatization
social (third-party) costs

Activities

Thinking/Inquiry

1. A firm's total revenue depends on the price it charges and the quantity it sells. But the most profitable firm is not necessarily the one that charges the highest price or makes the most sales. Explain why.

2. Explain how competition holds firms and the managers who run them accountable to both the firm's owners (shareholders) and its customers.

3. Under what conditions would a firm continue producing in the short run even if it were experiencing a loss?

4. John Maynard Keynes, one of the great economists of the 20th century, said, "In the long run, we are all dead." What could he mean with respect to the way decisions are made in firms?

5. Perfect competitors all produce an identical product that they all sell at the same price. If they do not compete on either a price or a non-price basis, why is this type of market considered "perfect" by economists?

6. Analyze the costs and benefits of a merger from the point of view of (a) the producer and (b) the consumer.

Communication

7. Assume you have been selected to be a member of a commission that is investigating a current issue related to how Canada produces the goods and services that Canadians need. Several current issues are described below as examples. Choose one of these or another issue related to private versus public delivery of services.

Possible topics:

• The government has been interested in entering into new "partnerships" with private sector companies as a way of providing necessary public services. The new plan calls for a private firm to build and maintain a public facility, such as a school or a hospital, that it would lease to the government. After a specified time, the government could purchase the facility for a pre-specified sum. Should the government proceed with this scheme?

• Drug companies are now able to obtain patent protection for 20 years for any new drug they develop. The yearly total cost of drugs, most of which is not covered by government, is now greater than the cost of publicly paid doctors. What, if anything, should be done to make drug care more accessible?

- Typically, roads in Canada are built, maintained, and operated at public expense. Recently, Highway 407 north of Toronto was sold to a private firm, which now charges motorists a toll to use it. Should more roads be privately owned and operated in this way?

- Traditionally, post-secondary tuition fees have been heavily subsidized by government. Tuition fees usually raised no more than 25 per cent of the cost of educating a student. Now some tuition fees have been deregulated so that universities are able to charge students whatever they want. How should post-secondary education be financed?

- Should provincial governments fund private schools?

After you have chosen a topic, take the following steps.

a) Thoroughly research and describe the nature of the issue you have chosen.

b) Describe the details of the various options that could be considered in relation to this issue. Be sure to consider both public and private solutions.

c) Analyze the costs and benefits of each solution from the point of view of each group of stakeholders involved.

d) Prepare and present an interim report in which you outline the facts and your analysis to another group working on a different issue. This group will act as your advisory board. Seek the opinions of your board members about what option or mix of options would result in the best solution.

e) Evaluate all the data and views you have collected, considering the overall economic goals of Canadian society to determine a policy to recommend. Write a detailed conclusion with supporting evidence and arguments, and present a short summary of its contents to your advisory group for its reaction. You may be asked to present this summary to your class.

8. In this activity, you will research and report on competition in an industry that produces a product that you probably use every day: oil. Assume you are in charge of a government committee—the Bureau of Competition—that is looking into the case of gasoline pricing at the gas pumps and whether or not the major oil companies are gouging consumers in Canada.

Step 1: Research how gasoline prices affect both consumers and businesses in Canada. A good starting point would be Canadian newspaper and news magazine articles on the issue of gasoline pricing beginning in 1994.

Step 2: Analyze your findings by answering the following economic questions:

- Are consumers simply frustrated in not being able to satisfy their desires? Consumers seek to maximize satisfaction at the lowest possible cost to themselves. Higher prices generally mean fewer people are able to satisfy their desires.

- Are firms seeking to maximize their profits? Higher prices generally mean higher profits for firms, *ceteris paribus*.

- Are oil companies fixing their prices above the price they would be charging if there were open competition?

- What is the best way to keep prices at a level that benefits consumers? Should the government get involved? Should it let market forces do what they do? When should the government get involved to protect the interests of the consumer?

Step 3: Write a report that answers the question of whether the oil companies are gouging consumers.

Application

9. Figure 7.18 illustrates a firm's cost schedule for its clock-radio production.

a) What is this competitor's fixed costs of production?

b) Calculate the total variable costs of producing four clock-radios.

c) At which level of output is the firm operating most efficiently?

d) Why might a firm not always choose to produce clock-radios at the point that is most efficient?

Quantity Produced	Total Cost ($)
0	35
1	59
2	74
3	96
4	120
5	155
6	199
7	245

Figure 7.18 A firm's cost schedule for clock-radio production.

e) What problem does the firm face? What would you recommend the firm do to overcome this problem?

f) What should this firm do if it could sell its clock-radios at each of the following price levels: (i) $40, (ii) $30, and (iii) $20? Explain your reasoning in each case.

10. Classify each of the following industries by type of market structure:

a) natural gas distribution
b) local telephone service
c) long-distance telephone service
d) Internet service providers in large cities
e) Internet service providers in small towns
f) the garment industry
g) fast-food restaurants
h) nuclear-generated electricity
i) gold mining
j) wheat production
k) automobile manufacturing
l) fibre-optic cable production
m) steel production

11. Advertising is one form of non-price competition. Assume the Milk Marketing Board conducts an expensive but successful "Milk Is Beautiful" campaign. How would such a campaign affect the market for milk? Analyze its effect on demand and supply as well as *elasticity* (how sensitive quantity demanded or supplied is to a change in price), and forecast the resulting change in market price and the quantity of milk consumed.

12. Select a business in your community or region. Assume you wished to start your own business to compete with it. Describe the barriers to entry that would make it challenging for you to get started.

13. Select two or more competing firms at which you might shop in your community.

a) Describe the ways in which they compete against each other, and try to differentiate their goods or services.

b) Rank-order the ways in which they compete, according to their effectiveness in influencing your buying decisions.

14. Every firm is subject to significant government regulation. Interview a business operator in your community.

a) Identify the different ways in which the particular business is regulated.

b) Determine which regulations the operator would like changed and why.

c) Identify any new or different regulations the operator wishes that government would introduce.

CHAPTER 8

RESOURCE ECONOMICS: THE CASE OF LABOUR ECONOMICS

Career-planning tool for youth launched in Charlottetown

CHARLOTTETOWN—
Canadian youth have a new way of getting the most up-to-date information about labour market conditions in order to make better career decisions.

Jane Stewart, Minister of Human Resources Development Canada, was in Charlottetown last Friday to launch Youth Outlooks, a career planning kit designed to meet the needs of young people, aged 15 to 24. The kit contains products explaining national labour market information and trends and how students can use that information to make better educational and career choices.

Youth Outlooks includes a video featuring live interviews with young Canadians, five booklets representing five educational routes and their labour market outcomes, as well as a set of four wall charts.

Stewart was accompanied by Shawn Murphy, Member of Parliament for Hillsborough, on a visit to Colonel Gray High School in Charlottetown where they discussed the benefits of the new kit with students.

"I am proud that the Government of Canada is helping young Canadians across the country acquire the skills and experience they need to fully participate in our society and economy," said Stewart in a news release. "Youth Outlooks is an excellent source of current labour market information and can be used by everyone involved in career planning."

Labour market information is a crucial part of the career planning process and includes data on employment wages, standards and qualifications, job openings, and working conditions, said the release.

The kit can help students learn about different occupational areas, find out about current and future labour market conditions, and make informed choices about their future.

Youth Outlooks will also help students come to a better understanding of links between education/training and work opportunities.

Source: "Career-planning tool for youth launched in Charlottetown" from *The Journal-Pioneer* (Summerside, PEI), 5 May 2001. Reprinted by permission.

QUESTIONS

1. According to the article, what is "labour market information"?

2. How do you think knowing about the trends in the labour market benefits you in the present?

3. How do you think knowing about the trends in the labour market benefits you in the future?

Chapter Goals

By the end of this chapter, you will be able to

• understand the forces that influence the market supply and demand of labour,

• explain how wage rates are determined in a perfectly competitive market and why there are different wage rates for different types of labour,

• identify current trends in the labour force market in Canada,

• explain the reasons for the development of labour unions in Canada,

• describe the major ways in which unions participate as stakeholders in Canada's economy.

Labour as a Resource Market

In the last chapter, we looked at how firms make their decisions about what level of output to produce and what price to charge. In previous chapters, we also looked at the basic factors of production that exist in the economy—land, labour, entrepreneurship, and capital goods. How do firms make decisions about how much of each factor to use? These decisions are made based on the relative price that the producers face for each of these inputs and how much additional revenue each is likely to provide. As a result, one must look at the markets for resource inputs in order to understand the behaviour of firms.

One of the resource markets in particular should be of interest to all high-school students because, one day soon, they will be active participants in this market—the labour market. Over the next few years, you will be making a series of important decisions about how best to prepare yourself for the labour market. It is not enough to say, "I want to become a dentist because I know that people will always have teeth and, therefore, there will always be a demand for dentists." The labour market is a complex system of interrelated factors based on supply and demand, just like the market for many other goods and services. The difference in this market, however, is that households are the suppliers, business firms are the consumers, and the price is the wage rate.

Demand for Labour

The concept of demand for labour is very similar to the concept of demand for goods and services in that both relate to a quantity that is demanded at a given price—the price of labour being the wage rate. There is a significant difference, however, in how each is demanded. The demand for goods and services is known as **direct demand** because consumers determine it directly as they use their dollars to indicate the value of utility that they receive from a good at various price levels. Demand for resources, including labour, is known as **derived demand** because it is dependent on, or derived from, consumer demand for the good or service being produced. The greater the quantity demanded of a particular good or service, the greater the quantity of labour demanded to produce it.

The demand for labour depends on more than just the demand for the product. It is also affected by how much each worker can produce in a specified period of time, a concept known as **productivity**. In fact, it is this productivity, tied to both the price of the good or service and the wage rate, that determines the demand for labour.

The **marginal revenue product of labour (MRPL)** is a concept that explains how the demand for labour is derived. The MRPL is directly related to the concept of marginal product. As an additional unit of labour is added to a firm's productive process, the additional output that is created is known as the marginal product. The marginal revenue product of labour is the amount of additional revenue that is generated from this marginal product.

For a firm operating in perfect competition, the MRPL is the price of the good multiplied by the marginal product because each new unit produced is sold at the market price. For example, Figure 8.1 (page 172) is the production schedule for a firm known as Paolo's Pizza Place. It shows what happens as the firm adds additional workers. In order to simplify the explanation, we will assume that the only cost incurred by the firm is the cost associated with labour input.

When Paolo has four employees, his firm produces an output of 180 pizzas per day. When an additional worker is hired, the marginal product of this fifth worker is 64 pizzas per day. If each pizza is sold for $10, the MRPL is 64 pizzas × $10, or $640. This is the total additional revenue that is generated by adding the fifth worker. As the schedule shows, adding additional workers creates additional output, but at a decreasing rate. The sixth worker adds only 32 pizzas and has a MRPL of $320. The decreasing MRPL is due to the law of diminishing marginal returns—each new worker contributes less marginal product and, therefore, less marginal revenue product.

In deciding how many workers to hire, the firm will consider the wage rate in relation to the MRPL. Let's assume that the wage rate is $40 per day. Would it make sense for the firm to hire the fifth worker? The additional cost is $40, but the additional revenue is $640. The firm would be wise to hire the fifth worker. What about the sixth worker? The additional cost is again $40 and its MRPL is $320, so the firm would again hire another worker. Looking at the schedule in Figure 8.1, you may safely conclude that this firm will continue to add workers up to and including the ninth worker, who contributes as much revenue as he or she costs. This worker would cost the firm $40 and generate an additional $40 in revenue. Thus, firms will hire additional workers as long as their marginal revenue product of labour is greater than the wage rate.

What if the wage rate were to change? If the wage rate were $80, the firm would hire eight workers. If it were $160, it would hire seven workers. As the price of labour goes up, the quantity demanded by the firm decreases. The result is the individual firm's demand curve for labour, which is graphed in Figure 8.2. In order to determine the market demand curve for "pizza labour," it would be necessary to add together the quantity of labour demanded at

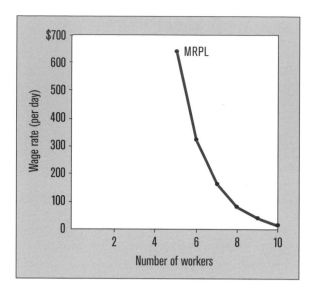

Figure 8.2 One firm's demand curve for pizza labour. This curve shows the number of workers demanded by a firm at each possible wage rate.

each of the possible wage rates by each firm in the pizza industry. Assuming that there are 20 identical pizza firms in the industry, the market demand curve for pizza labour is displayed in Figure 8.3. It shows the total number of workers that would be demanded at each wage rate. The **market labour demand curve**, then, is the quantity of labour demanded by all firms for a particular type of labour at each of the possible wage rates.

Factors That Shift the Labour Demand Curve

Just as in the market for goods and services, the demand curve shows the change in quantity demanded as the price of labour changes *ceteris paribus* (all else being equal). As other factors are allowed to change, however, the labour demand curve is subject to shifts. The demand curve for labour shifts primarily as a result of three factors:

• *A change in the demand for the product of labour.* Because the demand for labour is derived from the demand for the product of labour, it makes sense that a shift in the demand curve for the product will lead to a shift in the demand curve for workers involved in its production. If there is an increase in the

Units of Labour	Total Product (TP) (pizzas/day)	Marginal Product (MP) (pizzas/day)	Marginal Revenue Product of Labour (MRPL)
4	180	—	—
5	244	64	$640
6	276	32	$320
7	292	16	$160
8	300	8	$80
9	304	4	$40
10	306	2	$20

Figure 8.1 Worker productivity and production schedule for Paolo's Pizza Place.

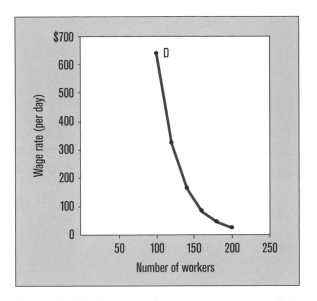

Figure 8.3 Market demand curve for pizza labour. This curve shows the number of workers demanded in the industry at each possible wage rate.

decrease. The price of land inputs, or raw materials, can be considered complementary to labour. If the price of raw materials increases, the demand for labour will see a decrease, and vice versa.

• *A change in worker productivity.* As workers become more productive—in other words, as they increase their marginal product of labour—the demand for labour will increase. This occurs because as each worker produces more output, his or her MRPL is higher. An increase in productivity can come from a number of sources. The introduction of capital equipment allows workers to be more efficient. Better worker training and improved worker management all have the potential to increase worker productivity and, therefore, the demand for labour. Once again, the opposite effect is also possible. A decrease in worker productivity leads to a decrease in the demand for labour.

demand for automobiles, there is a corresponding increase in the demand for automobile workers. This occurs because an increase in demand leads to a higher price for the product. The higher price for the product means that the same output now has a higher MRPL. The result is an upward shift of the labour demand curve. Conversely, a decrease in the demand for automobiles will result in a decrease in the demand for automobile workers.

• *A change in the price of other productive resources.* In the construction of our labour demand curve for Paolo's Pizza Place, we assumed that there were no other inputs. In reality, however, most products require inputs from land, labour, and capital. Capital is usually considered a substitute for labour. An automobile manufacturer might choose to produce automobiles using capital goods (e.g., robotic equipment) or using manual labour. If the price of using robotic equipment increases relative to the price of labour, the demand for labour will increase, as labour now appears relatively cheaper. On the other hand, as the price of using capital goods decreases, the demand for labour will

Supply of Labour

The **market labour supply curve** shows the number of people willing to offer their services to firms at each of the possible wage rates. The opportunity cost of working is the value of what individuals could have earned doing something else in the same time or the value they place on their leisure time. As the wage rate increases and becomes greater than the opportunity cost for more individuals, more of these individuals are willing to offer their services in the labour market. Therefore, at higher wage rates, the quantity of labour supplied is greater, and, as a result, the market supply curve is upward sloping.

There are other factors that influence the labour supply curve. The specific skills needed for certain jobs restrict some people from offering their services for labour in some markets. For example, most people cannot offer their services as a medical doctor because special skills must be learned before one can practise medicine. On the other hand, there are few special skills necessary in the delivery of newspapers, and, as a result, more individuals can offer their services at any given wage rate.

The geographic location of a market is also a factor. Labour markets that are in large population centres tend to have a greater quantity of labour supplied at each wage rate than those that are in more isolated areas. Jobs that are deemed unpleasant, distasteful, or dangerous also tend to have fewer people willing to offer their services at any given wage rate. For this reason, it must be understood that when we talk about labour markets, we are really talking about many different markets. These markets are influenced by the specific characteristics of the job, the specific skills necessary for performing the job, and the location in which the job is to be performed.

Factors That Shift the Labour Supply Curve

The factors that we have just discussed tend to be relatively stable over the long run. For example, oil drilling tends to occur in a market

Figure 8.4 Factors that influence the labour supply of oil-rig workers include the fact that such a job requires special skills and is specific to certain geographic areas. What other factor would influence this supply?

that is away from large population centres, and fire fighting is dangerous. The basic nature of these jobs means that the market supply curve is generally farther to the left than in markets where these restrictions do not exist. However, because these characteristics are relatively stable, they do not have much of a role in shifting the labour supply curve. Yet, a number of variable factors do cause shifts in the labour supply curve:

- *Changes in income tax rates.* An increase in income tax rates means the government takes away a greater proportion of the wage earned; the effect is the same as if the employer were to pay a lower wage rate. This will reduce the supply of labour, shifting the curve to the left. Likewise, a decrease in income taxes has the effect of increasing the supply of labour, shifting the curve to the right.

- *Changes in the size and composition of the population.* As the population increases or decreases, the relative number of people available to offer their services at a given wage rate also increases or decreases. This can also be influenced by the age distribution of the population. In the early 21st century, concern has arisen about the aging workforce and the fact that, as people retire, there will not be enough skilled workers to replace them. An increase in the workforce population, then, shifts the labour supply curve to the right, and a decrease in the workforce population shifts the labour supply curve to the left.

- *Changes in household technology.* As stated on page 173, the choice to work depends upon the opportunity costs involved in other productive work that could have been done in the same time period. Over time, the use of technology in the home has increased, and household chores can now be done much more quickly. The use of microwave ovens means dinners can be prepared more quickly. Dishwashers and automatic washing machines result in more efficient clean-up. There is now more time for individuals to offer their services to the labour markets because the opportunity cost is lower. As a result, the labour supply curve tends to increase, or shift to the right, as more household technology is introduced.

- *Changes in attitudes about work.* Another factor that has tended to increase the supply of

Figure 8.5 As attitudes about work have changed over time, more women have joined the labour force. How has this variable factor influenced the labour supply curve?

labour over time is changing attitudes about roles in society. For a long time, the role of women was seen to be in the household and not in the labour force. Over the past 100 years, these attitudes have steadily changed. According to Status of Women Canada, a federal government agency, in 1901, women made up 15 per cent of the labour force. A century later, in 1999, this figure had risen to 46 per cent. This has led to a shift of the labour supply curve to the right. Conversely, in the late 19th century and early 20th century, child labour was frequently used in manufacturing. As attitudes changed and laws were created that applied age restrictions to the use of labour, the labour supply was decreased, shifting the labour supply curve to the left.

Check Your Understanding

1. Explain the difference between direct demand and derived demand.

2. Why would a firm seek to equate its marginal revenue product of labour with the market wage rate?

3. Explain what the term productivity means and why an improvement in productivity shifts the market demand curve for labour.

4. What is the opportunity cost of someone offering his or her labour skills in the workplace?

5. Summarize the factors that can influence the labour supply curve.

Wage Determination

Equilibrium in the labour market is attained when the actual wage rate causes agreement between the amount of labour supplied by households and the quantity of labour demanded by firms. If the wage is too low, a shortage of labour occurs because the quantity demanded exceeds the quantity supplied. Firms will tend to offer higher wages in order to attract workers, pushing the wage rate higher and encouraging more labour to be supplied. If the wage is too high, a surplus occurs because the quantity of labour supplied exceeds the quantity demanded. In this case, workers who are willing to offer their services for less will tend to drive down the wage rate. The only rate that is "stable" is the rate at which there is no shortage or surplus and

the market is therefore in equilibrium. In Figure 8.6 (page 176), the market for pizza labour is in equilibrium when the wage rate is $160 per day and 140 workers are employed. Because Paolo's Pizza Place is only one small firm in a perfectly competitive market, it must accept the wage rate that is set by the labour market—$160 per day. As a result, according to its demand curve, Paolo will hire seven workers (see page 172).

Wage differentials, or differences in wage rates among different labour markets, are a function of labour supply and demand. All the factors mentioned previously that determine supply and demand influence the wage rates in individual labour markets. Non-monetary benefits in certain jobs influence supply and demand as well. Factors such as length of vacations, hours of work, working conditions, and

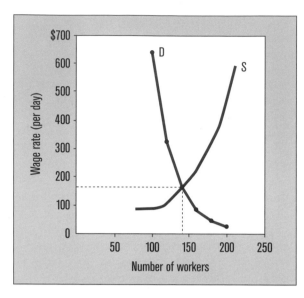

Figure 8.6 Market equilibrium in the pizza labour market. The equilibrium wage rate is established by the intersection of the labour demand curve (D) and the labour supply curve (S). In the market for pizza labour, firms will hire a total of 140 workers at a wage rate of $160 per day.

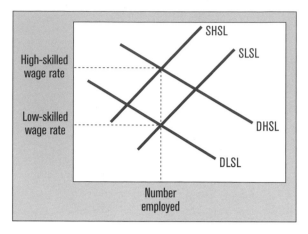

Figure 8.7 The equilibrium wage rate for high-skilled labour is higher than that for low-skilled labour. The vertical difference between the low-skilled and high-skilled curves is due to the value that is placed on attaining the skill.

fringe benefits all must be factored into individual labour markets. This makes labour market analysis very complex. In order to simplify analysis of the labour market, jobs are often described as being "high-skilled" or "low-skilled." The reason for these categories is that a significant factor in determining wage rates is the level of training that a worker has received.

As Figure 8.7 shows, the supply curve for high-skilled labour (SHSL) is above that for low-skilled labour (SLSL). The vertical distance between the two curves is the difference in the wage rate required to compensate the high-skilled worker for obtaining the higher skill (often achieved through some post-secondary education or apprenticeship). The demand curve for high-skilled labour (DHSL) is also above the demand curve for low-skilled labour (DLSL), reflecting the higher marginal revenue product (or productivity) of high-skilled labour. This results in higher equilibrium wage rates for high-skilled workers. The impact on earnings from investing in education can be seen in Figure 8.8 and the following case study.

Level of Study Completed	Average Full-time Earnings in 1992	Average Full-time Earnings in 1995
Trade/Vocational School	$24 200	$29 400
Community College	$26 700	$31 900
University Undergraduate	$32 200	$40 200
University Master's	$43 400	$53 300
University Doctorate	$46 600	$55 000

Source: Excerpts from Table 5.2.1: Labour Market Outcomes of Recent Graduates, from the Department of Human Resources Development Canada at <http://jobfutures.ca/doc/jf/lmo/part2/en/lm1.shtml>.

Figure 8.8 Impact on wage rates from attending various post-secondary institutions for students who graduated in 1990.

Concept of Human Capital

The importance of skill development is evident, not only in the earnings obtained by graduates of post-secondary education but also through the increasing attention being given to the concept of human capital by governments and employers. **Human capital** refers to the knowledge, skills, and talents that workers have, either through education or by nature. Education is an investment, then, in human capital, just as purchasing a computer is an investment in capital goods. Both help to improve the efficiency and output in the productive process.

Individuals invest in their own education in the hopes of making themselves more marketable in the future. They want to be able to offer their services in a specific area of the labour market where the demand for labour is high, while the supply of labour is low, and thereby obtain a higher wage rate. Firms also invest in human capital through on-the-job training, in-service training, and supporting further formal education for their employees in the hopes of raising productivity and thereby improving the marginal physical product of labour. Governments invest in human capital through subsidizing public education, some post-secondary education, and numerous job-training programs because improved efficiency expands the productive capacity of the economy and promotes economic growth. The impact of investing in one's own human capital in terms of lifetime employment earnings can be seen by comparing the education and career paths of two individuals who graduated from high school in the same year (see Figure 8.9).

	Ashley	Max
Educational/ work choice	Goes to university to become an electrical engineer.	Immediately enters the world of work as a machine operator. Starting salary: $17 700.*
Annual costs	$27 700: $10 000 for tuition, books, and living expenses *plus* earnings lost by not entering the labour market (i.e., $17 700*). Total cost of a five-year honours degree in electrical engineering is $138 500 ($27 700 × 5 years).	Living expenses.
Benefits	As an electrical engineer, Ashley is expected to earn $2 279 400 over her working life, from age 23 to 65.	As a machine operator, Max is expected to earn $1 372 600 over his working life, from age 19 to 65.
Net benefits	Ashley will earn $906 800 more in lifetime employment income than Max.	
Rate of return on post-secondary education	Ashley invested $138 500 and earned an additional $906 800—a 15.7% annual rate of return.	None.

*$17 700 is the average starting salary for a recent high-school graduate in this occupation.

Source: Table 3.2: Rate of Return to Education: Illustration of the case of two different educational profiles, from the Department of Human Resources Development Canada at <http://jobfutures.ca/doc/jf/factor/factor.shtml>.

Figure 8.9 The story of two students graduating from high school in the same year. Considering both the financial costs and benefits, research results from the Applied Research Branch of Human Resources Development Canada suggest that, in general, Canadians profit from investing in a post-secondary education. For example, over the course of their working lives, university graduates will realize an average financial gain of 10 to 15 per cent over and above what they would have earned with only a high-school diploma. This is based on rates of return estimated during the 1981–1996 period.

Trends in the Workforce Today

While knowledge of the economic dynamics of the labour market is important, it is also important to consider how this knowledge can be useful to high-school students who are planning on entering the workforce, or training to enter the workforce, over the next few years. Reviewing some of the projections made by Human Resources Development Canada provides useful information for those who want to be adequately prepared for today's job market. Knowledge about the kinds of skills that employers will be looking for, as well as where to obtain these skills, is invaluable because the rules that applied even just a decade ago are much different from those that apply today.

One can start the analysis with the radical changes in elementary and secondary education programs that have been occurring all over North America. These changes very closely reflect the changing essential skills that are considered to be required for success in the modern workplace (see Figure 8.10). Note that many of these skills are interconnected and also reflect the speed with which both technology and information change in today's economy. Adaptability and willingness to integrate new information and technology are absolutely necessary in the economy of the 21st century.

A second important element is an understanding of the employment outlook for various occupations and sectors in the economy. Between 1999 and 2004, economic growth in Canada is expected to account for 40 per cent of all new job openings while 60 per cent of openings are expected to be due to normal attrition—mainly retirements. Because 40 per cent of job openings will be new, a large proportion of jobs will be created in new and emerging industries. Of these new job openings, 80 per cent are expected to be in the service sector (mainly in the areas of business, information technology, health, accommodation and food services, and personal services industries) and 20 per cent are expected to be in the goods sector (mainly in construction).

Projections for occupational demand across Canada reflect these trends, as evidenced by the occupational outlook table in Figure 8.11.

Reading Text – The ability to read and understand complex sentences and paragraphs in the form of notes, letters, memos, manuals, specifications, regulations, books, reports, or journals.

Document Use – The ability to interpret and understand documents that include information in a variety of forms including words, numbers, icons, graphics, tables, lists, graphs, and schematics.

Writing – The ability to write textual material both on its own, such as memos, letters, notes, and reports, and in completing forms; this also includes using tools for writing, such as computers.

Numeracy – The ability to use numbers for numerical calculation and estimation in money, measurement, scheduling, and analysis of data.

Oral Communication – The ability to use speech in order to exchange thoughts and information in complex ways and through a variety of modes, such as speeches and presentations, in both small and large groups.

Thinking Skills – The ability to conduct independent cognitive skills such as problem solving, decision making, task planning and organizing, use of memory, and researching information.

Working with Others – The ability to work with others in carrying out tasks, and the self-discipline to meet targets while working independently.

Computer Use – The ability to use a computer in order to complete workplace tasks.

Continuous Learning – The ability to learn, to understand one's own learning style, and to gain access to a variety of materials and learning opportunities in order to continually upgrade skills and knowledge about your occupation.

Source: Excerpts from "Essential Skills" on <http://www15.hrdc-drhc.gc.ca/english/es.asp>.

Figure 8.10 Skills considered essential in the modern workplace.

National	Alberta (2000–2005)	Ontario (1999–2008)	Nova Scotia (1999–2003)	Newfoundland (1998–2003)
Aircraft Mechanics	Auditors, Accountants, and Investment Professionals	Chefs	Computer Programmers	Civil Engineers
Computer Systems Analysts and Programmers	Engineers	Computer Engineers	Computer Systems Analysts	Computer Programmers
Engineers	Contractors, Supervisors, and Trades-related Workers	Computer Systems Analysts and Programmers	General Practitioners and Family Physicians	Deck Officers, Water Transport
Health Care Professionals	Food Counter Attendants and Kitchen Helpers	Electrical & Electronics Engineering Technologists and Technicians	Graphic Designers and Illustrating Artists	Financial Auditors and Accountants
Heavy Equipment Operators	Mathematicians, Systems Analysts, and Computer Programmers	Machinists and Machining & Tooling Inspectors	Managers in Engineering, Architecture, Science, and Information Systems	General Practitioners and Family Physicians
Management, Advertising & Marketing Consultants	Medical Technologists and Technicians	Mechanical Engineers	Professional Occupations in Business Services to Managers	Pharmacists
Medical Technologists and Technicians	Nursing Supervisors and Registered Nurses	Mechanical & Industrial Engineering and Manufacturing Technologists/ Technicians	Nurse Supervisors and Registered Nurses	Registered Nurses
Plumbers and Pipefitters	Occupations in Food and Beverage Service	Registered Nurses	Pharmacists	Respiratory Therapists
Police Officers and Firefighters	Primary Production Labourers	Secondary & Elementary School Teachers	Retail Salespersons and Sales Clerks	School & Guidance Counsellors
Tool & Die Makers and Machinists	Secondary & Elementary School Teachers and Counsellors	Tool & Die Makers	Technical Sales Specialists, Wholesale Trade	Veterinarians

Source: Excerpts from "Job Futures 2000: World of Work," from the Department of Human Resources Development Canada at <http://jobfutures.ca/doc/jf/wow/en/>.

Figure 8.11 Occupations with a favourable employment outlook across Canada.

It is also interesting to note how this table highlights one of the elements of labour markets discussed earlier—namely, that different markets exist because of geographic mobility factors. Many people are tied to their location in the country by family, history, and personal preferences and are reluctant to pull up their roots and move elsewhere. The fact that there are different needs across the country highlights this situation. It would be expected, for example, that wage rates for chefs in Ontario are likely to move upward relative to wage rates for chefs in Newfoundland. If geographic mobility were not a factor, then there would be identical occupational outlooks in every province across the country.

Finally, one needs to consider how best to train for these trends in the labour markets. Human Resources Development Canada projects that over 70 per cent of all new job openings are expected to require some level of post-secondary training. Two sources of this training are university and community colleges. It is estimated that 23.4 per cent of new job openings will require university training, and 31.8 per cent of new job openings will require a community college or trade-school diploma or certificate. Most significantly, all broad fields of study at the university level are expected to show "fair" or "good" labour market conditions between the years 1999 and 2004, a characteristic that supports the global trend of further development of knowledge-based economies.

Check Your
Understanding

1. Explain why the labour supply curve for high-skilled labour is above the labour supply curve for low-skilled labour.

2. Which of the nine essential skills identified in Figure 8.10 (page 178) have you used to this point in this chapter?

3. Which segment of the economy is expected to see the largest job growth in the first few years of the 21st century?

4. What evidence and arguments have been provided in the first part of this chapter that the level of education you attain plays a significant role in your ability to make a living in the 21st century?

Labour Unions

A chapter on labour economics would not be complete without addressing the role of labour unions in the labour market. According to Statistics Canada, approximately 33 per cent of workers in Canada are members of labour unions, yet there are many misconceptions about the role of unions. A **labour union** is an organization of workers that collectively promotes the interests of its members and negotiates with their employers. While it is true that one role it plays affects the wage rate of union members, a union does much more than this. Unions have been responsible for shaping labour relations, laws, and working conditions in Canada over the past 150 years.

The three most common types of unions are trade unions, industrial unions, and public sector unions.

Trade unions, also known as **craft unions**, represent workers in a single occupation regardless of where they work. An example of a trade union is the International Brotherhood of Electrical Workers. Trade unions are very common in the construction industry.

Industrial unions represent all workers in a given industry regardless of the job that they perform. An example of an industrial union is the Canadian Auto Workers union (or CAW), which represents workers in the automobile industry, whether they are on the assembly line or sweeping the shop floor. The CAW, like many industrial unions, is also expanding its membership outside the original industry in which it was established and now represents workers in industries such as retail sales and fast food.

Finally, **public sector unions** represent workers who are employed by any of the levels of government in Canada. Two of the biggest unions in Canada are public sector unions—the Public Service Alliance of Canada (PSAC) and the Canadian Union of Public Employees (CUPE). Public sector unions began to develop throughout the 1960s as the services provided by government began to grow. As a result, so did the size of the civil service.

Collective Bargaining

The year 1943 was a benchmark year for labour unions in Canada. It saw the federal government pass legislation that restricted when unions were allowed to strike in exchange for the legal requirement that employers must bargain with a union if a majority of workers voluntarily agreed to have the union represent them. Prior to 1943, the role of unions in the workplace was fairly volatile. Strikes occurred for all sorts of reasons—day-to-day disputes with management, perceived mistreatment of individual workers, and general strikes against employers. Now, as long as there was a collective agreement between the workers and the employer, strikes were illegal.

Today, a union's most significant role is in negotiating wages and working conditions on behalf of all members. The process of arriving at this agreement is known as **collective bargaining**, and the contract that is negotiated is known as the **collective agreement**, which usually lasts for a period of one to three years. The collective agreement states the responsibility of both employees and employers concerning wages, vacations, job safety, fringe benefits, training, job security, hours of work, and grievance procedures (the process by which alleged violations of the collective agreement are settled between a company and its workers). **Cost-of-living allowances (COLA)** are often a factor in negotiations, as unions seek to protect their workers from rising prices levels by having their wages increase at the same rate.

Another element that is negotiated in the collective agreement is the union's own security clause. The union seeks to enroll as many workers as possible from each workplace. Not only is there strength in numbers but members also give the union a source of revenue—union dues—with which to finance its operations. **Union dues** are an amount of money that each member of the union pays in order to support its activities. The three basic types of union security clauses are the open shop, closed shop, and union shop.

In an **open shop**, union membership is voluntary. In a **closed shop**, the employer may only hire workers who are already members of the union. This is more common in trade unions, where there is an element of training controlled by the union, such as apprenticeship, in some sort of skilled trade. A **union shop** is somewhere between an open shop and a closed shop. In a union shop, an employer may hire whomever it wishes, but after some sort of probationary period, the employee is required to join the union.

A major breakthrough for unions and their security came in a 1945 arbitration decision in a dispute between Ford Motor Company of Canada and its workers. Mr. Justice Ivan Rand ruled that all workers in the workplace were required to pay union dues whether or not they were members of the union. The company was responsible for deducting these dues and remitting them to the union. This was because all workers, union members or not, benefited from the collective bargaining activities of the union. As a result, most Canadian industries now use some version of what is known as the **Rand Formula**.

Labour law is generally a provincial matter, so regulations vary from province to province, but all provinces have regulations that govern the process of collective bargaining. Most of the time, the union and the employer begin to negotiate a new collective agreement well before the old one has expired. If an agreement is not reached between the two parties before the old agreement expires, the old agreement continues to remain in force while further attempts are made to reach a new agreement. If an agreement cannot be reached, there are several options.

CASE Study

Collective Bargaining Simulation

The Situation

Ringaround Bathtubs Limited is a small firm employing 100 workers in Beachton, a small town of approximately 5000 inhabitants. A number of other small firms in Beachton produce a variety of consumer goods that compete in the provincial market. Beachton is a fairly prosperous town with a fairly low rate of unemployment.

Ringaround has been in the town for 15 years and, during that period, has enjoyed fairly good labour management relations. Most workers have been content working for this firm, but, recently, workers have felt that the wages the company pays have not kept pace with wages in other firms and with rises in the cost of living.

This year, for example, the consumer price index has indicated a 5 per cent rise in prices, and economists predict that this rate of price increases will continue into the next few years. Workers have formed Local 234 of the Canadian Bathroom Workers Union. Local 234 has been recognized as the bargaining agent for the workers at Ringaround. Workers are hopeful that their newly formed union will be able to gain increases in rates of pay and in the length of holidays with pay. Workers also expect their pay to keep up with any increases in the cost of living. Union officials also want the company to require all employees to become members of the union and to have union dues collected from workers' salaries.

Issues to Be Negotiated

Union Rights And Security

1. Should the firm be one of the following?
   a) *Union Shop:* All company employees must become members of the union after 30 days. Everyone in non-management positions is a member of the union.

   b) *Open Shop:* Employees are not required to join the union, nor will the company collect union dues.
2. Should the company deduct fees from all union members' paycheques and hand over the sum to the union? *yes*

Wages

1. An increase of 70 cents an hour.
2. An increase of 60 cents an hour.
3. An increase of 50 cents an hour.
4. An increase of 40 cents an hour.
5. An increase of 30 cents an hour.
6. An increase of 20 cents an hour.
7. An increase of 10 cents an hour.

Vacations

1. Three weeks after two years of service and four weeks after five years of service.
2. Three weeks after four years of service and four weeks after ten years of service.
3. Three weeks after five years of service and four weeks after 15 years of service.
4. Three weeks after five years of service.

Term of Contract (Length of Time Contract Is in Effect)

1. One-year agreement.
2. Two-year agreement.
3. Three-year agreement.

Cost-of-Living Allowance (COLA)

1. Any increase in the cost of living will be matched by an equal percentage increase in pay.
2. In any one month, any increase in the cost of living above 3 per cent will be matched by an equal percentage increase in pay.
3. With every 1 per cent increase in the cost of living, hourly wages will be increased by two cents.

Negotiation Information

Ringaround Bathtubs Limited financial information:

Profit Statement	Profit (Total Revenues – Total Costs)
Profit before taxes	$600 000
Less income and other taxes	$300 000
Net profit	$300 000

Note: Even though competition is stiff, the company expects modest profits in the coming years.

Cost of Various Wage Increases

Amount of Hourly Wage Increase	Annual Increase in Costs
$0.70	$255 000
$0.60	$244 000
$0.50	$224 000
$0.40	$185 200
$0.30	$152 000
$0.20	$141 000
$0.10	$80 000

Vacations

1. Three weeks after two years of service and four weeks after five years of service: Cost $80 000
2. Three weeks after four years of service and four weeks after ten years of service: Cost $68 000
3. Three weeks after five years of service and four weeks after 15 years of service: Cost $52 000
4. Three weeks after five years of service: Cost $20 000

Cost-of-Living Allowance (COLA)

	Estimated Increase in Cost		
	Year 1	Year 2	Year 3
Any increase in the cost of living will be matched by an equal percentage increase in pay.	$145 000	$200 000	$300 000
In any one month, any increase in the cost of living above 3 per cent will be matched by an equal increase in pay.	$0	$0	$0
With every 1 per cent increase in the cost of living, hourly wages will increase by two cents.	$24 000	$32 000	$52 000

Comparison with Other Firms in Beachton

Company Name	Average Wage per Hour	Years of Service for Vacation	
		3 Weeks	4 Weeks
Ringaround Bathtubs Ltd.	$10.25		
Brain Drain Plumbing Supplies	$10.75	5	12
Tim's T-Bar Company	$10.80	3	5
Electric Ways Ltd.	$15.00	6	12
WailBoard Trader Ltd.	$9.75	5	

Instructions

Divide into groups of 6 to 8 people. Each group should then subdivide equally into a management team and a union team.

Round 1

1. *Prepare Opening Position*
   - Each union team and each management team studies the issues to be negotiated and the negotiation information.
   - Each team decides what it wants to get from the bargaining process and how it is going to achieve its aims.
   - The union team draws up an initial set of demands, which it will present to the management team.
   - The management team draws up an initial "bottom line" for negotiation purposes.
2. *Negotiations (two sides meet)*
   - Union team presents its set of proposals to the management team.
   - Management team can ask questions.

Round 2

1. *Team Discussions*
   - Management prepares an explanation about why it cannot accept the union's position and prepares a counter proposal.
   - Union team prepares a defence of its own proposals and tries to anticipate counter arguments for what it believes will be management's position.

2. *Negotiations (two sides meet)*
   - Management explains why it cannot accept the union's proposals and presents its own counter proposals.
   - The union defends its own proposals and questions management on its proposals.

Rounds 3 and 4

Groups continue to discuss and negotiate the terms of an agreement until they come to a resolution or an impasse. Groups should be able to resolve their differences.

Final Round: Ratification

1. As groups reach agreements, the terms of each negotiating group are written on the board and the negotiators sign their agreements.
2. One representative from each negotiating group explains to the class why their agreement is best for both management and labour.
3. The class votes on which agreement they judge to be the best. Groups may not vote for their own agreement.

Source: Adapted from "Grade 12 Economics, 1996–1997," York Board of Education.

QUESTIONS

1. In what ways do you think this simulation reflected the realities of collective bargaining? What might be different in real life?
2. What did you learn about collective bargaining from this simulation?

Conciliation or **mediation** occurs when a third party is brought in to study the situation and suggest possible ways to reach an agreement, helping both parties to find some middle ground. Usually, some form of conciliation or mediation is required before a strike or lockout is allowed to occur. If conciliation or mediation fails, the parties may submit their dispute for voluntary arbitration. In **voluntary arbitration**, both sides agree to have a third party, who acts as a judge, make a decision about which position is more fair. The arbitrator does not seek a compromise but chooses only one side in an effort to get both parties to submit their most realistic proposals. Both parties must then abide by the decision. Occasionally, parties are forced to submit to **compulsory arbitration**, in which the government orders the two parties to submit their disputes to an arbitrator. This action is sometimes taken when a strike would be so disruptive to the general public that the government considers it undesirable.

Strikes and Other Job Action

Contrary to popular belief, the vast majority of collective agreements are settled without a strike or lockout. For example, in the period between 1998 and 2001, over 96 per cent of collective agreements in Ontario were achieved without a strike or lockout. Sometimes, however, the union and the employer are unable to find common ground, and each side uses a number of tools in an attempt to force the other's hand.

Probably the most well-known tool is the union's use of a strike. A **strike** is a temporary work stoppage by employees, designed to force an employer to meet the union's contractual demands. A strike can occur only after a majority of workers have approved of this action and only after certain conditions have been met, such as the expiry of the old collective agreement and the use of conciliation or mediation. An equivalent tool from the perspective of the employer is the lockout. A **lockout** occurs when an employer shuts down the place of employment in order to force workers to accept its contract offer. The use of either strike or lockout is fairly uncommon, but the threat of both provides incentive for the two parties to conduct successful negotiations.

The costs of both strategies are high. As well as direct costs, such as the lost wages employees suffer and the lost output resulting in lost sales and profits for the employer, there are indirect costs. Other related industries are often affected by strikes. For example, a strike at an auto parts manufacturing company may force an independent automobile producer that relies on these parts to lay off workers because it is unable to obtain materials to continue its own production. Another indirect cost is that borne by consumers, who are unable to obtain a good or service that they desire because a strike or lockout has stopped production. As a result, unions often use a number of other strategies before a strike is considered.

One such strategy is a **rotating strike**, which is usually used when the employer has a number of different workplaces. Instead of having all workers withdraw their services, the union organizes the withdrawal of services at individual work sites on a rotating basis, usually

Figure 8.12 In 2000, McDonald's workers picketed a McDonald's restaurant in Montreal. The picket was in support of union certification. Why do you think these employees would want to obtain such certification?

for a period of a day or two. The advantage to this strategy is that it causes disruption to the employer but limits the impact on union members in terms of lost pay.

Another strategy is the use of **work-to-rule**, where employees perform only the duties specifically stated in their contracts. This tool is particularly effective when employees find that they perform a lot of work after hours or in other situations (for example, when employee goodwill in the past has resulted in workers taking on many duties not specifically stated in the collective agreement).

Finally, a union may encourage a boycott of the employer's product by the members of other unions and the general public. In a **boycott**, people are asked not to purchase the product produced by the employer. In so doing, the union is hoping to lower sales to a point that lost revenues encourage the employer to reconsider its position.

Other Activities

While the best-known activity of unions is collective bargaining, they are involved in much more than this aspect of the labour market. One goal of unions is to improve the wage rate paid to their members. Simply negotiating with the employer has limits. The marginal revenue product of labour determines how high an employer is willing to raise wages. One of the best ways to improve compensation for members is to increase the demand for labour. Because the demand for labour is a derived demand, increasing the demand for the good or service can help to increase wage rates. Unions, therefore, sometimes act to increase demand for the product their workers produce. They sometimes campaign the public to "buy union made" in order to increase the demand for union-made goods. If you look at the labels of some goods, they may have "union made" or a "product of union labour" indicated on them.

Unions may increase the productivity of workers through training or encouraging employers to update capital equipment. As we learned earlier, improved productivity also serves to increase the demand for labour.

Unions may also attempt to raise wages by reducing supply (shifting the supply curve for labour to the left); entry into the workforce can be restricted through special training, certification, or apprenticeship. This would also shift wage rates upward.

In addition to these wage-related activities, unions lobby to influence government legislation regarding labour laws. Some examples of their successes include minimum-wage legislation, strike legislation, anti-scab legislation (that is, legislation against the use of replacement workers when a union is on strike), health and safety standards, institution of general statutory holidays, worker injury and illness compensation, and laws preventing unjust dismissal of workers. They have also been involved in lobbying for economic and social policies that affect workers (such as fair taxes, public education, pensions, maternity and parental leave, import restrictions through tariffs, and sexual harassment laws). Much of this general activity is pursued by large federations of unions working together, such as the **Canadian Labour Congress**, which lobbies the federal government, and the **Newfoundland and Labrador Federation of Labour**, which lobbies the provincial government of Newfoundland and Labrador.

Impact of Unions

There is much debate in society about the role that unions play and whether they are beneficial. Those who object to unions point out that they restrict labour mobility to some degree, whether through controlling labour supply or through job security clauses in collective agreements that prevent layoffs. It is claimed that these restrictions hamper the efficient allocation of resources. Furthermore, unions most often protect workers from layoffs on the basis of *seniority*, or years on the job, and not the competence of the individual workers, a practice that also prevents the efficient allocation of resources. Unions have been blamed for periods of inflation, as high wage increases end up being passed on to the consumer in the form of higher prices. They have also been blamed for contributing to the problem of unemployment, as they push wages higher than market equilibrium would naturally allow.

Others point out that higher wages and improved working conditions improve the incentive for workers and lead to better morale, which generates greater productivity. Unions protect workers from arbitrary dismissal and also hold employers accountable for safe working conditions. Investment in human capital is aided through training and education—functions that unions often take on. While it cannot be argued that the wide range of labour laws in Canada are solely the result of union lobbying, it can certainly be argued that labour laws, as well as many government programs for low-wage workers and other vulnerable groups in Canada, have been influenced by the lobbying of labour unions.

SKILL BUILDER
Thinking Like an Economist

Analyzing a Public Policy Issue

To analyze a public policy issue, economists use a decision-making model similar to that used by an individual (see Figure 1.3, page 9). They assess the costs and benefits of a number of choices. The major difference is that a public policy issue

has costs and benefits that affect a significant proportion of the population, either directly or indirectly. In this kind of analysis, each stakeholder needs to be identified and the relative value of the costs and benefits of each of the choices accounted for each of the stakeholders.

These are the steps that are taken in the analysis.

Public Issue/Controversy	
Political Consideration	**Economic Consideration**
• Value judgement leading to the exercise of choice in the interest of the greatest common good	• Systematic analysis based on a set of recognized criteria to determine the costs and benefits of each in order to substantiate judgement

1. Define the issue
Should unions continue to exist to protect the needs and interests of workers?

2. Identify the stakeholder groups and criteria

Workers
• Health and safety
• Wages and benefits
• Job security

Employers
• Allocative efficiency and freedom
• Impact on profit
• Long-term planning

Consumers
• Cost of goods and services
• Impact on delivery of goods and services

3. Analyze the choices
Set up a chart, like the one in Figure 8.13 (page 188), and use an assessment scale like that in Figure 8.14 (page 184) to organize the costs and benefits of each choice.

4. Conclusion

Unions should continue to be used to protect the needs and interests of workers. While both choices end up with a negative value, the best choice is the highest value. A completely free labour market has significant costs to workers but makes little difference to consumers. One factor that might be considered in reviewing the analysis is changes to the current system that negate, or at least limit, the costs that are incurred by making one choice over another. For example, if a mechanism were introduced that would allow for the dismissal of an employee who didn't achieve a certain level of efficiency, the weighting of this criterion might change from −4 to −1.

Choice	Cost/Benefit to Workers	Cost/Benefit to Producers	Cost/Benefit to Consumers	Total Weighted Cost/Benefit
Allow unions to continue operating in some labour markets	• Jobs lost as higher wages are negotiated (−4) • Individual freedom in working with employer is limited (−3) • More equitable income distribution (+5) • Healthier and safer working conditions (+5) • Seniority rights provide workers with greater job security (+3) Total = +6	• Reduced profit levels may decrease sustainability of enterprise (−5) • Sometimes unable to replace less productive workers (−4) • Because of wage increases, some workers command more goods and services, which increases demand (+3) • Long-term contracts allow for long-term planning (+2) Total = −4	• Price inflation triggered as a result of increased operating expenses being passed on to consumers (−3) • Work stoppages disrupt delivery of goods and services (−2) Total = −5	**−3**
Allow the free market to work without any outside interference on the labour market	• Current regulations protect workers, but there would be no force in place to assure regulations remain (−3) • Income differentials between high- and low-skilled labour will increase (−4) • Employer may terminate an employee without just cause (−4) • Increased employee freedom in negotiating (+3) Total = −8	• Unpredictable job action by workers could interfere with efficient production (−3) • Ability to terminate workers who are not efficient (+5) • Long-term planning of wage costs is more reliable (+4) Total = +6	• Work stoppages could still disrupt goods and services and would be more unpredictable (−4) • Impact of wage inflation would be limited by market forces (+1) Total = −3	**−5**

Figure 8.13 An example of a cost–benefit analysis.

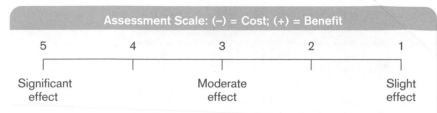

Assessment Scale: (–) = Cost; (+) = Benefit

| 5 | 4 | 3 | 2 | 1 |

Significant effect — Moderate effect — Slight effect

Note: When benefits and costs can be calculated in the form of quantifiable data, such as dollar amounts or employment statistics, relative significance can be attached to the comparative dollar value of benefits and costs. Often another kind of value judgement, more normative in nature, is required. The degree to which the analysis has relied on normative assessment should be noted in a concluding statement.

Figure 8.14 An assessment scale for cost–benefit analysis.

QUESTIONS

1. Review the preceding cost–benefit analysis. Do you agree with the weighting of the criteria? Explain your opinion. If you do not agree, re-weight the criteria. How does this re-weighting affect the final decision?

2. Are there other stakeholders or criteria that should be considered? If so, factor in this new information to the cost–benefit analysis.

3. Consider a third alternative: "Eliminate unions and allow the government to take on the role of unions as another 'social welfare' responsibility." You now need to add another stakeholder, establish the criteria for this stakeholder, and re-evaluate the decision.

Check Your Understanding

1. Explain the difference between a trade union and an industrial union.

2. List the items that are negotiated through collective bargaining.

3. What kind of help is available to unions and employers if they cannot reach a collective agreement on their own?

4. Besides a strike, what tools are available to a union in order to place pressure on an employer when negotiating a collective agreement?

5. How do unions attempt to raise the wages of their members besides negotiating collective agreements?

CHAPTER SUMMARY

- The demand for labour is considered a derived demand because it is determined by the demand for the product that labour produces.

- The marginal revenue product of labour (MRPL) is the additional revenue generated by adding one more unit of labour.

- A firm will hire workers until the marginal revenue product of the last unit of labour hired is equal to the additional cost of the worker, which is the worker's wage.

- The firm's labour demand curve is the number of workers that the firm is willing to hire at each of the possible wage rates.

- The market labour demand curve is the quantity of labour demanded by all firms for a particular type of labour at each of the possible wage rates.

- The labour demand curve will shift because of a change in the demand for the product that labour produces, a change in the price of other productive resources, or a change in the productivity of workers.

- The market labour supply curve shows the number of people willing to offer their services to firms at each of the possible wage rates.

- People will offer their services to the labour market once the wage rate is higher than the opportunity cost of the other activities they may perform in the same time, such as producing some other good or enjoying their leisure.

- The labour supply curve is influenced by such factors as education and skills necessary to perform the job, level of danger associated with the job, and geographic location of the market.

- The labour supply curve shifts because of such factors as income tax levels, changes in the size of the population, changes in household technology, and changes in social attitudes about work.

- The wage rate in a particular labour market is established when the quantity supplied is equal to the quantity demanded.

- Wage differentials between different job markets are due to key factors (such as skills and education necessary to perform the job) that influence the supply and demand curves.

- Human capital refers to the knowledge, skills, and talents that workers have either through education or by nature. Therefore, education is considered an investment in human capital.

- Changes in the labour markets over the past decade have led to changes in the types of skills that employers are looking for.

- Eighty per cent of all new job openings in Canada over the next five years are expected to be in the service sector.

- Seventy per cent of all new job openings are expected to require some form of post-secondary education.

- Trade, or craft, unions represent workers in a single occupation regardless of where they work.

- Industrial unions represent all workers in a given industry regardless of the job that they perform.

- Public sector unions represent workers who are employed by the levels of government in Canada.

- The most significant role that unions perform on behalf of their members is negotiating collective agreements with employers.

- Unions and employers may receive help in arriving at a collective agreement through mediation, conciliation, or arbitration.

- Unions may try to force an employer to meet their demands through strikes, rotating strikes, work-to-rule, or boycotts.

- Unions also attempt to raise the demand for their workers' product, provide training and certification, and influence government legislation regarding labour laws.

Key Terms

direct demand
derived demand
productivity
marginal revenue product of labour (MRPL)
market labour demand curve
market labour supply curve
wage differentials
human capital
labour union
trade unions (or craft unions)
industrial unions
public sector unions
collective bargaining
collective agreement
cost-of-living allowance (COLA)
union dues
open shop
closed shop
union shop
Rand Formula
conciliation (or mediation)
voluntary arbitration
compulsory arbitration
strike
lockout
rotating strike
work-to-rule
boycott
Canadian Labour Congress
Newfoundland and Labrador Federation of
  Labour

Activities

Thinking/Inquiry

1. Lawyers tend to have a higher hourly wage rate than retail store workers. What factors contribute to this higher wage rate? Explain this using supply and demand curve analysis.

2. The right to strike is a controversial one. Many people believe that some workers are "essential" and, therefore, should not have the right to strike.

   a) Make a list of occupations that you believe are essential and should, therefore, not have the right to strike. For each occupation, state why you believe it is essential.

   b) How do you think these workers should be able to resolve differences that they might have with their employers when negotiating a collective agreement? Can you see any issues of unfairness that might exist in your solution? Explain.

   c) Use the Internet to research your province's Ministry of Labour. What services does the ministry list as essential? What mechanisms does it have in place to help workers reach fair collective agreements?

3. Search the Human Resources Development Canada Web site for the latest predictions about the labour market. What jobs are reported to be in demand in your region?

Communication

4. Search the Ministry of Labour Web site for your province. From this site, choose an element of the labour market that the government regulates. Write a one-page report that explains the purpose of the government's involvement, the regulation(s), and the impact that it has on labour or the labour market. Include a list of definitions, if appropriate. Here are some suggested topics: minimum wage; parental/pregnancy leave; public holidays; termination and severance pay; vacations; hours of work and overtime; a particular health and safety measure; a regulation governing unions such as how to unionize a workplace; student workers.

5. Choose a specific union or federation of labour. Investigate its Web site to find out about one of its current policies. Complete a cost–benefit analysis that evaluates the impact of implementing the policy. You need to identify the stakeholders and criteria against which to judge the impact of the policy. Write a one-page report that explains this concern and your decision. Here are some suggested unions: Canadian Union of Public Employees; Canadian Auto Workers Union; Public Service Alliance of Canada; International Brotherhood of Electrical Workers; Fishermen, Food and Allied Workers Union; Teamsters Canada; Canadian Federation of Nurses Unions;

Canadian Labour Congress; Ontario Federation of Labour; Newfoundland and Labrador Federation of Labour.

Application

6. Figure 8. 15 shows the production schedule for Risa's Silk Shirt Company. If Risa's shirts sell for $25 each and the workers can be hired in a competitive labour market for $100 each per day, how many workers should be hired? What if the wage rate in the market were to rise to $200 per day due to a decrease in the supply of workers? Clearly explain your answers.

Number of Workers	Total Shirts Produced per Day
0	0
1	10
2	18
3	24
4	28
5	30
6	32

Figure 8.15 Production schedule, Risa's Silk Shirt Company.

7. Using supply and demand curves, explain the impact of each of the following events on the wage rate in the labour market for landscape workers.

a) The federal government lowers personal income tax rates.

b) A new trend for "natural gardens" that require no maintenance is promoted by gardening magazines.

c) New innovations in leaf blowers and lawn mowers allow workers to become more efficient.

d) A new high-tech automated robotic lawn mower is introduced whose cost is relatively cheaper than that of labour.

e) The cost of gasoline, disposal bags, and rakes rises.

f) The government increases the minimum age that students are allowed to work from 16 to 18 years.

8. Refer to Figure 8.10 (on page 178) and make a list of the "essential skills" identified by Human Resource Development Canada. Choose a course that you are currently taking. Beside each of the skills that you identified, list an assignment or activity from your course that is encouraging you to develop the skill.

9. a) Refer to Figure 8.16. Graph the supply and demand curves for taxi drivers.

Number of Drivers Demanded	Wage in Dollars per Hour	Number of Drivers Supplied
1000	$5.00	300
900	$6.00	400
800	$7.00	500
700	$8.00	600
600	$9.00	700
500	$10.00	800
400	$11.00	900
300	$12.00	1000

Figure 8.16 Supply and demand for taxi drivers.

b) What is the equilibrium wage, and how many workers would be hired at this wage?

c) Explain two factors that might shift the labour demand curve to the right. What would be the impact on the wage rate?

d) Explain two factors that might shift the labour supply curve to the right. What would be the impact on the wage rate?

e) If the government instituted a minimum wage of $10 per hour, how would this change the employment situation in the taxi driver labour market?

10. It is sometimes argued that labour unions, by demanding wages higher than the market equilibrium wage rate, sometimes hurt their members more than they help them. Using labour supply and demand curves, explain this reasoning.

Unit 2 Performance Task: Investigating Market Impact

The chapters in this unit have explored how market forces address the questions of what, how, and for whom to produce as well as the theoretical roles and influences of consumers, workers, producers, and gov-ernment in addressing these questions. In this perform-ance task, you will examine current news stories about the Canadian economy and apply some of the theories that you have learned to the operation of a market.

Your Task

You are an economist for a corporation or a labour union. Your job is to research current events and report on their possible impact in a particular market or industry in Canada. The focus of this investigation is a cost–benefit analysis of the impact on the marketplace of a government initiative or of an economic deci-sion by a large business or labour union.

Task Steps and Requirements

1. Choose an economic decision or proposal made by a business or labour union or by a government initiative in a particular market or industry that is intended to achieve a specific economic goal. Some suggested topics include corporate acquisitions and mergers; regulation of anti-competitive behaviour; advertising; consumption taxes on gas or tobacco; price floors and subsidies in agriculture; production technology, inno-vation, and productivity; collective bargain-ing; labour disputes; and privatization and deregulation of government services.

2. Research the various opinions on the deci-sion or proposal using electronic newspaper databases at the library and on the Internet.

3. Identify the criteria that at least three stake-holders (producer, consumer, labourer, labour union, government, etc.) would use to evalu-ate the impact of the decision on the market-place. The criteria might include the impact on the markets involved in terms of prices, the quantity and quality of what is produced, and other intangible factors that market sup-ply and demand analysis might not consider (such as the impact on citizens forced to make do without a particular good).

4. Complete a cost–benefit analysis to assess the impact on stakeholders. Follow the model presented on pages 187 to 189 in Chapter 8.

5. Write a memo in the form of an argumen-tative essay that clearly states your position based on the conclusions reached in your cost–benefit analysis. Support your position using the criteria established in the cost–benefit analysis, as well as supply and demand diagrams, where appropriate.

Adapting the Task

Consider creating a Web page that the stake-holder might add to its Web site to inform interested parties. This task could also be set up as a debate, with various groups taking the posi-tions of different stakeholders participating in an economic symposium on the health of a partic-ular market or industry. Share drafts of your cost–benefit analysis with your teacher, class-mates, and parents or guardians in order to obtain useful feedback.

Assessment Criteria

The following criteria will be used to assess your work:

- *Knowledge*—appropriately and accurately using economic concepts, principles, and terminology related to microeconomics
- *Thinking and Inquiry*—evaluating the impact and effectiveness of a proposed change; con-ducting research effectively in order to locate information from a variety of sources
- *Communication*—presenting economic infor-mation and analysis clearly, in an appropriate format and style
- *Application*—applying the cost–benefit method of inquiry effectively using stakeholder criteria and economic goals; illustrating how the con-flicting self-interests of different stakeholders affect the achievement of economic goals; building and supporting an effective argument

UNIT 3

MACROECONOMICS: PRODUCTION AND MONETARY FLOWS IN THE ECONOMY

The Bank of Canada, with the Parliament Buildings reflected in the glass. Throughout the 20th century, the role of these two institutions in managing the economy expanded significantly. How might their actions influence economic activity?

Unit Overview

Over the course of the 20th century, the expectations that Canadian citizens had for the government with regard to its role in the economy grew considerably. When unemployment increases or prices rise too rapidly, Canadians often hold the government accountable for these problems and look to the government to solve them. In Unit 3, we'll explore how the government attempts to live up to these expectations.

We'll begin by looking at the main economic measures that the government uses in order to determine current economic conditions and concerns. We'll examine how the economy tends to move in cycles and what influences these cycles. Then, we'll consider how the government attempts to stabilize the economy using spending and taxation policies. In conclusion, we'll look at how the government uses the Bank of Canada and the tools at its disposal in order to stabilize the economy.

Learning Goals

In this unit, you will

- define and calculate statistical measures for economic output, economic growth, price stability, and unemployment and evaluate the validity of these as measures of economic well-being,
- describe the characteristics and causes of economic instability in each phase of the business cycle,
- predict the economic impact of an event by applying the process, skills, and concepts of economic inquiry,
- analyze the causes and consequences of economic instability and the use of government fiscal and monetary policies to stabilize the business cycle,
- apply the model of aggregate demand and supply to identify and analyze choices, forecast economic change, and explain the impact of government fiscal and monetary policies,
- demonstrate an understanding of the major ideas and theories of John Maynard Keynes and Milton Friedman in applying stabilization policies,
- describe the forms and functions of money in Canada's economy and the ways in which the Bank of Canada controls the money supply,
- describe the role of Canada's different types of financial institutions as financial intermediaries and their involvement in conducting monetary policy,
- explain the nature and economic functions of Canada's public institutions,
- identify the types, causes, and effects of inflation, deflation, and unemployment.

Skill Builder

Thinking Like an Economist

In this unit, you can develop some of the skills that economists use. These include

- estimating the size of the Gross Domestic Product gap by applying Okun's law,
- constructing a price index,
- indexing to the Consumer Price Index,
- explaining the multiplier effect,
- using the deposit (money) multiplier.

Unit Performance Task

The activity at the end of this unit provides a focused opportunity for you to

- conduct research to locate information about the changes in output, employment, and price level in the Canadian economy over the past three years,
- produce an analysis of the current economic situation, the trends in the economy, and the strengths and weaknesses of the economy, using the skills developed in this unit,
- identify and explain the appropriate fiscal and monetary policies to address the needs of the current economic climate, and
- communicate the above findings in a written report to the minister of finance.

CHAPTER 9

AN INTRODUCTION TO MACROECONOMICS

Buoyant economy seen gathering steam

Reports predict added jobs, spending boom

MORE JOBS and a boom in consumer spending were a few of the cheery predictions included in a pair of reports released yesterday on the buoyant Canadian economy.

Those predictions, coupled with a StatsCan report that the annual inflation rate dropped to 1.6 per cent in May, down from 1.7 per cent the previous month, reveal a bright economic outlook.

Economists at la Caisse de dépôt et placement du Québec said favourable economic conditions will translate into a drop in the national jobless rate to 7.5 per cent by year-end.

And Scotiabank said the thriving economy will continue to get a boost as increasingly confident consumers open their wallets and spend.

While the economy has grown over the last two years, much of that growth has been fuelled by exports to the United States.

But in recent months, higher consumer spending has become an increasingly important factor.

The unemployment drop predicted by the Caisse would mean a remarkable increase in jobs across Canada over the next half year, given that unemployment was 8.1 per cent in May.

The giant Quebec public pension fund also predicted the economy will grow at a robust rate of 3.2 per cent this year. . . .

The Scotiabank report, by chief economist Warren Jestin, was equally optimistic, predicting economic growth this year of about 3.5 per cent.

This prediction is closer to Bank of Canada governor Gordon Thiessen's expectations that the economy could grow at a rate as high as 3.75 per cent this year—much higher than expected. . . .

Both economic reports attributed Canada's economic success to the surging growth in the United States, Canada's largest trading partner and buyer of about a third of everything produced in this country. . . .

Scotiabank also predicted that solid inflation and balanced budgets were contributing to a stronger Canadian dollar. And the fact that the Bank of Canada will probably not follow an expected boost in American interest rates by the US Federal Reserve will push Canadian borrowing rates even lower.

The Caisse report agreed, predicting that with inflation under control at 1.2 per cent, "further monetary easing seems unlikely for the time being.". . .

"In general, most core components of the (consumer price index) remain well-behaved," said Adrienne Warren, an economist at Scotia Capital Markets.

On a monthly basis, the CPI rose 0.3 per cent between April and May with cheaper prices for women's clothing and baked goods helping to offset higher energy costs.

Source: Abridged from "Buoyant economy seen gathering steam" from *The Toronto Star,* 19 June 1999. Reprinted by permission of The Canadian Press.

QUESTIONS

1. What organizations were involved in collecting the data reported in this article?
2. Why do you think these organizations might be interested in the data?
3. What measures were used to support the prediction that the economy was "gathering steam"?

Chapter Goals

By the end of this chapter, you will be able to

- understand what is meant by the term macroeconomics,
- examine the components and weaknesses of the Gross Domestic Product (GDP) as a measure of economic output,
- understand why unemployment occurs, how the unemployment rate is calculated, and the impact of unemployment on the economy and citizens of a country,
- explore the components of the Consumer Price Index (CPI) and how the CPI is used to adjust for the effects of inflation.

Defining Macroeconomics

So far in this book we have concerned ourselves with microeconomic issues. Among other topics, we have looked at individual markets and how they operate, and we have concerned ourselves with the ideal output for firms and the characteristics of the industries in which they operate. However, this kind of analysis does not tell us much about the economy as a whole. For example, the computer industry may be thriving while the auto industry is laying off large numbers of workers. Based on this information, what can we say about the economy as a whole? Is it in good shape or not?

The study of the economy as a whole is known as **macroeconomics**. To use a modern analogy, microeconomics is rather like the pixels on a computer monitor. Individually, one can look at a pixel and say that it is "red" or "blue," but to understand the complete picture, one must look at all of the thousands of pixels together. The manner in which these pixels combine gives us the picture on the screen. This complete picture is like macroeconomics. All the markets—consumers, workers, and firms together—create the "big picture" of our economy.

Why Measure Performance?

An understanding of some of the key measures of overall economic performance of the national economy is important in investigating macroeconomic issues. While there are many different macroeconomic measures, we shall focus on the three that receive the most attention in our economy: output, employment levels, and price stability.

Why is measuring national economic performance important? A few answers include the following:
- Measuring the national economy's performance helps governments decide on tax policies and spending priorities.
- Governments use this information to measure the effect of their economic policies.
- Performance measures allow us to compare our economy to the economies of other countries.
- Performance measures allow us to look at the role and impact of specific industries on the whole economy.
- Unions and wage earners use economic measures in contract negotiations.
- Individuals and businesses use economic measures to help them make investment decisions.

Gross Domestic Product: A Way to Measure Output

The most commonly used measure of a country's output is **Gross Domestic Product** or **GDP**. GDP is the total market value of all final goods and services produced within a country in one year. The GDP can be calculated in two ways. The first is to add up the total that is spent on all final goods and services in one year—the **expenditure approach**. The other is to add up all the income that is earned by the different factors of production (wages, rent, interest, profit) in producing the final goods and services—the **income approach**. The GDP in each case should be the same, as what is an expenditure for one person in the economy is an income for someone else.

Consider purchasing an automobile. If the entire economic activity for one country were the selling of one automobile for $50 000, the expenditure approach would say that the value of the GDP was the money that was spent to purchase the car—$50 000. Conversely, the income approach would measure the income earned by those who made and sold the car— also $50 000.

Of course, even in a one-car economy the money flows would be a little more complicated than this. What about all the components that went into producing the car, such as the tires, the engine, the seats, and the windshield? This is why GDP measures only the *final* value of goods and services that an economy produces. It is to avoid what is known as **multiple-counting**. The cost of these components is included in the final price of the car. If they were counted when they were sold to the company that built the car and then counted again when the car was sold to the consumer, they would be counted twice, which would make the output of an economy appear higher than it actually was. To get an accurate figure for the total value of an economy's total output, the only goods and services that are counted are the ones being purchased for final use. In other words, they are purchases that are not going to be re-sold.

The Expenditure Approach

In order to understand the following chapters on fiscal and monetary policy, it is important to develop the concept of the expenditure approach a little further. Statistics Canada is the federal government organization responsible for gathering data about the Canadian economy and its people. To calculate the GDP using the expenditure approach, the final value of goods and services produced in Canada is tabulated by Statistics Canada through gathering expenditure information on a nationwide basis and then using a formula to arrive at the GDP. A simplified version of the formula is:

$$GDP = C + G + I + (X - M)$$

In the formula, C represents **consumption**, or what households spend on goods and services. It is the total spent on durable goods (goods that last a long time, like cars and household appliances), semi-durable goods (goods such as clothing that last a reasonable amount of time but not as long as durable goods), non-durable goods (goods that are used up very quickly, such as food and gasoline), and services, such as haircuts, car tune-ups, and eating out at restaurants.

The letter G represents government purchases. This comprises the value of expenditures on goods and services by all levels of government and includes spending on wages to employees, office supplies, and public capital goods (such as schools, highways, and hospitals).

The letter I represents **investment**. In economics, this refers to the purchase of new capital goods for use in the production process, construction of new buildings, and changes in business inventories. Statistics Canada refers to the first two components as "fixed capital formation." The third component—changes in

business inventories—is included because it is output that has been produced in the time period and has value but has not yet been sold.

Finally, $(X - M)$ represents the value of net exports in Canada. In considering consumption, investment, and government spending, Statistics Canada includes purchases of all items, some of which are produced outside Canada. These items are known as imports (M); they must be subtracted from GDP because they do not represent Canadian production. On the other hand, there is also production that originated in Canada but is purchased by individuals, businesses, and governments in other countries. These items are known as exports (X) and must be added to the GDP. Statistics Canada's expenditure approach for calculating the GDP in the year 2000 can be seen in Figure 9.1.

Until 1986, Canada used a slightly different method of measuring output, known as **Gross National Product** or **GNP**. The GNP was the total value of all final goods and services produced by Canadian-owned factors of production in Canada and anywhere in the world. Under this measure, a Japanese-owned factory that was paying Canadian workers, buying Canadian raw materials, and selling to Canadian customers was not included as Canadian output while a Canadian firm operating under similar conditions in Japan was included. Canada began using GDP as its main measure of output because it gives a better indication of Canadian output. That is, it includes the production from the Japanese-owned firm but excludes the production from the Canadian-owned firm, which is really more reflective of Japanese output.

Because GDP is calculated based on the market prices at the time the goods are sold, changes in the level of prices from year to year mean that comparing different years can produce misleading results. If prices increase rapidly, the growth in GDP may not actually be a result of increased output. Removing the effects of price increases can correct for this. A discussion on using the *GDP deflator* and the *chain Fisher volume index* to achieve this appears later in this chapter. At this time, however, it is important to understand that real GDP (also known as constant-dollar GDP or chained-dollar GDP) results from removing

Component	Real GDP (in billions of chained* 1997 dollars)	Percentage of GDP
Personal Consumption Expenditures (C)	**566.2**	**56.1**
Durable goods	81.9	8.1
Semi-durable goods	50.5	5.0
Non-durable goods	130.3	12.9
Services	303.7	30.1
Gross Private Investment (I)	**190.0**	**18.8**
Fixed capital formation	180.9	17.9
Inventory change	9.1	0.9
Government Purchases (G)	**207.6**	**20.6**
Net exports (X – M)	**45.7**	**4.5**
TOTAL Gross Domestic Product	**1009.2**	**100.0**

Note: Numbers may not add exactly due to rounding and are estimates readjusted annually.
*The chain Fisher volume index is addressed on page 212.

Source: Adapted from the Statistics Canada publication, *The Daily*, Catalogue 11–001, 28 February 2001.

Figure 9.1 Components of Canada's GDP, 2000: The expenditure approach.

the effect of price increases from nominal (or current-dollar) GDP.

GDP is most commonly used as a tool for measuring the **economic growth** of a country—how much a country's economy has expanded from one year to the next. The change in GDP figures for two successive years (or sometimes *quarters*, which are three-month periods of the year) are compared and expressed in terms of a percentage of growth. The formula to express this is:

$$\text{real GDP growth rate} = \frac{(\text{real GDP year 2} - \text{real GDP year 1})}{\text{real GDP year 1}} \times 100$$

For example, Canada experienced a real GDP of $966.4 billion in 1999. By the year 2000, real GDP had risen to $1009.2 billion. The

Canadian economy was said to be growing at a rate of 4.4 per cent. The growth rates of Canada's real GDP from 1982 to 2000 are displayed in Figure 9.2 (page 200).

As you learned in Chapter 6, many people also use the GDP figures of countries around the world to compare **standards of living**, which is the quantity and quality of goods and services that people are able to obtain to accommodate their needs and wants. The basic premise comes from the income approach in calculating GDP. If the real GDP represents the total amount of income that is earned in a country, comparing the real GDP on a per capita basis (dividing the total real GDP by the country's population) provides an average income for each person living in that country. It is presumed that the higher the per capita real GDP, the more well-off citizens are and, therefore, the higher their standard of living.

Drawbacks to GDP

The use of GDP as a measure of economic welfare and well-being has been criticized because of a number of limitations:

• *Population size.* Comparing the GDP for different years may be misleading if the population of the country has changed significantly. A country where GDP has grown by 5 per cent may seem to have had substantial growth, but if the population has grown by 7 per cent, there is actually less output per person. Dividing a country's GDP by its population reveals its **per capita GDP**. This removes the effect of a population change on the GDP.

• *Non-market production is not measured.* GDP does not count output that has no dollar

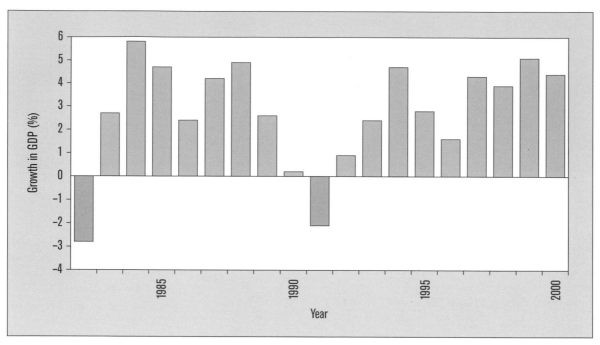

Source: Created from the Statistics Canada CANSIM II database at <http://cansima.statcan.ca/cgi-win/CNSMCGI.EXE>, Table 384-0002.

Figure 9.2 GDP growth rate in yearly percentage change for Canada, 1982–2000 (in chained 1997 dollars).

value attached to it. This means, for example, that the contributions of people who create output by renovating their own homes, the productive services of homemakers, and voluntary services to charitable organizations are not counted. This omission seriously weakens GDP as an accurate measure of a country's output.

• *Underground economy.* Another type of economic activity that is not measured by the GDP is transactions for which no "paper trail" exists. Illegal activities such as selling drugs and prostitution are included in this category, as are "under-the-table" transactions that occur so parties can avoid paying taxes. Statisticians have estimated that the value of these activities would add between 3 and 20 per cent to the value of the GDP. (Together, non-market and underground activities constitute what economists often refer to as the **hidden economy.**)

• *Types of goods produced.* The inclusion of all types of goods and services that are produced weakens the GDP as a measure of well-being. Some would argue that the production of

guns or the cost of policing riots (such as those that occurred at the World Trade Organization meeting in Seattle in 1999) do very little to improve society's well-being.

• *Leisure.* Theoretically, the GDP could grow significantly if all workers began to work 24 hours a day, seven days a week, but few would argue that a society with this workload had a higher standard of living than one in which its workers had at least some free time. An effective measure of well-being would take leisure time into account.

• *Environmental degradation.* The GDP does not take into account the negative effects of our economic production. Water pollution, air pollution, and solid waste disposal do not make us better off, yet the production of the goods and services that create these problems add to our GDP. In an ironic twist, environmental disasters, such as oil and chemical spills, actually increase the GDP as money is spent to clean them up.

• *Distribution of income.* GDP does not take into account how evenly the income in a country is distributed among citizens. A country can

Case Study

Grossed Out (Gross Domestic Product)

A University of Alberta academic says the GDP is an outdated gauge of economic performance.

As a global measure of progress, Gross Domestic Product (GDP) has become almost as popular as Coca-Cola. Whenever national economies release their GDP data, financial pundits invariably cheer when the GDP goes up—and boo when it goes down.

Mark Anielski doesn't buy into that herd mentality. Together with a growing cadre of North American economists, the 38-year-old director of the Centre for Performance Management at the University of Alberta's faculty of business argues that GDP is not only an anachronism, it's a downright stupid gauge of economic performance. As a senior fellow with Redefining Progress (he's the only Canadian serving on the ten-member San Francisco-based think-tank), Anielski has played an active role in creating what he says is a better tool for measuring economic well-being: the Genuine Progress Indicator (GPI). Unlike GDP, this alternative yardstick paints a very different picture of prosperity. In fact, 1998's GPI update for the US, penned by Anielski and a colleague, shows a rapid decline in economic health and indicates that our booming neighbour to the south "is living off its capital—social and environmental, as well as financial."

The GDP, a legacy of John Maynard Keynes, could never measure the downsides to growth, let alone conceive of such a thing. Way back in 1939, Keynes, a spend-more economist, needed a planning tool—a record of all money transactions—to help the British government allocate resources for the war effort. His Gross National Product (GNP) and its successor, the GDP, became something of international happy faces in government accounting. But because the GDP works like "a gas gauge that goes up as the car burns gas," Anielski argues, it was always a lopsided measurement. "It only adds and never subtracts."

As such, says Anielski, the GDP's ideal economic hero is a "chain-smoking terminal cancer patient going through an expensive divorce whose car is totalled in a 20-car pile up." But no household or business could ever thrive economically by using such bad accounting practices. "Coca-Cola just wouldn't be in business today if it only counted revenue and ignored depreciating assets," Anielski explains.

In contrast, the GPI not only adds and subtracts but also considers the future. It still measures growth because growth matters, but it puts a cost column on the ledger. Good marriages, friendly communities, clean water, leisure time, and wild places are treated as pluses. But when economies spend a lot on crime, pollution, commuting, and family breakdown, those expenditures are counted as negatives rather than more great economic news. Although placing a value on safe communities or clean air stretches the parameters of priced-based thinking, the GPI doesn't blindly assume, as the GDP does, that buying guns, for example, is progress just because money changes hands.

For these very reasons, GPI for the US (the Canadian government is now toying with the idea of creating a similar index) has been sinking since the 1970s while the GDP has been rising. The negative costs include disappearing natural resources (oil and coal), a downsized middle class, underemployment, ozone depletion, and a drop in leisure time. This last cost means people have less time for kids and families as well as for civic and community needs. That loss, in turn, says Anielski, translates into "a depletion of the social capital upon which an economy depends."

Anielski isn't suggesting that a better accounting system such as the GPI might lead to smarter economic policies. But retiring the last of Keynes's economic ghosts would at the very least guarantee that governments get better information. Changing economies, Anielski concludes, simply need accounting tools that keep pace with changing times.

Source: Andrew Nikiforuk, "Grossed out (gross domestic product)," *Canadian Business*, 9 April 1999, 72(6), 17.

QUESTIONS

1. What does Mark Anielski mean when he says that the GDP's ideal economic hero is a "chain-smoking terminal cancer patient going through an expensive divorce whose car is totalled in a 20-car pile up"?

2. What do you think Anielski means by the phrase "a depletion of the social capital upon which an economy depends"? Do you agree with him?

3. What are some examples of negative costs that the GPI would take into account?

4. What are some examples of factors that would be considered pluses?

5. A project by the Pembina Institute found that between 1961 and 1999 GDP in Alberta increased by 4.4 per cent annually on average while well-being measured by GPI declined by 0.5 per cent annually. Create a T-chart in your notebook. On one side of the chart, list the arguments that might be made in favour of adopting the GPI; on the other side, list the arguments that might be made against.

---

have significant economic growth and the appearance of rising living standards for its population, but if the growth is so unevenly distributed that a very small segment of the population is reaping most of the rewards, it cannot be said that the standard of living has actually risen for most of the citizens in that country.

United States Senator Robert Kennedy once summed up the drawbacks of measures of output such as the GDP and GNP in this way:

> *GNP [GDP] … counts air pollution and ciga-*
> *rette advertising, and ambulances to clear our*
> *highways of carnage. It counts special locks for our*
> *doors and the jails for those who break them. It*
> *counts the destruction of our redwoods. Yet the*
> *gross national product does not allow for the*
> *health of our children, the quality of their educa-*
> *tion, or the joy of their play. It does not include*
> *the beauty of our poetry or the strength of our*
> *marriages … it measures everything, in short,*
> *except that which makes life worthwhile.*

Source: Robert Kennedy, "Recapturing America's Moral Vision," in *RFK: Collected Speeches* (New York: Viking Press, 1993), 329–330.

Noting the drawbacks and limitations of the GDP does not necessarily make it a useless measurement tool, but it should remind us that all statistics have their limitations. It is important for anyone using statistics, economic or otherwise, to be aware of this. The user should be able to identify these limitations and understand their impact on any conclusions reached.

Check Your
Understanding

1. Why are there two methods for calculating the GDP?

2. Why is it important that only the final value of goods and services is measured in calculating the GDP?

3. Describe the components of the formula used to calculate the GDP using the expenditure approach.

4. Why should one be cautious in using per capita GDP as a means of comparing standards of living.

Measuring Employment: The Unemployment Rate

The unemployment rate is the economic measure that receives the most attention in Canada. This is likely due to the personal and easily observed nature of the problem. Most of us have had to look for a job at one time or another, and the impact of not finding a job is easy to imagine. It is also obvious that if someone is not working, that person is not contributing to economic output, so a high unemployment rate is a clear sign that the economy is not using all its resources very efficiently.

The **unemployment rate** is the percentage of the labour force not working at any given time. Statistics Canada calculates this figure once a month. It starts by conducting a nation-wide Labour Force Survey of 59 000 households, asking a series of questions about each member of the household and his or her role in the economy.

The population is then grouped into a number of categories. The first category includes those under the age of 15 and those who are institutionalized (for example, in a prison)—those who are, therefore, not legally eligible for the workforce. The second category is people who are eligible to be part of the workforce but have chosen not to participate. Some examples would include homemakers, students older than 16 years of age and in school full-time, and those who are retired. The third category is the **labour force**—people who are either employed or who are willing and able to work and actively seeking employment. Those that are unemployed, then, are those members of the labour force who are without work and seeking work. The unemployment rate, therefore, is:

$$\text{unemployment rate} = \frac{\text{number unemployed}}{\text{labour force}} \times 100$$

This definition of the labour force gives rise to some criticism of Statistics Canada's unemployment rate as an accurate measure of unemployment. First, it includes anyone who has any type of wage-earning job as being "employed." Yet many workers who want to be employed in full-time jobs accept part-time jobs. In reality, they are only partially employed, but for the purposes of the unemployment rate, they appear to be fully employed. Second, the unemployment rate does not include those workers who have been looking for a job for so long that they may have just "given up." If they are not actively looking for work, they are not counted as part of the labour force and, therefore, are not counted as unemployed. Both these factors contribute to the Statistics Canada unemployment rate being "understated." In other words, the actual unemployment rate is really higher than the official figure suggests. Third, there are many people who accept jobs for which they are overqualified, such as a person who graduates as a teacher but can find work only as an educational assistant. These people are said to be "underemployed," that is to say, their skills are not being fully utilized. Underemployment means the economy falls short of its full productive capacity.

Full Employment

One would think that full employment means an unemployment rate of zero, but that is not necessarily the case. Most economists believe that, in an active and free economy at least, some structural and frictional unemployment will always exist (see Figure 9.3 on page 204). Indeed, the only way to eliminate frictional unemployment is for the government to decide where and when workers can move from job to job.

Figure 9.4 (page 204) shows that over the past few decades, even when the economy has been in a period of significant growth, the unemployment rate has been no lower than in the range of 6 to 7 per cent. Workers

Type	Description
Structural Unemployment	Occurs when the skills or location of workers no longer matches the patterns of demand in the economy. This type of unemployment occurred in the 1990s in Atlantic Canada with the shut-down of the cod fishery due to declining fish stocks.
Technological Unemployment	Results from industries using more technology in the production process and thus reducing the need for workers. Increased automation in industries such as the automobile industry leads to technological unemployment.
Replacement Unemployment	Results as firms move labour-intensive production to other countries where labour rates are lower. Workers producing in another country replace the local Canadian labour.
Frictional Unemployment	Results from people moving between jobs. It includes both students who are graduating from school and looking for jobs, and workers who have made a choice to move from one job to another. A certain amount of frictional unemployment is natural in an economy.
Cyclical Unemployment	Results from a reduction in overall consumer spending. As overall demand for goods and services declines in all industries, fewer workers are needed in all industries. This is the type of unemployment that was predominant in the Great Depression of the 1930s.
Seasonal Unemployment	Caused by variation in climate over the course of the year. Fishing, farming, construction, and recreational camps are all examples of industries that see a decline in employment over the winter months. Statistics Canada adjusts for this type of unemployment when it calculates its "seasonally adjusted" unemployment rate.

Figure 9.3 Types of unemployment. Suggest at least one possible course of action that might ease or eliminate each of the types of unemployment listed above.

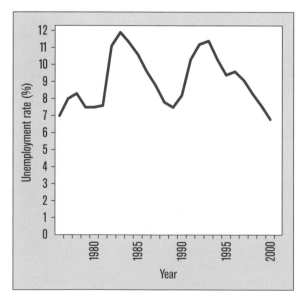

Source: Created from the Statistics Canada CANSIM II database at <http://cansima.statcan.ca/cgi-win/CNSMCGI.EXE>, Series D98075.

Figure 9.4 Seasonally adjusted unemployment rate for Canada, 1976–2000.

tend to feel more confident about leaving their positions and seeking better employment opportunities when the economy is doing well, and, therefore, the amount of frictional unemployment during this time is probably at its maximum. Other types of unemployment are minimized because the economy is doing very well. As a result, **full employment** in Canada is considered by many to be when the unemployment rate is in the range of 6 to 7 per cent. This is also known as *the natural rate of unemployment.*

A high unemployment rate also entails the financial cost of programs such as Employment Insurance, which help alleviate the problem of unemployment. The financial cost is compounded by lost taxation revenues due to lower incomes and decreased spending on goods and services. There are also significant social costs involved. People who suffer from unemployment face a loss of self-esteem, a loss of job skills, and an increase in family

Social Pathology	Increase in Rate of Pathology (%)
Mortality	1.2
Mortality due to cardiovascular diseases	1.7
Mortality attributable to cirrhosis	1.3
Homicide rate*	1.9
Suicide rate	0.7
Admissions to psychiatric hospitals	4.2
Incarcerations*	6.0
Arrests	4.0

*Increases in the rates for homicides and imprisonments are related to an increase in the unemployment rate for young men (18–24 years old), expressed as a percentage of the total unemployment rate.

Source: Human Resources Development Canada, *Tallying the Economic and Social Costs of Unemployment,* Volume 2, Number 2 (Summer–Fall 1996).

Figure 9.5 Estimates of direct effects of a 10 per cent increase in the unemployment rate on the incidence of social pathologies in the United States (results of Brenner Study, 1984).

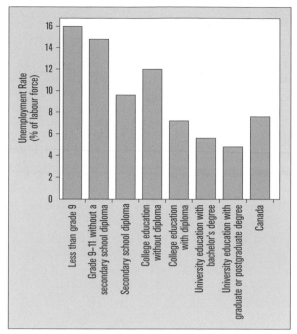

Source: Created from the Statistics Canada "Labour Force Survey" Microdata File, Catalogue 71M0001, May 2002.

Figure 9.6 Unemployment rates in Quebec, 1999, according to highest level of schooling attained.

tension. Periods of high unemployment have also been linked to periods of social unrest, crime, and political upheaval. One such study by Dr. M. Harvey Brenner, conducted for the United States Congress in 1984, estimated the direct relationship between a number of social problems and a 10 per cent increase in the unemployment rate. Some of the results of his study can be found in Figure 9.5.

The problem of unemployment is also more significant when you consider that certain groups in Canada shoulder a greater degree of the problem. As indicated in Figures 9.6 and 9.7, people living in Atlantic Canada and individuals with lower education levels consistently face higher levels of unemployment than the average Canadian.

Province	Unemployment Rate (%)*
Newfoundland	16.7
Prince Edward Island	12.0
Nova Scotia	9.1
New Brunswick	10.0
Quebec	8.4
Ontario	5.7
Manitoba	4.9
Saskatchewan	5.2
Alberta	5.0
British Columbia	7.2
Canada	**6.8**

*Both sexes; 15 years and over

Source: Created from the Statistics Canada CANSIM II database at <http://cansima.statcan.ca/cgi-win/CNSMCGI.EXE>, Table 279-0004.

Figure 9.7 Average annual unemployment rate by province, 2000.

Applying Okun's Law

Unemployment above the *natural rate* of unemployment has both financial and social costs associated with it. The financial cost of unemployment is the lost output that results from the labour resources that are sitting idle. If you think back to Chapter 1 (see Figure 1.12 on page 18), a point somewhere inside the production possibilities curve represents falling short of what the economy is actually able to produce. This lost output is known as the **GDP gap**. It is the difference between the actual GDP produced by the economy and the **potential GDP** that could be produced if the unemployment rate was not higher than the natural rate.

An economist, Arthur Okun, created a formula that is used to estimate the size of this gap. **Okun's law** states that for every percentage point that the actual unemployment rate exceeds

the natural rate, a GDP gap of 2 per cent occurs. Expressed as a formula:

$$\frac{GDP}{gap} = \frac{actual}{GDP} \times \frac{(unemployment\ rate\ -\ natural\ rate)}{100} \times 2$$

In Canada in 1993, the unemployment rate was 11.4 per cent. If the natural rate of unemployment is assumed to be 6.5 per cent then the real unemployment rate exceeded this by 4.9 per cent (11.4 minus 6.5). This means that the GDP could have been 9.8 per cent higher (4.9 per cent $\times$ 2). The actual GDP in 1993 was $769.1 billion, but it could have been 9.8 per cent higher or $75.4 billion more in terms of dollars ($769.1 $\times$ 0.098). This figure represents the GDP gap. The potential GDP of the Canadian economy was $844.5 billion—if only it had been able to achieve full employment.

QUESTIONS

1. Canada's GDP in the year 2000 was measured at $1009.2 billion when the unemployment rate was 6.8 per cent. If the natural rate of unemployment is 6.5 per cent, how much was Canada's GDP gap in the year 2000?

2. Calculate the GDP gap for the countries in Figure 9.8.

Country	GDP ($ billions)	Unemployment Rate (%)	Natural Rate of Unemployment (%)	GDP Gap
A	550.0	10.0	8.0	?
B	728.0	7.4	3.0	?
C	325.7	13.7	4.8	?

Figure 9.8

Check Your Understanding

1. How does Statistics Canada determine the unemployment rate?

2. What are the criticisms of the method used by Statistics Canada for calculating the unemployment rate?

3. What is the natural rate of unemployment considered to be in Canada?

4. What are the social and economic costs of unemployment?

Measuring Price Stability: The Consumer Price Index

One of the main economic goals of the federal government has been to maintain price stability. If the prices of goods and services are allowed to rise and consumers' incomes stay the same, it is as if consumers have less income. For example, if you earn $1 per day, and the only item that you ever buy is a chocolate bar that is priced at $1, you would be shocked if one day you went to the store and the bar was $2. Not only would you be shocked, you would be hungry because you could not afford to buy it. Even though your actual income has not changed, the price change makes it seem as though your income is less. (Remember the income effect from the introduction to demand in Chapter 4.)

The term **inflation** is used to describe the persistent rise in the general level of prices. Every year, prices tend to increase a little for a variety of reasons, which include increased consumer demand and increases in the prices of productive resources. These reasons will be further explored in Chapter 14.

Calculating the CPI

In Canada, the task of measuring inflation is the responsibility of Statistics Canada. It uses a device known as the **Consumer Price Index**, or **CPI**, to track inflation. The CPI is a price index that measures the changes in the prices of consumer goods.

It would be nearly impossible to monitor every single good and service used by every single Canadian throughout a given year. Consequently, Statistics Canada uses a type of "representative basket" of goods and services. It monitors the consumption of over 600 goods and services in cities across Canada and, from this information, determines the spending habits of households. The households are defined as urban, with a size of four members. The items are put into one of eight categories and then "weighted" to reflect how important they are in a typical household's "shopping basket." This weighting is based on how much the

typical household tends to buy in a particular category. Figure 9.9 indicates that the typical Canadian household tends to spend 27.9 per cent of its consumption expenditures on costs associated with shelter, so these prices are weighted at 27.9 per cent in the CPI basket.

Using the CPI

The primary use of the CPI is to calculate the **inflation rate**. This is the annual percentage by which the CPI has risen. Any two back-to-back years can be used to calculate an inflation rate. The formula for this is expressed as:

$$\text{inflation rate} = \frac{(\text{CPI year 2} - \text{CPI year 1})}{\text{CPI year 1}} \times 100$$

Figure 9.10 (page 208) displays the annual inflation rate in Canada between 1915 and 2001. For example, in September 2000 the CPI was 114.4 and in September 2001 it had risen to 117.4. The inflation rate was therefore:

$$\frac{(117.4 - 114.4)}{114.4} \times 100 = 2.6\%$$

This tells us that between 2000 and 2001 prices rose 2.6 per cent. Why is it helpful for people to know this? Governments, unions,

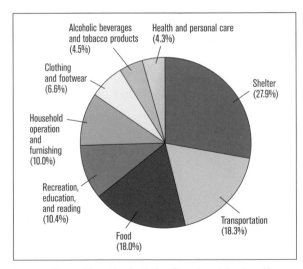

Source: Created from the Statistics Canada publication, *Your Guide to the Consumer Price Index,* Catalogue 62-557, 1996.

Figure 9.9 Consumer Price Index weights by major components for Canada, 1992, expressed in percentages.

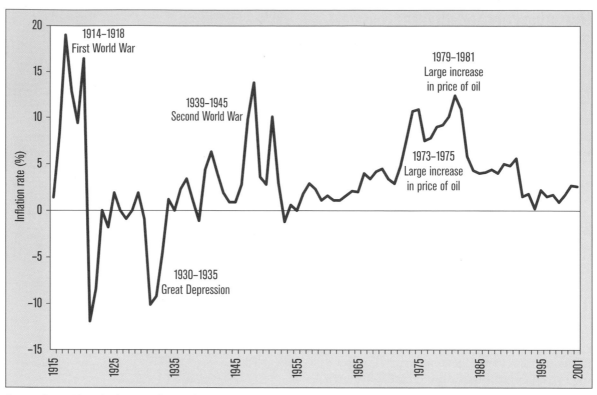

Source: Created from the Statistics Canada CANSIM II database at <http://cansima.statcan.ca/cgi-win/CNSMCGI.EXE>, Table 326-0001.

Figure 9.10 This graph shows the percentage inflation rate in Canada from 1915 to 2001. Using the labels on the graph, in addition to other knowledge that you may have about Canadian history, make some judgements about what factors have influenced the inflation rate in Canada.

Constructing a Price Index

In order to establish a basis for the comparison of prices from year to year, Statistics Canada sets a base year for which it fixes the representative basket value at 100 (or 100 per cent). The most recent base year set by Statistics Canada is 1992. The value of the representative basket is then totalled for each succeeding year and expressed as a percentage in terms of the base year.

Let's look at a simple "Student Price Index." In 1992, Cathie found that she bought only hamburgers, T-shirts, and basketball tickets. By 1993, she found that the prices for all these goods had

risen. The prices that she paid are displayed in Figure 9.11.

Item	Price in 1992	Price in 1993
Hamburger	$2	$3
T-shirt	$10	$13
Basketball ticket	$25	$30
Total of basket	**$37**	**$46**

Figure 9.11 Cathie's expenditures without weighting.

Item	Weight	Price in 1992	Total Spent	Price in 1993	Total Spent
Hamburger	21	$2	$42	$3	$63
T-shirt	7	$10	$70	$13	$91
Basketball ticket	2	$25	$50	$30	$60
Total of basket		**$37**	**$162**	**$46**	**$214**

Figure 9.12 Cathie's expenditures with weighting.

The formula for calculating the price index is:

$$\text{price index} = \frac{\text{price of basket in current year}}{\text{price of basket in base year}} \times 100$$

The index in the base year is always 100.

$$\frac{37}{37} \times 100 = 100$$

The price index for 1993 is then

$$\frac{46}{37} \times 100 = 124.3$$

The basket of goods increased in price by 24.3 per cent.

To make it a more realistic price index, however, a weighting system needs to be created. Cathie did not buy one of each of the items. She needed more hamburgers than T-shirts, and she needed more T-shirts than basketball tickets. Assume that, over a period of a week, she consumes 21 hamburgers and buys seven T-shirts and two basketball tickets. The effect of the price increase in hamburgers will be more important to her basket than the effect of price increases for the other two goods. The value of the baskets has now changed (Figure 9.12).

The base year of 1992 is still 100.

$$\frac{162}{162} \times 100 = 100$$

The weighted price index for 1993 is now

$$\frac{214}{162} \times 100 = 132.1$$

The weighted basket of goods increased in price by 32.1 per cent.

The reason for the difference is that Cathie buys a lot of hamburgers, and the weighting of the basket takes this change into account. The price increase of hamburgers was more significant than the price increase of the other goods.

QUESTIONS

1. The only goods sold in the country of Ekaj are stuffed purple dinosaurs, bags of lemon drops, and bags of gumdrops. Each of these items is given a weight based on the purchasing habits of a typical household. If the base year is 1999, calculate the CPI in the year 2001 for the statistics given in Figure 9.13.

Good	Weight	1999 Price	2001 Price
Stuffed dinosaur	4	$20.00	$24.00
Bag of lemon drops	6	$4.00	$5.00
Bag of gumdrops	9	$4.50	$5.25

Figure 9.13 Price of goods in Ekaj.

and wage earners (among others) use the CPI to help judge how wage and pension payments should be adjusted to offset year-to-year price increases. This is known as **indexing**. Using the chocolate bar example mentioned earlier, if your daily wage increased to $2, you could buy the chocolate bar and be in the same situation you were in when your wage and the chocolate bar were both $1. These adjustments can be made to remove all of the effect of a price increase by increasing wages and pensions at the same rate as prices rise (fully indexed), or they can be set to only increase by some amount that is smaller than the full price increase (partially indexed).

Limitations of the CPI

No statistic is without its limitations, and the CPI is no exception. One issue that needs to be considered is the weighting of the categories shown in Figure 9.9 (page 207), and the items included in these categories. While Statistics Canada goes to great lengths to ensure that the categories represent the spending habits of the typical Canadian household, not every household's spending habits reflect the index weights of the CPI. (Some households may spend no money on tobacco and alcohol while spending an above average amount on housing. An increase in the CPI due to a price increase in tobacco does not really affect such a household.) This is especially true when you consider the family-size definition of the CPI. Many households in Canada do not match the norm of four members set by Statistics Canada. A household with more members, for example, will likely spend disproportionately more on housing, food, and clothing. As a result, changes in the CPI may not reflect reality for many individuals in the economy.

Another problem is the individual items in the base year basket. A computer that is being sold today is very different in its quality, price, and composition than a computer sold when the base year basket was created. In fact, people may switch their purchases to entirely new products, such as the increasing trend over the past few years of buying DVD instead of VHS players. Statistics Canada tries to solve some of these problems by updating the spending patterns of Canadians periodically and revising the weights of the items in the CPI basket. They also occasionally set a new base year in order to reflect current costs as well as goods and services.

Cultural diversity is also an important area of concern. Toronto and Vancouver are both multicultural cities, more so than most other urban areas in Canada. Consumption patterns are often culturally unique because housing, recreation, food, and clothing all take on varying degrees of importance in the domestic budgets of different cultures. For a family that maintains its cultural traditions, the CPI may not be a true measure of the impact that price changes have on households. This is of special concern if the CPI is being used to index wages and pensions. A family that finds the CPI "understates" the impact of price increases on their budget may find that their income increases are not enough to compensate them for the increase in their cost of living.

Real GDP

The existence of inflation brings up an interesting problem in measuring GDP and its annual growth rate. If we are measuring output value in prices and then the total value of our output increases, how much of this increase is because the economy is growing and how much is because prices have increased? To use our example of the chocolate bar again, in the first year the price of the chocolate bar was $1. If the price of the chocolate bar rose to $2, and it was the only output of the economy, it would appear that the GDP doubled. In reality, however, we are still producing only one chocolate bar; the only reason GDP has increased is because prices have increased. It is necessary to use some tool to remove the effect of inflation to compare year-to-year output effectively.

Until May 2001, Statistics Canada used a tool very similar to the CPI known as the **GDP deflator**. This was a price index that was based on a representative basket of all the goods and

Indexing to the CPI

You can think of indexing to the CPI as working with two fractions that must be kept in the same ratio. The ratio looks like the following:

$$\frac{\text{CPI year 1}}{\text{CPI year 2}} = \frac{\text{wage or pension amount year 1}}{\text{wage or pension amount year 2}}$$

If you know three of the values then the fourth value can be calculated through cross-multiplication. What follows is an example.

Alma earns a salary of $30 000 per year when the CPI is 103. How much would her salary be if the CPI is currently 112 and her salary is to be fully indexed to the CPI?

$$\frac{103}{112} = \frac{30\,000}{\text{current salary}}$$

$$\text{current salary} \times 103 = 112 \times 30\,000$$

$$\text{current salary} = \frac{112 \times 30\,000}{103}$$

$$\text{current salary} = \$32\,621.36$$

QUESTIONS

1. Your grandmother's annual pension was $25 000 in 1995 when the CPI was 110. How much would her fully indexed pension be in 2002 if the CPI is 115?

2. Danny's annual salary was $45 000 when the CPI was 115. If his salary is now $60 000 and the increases were due only to inflation, what is the current CPI?

---

services in the GDP—not just consumer goods and services. It was used to determine if there had been a real increase in the GDP from year to year, or if the increase was due just to an increase in the level of prices. The job of the GDP deflator was to remove the effect of price increases in measuring the GDP.

Nominal GDP (also known as current-dollar GDP or **money GDP**) is the total value of the output of an economy before the effect of price increases is removed. The GDP deflator was applied to remove the effect of inflation and create what is known as **real GDP** (also known as **constant-dollar GDP**). Once again, it is necessary to use a simple formula in order to calculate real GDP using the GDP deflator:

$$\text{real GDP} = \frac{\text{nominal GDP}}{\text{GDP deflator}} \times 100$$

To compare the GDP between two years to see whether real growth occurred, the nominal GDP for each year must be converted into real GDP; this basically compares the two years in constant dollars. The value of these dollars is set by the base year of the GDP deflator. For example, in Figure 9.14 (page 212) the nominal GDP in 1999 was $957.9 billion. This appeared to be 6.2 per cent higher than the GDP in 1998. This would be very significant economic growth. However, once the GDP deflator is applied to both 1998 and 1999, the growth rate is not quite so high. In fact, 1.6 percentage points of the apparent increase was due to an increase in the level of prices. The real growth was a rather healthy 4.6 per cent.

In May 2001, Statistics Canada made a change to its method of calculating the real GDP. The new method of calculation is known as the chain Fisher volume index and is in line with practices in the United States and those suggested by the United Nations in its guide, *System of National Accounts, 1993*.

The problem with the GDP deflator was its use of a base year. While it worked well

Year	Nominal GDP ($ billions)	Change from Previous Year (%)	GDP deflator	Real GDP ($ billions of 1992)	Change from Previous Year (%)
1997	877.9	—	107.7	815.1	—
1998	901.8	2.7	107.1	842.0	3.3
1999	957.9	6.2	108.8	880.4	4.6
2000	1038.8	8.4	112.7	921.7	4.7

Source: Adapted from the Statistics Canada publication, *The Daily*, Catalogue 11-001, 28 February 2001.

Figure 9.14 Impact of the GDP deflator in Canada, 1997 to 2000.

throughout the 1970s and 1980s, the rapid expansion of information and communications technology industries has produced biased results that overstated economic growth in Canada during the 1990s. Because the base year of 1992 set the weighting of categories based on the prices in 1992 and the prices of technology have declined drastically since this time, the GDP deflator no longer effectively accounted for the effects of inflation.

The **chain Fisher volume index** eliminates the use of a base year and uses a formula to "rebase" the GDP each quarter that it is measured. Under the old measure, GDP growth in Canada was measured at 3.3 per cent in 1998, 4.6 per cent in 1999, and 4.7 per cent in 2000. As can be seen in Figure 9.15, the chain Fisher volume index more accurately measured growth at 3.9 per cent, 5.1 per cent, and 4.4 per cent, respectively. While the actual method of calculation is more complicated than the GDP deflator, it is said to be a more accurate measure of the changes in GDP and its components. Ultimately, its use is similar to that of the old GDP deflator—it is used to remove the effects of changes in price levels on the GDP.

Year	GDP in Chained 1997 Dollars ($ billions)	Change from Previous Year (%)
1997	885.0	—
1998	919.8	3.9
1999	966.4	5.1
2000	1009.2	4.4

Source: Created from the Statistics Canada CANSIM II database at <http://cansima.statcan.ca/cgi-win/CNSMCGI.EXE>, Table 380-0002.

Figure 9.15 Impact of the chain Fisher volume index on real GDP in Canada, 1997 to 2000.

Check Your Understanding

1. How does Statistics Canada measure the change in the level of prices in Canada?
2. What are the three largest components of the CPI?
3. Why is indexing an important use of the CPI?
4. Why can it be said that the CPI is a good measure for the country but not a very good indicator for individuals?

CHAPTER SUMMARY

- Macroeconomics is the study of all of the segments of the economy as a whole.
- A number of economic measures are used to gauge the performance of the economy.
- Gross Domestic Product measures the total market value of all goods and services produced for final use in an economy.
- The expenditure approach for measuring GDP uses the formula C + I + G + (X – M).
- Comparing the GDP in two successive years reveals the growth rate of an economy.
- Gross Domestic Product is frequently used as a measure of well-being for a country.
- There are a number of drawbacks to using GDP as a measure of economic output and well-being of a country.
- The labour force consists of those people who are employed or who are willing and able to work and are actively seeking employment. The unemployment rate is the percentage of the labour force not working at any given time.
- The unemployment rate in Canada is understated because the method used by Statistics Canada ignores people who have given up looking for work and those who have accepted part-time employment.
- The reasons for unemployment are classified under a number of categories.
- Full employment is considered to be achieved when only frictional and some structural unemployment exist. This is also known as the natural rate of unemployment. In Canada, this is considered to be between 6 and 7 per cent.
- The lost output due to unemployment above the natural rate is known as the GDP gap. The value of this gap can be calculated using Okun's law; it is said to be 2 per cent of GDP for every 1 per cent the unemployment rate exceeds the natural rate of unemployment.
- Inflation refers to the persistent rise in the general level of prices.
- The Consumer Price Index (CPI) is used to measure the changes in the prices of consumer goods.

- The CPI is primarily used to calculate the inflation rate over two successive years.
- Unions, wage earners, and governments (among others) use the CPI to index wages and pensions.
- A number of drawbacks limit the usefulness of the CPI as a measure of the effect of price increases on individual households. These drawbacks include the weighting of the basket, changes in the types of products, and the cultural make-up of Canada.
- The GDP deflator and chain Fisher volume index are measures similar to the CPI that allow the effect of price increases to be removed from the calculations of change in GDP. Applying these tools allows one to convert the nominal (or money) GDP into real (or constant-dollar) GDP.

Key Terms

macroeconomics
Gross Domestic Product (GDP)
expenditure approach
income approach
multiple-counting
consumption
investment
Gross National Product (GNP)
economic growth
standard of living
per capita GDP
hidden economy
unemployment rate
labour force
full employment
GDP gap
potential GDP
Okun's law
inflation
Consumer Price Index (CPI)
inflation rate
indexing
GDP deflator
nominal (or money) GDP
real (or constant-dollar) GDP
chain Fisher volume index

Activities

Thinking/Inquiry

1. Examine the information in Figure 9.16.

   a) By what percentage did real GDP grow between 1985 and 1995?

   b) By what percentage did it grow between 1990 and 2000?

   c) What is the average growth rate per year of these two time periods?

Year	1985	1990	1995	2000
Nominal GDP ($ millions)	235	360	510	700
GDP deflator	104	119	139	152

Figure 9.16

2. Why is the work of volunteers not included in the calculation of the GDP? Do you think it should be? Prepare a defence of your position.

3. Which of the following transactions are included in the GDP, and to which component of expenditure GDP does each belong?

   a) The purchase of building materials by a contractor who is working on your kitchen.

   b) The purchase of building materials by you for the basement renovation project that you are completing.

   c) The sale of a dozen ears of corn in the supermarket.

   d) The sale of a basket of tomatoes at a roadside stand.

   e) Your purchase of a Swiss-made watch.

4. What type of unemployment is each of the following?

   a) A high school graduate looking for her first job.

   b) Workers laid off by Chang Incorporated, a doughnut shop company, because consumers have shown a tendency to eat more bagels than doughnuts.

   c) Lift operators laid off from a ski resort for the summer.

   d) Workers laid off by General Motors as it brings new automation to its assembly line.

   e) Workers dismissed by a large number of companies because of a general decline in demand for goods and services.

   f) Workers losing their jobs when Hoyt Enterprises, a hockey stick manufacturing company, closes its plant in Canada, preferring to manufacture its sticks in Sweden and import them.

5. "Not all Canadians feel the impact of inflation equally." Explain this statement, referring to the limitations of the CPI.

6. Compare Figures 9.2 (page 200), 9.4 (page 204), and 9.10 (page 208). Can you see any relationship among the three measures? Speculate as to why any relationships you find exist.

7. There are many economic measures other than those described in this chapter that Statistics Canada monitors. Search either the Statistics Canada Web site or back issues of newspapers to find at least two other macroeconomic measures. Explain what the measure is and how it might help you assess the state of the economy.

Communication

8. Collect five articles from newspapers, magazines, or online databases that you believe relate to the concepts taught in this chapter. For each of the articles, write a brief summary and explain how it relates to what you learned in this chapter.

9. Divide a group of four people in half. Discuss the pros and cons of the value of adopting the GPI as an economic measure, with each pair taking one side of the argument.

10. Find a partner and go to the Web site hosted by the Organization for Economic Cooperation and Development (OECD). Collect and compare the data provided—regarding the three main economic measures described in this chapter—in the same year

for any five countries and Canada. Create one set of bar graphs for each measure that displays the results of your research. If you notice significant differences in the main measures, conduct some further research to determine why the data are different for different countries. Write a summary of your findings.

Application

11. Go to the Statistics Canada Web site and find the real growth rate, unemployment rate, and inflation rate for the last two years. You may have to do your own calculations from the information provided to find these answers.

12. Explain the effect of each of the following on the size of the GDP and the well-being of Canadians.

    a) War breaks out overseas and Canadians are involved.

    b) Because of increasing concerns about international terrorism, the Canadian government increases its border security measures by hiring more border guards.

    c) The work week is lengthened from 40 hours to 50 hours.

    d) More people engage in home renovation projects.

    e) Ontario introduces an environmental protection program that requires drivers to have their cars pass pollution emission tests before they can renew their licences.

13. a) The fictional economy of Werdna measures its GDP at $540 billion in a year when their actual unemployment rate is 9.3 per cent. Economists estimate the natural unemployment rate as 4 per cent. What is the GDP gap of Werdna?

    b) Werdna government economists estimate that if the Ministry of Labour had spent $10 billion on programs to create employment, they would have lowered the unemployment rate to 7 per cent. From a financial point of view, would it have been wise for the Ministry to go ahead with this program? Explain your answer.

14. Koskins Inc. has negotiated a collective agreement with its workers that fully protects them against the effects of inflation by fully indexing wages to the CPI. If the wage rate in the first year of their contract was $13.25 per hour when the CPI was 127, what is the wage rate at the end of the third year of the contract when the CPI is 145?

15. The federal government decides to give a tax deduction (income that a person is not required to pay tax on) for the purchasing of educational books. In the year 2002, the deduction is valued at $1000, and in 2005, the deduction is $1100. The CPI in 2002 is 128, and in 2005, it is 145. Is the deduction fully or partially indexed? Explain your answer.

16. Calculate the unemployment rate for each of the countries in Figure 9.17.

Country	Labour Force (year)	Number Employed
Canada	16 100 000 (2000)	15 000 000
Bangladesh	64 100 000 (1998)	41 500 000
United Kingdom	29 200 000 (1999)	27 600 000
Vietnam	38 200 000 (1998)	28 650 000
Australia	9 500 000 (1999)	8 900 000

Figure 9.17

CHAPTER 10
THE BUSINESS CYCLE AND FISCAL POLICY

In response to a sudden economic downturn in 2001, the Canadian federal government took the unusual step of making a special fiscal statement.

This statement, by Paul Martin, the finance minister, captured the essence of the use of fiscal policy in responding to a recesssion.

Actions Supporting the Canadian Economy

In the February 2000 budget and the October Statement, we outlined a number of actions which are part of our ongoing strategy to protect Canadians, a strategy to invest in the social fabric of our country, reduce taxes, and pay down debt. These actions are not only the kind of initiatives that will contribute to the long-term strength of our economy— they also provide stimulus in the short term when we need it now, by putting more money into the hands of Canadians, by spurring business, sparking investment, and creating jobs.

First and foremost, there are tax cuts—the largest in Canadian history....

What do all these tax measures mean for Canadians?...

This year alone these tax measures will provide the Canadian economy with $17 billion in added stimulus.

Furthermore, in addition to the tax reductions, which are largely focused on middle- and low-income earners, a number of strategic investments are being made in areas that are also of great importance to Canadians—areas like health care, education, and innovation....

Taken together, all of the expenditure initiatives announced ... amount to almost $7 billion in stimulus for the Canadian economy this fiscal year. When combined with the $17 billion in tax measures, the total impact this year alone will be close to $24 billion—this is one of the most, if not the most, stimulative packages introduced into its economy by any government of a major industrialized country this year....

Source: Department of Finance, 17 May 2001,
<http://www.fin.gc.ca/ec2001/ec01speeche.html>.

QUESTIONS

1. What specific actions taken by the government of Canada in response to the recession does Mr. Martin cite?

2. Why might spending increases and tax cuts be helpful in the face of a sluggish economy?

3. Why is spending in areas such as education and innovation important for economic growth? (Think about how this might be explained using the production possibilities curve.)

Chapter Goals

By the end of this chapter, you will be able to

• explore the macroeconomy through aggregate demand and supply analysis,

• understand the fluctuations of the economy as explained by the business cycle,

• describe how the Great Depression led to the development of the Keynesian view of government in economic intervention,

• understand the use of fiscal policy to influence the business cycle,

• explain the limitations and drawbacks of using fiscal policy to manage the economy.

Introduction to Fiscal Policy

The last chapter introduced critical macroeconomic indicators such as the unemployment rate, the inflation rate (measured as an annual percentage change in the CPI), and economic growth (measured as an annual percentage change in the GDP). In Chapter 1, we examined how the production possibilities curve helps to describe the choices that an economy faces and the potential that exists if all its resources are used to maximum efficiency. In other chapters, we also explored how equilibrium is determined in the product, labour, and capital markets. These concepts form the foundation necessary to understand how the macroeconomy works and to examine a long-standing economic debate: what is the best way to ensure the economic well-being of our society?

Aggregate Demand and Supply

In previous chapters, we looked at supply and demand as a way to explain how equilibrium is established in individual markets. Our explanation of equilibrium at the macro level begins with a similar analysis. If, in theory, we could add up all consumer demand, at all the various price levels, for all markets, we should be able to determine the total demand schedule for an economy. By the same token, if we could add up all of what producers are willing to supply, at all the various price levels, for all markets, we should be able to determine the total supply schedule for an economy. When we combine all markets for individual goods and services in society, we are looking at the *aggregate*, or total, for the entire economy.

Aggregate Demand

Aggregate demand (AD) is the total demand for all goods and services produced in a society. The aggregate demand schedule in Figure 10.1 displays the total amount of goods and services purchased at each price level, as measured by the chain Fisher volume index, in a particular economy. The graphic representation of its aggregate demand curve is shown in Figure 10.2 (page 218). Note that the aggregate demand curve looks very similar to the market demand curve studied in microeconomics—as price levels rise, the total real output (or aggregate quantity demanded) falls.

Finally, it should be pointed out that the aggregate demand at each of the price levels is really equivalent to the GDP that would occur at that price level, or the sum of all consumption, investment, government spending, and net exports in the economy. In the last chapter, we defined this by the formula

$$GDP = C + I + G + (X - M)$$

For real economic growth to occur, the real GDP must grow—in other words, the aggregate quantity demanded must increase at each of the price levels. This means that one or more of the variables in the GDP formula must increase in value.

Price Level (chain Fisher volume index*)	Real GDP Demanded ($ millions)
160	77
150	82
140	87
130	91
120	96
110	101
100	105
90	110
80	115
70	119
60	124
50	129

*See page 212 in Chapter 9

Figure 10.1 Example of total amount of goods and services purchased at each particular price level in an economy (aggregate demand).

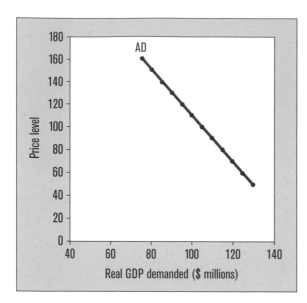

Figure 10.2 Aggregate demand curve for the statistics in Figure 10.1.

Aggregate Supply

Aggregate supply (AS) is the total supply of all goods and services produced in a society. The aggregate supply curve displays the total amount of goods and services that would be supplied at each price level, as measured by the chain Fisher volume index, in an economy. Figure 10.3 is an aggregate supply schedule for a particular economy. The graphic representation of its aggregate supply curve is shown in Figure 10.4.

While similar in shape to the supply curve that you are familiar with from microeconomic supply and demand analysis, the aggregate supply curve does feature some important differences. The first important characteristic is the very elastic portion that occurs at low output levels. At very low outputs, most of a society's resources are sitting idle. Consider unemployed workers, for example. When there are many people unemployed, there is too little competition for workers among producers to force the price of wage labour higher (surpluses force prices down). Therefore, there is little increase in the average costs of production when new workers are hired and output is increased. Price levels would consequently stay fairly low

even as output increases. As more output is produced, however, more competition occurs among producers for limited amounts of land, labour, and capital inputs. As these resources become scarcer, their prices go up and put

Price Level (chain Fisher volume index)	Real GDP Supplied ($ millions)
160	140.0
150	140.0
140	139.5
130	137.5
120	134.0
100	123.0
90	110.0
85	80.0
84	60.0
83	40.0

Figure 10.3 Example of total amount of goods and services supplied at each particular price level in an economy (aggregate supply).

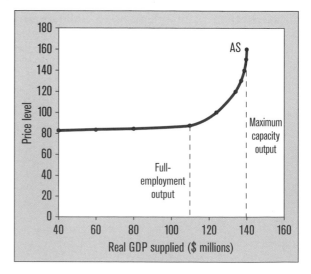

Figure 10.4 Aggregate supply curve for the statistics in Figure 10.3.

upward pressure on the prices of all goods and services.

At higher output levels, then, prices tend to rise much more rapidly. At some point, the economy would run out of resources altogether. Then, any attempted increase in output would simply result in producers "bidding up" input prices to higher levels without actually producing any more output. The aggregate supply curve becomes *perfectly inelastic*, or vertical, at this level of output. In theory, an economy producing at that level of output is producing at a point on its production possibilities curve—it cannot physically produce more output without improvements in technology or the discovery of new physical inputs.

Equilibrium Output and Price Level

The point at which the AD curve intersects the AS curve is the equilibrium level of price and output for the economy (see Figure 10.5). When the economy is at **full-employment**

equilibrium, the two curves intersect at a point on the AS curve where prices start to rise more rapidly, but the curve is not yet vertical. As the economy approaches full employment, competition for scarce resources starts to push price levels up. The economy still has room for further increases in real GDP because of frictional unemployment and the possibility of increasing output beyond the full-employment level (by having employees work overtime). At some point, however, the curve would become vertical as an absolute capacity is reached. Full-employment equilibrium is, therefore, the point at which price levels start to rise more quickly but below the absolute capacity of the economy.

Two other possibilities exist for an economy. Below full employment equilibrium occurs when the AD curve intersects AS to the left of full-employment equilibrium. At this point, real GDP is lower and price levels are rising very slowly. The low level of output leads to higher unemployment levels and what is known as a

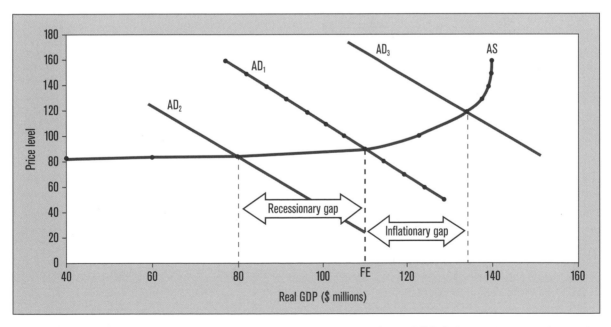

Figure 10.5 Full-employment equilibrium occurs when the aggregate demand (AD₁) intersects aggregate supply (AS) at full-employment output (FE). If aggregate demand (AD₂) intersects below full-employment output, a recessionary gap exists with low employment levels, low output levels, and low inflation. If aggregate demand (AD₃) intersects above full-employment output, an inflationary gap exists with high employment levels, higher output levels, and higher inflation.

recessionary gap. This situation is characterized by high unemployment, low inflation, and low GDP growth. Above full employment, equilibrium occurs when the AD curve intersects AS to the right of full-employment equilibrium. At this point, real GDP is very high, as are employment levels. Price levels, however, are rising very rapidly. This is known as an **inflationary gap.** High inflation, high employment levels, and high levels of GDP growth are characteristics of inflationary periods.

Check Your
Understanding

1. How are aggregate demand and aggregate supply similar to the microeconomic concepts of demand and supply?

2. What are the components of aggregate demand?

3. Why is the aggregate supply curve elastic at low levels of output and inelastic at high levels of output?

4. Describe the characteristics of an economy suffering from a recessionary gap.

Changes in Aggregate Demand

Just as the demand curve might shift in microeconomic analysis, the aggregate demand curve will shift as changes in economic activity are considered. Shifts in the aggregate demand curve can be attributed directly to changes in the variables that make up the GDP—consumption (C), investment (I), government spending (G), and the balance of foreign trade (X − M).

Changes in consumption

Consumer income can be divided into four possible uses. It can be used for consumption, go to the government through taxes, be saved for future use, or be spent on imports. In terms of the impact on aggregate demand (AD), we are most concerned about the consumption component as it makes up 60 per cent of GDP. The amount that is available for consumption is whatever is left over after the other three components are considered. As a result, an increase in AD will occur when consumption increases. This may be the result of either an increase in the level of income or a decrease in one or more of savings, taxes, and import spending. Such an increase in consumption is represented by a rightward shift of the AD

curve because, at each price level, a higher level of real GDP is demanded.

In Figure 10.5, a move of the AD curve from AD_2 to AD_1 would reflect an increase in AD. The result is an increase in the equilibrium level of prices, real GDP, and employment. A decrease in consumption (or an increase in savings, taxes, and import spending) will likewise decrease AD, shifting the curve to the left (for example, from AD_3 to AD_1), decreasing price levels and real GDP, and increasing unemployment.

Changes in investment

Since profits are equal to revenue minus costs, expected profits are equal to expected revenue minus expected costs. The overall level of investment spending is related, then, to the expectation of future profits. For instance, if business profits are expected to increase and the economic climate looks strong, investment will increase and the AD curve will shift to the right. However, if businesses foresee a downturn in economic profits, investment will decrease and the AD curve will shift to the left.

These movements are also closely tied to the interest rate. Because any investment is likely to necessitate the borrowing of funds, if the interest rate goes up, the costs associated with the investment also go up. This would reduce the potential for profit. Therefore, increases in interest rates also tend to reduce investment spending, shifting the AD curve to the left. Decreases in interest rates have the opposite effect.

Changes in government spending

If a government increases its spending or transfer payments, this will shift the AD curve to the right by acting on the G component of the GDP equation. If governments reduce spending, this will shift the AD curve to the left. These changes are at the heart of fiscal policy and will be dealt with in greater detail later in the chapter.

Changes in export demand (foreign trade)

There are three major factors influencing demand for Canadian-produced exports: the domestic rate of inflation, the relative levels of income in other countries, and the value of the Canadian dollar. Because inflation (or a general increase in the level of prices) affects only domestic and not foreign goods and services, a general increase in the price of Canadian goods and services makes them relatively more expensive than foreign-made goods and services. A rapid rise in inflation will then reduce export demand as foreign consumers will purchase fewer Canadian products. Conversely, a decline in the rate of inflation will make Canadian goods relatively less expensive and thus increase export demand.

A similar effect is felt as the income levels rise for consumers in countries that are trading partners. Their demand for goods will increase and, as a result, Canadian exports to these countries will rise. The opposite would be true for a decrease in the level of foreign incomes.

Increases in the value of the Canadian dollar will increase the cost of Canadian products for

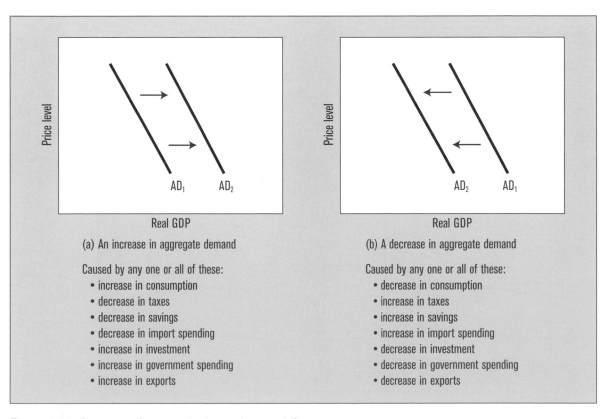

(a) An increase in aggregate demand

Caused by any one or all of these:
- increase in consumption
- decrease in taxes
- decrease in savings
- decrease in import spending
- increase in investment
- increase in government spending
- increase in exports

(b) A decrease in aggregate demand

Caused by any one or all of these:
- decrease in consumption
- increase in taxes
- increase in savings
- increase in import spending
- decrease in investment
- decrease in government spending
- decrease in exports

Figure 10.6 Summary of aggregate demand curve shifts.

those buying them in other countries, making them less attractive to foreign buyers. An increase in the value of the Canadian dollar can translate into a decrease in AD because we are selling fewer exports. Decreases in the value of the dollar, on the other hand, make the relative price of Canadian products more attractive to foreign consumers, thus increasing AD.

Changes in Aggregate Supply

Just as events in the marketplace can shift the AD curve, the AS curve is subject to movements as well. There are three basic reasons why the AS curve might shift: a change in the price of any of the basic inputs (land, labour, and capital), a change in the amount of basic inputs available, or a change in the efficiency of the production process.

Changes in price of inputs

If the prices for land, labour, or capital increase, firms will be able to produce less at each price level. As a result, the AS curve will shift upward and to the left at all points to the left of its perfectly inelastic section (see Figure 10.7a). The perfectly inelastic section of the curve will not move because, while prices are higher, the same amount of inputs are available, and, therefore, the maximum real GDP possible is the same as it was before the price increases. Decreases in the price of inputs will shift the AS curve downward.

Changes in the amount of inputs available

If new resources are discovered, more capital goods are made available, or the workforce grows, there are more inputs available for use. Just as these changes would shift the production possibilities curve outward, they would increase the maximum capacity of the economy. The availability of more resources also reduces competition for them, pushing down the costs of basic inputs. The effect on the AS curve is to shift the relatively elastic, horizontal portion downward, reflecting decreased input prices, while shifting the vertical portion to the right, reflecting the increased capacity of the economy (see Figure 10.7b).

Changes in efficiency

Improvements in technology make the workforce more productive. As the workforce becomes more efficient, it can produce more output with the same resources. The resulting effect on the AS curve is the same as increasing the amount of resources available. The curve shifts downward, with the vertical portion moving farther to the right (see Figure 10.7b).

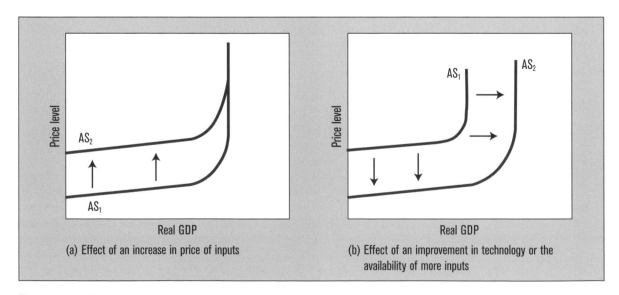

(a) Effect of an increase in price of inputs

(b) Effect of an improvement in technology or the availability of more inputs

Figure 10.7 Summary of aggregate supply curve shifts.

Check Your

Understanding

1. Explain why decreases in income taxes, savings, and import spending all increase aggregate demand.

2. How does a change in the interest rate influence the aggregate demand curve?

3. If the value of the Canadian dollar decreases, what is the likely impact on aggregate demand?

4. Why is a shift of the aggregate supply curve to the right like an outward shift of the production possibilities curve?

The Business Cycle and Aggregate Supply and Demand

In order to understand the purpose of fiscal policy, we must first understand what a business cycle is. A **business cycle** covers periods of alternating economic growth and recession (or negative economic growth) as measured by changes in real GDP. In other words, business cycles are the ups and downs of the economy. The duration in time of a business cycle and its size (in loss or gain of real GDP) vary from one cycle to the next. Some expansionary or growth periods are extended while others are not. Some recessionary periods can last a long time; others seem to disappear before we notice them.

A business cycle occurs because of the fluctuations that economies experience over time. These fluctuations result from changes in economic growth and patterns of consumption. In the previous section, we explained such changes as shifts of the aggregate demand and supply curves. Business cycles, then, are at the heart of macroeconomics. Economists try to determine how well the economy is doing and, more importantly, where it is heading. Forecasting the coming economic climate allows economists to advise political and business leaders on how to deal with possible adverse future economic events. When the economy is heading in an undesirable direction, economists may advise a nation's leaders to apply fiscal or monetary policy tools to try to change the course of the economy.

The Dynamics of the Business Cycle

The causes of these fluctuations in economic activity are varied. The cyclical nature of the marketplace is dynamic, and it is not possible to detail all the reasons for cyclical fluctuations in the economy. Here we will look at two examples to illustrate how a simple macroeconomic model works.

An *expansion period* begins when consumer spending increases and production increases. As Figure 10.8 (page 224) shows, expansion is represented by an upward trend in the business cycle. Let's assume the Canadian economy is on an upswing—that is, unemployment is declining, business activity is increasing, and there is increased production. Generally, increased production leads to more workers being hired. New employment leads to a general rise in consumer incomes, which, in turn, has a tendency to generate increased levels of consumption spending. Consumer psychology that is influenced by positive economic news can also contribute to increased spending. Increased spending translates into an increase in the demand for goods and services. As we described earlier in this chapter, an increase in aggregate demand leads to higher levels of output and employment as well as higher prices. This higher demand leads to increased production, more workers being hired, and so on. As Figure 10.9 (page 224) shows, this **prosperity cycle** is the result of aggregate demand feeding itself.

At first glance, it would appear that, as long as resources are available, this trend for greater and greater economic expansion should continue. However, at some point this will change. The economy will peak, and then the trend will begin to reverse. The reasons for the turnaround at the peak of a business cycle are varied. Consumers may simply have exhausted the purchasing patterns that pushed up aggregate demand. After all, many of the expensive

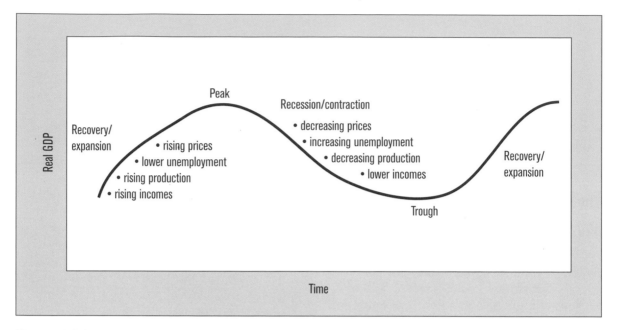

Figure 10.8 Business cycle. The definition of an economic business cycle is a time period of alternating growth and recession. In this figure, the horizontal axis measures time while the vertical axis yields the real GDP growth rate. While the cycle appears to be even and regular, it is drawn this way only to show the general trend. Sections of actual business cycles vary in length and slope. The trend over the past 30 years has been seven to eight years of growth followed by one to two years of recession.

durable goods (such as automobiles, appliances, and new homes) that drive a booming economy do not need to be replaced very often. Demand begins to decrease when many con-

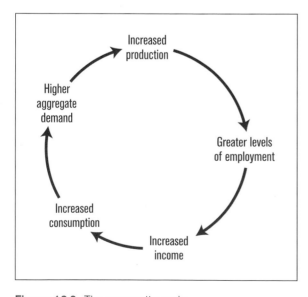

Figure 10.9 The prosperity cycle.

sumers' wants are satisfied. Sometimes, the turnaround is linked to an event, such as the stock market crash that occurred on 29 October 1929. When this was combined with restrictive trade policies, the dependence of the Canadian economy on the market for natural resources, and reduced government and investment spending, the result was a huge drop in aggregate demand.

The increase in producers who are competing for capital funds to support business expansion tends to put upward pressure on interest rates. As interest rates increase, consumers are less likely to buy goods for which they need to borrow money—the durable goods that make up almost 10 per cent of our GDP. Finally, if demand shifts too far to the right, it will exceed the economy's capacity to produce. At this point, according to aggregate supply and demand analysis, more severe inflation begins to occur. As prices rise, higher inflation levels have the effect of reducing the real income of consumers. As a result, demand begins to decline. Together, these

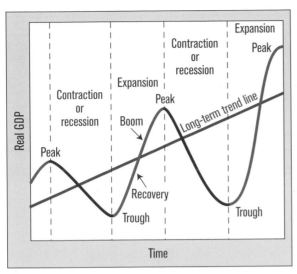

Source: From *Economics: A Canadian Perspective* by James D. Thexton. Copyright © Oxford University Press Canada 1992. Reprinted by permission.

Figure 10.10 The phases of the business cycle can vary in intensity and duration. Over time, however, a steady upward growth trend is apparent.

factors have the effect of reversing the direction of shift in the aggregate demand curve. Instead of moving to the right, as it did while the economy was expanding, it now begins to shift to the left. This trend is reflected in the recessionary part of the business cycle, which has a negative slope.

The events we just outlined begin to occur in reverse as we move past the peak of the business cycle. In our simple model, reduced demand for domestic goods leads to an accumulation of business inventories. That is, firms tend to be overstocked with goods. An increase in business inventories indicates to firms that they should cut back production. Production cutbacks generally lead to worker layoffs, which in turn lead to lower incomes. Decreased incomes can lead to a decrease in consumer demand for goods and services, shifting aggregate demand to the left. If this occurs, the revenues of firms will tend to decline. Some firms will be forced to cut back production in order to control costs, others may lay off workers, and still other firms that cannot reduce their costs may go out of busi-

ness. When this type of downward spiral in economic activity occurs, it is referred to as a recessionary trend. Officially, a **recession** occurs when real GDP growth is negative, or declines for two consecutive quarters (two consecutive three-month periods). The recessionary, or contractionary, part of the business cycle is characterized by increasing levels of unemployment, low (or negative) levels of real GDP growth, and low levels of inflation or even falling prices (deflation).

The recessionary period is often influenced heavily by consumer psychology. As media reports of layoffs (and the threat of more layoffs) occur, those who still have jobs reduce their levels of consumption spending. Sometimes individuals begin to save in order to provide a "cushion" in case they should find themselves out of work—an increasingly likely prospect, according to the news reports. Others may cut back on the purchase of "big ticket" durable goods, fearing to increase their debt load at a time when wage increases are unlikely and loss of income is possible. These changes in the level of consumption spending make the recessionary period worse as they tend to pull aggregate demand farther to the left. If the recessionary period becomes prolonged, with very high unemployment and very low output levels, it is known as a **depression**.

At some point, events will occur that will stop the downturn in economic activity and will generate increases in consumer spending. For instance, prices may fall to a point where consumers start to spend again, and the upward movement of the business cycle resumes. Also, consumers can postpone the purchase of some items only for a certain length of time. A new automobile or refrigerator is bought when it is no longer worthwhile to repair it. Clothes wear out. As these purchases occur, inventories of firms begin to dwindle and, in most cases, firms increase production again.

While these regular fluctuations of economic activity occur over varying durations and to varying degrees, over time the level of business activity in an economy tends to increase steadily (Figure 10.10).

Leakages and Injections

Another explanation of the business cycle centres on the money payments that flow through the economy. This **circular flow of income** sees the GDP as a total of all money payments in the economy. Businesses hire individuals from households to work for them and pay them a wage in exchange. Businesses also pay individuals money through interest payments on the capital that they borrow for expansion. Individuals, in turn, spend the money that they earn on goods and services that the businesses produce. This simplified circular flow model can be seen highlighted in green in Figure 10.11.

Another way to look at the changes in aggregate demand is through leakages and injections in the circular flow of income (see Figure 10.11). **Leakages** can be described as

any uses of income that cause money to be taken out of the income–expenditure stream of the economy. The income generated by production is subject to three leakages as it is returning to generate more production. These are taxes (T), savings (S), and imports (M). Taxes must be paid, some of the income generated by production will be saved, and some will be used to buy imported goods. Note that the amount of each of these leakages will rise and fall with the level of production.

Often, "leaked" money ends up getting respent in the economy. The problem is where and how. For instance, governments might spend the money they take in taxes. On the other hand, they might also spend more or less than the amount they actually receive in tax revenues. Other countries' export earnings might be used to purchase imports, but there is

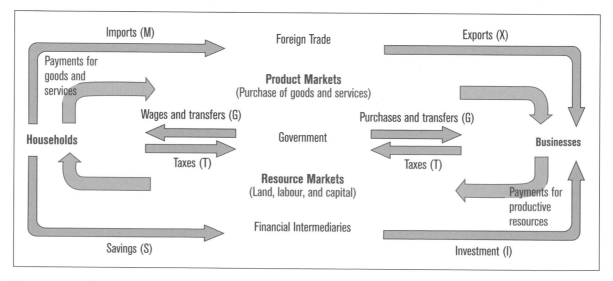

Figure 10.11 The circular flow of income (shown in green) with leakages (shown in blue) and injections (shown in red).

no guarantee that trade will be balanced, or that they will purchase Canadian goods. The money we save might be borrowed for business investment inside Canada, but then again, it might not.

As stated above, each of the leakages may be re-injected into the economy. An **injection** can be defined as any expenditure that causes money to be put into the income–expenditure stream. The three major injections into the economy are government spending (G), investment spending (I), and exports (X). Note that consumption is not considered an injection; however, it is hidden in the leakages and injections model. Since consumer incomes are disposed of through consumption, taxes, savings, and import spending, if leakages are going up, they reduce consumption spending; if they are going down, they help to increase such spending.

The relationships among the three leakages and three injections determine whether overall demand is growing or shrinking. If the sum of the leakages is greater than the sum of the injections, aggregate demand will shrink. But it will not shrink forever. As production falls, consumers will pay fewer taxes, save less, and buy fewer imported goods. When the total of the leakages falls to the level of the total injections, the economy generally stops shrinking. At this point, the economy is in equilibrium. The equilibrium level may be below full employment (a recessionary gap), at it (full employment), or above it (an inflationary gap).

When the total of the injections is larger than the total of the leakages, the economy will grow as aggregate demand increases. But as production and incomes rise, so do taxes, savings, and imports. When the three leakages are, together, as large as the injections, growth will generally stop. Once again, this may be at, above, or below full-employment equilibrium.

Some have likened this model to filling a bathtub. If the amount of water coming in (the injection) is greater than the amount going down the drain (the leakage), the bathtub fills up (the GDP gets bigger). If the amount of water coming in is less than the amount that is leaking out, the bathtub empties (the GDP shrinks). Finally, if the water coming in and the water

leaking out are equal, the amount of water in the tub remains the same (equilibrium).

This model can be expressed as a formula:

$$\text{If } T + S + M > G + I + X,$$
then AD will shrink until such time as
$$T + S + M = G + I + X.$$

$$\text{If } T + S + M < G + I + X,$$
then AD will rise until such time as
$$T + S + M = G + I + X.$$

Fiscal Policy

Most mixed economies go through upheavals caused by the ups and downs of the business cycle. Should we as a society do anything about these economic booms and recessions, or should we let the market make its own adjustments? As you learned in Chapter 3, the economist John Maynard Keynes believed that the business cycle should be managed and advocated government intervention. Governments intervene in the economy through the use of **stabilization policies**. One way that a government can intervene is through applying the tools of fiscal policy. We will start our exploration of fiscal policy with a look at how it developed (see the Case Study on page 228).

Keynes's Ideas

By examining the relationships among the various forms of demand and income, Keynes was able to explain the Great Depression in a way that classical economists could not. A collapse of investment spending brought consumer spending down with it; with low levels of consumer spending, it was unlikely that investment spending would soon recover. An auto company that is running at only 50 per cent of capacity has no reason to build new factories. But Keynes's ideas went far beyond simply explaining depressions and recessions. If government policy could affect the sizes of the leakages (taxes, savings, and imports) and the injections (investment spending, government spending, and exports), aggregate demand could be managed.

Case Study

The Birth of the Keynesian School

Classical Laissez-faire Economics

The classical school of thought (led by Adam Smith and David Ricardo) had a significant influence on how the economy was run prior to the 20th century. Its use had several important implications:

- The government played a minimal role in determining the condition of the economy; extensive government intervention was thought to hinder the efficient operation of the market in the determination of prices of goods and services and in the allocation of resources toward their production.
- The normal state of the economy was considered to be full employment. This assumption implied that all workers who desired jobs would have them and that those who were unemployed voluntarily chose to be so.
- The government had a minimal role in the course of the business cycle. Left alone, the economy would gravitate toward full employment.

The Great Depression

Classical economists believed that economic recessions, even depressions, were temporary in nature. Left alone, the economy would return to a level consistent with its potential output. During a recession or a depression, economists belonging to the classical school would argue as follows: Flexible and falling prices, wages, and interest rates could offset an economic slow-down in several ways. Layoffs and a decrease in labour demand lead to a decrease in wages. Lower wages reduce the price of employing labour relative to employing capital goods and, therefore, create an offsetting increase in the demand for labour. If prices fall farther than wages then purchasing power increases. This leads to increased consumption, offsetting the initial decrease in aggregate demand that caused the economic downturn in the first place.

Lower interest rates improve the return on investment, resulting in an increase in business investment and an increase in aggregate demand.

The Great Depression of the 1930s saw output plummet and unemployment rates soar in many industrialized nations. In Canada, unemployment reached between 20 and 30 per cent and output dropped by more than 30 per cent from the level reached in 1929. Several important factors combined to make the 1930s a decade of extreme economic depression, and one that did not fit the models that had been created by the classical school.

During the 1920s, corporate, bank, and individual participation and speculation in the stock markets were very high. Investors, including banks, could buy stocks on margin, paying only a small percentage (for example, 10 per cent) of the stock's street value, with the promise to pay back the money borrowed after the stock increased in value. This led to high demand for stocks and, as a result, pushed stock prices higher. In addition, banks could use customer deposits to buy stocks, further driving up share prices and increasing the potential fall in prices. And prices did fall. From October 1929 to the early 1930s, many stock prices lost over 90 per cent of their value. For many Canadians, their savings and wealth evaporated almost overnight as their shares lost value, and the lenders put out margin calls, demanding that the borrowed money be paid back.

With the business downturn, demand for goods and services plummeted. US corporations responded by lobbying the government for increased protection. They wanted tariff taxes on imported foreign-made goods, hoping to increase demand for their own products. In response to the crisis and to tariffs placed on Canadian goods (especially in the United States), the Canadian government erected their own tariff barriers that hampered trade. Since a tariff acts as a tax, this led to a corresponding increase in the price of imported goods to the Canadian consumer. As more and more foreign countries erected their own tariff barriers, global trade contracted, leading to a further deterioration of the world economy.

With the economic downturn, incomes—and, therefore, tax payments to the government—declined. Believing a balanced budget was of primary importance, the Canadian government raised income and corporate taxes, creating a leakage that further decreased disposable incomes, aggregate demand, and jobs.

The classical argument that falling prices and interest rates would restore economic prosperity proved faulty. The economy remained stuck in a recession, which, as it became prolonged, turned into a depression. With high unemployment, there was not enough consumer income to stimulate consumption and aggregate demand. With falling demand for output, business investment sank, and high tariffs prevented increasing aggregate demand through selling goods abroad.

Stunned by the magnitude and duration of the Great Depression, classical economists did not know how to respond. The traditional classical solution to the business cycle—allow prices, wages, and interest rates to adjust, and wait it out—was not working. Wages, prices, and interest rates did fall, but output continued to fall farther while the unemployment rate skyrocketed. All the usual catalysts for economic growth—consumption, investment, and international trade—stabilized at levels far below a recovery. Massive unemployment, coupled with a devastating loss in wealth, left consumption much smaller. Businesses had no reason to expand productive capacity when demand for their goods and services had fallen drastically. Finally, international tariffs led to a substantial contraction in foreign-trade activity as well as in the injections that export markets in other countries could have provided.

In hindsight, it seems obvious that the only sector left available to stimulate economic

growth and activity was the government. But it was left to John Maynard Keynes to point out the obvious—when traditional methods of economic stimulus fail, use the government as a last resort, and use it forcefully.

Keynes pointed out several problems with classical theory. An important point was that wages tended not to fall as much as prices during economic downturns. The result was an increase in real wages and a decrease in the demand for labour as the real cost of labour inputs increased. Keynes also developed the idea that, during periods of economic weakness, investment tends to be relatively interest-inelastic—that is, investment is relatively unresponsive to changes in the interest rate, especially if aggregate demand is not increasing. Thus, a decrease in the rate of interest will have little or no stimulative impact on the investment component of aggregate demand.

Figure 10.12 During the Great Depression, thousands of men "rode the rails," searching for work, from one end of Canada to the other. What were the circumstances that led to this upsurge in unemployment?

QUESTIONS

1. Why did classical theory fail during the 1930s?
2. What fundamental error is there in the classical economists' argument that "lower wages reduce the price for labour relative to employing capital goods and, therefore, create an offsetting increase in the demand for labour"?
3. Knowing what you do about the components of the GDP equation, how do you think the government might have been able to prevent the recession from turning into a deep depression?

Aggregate demand could be purposely increased in a recession or depression and purposely reduced when excessive demand was leading to inflation. This was a revolutionary way of thinking that would influence economic thought for the rest of the 20th century. For example, the stock market fell in October 1987 and after the terrorist attacks in New York and Washington, DC, on 11 September 2001 much more rapidly than it did in 1929, yet the rate of economic growth was not greatly affected, partly because governments applied Keynesian theory. Governments were expected to implement policies that would influence the direction of the economy when necessary.

Government policies to manage aggregate demand fall into three areas: fiscal policy, monetary policy, and trade policy.

The Basics of Fiscal Policy

Fiscal policy is the use by a government of its powers of expenditure, taxation, and borrowing to alter the size of the circular flow of income in the economy so as to bring about greater consumer demand, more employment, inflationary restraint, or other economic goals. If spending by households and business firms is too small, government can increase aggregate demand by increasing its own spending or by encouraging private spending. If private spending is too large, so that the economy is threatened with excessive inflation, government can reduce aggregate demand. It can do this by restricting its own spending and by discouraging private spending. When the government takes deliberate actions through legislation to alter spending or taxation policies in order to influence the level of spending and employment, it is using **discretionary fiscal policy**. Our basic framework of analysis is the aggregate demand and aggregate supply model.

Expansionary policy

When the economy is in a recession, aggregate demand is too low. Unemployment is high, and there is little, or negative, growth in output. The government may wish to increase aggregate demand by using an **expansionary fiscal policy**. This would entail a tax cut, an increase

in government spending, or both, to stimulate economic growth and lower unemployment rates. Figure 10.13 illustrates how this mechanism would work.

If the government decided to cut taxes, it would effectively increase the disposable income of consumers. Assuming that consumers did not save this increase, or spend it on imports, they would increase the aggregate demand in the economy through the consumption portion of the GDP equation. The increase in aggregate demand from AD_1 to AD_2 would lead to both an increase in employment levels and an increase in the growth of GDP as the equilibrium moved closer to full-employment output. Note that there would be little increase in the general level of prices as long as the equilibrium remained below full-employment equilibrium.

The same stimulation of the aggregate demand curve would occur, although for different reasons, if the government decided to enact an expansionary policy through an increase in the level of government spending. As one of the four components of GDP and, therefore, of aggregate demand, an increase in government spending would directly shift the aggregate demand curve to the right through the G portion of the GDP equation. Note that this influence is direct and has the intended effect. A reduction in the level of taxes requires

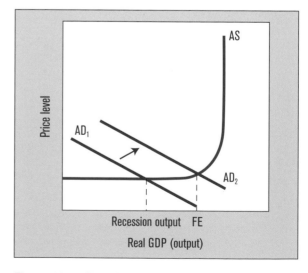

Figure 10.13 The effect of an expansionary fiscal policy.

consumers to follow through by spending their increase in income, which they may choose not to do. If they choose not to increase consumption, aggregate demand will not increase. Because an increase in government spending acts directly on aggregate demand, there is no risk that the policy will not have the desired effect.

Finally, if the government wanted to maximize the effect of its expansionary policy, it could use both a tax cut and a spending increase in order to stimulate aggregate demand as much as possible.

Contractionary policy

When the economy is suffering from inflation, aggregate demand is too high. Employment is high, and there is high growth in output. The government may wish to decrease aggregate demand by using a **contractionary fiscal policy**. This would entail a tax increase, a decrease in government spending, or both to reduce upward pressure on prices. Figure 10.14 illustrates how this measure would work.

If the government decided to increase taxes, this action would effectively decrease the disposable income of consumers. In turn, this would decrease the aggregate demand in the economy through the C portion of the GDP equation. The decrease in aggregate demand

from AD$_1$ to AD$_2$ would lead to a decrease in the inflation rate. However, the decrease would also have the trade-off of lowering GDP and employment levels as equilibrium moved back toward full-employment output.

The government could also address this problem by altering its spending. A reduction in government spending would reduce aggregate demand. As in expansionary policy, the use of both tools would increase the overall effect.

The overall goal of expansionary and contractionary fiscal policy (known as fiscal stabilization policy) is to smooth out the ups and downs of the business cycle, as indicated in Figure 10.15 (page 232).

Tools of Fiscal Policy

Changes in spending

If the government wants to stimulate the economy, it can increase general spending in all areas of its normal budgetary programs—health and welfare, culture, education, and so on. It can also undertake infrastructure programs. **Infrastructure** is the underlying economic foundation of goods and services that allows a society to operate. These programs might include the building of roads, hospitals, schools, and communications systems, such as the laying of fibre-optic cable. The added advantage of spending in these areas is that they add to the stock of capital goods and, therefore, promote the outward shift of the production possibilities curve in the future.

Changes in taxation

To restrain or stimulate economic activity, the government can also change the amount of tax that it collects. It has a number of options that it may consider in pursuing this policy. It could
• raise or lower personal and corporate income taxes and/or sales and excise taxes,
• alter tax exemptions or tax credits,*
• provide special tax incentives for investment, such as larger capital cost allowances on new buildings and equipment; this would influence aggregate demand through the I portion of the GDP equation.
(*Exemptions and credits are applied to uses of income on which you are not required to pay taxes,

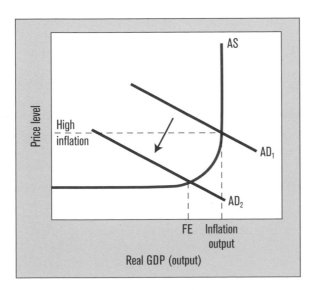

Figure 10.14 Effect of a contractionary fiscal policy.

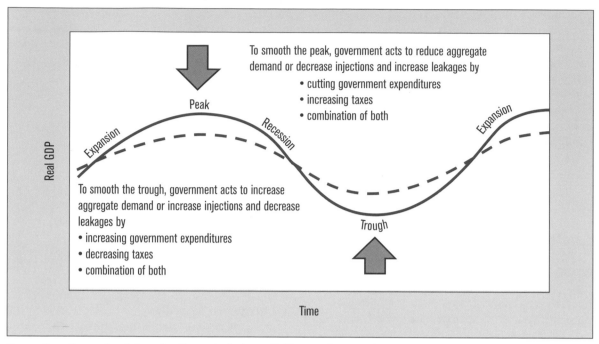

Figure 10.15 The effect of fiscal policy on the business cycle. A well-managed fiscal policy reduces the wide variations between the peaks and troughs of the business cycle, making the economy relatively more stable while encouraging steady growth.

such as tuition fees for post-secondary education and contributions to Registered Retirement Savings Plans—better known as RRSPs.)

Automatic stabilizers

So far we have looked at discretionary fiscal policies, which require that the government make specific decisions to implement the necessary changes to its spending and taxation policies. **Automatic stabilizers**, however, already exist and are acting on aggregate demand before a recession or inflationary trend takes hold. These stabilizers are mechanisms built into the economy that automatically increase aggregate demand when needed and decrease aggregate demand when the economy is too inflationary. They require absolutely no direct action or legislation by policy makers because they are already legislated.

Employment Insurance and welfare are automatic stabilizers. During periods of economic downturn, Employment Insurance payments increase as more people become unemployed. Since unemployment increases during recessionary periods, Employment Insurance payments help to maintain incomes and, thus, the consumption portion of GDP. If the recessionary period is prolonged, the number of people on welfare rolls also increases. The purpose of welfare is to ensure people a level of income so that they may survive, but these payments also help to increase consumption so that downward pressure on aggregate demand is somewhat cushioned. This either slows the leftward shifting of the AD curve or begins to increase AD.

Another common type of automatic stabilizer is tax rates that vary with levels of income. A **progressive tax** acts as a stabilizer in that it rises as incomes rise and has the effect of increasing a leakage as incomes grow. At lower levels of income, the tax rate may be 20 per cent, but as a person's income rises, it may start to be taxed at 30 per cent. These increases in the amount of tax collected slow down increases in consumption and, therefore, stop the aggregate demand curve from shifting too quickly to the right, which could lead to inflation.

Any built-in mechanism that increases or decreases government spending or taxation as the business cycle fluctuates is considered an automatic stabilizer. It is important to note that there is also a discretionary element to automatic stabilizers. At any time, the government may make a decision to change the level of spending or taxation. When these changes are made, they are considered discretionary fiscal measures.

Check Your Understanding

1. List the three leakages and the three injections that exist in an economy.

2. How do leakages and injections influence the aggregate demand curve?

3. How was Keynesian economics a radical departure from the classical school?

4. What is the difference between discretionary fiscal policy and automatic stabilizers?

5. Under what conditions would expansionary fiscal policy be used? Contractionary policy?

6. What three options are available to a government in pursuing fiscal policy?

Government Budget Options

Governments in Canada usually announce their changes in revenue and spending plans in the spring by outlining the coming year's budget. In establishing their budget, a government can end up in one of three situations:

• A **deficit budget** occurs when the government spends more than it collects in tax revenue. It must borrow the money to cover the shortfall.

• A **surplus budget** occurs when the government collects more in tax revenue than it spends. Consequently, it has money left over.

• A **balanced budget** results when the government spends an amount equal to what it has collected in tax revenue.

A term related to deficit budgets is debt. The **debt** is the total amount that a government owes on money it has borrowed to fund deficit budgets. For instance, if a government spends $150 billion in year 1 but takes in only $130 billion in revenues, it has a shortfall, or budget deficit, of $20 billion. In order to make up that shortfall, it must borrow the $20 bil-

lion. In year 2, the government still spends $150 billion (including interest on the debt incurred the previous year) and takes in $140 billion in revenues. This year it has a deficit of $10 billion and an accumulated debt of $30 billion ($20 billion from year 1 plus $10 billion from year 2).

Changing Opinions About Government Budgets

Over the past century, a number of opinions have been expressed as to how fiscal policy should be used; when the government should have deficit, surplus, and balanced budgets; and why these decisions should be made.

Annually balanced budget

Until the 1930s, the primary aim of fiscal policy in Canada was to ensure that government expenditure each year did not exceed revenue—in other words, to balance the annual budget. During the Great Depression, the problem with a balanced budget policy—that it may exacerbate an existing problem in the economy—became obvious. If the government seeks to balance the budget during recessionary

The Multiplier Effect

Increasing government spending to help boost economic output seems rather like trying to fill an ocean with an eyedropper. In a country with a real GDP that is close to $1000 billion, how much of an effect could an increase in government spending have? Even if government spending increased by $5 billion, that amount is only a small fraction of the GDP.

The above argument would be true if it were not for the impact that the multiplier has on increases in government spending. The **multiplier effect** is easier to understand in the context of **marginal propensity to consume (MPC)** and **marginal propensity to withdraw (MPW)**. These terms refer to a person's likelihood to spend extra income on domestically produced goods and services or to withdraw extra income from the circular flow of income in the form of savings, taxes, or imports.

MPC measures the change in consumption spending that occurs with a rise or fall in domestic income. By measuring how consumption changes in response to a rise in income, economists can make predictions about how a rise in income will affect the economy as a whole. MPC is calculated as follows:

$$\frac{\Delta \text{ consumption}}{\Delta \text{ income}} = \text{MPC}$$

"Δ" is read as "change in." This would be calculated by subtracting the new value from the old value. For example, a change in income would be: (income in year 2 − income in year 1).

MPW measures the change in withdrawals due to savings, taxes, and buying of imports that occurs with a rise or fall in domestic income. MPW is calculated as follows:

$$\frac{\Delta \text{ withdrawals}}{\Delta \text{ income}} = \text{MPW}$$

Now try a simple numerical example. Let us say a household's income rises by $10 000, and the family chooses to spend $8000 of it on consumer items and $1500 on imports and saves the last $500. In this example, the MPC would be 0.8 and the MPW would be 0.2. These values are calculated as follows:

$$\frac{\Delta \text{ consumption}}{\Delta \text{ income}} = \frac{\$8000}{\$10\ 000} = 0.8$$

$$\frac{\Delta \text{ withdrawals}}{\Delta \text{ income}} = \frac{\$2000}{\$10\ 000} = 0.2$$

The family in the above example spent 80 per cent of the increase in their income. If all families in the economy did this, there would be a cumulative impact. For example, family 1 spent $8000 of their increase in income. This $8000 represented an increase in income to whomever received it. This person would then spend 80 per cent of this sum, or $6400. This amount would be received by another family, who would spend 80 per cent of it, or $5120. This re-spending would continue until the fraction becomes so small that the increase in income is finally exhausted.

If one were to add up all the re-spending in the economy that came from this initial increase in income, it would be possible to estimate the final increase in the GDP. The factor by which it increases is known as the multiplier. The magnitude of the multiplier depends on the size of the leakages from the flow of spending. The formula to determine the multiplier is:

$$\frac{1}{\text{MPW}} = \text{multiplier}$$

The multiplier in the above example is:

$$\frac{1}{0.2} = 5$$

This means that if all the rounds of spending were added together, the GDP would increase by a total of five times the initial increase in income. For our example above, that would mean an increase in GDP of $5 \times \$10\ 000$ or a total of $\$50\ 000$. As for the $5-billion increase in government spending that was indicated at the beginning of this section, the multiplier would turn this into a $25-billion increase in GDP.

The multiplier in Canada has been estimated at between 1.4 and 2, largely because of the leakage role that taxes play on increased incomes. This means that reductions in taxation levels could have a significant impact on GDP. Not only do reductions increase disposable income for con-sumption spending; they also decrease the MPW, which would increase the multiplier.

QUESTIONS

1. The Morris family has an income of $50 000 and uses $40 000 of it for consumption. They receive an increase in income to $75 000 and now spend $60 000 on consumption. What is their marginal propensity to consume?

2. If the above scenario held true for all individuals in the economy, and the source of the increase in income was a $50-million rise in government spending, by how much would the GDP increase after the full effect of the multiplier?

periods, it must either cut back spending or increase taxes. Both policies serve to intensify the effects of the recession by holding back aggregate demand. By cutting back spending, the G portion of GDP is reduced. By increasing taxes, the government reduces incomes due to increased tax leakages, which would reduce the C portion of GDP. Either way, the current economic problem is intensified—the recession is made worse. Conversely, during inflationary periods, tax revenues rise, and the government is forced to increase spending or lower the tax rate in order to balance the budget. Either way, more income is put back into the circular flow, causing upward pressure on aggregate demand and subsequently causing further inflation.

Cyclically balanced budget

According to Keynesian economists, governments should use their fiscal policy to achieve a high, stable level of national income with neither unemployment nor inflation. If an economic recession begins, the government should start to spend more than it receives in tax revenues. Such a policy is centred on altering fiscal decisions according to changes in the business cycle. During a recessionary phase, governments should run deficits by increasing government spending, decreasing taxes, or both. During an inflationary phase, govern-ments should run surpluses by decreasing government spending, increasing taxes, or both. The idea is that during weak economic times governments should work to stimulate the economy; during expansionary and peak periods of economic activity the government should work to slow the economy. Over the whole cycle, the deficits and surpluses should balance. The government's role, then, is to act as a stabilizer.

This type of budgetary fiscal policy, which was introduced after the Great Depression, was criticized for not recognizing that the economy can sink into long periods of economic recession and unemployment, as happened in the 1930s, while subsequent expansionary phases may be relatively short. Because of these factors the budget may not be balanced over the business cycle, which would mean a possible steady growth in the debt.

Deficit and surplus budgets as necessary

An extension of Keynesian theory held that fiscal budgets could be managed from the perspective of running deficits or surpluses when necessary. A deficit budget would be used only when the economy needed a boost. If a debt was accumulated as a result, so be it. The general health of the economy was more important than the balancing of budgets over the business cycle. Since the Great Depression, the expansionary periods have been longer than the contractionary periods, so a large debt should not be an issue. But by the year 2000, Canada had a federal debt of $564.8 billion. What had happened? One theory is that there is a conflict between election cycles in Canada and the business cycle.

Between 1967 and 1997, the federal government posted a deficit budget in 24 of 31 years. Many of these years were periods of economic boom when, according to the "budget as necessary" theory, there should have been budget surpluses. It is hard for governments to make budget cuts in general, but it is even harder when they are thinking about being re-elected. Generally, in the first two years of their mandate, governments make the toughest spending cuts—long before voters have to cast a ballot.

The nearer the time for an election, the harder it is to make spending cuts. In fact, a government that wants to be re-elected is more likely to increase spending and decrease taxes, possibly running a budget deficit even when the economy does not need it. The result may be increased inflation, but it also certainly means an increase in the federal debt. Figures 10.16 and 10.17 show the history of Canada's federal debt from 1980 to 2000.

Economists have identified two components to budget deficits. The **cyclical deficit** is that part of the deficit that is incurred in trying to pull an economy out of a recession. It would include spending on infrastructure projects and programs that invest in human capital, such as job retraining or the upgrading of skills. The second component, the **structural deficit**, is the amount above the cyclical deficit that would exist even if the economy were operat-

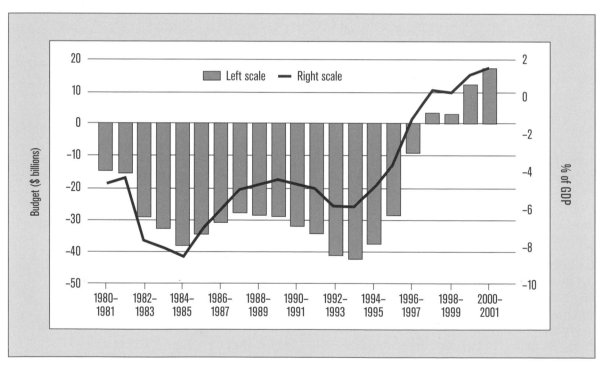

Source: "Federal Budgeting Balance (Public Account Basis)" from *The Budget Plan 2001*. Reproduced with the permission of the Minister of Public Works and Government Services Canada, 2002.

Figure 10.16 Federal budgetary balance, 1980–2000. The bar graphs show the amount of the deficit (below the line identified as 0, which would be a balanced budget) or surplus (above the line) in each of the years between 1980 and 2001. The line graph displays the percentage that the deficit or surplus was of the Gross Domestic Product. For example, the deficit in 1984–1985 was approximately $38 billion, which represented about 8 per cent of the GDP that year.

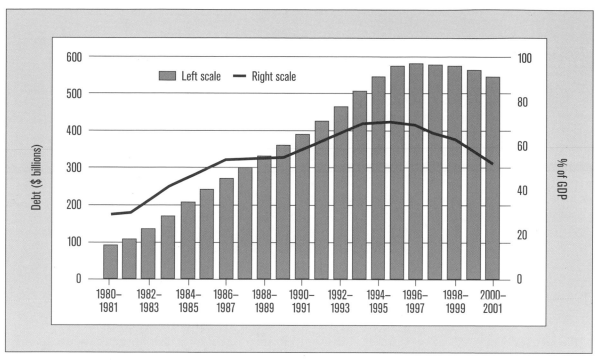

Source: "Federal Net Debt (Public Account Basis)" from *The Budget Plan 2001*. Reproduced with the permission of the Minister of Public Works and Government Services Canada, 2002.

Figure 10.17 Federal net debt, 1980–2000. The bar graphs show the growth and decline of the federal net debt from 1980 to 2000. The line graph shows the amount of this debt expressed as percentage of the Gross Domestic Product. Many economists feel that this debt-to-GDP ratio is the most appropriate measure of debt because it measures debt relative to the country's ability to finance it in terms of economic output.

ing at full employment. In general, economists agree that cyclical deficits are good because they help to stabilize the business cycle. However, many economists consider the presence of a structural deficit to be a sign of financial mismanagement. Over the long term, if a government runs a structural deficit, it is not able to control spending in line with the needs of the economy.

Full-employment budget

The latest thinking on fiscal policy is that governments should try to achieve a non-inflationary, full-employment level of output. That is, they should intervene with fiscal policy only when the economy falls below its full-employment targets. As discussed in Chapter 9, full employment in Canada is considered to be achieved when the unemployment rate is in the range of 6 to 7 per cent. In theory, full

employment would entail using just the right amount of government spending, taxation, or both, combined with the multiplier effect, to shift the aggregate demand curve so that it intersects aggregate supply at full-employment equilibrium. In doing so, the government would run only cyclical deficits; structural deficits would not exist.

Drawbacks and Limitations of Fiscal Policy

While the application of fiscal policy has increased since the 1930s, it is still controversial. There are a number of drawbacks and limitations in its use that must be considered:
• *The time lags that exist in utilizing fiscal policy are significant.* First, there is the **recognition lag**, or the time the government takes to recognize a problem in the economy. Second,

A Matter of Opinion | Why Debt Reduction Is a Tax Increase

" Finance Minister Paul Martin has made a virtue of the Liberal plan to use surpluses to pay down federal debt. In his last Official Overhead Slide Projection of All the Budget Numbers We Think You Need, Mr. Martin announced $15 billion in debt reduction, a worthy act that he said will "reduce the burden on future generations." Most economists approve, as do a large majority of Canadians. Various business groups, along with the Canadian Alliance, also routinely urge Ottawa to set debt reduction as a priority. Paying down debt is one of those things that just sounds like the right thing to do. But it isn't, at least not the way Ottawa is going about it.

Reducing debt smacks of good financial management. Every Canadian can identify with the idea that too much debt is a dangerous burden that should be eliminated. But the arguments in favour of debt reduction are mostly misleading. What we have in Ottawa, moreover, is not so much removal of debt as the creation of new spending room. In other words, debt reduction is turning into a vehicle for long-term spending increases and the maintenance of higher tax rates.

Paying down debt is also not necessarily good financial management. Canadians generally like the idea because it fits with their own personal financial views. Mortgages should be paid down, credit card balances should be reduced, you don't want to die destitute. Mr. Martin plays to this theme. "Just as individual Canadians pay down their credit cards when times are better, governments must do the same."

Governments, however, are not mortal individuals with limited lifetimes and tightly defined income cycles. You work, spend, borrow, save, pay off debts, then you die. The economy, by contrast, is a perpetual machine that has unlimited growth and expansion potential. High debt levels, even when they exceed prudent ratios as they have in Canada, quickly disappear with growth and the passage of time.

Ottawa's net public debt is already in steep decline as a percentage of the economy, but this has almost no relation to debt paydown activity. From a peak of more than 71 per cent of GDP five years ago, net debt has dropped to below 53 per cent, a decline of 18 percentage points. Mr. Martin likes to spin that reduction as a major government achievement. "In recent years no country has reduced this ratio as much as Canada." But only about 3 points of that 18-point decline can be attributed to the Liberal debt reduction scheme.

The real driver of debt reduction as a percentage of GDP is growth in the economy. In fact, with every year of 5 per cent nominal growth in the economy, Canada's debt-to-GDP ratio will automatically fall by 3 percentage points a year and would reach 40 per cent by 2005—without one cent of formal debt reduction payments. And at 40 per cent, even cautious economists would agree there is minimal distortion and risk to the economy.

If Ottawa's debt-to-GDP ratio is already on automatic pilot downward, why bother using surpluses to pay it down even further, especially when the incremental impact on debt ratios is marginal? Mr. Martin has already provided the answer. In his peek-a-boo financial show the other day, he said the $15 billion paid toward the debt is part of a plan. "This means that we will have retired more than $33 billion of debt in the last four years ... saving Canadians close to $2 billion a year in interest payments—money that can be used for other priorities such as health care and education, year in and year out."

Year in and year out, in other words, direct debt reduction so far will give the government an extra $2 billion to spend. That's the real reason Ottawa is keen on debt reduction. Instead of giving $33 billion in surpluses to Canadians as tax reductions, and letting the debt ratio slide nicely on its own, Ottawa has found a way to hold on to the tax revenue associated with the debt. The interest savings do not go to Canadians, as Mr. Martin put it; they are retained by the government to maintain taxes and renew spending.

Much is made of tax-cutting operations in Ottawa and the provinces. But there is little evidence that total government taxation is in decline as a share of the economy. Maybe the tax line will start to shift down in coming years. To date, however, taxation is at near-record highs and high-profile debt reduction plans are just another Ottawa technique for holding on to the record. **,,**

Source: Terence Corcoran, "Why debt reduction is a tax increase" from *National Post*, 31 May 2001. Reprinted by permission of National Post.

QUESTIONS

1. Why does the author say that the debt incurred by governments is different from that incurred by individuals?
2. The author claims that debt reduction as a percentage of GDP has little to do with controlling government spending. Explain his reasoning.
3. Explain the "real reason" for debt reduction, according to the author. Do you agree? What reasons might the author have for making his claims?

there is the **decision lag**, the time required for the government to determine the most appropriate policy. Third, there is an **implementation lag**: once the decision has been made, various government departments have to figure out just how to implement the new directives regarding spending and taxation. Finally, there is the **impact lag**. Once the policy is in place, time is required before its full effects can be felt through the multiplier effect. The total time lag may amount to years. In fact, the problem may already have self-corrected before the fiscal policy takes hold. Automatic stabilizers help to minimize the impact of these lags.

- *The government might have difficulty changing spending and taxation policies.* Raising taxes is often unpopular. Cutting spending may be impossible if there are long-term contracts or the programs are very popular with citizens. The timing of government elections may also influence spending and taxation policies.
- *Conflict between the various levels of government regarding the appropriate fiscal policy might limit effectiveness.* If the federal government is reducing spending and increasing taxes in an effort to slow down economic growth, and a powerful provincial government is increasing spending and cutting taxes in order to gain

political support, the two policies may offset each other.
- *Regional variations may exist that interfere with the implementation of fiscal policy.* If part of the country is doing well while another region is suffering from a slowdown, what policy should be used? An expansionary policy would likely cause inflation in the region doing well, yet a contractionary policy would make the recession worse in the part of the country suffering a slowdown.
- *The size of the debt can also limit the use of fiscal policy as an effective tool.* In recent years, the federal debt in Canada has grown so large that there is much political pressure not to increase it further. If an expansionary policy were desired, the government would have little room to increase spending and cut taxes without further additions to the debt. Recently, discretionary fiscal policy has played a less significant role when dealing with the overall management of the economy. The federal government and most provincial governments made deficit reduction the primary focus of fiscal policy during the latter half of the 1990s and let the Bank of Canada take the economic reins through monetary management.
- *Some economists believe that a **crowding out** of private investment occurs when the government*

competes with the private sector to borrow funds to finance the debt. They argue that this policy drives up interest rates and reduces the amount available for private investment. As a result, investment in capital goods decreases and the rate of economic growth slows.

• *Deficits redistribute income from all taxpayers to bondholders.* In a sense, the deficit creates a debt that we owe in large part to ourselves. The government sells bonds and treasury bills in order to finance some of that debt. This is known as the marketable debt. Canada's Department of Finance estimated in 2001 that approximately 80 per cent of the federal marketable debt was in the hands of Canadians while 20 per cent was held by foreign investors. However, only some Canadian citizens are the government's creditors. The government pays interest on the debt but does so with tax dollars. In reality, the people who hold bonds are receiving a portion of the tax dollars paid by all Canadians. Most government bondholders are corporations or those with above-average incomes. Creating debt and financing it through bonds redistributes income from the poor in society to the rich—because most income earners pay taxes, yet the interest payments go only to bondholders.

• *Deficits impose a net burden on future generations because the foreign-owned portion of the debt removes capital from the country when interest is paid.* Here, it depends on what the deficit is used for. If the money is spent on economic infrastructure, such as roads or buildings, then future generations will get the benefit of using those expenditures. If, however, the deficit is created because of current expenditures, such as employee salaries or Employment Insurance payments, then future generations will derive no net benefit from the debt that is created.

Check Your Understanding

1. Describe the three options that exist in establishing a government budget.

2. How is the "debt" different from the "deficit"?

3. Why is structural deficit considered a sign of financial mismanagement in the application of fiscal policy?

4. How do automatic stabilizers help to deal with the problem of time lags in fiscal policy?

CHAPTER SUMMARY

- Aggregate demand is the total demand for all goods and services produced in a society at any given price level.

- Aggregate supply is the total supply of all goods and services produced in a society at any given price level.

- Full-employment equilibrium occurs when the aggregate demand curve intersects the aggregate supply curve at a level of output consistent with full employment.

- An economy that has too little aggregate demand will have a recessionary gap that reflects unemployment, low inflation, and low levels of GDP.

- An economy that has too much aggregate demand will have an inflationary gap that reflects high employment, high inflation, and high levels of GDP.

- The aggregate demand curve will shift if any of the GDP equation components are changed.

- The aggregate supply curve will shift as changes occur in the amount of inputs available, efficiency, and the price of inputs.

- All economies face business cycles that reflect alternating periods of economic growth and contraction.

- The movements of the aggregate demand curve explain these alternating periods of growth and contraction.

- Changes in aggregate demand can also be explained by leakages and injections in the circular flow of income.

- The government may choose to influence aggregate demand by changing spending and taxation policies, an action known as fiscal policy.

- Fiscal policy includes both discretionary and automatic tools.

- The multiplier effect magnifies the impact of fiscal policies on the final change in output.

- Government budgets are used to implement fiscal policy and are classified as deficit, surplus, or balanced budgets.

- The debt is an accumulation of money owing because of yearly deficit budgets.

- The application of fiscal policy has a number of drawbacks and limitations that must be considered.

Key Terms

aggregate demand (AD)
aggregate supply (AS)
full-employment equilibrium
recessionary gap
inflationary gap
business cycle
prosperity cycle
recession
depression
circular flow of income
leakage
injection
stabilization policies
fiscal policy
discretionary fiscal policy
expansionary fiscal policy
contractionary fiscal policy
infrastructure
automatic stabilizers
progressive tax
deficit budget
surplus budget
balanced budget
debt
multiplier effect
marginal propensity to consume (MPC)
marginal propensity to withdraw (MPW)
cyclical deficit
structural deficit
recognition lag
decision lag
implementation lag
impact lag
crowding out

Activities

Thinking/Inquiry

1. In a situation of declining GDP, rising unemployment, and a budget that already has a small deficit, explain the effect that each of the following government actions would have on the economy, the current year's budget, and the national debt:

   a) a reduction in personal income taxes
   b) a reduction in social welfare payments
   c) an increase in public works projects
   d) an increase in corporate taxes

2. Suppose an economy is operating at full-employment equilibrium. What will happen to output and price levels in the face of each of the following events?

   a) a cut in income taxes
   b) a decrease in business investment
   c) introduction of new technology that improves productivity
   d) a decrease in the value of the Canadian dollar that increases exports
   e) an increase in Canadians' level of saving

3. One of the dangers of using expansionary fiscal policy is that it can cause inflation. Under what circumstances is an expansionary fiscal policy likely to cause inflation?

4. Conduct research into any two other economic measures that change with the business cycle. How do changes in these measures relate to the business cycle? Assess whether these measures could be used to predict changes in the business cycle before they actually occur.

5. Analyze the data presented in Figures 9.2 (page 200), 9.4 (page 204), and 9.10 (page 208), and sketch a business cycle that is consistent with the data. For each of your "peaks" and "troughs," record the growth rate, unemployment rate, and inflation rate.

Communication

6. Go to the Canadian Department of Finance Web site. Write a summary of the main points in the Minister of Finance's latest budget statement. Identify the spending and taxing priorities. What kind of fiscal policy do you think is being followed? Assess the impact these policies will have on the national debt.

7. Write a response to the author of the article "Why Debt Reduction Is a Tax Increase" (page 238) in the form of a letter to the

editor. Explain why you agree or disagree with the author, using what you have learned in this chapter.

8. Figure 10.9 (page 224) displays the prosperity cycle that occurs when there is a boom. Create a flow chart that shows what a depression cycle would look like when a contraction is occurring.

9. The country is suffering from a recessionary phase in the business cycle, and the federal government is carrying out an expansionary fiscal policy. The government of one of the more populous provinces is increasing taxes and decreasing government spending in order to get its provincial debt under control. As the minister of finance, write a letter to the premier of this province explaining the problem with this situation. Use aggregate supply and demand curves to further your argument. How might you convince the premier that following a slightly expansionary policy could help the provincial government achieve its goal?

Application

10. A fiscal policy is introduced because a recession seems to be starting. Describe what would happen to aggregate supply and demand and the three main economic measures if time lags cause the fiscal policy to take hold after the recession has already corrected itself.

11. Explain the impact of each of the following fiscal policies on economic output and price levels, using aggregate supply and demand analysis:

a) Increase government expenditures and leave tax revenues unchanged when the economy is in a recession.

b) Increase tax revenues and leave government expenditures unchanged when the economy is suffering from inflation.

c) Increase government expenditures and increase tax revenues when the economy is in a recession.

12. What would be the objective of a government fiscal policy that results in increases in government spending and decreases in personal taxes? Illustrate using AD and AS curves.

13. Use aggregate demand and aggregate supply analysis to explain why a significant increase in the price of inputs is such a serious problem that even the application of fiscal policy may fail to address it.

14. On a trip to the East Coast, you discover that the local economy has been depressed because of restrictions on fishing. You spend over $3000 on hotels, restaurants, and entertainment. What factors will influence the actual amount by which total GDP rises in the region because of your expenditures?

15. If the marginal propensity to withdraw is 0.4 and your government wants to raise the GDP by a total of $300 million, by how much must you increase government spending?

CHAPTER 11

MONEY AND BANKING

Record Price Expected for Rare Note

It may once have been a gambler's emergency grubstake or a bootlegger's booty.

But whatever its history, an American auction house is hoping a rare Canadian $500 bill from 1911 will fetch a record price at an auction in Florida next month.

Dallas-based Heritage Numismatic Auctions Inc. is suggesting the Dominion of Canada note could bring at least US$125 000, about Can$187 000.

"The problem with rarity is that it's hard to determine value," says Bob Korver, director of the company.

"What is it worth? The real answer to that question will be decided at the auction."

He said the previous auction record for Canadian paper currency is likely the US$35 000—about Can$52 500—that a 1935 Canadian $500 bill fetched just last year....

The only two known specimens of the 1911 $500 bill are both in the hands of US collectors.

Source: Excerpts from "Record price expected for rare note" reprinted by permission of The Canadian Press.

QUESTIONS

1. Why are people willing to pay so much for this bill? Use demand and supply analysis to determine your answer.

2. Have you ever seen or handled a $500 bill? What kind of money has largely replaced the use of large bills?

3. The government recently phased out $1000 bills. Speculate on the reason for this action.

4. What are your feelings about the fact that the owners of these rare pieces of Canadiana are not Canadian? Should our government step in to buy these notes? Explain.

Chapter Goals

By the end of this chapter, you will be able to

- understand the purpose, history, and functions of money in an economy,
- recognize how banks create money by their lending activities,
- identify the differences between the Canadian and US banking systems,
- explain how the Canadian money supply is measured,
- describe how the nature of banking and money is changing.

The Role of Money in an Economy

In the previous chapter, we learned how government fiscal policy attempts to stabilize the economy by influencing our spending on goods and services. We use **money** to pay for these goods and services, which we purchase from individuals or businesses. In this chapter, we shall examine the origin and development of money from very early times to the present. We'll see that banks began first as storehouses to safeguard gold and silver coins. Later, banks discovered that they could create a new type of money, bank deposits, which today comprises almost all our economy's money supply. In the next chapter, we'll find out how the government attempts to influence the size of that money supply, and thus our spending, through its monetary policy.

The History of Money

Money was not invented at one time or in one place. As societies progressed from producing a few goods that sustained life to producing many goods that also enriched life, money came about as a necessity. Thousands of years ago, small groups dependent on hunting and gathering spent most of their time trying to provide themselves with enough food, shelter, and clothing simply to survive. Few goods were produced, and any exchanges of goods between people were carried out through barter. The value of a good was determined in relation to another good, usually in terms of weight. It might be agreed, for example, that two goats were equal to one cow or to a given amount of wheat. Although it worked well enough for exchanges between these hunter-gatherers, barter still faced the **double coincidence of wants** problem. This meant that if a person wanted to exchange wheat in return for goats, that person had to find someone who had goats and wanted wheat. This is a key problem in the system of barter—one that led people to invent money.

As far as we know, cattle were the first type of money. Initially bartered for other goods, cattle came to be the *measure of value* for all other goods and, eventually, the *medium of exchange*, a type of money that was used to buy a good from a seller. No longer did a person have to offer what another wanted and want what the other offered.

As hunting and gathering societies evolved into agricultural economies, settling in the great river valleys of the Middle East, India, and China, farmers were able to produce surpluses of food. These surpluses allowed some people to shift their energies from working the land to taking on other occupations. They became artisans, merchants, soldiers, government officials, priests, and so on. These specialists needed a way to obtain food, shelter, and clothing. For example, it was difficult for someone who produced metal agricultural tools to barter or to obtain cattle (which could then be used as a form of money to purchase necessities). Thus, money became vital to acquiring the growing number of goods that these more developed economies were producing. As societies continued to advance, money took on different forms. We see this pattern throughout economic history: money continues to evolve as economies become more developed and more complex.

The evolution of currency

Commodities

Money can be defined as anything that is generally acceptable in purchasing goods or settling debts. We are most familiar with coins and notes, but cattle, oxen, wheat, shells, salt, amber—even whisky—have all served as money in various societies. These items are called **commodity money** because they had value in themselves. Although cattle were most commonly used as money in early agricultural societies, they were not practical for small transactions because they are not divisible while they are alive! As various societies discovered metals, cattle were usually replaced by smaller commodities such as metal picks, hoes, and fishhooks.

About 5000 years ago, gold, silver, and copper were introduced as commodity money. They were first used in the form of ornaments or jewellery then were given value by weight and made into ingots, usually oblong pieces of metal. By 3000 BCE, Babylonia was using silver as money, measuring it by units of weight (known as shekels and talents) that had originated for grain measurement. Today, the shekel is the principal unit of money in Israel. The British pound dates from the time when precious metals were circulated by weight. The pound was originally an amount of silver weighing a pound; in 1816, Britain switched to the gold standard, a concept we'll explore later in the chapter.

Coinage

The next stage was to mint the metals into coinage. The use of gold and silver as money, which merchants measured using grain on their scales, began to supersede their use as commodities. The ancient Lydians, a people living in what is now modern-day Turkey, are credited with minting the first coins in the seventh century BCE. The Greeks copied the Lydian idea and produced their own coinage, spreading it throughout their Mediterranean trading empire.

After Alexander the Great amassed his empire, the custom began of imprinting the head of the ruler on coinage as a guarantee of the purity and weight of the metal. Even these coins, however, could not deter the ruler's subjects—or even the ruler—from the temptation to cheat. Small slivers of gold or silver were collected by shaving the edges of coins, a process called *clipping*. *Sweating* was another method of collecting gold or silver slivers and dust, done by shaking the coins vigorously in a bag. The slivers and dust were then melted down and either formed into new coins or sold for making jewellery.

Rulers often *debased* the coins they issued by reducing their stated gold or silver content. They would then mint new coins that indicated the same stated value but that actually contained a smaller portion of gold or silver in order to provide extra revenue for themselves.

Paper

Paper money was the next stage in the evolution of money. The Chinese were the first people to develop paper money and did so in the seventh century CE. From the seventh to the 11th centuries CE, paper receipts were issued by Christian monastic orders for coinage deposited for safekeeping in monasteries and churches. By the 13th century, Italian merchants in Venice, Genoa, and Florence had taken their place, operating as merchant-bankers. The paper receipts were used to transfer ownership of coinage from one person to another, but it was not until the 17th century that goldsmiths in England introduced paper receipts as a form of money that could be used to purchase goods.

Travelling merchants and people who held large numbers of coins or precious metals in bulk found it safer to deposit their money with a local goldsmith and accept a receipt for the amount deposited. These receipts then could be transferred to another person as payment for a good or service, with the assumption that, at any time, the holder could redeem the receipt for the metals stored safely in the goldsmith's vault. As long as the goldsmith was reliable, the receipts were "as good as gold." By the 17th century, the idea that paper could represent monetary value was accepted in England and then in continental Europe. It was a short step from paper receipts to paper **currency**, which promised the holder gold on demand.

The origins of banking and money creation

The goldsmiths discovered that the holders of their receipts seldom returned for payment of the full amount of gold or silver because the receipts themselves were safer and easier to use as a form of money. While small amounts of the precious metals or coins might be withdrawn, generally, the store of valuable metals in the vaults continued to pile up. A wonderful opportunity to make money now presented itself.

A goldsmith could make a loan from the untouched coinage or metals in the vault and charge the borrower interest on it. The goldsmith would insist that the borrower secure the loan by pledging property or other valuable assets that would be surrendered if the loan was not repaid. The loan itself would be granted in the form of a simple notation in the goldsmith's account books. Borrowers might use a loan for a good or service by transferring some or all of it to the account of another customer of the goldsmith. They might also take the loan in the form of paper certificates that promised payment in gold or coinage and use these certificates for payment.

Goldsmiths felt secure in the knowledge that borrowers, like the original depositors of the coinage, tended to leave most of the coinage to which their paper certificates entitled them untouched and idle in the vaults. Now there was more paper in circulation than there was coinage and metal to back it up. With the creation of paper currency, along with the notations in their account books, goldsmiths had, in reality, created money.

In their lending and deposit-accepting roles, goldsmiths had also created banking, based on the discovery that only a *fraction* of the total amount of money deposited for safekeeping needed to be kept on *reserve*. The rest could be lent in the form of paper. Thus, **fractional reserve banking** was born, ushering in a change in the nature of money. We'll learn more about this system later in the chapter when we look at Canadian banking.

Central banks

There is no doubt that if the holders of the goldsmiths' paper receipts or the borrowers with notations in the account books had all wanted to cash in at the same time, there would have been insufficient coins and metals to pay them. Indeed, this situation has occurred in every country at one time or another. When a financial crisis developed—as the result, possibly, of a war or a poor harvest—a "run on the banks" took place as note holders demanded payment in "hard money." The banks, unable to pay all the holders of their notes, were forced to close their doors and declare bankruptcy. During the 19th and early 20th centuries, many banks collapsed in Europe, Canada, and the United States, taking with them the savings of their depositors. Between 1867 and 1900, for example, there were 51 banks in Canada; by 1900, 17 had failed or had been stripped of their charters.

The collapse of these banks, along with the problems associated with coinage and paper money, led to demands for federal governments to establish central banks and regulate the issue of coins and paper money. The Bank of England, founded in 1694, was one of the first central banks to be established with the support of its national government. Canada's central bank, the Bank of Canada, was established in 1934. By the 20th century, most nations had central banks to regulate private banks, provide security for depositors, and issue currency. Paper currency, once issued by the private banks, was now issued by the central banks.

Like the goldsmiths' paper receipts, most national currencies were convertible into gold, until the 1930s. Nations that promised to pay gold on demand for their notes were said to be on the **gold standard**. Central banks counted on the fact that all the national currency would not be presented for payment in gold at the same time. Thus, like the goldsmiths, they could issue more currency than the amount of gold held in reserve—within limits. But with the Great Depression of the 1930s, most nations "unhooked" their currencies from gold, abandoning the gold standard. The terrible insecurity of the Depression had undermined people's confidence in the soundness of their currency. Governments feared that their citizens might suddenly demand gold for their currency—gold that governments did not have in sufficient quantity to meet demand. Currencies became known as **fiat money**—in other words, money that is accepted not because it can be exchanged for gold but because governments declare that it is **legal tender** and, therefore, must be accepted for all payments.

Bank deposit money

So far in our description of money, we have concentrated mostly on currency—coins and paper. Although currency is the most visible type of money that we use, it is not the most important. In fact, currency comprises only about 7 to 8 per cent of the total money supply in more developed countries. The rest of the supply is called **bank deposit money**, most of which is created by the banks when they grant loans (in the same way the goldsmiths did in earlier times). We shall discover how this money is created when we examine the Canadian banking system.

A MATTER OF OPINION | Will Electronic Money Replace Cash?

As we move ever further into the Information Age, technology continues to redefine what constitutes money, as the following article illustrates.

" Electronic money offers the user the choice of keeping money in dollars, marks, yen, or any combination of currencies. In the near future, financial corporations may begin to offer their own electronic money to compete with the national currencies in use today. Private currencies may be invented based on gold, on a particular mixture of commodities or currencies, or simply on the reputation and financial strength of a particular money-issuing entity. We might have Citicorp Currency, Yamamoto Yen, or Dresdener Talers, each based on the financial strength and reputation of its backer.

The electronic network allows money to become more personalized even as it makes the ties between customers and merchants less personalized. Electronic money comes in far greater varieties than traditional currency— e-cash, e-money, cyber cash, DigiCash, cyberbucks, and as many other forms as people care to create and float. Market forces will push many of these currencies out of use, but rather than just reducing money to a few name brands—the way credit cards were reduced to Visa, Discover, MasterCard, and a few others— the new currencies will likely become special-purpose moneys. Consumers in the near future are likely to use several types of electronic money, depending on the kind of service or product they are purchasing. In addition to the live forms of electronic money on the wire, they will have several forms of cash cards in their pockets or, at least, several kinds of accounts on a single card....

[In the past] each technological change in money production added a new type of money and spread its use into new areas, but the changes did not eradicate the old types.... Paper money altered the role of gold and silver coins but did not end their usefulness. Similarly, electronic money has added yet more types but without destroying paper or coins....

Electronic money promises to expand the role of money in our society even farther than metal, paper, and plastic were able to do. People will create new uses for electronic money that we cannot even imagine and that could not have been possible with the earlier forms of money. "

Source: Excerpts from *The History of Money* by Jack Weatherford. Copyright © 1997 by Jack Weatherford. Used by permission of Crown Publishers, a division of Random House, Inc.

QUESTIONS

1. According to the writer, how will electronic money make money more personalized?

2. Devise a scenario in which a business or an individual could create a special-use currency.

Check Your Understanding

1. a) Why can the barter system work in small economies with few goods?
   b) Why does it become difficult to barter as economies produce more goods?

2. Why did metals serve as a better form of money than commodity money?

3. a) Why were people willing to accept paper receipts?
   b) What advantages did paper receipts have over gold and silver as money?

4. Why could goldsmiths lend more money than they had in their vaults? What risks were involved?

5. Why would people have more confidence in the paper currency issued by a central bank than in that issued by individual banks?

6. Suppose that banks today were required to keep 100 per cent reserves against their deposits. What would be the result?

What Is Money?

We have defined money as anything that is generally acceptable as payment for goods and services. Our study of the history of money reveals that as money evolves, it becomes steadily more abstract. From being acceptable only as a valuable commodity in itself, money progressed to coins and paper backed by gold and silver, to fiat money representing value, to notations in bank accounts. Today, we are moving into another stage dominated by **electronic money** (which was discussed in the feature "Will Electronic Money Replace Cash?" on page 248).

The Functions of Money

It is said that "money is what money does." People will accept anything as money as long as it performs the three functions for which it is designed. We'll examine each of these functions in turn, starting with the most important.

A medium of exchange

Barter, as you will recall, requires a double coincidence of wants. For example, your desire for a new sound system can be met only if the good you are willing to trade, say a computer, is wanted by someone else who has a sound system. It would require much time and effort to find someone who wanted what you have and who also had what you wanted—time that both of you could be using for some other productive activity. Using money as a **medium of exchange**, you save time: you can sell the computer to any willing buyer then use the money to buy a sound system from any seller.

The time and effort wasted in barter force people to try to become as self-sufficient as possible because they cannot be assured of obtaining through trade the goods they may need. Money, however, gives people the freedom to specialize in the goods and services they produce because they can then obtain the other goods they need through purchase. When people specialize, they become more skilled and productive at what they do, contributing to an increase in their community's total wealth.

As a medium of exchange, cash is legal tender in Canada. Strictly speaking, bank deposits that are exchangeable by cheque or debit card are not legal tender because they may not be accepted for all payments. Their acceptance depends on people's confidence that deposits can be converted into cash.

A measure of value

As a **measure of value**, or **standard unit of account**, money allows us to compare the value of various goods in our economy. In the barter system, the value of any good would be expressed in terms of many other goods; for example, a loaf of bread would be worth so many eggs, so much milk, and so forth. In a money system, there is a unit of currency that serves as a standard against which we can measure the value of a good or service and compare its value with that of another good or service. For example, if the cost of a trip to a beautiful Caribbean island is equal to the cost of a certain make of used car, money makes the comparison easy because the items are the same price.

A store of value

Money also serves as a **store of value**, or an instrument for storing purchasing power for the future. With barter, some good must be accepted in exchange for another; with money, a good can be sold today, and the money received for that good can be stored until it is needed. While other items known as assets (jewellery, rare paintings, antiques, real estate, stocks, and bonds) can store value as well, money is the asset that allows us to pay most easily for a good or service. The term **liquidity** refers to the relative ease with which an asset can be used to make a payment. Money is the most liquid of assets. Other assets are less liquid because, although they have value, they are not so easily exchanged for goods since they must first be sold in order to obtain money.

The Characteristics of Money

In order for money to serve as a medium of exchange, it must above all be generally acceptable. There are several other characteristics that

"Smart Cards" Need to Convince Consumers They'll Work

On the road to a cashless economy, smart cards seem to have hit some speed bumps.

Smart cards are kind of like electronic money —they're able to store cash that is essentially downloaded into them. They're not really all that smart when compared with a computer, but do have an embedded microchip that can store data.

The chip's key feature, and what really sets it apart from a credit card, is its ability to communicate with an online network to get authenticating information from a bank or other institution.

Recent trials showed that consumers aren't quite ready to give up their hard cash for the electronic version just yet. A 20-month trial in Sherbrooke, Quebec, was pulled last May [2001] after participants said they didn't like having a separate card for credit, banking, and electronic cash. A similar 1998 trial in Guelph, Ontario, was cut short due to lack of interest.

"There's the issue of perfecting the technology: getting people comfortable with what it is and how to use it," said Robert Gold, managing partner at Bennett Gold chartered accountants and editor of E-CommerceAlert.com.

Mondex, the "stored-value" or e-cash system developed by a group of major banks in partnership, just didn't cut it with either customers or retailers. But Mondex has vowed that theirs is the payment system of the future.

"It's not if, it's when," Mondex president Joanne De Laurentiis said at the end of the Guelph trial.

But for consumers to really embrace these cards, there has to be some value in it for them, says e-commerce author Rick Broadhead. User fees might also have to offset the huge capital investment required to get an electronic cash system off the ground. "Banks and stores will have to spend a fortune upgrading equipment...," Broadhead says. "Once they're here and accepted, I think we'll look back and say 'Why did it take so long?'"

Commercial smart cards could revolutionize the way we pay: from use in parking meters to convenience stores, they would eliminate the hunt for loose change and the mad dash for a cash machine. They would also be a secure payment option for Internet shoppers who want to pay cash for goods or services without giving out credit card information. Here's one scenario: an electronic reading device connects to a home computer, enabling the consumer to load cash directly from a bank account into the card. The consumer then uses the card to order a product over the Internet, or takes it out into the street to shop at a retail store that has a card reader and access to an authorized financial network.

It sounds simple, but there are drawbacks. For one, if you lose the card, you lose the cash on it.... And in order for everyone to use the cards, banks and merchants (bricks-and-mortar and online) have to be on a universal system that can read the cards and process the transactions.

"I don't think you're dealing with technologically adept society yet." says Gold. "I think it's got to pass the mom test. When your mom says 'I've got my smart card and I'm using it,' we'll be there."

Source: Excerpts from "Long-promised 'smart cards' still need to convince consumers they'll work" reprinted by permission of The Canadian Press.

QUESTIONS

1. To what degree does electronic money perform the three functions of money described on page 249?

2. List the six characteristics of money described on page 251. For each one, state whether you believe electronic cash is more or less effective in achieving the characteristic. Explain your answers.

3. Complete a brief cost–benefit analysis to weigh the advantages and disadvantages of having smart cards replace cash.

enhance money's acceptability, particularly when we examine coins and bills:

- Since we use money on a daily basis, it should be portable and easy to use. Heavy, cumbersome coins or large-sized bills that are difficult to pocket will not be popular.
- Money must be durable because it is passed from hand to hand countless times, stored in wallets and purses, and used in vending machines.
- Money must be easily divided into units to facilitate both small and large purchases.
- The various units of coins and bills should be readily recognizable by shape and colour in order to avoid mistakes during monetary transactions.
- Counterfeiting is a universal problem in money systems. In the past, counterfeiters needed considerable skills to design the metal plates used in offset printers to produce

cour
pute
copi
crim
den
to c
diffi

- Mo
of c
ove
wh
mo
cha
in
pri
po
mo

Components of the Money Sup

- **Demand deposits** ca
als, businesses, and g
holders to transfe
demand," by ch
ous types of
below.
—Cheq
est

is vigilant about inflation and is quick to warn the public and politicians of its impending appearance.

Check Your
Understanding

1. Of the three functions of money, which one do you regard as most essential? Why?
2. Which of the three functions of money does a rise in inflation tend to undermine most severely?
3. a) What is meant by liquidity?
   b) Rank the following assets in terms of their liquidity: a rare painting, gold jewellery, a diamond ring, shares in a large corporation, a Canada Savings Bond.
4. Compare the characteristics of our currency, in terms of its acceptability, with that of the United States or of another country. Do you think our currency meets the tests of acceptability, as described above, more or less satisfactorily than the other nation's currency? Explain.

Measuring Canada's Money Supply

We have defined money as anything that is generally acceptable to people as payment for goods and services. The total **money supply** of a modern economy is defined as the total amount of cash in circulation outside the banks plus bank deposits. As well as fulfilling the essential *medium of exchange* function described on page 249, money also serves to measure and store value. Currency serves all these functions at the same time, but what about all the various types of bank deposits? If they don't perform the *medium of exchange*

function, should they be included in the money supply?

People now hold different types of bank deposits, along with other financial assets. This variety makes it difficult to put forward an exact definition of what should be included in the money supply. The term **near money** is used to define these other types of deposits or assets that act as a store of value and can be converted into a medium of exchange but are not themselves a medium of exchange. In order to understand the problem of measuring the money supply, we need to define the main types of deposits and financial assets.

...ply

... be held by individu-
...vernments and allow
... money immediately, or "on
...eque or debit card. The vari-
...demand deposits are outlined

...**ing accounts** pay little or no inter-
...and usually charge service fees. They are
...sed primarily as a medium of exchange.

– **Current accounts** are set up for businesses
   but operate in much the same way as
   chequing accounts; they are also used as a
   medium of exchange.

– **Savings accounts** allow holders to save
   money for the future and earn interest. They
   are not generally used for making immediate
   payments, although some savings accounts
   have chequing privileges. Banks reserve the
   right to require notice of withdrawal on
   these deposits but, in practice, allow people
   to make withdrawals at any time.

• **Term deposits** are accounts in which the
   customer agrees to deposit a fixed amount of
   money for a fixed period of time (usually
   ranging from one month to several years) in
   return for a higher rate of interest, which is
   surrendered if the deposit is cashed in.

• **Notice accounts** require the depositor to
   give notice to the bank before withdrawal.
   These accounts pay some interest and are
   used primarily by businesses, in which case
   they are called *non-personal accounts*.

• **Money market mutual funds** are mutual
   funds specializing in short-term (less than a
   year) securities issued by governments (for
   example, treasury bills) and corporations (for
   example, bonds).

Definitions of the Money Supply

The Bank of Canada has broken down the
money supply into several categories ranging
from a narrow definition to a very broad one:

1. **M1** is the narrowest definition of the
   money supply. It is money that is used primarily as a medium of exchange to make
   payments. It includes all currency in circulation outside the banks as well as demand

deposits held in chequing and current
accounts. Currency that is out of circulation
and held in bank vaults or automated teller
machines (ATMs) is excluded because
when this currency is deposited, it becomes
a bank deposit. If M1 included the currency
held by banks in vaults or ATMs, as well as
bank deposits, the money would be
counted twice.

2. **M2** is a larger measure of the money supply. It includes all M1 plus personal savings
   accounts, including chequing–savings
   accounts, term deposits, and non-personal
   notice deposits. This is a broader definition
   because it includes two types of deposits—
   term deposits and non-personal notice
   deposits—not generally used for making
   immediate payments. These deposits are
   examples of near money.

3. **M2++** includes all M2 as well as deposits
   at non-bank deposit-taking institutions
   (for example, credit unions, trust companies, and caisse populaires), money market
   mutual funds, and individual annuities at

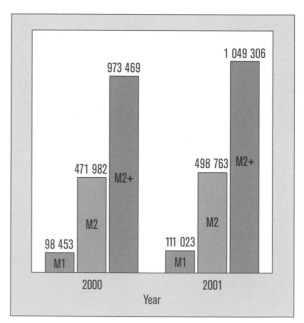

Source: Excerpts from Table 36: Money supply and credit, from
the Statistics Canada publication, *The Canadian Economic
Observer*, Catalogue 11-001, December 2001.

Figure 11.1 The composition of the official money supply
in January 2000 and January 2001 (in $ millions).

life insurance companies. These assets are used primarily as a store of value but typically can be turned into cash in one to two business days.

4. **M3** comprises M2++ as well as large term deposits held by businesses and foreign currencies held by Canadians. Although both types of deposits are used primarily as a store of value, they can be converted into cash.

As we shall see in Chapter 12, the Bank of Canada must have an accurate measurement of the money supply that is actually being used for transactions in the economy. Based on this measurement, it adjusts policies (such as the level of interest rates) to support our economy's growth. The problem for economists revolves around the question of what account or asset can be used for immediate payment by most people.

Should the money supply include only M1, the narrowest definition? M1 includes currency about which there is no argument because it is legal tender that must be accepted for payment. M1 also includes chequing accounts, which people use for payment as readily as they do currency—increasingly so with the advent of debit cards. However, there is a strong argument for including M2 in the money supply, especially because most people now use ATMs as well as telephone and Internet banking. These systems allow easy transfer of funds between the various accounts—from savings to chequing, for example. Does the fact that systems are in place to facilitate immediate payment encourage people to ignore the divisions between different accounts and assets? If so, a broader definition of the money supply—M2 or even M3—is most accurate.

Check Your Understanding

1. Which of the following assets serve primarily as a medium of exchange: coins and bills, a term account, a savings account, a chequing account, and a money market mutual fund? Which serve as a store of value?

2. Examine the graph in Figure 11.1. Can you tell if money appears to be used more as a medium of exchange or as a store of value? Explain.

3. Should a $50 bill found stuffed in a mattress be counted as part of M1? Explain.

Canada's Financial System

Up to this point in the chapter, we have examined money and its association mainly with banks. However, as important as they are, banks are actually part of a larger financial system in Canada that includes approximately 9000 banks, trust companies, credit unions, insurance companies, and brokerages. Until the 1960s, these institutions were restricted by law to carrying out specific functions. For example, banks could not sell insurance, and trust companies could not sell shares of corporations, because that was the function of brokerages. By 1992, these barriers had been removed; today, financial institutions offer several services.

While financial institutions can be divided into three broad categories, keep in mind that they cross over to perform other functions:

• *Deposit-taking and lending institutions.* These include chartered banks as well as near banks, which comprise trust companies, mortgage companies, and credit unions. Chartered banks have a close association with the Bank of Canada; we'll learn more about them shortly. The near banks now closely resemble the chartered banks in their operations, but they are not allowed to use the word bank in their names. In addition to accepting deposits, trust companies administer estates and trusts, mortgage companies invest depositors' assets in real estate, and credit unions are co-operatives that offer banking services to their members.

- *Insurance companies and pension funds.* Insurance companies cover individuals and businesses against fire, damage, automobile accidents, and other risks. Pension funds are pools of capital invested in financial assets, such as shares, bonds, and real estate, in order to provide retirement income for contributing members.
- *Investment dealers and sales and finance companies.* Investment dealers sell new issues of company shares to the public and act as brokers for investors in the stock market. Sales, finance, and consumer loan companies lend money to businesses and individuals.

Since the chartered banks are the largest of these financial institutions, we shall focus on the banking system. The six largest banks in Canada dominate our financial system, owning 70 per cent of its total assets. Their lending activities create the money necessary to purchase the goods and services produced by our economy.

The Canadian Banking System

Two types of banking systems operate in modern economies. The *unit banking* system allows many independent banks to exist, sometimes with restrictions on the number of branches each can establish. The **branch banking** system restricts the number of banks that can operate but allows these banks to establish as many branches as they want. The United States, with over 14 000 banks, is an example of the first system. Canada, on the other hand, follows the British model and has a branch banking system with few banks but many branches.

In the past, the advantage of a branch banking system was primarily one of security for depositors. If one bank branch faced an unexpected withdrawal that could lead to a "run on the bank" by customers fearful of losing their deposits, the other branches could supply the necessary cash and restore confidence. A bank facing the same situation in the United States might have collapsed because it would have no branches to support it.

For much of the 20th century, the Canadian branch system held up well in comparison to the US unit system. Only three banks failed in Canada between 1923 and 1985. No Canadian banks failed during the Great Depression of the 1930s, the debt crisis of less developed countries in the early 1980s, or the real estate bust in Canada and the United States in the early 1990s. In contrast, 2200 US banks failed in 1932 alone. (In 1982—a more recent example—42 banks failed.) Today, government deposit insurance, instituted in both countries after the Great Depression, protects the deposits of bank customers.

The Canadian banking system may be safe, but it has been criticized for being too concentrated among a few large banks in comparison to the highly competitive US banking system. In 1998, four of the largest Canadian banks attempted to win approval to merge into two large banks, claiming they needed to be larger in order to compete internationally. The government turned down the proposal, sensing the public was against further concentration. Instead, the government moved ahead in 2001 with plans to stimulate further competition in Canadian banking (as we shall see shortly).

The chartered banks

At present, Canada has 13 **chartered banks**, or banks established by a charter passed by the federal Parliament. Six of these banks—with over 90 per cent of Canadian banking assets and about 8000 branches across the country—dominate the Canadian banking system (see Figure 11.2).

The remaining seven are the Laurentian Bank, Canadian Western Bank, the Manulife Bank of Canada, CS Alterna Bank, President's Choice Bank, First Nations Bank of Canada, and Citizens Bank of Canada. The Citizens, President's Choice, and Manulife Banks are among the first "virtual" banks, operating solely through telecommunications. Another bank within this group, the First Nations Bank of Canada, is a joint venture of the Toronto-Dominion Bank and the Saskatchewan Equity Foundation. The Federation of Saskatchewan Indians, representing 73 First Nations, will wholly own this bank by 2006 and plans to

Bank	Assets ($ billions)
Royal Bank of Canada	291
Canadian Imperial Bank of Commerce	268
Toronto-Dominion Bank Financial Group (including Canada Trust)	265
The Bank of Nova Scotia	253
Bank of Montreal	233
National Bank of Canada	76

Source: "Canada's Banks", Department of Finance Canada, updated version (August 2001) at <http://www.fin.gc.ca/toce/2001/ bank_e.html>.

Figure 11.2 The top six banks in Canada by total assets, 31 October 2000.

offer services to Aboriginal peoples across Canada.

The top six banks have several international branches, particularly in the United States, Latin America, the Caribbean, and Asia. These foreign operations are an important source of revenue for these banks. In 2001, they earned 50 per cent of their net revenue from business outside Canada. In the 1980s, these six banks

Figure 11.3 As the First Nations Bank of Canada further develops its proficiency and expertise, First Nations investors will take over ownership and control from the Toronto-Dominion Bank, conditional upon regulatory approval.

were ranked among the top 25 banks in the world in terms of assets. Recently, however, they have slipped below 50th place in the ranking. This slippage was used as an argument in 1998 for merging four banks into two (Bank of Montreal/Royal Bank and Toronto-Dominion Bank/Canadian Imperial Bank of Commerce) in order to increase their size and regain their higher ranking. As mentioned previously, the argument was unsuccessful.

How Banks "Create" Money

In order to understand how bank deposit money is created in a banking system, we shall begin by looking at the operations of a fictitious bank serving an isolated community. We'll assume that no other banks are operating in this community, so residents who want to deposit money or obtain loans must deal with this **monopoly bank**. First, we have to understand how to read its books.

As with other businesses, a bank maintains a **balance sheet**, which is a snapshot of its financial health. A balance sheet is divided into two columns: assets appear in the left column; liabilities in the right column. An **asset** is something the bank *owns* or *is owed*. A **liability** is something the bank *owes*. Figure 11.4 shows the balance sheet of our monopoly bank. A customer who has $10 000 in cash wants to deposit it in the bank for safekeeping. The bank now has $10 000 in cash; in other words, it now owns an asset. When the customer handed over the $10 000, the bank credited the customer by creating a bank deposit, so the deposit is also a liability for the bank because it owes $10 000 to the customer. In other words, a deposit of cash creates both an asset and a liability for the bank and is recorded as such on the balance sheet.

The bank realizes that the depositor will likely withdraw only a fraction of the deposit

Assets		Liabilities	
Cash	+$10 000	Deposit	+$10 000

Figure 11.4 Initial balance sheet of the monopoly bank.

in cash. The rest of the cash to which the depositor is entitled will not be withdrawn. Thus, the bank needs to keep only a fractional reserve against the deposit. The depositor will likely spend the new deposit by writing cheques or using a debit card. Since it is a monopoly bank, cheques will be redeposited in the bank, and the amounts will be simply transferred to the account of another bank customer. If the depositor uses a debit card, the bank will again transfer the amount from the depositor's account to another account.

Fractional reserves allow the bank to make loans and create new money. Let's suppose that the bank normally keeps 10 per cent of a cash deposit as a reserve. This means that the monopoly bank keeps $1 of reserves for every $10 of deposits, a concept known as a **reserve ratio**. In this way, it can expand its deposits to *ten times* the original amount of cash deposited. How is this possible?

The bank created a deposit of $10 000 for the initial depositor of cash. Through long experience, it realizes that the depositor will withdraw only 10 per cent of the $10 000, or $1000, in cash. The bank has $9000 in cash left in the vault as **excess reserves**, that is, the amount of cash over and above what is needed to meet normal demands from the depositors. It is now in a position to lend $90 000 in the form of a new deposit for a borrower because the borrower will, at the most, withdraw only 10 per cent of the $90 000 deposit, or $9000. Thus, the total cash withdrawn ($1000 + $9000 = $10 000) equals the total amount originally deposited. As a safety net, the bank also has cash deposited by other customers.

Let's check the balance sheet after the loan by examining Figure 11.5. The loan is recorded as an asset because the borrower has signed a contract, usually called a *promissory note*, backed by collateral—something of value (for example, real estate, bonds, or stocks) that the bank would take if the loan were not repaid. At the same time, because the loan has been granted to the borrower in the form of a new deposit, it is recorded as a liability because the bank owes the amount to the borrower.

It may seem that some sort of numerical trick has been performed because the amount of money created by the loan is so much greater than the amount of "real money" the bank has in its vault. However, there are three key points to keep in mind:

- The loan is in the form of a bank deposit—a figure (noted in an account book in the past, imprinted on a chip in the bank's computer system today) that is money. It is considered money because it can be exchanged for goods by writing a cheque or by using a debit card. In the case of our monopoly bank, none of this money leaks out to another bank. All of it returns in the form of cheques or credits to other accounts in the same bank.
- Generally, people demand little cash relative to the size of their deposits. In a sense, the bank can "get away" with creating loans much larger than its cash reserves. The loans, in turn, create the bank deposits that compose the greatest part of the economy's money supply.
- The bank has a constant flow of incoming cash deposits that give it a safety hedge of cash against occasional customers who draw out more than 10 per cent of their deposits in cash.

Modern economies have many banks, making the process of money creation more complicated, but the result is still the same: a given amount of reserves can support a much greater expansion of the money supply measured in newly created bank deposits. Before we turn to a modern multi-bank system to see how this is accomplished, we have to make two assumptions. First, each bank lends the fullest possible amount from its reserves. Second, each borrower uses the total amount of a loan to repay a debt, and the amount is immediately redeposited by the person who has been repaid.

Assets		Liabilities	
Cash reserves	$10 000	Initial deposit	$10 000
Loan	+$90 000	New deposit	+$90 000
Total	$100 000	Total	$100 000

Figure 11.5 Balance sheet of the monopoly bank following a loan.

Bank A			
Assets		**Liabilities**	
Cash	+$10 000	Deposit	+$10 000
Required reserves	$1000		
Excess reserves	$9000		
Total	$10 000	Total	$10 000

Figure 11.6 Bank A's balance sheet. It now has excess reserves that it can use to make a loan.

Bank A			
Assets		**Liabilities**	
Cash reserves	$10 000	Initial deposit	$10 000
Loan	+$9000	New deposit	+$9000
(owed by Ms. Yeung)		(owed to Ms. Yeung)	
Total	$19 000	Total	$19 000

Figure 11.7 Bank A makes a loan of $9000 from its excess reserves to Ms. Yeung.

We'll go through the process of money creation in the banking system by looking at a series of transactions. Let's begin with Bank A, which has the same balance sheet as our monopoly bank and the same reserve requirement—10 per cent. It has $9000 in excess reserves (see Figure 11.6).

Bank A is now in a position to use its excess reserves to make a loan of $9000 to Ms. Yeung. It grants the loan in the form of a new bank deposit in the borrower's (Ms. Yeung's) chequing account (see Figure 11.7).

Ms. Yeung spends the loan by writing a cheque or using a debit card. Let's assume that she buys new furniture and writes a cheque to the local furniture store for the full amount of the loan. The store's account is with another bank, Bank B, where the cheque is deposited. Bank A must pay Bank B $9000. Figures 11.8 and 11.9 show the new balance sheets for Banks A and B.

Bank A's reserves and deposits have been reduced by $9000, but Bank B now has a new deposit of $9000. When it allows 10 per cent (or $900) for its required reserves, it will have $8100 in excess reserves. Suppose Bank B then

lends all of the excess to another customer, Mr. Papas.

Mr. Papas writes a cheque for the full amount of the $8100 loan to another person, Ms. Bray, who deposits it in Bank C. Setting aside 10 per cent of the new deposit for required reserves, Bank C has $7290 in excess reserves that it can lend to another customer, Mr. Khan (see Figure 11.10 on page 258).

Mr. Khan then writes a cheque for the full amount to another person who, in turn, deposits it in Bank D. Once again, Bank D will keep 10 per cent of the deposit on hand as a reserve and lend the rest. Thus, the process of lending and deposit creation will continue through other banks.

Banks A, B, and C created new deposits totalling $27 100 ($10 000 + $9000 + $8100). As the process continues through the rest of the banks in the system, more deposits will be created. How much in total will be created if we

Bank A			
Assets		**Liabilities**	
Cash reserves	$1000	Initial deposit	$10 000
Loan	$9000		
Total	$10 000	Total	$10 000

Figure 11.8 When Ms. Yeung spends her $9000 loan, Bank A's cash reserves and deposits fall by $9000.

Bank B			
Assets		**Liabilities**	
Cash reserves	+$9000	Initial deposit	+$9000
Required reserves	$900	New deposit	+$8100
Excess reserves	$8100	(owed to Mr. Papas)	
Loan (owed by Mr. Papas)	+$8100		
Total	$17 100	Total	$17 100

Figure 11.9 The furniture store's deposit has increased the excess reserves of Bank B, allowing the bank to give Mr. Papas a loan of $8100.

Bank C			
Assets		**Liabilities**	
Cash reserves	+$8100	Initial deposit	+$8100
Required reserves	$810	New deposit	+$7290
Excess reserves	$7290	(owed to Mr. Khan)	
Loan (owed by Mr. Khan)	+$7290		
Total	$15 390	Total	$15 390

Figure 11.10 Ms. Bray's deposit has increased the excess reserves of Bank C, allowing it to lend $7290 to Mr. Khan.

trace the process through Banks D, E, F, G, and so on? The monopoly bank created $100 000 in new deposits from a $10 000 cash deposit. We have already noted that the result of a multi-bank lending process will be exactly the same. With a 10 per cent cash reserve ratio and the same initial cash deposit, a modern banking system will create $100 000 in new deposits. If we subtract the initial $10 000 in cash that was already circulating in the economy, the banks have created $90 000 ($100 000 − $10 000) in new money. In the Skill Builder on page 260, we'll learn the formula for calculating the total amount of new deposits that could be created by a multi-bank banking system.

The realities of money creation

Before we traced the process of deposit creation, we made two rather extreme assumptions: first, that each bank lent all its excess reserves, and, second, that all borrowers immediately withdrew and spent the total amount of the deposits created for them. At this point, we need to withdraw these assumptions and consider a more realistic situation for the banks and the borrowers by examining the following two limitations: excess reserves and cash drains.

Excess reserves

If banks do not lend all their excess reserves, the total amount of new deposits that can be created is reduced. There are two reasons all reserves might not be loaned. First, there must be a sufficient number of people borrowing

from the banks in order for their excess reserves to be fully lent. However, there is no guarantee that this will happen. The economy could be suffering job losses, declining retail sales, and uncertain economic forecasts, all of which discourage people from borrowing money. The banks may want people to borrow, but people cannot be forced to do so!

Second, banks may not be willing to lend up to their maximum in excess reserves if they perceive that the risk of borrowers defaulting on repayment of their loans is too great. This reluctance on the banks' part is understandable since the loans they grant are obtained from other people's money. Bank managers are very aware that they must safeguard the deposits of their customers. Banks must be prudent in their lending practices, particularly so when economic conditions are not favourable. Individuals who lose their jobs are likely to default on repayment of their loans. Businesses that borrow when times are good may not be able to repay their loans if economic conditions reverse and their sales decline.

Cash drain

Not all people hold money in bank deposits. If our original depositor, Ms. Yeung, had kept a portion of her $9000 in cash on her person or at home, the amount of her deposit would have been reduced. Bank A would have less in excess reserves to lend, which, in turn, would reduce the reserves, loans, and deposits of all the other banks. Similarly, if other borrowers down the line drew a portion of their loans out in cash, the banking system's lending potential would be decreased. These **cash drains** limit the banks' capacity to create new deposits.

These two limitations mean that the ability of the banking system to create deposits is somewhat more restricted than in our example on page 257. However, a multi-bank system can still expand bank deposits—and thus the money supply—many times more than the amount of currency issued.

How Banks "Destroy" Money

A banking system not only can create money but can also destroy it by contracting deposits and, therefore, the money supply. Let's return to Bank A to see how this happens. Suppose the original depositor withdraws the $10 000. Bank A has $1000 in its reserves, but the person withdrawing the deposit demands $10 000. The bank is now short $9000. How would Bank A make up the shortfall in its reserves?

First, Bank A would cease lending money until new deposits of cash replenished its reserves. Second, it would count on its cash reserves being replenished from existing loans that are in the process of being repaid. Its borrowers would probably make withdrawals from other banks in the system in order to make loan payments. If Bank B, for instance, loses $9000 to withdrawals that a borrower makes to repay Bank A then Bank B must cease its lending and count on its loans being repaid to replenish its reserves. Since Bank B has $900 in reserves, the withdrawals leave it with a $8100 shortfall. Bank B's borrowers, in turn, would repay their loans by drawing on Bank C, and so the chain of withdrawals would continue, contracting deposits and reducing the money supply. Figure 11.11 shows how the balance sheet of Bank A would be affected. The balance sheets of the other banks would be affected in a similar way.

Foreign Banks in Canada

For most of Canada's history, our federal government has ensured that, by law, ownership of Canadian banks was restricted to Canadian investors. Government regulations also ensured that bank shares were widely held by Canadian investors to avoid one investor, or a small group, from controlling a bank. Canadian laws also prevented foreign banks from establishing branches or subsidiaries in Canada. However, under legislation passed in 2001, foreign banks can now establish either full-service or lending branches in Canada. Full-service branches are permitted to take deposits greater than $150 000 while lending branches are not permitted to take any deposits and are restricted to borrowing only from other financial institutions. Forty foreign banks now operate in Canada.

To further encourage more competition in Canada and to reduce the amount of concentrated control by the top six banks, other changes have come into effect. The new legislation divides Canadian chartered banks into three categories based on their size. Each category stipulates certain ownership regulations. The top six fall into the large-size category; the other seven, into the medium- and small-

Bank A				
a) Loss of Deposit			**b) Reduction in Loans**	
Assets		**Liabilities**	**Assets**	**Liabilities**
Cash reserves	−$10 000	Deposits −$10 000	Loans −$9000 Cash reserves +$9000	
Actual reserves −$10 000 Required reserves −$1000 Excess reserves −$9000			Actual reserves $9000 Required reserves — Excess reserves $9000	
Total	−$10 000	Total −$10 000	Total —	Total —

Figure 11.11 Bank A's balance sheets, showing contraction of deposits. Balance sheet (a) shows a $10 000 deposit withdrawal, which causes required reserves to fall $1000, while its actual reserves drop by $10 000. Thus, its excess reserves are short by $9000. Balance sheet (b) shows a loan reduction of $9000, which increases its reserves by $9000. The loan would be repaid through a withdrawal from Bank B, which would have similar effects on its balance sheet. This process would continue through the other banks, reducing deposits and thus contracting the money supply.

SKILL BUILDER
Thinking Like an Economist

The Deposit (or Money) Multiplier

A simple formula can be used to determine the total amount of new deposits that can be created from an initial deposit. The **deposit (or money) multiplier** is the amount by which a change in the monetary base is multiplied to determine the resulting change in the money supply. The deposit multiplier is calculated as follows:

$$\frac{\text{change in}}{\text{deposits (D)}} = \frac{1}{\text{reserve ratio (R)}} \times \frac{\text{change in}}{\text{reserves (C)}}$$

Example 1
If $100 is deposited in a bank that is part of a multi-bank system with a reserve ratio of 10 per cent, how much could total deposits increase?

$$D = \frac{1}{0.10} \times \$100 = \$1000$$

Total deposits will increase by $1000.

Example 2
If $500 is deposited in a bank that is part of a multi-bank system with a reserve ratio of 5 per cent, how much could total deposits increase?

$$D = \frac{1}{0.05} \times \$500 = \$10\ 000$$

Total deposits will increase by $10 000.

What is the total amount of new money that has been created in both examples? Remember that the money supply is defined as cash in circulation plus bank deposits. When cash is deposited, it is subtracted from the money supply because it is no longer in circulation. Keep in mind that the bank credits the cash depositor with a bank deposit. Thus, we subtract the initial cash deposit from the total of bank deposits created to determine the total addition to the money supply:

$$\frac{\text{total increase}}{\text{in money}} = \frac{\text{total new}}{\text{deposits}} - \frac{\text{initial cash}}{\text{deposit}}$$
$$\text{supply}$$

Example 1
Total new deposits   = $1000
Initial cash deposit   = $100
Total increase in money supply = $1000 − $100
                                 = $900

Example 2
Total new deposits   = $10 000
Initial cash deposit   = $500
Total increase in money supply = $10 000 − $500
                                 = $9500

QUESTIONS

1. If $5000 in cash is deposited in a bank that is part of a multi-bank system with a reserve ratio of 10 per cent, how much could be created in (a) new deposits and (b) new money?

2. If $10 000 in cash is deposited in a bank that is part of a multi-bank system with a reserve ratio of 8 per cent, how much could be created in (a) new deposits and (b) new money?

3. Suppose a person withdraws $1000 in cash from an account. How much would total deposits decrease if the reserve ratio is 20 per cent?

4. Create a balance sheet for Bank A and Bank B showing the effect of a $10 000 withdrawal on deposits and the money supply.

---

size categories. These new ownership regulations also allow for the creation of community-based banks, with services tailored to the needs of a specific clientele, such as the First Nations Bank of Canada. They also permit commercial enterprises (for example, those with a significant retail presence) to own a bank (for example, the President's Choice Bank, a partnership between Loblaws and the Canadian Imperial Bank of Commerce). The future will likely see more small and medium-sized Canadian banks being established, which, along with the foreign banks, should give Canadians a reasonable amount of choice for their banking needs.

Check Your Understanding

1. Contrast the branch banking system with the US system. Which do you think was more desirable in the past? Which do you think is more desirable today? Why?

2. What tendency among its depositors is a bank in a multi-bank system counting on to be able to lend its excess reserves?

3. An individual deposits $1000 in cash in the local bank. Why does it become both an asset and a liability for the bank?

4. a) In a monopoly bank, one person deposits $5000 while another deposits $18 000. How much could the bank lend if the reserve ratio were 10 per cent for each deposit?

   b) Draw up the bank's balance sheet to show how much the bank would be able to lend for each deposit.

   c) Suppose the reserve ratio were 20 per cent. How much would the bank be able to lend for each deposit?

5. A deposit of $5000 is made in one bank that is part of a system of three banks. The reserve ratio is 10 per cent. Draw up three balance sheets and trace the amount of (a) new deposits and (b) new money that would be created if each bank lent all its excess reserves and there were no cash drains.

6. State two recent changes that were implemented to open up banking in Canada to more competition.

CHAPTER SUMMARY

- The invention of money was a universal response to the problems posed by barter, in particular the problem of finding two people who each want goods the other possesses and of determining the exchange value of each good.

- The first form of money was commodity money, which included useful items valuable in themselves, for example, cattle, wheat, and metal tools followed by gold and silver ornaments and jewellery.

- Gold and silver, measured with grain, was followed by coinage made from the same metals, often stamped with a likeness of the ruler's head.

- Paper money began with merchants who found that receipts for valuable coinage left in a gold-smith's vault were safer and easier to use in monetary transactions.

- Goldsmiths discovered that because depositors preferred using paper receipts rather than coinage as money, they could lend the unused coinage (fractional reserves) for profit. This discovery led to the beginning of banking and money creation.

- Problems with coins, a surplus of paper currency, and bank failures led to the establishment of central banks to issue currency, support it with gold, and regulate banks.

- Money, in whatever form it takes, functions in three important ways: as a medium of exchange, as a measure of value, and as a store of value.

- Currency must be durable, easily divisible, recognizable, and difficult to counterfeit; most importantly, it must retain its value over time. Inflation is the greatest threat to any currency.

- Canada's money supply is divided into four categories—M1, M2, M2++, and M3—based on types of bank accounts and financial assets. There is debate over which category is the most accurate measure of the money supply.

- Canada's financial system is divided into three categories: deposit-taking and lending institutions, insurance companies and pension funds, and investment dealers and sales and finance companies.

- Canada developed a branch banking system in contrast to the unit system used by many independent banks in the US. The Canadian system is noted for its security and for being highly concentrated, with 90 per cent of the banking industry dominated by six banks.

- The modern multi-bank system can create, from excess reserves, new deposits totalling much more than the amount of cash deposited in the banks.

- Not all excess reserves are loaned. There are two reasons for this: the banks' reluctance to lend during uncertain economic times, and the willingness of depositors or borrowers to use cash and drain the banks' reserves.

- Bank balance sheets, divided into assets and liabilities, place cash deposits under assets as well as under liabilities.

- Recent legislation has opened up Canadian banking to foreign banks and has facilitated the establishment of new banks.

Key Terms

money
double coincidence of wants
commodity money
currency
fractional reserve banking
gold standard
fiat money
legal tender
bank deposit money
electronic money
medium of exchange
measure of value (or standard unit of account)
store of value
liquidity
money supply
near money

demand deposit
chequing account
current account
savings account
term deposit
notice account
money market mutual fund
M1   M2   M2++   M3
branch banking
chartered bank
monopoly bank
balance sheet
asset
liability
reserve ratio
excess reserves
cash drain
deposit (or money) multiplier

Activities

Thinking/Inquiry

1. a) At one time, central banks supported their currencies with gold, but not any longer. What supports our money today?

   b) Describe a set of circumstances that could undermine Canadians' faith in their money.

2. In a comparison organizer, list any five items that serve as money today, or have in the past, and assess how well they perform. Use at least five performance criteria.

3. How strongly does a nation identify with its currency? Is there a sense of identity derived from distinctive coins and bills that e-money might undermine? What is your opinion?

4. "Money has steadily become more abstract." Explain this statement with reference to the past, present, and future of money.

5. As a result of the run on banks by depositors during the Great Depression, the United States and, later, Canada introduced government-backed deposit insurance. How would government insurance for deposits reduce the likelihood of runs on the banks?

6. Suppose interest rates for loans triple. What would happen to the public's willingness to borrow money? What would then happen to the size of the money supply in the economy?

Communication

7. Using the Internet, research different types of e-money that are now being used. Find out about the security issues surrounding e-money. Present your report to the class.

8. Using the Internet, research several of Canada's new chartered banks, and report on how they are trying to distinguish themselves from the larger established banks.

Application

9. Draw up four balance sheets representing four banks. Assume that a person deposits $4000 in the first bank. Each bank lends all its excess reserves, and the reserve ratio is 10 per cent.

   a) How much in new deposits will be created by the four banks? How much will be created in new money?

   b) Using the deposit multiplier, determine how much would ultimately be created in new deposits and new money if the process continued through other banks in the system.

10. Suppose an economy uses barter to trade 100 goods. Each good could be priced in terms of 99 other goods. For example, a baseball glove could be measured as being worth 12 baseballs, or two baseball bats, or 100 packs of sunflower seeds, or any number of the other 96 goods that the economy trades. How many different price combinations where one good is measured in terms of another would there be? Use the following formula to figure it out:

$$\frac{n\,(n-1)}{2} \text{ (where n is the number of goods)}$$

In contrast, how many prices would there be in a money system?

11. Amir withdraws $1000 from his chequing account and puts the cash under his mattress. His bank's reserve requirement is 10 per cent. How much will Amir's withdrawal reduce the money supply?

CHAPTER 12

MONETARY POLICY

Monetary Policy: Just a Monopoly Game

Ever played the Hasbro board game Monopoly? If you recall, the purpose of the game is to accumulate as much wealth as possible through financial transactions involving real estate properties. The board is divided into properties of different values. When a player rolls the dice and lands on a property, he or she may buy it and then charge rent to any other player who lands on the property. Property owners can auction their holdings whenever they need cash.

Let's imagine that a group of 12 friends decides to play Monopoly on three boards (four players at each board). The only difference in the starting positions for each group involves the amount of money that the players are provided before the game starts:

• In Game A, each player begins with $10 000.
• In Game B, each player begins with double the amount given the Game A players, $20 000.
• In Game C, each player begins with half the amount given the Game A players, $5000.

Think about how this one variable will influence the game. How might it affect the average resale prices paid for properties in each game? If you like, try playing Monopoly with your classmates to see the differences. Otherwise, speculate on how Game A's average resale price level for properties would compare with those of Game B and Game C.

QUESTIONS

1. Did doubling the amount of money in Game B allow players to buy more property and become better off? If all Canadians had their incomes doubled, would everyone be better off? Explain.

2. If all Canadians had their incomes cut in half, as in Game C, would their economic situation be the same, better, or worse? Explain.

3. Suppose a number of new properties were added to the board. What would happen to the average resale price level in Game A? Game B? Game C? Explain.

4. If new properties were added, would the real wealth of people rise or fall? Why?

5. Which game represents inflation in an economy? Which represents deflation? Why?

6. Why is it important for an economy to try to achieve an appropriate level of money?

Chapter Goals

By the end of this chapter, you will be able to

• define and understand the general purpose of monetary policy,
• understand the purpose and organization of the Bank of Canada,
• appreciate the importance of interest rates to the economy, and understand how they are set,
• define and explain easy and tight monetary policy.

The Bank of Canada

We learned in the previous chapter how the banking system, through its bank deposits, bank reserves, and lending practices, actually creates money beyond paper and coin currency. The size of this money supply is vitally important to the economy. As we saw in the Monopoly scenarios outlined in the introduction to this chapter, an increase in the money supply without an increase in the output (represented by new properties in the game) does not make people better off. Instead, it inflates the prices everyone must pay for goods and services. Worse, real hardship is experienced by those people whose incomes do not increase. A situation in which too little money is created can also cause problems. If the economy does produce more output, and the money supply is not allowed to grow, people may not purchase the total output. Prices will fall, and the economy will enter a painful period of deflation.

To ensure that Canada's economy has just the right amount of money to purchase goods and services without causing inflation or deflation, the government uses monetary policies to adjust **interest rates** (the "price" charged for borrowing money) and thereby the size of the money supply. We can define **monetary policy** as a process by which the government affects the economy by influencing the expansion of money and credit. The agency through which these policies are delivered is our central bank, the Bank of Canada.

The Founding of the Bank of Canada

The Bank of Canada was founded by Parliament in 1934 at the height of the Great Depression for the purpose of stabilizing the Canadian economy and providing security for the banking system. It was believed that the banks had allowed too many people to build up too much credit during the 1920s, leading to the 1929 crash that ushered in the Great Depression of the 1930s. Banks throughout the Western world were unstable; as mentioned earlier in this book, several thousand US banks suffered runs on their deposits by panicked customers who lost their life savings when the

banks had insufficient cash reserves to pay them all.

Canadians hoped that a government-run central bank could prevent the mistakes that had been made previously and maintain confidence in the Canadian banking system. Examples of other countries' central banks were close at hand: Britain's Bank of England had been operating since the 18th century while, in the United States, the Federal Reserve System (an association of 12 regional central banks) had been established in 1904.

At first, there was considerable opposition from the chartered banks to the Bank of Canada. You will remember from the previous chapter that **chartered banks** are privately owned institutions that operate according to the rules of the Bank Act. These banks feared that politicians would use a government-run central bank to manipulate them. To calm these concerns, the Bank of Canada was set up as a private corporation that sold shares to the public, with limits placed on the number of shares one individual could own. The only connection to the government would be the deputy minister of finance, who sat on the corporation's board as a non-voting member. By 1938, however, the government of Prime Minister Mackenzie King bought all the shares to form a Crown corporation. (To find out more about Crown corporations, see Chapter 6.) Nonetheless, the corporation has always maintained the original intention of operating at arm's length from the government.

The chartered banks had a second reason to resist the formation of a central bank. Every chartered bank had the power to issue their own **bank notes** (paper money), a function that had been a profitable part of their business and a significant source of prestige. These bank notes looked just like the currency issued by the federal government, called Dominion notes. (A large denominational example of a Dominion note is shown on page 244 at the beginning of Chapter 11. Bank notes looked similar but had the issuing bank's name on them.) Once formed, the new central bank moved swiftly to control Canada's currency. The day the Bank of Canada began its operations (11 March 1935), it replaced the

Dominion notes with notes of its own. The Bank also moved to phase out the right of the chartered banks to issue their own bank notes, all of which finally went out of circulation in 1945.

The Bank's original mandate

The Bank of Canada was given a broad and ambitious role in the Canadian economy as outlined in the Bank Act passed in 1934. The Bank was expected to "regulate credit and currency in the best interests of the economic life of the nation, to control and protect the external value of the national monetary unit [the Canadian dollar] and to mitigate [reduce] by its influence fluctuations in the general level of production, trade, prices, and employment" (*The Canadian Bank Act*, 1934, Chapter B-2).

At the time these words were written, Canada's production, foreign trade, prices, and employment had all fallen to their lowest levels in the century. Much faith was placed in the new central bank; everyone from economists and politicians to ordinary people hoped that the Bank would be able to achieve the targets outlined in the Bank Act, and pull Canada out of the Depression. This expectation was probably unreasonable considering that John Maynard Keynes's theories—the ones you studied in Chapters 3 and 10—were not known at this time. These theories would have explained how depressions could be ended through appropriate fiscal policies. Nonetheless, the new central bank, which many Canadians wanted, was at least a beginning in the battle to haul the country out of economic depression.

The Functions of the Bank of Canada

Today, the Bank of Canada performs four functions in the economy:

• *Director of monetary policy.* First and foremost, the Bank is responsible for controlling the growth of the money supply in Canada by regulating credit, currency, and interest rates. Later in this chapter, we will examine how the Bank carries out this primary function.

• *Banker to the chartered banks.* Just as people and businesses have deposit accounts with the chartered banks, the chartered banks have deposit accounts with the central bank. The chartered banks use their accounts at the Bank to settle debts among themselves. The Bank of Canada also lends money to the chartered banks for short periods of time for investment purposes. If a chartered bank is threatened by a loss of confidence—in which case many depositors may attempt to withdraw all their money at once—the central bank can support it with cash advances.

• *Banker to the federal government.* The federal government's revenues are on deposit in two locations: the Bank of Canada and the chartered banks. These deposits are regularly shifted between the two locations, as we shall see when we examine monetary policy. The central bank also buys and sells federal government bonds and makes interest payments on them to bondholders. Finally, the Bank handles **foreign exchange reserves**—holdings of foreign currencies such as the US dollar—and uses them when it intervenes in the foreign exchange market to manage the Canadian dollar, a topic we will examine in Chapter 18.

• *Issuer of currency.* The Bank of Canada is responsible for the issue of paper currency. It decides on the design of the notes, gauges the amount required at various times of the year (Christmas time requires more notes than other times), and tries to eliminate the problem of counterfeiting. Coinage is the responsibility of another Crown corporation, the Royal Canadian Mint.

The Bank's Organization

The Bank of Canada is run by a board of directors appointed by the government. The board appoints a governor and deputy governor for a seven-year term with the approval of the federal government. (The signatures of these two officials are on every bank note.) These officials cannot be removed from their posts without a special act of Parliament passed by both the House of Commons and the Senate. The question arises: how independent from government and democratic control is the governor and the Bank of Canada? Some critics believe that the Bank of Canada has too much power.

On the one hand, it is desirable to have a central bank that functions independently of government so that it can control the nation's money supply without political interference. History has numerous examples of governments that paid their bills by literally "running the printing presses" to create money. Germany did this in the early 1920s, triggering a massive inflation that caused the currency to lose so much value that it eventually became worthless. In 1920, one US dollar was worth about 50 German marks. By 1923, one US dollar was worth about 4200 billion marks. The reasons for this are the same as in the Monopoly game example at the beginning of this chapter. The greater the supply of money in the game, the less value the money has (it takes more to buy the same piece of resale property). An independent central bank protects the value of money by separating the power to spend money—held by government—from the power to create money, a power held by the central bank and the banking system.

Case Study: Meet the Money Man

David Dodge, the new governor of the Bank of Canada [appointed in December 2000], is stepping into the spotlight at a tricky time. The "Goldilocks" economy ("not too hot, not too cold, just right") is softening, and the decisions he makes may determine whether it's a short-lived downturn, or something worse.

"I think the governor of the Bank of Canada is probably the most influential person in the economy because he has direct control over two key instruments: interest rates and the exchange rate, and there's hardly a person in the economy that is not affected by one, if not both of those levers," says economist Jeff Rubin of CIBC World Markets....

Now [Dodge] watches every economic statistic and indicator, and he must anticipate the necessary monetary policy action. And that's the tricky part. Statistics often take weeks or months to be compiled, making Dodge's task all the more difficult....

Dodge spends much of his time meeting with economists and number crunchers, constantly surveying the economic landscape for signs of inflation and the general health of our economy and those around the world. His computer screen is updated every two minutes with market information and notes from his staff. The Bank of Canada controls the money supply and sets the trend-setting Bank rate, and the information he gathers is critical to making policy decisions.

Dodge says he will be the most open and accessible governor the Bank has ever seen. He intends to share information because "it is absolutely critical for business, governments and even more important that ordinary Canadians understand what it is we're trying to do and to be able to anticipate a little bit what we're trying to do" because "if people correctly anticipate what's going to happen they don't make mistakes."...

So all eyes will be on Dodge as he makes his first big decision on interest rates on 6 March. He will need a deft hand on the tiller to steer our economy through the tricky waters ahead.

Source: "Meet the Money Man," *Venture*, 27 February 2001, <www.cbc.ca/business/programs/venture/onventure/022701.html>.

QUESTIONS

1. According to this article, why is David Dodge the most important person in the economy?

2. Why is his job not an easy one?

3. Why might Mr. Dodge want Canadians to anticipate what the Bank is going to do?

Ensuring accountability

On the other hand, critics believe the Bank and its governor lack accountability in their management of monetary policy. The issue of accountability was at least partly settled by Louis Rasminsky, an early governor. He stated that "(1) In the ordinary course of events, the Bank has the responsibility for monetary policy, and (2) if the government disapproves of the monetary policy being carried out by the Bank, it has the right and responsibility to direct the Bank as to the policy which the Bank is to carry out" (*Bank of Canada Annual Report*, 1961). With that statement, it appears that monetary policy became a dual responsibility of both the Bank and the government.

Today, clear procedures have been established to ensure accountability. The finance minister meets regularly with the governor to discuss the economy. If disagreements arise between them that cannot be resolved, the finance minister has the right to issue a directive—a letter—indicating the specific change in monetary policy that the government wants to see implemented. The directive is published for the general public and must be brought before Parliament within 15 days.

Most likely, the governor would resign if such sharp differences between the government and the Bank occurred. In the unlikely event that the governor would not resign, the government would have the legislative power to revise the Bank Act and dismiss the governor. Because the governor knows of the government's ultimate power, he or she would resign instead. The resignation of the head of a central bank is a serious matter for a country; confidence in the banking system and the currency can be shaken, at home and abroad. Both the government and the Bank realize the consequences of issuing a directive and would therefore do their best to reach agreement. The underlying effect of the directive procedure, however, is to clarify who has the final authority in monetary matters: the government. Even though the government would never exercise its authority except as a last resort, it definitely has the last word.

Although the government has the ultimate power, it is the governor of the Bank of Canada who is, in a sense, the instrument of the government. The governor exercises such power on a daily basis that he or she is considered by many to be the most influential person in the Canadian economy. The Case Study on page 267—an article based on a 2001 episode of the business news television show *Venture*—describes the career, views, and function of the current governor of the Bank of Canada, David Dodge.

Check Your Understanding

1. Why would the Bank of Canada insist on the right for it, not the government or other banks, to issue the Canadian currency?

2. Why do the federal government and the chartered banks both need accounts at the Bank of Canada?

3. In what ways does the Bank of Canada provide security to the banking system?

4. Why must the power to spend money be kept separate from the power to create money?

5. Does the governor of the Bank of Canada or the minister of finance appear to be less accountable? Explain your reasoning.

6. Why would both the governor and the government want to avoid the issuance of a directive?

What the Bank of Canada Tries to Do

In Chapter 10, you were introduced to the idea of the business cycle. The diagram in Figure 12.1 shows the business cycle as it revolves through expansion, recession, and expansion once again. Let's suppose that the Canadian economy is on an upswing in the business cycle, as illustrated by the rising line at the left in the diagram. With the higher incomes and increased number of jobs that accompany an upswing, Canadians will want to borrow more to buy a house, new appliances, or a new car. Businesses will want to borrow to expand their facilities, build a new plant, or buy more stock to cash in on the increased demand by consumers for their goods. The chartered banks will be only too happy to lend money to credit-worthy consumers and businesses. As we learned in the last chapter, the result is that the money supply expands as more bank deposit money is created to support the desire of individuals and businesses to spend more.

But economic good times always carry a price—higher prices in this case—as inflation begins to creep into the economy. At this point, the Bank of Canada must play the "spoiler of the party" by raising interest rates to restrain borrowing and slow the growth of the money supply. Otherwise, consumers and businesses will fuel the demand for goods and services so much that price increases will accelerate throughout the economy, causing serious inflation. However, the Bank must be careful; too much restraint, badly timed, and the economy could be thrown back into a recession. The Bank's goal is to slow growth, not to end it.

Let's now suppose that the Canadian economy is on a downswing in the business cycle, as illustrated by the dropping line at the centre of the diagram in Figure 12.1. Such a recession brings falling levels of production, consumption, and investment and brings high levels of unemployment. At such a time, the Bank will attempt to increase spending by lowering interest rates to encourage borrowing by consumers and businesses.

The term used to describe monetary policies of low interest rates, easy availability of credit, and growth of the money supply is **easy money**. Easy money policies are used to curb recessions. The term used to describe monetary policies of high interest rates, more difficult availability of credit, and a decrease in the money supply is **tight money**. Tight money policies are used to restrain the economy in times of expansion. The diagram in Figure 12.1 indicates where easy and tight money policies should be applied. Later, we will explain in

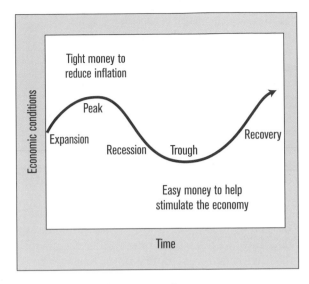

Figure 12.1 The business cycle.

more detail how the Bank of Canada brings about easy or tight money. First, though, we have to understand more about interest rates.

The Role of Interest Rates

Interest rates play a key role in the economy because they affect our decisions as consumers about both saving money and borrowing money. The higher the interest rate, the less likely we are to borrow. Interest rates influence the decisions made by businesses to invest by purchasing new machinery, expanding, or building a new plant. They also influence the value of the Canadian dollar internationally, as higher interest rates attract more foreign investors and, therefore, increase the demand for Canadian dollars. The budgets of governments are affected as well because the more they have to spend on interest on their debts, the less money they have available for social or other programs.

Supply and demand for loanable funds

Interest is a price paid for a loan. We can use a simple demand and supply graph, like the one in Figure 12.2 (page 270), to examine how interest rates are set.

The demand for loanable funds comes from three sources: consumers, businesses, and government. The downsloping demand line in

Figure 12.2 shows that as interest rates decrease, more loanable funds are borrowed; if rates rise, less is borrowed. The following three examples show how interest rates can affect various purchases:

• Many consumers considering major purchases, such as a house, an automobile, appliances, and furniture, have to borrow money. Lower interest rates mean that they pay less for these goods than they would if rates were higher. When rates rise, major purchases cost more, and consumers postpone their purchases if they can.

• Businesses considering a new investment must take into account how much more they will earn with new machinery or an expanded plant. If they estimate the **rate of return**—the amount of extra revenue the investment will bring in—as 7 per cent and the interest rate on the loan as 4 per cent, they may well go forward with their plans. If interest rates rise to, say, 7 per cent and the rate of return stays the same as without the investment, investment plans become problematic.

• Governments borrow money as well, but their decisions are not usually affected by the interest rate. Higher or lower rates, however, mean higher or lower interest costs for the government, an expense paid ultimately by taxpayers.

The supply of loanable funds comes from individuals, businesses, and chartered banks. The upsloping supply line in Figure 12.2 indicates that as interest rates rise, more loanable funds are supplied; when rates fall, less is supplied. How does the amount of loanable funds increase or decrease? Let's look at the situation for each of the three suppliers of loanable funds:

• Individuals affect the amount of loanable funds by increasing or decreasing the amount of money in their deposit accounts. The higher the amount of money in deposit accounts, the more money the bank has to lend. Individuals save for a variety of reasons. They may save to spend at a later date, thereby avoiding the costs of borrowing. They may simply have no major purchase to make at the present time. Others may save their money because they expect a downturn in the economy that may adversely affect their income or employment status. The upsloping line indicates that when interest rates rise, people are encouraged to save more; when rates fall, they save less.

• Businesses affect the amount of loanable funds in the same way that individuals do—by increasing or decreasing the amount of money in their deposit accounts. Businesses tend to save money to cover future expenses, such as the cost of replacing machinery that wears out. Instead of distributing all their profits to shareholders, businesses may save a portion for future expansion. They, too, tend to save more money during periods of high rates.

• Banks, as we learned previously, are the agents that use the money deposited by consumers and businesses to lend to individuals and to businesses that want to borrow. Through this process, banks create new money. If interest rates rise, chartered banks, as lenders, will want to supply more so they can increase their interest income.

Changes in interest rates

While interest rates can affect both the supply of and demand for loanable funds, the inverse applies as well: the supply and demand for loanable funds can affect interest rates. The

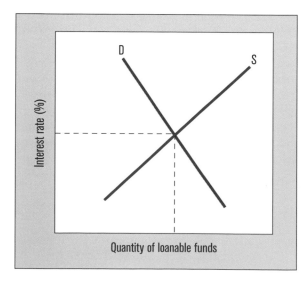

Figure 12.2 How interest rates are set.

demand for loans can increase when employment levels are high, incomes are rising, and people want to purchase goods immediately. Businesses may believe that the investment climate is favourable and will therefore increase their demand for loans. As indicated in Figure 12.3, this eagerness to borrow will shift the demand line to the right (D_1 to D_2 or D_3 to D_1), increasing the rate of interest. At another time, when the economy is in a recession or the economy's future looks uncertain, both individuals and businesses will lower their demand for loans, causing the demand line to shift to the left (D_1 to D_3 or D_2 to D_1) and the interest rate to fall.

The supply of loanable money can increase or decrease as well. If the economy is doing well, with rising employment and incomes, people tend to spend more but also save more. Similarly, higher profits for business will encourage them to save a greater percentage of their profits. Changes such as these increase the amount of funds available to chartered banks for lending. Therefore, as in Figure 12.4, the supply line shifts to the right (S_1 to S_2 or S_3 to S_1), causing the interest rate to fall. Alternatively, a recession causing unemployment and falling incomes means individuals and businesses are unable to save as much as they could

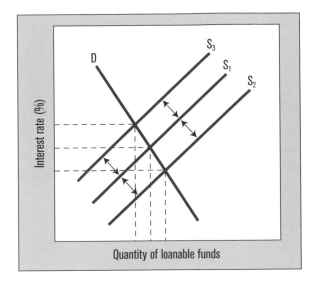

Figure 12.4 Change in supply for loanable funds. Supply falls in recessionary times (to S_3) and rises in expansionary times (to S_2).

when times were good. Many withdraw funds from their deposit accounts, decreasing the amount that chartered banks have available for loan. This causes the supply line to shift to the left (S_1 to S_3 or S_2 to S_1), causing interest rates to rise.

Different Types of Interest Rates

Different types of interest rates exist, serving a variety of purposes. It is important to grasp that they all tend to rise and fall together over the long run. You might be familiar with the interest rate charged on credit cards. (The issue of excessively high credit card interest rates is examined in the Economics in the News feature on page 272.) Another important lending rate is the **prime rate**, which is the lowest rate of interest a financial institution offers to its best customers (such as large corporations). The prime rate serves as a benchmark for the other lending rates that the institution offers to its other customers. If approved for a loan, a customer will be offered an interest rate that is a certain number of points "above prime," a number that varies depending on the customer's credit-worthiness, the amount of the loan, the term of the loan, and the amount of other business that the individual does with the institution.

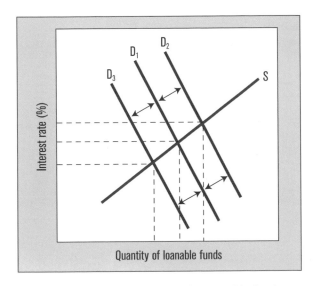

Figure 12.3 Change in demand for loanable funds. Demand falls in recessionary times (to D_3) and rises in expansionary times (to D_2).

Economics in the News

Credit Card Users Get a Welcome Champion

John McCallum [appointed federal minister in charge of financial institutions in 2002] has done consumers a favour by speaking out about the "grotesquely high" rates charged on credit cards.

If a former Royal Bank of Canada economist can't understand why credit card rates remain lofty while the Bank rate falls to record lows, how can anyone else?

He's legitimized what many of us have been thinking for quite a while. It's time for credit card issuers to open the books on their operations.

Here are a few questions I'd like federal politicians to ask credit card issuers:

• Do credit card rates track the Bank of Canada rate? If not, why not?

The link between credit card rates and the Bank rate is gradually breaking down. Major retailers, such as Sears, the Bay, and Canadian Tire, started the trend when they raised their card rates to 28.8 per cent in the early 1980s.

That made sense at a time when the Bank rate hit a record high of 21 per cent, but the retailers haven't budged since. We've had 17 years of flat-lining.

Banks have kept premium card rates stuck at 18 per cent to 20 per cent since the mid-1990s, though their low-rate cards tracked the Bank rate closely until last year. Now they, too, are decoupling.

When asked why credit card rates haven't dropped, bankers continually refer to administrative costs: delinquencies, fraud, replacing lost and stolen cards, marketing budgets, the cost of adding new features.

"What people don't appreciate is that the internal cost of funds is only about 30 to 35 per cent of the overall cost of providing cards,"... a spokesperson for the Royal Bank [said].

But if banks are doing a good job of keeping expenses under control, they can still give consumers a break when their cost is cut in half. Otherwise, they're making more profit every time the Bank rate falls.

• Why do administrative costs keep growing? And, is there a plan to bring them down?

Let's agree, for now, with the banks' claim that customers demand all the features that have been added to credit cards in recent years.... This means you get more for your money with a premium Visa or MasterCard than with a low-rate one. Someone has to pay for the piled-on perks.

But other costs seem outside the customer's control.

In their zeal to attract students and young people, banks seem to be loosening the criteria for giving out cards. They're certainly eager to extend more credit to existing customers, even those who never asked for it and may not be able to handle it responsibly.

Let's hope McCallum succeeds in getting a renewed investigation into these issues.

Source: Excerpts from "Credit card users get a welcome champion" by Ellen Roseman, *The Toronto Star*, 18 January 2002. Reprinted with permission— The Toronto Star Syndicate.

QUESTIONS

1. Explain why the author believes there is less justification for high credit card rates today than there was in the past.
2. What defence do the chartered banks offer for their high rates?
3. How can you avoid paying high interest rates on cards?

Another type of interest rate is the **Bank rate**. This is the rate of interest charged by the Bank of Canada for loans made to the chartered banks and other financial institutions. If the Bank rate rises, financial institutions will usually raise the rates they charge their borrowers; if it falls, they lower the rates. The Bank rate is set at 0.25 per cent above the overnight rate target (a tool of the central bank that you will learn about in the section on Tools of Monetary Policy on page 274).

One of the most important factors built into all interest rates is the allowance for inflation, called the **inflation premium**. Let's examine how this works.

Suppose you borrow $1000 from your parent or guardian with the understanding that you will repay the loan in one year. During that year, Canada's general price level rises 4 per cent. This means that the $1000 you borrowed is worth 4 per cent less when you repay the loan, or $960 [$1000 − ($1000 × 4%) = $960]. Your parent or guardian receives dollars that are worth less in purchasing power than they were when he or she granted you the loan. You have benefited because you are repaying dollars worth less than when you borrowed them. Inflation hurts lenders— your parent or guardian, in this case—and benefits creditors. The only way to avoid the effects of inflation is to set the interest rate at a level that compensates for the loss of purchasing power.

If, for example, your parent or guardian was aware of inflation's damaging effect, he or she should charge you a rate of interest that would cover the loss in purchasing power—an inflation premium of 4 per cent. You would be required to repay $1040 [$1000 + ($1000 × 4%) = $1040]. Your parent or guardian, however, doesn't know for sure that inflation will raise prices by 4 per cent. If it stands at only 2 per cent, your parent or guardian would come out ahead. If it stands at 5 per cent, however, he or she would lose.

Financial institutions that lend money build an inflation premium, based on future inflation estimates, into all the rates they charge borrowers. The interest rate that includes an inflation premium plus an allowance for risk and credit-worthiness is called the **nominal interest rate**. If the expected rate of inflation is subtracted from it, we have the **real rate of interest** on the loan. Here is a simple formula demonstrating the relationship:

$$\begin{array}{ccc} \text{real rate} \\ \text{of interest} \end{array} = \begin{array}{c} \text{nominal rate} \\ \text{of interest} \end{array} - \begin{array}{c} \text{expected rate} \\ \text{of inflation} \end{array}$$

If you borrow from a chartered bank and it allows 2 per cent for the risk of granting you a loan plus 4 per cent for inflation, the nominal rate would be 6 per cent. If the rate of inflation for the year turned out to match the predicted 4 per cent, the real rate of interest for the bank would be 2 per cent. We see, then, that inflation raises interest rates, making borrowing more expensive. When inflation rates are low, as they were in the early 2000s, Canadian interest rates are low as well. There is one exception to this situation, however, which was examined in the Economics in the News feature on page 272.

Check Your Understanding

1. Refer to Figure 12.2 (page 270). Why is the demand line for loans downsloping? Why is the supply line for loanable funds upsloping?

2. Refer to Figure 12.3 (page 271). What causes the demand line for loanable funds to shift right? to shift left? What happens to the interest rate in each case?

3. Refer to Figure 12.4 (page 271). What causes the supply line for loanable funds to shift left? to shift right? What happens to the interest rate in each case?

4. A chartered bank offers a one-year loan at "3 points above prime." Prime is 4 per cent.

   a) What is the nominal interest rate?

   b) If expected inflation is 3 per cent for next year, what is the real rate of interest?

   c) Suppose inflation rises to 4 per cent. What is the real rate of interest?

5. Explain why lenders build an inflation premium into their lending rates.

The Tools of Monetary Policy

The Bank has repeatedly stated that it considers price stability—a consistently low inflation rate—as its primary goal. In 1991, the rate stood at 5.9 per cent, but the Bank's tight money policies finally brought it down to 2 per cent by 1993. Since then, it has never risen above 3 per cent. The Bank's goal is to keep it within a 1 to 3 per cent band, never allowing it to fall or rise below or above the band. If it falls close to 1 per cent, the Bank decreases short-term interest rates to nudge it up with an easy money policy. If it rises close to 3 per cent, the Bank raises rates to pull inflation down with a tight money policy.

The Overnight Rate Target

The main tool used by the Bank of Canada to control the inflation rate is the ability to change its **overnight rate target**, which is an indispensable tool of monetary policy. Financial institutions know that they can always borrow money from the Bank of Canada at the Bank rate. The rate at which the Bank of Canada pays interest on its deposits is half a percentage point lower than the Bank rate. The 0.5 per cent range between these two rates is called the **operating band**. The overnight rate target always lies at the midpoint within the operating band. For example, if the central bank sets the overnight rate target at 3.75 per cent, it will charge a Bank rate of 4.0 per cent for loans and pay 3.5 per cent for interest on deposits. The operating band would be between 3.5 and 4 per cent.

Chartered banks and other financial institutions pay one another a rate within the operating band when they borrow money from one another for very brief periods. The actual rate they charge one another becomes the **overnight rate**, which the Bank of Canada attempts to control by stating its overnight rate target. It makes no sense for financial institutions to lend funds to each other outside of the operating band because they know they could get a better deal with the Bank of Canada.

By changing the overnight rate target, the Bank tells the chartered banks and other financial institutions the direction that it wishes monetary policy to take. An increase in this target usually encourages chartered banks to increase their own interest rates to higher levels.

Part of the reason for this increase is the Bank rate, which moves whenever the overnight rate target is moved. To lend money to customers, the chartered banks often need to borrow money at the Bank rate from the Bank of Canada. To make a profit, the interest rate they charge their customers must be higher than the Bank rate. In this manner, then, the Bank of Canada effectively controls interest rates. You can see the effect that a

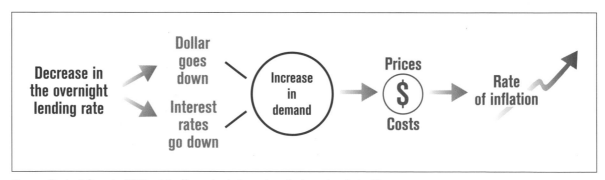

Source: Bank of Canada, 2002, <http://www.bankofcanada.ca/en/monetary/index.htm>.

Figure 12.5 Easy money. This is how the Bank of Canada keeps the rate of inflation above 1 per cent. How does decreasing the overnight rate target affect the economy?

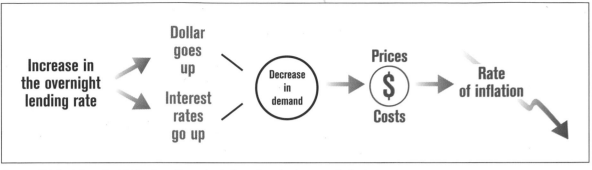

Source: Bank of Canada, 2002, <http://www.bankofcanada.ca/en/monetary/index.htm>.

Figure 12.6 Tight money. This is how the Bank of Canada keeps the rate of inflation below 3 per cent. How does increasing the overnight rate target affect the economy?

change in the overnight rate target can have on the economy in Figures 12.5 and 12.6.

The Bank's Balance Sheet

Just as the chartered banks have a balance sheet (as we saw in the previous chapter) so does the Bank of Canada.

The central bank's balance sheet consists of three types of assets and three types of liabilities, as you can see in Figure 12.7. These constitute tools of monetary policy, as outlined below.

Assets:

1. *Government of Canada bonds.* A **bond** is an IOU issued by a borrower to repay a certain amount of money by a fixed date. The lender receives interest on the loan

from the borrower. Sometimes the Canadian government sells bonds to the Bank of Canada. When this happens, the central bank is the lender and the Canadian government is the borrower because the Canadian government receives money in exchange for the bonds, which are a promise to pay back the Bank of Canada. Through the Bank of Canada, the government also sells bonds to Canadian individuals, businesses, chartered banks, financial institutions, and foreign buyers.

2. *Foreign exchange.* This is the stock of foreign currencies used to defend the Canadian dollar on international money markets. Consisting mainly of US dollars, along with some gold holdings, these currencies are used on occasion to purchase Canadian dollars, an action that props up the dollar's price.

3. *Advances to the chartered banks.* The Bank lends money to chartered banks and other financial institutions for their investment purposes. It charges interest—the Bank rate—to all such borrowers.

Liabilities:

4. *Currency outstanding.* This item consists of the bank notes issued by the Bank. All paper money in circulation in Canada is really a liability to the bank because it is an asset to you.

Balance Sheet of the Bank of Canada	
Assets	**Liabilities**
1. Government of Canada bonds	4. Currency outstanding
2. Foreign exchange	5. Deposits of the chartered banks
3. Advances to the chartered banks	6. Deposits of the federal government

Figure 12.7 Balance sheet of the Bank of Canada.

5. *Deposits of the chartered banks.* These are balances held by the chartered banks at the central bank for the purpose of settling debts among them and to act as reserves for them. The central bank pays interest on these deposits.

6. *Deposits of the federal government.* This item constitutes the "chequing account" of the federal government. The government deposits its revenues here and makes payments from this account for expenses such as paying its employees and employment insurance claimants.

By shifting deposits and by buying or selling bonds, the Bank can lower or raise short-term interest rates and speed up or slow down the growth of the money supply.

Figure 12.8 In 2002, Argentinians take to the streets to protest mismanagement of their country's economy. For years, the Argentinian central bank tied its peso to the US dollar, a strategy aimed at curbing the hyperinflation of the 1980s. Although the strategy did curb inflation, it also decreased the central bank's ability to control monetary policy. When recession hit, the government was unable to stimulate economic activity, leading eventually to economic crisis. How is the Canadian approach different?

Check Your Understanding

1. How does the Bank of Canada keep the inflation rate within a range of 1 to 3 per cent? Why is this its goal?

2. Explain the relationship between the overnight rate target, the operating band, and the overnight rate.

3. Which assets and liabilities of the Bank's balance sheet act as tools of monetary policy?

Monetary Policy at Work in the Economy

How Monetary Policy Works

We will use a model you studied in Chapter 10—the aggregate (or total) demand (AD) and aggregate supply (AS) model—to see how monetary policy, properly used, can help the economy. Let's suppose the Canadian economy is in a recession, as illustrated in Figure 12.9. Aggregate demand is at AD_1, below the level of full employment (FE). The minister of finance will use various fiscal tools, such as increased government spending and tax cuts, to try to

move AD_1 to AD_2. You will remember that increasing aggregate demand increases real GDP and encourages employment levels closer to full employment. Acting in concert with the government's actions, the Bank of Canada will engage in an easy money policy, by lowering interest rates and increasing money supply growth.

Ideally, the easy money policy of the Bank will put into action a series of four consequences that conclude with an end to the recession:

• *Stage 1.* The Bank shifts its government deposits to the accounts of the chartered

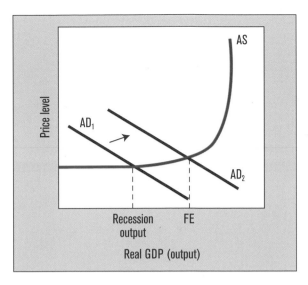

Figure 12.9 Aggregate demand and aggregate supply model illustrating a recession.

banks, thereby increasing their reserves. With extra reserves, the chartered banks are able to lend more. To attract potential borrowers of these extra reserves, the banks lower their interest rates.
• *Stage 2*. Lower interest rates encourage consumers to borrow for large purchases such as houses, appliances, and cars. Businesses respond to increased consumer spending by borrowing more to invest in new stock, equipment, and plants.
• *Stage 3*. New borrowing by consumers and businesses increases money supply growth (through increased bank deposits and reserves), allowing the increased output to be purchased throughout the economy.
• *Stage 4*. The increased spending by consumers and businesses pushes AD_1 to AD_2, increasing GDP and thereby ending the recession and leading to full employment at FE.

Let's suppose now that the economy is experiencing a period of high inflation, as illustrated in Figure 12.10. Aggregate demand is at AD_1. The minister of finance will use fiscal measures such as tax increases and lower government spending to try to move AD_1 down to AD_2. Acting in concert with the government's fiscal policies, the Bank of Canada will use a tight money policy by raising interest rates and reducing the rate of money growth.

Ideally, the tight money policy of the Bank will put into action a series of four consequences that conclude with an end to high inflation:
• *Stage 1*. The Bank shifts government deposits from the government accounts at the chartered banks back to the government account with the Bank of Canada. With reserve levels down, the chartered banks do not have as much money to lend out to potential customers. With the decreased supply, banks can raise interest rates for the money they do lend out and still maintain the level of customers they need.
• *Stage 2*. Higher interest rates discourage consumers from borrowing for large purchases. Businesses respond to both the higher interest rates and the fall in consumer spending by cutting investment in new stock, machinery, and plants.
• *Stage 3*. Less borrowing by consumers and businesses decreases the money supply growth as chartered banks find it more difficult to lend based on their reserves, a situation that contributes toward the desired fall in spending.
• *Stage 4*. Decreased spending by consumers and businesses pushes AD_1 down to AD_2; prices decline, thereby ending the period of high inflation.

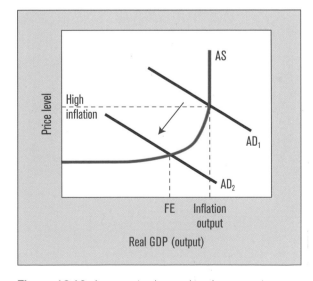

Figure 12.10 Aggregate demand and aggregate supply model illustrating a period of inflation.

Quiet shifts in monetary policy can have a profound effect on Canadian industries and on the lives of individual citizens. To find out how the monetary policy of Canada's central bank has affected the housing industry and home buyers, have a look at the Economics in the News feature below. As you read, consider the ways that interest rates can affect us, either directly or indirectly, through the economy.

The Bank of Canada's Recent Record

Central banking has changed greatly throughout the world over the last century. At one time, an air of mystery surrounded the operations and decisions made by central banks, and few people understood how they operated. The heads of central banks were often rather lofty, remote figures who held themselves at a distance from the general public and seldom communicated their policy objectives.

In most countries, this style has changed as central banks embrace a new, transparent approach. Central banks now want the general public to understand fully why they pursue particular policies, when they intend to change course, and what strategies they will use to meet their objectives. To better commu-

Low Interest Rates Keep Housing Market Buoyant

The Canadian housing industry ended 2001 at its strongest in almost a decade, data released yesterday showed.

Buttressed by rock-bottom interest rates, housing starts jumped 4 per cent to an annualized 175 500 units in December—the highest annual rate since February 1992, the Canadian Mortgage and Housing Corp. said. [Mortgages are loans homebuyers take out to buy a house.]

For the year as a whole, preliminary data show housing starts totalled 163 200 units, a 7.6 per cent gain over 2000 and also the highest level since 1992.

While warm weather likely boosted building in December, the housing industry has remained a hive of activity for an otherwise languid Canadian economy.

"Many had looked for the market to weaken, but it hasn't," said Derek Burleton, senior economist at Toronto-Dominion Bank. "The word 'affordability' takes care of it. Rates are low and it's keeping first-time buyers in the market."

Interest rates dropped to 40-year lows in Canada in 2001 as the Bank of Canada moved aggressively to fend off the US economic down-

turn. The central bank's overnight rate ended the year at 2.25 per cent, down from 5.75 per cent at the beginning of the year, sending mortgage rates tumbling.

"What's amazing in 2001 is how well the interest-sensitive sectors held up," Mr. Burleton added. "For those that believe monetary policy doesn't have much impact, the ongoing strength of the housing market through 2001, despite a lot of economic uncertainty, as well as auto sales, indicate that interest rates do continue to work magic."

Source: Excerpts from "Low interest rates keep housing market buoyant" by Jacqueline Thorpe from *Financial Post*, 10 January 2002. Reprinted by permission of National Post.

QUESTIONS

1. The article uses the term "interest-rate sensitive" in describing the housing market. What is meant by this term? Can you think of other consumer purchases that are sensitive to interest rates?

2. How is aggregate demand and employment affected by a good housing market?

Figure 12.11 In the 1980s, the central bank ended the speculation in the housing market in central Canada using the strategy of high interest rates. In Atlantic Canada, homes like these on Gower Street in St. John's took forever to sell because the region was experiencing high unemployment. What strategy would have been more helpful for Atlantic Canada?

nicate with the public, the Bank of Canada uses several means of providing information. For example, it maintains a Web site that explains in clear, non-technical language what its goals are and what tools it uses to achieve those goals. The governor frequently communicates with the public by distributing press releases, giving speeches, and speaking with the media.

Why does the Bank believe in a transparent approach? It believes that if the public knows how the Bank will respond to particular economic indicators, the public will be empowered to make better economic choices.

When the public knows that the Bank is determined to ensure that the Canadian economy will have low inflation and low interest rates, it can make easier decisions about spending and saving. Knowing that the Bank has inflation under control, people generally feel less pressure to buy goods immediately to avoid price increases. People no longer fear that the purchasing power of their money will decline quickly, eroding their incomes and standard of living. This allows for low interest rates, which in turn encourage home ownership (with low mortgage rates) and productive business investment in new technology and plant improvements.

Low interest rates have been a contributing factor behind the slide of the Canadian dollar from US$0.87 in 1990 to US$0.62 in 2002. Canada's exports, particularly to the United States, have benefited from this low dollar, but people across the country are concerned that this exchange rate is too low. Even exporting companies express concern when they have to pay high prices to purchase specialized machinery, for example, from the United States.

Check Your
Understanding

1. Is easy money policy or tight money policy most likely to cause unemployment and lost income for some people? Explain.

2. How does easy money affect (a) interest rates, (b) the money supply, and (c) aggregate demand? How does tight money affect them?

3. How does the Bank of Canada communicate with the public?

4. How does a transparent monetary policy benefit an economy?

CHAPTER SUMMARY

- Monetary policy is the process whereby the government, through the Bank of Canada, affects the economy by influencing the expansion of money and credit.

- The Bank of Canada was founded in 1934 for the purpose of stabilizing the Canadian economy and providing security for the banking system.

- The Bank moved swiftly to issue its own currency and end the right of the chartered banks to issue theirs.

- The Bank of Canada's prime function is to control the growth of the money supply by regulating credit, currency, and interest rates.

- The Bank also is a banker to the chartered banks and the federal government.

- The Bank's board of directors appoints the governor of the Bank. The government employs several measures to ensure the Bank's accountability.

- Easy and tight money refer to monetary polices followed by the Bank either to lower or to raise interest rates, to make credit easier or more difficult to obtain, and, ultimately, to raise or to lower money supply growth.

- Interest rates are set by the demand for and supply of loanable funds.

- The demand for loanable funds comes from consumers, businesses, and government. The first two groups borrow more as the interest rate declines but less as the rate increases.

- The supply of loanable funds comes from individuals, businesses, and chartered banks. The amount they supply varies with the interest rate.

- Interest rates change because of shifts in the demand and supply of loanable funds.

- When calculating their interest rates, chartered banks take into account the effect of inflation. They do this because rising prices undermine the value of the dollars that the borrower ultimately pays back.

- The overnight rate is, today, the most influential interest rate because of its effect on other rates.

- The Bank of Canada shifts government deposits back and forth between the government account and those of the chartered banks to increase or decrease reserves.

- As the reserves rise or fall, the chartered banks lower or raise interest rates, thereby increasing or decreasing their lending activities.

- Ideally, monetary policy works along with fiscal policy to influence aggregate demand to rise if the economy is in a recession or to fall if it is experiencing excessive inflation.

- A recession will call for easier money, with lower interest rates and an expansion of the money supply.

- An inflationary economy will call for tighter money, with higher interest rates and a contraction in the money supply.

Key Terms

interest rate
monetary policy
chartered bank
bank note
foreign exchange reserve
easy money
tight money
rate of return
prime rate
Bank rate
inflation premium
nominal interest rate
real rate of interest
overnight rate target
operating band
overnight rate
bond

Activities

Thinking/Inquiry

1. Explain why a modern economy needs a central bank such as the Bank of Canada.

2. In Alberta, the Social Credit party won the election of 1935 in the middle of the Depression by promising to give every citizen $25 a month in the form of a paper notes called "prosperity certificates." The party promised that this policy would revive the battered Albertan economy, but the plan never worked.

   a) Why do you think Albertans voted for this policy?

   b) What problems would the "prosperity certificates" have when people tried to spend them?

   c) After 1935, why could the federal government rule these paper notes illegal?

3. Suppose the Bank of Canada tried to target a tight money policy to parts of the country where inflation was particularly high by insisting that chartered banks charge higher interest rates where inflation is high and lower rates where inflation is low. What problems would this hypothetical monetary policy face?

4. Why do governments choose fiscal policies over monetary policies when they wish to target economic conditions particular to only certain regions of Canada?

5. Inflation must be taken into account when parties lend or borrow money.

   a) Why does inflation tend to benefit the borrower and penalize the lender?

   b) How does inflation affect interest rates?

   c) Why is inflation particularly unwelcome to the financial community, even more than unemployment?

6. Visit the Bank of Canada's Web site to find answers to the following questions:

   a) How does the Bank set the overnight interest rate?

   b) What is the monetary conditions index, and how is it used?

   c) How does the Bank define *core inflation* and the *consumer price index (CPI)*?

   d) How and why does it distinguish between these two terms?

7. A political power struggle between the government and a governor of the Bank of Canada highlighted the need to establish who controls monetary policy. Research the events of 1961 involving James Coyne and his struggle with parliament.

Communication

8. Divide into small groups, with each member assuming the role of one of the individuals listed below:

   • a real estate agent
   • a well-off individual with holdings of government bonds
   • a retired person living on a fixed pension plus a modest level of savings invested in term deposits
   • an automobile salesperson
   • a construction worker
   • a banker

What would be your attitude toward (a) a tight money policy and (b) an easy money policy? Explain to the others in your group why you would either support or oppose each policy.

9. Take one of these two positions:
   • "It would be better for Canada's economy if the Bank of Canada became more independent of the government."
   • "It would be better for Canada's economy if the Bank of Canada became less independent of the government."

   After finding information in this chapter to support your chosen position, be prepared to debate the issue in class.

10. Do some research to find out what monetary policies the Bank of Canada has followed during one of the following four periods:
   • 1960–1961
   • 1974–1976
   • 1981–1983
   • 1989–1991

   For the period you choose, determine the following:

   a) What were the economic conditions in Canada at the time? Where in the business cycle was the Canadian economy?

   b) Did the Bank follow an easy or tight policy, and what was their objective?

   c) How were employment and the inflation rate affected by the policy?

   d) Was the strategy of the Bank of Canada helpful for your particular region of the country? Why or why not?

   e) Was the policy generally successful, in your opinion? Would it bear repeating? Explain.

   Present your findings in the form of a brief written report, the script of an "interview" with a hypothetical individual who lived during that time period, or an oral presentation.

Application

11. It is often said that easy money policies are like "pushing on a string" in their ability to encourage people to borrow and spend. Explain this saying. In contrast, tight money policies are likened to "pulling on a string." Explain.

12. Suppose you are considering buying a guaranteed investment certificate that will pay a set amount of interest per year. If it is cashed in before its term, the interest is forfeited, meaning that you only get back the principal—what you originally invested. You have to decide whether to buy for a two- or three-year term. What factors about inflation and interest rates would you consider before purchase? Explain how these factors would affect your decision.

Unit 3 Performance Task: Dealing with an Economic Problem

Throughout this unit of study, we have explored the dynamic nature of the Canadian economy, and how the interaction of various stakeholders influences the ups and downs of economic activity. We have also examined the expectations of the government's role in influencing this economic activity. In this performance task, you will investigate the current state of the Canadian economy and then propose an appropriate stabilization policy.

Your Task

Your job is that of policy adviser in Canada's federal Department of Finance. Your employer has asked you to assess the current economic trends in Canada, using the principal economic measures. Once you have completed your assessment, you will produce a report outlining your policy recommendations to the minister of finance, who will then deliver these recommendations to the prime minister and the Cabinet.

Task Steps and Requirements

1. Research the three principal economic measures (the GDP growth rate, the unemployment rate, and the inflation rate) and their fluctuations over the past three years. Some possible sources of information include the Web sites of the Department of Finance Canada or Statistics Canada.
2. Using the business cycle and aggregate supply and demand analysis, explain the direction in which the economy is moving and suggest the dangers that lie ahead if it should continue to move in the same direction.
3. Identify the appropriate fiscal and/or monetary policies that should be used to deal with the current economic climate.
4. Outline the appropriate economic tools to implement your policy recommendations, using the economic language you learned in this unit.
5. Provide specific, appropriate, and reasonable examples of how your policy recommendations could be achieved, addressing the impact (both positive and negative) on all economic stakeholders—consumers, producers, investors, exporters, and importers.
6. Present your findings in a well-organized written report addressed to the minister of finance.

Adapting the Task

You may choose to organize your findings in an audio-visual multimedia report or a PowerPoint slide presentation, which could then be presented to Cabinet. Discuss the selection of a format for your report with your teacher. Keep the language appropriate for the intended audience. Share drafts with your teacher, classmates, and parents or guardians in order to obtain useful feedback.

Assessment Criteria

The following criteria will be used to assess your work:
- *Knowledge*—appropriately and accurately using terminology related to macroeconomics and fiscal and monetary policy
- *Thinking and Inquiry*—researching the relevant evidence and interpreting it effectively; applying sound economic reasoning
- *Communication*—clearly presenting and communicating your recommendations to the intended audience, using an appropriate tone
- *Application*—stating the appropriate conclusions regarding economic policy; planning a clear course of action for the government

UNIT 4

ECONOMIC DECISION MAKING

Members of the BC Nurses Union, in April 2001, after voting in favour of a strike by an over-whelming majority. How are these Canadians attempting to influence public policy decisions? What economic strategies should be used to deal with this problem? What are the economic costs associated with these strategies? Are these strategies worth the costs?

Unit Overview

In Unit 4, we'll focus our attention on collective decision making in order to understand how the Canadian economy works and why a balance between self-interest and the common good is necessary. We'll explore public policy issues arising from the diverse and sometimes conflicting economic interests and goals of different stakeholders. Even when goals are complementary, there are often conflicting opinions about the best course of action to achieve them.

First, we'll examine the role of government in the Canadian mixed-market economy. We'll then consider the relationships that exist between aggregate national production, unemployment, and price inflation in order to get a better sense of employment issues and prospects. Next, we'll turn our attention to the economic goal of equity and investigate government attempts to redistribute incomes and combat poverty. Finally, we'll explore how economists explain the impact of economic activity on the environment and how this impact should be addressed by both the public and private sectors.

Learning Goals

In this unit, you will
- describe how government is involved in the economy as a provider of goods and services, a supplier of infrastructure (roads, schools, etc.), an employer of resources, a regulator of competition and of aggregate demand, and a redistributor of income,
- identify the most important sources of local, provincial, and federal government revenues and classify government spending by purpose,
- describe the characteristics and causes of economic instability in each phase of the business cycle,
- identify the types, causes, and effects of inflation, deflation, and unemployment,
- explain how government fiscal policy (e.g., government spending or taxation) and monetary policy (e.g., increasing or decreasing interest rates) can help stabilize the business cycle and prices and lower the unemployment rate,
- illustrate how tools such as the Human Development Index, the Lorenz curve, and poverty lines can be used as indicators of socio-economic well-being,
- explain the concepts of responsible stewardship and economic externalities as they apply to marginal cost and marginal benefit analysis and to economic decisions in terms of environmental impact, income distribution, resource allocation, and sustainable growth,
- explain the benefits and costs of economic growth and evaluate strategies based on regulation, taxation, and market incentives to reduce negative externalities of growth such as pollution and resource depletion,
- evaluate the effectiveness of government legislation and programs, including education, health care, social services, and transfer payments, designed to enhance the economic security and well-being of all Canadians,
- analyze the costs and benefits of economic decisions related to public policy issues (regarding recession, employment, inflation, environmental protection, and income redistribution) for different stakeholder groups with diverse and sometimes conflicting interests and goals.

Skill Builder
Thinking Like an Economist

In this unit, you can develop some of the skills that economists use. These include
- working with indicators to make comparisons and detect patterns and trends,
- reading and making Lorenz curves.

Unit Performance Task

The activity at the end of this unit provides a focused opportunity for you to
- assume the role of a social advocate,
- apply economic knowledge and skills to outline the most appropriate role of government in the Canadian economy today,
- prepare and present a persuasive argument, and
- use a performance task rubric and feedback to prepare high-quality work.

CHAPTER 13
THE ROLE OF GOVERNMENT

The important thing for government is not to do things which individuals are doing already, and to do them a little better or a little worse; but to do those things which at present are not done at all.

—John Maynard Keynes, British economist

Government is the illusion of service masking the corruption of power. It is a mechanism controlled by the rich and powerful to trickle down just enough power and wealth to the poorer masses to help ensure that they will not rise in revolt.

—A political activist

We expect our elected representatives to be responsible stewards of the public purse, to show compassion for those at the margins of Canadian society, and to make decisions for the common good of all Canadians.

—A senior citizen

Be thankful that we are not getting all the government we are paying for!

—Will Rogers, American humourist

Perspectives on Government

What role should government play in a mixed-market economy? Is society best served when government involvement in the economy is maximized or minimized? The quotations and political cartoon presented here reflect five interesting perspectives on government. Examine each quote and consider the speaker's frame of reference. According to the cartoonist, in what balancing act was the federal government engaged in 1997?

ZAZULAK, The Hill Times, Ottawa

QUESTIONS

1. What pattern can you detect between each perspective and its source? To what extent do you agree with each perspective?

2. Write your own perspective on the role of government in society. Review your perspective once you have completed this chapter.

Chapter Goals

By the end of this chapter, you will be able to

- explain the different roles that government performs in the Canadian economy,
- evaluate the effectiveness of government legislation and programs designed to increase the economic security of Canadians,
- use supply and demand curves to explain the impact of taxation on different markets.

Government Involvement in the Economy

As Canada entered the 21st century, the issue of government involvement in the economy continued to attract controversy. While both federal and provincial governments in Canada reduced their spending and scaled back their involvement in the economy, critics lamented the systematic dismantling of the social welfare safety net that had distinguished Canada among industrialized nations. Today, many Canadians embrace a more "Americanized" model of government that features less government and reduced taxes. Through such government-reducing programs as privatization (which we explored in Chapter 6) and **deregulation** (a reduction of protective rules on certain industries), government becomes less involved in economic matters, and individuals and groups assume more economic freedom and responsibility.

However, fundamental questions continue. How can the common good prevail in an environment driven by individual self-interest? Can an economy correct itself sufficiently and quickly enough to eliminate the need for government involvement? What is the appropriate amount of government involvement? Should government involvement be limited to certain areas and methods of intervention? Currently, attitudes range from a strong advocacy of laissez-faire to unqualified support for substantial government involvement in order to ensure economic stability and a fair distribution of wealth. In this chapter, we shall look at the role of government in the Canadian economy to better understand its complexities.

The Great Depression

Among industrialized countries, few human tragedies parallel the pain and suffering inflicted by the Great Depression of the 1930s. Between 1929 and 1933, production in the United States dropped an estimated 42 per cent. Approximately 85 000 businesses failed, and some 5000 banks closed. Unemployment, which had been 3 per cent prior to the stock market crash of 29 October 1929, rose to an alarming 25 per cent.

In Canada, unemployment soared to a record level of 20 per cent as national production levels dropped an estimated 37 per cent. How could all this have happened? How long would it take the economy to recover? Could anything be done to speed up this recovery?

The frightening thing was that the "classical" answers were no longer valid. Prices had dramatically declined, but so too had national production and employment levels. This was not supposed to happen because falling prices, lower wages, and lower interest rates were all presumed to return the national economy to its normal state of full employment and capacity production. Glitches in the economy were supposed to be short-lived and self-correcting, but by 1933, the economy had yet to recover. It became apparent that something radically different had to be done before economic conditions deteriorated further.

Reconsidering laissez-faire capitalism

John Maynard Keynes was one of the first economists to propose that governments had to spend their way out of the Depression by hiring unemployed workers in major public works projects. He believed that this strategy would restore consumer spending and stimulate increased economic activity in the private sector. At first, Keynes's views were considered heretical, but as governments experimented with his new theory, economic activity eventually began to pick up. The government spending and the private investment that resulted from the Second World War returned the Canadian economy to full employment.

The Canadian welfare state

Since there was no formal welfare system and no Unemployment Insurance program, neither the federal nor the provincial government was obliged to provide financial help to those in need at the start of the Great Depression. It was usually left to local governments to help residents faced with unemployment and severe financial hardships. However, in provinces like Saskatchewan, where a lot of people needed assistance, the provincial governments had to provide organized relief services. As economic conditions worsened and millions of Canadians became unemployed, governments in Canada began to spend more on relief programs, or *social assistance*, that consisted of government transfer payments to needy individuals and families.

From the 1930s to the 1970s, the role of government (especially the federal government) in attending to the socio-economic welfare of its citizens continued to expand. During the second half of the 20th century, Canada transformed itself into a welfare state. In a **welfare state**, the government plays a significant role in attempting to ensure the economic well-being of its residents. The welfare state represents a radical departure from the laissez-faire capitalism supported by the more traditional schools of economics. Figure 13.2 (page 291) outlines the principal components of Canada's **social welfare safety net**. By the end of the 20th century, government spending on income security, health, and education represented the three main pillars of the Canadian social welfare system.

A critical look at the welfare state

Critics of the welfare state and of **transfer payments**—the transfer of monies from the state to disadvantaged individuals and households—generally point to three main problems, as outlined below:

• *Incentive to work.* One major criticism of Canada's social welfare programs is that they often reduce an individual's incentive to work and, therefore, to be self-supporting. For every dollar that a welfare recipient earns by working, welfare benefits are reduced. Although the purpose of this policy is to provide finite government assistance where it is most needed, it also has the unintended effect of discouraging some recipients from finding full- or part-time jobs. The **marginal tax rate**, or the tax rate paid on any increases in income, also acts as a disincentive. Since, as a general rule, welfare recipients are low-income

A Matter of Opinion | What Is Government's Role in the Economy?

Political Perspective	Right-wing View	Left-wing View
Orientation	• Conservative; traditionalist	• Progressive; liberal-minded
Market preference	• Laissez-faire free-enterprise capitalism	• Mixed market (capitalism with government enterprise and a social conscience)
Sample political affiliation in Canada	• Progressive Conservative; Canadian Alliance	• New Democratic Party
Fundamental economic beliefs	• Values the classical school of economics founded by Adam Smith. Self-interest and competition serve as an invisible hand that guides decision making in a free market toward a self-regulated balance; government intervention upsets this natural balance. • Free-enterprise capitalism can best satisfy human wants while making efficient use of available resources. • The free-enterprise system is most able to correct itself and promote prosperity.	• Challenges the classical school of economics and its contention that the free market is fair and self-correcting. • Uncontrolled capitalism has a tendency to be exploitative—acting out of self-interest, the powerful can and will exploit and oppress the weak. • Free markets are vulnerable to cyclical downturns, which tend to victimize the weak. During a recession, firms generally lay off workers to protect the profit levels of wealthy investors.

Continued

Political Perspective	Right-wing View	Left-wing View
Role of consumers	• In a free-market economy, competition ensures that the consumer is sovereign. By generally choosing the best quality at the lowest price, consumers rule the market place by rewarding firms that efficiently produce what is demanded and by rejecting firms that do not.	• In a free-market economy, big business can manipulate consumer choice through production, pricing, and marketing strategies that influence product demand and selection and that limit the entry and effectiveness of competing firms.
Distribution of wealth	• Driven by self-interest, the incentives of private ownership and profit promote efficiency and wealth. • Market forces facilitate a fair distribution of wealth—individuals get a share of national wealth based on merit and effort.	• Uncontrolled capitalism contributes to the maldistribution of wealth—as employers and investors receive the lion's share of wealth, workers receive a disproportionate share. • Market forces facilitate the concentrated accumulation of wealth and capital—the rich get richer as the poor become more desperate.
Role of government	• Government involvement in the free marketplace is an intrusion that is generally inefficient or ineffective. It should be kept to a minimum and focused on the areas of administration of law and justice, national defence, public works, and public institutions. • The more people expect from their government, the more dependent and, therefore, less self-sufficient they become.	• Beyond the areas identified by laissez-faire advocates, government involvement is necessary to address the excesses of the free-market system (that is, to provide goods and services that the private sector will not because of low profit margins); to regulate business practices and protect competition, especially in key industries; and to facilitate a more equitable distribution of wealth. • The government must look after the common good (especially when individual decisions act against it) and serve the needs of those least able to care for themselves.

Figure 13.1 Conflicting viewpoints about the government's role in the economy. The spectrum of political viewpoints was introduced in Chapter 2. The left and the right of the political spectrum in Canada have significantly different views regarding the rightful role of government in the economy. This comparison chart outlines some of the key differences in these viewpoints.

QUESTIONS

1. For each of the following government strategies, write two statements of opinion—one reflecting the viewpoint of the political right, the other of the political left. Explain why each view is held by its respective group.

   a) an increase in tuition fees for post-secondary education

   b) raising taxes on investment income (interest, dividends, and capital gains) in order to reduce the cost of day care for low-income earners

   c) increased government spending on public broadcasting

   d) a decrease in corporate income tax rates

   e) charging user fees for medical services and prescription drugs

   f) borrowing in money markets in order to finance expanded social programs

2. Which viewpoint best describes your position regarding the role of government in the economy? Explain where you agree and disagree with these views.

3. Re-examine these opposing viewpoints at the end of this chapter to assess whether your position has changed or has been reinforced.

earners, they pay very little income tax. Many welfare recipients gain little from taking on work because they have to pay a relatively high marginal tax rate. As much as 80 per cent of their extra income can be lost to taxes. In comparison, the highest income earners in Canada pay a marginal tax rate of close to 50 per cent.

In order to escape this high rate of marginal tax, welfare recipients must move beyond the low-income levels. Unfortunately, it is quite difficult for untrained and inexperienced persons to get these well-paying jobs. The self-interest that drives most Canadians to improve their economic circumstances through hard work offers little motivation for the poorest sector of the population.

Canada's Employment Insurance (EI) program has been criticized for actually contributing to unemployment by allowing repeated claims for benefits, after a brief work period. This can reduce the incentive to find more permanent employment in a different industry or region of Canada. In addition, employers' EI contributions increase each time an additional worker is hired—a factor, critics argue, that may discourage employers from increasing their workforce.

- *Inequities, abuses, and inefficiencies.* The welfare system is designed to redistribute income from higher-income Canadians to lower-income Canadians. However, under the present system, some disadvantaged Canadians fail to receive enough assistance while billions of dollars of benefits are paid out, instead, to less disadvantaged people. This is a direct result of **universality**, a long-standing principle of the Canadian welfare system. It recognizes that some benefits, such as Employment Insurance, Old Age Security, and Medicare, should be available to all Canadians regardless of income. In recent years, in order to combat the escalating cost of social welfare programs, which contributed greatly to government deficits, there has been a move toward means testing. Under **means testing**, transfer payments vary according to each recipient's income. Examples of means-tested programs include the Guaranteed Income Supplement

for older people and the Child Tax Credit for parents.

Advocates for low-income people challenge the use of means testing because, by raising the requirements, many Canadians who need social assistance are disqualified from receiving full benefits. On the other hand, critics note abuses of programs such as Employment Insurance and Medicare. For example, the cost of Medicare is greatly increased by abuses of the system linked to the fraudulent use of health cards and the charging of unnecessary expenses and procedures.

It is generally agreed that Canada's social welfare system is too complex and inefficient; there are too many programs with too many levels of government administering them. Critics point to the uncertainty about the benefits to which individuals and households should be entitled, to program overlaps and costly duplication, and to the levels of expensive government **bureaucracy** (or administrative structure) as proof of systemic inefficiency.

- *Effectiveness and cost.* Despite the spending of billions of dollars annually on social welfare programs, the distribution of income in Canada has remained virtually unchanged even as the welfare system has been expanded over the past 40 years. Many Canadians still live in poverty, with the poorest segment (20 per cent) of the population continuing to receive about 4 per cent of all income. Critics conclude that the present system has been relatively ineffective as a tool to redistribute income. Pointing to such evidence as the increased number of homeless people since 1995, advocates suggest that lower income levels would drop even further if existing programs were scaled back.

After the 1970s, government spending in Canada increased much faster than tax revenues. This led to annual budget deficits and increased borrowing in order to support growing social welfare programs. By the 1990s, it was clear that neither the Canadian economy nor the Canadian government could continue to absorb these rising costs.

Component	Description
Unemployment Insurance (UI)	This federally run program was started in 1942. It provides assistance to Canadians who have paid benefits for at least one year and who now find themselves temporarily out of work because of job loss, illness, or the birth or adoption of a child. All working Canadians and their employers make compulsory contributions in order to build up the fund. Any shortfalls are made up by the federal government. In 1996, the program was updated and its name was changed to **Employment Insurance (EI)** in order to reflect a more positive outlook. Although premiums were increased, benefits were decreased; by 2000, the fund had developed a $30-billion surplus, prompting renewed calls for a reduction in premiums, especially from employers who create jobs.
Family Allowance	Starting in 1945, all families received a standard amount of monetary support for each child under 18 years of age. Also known as the "baby bonus," this was a universal benefit paid to all families, regardless of family income. In 1978, the program was replaced by a **Child Tax Credit**, available only to low-income households.
Old Age Security (OAS)	This federal program, started in 1952, provides monthly benefits to all residents of Canada once they reach the age of 65. These benefits are considered taxable income. The **Guaranteed Income Supplement (GIS)** was introduced in 1966 to help boost the monthly income of older Canadians whose primary source of income is Old Age Security.
Canada Assistance Plan (CAP)	In 1965, the federal government initiated this cost-sharing program to help fund the welfare services provided by provincial, territorial, and local governments to individuals and households that cannot support themselves. As of 1997, the federal government significantly decreased its contributions to this plan in order to reduce spending.
Canada Pension Plan (CPP)	Along with the **Quebec Pension Plan (QPP)**, the CPP was started in 1966 to provide monthly payments to retired workers who made regular contributions to the plan during their working years. Employers and employees pay an equal share of Canada Pension premiums.
Medicare	In this program, launched in 1968, the cost of medical services for Canadians is shared by the federal and provincial governments, instead of being paid directly by the individuals receiving the service. Through Medicare, Canadians receive quality medical services without the burden of large, unexpected bills. Even though health care costs as a percentage of GDP doubled in Canada from the 1950s to the 1990s, many Canadians are still concerned about the quality of health care available. Reports of hospital emergency wards turning away patients because of a lack of beds and staff, as well as recent provincial initiatives to reintroduce private health care, remain matters of public concern, in spite of increased annual spending on socialized health care.
Publicly funded education	Primary and secondary education are financed entirely by tax revenues. Post-secondary education is still heavily subsidized by the both federal and provincial governments. Despite rising tuition fees during the late 1990s, governments continue to contribute the majority of the funds needed to sustain Canada's post-secondary institutions. Government support of post-secondary education is generally accepted on two grounds. First, this investment in "human capital" is necessary in an increasingly complex and competitive society. Second, public funding provides greater equality of opportunity for Canadians who might not otherwise be able to afford the costs of higher education. By the end of the 20th century, Canada was spending more on public education (as a percentage of GDP) than virtually any other nation.

Figure 13.2 Canada's social welfare safety net.

Case Study

How the Great Depression Ruined Mr. Wye and Mrs. Knott

Curtis Wye

In 1920, Curtis Wye was hired to work in the shipping department of the Timothy Eaton Catalogue Company. His salary was $10 a week. In 1922, based on advice from his manager, Mr. Wye decided to buy shares in Allied Canadian, a successful chemical company. He bought 100 shares at $0.50 each, for a total investment of $50. By 1925, Allied Canadian was prospering, and its shares were now selling on the Toronto Stock Exchange at $2.50 per share. On paper, Mr. Wye's stock holdings represented half a year's wages. He borrowed $500 from the bank and bought 200 additional shares of Allied Canadian at $2.50 per share. He intended to pay off the loan with his profits.

By October 1929, rumours began to surface that stock prices had climbed too high and the bubble was about to burst. Allied Canadian was still holding firm at $3 per share. A large number of investors decided that it was time to sell before stock prices began to fall. More and more investors followed suit as they saw others getting rid of their stock. In order to find someone willing to buy the stock, holders had to settle for a lower selling price. On Thursday, 24 October 1929, an avalanche of sales flooded the New York Stock Exchange as prices plummeted. This day became known as "Black Thursday." The Toronto market followed this rapid decline. Bankers and stockbrokers began to insist that investors pay back the money they had borrowed to buy stock. The panic continued as investors rushed to sell their shares before the price dropped further. On Tuesday, 29 October 1929 ("Black Tuesday"), the New York stock market crashed. In Toronto, similar panic unfolded. Mr. Wye sold all his shares for $0.20 each, making only $60 on the transaction. The $500 he had borrowed was lost. Like many other Canadian investors, Mr. Wye suddenly found himself without savings and deeply in debt. He owed the bank a year's wages. The economy had shifted from boom to bust.

As individuals like Mr. Wye failed to repay their loans, large chartered banks began to seize personal property in order to recover as much money as possible. Many small banks in the United States folded because people failed to repay their loans. Those who had accounts in these banks lost their life savings. Consumers in both Canada and the United States became very worried about their economic prospects, and, as a result, consumer spending declined. In addition, investment declined sharply as firms became concerned about declining sales. Like many others, Mr. Wye found himself out of work by 1930. The company promised to hire him back as soon as catalogue sales picked up, but as more workers were laid off each month, consumer spending declined even further, creating a vicious circle.

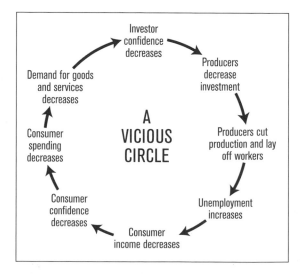

Figure 13.3 A vicious circle. With each repetition of this downward spiral, the economies of Canada and the United States lapsed deeper into economic depression.

Mr. Wye could not find steady work for almost ten years.

Stephanie Knott

Stephanie Knott and her husband worked a wheat farm in southern Saskatchewan that had been in the family since 1905. After a difficult start, the Knotts' farm eventually produced bumper crops of wheat, the result of sunshine, rich soil, rain, and hard work. When the Russian Revolution of 1917 disrupted wheat farming in that country, Canadian wheat found a ready market. The Knott family joined a co-operative wheat pool to collect and sell their wheat. The pool bought the wheat from farmers at close to market prices, stored it, and then sold it in bulk to Canadian and foreign buyers. By 1928, Canada was supplying 40 per cent of the world's wheat at a price of $37 per tonne. The Knotts borrowed heavily to purchase additional farm machinery, which would allow them to increase their harvest.

By 1929, crops in other countries were thriving, and there was a surplus of wheat in the world. Canadian grain elevators were still filled with the 1929 crop when the 1930 crop arrived. As the Depression worsened, world trade declined and then stopped as a result of the high tariffs most countries had placed on imported goods. The Knotts were unable to sell the wheat they had produced in 1930. They had borrowed money to buy seed and farm machinery in the spring, with a promise to repay the loans after the fall harvest. With no income from sales, the Knotts could not fulfill this promise. To make matters worse, southern Saskatchewan was hit by drought in 1929, and the rains did not return until 1939. The winds blew the thin, brown topsoil across the prairies, turning the farms into dust bowls. In areas where crops did grow, swarms of hungry grasshoppers attacked and destroyed much of the harvest.

By 1938, the world price of wheat had climbed back up to $37 a tonne; however, prairie farms were producing only one-third the amount of wheat they had produced a decade earlier. Thousands of hectares were abandoned to the dust and grasshoppers as farmers moved on to other parts of Canada. Some farmers decided to stay on, struggling to live on their life savings; their meagre, unpredictable earnings; government relief payments; and donations from other Canadian farmers who had not been hit as hard by the Great Depression. For the Knott family, the debt load proved too much to bear. The bank foreclosed on the family's defaulted mortgage, and the Knotts lost their farm. Between the drought, the dust, the plague of locusts, and the bank foreclosure, prairie farmers could be forgiven for thinking that the Depression was their own personal hell.

Figure 13.4 Prairie farmers lined up for relief supplies to help them through a long, cold winter. Needy families received coupons that could be used to obtain basic necessities.

QUESTIONS

1. How much profit did Mr. Wye appear to make on paper as a result of his original investment? What effect did this have on his investment strategy?

2. Draw a graph to help explain why stock prices fell as more and more investors attempted to sell their shares. Use your graph to illustrate shifts in both supply and demand schedules.

3. Draw a flow chart similar to Figure 13.3 to help explain the vicious circle that Saskatchewan wheat farmers found themselves in during the Great Depression.

4. Why did Canada and almost all trading partners raise tariffs (taxes on imported goods) during the Depression? Explain the economic reasoning and why it backfired.

By restraining federal spending, increasing the use of means testing, and downloading more health and welfare costs to the provincial governments, the federal government was able to balance its annual budget. A budget surplus was achieved by the end of the 1990s. In turn, provincial governments reduced their spending on programs and downloaded some welfare costs to local governments in order to bring spending in line with revenues. While social advocates lament the adverse effect that this has had on the most needy of Canadians, advocates of free-enterprise capitalism continue to question the overall effectiveness of Canada's expensive social welfare safety net.

During the "nasty 90s," many Canadians began to fear the systematic dismantling of the social welfare safety net as a means of reducing the huge government deficits. As the federal government began to experience a budget surplus during the late 1990s, public debate focused on whether to use the extra money to pay down the accumulated national debt, to increase spending on social programs, or to cut taxes for Canadians. After the terrorist attacks of 11 September 2001, the need for additional spending on national security consumed a significant portion of this surplus.

Check Your Understanding

1. How did government relief programs during the Great Depression set the foundation for the Canadian welfare state?

2. Identify and explain the three main pillars of the Canadian welfare system.

3. Compare the principles of universality and means testing.

4. What are the main problems identified with Canada's complex social welfare system? What reforms have been introduced to address these concerns?

Taxation and Government Spending

The main purpose of taxation is to
• finance state activity (such as national security and social welfare),
• promote income equity, and
• influence conditions in specific markets.
The taxes collected by all three levels of government in Canada have increased significantly over the past decades, relative to national production figures. While taxes represented close to 10 per cent of Gross National Production in 1926, by the end of the century, this ratio had increased to approximately 38 per cent.

The principles of benefits received (as applied to gasoline consumption taxes) and ability to pay (as applied to income taxes) are generally used to determine how the burden of tax is distributed to taxpayers.

Taxes are related to income in one of three possible ways, as shown in Figure 13.5. In each of the taxes outlined in Figure 13.5, the amount of tax paid by the person earning $40 000 is greater than the tax paid by the person earning $10 000, but the difference varies greatly between each tax. A progressive tax generally provides the greatest proportional difference between what high- and low-income earners will pay. Progressive taxes are politically popular because they are based on the principle of ability to pay.

When a government tax is imposed, the individual or firm for whom the tax is intended may actually assume the burden of payment. However, in some cases, the burden of payment can be passed on to others. When the burden of payment is considered, economists recognize two different forms of taxa-

Economic Concept	Progressive Tax		Regressive Tax		Proportional Tax	
Taxable income	$10 000	$40 000	$10 000	$40 000	$10 000	$40 000
Tax rate	10%	20%	10%	5%	10%	10%
Tax payable	$1000	$8000	$1000	$2000	$1000	$4000
Relationship between tax and income	Tax rate takes a proportionately higher percentage from higher income earners.		Tax rate takes a proportionately lower percentage from higher income earners.		Tax rate takes a constant percentage from all income earners.	

Figure 13.5 Taxes (**progressive**, **regressive**, and **proportional**) and income.

tion. With **direct taxes**, the real burden of payment falls directly on the individual or firm immediately responsible for payment and cannot be passed on to others. Taxes collected on the income earned by individuals and firms are an example of direct taxes. With **indirect taxes**, the real burden of payment is added to the selling price and is, therefore, passed on to the buyer. Taxes on goods and services are an example of indirect taxes. In this case, producers may prepay the tax and then recover all or part of this payment from their customers.

Types of Taxation

Canadian governments use five main types of taxes to generate revenues:
- **Personal income taxes** are payable to both federal and provincial governments on the income individuals earn from wages and salaries, interest (from savings certificates deposited in financial institutions), dividends (from profits earned by stock holdings), capital gains (from the difference between the purchase and selling prices of assets such as land, property, and stock), and transfer payments (from governments for social assistance). Generally speaking, Canadians earning higher incomes pay higher percentage rates of income tax. Income taxes are, therefore, said to be progressive taxes.
- **Corporate income taxes** are directly payable to federal and provincial governments as a percentage of a company's annual profits

after all available deductions have been applied. Corporations, as we learned in Chapter 6, are treated as distinct persons under Canadian law.
- **Sales taxes** are payable to both federal and provincial governments on the purchase and consumption of goods and services by the end user. **Provincial Sales Tax (PST)** is charged by provincial governments on a wide range of goods and services as a set percentage of the selling price. **Goods and Services Tax (GST)** is charged by the federal government on a wide range of goods and services as a set percentage of the selling price (harmonized into one in some provinces, including Newfoundland and Labrador).
- **Excise taxes** are payable to federal and provincial governments, as a set dollar amount per unit, on particular products such as gasoline, liquor, and tobacco. **Custom duties**, or **tariffs**, charged by the federal government on foreign goods entering Canada, are a special type of excise tax used to protect Canadian producers. (Tariffs will be explained more fully in Chapter 17.) Excise taxes are a good example of an indirect tax because they are ultimately added to the selling price and paid by consumers.
- **Property taxes** are payable to local governments on the value of buildings and land. First, these holdings are assessed to establish a set value, intended to approximate the market value at a specific time. Then, each year, the local government establishes a **mill rate** that represents the property tax rate as a fraction

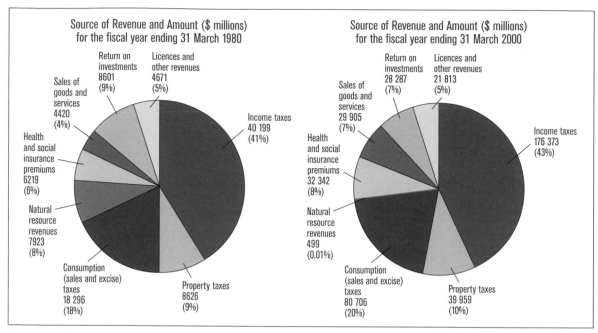

Source: Data from Statistics Canada Public Finance Historical Data No. 68–512, pp. 162, 163; CANSIM II, Table 385-0001.

Figure 13.6 Consolidated revenues for all levels of government in Canada, 1980–2000. What changes are evident over time?

For the fiscal year ending 31 March 2000

	Level of Government					
	Federal		Provincial/Territorial		Local	
Source of Revenue	in $ millions	%	in $ millions	%	in $ millions	%
Income taxes	112 196	61.4	64 176	32.7	0	0
Property taxes	0	0	8070	4.1	23 845	64.9
Consumption (sales and excise) taxes	36 011	19.7	44 633	22.7	61	0.2
Natural resource revenues	0	0	499	0.3	0	0
Health and social insurance premiums	18 933	10.4	8481	4.3	0	0
Sales of goods and services	4243	2.3	6221	3.2	9526	26.0
Return on investments	6264	3.4	19 434	9.9	2246	6.1
Licences and other revenues	5131	2.8	44 829	22.8	1041	2.8
TOTAL	182 778	100.0	196 343	100.0	36 719	100.0

Source: CANSIM II Tables 385-0002 and 385-0004.

Figure 13.7 Revenues by level of government. What revenue patterns does this table confirm?

of the assessed value. For example, if the mill rate is set at 0.0123, for every $100 000 of assessed property value, the owner will be charged $1230 (0.0123 × $100 000) in property taxes. Property taxes are affected by changes in the assessed value as well as by changes in the mill rate. Toward the end of the 20th century, property taxes in many communities across Canada increased as the operating expenses of local government grew.

Taxation and the Marketplace

The imposition of an indirect tax will affect market conditions for that specific good or service. The graphs in Figure 13.8 (page 298) help to illustrate the specific effects of taxation on the market price and the quantity transacted for pork (representing goods with an elastic demand) and gasoline (representing goods with an inelastic demand). Review the concept of elasticity of demand, developed in Chapter 5, to help you understand the elasticity of demand for each sample commodity.

Let's assume that the federal government imposes a special excise tax amounting to $1.00 per kilogram on pork and $0.50 per litre on gasoline. Figure 13.8 demonstrates that the effect of indirect taxes depends on the elasticity of demand for the good or service being taxed. In the case of the pork market, the new tax acts as a tax on production and may seriously affect the ability of some pork producers to stay in business. In the case of the gasoline market, the new tax acts as a tax on consumption and may affect both driving habits and the sale of more energy-efficient vehicles. Which of these two taxes is the Canadian government more likely to impose?

Anyone operating a motor vehicle today will quickly recognize that the excise taxes already imposed on gasoline account for close to half of the per-litre price paid by Canadian consumers at the pump. Governments prefer to impose these indirect taxes on goods such as tobacco, gasoline, and alcohol to generate steady revenue streams and to tax and regulate consumption. Some of the revenues generated from gasoline excise taxes can then be used by

governments to build and maintain the infrastructure of roads and bridges needed by both individuals and industry.

Tax Reform in Canada

Generally speaking, governments can generate revenues by taxing incomes, assets, and spending, but, in doing so, there are always economic costs. High income taxes can be a disincentive to work, save, and invest and can, therefore, have an adverse effect on national production levels. Personal income tax was introduced in Canada during the First World War as a temporary means of raising funds. By the 1990s, over half of federal government revenues came from personal income tax.

Property taxes discriminate against those who hold property assets instead of other assets. Since property taxes consume a larger portion of the income earned by lower-income residents, property taxes are recognized as a regressive tax. Sales taxes are also more burdensome on low-income households. Since both low- and high-income earners pay the same amount of tax on the goods and services they consume, sales taxes make up a higher percentage of the incomes of low-income households. For this reason, economists also consider sales taxes to be regressive taxes.

Taxes collected by all three levels of government in Canada increased steadily during the 20th century relative to the size of the national economy. Where total taxes represented approximately 12 per cent of the Gross Domestic Product in 1926, by the end of the 1990s, they represented closer to 40 per cent of the value of national production. This increase was needed to build and administer the social welfare safety net that Canadians wanted from their governments. Since the late 1980s, the federal government has attempted to address this concern about overtaxation by introducing a series of reforms intended to focus on three important aspects of taxation:

• Marginal tax rates on personal incomes were reduced so that if Canadians earned extra income, they could keep more of it to spend, save, or invest.

	Effect of a $0.50 Tax on the Gasoline Market	Effect of a $1.00 Tax on the Pork Market
Elasticity of demand	The demand for gasoline is relatively insensitive to price changes because gasoline is an essential source of fuel for automobiles, with very few substitutes readily available.	The demand for pork is sensitive to price changes because pork is a non-essential source of protein, with substitutes such as beef, fish, and poultry readily available.

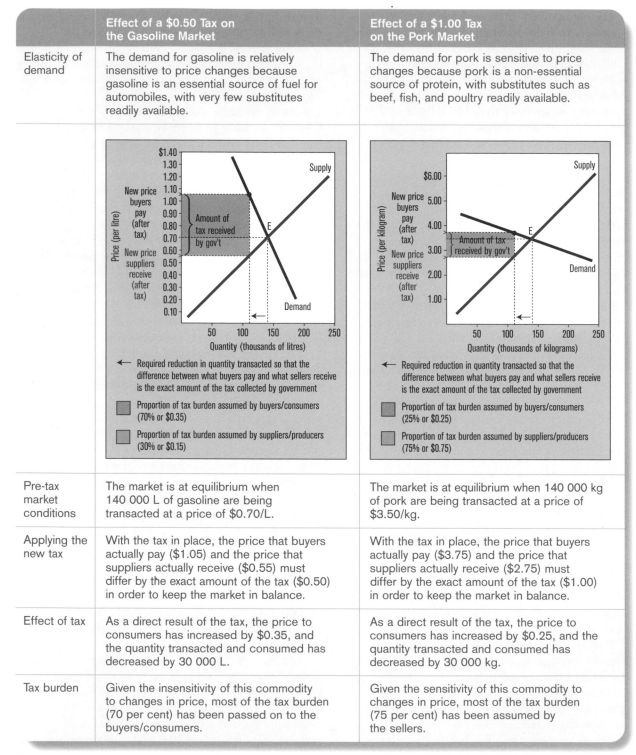

Pre-tax market conditions	The market is at equilibrium when 140 000 L of gasoline are being transacted at a price of $0.70/L.	The market is at equilibrium when 140 000 kg of pork are being transacted at a price of $3.50/kg.
Applying the new tax	With the tax in place, the price that buyers actually pay ($1.05) and the price that suppliers actually receive ($0.55) must differ by the exact amount of the tax ($0.50) in order to keep the market in balance.	With the tax in place, the price that buyers actually pay ($3.75) and the price that suppliers actually receive ($2.75) must differ by the exact amount of the tax ($1.00) in order to keep the market in balance.
Effect of tax	As a direct result of the tax, the price to consumers has increased by $0.35, and the quantity transacted and consumed has decreased by 30 000 L.	As a direct result of the tax, the price to consumers has increased by $0.25, and the quantity transacted and consumed has decreased by 30 000 kg.
Tax burden	Given the insensitivity of this commodity to changes in price, most of the tax burden (70 per cent) has been passed on to the buyers/consumers.	Given the sensitivity of this commodity to changes in price, most of the tax burden (75 per cent) has been assumed by the sellers.

Figure 13.8 Market comparison table for gasoline and pork.

- Tax credits were increased for lower-income earners to help offset the regressive effects of sales and property taxes and reduce the tax burden on low-income Canadians.
- The Goods and Services Tax (GST), a broadly based 7 per cent tax on consumption, was introduced in 1991 to replace the Federal Sales Tax (FST) on manufactured goods.

Revenue from the GST was intended to make up for the lost revenues incurred by the other tax reforms and also to help pay down the growing national debt. The GST is different and more complicated to administer than other sales taxes because producers do not have to pay GST on the materials needed for production. GST payments made on the purchase of production materials are refunded to manufacturers when they sell their final products. Therefore, unlike the old FST, there is no increase in production costs and no reduction in global competitiveness.

The GST is ultimately paid by the consumers of goods and services at the point of purchase. To help offset the regressive nature of this tax, a GST tax credit plan was introduced. Under this plan, low-income households receive GST rebates four times a year—in advance of actually paying the GST on their purchases.

During the late 1990s, provincial governments in Ontario and Alberta also attempted to stimulate their provincial economies by reducing income taxes in order to increase consumption. Increasing consumer spending was seen as one way to promote more employment and production. To fund these tax cuts, government spending on such programs as health care, education, welfare, and the environment was reduced.

Critics still maintain that Canadians today are greatly overtaxed relative to their US neighbours and trading partners. The Canadian Alliance Party, for example, continues to claim that high taxation is one main reason for the *brain drain*, or exodus of highly educated and talented Canadians to job opportunities in the United States. Many Canadians are prepared to pay current tax levels to preserve their quality of life; however, according to recent public opinion polls, most Canadians would like to see a reduction in what they perceive to be wasteful spending by government. Every year, for example, the federal Auditor General's report outlines examples of the inefficient or wasteful use of public funds.

A 1998 research study comparing tax rates in Ontario to those in New York State revealed that the difference in tax rates is relatively small. In fact, at lower income levels, tax rates are relatively lower in the Canadian welfare state than in the United States. For moderate income levels, the rates on both sides of the border seem comparable. Only at higher income levels do US households experience lower rates of taxation. Similar global comparisons indicate that taxation rates in Canada compare favourably to the rates found in most industrialized, or G7, nations.

Since 1995, the tax reform movement in Canada has focused its attention on

- reducing the tax burden of working- and middle-class Canadians,
- reducing government waste and inefficiency to make the best use of tax dollars, and
- further reducing marginal income tax rates to make it in the best interest of all Canadians to increase their own incomes.

Reducing tax rates is seen by some economists as a good way to stimulate consumption, production, investment, and employment.

How Tax Dollars Are Spent

Figure 13.9 (page 300) outlines how government spending patterns changed over the latter part of the 20th century. Clearly, almost half of all government spending in Canada is allocated to the "three pillars" of health, social services, and education.

Poverty in Canada

Every society in human history has had to deal with the issue of fair distribution of available wealth. In Canada, the economic goal of income equity is to reduce the number of people living in poverty. Social critics are quick to point out that additional structural

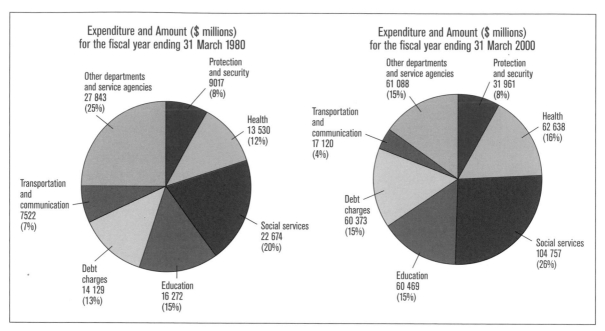

Source: Data from Statistics Canada Public Finance Historical Data No. 68–512, pp. 164, 165; CANSIM II, Table 385-0001.

Figure 13.9 Consolidated expenditures by all levels of government in Canada. What spending patterns are evident over time?

For the fiscal year ending 31 March 2000						
	Level of Government					
	Federal		Provincial/Territorial		Local	
Expenditure	in $ millions	%	in $ millions	%	in $ millions	%
Protection and security	18 442	10.7	7676	3.9	7275	15.9
Health	1723	1.0	56 891	29.2	916	2.0
Social services	50 384	29.2	31 398	16.1	5782	12.6
Education	4507	2.6	39 654	20.3	193	0.4
Debt charges	44 139	25.5	27 962	14.4	2717	5.9
Transportation and communication	1719	1.0	9732	5.0	9104	19.9
Other departments and service agencies	51 856	30.0	21 595	11.1	19 885	43.3
TOTAL	172 770	100.0	194 908	100.0	45 872	100.0

Source: CANSIM II Tables 385-0001 and 385-0004.

Figure 13.10 Expenditures by level of government. What spending patterns does this table confirm?

adjustments, government spending, and income redistribution will be necessary in order to reduce further the amount of poverty that now exists in Canada. In Chapter 15, we shall explore these issues of income distribution and poverty.

Deficit Reduction and the Accumulated Public Debt

With government spending levels generally exceeding revenues each year, governments in Canada had to borrow increasingly larger sums of money in order to finance their spending programs. This practice had an adverse effect on interest rates because, in order to secure the needed funds, governments had to offer attractive rates of interest. In addition, as annual deficits grew, the proportion of government spending required to make interest payments on the total accumulated debt continued to climb. Critics of deficit budgeting also linked inflation (general price increases) to unrealistic levels of government spending. Advocates of deficit budgeting were quick to point out that, as the Canadian economy continued to grow, the accumulated public debt would remain manageable and slowly lose significance relative to the volume of national production. For many Canadians, this was seen as a reasonable price to pay for Canada's social welfare safety net.

By 1996, the accumulated public debt in Canada had once again become a significant portion of Gross National Production. The interest being paid to carry the public debt burden consumed close to one of every four dollars spent by government. Government spending was scaled back considerably in order to reduce deficits and begin the process of slowly repaying the accumulated public debt. Many Canadians remain convinced that increasing public debt in order to fund social programs, as was the case during the second half of the 20th century, may no longer be a viable option.

Check Your
Understanding

1. Which of the following principles of taxation is the most fair—ability to pay or benefits received? Explain. Which principle is the easiest to implement? Explain.

2. For each of the five types of taxes collected by governments in Canada, determine whether each is an example of direct or indirect taxation and whether each is a progressive or a regressive tax.

3. Use supply and demand graphs to explain how the elasticity of demand helps to determine the effect of an indirect tax on the market price and on consumption.

4. List the economic and political advantages and disadvantages of using each of the following methods to increase government revenues: personal income taxes, corporate income taxes, gasoline excise taxes, tobacco excise taxes, and consumption/sales taxes.

5. List and explain the tax reforms introduced since 1990. Explain the effect of the GST on the ability of Canadian firms to compete in global markets.

Regulation of Competition in the Economy

We have seen how governments can influence or regulate the production and consumption of certain goods and services by imposing special taxes. In Canada, government regulation is also useful for maintaining safe drinking water, for inspecting and grading agricultural produce intended for human consumption, for maintaining the quality of hospitals and schools, and for providing healthy levels of competition in the economy.

Competition is seen as a positive factor in a market economy for the following reasons:

- *Competition increases consumer choice.* In a competitive market, both the quantity and the variety of goods available to consumers are increased. By choosing among the products available, consumers determine whether firms succeed or fail. For example, the styles, models, and optional features of automobiles provide consumers with ample choice at different price levels. Unpopular models are quickly discontinued and replaced by manufacturers.
- *Competition increases entrepreneurial freedom.* In a competitive marketplace, there are few obstacles barring producers from getting into an industry. Entrepreneurs will be attracted to industries where profit potential is seen to be relatively high. For example, many entrepreneurs have recently chosen to enter the growing field of information technology by developing and marketing specialized computer software.
- *Competition encourages investment and growth.* When there is healthy competition in an industry, products and services often improve. Improvements and innovations in the production process are rapidly implemented across the industry in order to improve efficiency or increase a firm's share of the market. To maintain competitiveness, firms are motivated to invest in and develop new technology. For example, in recent years, Ontario winemakers have invested heavily in new varieties of grapes and production processes, such as the development of ice wine and other award-winning products.
- *Competition keeps prices down and product quality high.* In a competitive environment, there is increased pressure on firms to provide high-quality products at competitive prices. Firms have less ability to manipulate prices upward because doing so will drive buyers to other competitors. For example, as a result of increased competition, today you can make an overseas phone call for a fraction of what it would have cost you in 1980.
- *Competition improves resource allocation and efficiency.* The efficient use of productive resources allows firms to generate profits in a competitive environment. Available resources are allocated based on market demand, as production shortages and surpluses are immediately corrected. For example, DaimlerChrysler AG quickly moved to cut production of its minivans and full-sized cars in 2001 when faced with rapidly declining sales in North America. Resources were freed up to increase production of the firm's popular PT Cruiser, reducing the three- to six-month waiting period for buyers.

Competition Legislation

Where one or more firms are able to influence the marketplace by fixing prices, limiting production, or controlling distribution so as to limit competition to the detriment of consumers, it is considered "combinations in restraint of trade." The **Combines Investigation Act** was passed in 1889 to prevent firms from taking actions that would "unduly lessen competition." This legislation was largely ineffective because it failed to define clearly what was meant by "unduly lessening" competition. Furthermore, since the Combines Investigation Act was based on criminal law, proof beyond reasonable doubt was needed in order to secure a conviction. Very few cases were successfully prosecuted because agreements to lessen trade were rarely put in writing; in addition, absolute physical proof that actions were "detrimental to the public interest" was required.

Prior to 1986, competition legislation was based on the premise that large corporations were able to exercise unfair influence on the domestic marketplace. With the evolution of freer global trade, especially during the 1970s and 1980s, the focus of attention gradually shifted to a consideration of whether Canadian firms were actually large enough to compete effectively in global markets. Large foreign firms were also recognized as sources of increased competition for Canadian companies. Some smaller Canadian companies could better compete in the global economy if they were allowed to join forces or merge with their competitors. With a steady decrease in trade tariffs, the competitive balance would be maintained by opening Canadian markets to large foreign corporations.

In 1986, the Combines Investigation Act was replaced by the **Competition Act**. The purpose of this new legislation was to encourage competition in Canada while promoting economic efficiency and the ability of Canadian firms to compete effectively in larger global markets. Three main goals were identified:

• Recognizing the role of foreign competition in Canada while at the same time recognizing opportunities for Canadian firms to compete effectively in global markets.
• Ensuring that small and medium-sized businesses have an opportunity to participate fairly in the Canadian economy.
• Providing consumers with competitive prices and product choices.

The Act is administered by the **Bureau of Competition Policy**, which is attached to Industry Canada. The process created by this Act was designed so that matters could be addressed outside the criminal courts. Most concerns are dealt with through negotiations between the Bureau and the corporations involved. When the parties are unable to reach an agreement, the matter is taken to the **Competition Tribunal**. Tribunal decisions may be appealed to the Federal Court of Canada.

Of the 340 merger deals that the Bureau of Competition was required to examine during its first three years in operation, most were accepted without challenge. In nine cases, the Bureau negotiated a restructured proposal with the merging companies. In 19 cases, the Bureau decided to monitor market conditions after approving the merger. In seven cases, the proposed mergers were voluntarily abandoned as a result of the objections raised by the Bureau. Only four cases were forwarded to the Competition Tribunal for a formal ruling.

In 1989, four commercial printing companies were each fined a record $400 000 for fixing what were supposed to be competitive bids on work contracts. As a result of this case and others like it, many economists have concluded that the Competition Act is more effective than its predecessor in combating price fixing. With its focus on economic and competitive factors, instead of on legal factors involving the existence of criminal conspiracies, the Competition Act is also seen as more effective than the Combines Investigation Act in dealing with mergers and acquisitions.

Check Your Understanding

1. List the benefits of competition for consumers by order of importance. Justify your ranking.

2. Produce a comparison chart to summarize the similarities and differences between the Combines Investigation Act and the Competition Act.

3. How effective has the Competition Act been in dealing with mergers, acquisitions, and price fixing?

4. Why did government policy regarding mergers and acquisitions change in Canada around 1986?

CASE Study

Protecting Competition While Permitting Mergers and Acquisitions

In 1989, Imperial Oil made a substantial bid to take over Texaco (Canada). At the time, Imperial was Canada's second largest oil company, with over 3000 gasoline service stations, five refineries, 32 distribution terminals, and several product pipelines. Texaco (Canada) was the fourth largest oil company, with over 2000 service stations, two refineries, 21 distribution terminals, and two product pipelines. Given the size of both companies involved, under the Competition Act of 1986, this acquisition had to be reviewed by the federal government's Bureau of Competition Policy.

The Bureau approved the acquisition, subject to certain conditions. While agreeing that Imperial Oil's takeover of Texaco would remove a "rigorous and effective competitor" from the Canadian gasoline and home-heating fuel markets, the director of the Bureau made two observations. First, by requiring Imperial Oil to sell off certain assets, consumers could rest assured that the decrease in competition would not result in price hikes. Second, concentration in the petroleum refining industry was "unavoidable if Canada [were] to obtain the benefits of economies of scale." Imperial was required to sell off 543 Esso service stations, mostly in parts of Canada where competition would be reduced significantly because of the disappearance of Texaco. In addition, Imperial Oil was required to sell off one refinery and 14 distribution terminals.

While the Bureau negotiates with the parties in a merger or acquisition to ensure that com-

Figure 13.11 The merger between Imperial Oil and Texaco was widely recognized as being a possible threat to competition in the Canadian oil industry. Consider the gasoline service stations in your area. Would you say adequate competition exists? Are there many independent operators?

petition is not diminished significantly, the Competition Tribunal gives final approval. At the Tribunal, critics argued that the deal was dangerous because it gave Imperial Oil too much power in Atlantic Canada, Quebec, and Ontario. Imperial could use this dominant market power to increase the prices of gasoline and heating oil. Reflecting on these concerns, the Tribunal refused to approve the takeover deal unless Imperial agreed to

- sell an additional 95 Esso service stations (bringing the total to 638),
- sell all of Texaco's assets in Atlantic Canada, and
- guarantee gasoline supplies to independent retailers (especially in central Canada).

| | Percentage of Total in the Industry | |
Corporation	Gasoline Service Stations	Refining Capacity
Imperial Oil	24 (Esso)	27
Petro-Canada	24	22
Shell	18	15

Source: From *Economics: A Canadian Perspective* by James D. Thexton. Copyright © Oxford University Press Canada 1992. Reprinted by permission.

Figure 13.12 The three largest oil companies in Canada (prior to Imperial Oil's forced sale of assets). With Imperial Oil's takeover of Texaco, the three largest oil companies controlled the lion's share of the country's gas stations and refinery capacity.

Imperial Oil accepted all the conditions imposed by the Tribunal and the Bureau, and the deal was given final approval in 1990.

By 1998, many consumers living in central and eastern Canada were convinced that large oil companies were systematically raising prices, especially during summer weekends. The Ontario government also became a vocal critic of gasoline price fluctuations. Adding to these concerns, the number of independent operators in central Canada had decreased significantly since 1990. As global oil prices continued to climb during 2000, gasoline prices in Canada reached new levels. Oil company executives were quick to point out that half of the price of a litre of gasoline consisted of excise taxes payable to government. Early in 2001, the federal government reported that their investigation produced no proof of price fixing or any other actions intended to lessen competition and hurt consumers.

Source: Adapted from *Economics: A Canadian Perspective* by James D. Thexton. Copyright © Oxford University Press Canada 1992. Reprinted by permission.

QUESTIONS

1. a) With Imperial Oil's takeover of Texaco and without the forced sale of assets, the three largest oil companies would have controlled what percentage of service stations and refinery capacity in Canada?

   b) Is abuse of dominant market position possible in the Canadian oil industry?

2. a) Without the conditions imposed by the Bureau and Tribunal, how might this takeover become disadvantageous to consumers and independent gas station operators?

   b) How far, in your opinion, do the conditions reduce the risk of these disadvantages? Explain.

3. In February 2001, Imperial Oil announced plans to spend $1 billion to expand its heavy-oil operations at Cold Lake in northern Alberta. The proposed expansion would result in the production of 180 000 barrels of bitumen (heavy oil) per day by the end of the decade. At present, 119 000 barrels are produced each day. Calculate the percentage rate of change in oil production reflected by this planned expansion.

4. Why is Imperial Oil better able to take on this expansion? Consider the ruling of 1990 as well as global market conditions at the time the announcement was made.

5. Research the assets and/or annual revenues of Canada's three largest oil companies to determine whether their size and market share have changed significantly since 1990.

CHAPTER SUMMARY

- The political right in Canada generally favours laissez-faire free-enterprise capitalism, with limited government involvement; the left prefers a mixed-market economy, with considerable social programs and government enterprise.

- Since the Great Depression, Canada has transformed itself into a welfare state by developing a complex system of social programs, including Employment Insurance, Family Allowance payments, Old Age Security, national pension plans, and Medicare. The three main pillars of the Canadian welfare state are income security, socialized health care, and publicly funded education.

- Critics of the welfare state question the transfer of monies from governments to needy households because they claim that these transfer payments discourage employers from hiring, reduce the incentive to work and be self-sufficient, lead to inequities and abuses, and are not cost effective. The principle of universality provides transfer payments to all Canadians, but those most in need receive less assistance as a result.

- Since 1985, welfare reforms have focused on the increased use of means testing (to reduce costs and direct more assistance to disadvantaged Canadians); on increased incentives for individuals to maintain full-time employment; on the reduction of government bureaucracy and spending and on the reduction of sales and property taxes that are particularly burdensome for low-income earners.

- Personal and corporate income taxes as well as sales, excise, and property taxes generate the largest portion of revenues for governments in Canada.

- In the case of a commodity with a relatively inelastic demand, such as gasoline, most of an indirect tax is paid by consumers. In the case of a commodity with a relatively elastic demand, such as pork, most of the tax is paid by producers. Both markets experience a decline in the quantity transacted as a result of taxation.

- Since 1990, tax reform has focused on the reduction of marginal tax rates on personal incomes (so that if Canadians earn extra income, they can keep more of it to spend, save, or invest) and on the increased use of tax credits to offset the regressive effects of sales and property taxes and to reduce the tax burden on low-income earners. A broadly based Goods and Services Tax (GST) was introduced in 1991.

- The GST is a 7 per cent tax on consumption, which replaced the Federal Sales Tax (FST) on manufactured goods. It was imposed to help pay down the federal debt, and to improve the global competitiveness of Canadian manufacturers.

- Close to half of total government spending in Canada is allocated to health, social services, and education. The next largest block of spending (close to 20 per cent) is allocated to paying interest charges on the national debt. Since 1996, there has been a concerted effort to bring government spending in line with revenues.

- Some Canadians advocate using government surpluses to pay off part of the national debt. Others advocate the reduction of taxes to stimulate the economy. A third group advocates using surpluses to increase spending on social programs.

- In Canada, government regulation is useful for maintaining safe drinking water, inspecting and grading agricultural produce, maintaining the quality of hospitals and schools, and providing healthy levels of competition in the economy. Competition is good because it expands consumer choice, increases entrepreneurial freedom, encourages investment and growth, keeps prices down and product quality high, and improves resource allocation and efficiency.

- The Competition Act, administered by the Bureau of Competition Policy through Industry Canada, encourages competition while promoting economic efficiency and the ability of Canadian firms to compete globally. Matters are dealt with mostly through negotiations between the Bureau and the corporations involved. When the parties are unable to come to an agreement, the Competition Tribunal is required to make a formal ruling. Tribunal decisions may be appealed to the Federal Court.

Key Terms

deregulation
welfare state
social welfare safety net
transfer payments
marginal tax rate
universality
means testing
bureaucracy
Unemployment Insurance (UI)
Employment Insurance (EI)
Family Allowance
Child Tax Credit
Old Age Security (OAS)
Guaranteed Income Supplement (GIS)
Canada Assistance Plan (CAP)
Canada Pension Plan (CPP)
Quebec Pension Plan (QPP)
Medicare
progressive tax
regressive tax
proportional tax
direct tax
indirect tax
personal income tax
corporate income tax
sales tax
Provincial Sales Tax (PST)
Goods and Services Tax (GST)
excise tax
custom duty (or tariff)
property tax
mill rate
Combines Investigation Act (1889)
Competition Act (1986)
Bureau of Competition Policy
Competition Tribunal

Activities

Thinking/Inquiry Skills

1. Research the current state of the health care system in your province. Prepare a report on the economic realities affecting the demand for nurses and doctors, as well as the supply of services, under the current fee structure. Draw a supply and demand graph to help explain the current market for health care services.

2. Each fiscal year, federal and provincial finance ministers present a budget summarizing the government's revenues and expenditures for the past year and outlining their plans for the coming fiscal year. Research a current budget to prepare an oral report that addresses the following topics:

   a) revenue sources and amounts recorded for the past year and projected for the next year

   b) expenditures and amounts recorded for the past year and projected for the next year

   c) new budget initiatives and a rationale for their adoption

   d) assessments from critics and supporters

   e) your overall assessment of the budget

3. Visit the reference section of the local public library to find a recent copy of the *Public Accounts of Canada*, published annually by the Auditor General of Canada. Research specific examples of questionable spending, then prepare a written report outlining the examples you found and recommending actions to prevent future occurrences.

4. In order to reduce government involvement in the economy, governments have decided to turn over certain activities to private companies. One recent example in Ontario is the generation and supply of hydro-electricity. Research the results of electrical energy privatization in California, as well as in other jurisdictions, to support your position on the privatization of these important activities.

Communication

5. Write a one-page position paper or a letter to the editor that advocates either universality or means testing in order to best allocate Canada's limited social assistance funds.

6. Draw a causation cycle diagram, similar to Figure 13.3 (page 292), to explain the effect of a general reduction in taxes on gross domestic

production in Canada. Explain the trade-offs, or opportunity costs, involved in achieving the benefits as shown in your diagram.

7. a) Complete the following cost–benefit chart, outlining four ways to use government surpluses.

Option	Benefits (advantages)	Costs (drawbacks)
Pay down debt		
Increase social spending		
Cut taxes		
Increase spending on security		

b) Prepare an argument for the most effective use of government surpluses from the perspective of one of the following stakeholders: unemployed student, stock market investor, worker permanently disabled by a workplace accident, bank manager, social worker, and small-business entrepreneur. Share your argument with classmates in order to compare the views of different stakeholders.

8. Right-wing advocates of free-enterprise capitalism are generally less sympathetic to people with low incomes, believing that they should do more to help themselves and that, unless they do so, the help that others provide is of limited benefit. Use economic reasoning to defend or refute this position.

9. You are a politician faced with a budget deficit. Would you choose to reduce spending, increase taxes, or increase borrowing to maintain the deficit? In defending your choice, explain the economic costs of each strategy.

10. It has been widely speculated that baby boomers (Canadians born between 1946 and 1966) will exhaust social welfare programs such as Medicare and the Canada Pension Plan as they age in large numbers. Research this topic to produce a position paper recommending a specific course of action

to the Government of Canada and to aging baby boomers.

11. Prepare a video news report outlining how and why the role of the government in Canada changed during the second half of the 20th century. Assess the increased role of the public (government) sector in the Canadian economy since 1966.

Application

12. In the United States, property owners can deduct mortgage payments from their taxable income. Who would benefit most from this deduction? Who would benefit least? What specific effects would this deduction have on the housing market? In your opinion, should Canada adopt a similar plan? Explain.

13. Assume that Canadian hog producers are experiencing economic hardships and many are going bankrupt. In order to protect the supply of pork to Canadian consumers, the government decides to provide a $1-per-kilogram support payment, or *subsidy*, to hog producers. Use the pork market graph in Figure 13.8 (page 298) to determine the effect of this government subsidy program on the pork market. Who receives most of this subsidy? Explain why. Draw a market graph to confirm your reasoning.

14. Some economists argue that there should be more rather than fewer mergers and acquisitions in the Canadian economy. Use economic reasoning to support or refute this position.

15. During the 1980s, taxes on cigarettes were increased as part of the government's anti-smoking program. In February 1994, taxes were slashed by Ottawa (in concert with Ontario, Quebec, Nova Scotia, New Brunswick, and Prince Edward Island) in a bid to halt cigarette smuggling. Draw a market graph to help explain the effect of the self-interest of cigarette smugglers, operating in the "hidden economy," on the supply of cigarettes to Canadian consumers, on the market price, on profits of organized crime, and, ultimately, on the effectiveness of the government's anti-smoking program.

CHAPTER 14
EMPLOYMENT, RECESSION, AND RECOVERY

What's Wrong with This Picture?

In this chapter, we shall investigate the relationships that exist among aggregate national production, unemployment, and price inflation. Unemployment rates and inflation rates are said to be inversely related. For many years, this inverse relationship was visualized in a graph known as the Phillips curve. This curve presumes a trade-off between inflation and unemployment: the lower the inflation rate, the higher the unemployment rate, and vice versa. In the given example of the Phillips curve (at right), as the inflation rate rises from 2 to 4 per cent, unemployment decreases from 10 to 6 per cent.

The political cartoon below, which dates back to 1979, shows a visibly upset Prime Minister Trudeau taking his young finance minister, Jean Chrétien, to task. Study this cartoon carefully.

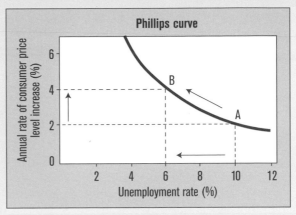

Source: Adaption of The Phillips Curve from *Economics: A Canadian Perspective* by James D. Thexton. Copyright © Oxford University Press Canada 1992. Reprinted by permission.

QUESTIONS

1. What's wrong with the assembled economic seesaw?
2. Why has the artist chosen a seesaw to get his point across? How have inflation and unemployment been personified?
3. Why do you think that inflation and unemployment are inversely related?
4. How does the present inflation rate compare to the unemployment rate? Has the economic seesaw been fixed? Explain.

Chapter Goals

By the end of this chapter, you will be able to

- identify the types, causes, and effects of inflation, deflation, and unemployment,
- describe the characteristics and causes of instability in each business phase,
- apply economic inquiry to assess indicators and to analyze public policy issues related to unemployment, inflation, and recession.

Monitoring Employment

In this chapter, we shall look more closely at the relationships among aggregate national production, unemployment, and price inflation in the Canadian economy in order to get a better sense of unemployment issues and future prospects. However, before proceeding, it would be useful to refresh your understanding of such fundamental concepts as the economics of labour (Chapter 8), labour force (Chapter 9), the elasticity of demand (Chapter 5), and the unemployment rate (Chapter 9).

Employment and Unemployment Rates

In Chapter 9, the *labour force* was defined as all residents of Canada who have jobs as well as all those who are actively seeking employment. Through its Labour Force Study (LFS), Statistics Canada keeps track of fluctuations in the labour force by surveying a random sample of approximately 50 000 representative households each month. National figures are computer-projected, based on the survey data collected. Interviewers gather employment information on all household members who are 15 years of age and older. Those individuals who did any part-time or full-time work during the month are considered to be employed. All those who had jobs but did not work because of labour disputes, vacations, or illness are also included in the employed category.

The employment rate
In 2000, the total number employed in Canada was 14.9 million. This amounts to a 93.2 per cent national employment rate. The following formula is used to calculate the **employment rate**:

$$\text{employment rate} = \frac{\text{number employed}}{\text{labour force}} \times 100$$

$$= \frac{14\ 909\ 700}{15\ 999\ 200} \times 100 = 93.2\%$$

The unemployment rate
The unemployed group consists of all those who are not working and who are actively seeking and presently available for work. Workers who are on temporary layoff are also included in this category. In 2000, the total number of unemployed Canadians was slightly over 1 million. This amounts to a 6.8 per cent national unemployment rate. Applying the formula used to calculate the *unemployment rate* in Chapter 9 (see page 203):

$$\text{unemployment rate} = \frac{1\ 089\ 500}{15\ 999\ 200} \times 100 = 6.8\%$$

Statistics Canada calculates two unemployment rates: an actual unemployment rate and a seasonally adjusted rate. The **seasonally adjusted rate** eliminates short-term or seasonal fluctuations, such as the noticeable rise in unemployment each winter when many employed in farming, fishing, construction, and other seasonal industries are temporarily out of work.

The participation rate
The total labour force includes both the employed and the unemployed, with the exception of full-time military personnel, inmates of penal institutions, full-time students, retired workers, and homemakers. In 2000, the Canadian labour force consisted of approximately 16 million people. When the labour force is expressed as a percentage of the total employable population (all those 15 years of age and over), that percentage is known as the **participation rate**. In 2000, the participation rate was:

$$\text{participation rate} = \frac{\text{total labour force}}{\text{total employable population}} \times 100$$

$$= \frac{15\ 999\ 200}{24\ 277\ 997} \times 100 = 65.9\%$$

The higher the participation rate, the higher the proportion of available human resources actually employed and contributing to a nation's aggregate production. The inclusion of all persons 15 years of age or older in the participation rate is challenged by some who believe that those 65 and older should not be included. Do you agree?

The Limitations of Employment Data

As with GDP, it is important to recognize that the accuracy of national employment figures can be at issue because of the way they are calculated. Critics often cite the three factors of underemployment, discouraged workers, and dishonesty when they question the accuracy of employment data.

Unemployment figures may understate the true level of unemployment because part-time workers are recorded as fully employed workers. Although some people work part-time by choice, others would prefer full-time work but cannot find it. They are statistically recorded as fully employed but they are, in fact, only partially employed. Furthermore, during tough economic times, some workers may have to work at jobs that do not fully utilize their skills and education. In both examples, **underemployment** is evident.

Discouraged workers are those who would like to work but have stopped looking because they believe nothing is available for them. Since they are not actively seeking employment, these discouraged workers are not considered part of the labour force and not included among the unemployed.

It has been suggested by some economists that the numbers of underemployed and discouraged workers, sometimes referred to as the **hidden unemployed**, would increase the official unemployment rate in Canada by as much as 70 per cent. If accurate, this would mean that during the economic recession that peaked in 1992, the true unemployment figure would have been closer to 19 per cent rather than the 11.2 per cent reported by Statistics Canada.

Dishonesty can also be a problem for Statistics Canada. Respondents to the monthly Labour Market Survey may claim to be actively seeking work when, in fact, they are not. It is extremely difficult to verify how seriously respondents are actually looking for work or to check whether they have unreported jobs.

Considering these three factors, it can safely be concluded that national and regional unemployment figures are "best estimates" and, thus, not absolutely accurate. However, since these figures are recorded in the same manner each month, they provide useful comparative data.

Types of Unemployment

Six types of unemployment were introduced in Chapter 9 (see Figure 9.3 on page 204). Economists use the terms frictional, seasonal, structural (including technological and replacement), and cyclical unemployment to help clarify the causes of unemployment.

Frictional unemployment refers to the short-term unemployment of those workers who are presently between jobs or who are entering or re-entering the labour market. Examples include parents re-entering the labour force after staying home to raise children and workers who have left their jobs to look for higher-paying or more suitable employment. Where workers are free to change jobs, some 3 per cent of the labour market may be between jobs at any time. Given its short-term nature, this type of unemployment is considered the least serious.

Seasonal unemployment is the result of climatic changes that may leave workers unemployed for specific periods each year. As a result of Canada's climate, the construction, lumbering, fishing, farming, and tourism industries all experience seasonal fluctuations in employment. These fluctuations are less significant today than they were in the past. Technological advances now permit increased construction activity in winter. The demand for workers in the tourism industry in winter has risen because of growing interest in winter sports and recreational activities. Furthermore, today a smaller proportion of the Canadian labour force is employed in seasonally affected primary industries. As mentioned earlier, in order to minimize seasonal fluctuations in unemployment data, Statistics Canada calculates a *seasonally adjusted* unemployment rate.

Structural unemployment is the direct result of structural changes in the economy. As the Canadian economy evolves, some industries grow while others decline and even disappear. For example, the depletion of natural resources may cause miners to lose their jobs

SKILL BUILDER
Thinking Like an Economist

Working with Indicators

Although they are often best estimates, indicators are used by economists to make comparisons and detect patterns and trends. Changes in these indicators help economists recognize and confirm important employment patterns. The employment indicators that we examined in the previous sections are presented in Figure 14.1. The data, which cover the period between 1990 and 2000, were collected from various Statistics Canada publications. To help you understand what happened to employment and production levels during the 1990s, answer the questions on page 313, using the data in Figure 14.1.

	1990	1992	1994	1996	1998	2000
Population (15+ years)	21 223 547	21 860 274	22 433 589	23 028 593	23 683 103	24 277 997
Labour force	14 241 000	14 362 200	14 626 700	14 899 500	15 417 700	15 999 200
Participation rate	67.1					65.9
Total Employed	**13 084 000**	**12 760 000**	**13 111 700**	**13 462 600**	**14 140 400**	**14 909 700**
Employment Rate (%)	**91.9**	**88.8**	**89.6**	**90.4**	**91.7**	**93.2**
Self-employed workers		15	15.5	16.1	17.2	16.2
Temporary/contract workers	—	—	—	11.2	11.8	12.5
Those working 40+ hrs/wk	—	20.3	21.7	21.2	18.9	18.0
Unionized workers	34.7	34.9	34.5	33.9	31.8	29.9
Total Unemployed						**1 089 500**
Unemployment Rate (%)	**8.1**	**11.2**	**10.4**	**9.6**	**8.3**	**6.8**
Among those aged 15–24	12.4	17.1	15.8	15.3	15.1	12.6
Among those aged 25–54	7.1	9.9	9.2	8.5	7.0	5.7
Among those with high-school education or less	12.2	14.0	13.1	12.4	11.1	9.3
Among those with post-secondary certificate or diploma	6.4	9.3	8.9	8.1	6.5	5.2
Among those with university degrees	3.8	5.5	5.4	5.2	4.4	3.9
Consumer Price Index (% increase)	4.8	1.5	0.2	1.6	0.9	2.7
Gross Domestic Product (in billions of 1992 dollars)	609.2	604.3	645.9	672.8	721.9	786.9
GDP (annual % change)	0.3	0.7	4.5	1.5	3.1	4.5

Source: Statistics Canada, Canadian Economic Observer, 2000/2001 #11-210; Labour Force Historical Review, 2000 # 71-201.

Figure 14.1 Employment indicators.

QUESTIONS

1. Explain the relationship between the employment and unemployment rate for any given year. Use a pie chart to illustrate this relationship.

2. Calculate the number of unemployed Canadians from 1990 to 1998.

3. Calculate the participation rate for 1992 to 1998. Compare the usefulness of this indicator to the employment rate calculation. In 1996, employment increased sharply while the participation rate actually decreased. Explain how this is possible.

4. Explain the relationship that exists between unemployment and education.

5. Explain the changes in the labour market during the 1990s by referring to changes in the percentage of workers working longer hours, the percentage of workers employed in temporary or contract positions, and the percentage of workers belonging to labour unions.

6. When was the unemployment rate highest during the 1990s? Based on the reported changes to the GDP figures at this time, explain what happened to the Canadian economy in the early 1990s.

---

permanently. On the other hand, it may become profitable for a firm to employ more capital-intensive methods of production, replacing workers with automation technology. This type of structural unemployment is often classified as **technological unemployment** in order to identify the cause.

Structural unemployment occurs when the skills and location of available workers do not match the skill requirements and location of employment opportunities. For example, automobile assembly-line workers who lose their jobs in Ontario because of automation may also require retraining and relocation in order to find new employment. Learning new skills, moving elsewhere to find work, and developing new industries in a region where the traditional industries are in decline all take time. As a result, structural unemployment can persist for long periods.

Some structural unemployment is created when workers permanently lose their jobs because of competition from lower-priced foreign imports. As firms move labour-intensive production to countries where labour rates are cheaper, workers in another country effectively replace Canadian labour. This type of structural unemployment, also referred to as **replacement unemployment**, is one of the costs that Canada and other industrial nations will face in moving to a global economy.

(However, as we'll learn in Chapter 17, there are also considerable benefits.)

Market economies typically experience periodic upswings and downturns known as *business cycles*. **Cyclical unemployment** is caused by reduced employment opportunities during periods of economic decline. As overall consumer confidence and spending decrease, the overall demand for goods and services declines and fewer workers are needed in most industries. As we learned in Chapter 13, during the Great Depression of the 1930s, unemployment levels in Canada reached 20 per cent. During the recession of 1982–1983, unemployment levels reached 12 per cent, while the downturn of 1990–1992 produced unemployment levels of 11 per cent. In periods of high consumer demand, auto workers may work overtime, but in periods of low demand for new cars, they may be laid off.

Cyclical unemployment is largely the result of declining demand during periods of economic downturn. For this reason, it is sometimes referred to as **inadequate demand unemployment**. Sometimes government policy contributes to cyclical unemployment. If the Bank of Canada restricts the money supply and raises interest rates in order to combat inflation, the level of consumer demand is adversely affected, investment is reduced, and unemployment may increase.

Full Employment

From what we have learned about the nature of unemployment in Canada, it is unreasonable to expect 100 per cent employment. Economists believe that structural, seasonal, and frictional unemployment are inevitable. For economists, then, *full employment* is the lowest possible rate of unemployment, making allowances for the portion of unemployment that is inevitable and necessary to keep the rate of price inflation from accelerating.

In effect, full employment is the highest reasonable expectation of employment, sometimes referred to as the **natural employment rate**. The full employment rate traditionally includes frictional and structural unemployment and excludes cyclical and seasonal unemployment. Cyclical unemployment is excluded because this type of unemployment can be effectively controlled by stabilizing the downturns and upswings of the business cycle. Cyclical unemployment is neither inevitable nor necessary. Seasonal unemployment is automatically excluded from all seasonally adjusted data.

The full employment rate has been adjusted over time. In the 1960s, the Economic Council of Canada concluded that a 3 per cent rate of unemployment was reasonable. This goal was almost reached in 1966, when unemployment in Canada reached 3.4 per cent. By 1980, the full employment rate was doubled to 6 per cent in order to reflect increases in the rates of frictional and structural unemployment. By the mid-1990s, most definitions of full employment included a natural unemployment rate between 6 and 7 per cent. Frictional unemployment alone is now estimated to create 3 per cent unemployment at any given time.

The Costs of Unemployment

Chronic unemployment can hurt both individuals and the Canadian economy as a whole. There are human and economic costs associated with joblessness, especially unemployment lasting for extended periods of time. Unemployment can create stress, financial hardship, discouragement, and low self-esteem for jobless workers and their families.

Chronically high unemployment rates can lead to social unrest and produce negative attitudes toward the government in power and toward immigration policy. Some unemployed Canadians believe that immigrants take jobs away from them, even though economists have demonstrated that immigration creates additional job opportunities. During periods of high unemployment, the call for reduced immigration can still be heard.

Although these human and social costs are difficult to calculate in terms of dollars and cents, they must be carefully considered in any assessment of the full impact of unemployment. Too often the emphasis is placed on costs that affect the economy as a whole rather than on individual well-being. We will investigate these human costs in Chapter 15.

The cost of unemployment for the entire economy, as introduced in Chapter 9, is reflected by the *GDP gap*. This is the amount by which the **potential output** (associated with full employment) exceeds the **actual output**, measured in dollars. The greater the GDP gap, the greater the value of national production lost because of the underemployment of labour resources. Okun's law states:

For every 1 per cent that the actual unemployment rate exceeds the full employment rate, there is a 2 per cent gap in the GDP.

During the recession of 1983, unemployment reached 11.8 per cent while the GDP (in 1986 dollars) was determined to be $439.5 billion. Assuming a 7 per cent full employment rate, we can estimate the GDP gap during that recession by using Okun's law (see page 206 in Chapter 9):

$$\text{GDP gap} = \$439.5 \text{ billion} \times \frac{(11.8 - 7) \times 2}{100}$$

$$= \$42.19 \text{ billion}$$

Therefore, the lost national production that resulted from the unemployment of labour resources in 1983 amounted to $42.19 billion, or $1700 in lost income for every single Canadian. Unfortunately, since the costs of unemployment are not shared equally in Canada, the losses suffered by some individuals and families in 1983 were far greater.

Check Your
Understanding

1. What is the labour force status—employed, unemployed, or officially not in the labour force—of each of the following persons? Explain why in each case.

   a) A university graduate is seeking her first job.

   b) A male homemaker stays home full-time to care for three small children and an ailing parent.

   c) A mechanical engineer has left her job to look for a better position.

   d) A computer operator has a job but is too ill to work.

   e) An unemployed fisheries worker has given up looking for work after ten months of trying.

   f) A new Canadian with a PhD in microbiology has to drive a cab to make a living.

2. Identify the type of unemployment represented by the following examples.

   a) Declining salmon stocks in the Pacific Northwest have produced a sharp decline in the number of people employed in the fishing industry in British Columbia.

   b) Employees who are tired of working for an unreasonable boss decide to quit and look for better jobs.

   c) Foreign automobile manufacturers have increased their market share in Canada since 1980. As a result, some Canadian auto workers have lost their jobs.

   d) Retailers who hire extra staff for the Christmas period lay them off after the Boxing Week sales.

   e) As labour unions succeed in negotiating higher wages for their members, it becomes more attractive for firms to use machines instead of unionized workers. As a result, some workers are laid off.

   f) Increases in interest rates cause mortgage rates to climb. As a result, consumer demand for new houses decreases and construction workers are laid off.

3. What is meant by the *hidden unemployed*? What effect do they have on unemployment data?

4. Assuming a full employment rate of 7 per cent, use the data in Figure 14.1 (page 312) to calculate the GDP gap for the years 1990 to 2000. Which year had the greatest GDP gap? Develop a general rule to explain when the GDP gap is greatest and when it is at a minimum.

Economic Instability: Business Cycles and Employment Patterns

Canadian Unemployment Patterns, 1966–2000

Despite its limitations, the annual unemployment rate is often used as an indicator of general economic health. Furthermore, comparing rates from one year to the next provides a relative indication of how effectively the economy is creating new jobs for Canadian workers. In net terms, new jobs require growth or expansion in economic activity. Therefore, periods of relatively low unemployment (that is, relative to the years that precede or follow) identify intervals when the economy has been able to create more new jobs than it lost. These are considered periods of economic expansion or recovery, even if the impact is only modest.

Figure 14.2 (page 316) clearly presents the fluctuations in the average annual unemployment rates in Canada (and, therefore, the general health of the Canadian economy) from 1966 to 2000. Over this 33-year period, changes in the level of unemployment seem to follow a cyclical pattern of peaks and valleys. Unfortunately, the general trend has been upward. Rates averaged about 4 per cent during the late 1960s and climbed to 10 per cent during the 1990s. The following are some of the reasons offered to explain this gradual escalation of unemployment rates:

• Globalization has led to increased replacement unemployment as manufacturing jobs continue to migrate to countries with cheaper labour costs.

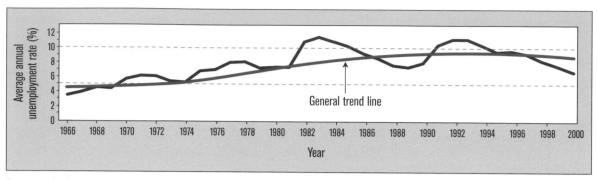

Source: Adaption of Figure, Average annual unemployment rates in Canada, 1966–1991, from *Economics: A Canadian Perspective* by James D. Thexton. Copyright © Oxford University Press Canada 1992. Reprinted by permission.

Figure 14.2 Average annual unemployment rates in Canada, 1966–2000.

• High Employment Insurance benefits act as a disincentive to permanent employment.
• Automation has created technological unemployment as workers continue to be replaced by machines.
• Greater economic freedom and worker mobility have resulted in an increased number of Canadians who are between jobs during any reporting period.

Periods of relatively high unemployment (1971, 1978, 1983, and 1992) are noticeable in Figure 14.2 as peaks, or upward bulges. Periods of relatively low unemployment (1969, 1974, 1979, and 1989) appear on the graph as troughs, or downward bulges. These downward bulges correspond with peaks in the GDP, identifying periods of relative economic growth or expansion (see Figure 4.1 on page 312). In absolute terms, the lowest unemployment rate during this period was observed in 1966; the highest rate was observed in 1983. By extending the general trend line, a reasonable forecast can be made about future unemployment rates in Canada. What would you expect the unemployment rate to be in ten years?

Fluctuations in the Canadian Economy

Expansion and contraction

Since the Canadian government began to collect economic performance data in 1926, national production records reveal a continuously alternating pattern of economic slow-down, recovery, and expansion. These fluctuations are generally referred to as **business cycles**. Figure 10.10 (see page 225 in Chapter 10) illustrated the four general phases present in each cycle: peak, contraction, trough, and expansion (although business cycles may vary significantly in severity and duration).

As we have learned, the most significant economic downturn since 1926 occurred during the Great Depression of the 1930s. In Canada, between 1929 and 1933, unemployment approached 20 per cent and real GDP declined by 30 per cent. Clearly, this was a period of significant economic contraction in Canada and abroad. As the economy declines, workers are laid off in response to the decreasing demand for the goods and services being produced. Therefore, unemployment rates climb sharply during a period of contraction. If this contraction is seen to last longer than six consecutive months (two business quarters), the economy is said to be in **recession**. A recession is a pronounced contraction. A *depression* is a severe and lengthy recession.

Periods of *expansion* (increasing national production) generally follow recessionary periods. During the first part of an expansionary period, the economy is said to be in the **recovery** mode.

Since expansion phases represent periods of sustained increases in real aggregate output, generally speaking, employment rates increase as the economy expands. There is a direct relationship, therefore, between GDP and employment. There is an inverse relationship between GDP and unemployment. You will notice in comparing the patterns shown in Figure 14.1 (page 312) that peak unemployment occurs during the same years that GDP patterns bottom out. To put it succinctly, unemployment peaks as economic production bottoms out. Unemployment bottoms out as aggregate production peaks.

Inflation and employment

In his analysis of business cycles, Keynes also linked employment to price inflation. According to Keynesian theory, the business cycle model implies that fluctuations in aggregate production levels will cause economies to alternate between periods of inflation or unemployment. During a recession, levels of unemployment are relatively high. With more workers unemployed, consumer spending is adversely affected. Both the amount of money in circulation (*money supply*) and the rate at which money changes hands through business transactions (*velocity of money*) are also adversely affected. All these economic adjustments act to reduce aggregate demand and inflationary pressures in the economy; thus, prices generally stabilize.

During periods of economic expansion, the opposite happens. Levels of unemployment are reduced because more of the labour force is able to find work. With more workers employed, the demand for consumer goods increases. As economic activity increases, both the supply and the velocity of money increase. If the production side of the economy does not keep pace with this increased demand, prices will rise as more dollars attempt to chase after available goods and services. Economic expansion can produce inflationary pressures in the economy.

Two distinct types of inflation are identified by economists. **Demand-pull inflation** results from excessive increases in consumer demand, relative to available aggregate production. **Cost-push inflation** results from the passing down of increased operating costs from producer to consumer. Thus, rapid expansion is synonymous with inflation, and recession is synonymous with unemployment. Price deflation is usually synonymous with a depression.

Continuing in the Keynesian tradition, in the early 1960s, at the London School of Economics in Britain, the economist A.W. Phillips researched the link between inflation and unemployment rates. What eventually evolved from these studies was a diagram, known as the **Phillips curve**, showing a stable and predictable inverse relationship between inflation and unemployment rates. According to this curve, as inflation rises, unemployment declines, and vice versa. This curve was used to introduce this chapter (see page 309).

When an economy adopts an *easy money policy* (low interest rates) and an *expansionary fiscal policy* (cutting taxes while increasing government spending) in order to combat unemployment, it must accept a higher rate of inflation as a consequence. The converse can also be forecasted. A tight money policy and a contractionary fiscal policy (raising taxes while cutting government spending) will combat inflation at the cost of increased unemployment. This trade-off between inflation and unemployment was thought to exist in both the short and the long term.

Until the 1970s, many economists agreed that Keynes and Phillips had provided an accurate model of how a market economy fluctuates. However, by the mid-1970s, an interesting economic phenomenon was occurring. Although inflation and unemployment were previously seen as opposites, the Canadian economy began to experience the unexpected: simultaneous increases in unemployment and inflation. (This situation was lampooned in the 1979 cartoon presented at the beginning of this chapter.) These periods of economic stagnation, where aggregate production slows down and both unemployment and inflation rates increase, became known as **stagflation**. This particular period of stagflation was caused by aggregate supply not being able to keep pace with increases in aggregate demand. Figure 14.3 (page 318) outlines some of the principal causes for the stagflation that occurred during the 1970s.

Factor	Effect on Production/Supply	Effect on Unemployment	Effect on Inflation
Sharp increases in global oil prices The price of crude oil was more than ten times higher in 1982 than it was in 1972 as a result of the actions of the Organization of Petroleum Exporting Countries (OPEC), a cartel that includes many of the world's major oil producers.	Since oil is an important resource to many industries and a fuel for transportation and heating, production costs increased significantly. Many firms responded by decreasing their output.	Fewer workers were needed when firms cut production.	Prices were increased to cover increases in production costs (i.e., cost-push inflation).
Poor harvests in Eurasia Climatic and technological problems resulted in poor harvests in China and the Soviet Union in the 1970s.	The global food supply decreased as a result of low crop yields. Canadian production levels remained constant.	The percentage of the Canadian labour force employed in agriculture continued to decline during the 1970s and 1980s.	Prices of agricultural products increased as the global food supply decreased.
Devaluation of the Canadian dollar The value of the Canadian dollar decreased in foreign money markets during the 1970s and 1980s.	Prices of foreign supplies and materials increased, raising production costs and adversely affecting production levels.	Fewer workers were needed when firms cut production.	Prices of foreign goods increased as a result of a weaker dollar.
Push for higher wages by Canadian labour With inflation rates climbing and expected to continue to climb, workers began to push for higher wages and cost-of-living adjustments in labour negotiations.	Wage increases were not based on increased worker productivity but rather on keeping up with inflation. Rising wages increased operating costs. Many firms responded by cutting production.	Higher labour costs meant that firms made do with fewer workers. As a result, unemployment increased.	Firms raised prices to recover their increased labour costs and protect their profit margins.
Government policy Regulations (e.g., minimum-wage legislation, mandatory vacation pay, and worker's compensation premiums) increased production costs. Policies protecting declining enterprises in their waning years led to reduced productivity.	Aggregate supply did not reach maximum potential as producers sought to reduce labour costs and declining enterprises operated at reduced efficiency.	Employers made do with fewer workers as labour costs increased. Jobs in declining industries and depressed economic communities were protected.	Increased labour costs and decreased efficiency in declining industries caused prices to increase.
Bank of Canada interest policies High interest rate policies were designed to control consumer spending and reduce inflationary pressures.	High interest rates discouraged investment and adversely affected productivity.	With less investment spending, fewer new jobs were created for Canada's growing labour force.	Demand-pull inflation was reduced slightly, but cost-push inflation and inflation imported from other countries continued to grow.

Figure 14.3 Factors causing stagflation in Canada from 1973 to 1982. Most point to a downward shift in the aggregate supply curve.

"Jobless" Recovery: Short-Term Adjustment or Long-Term Reality?

The Paradox of Collective Bargaining

During the 1990s, inflationary pressures were effectively reduced. However, unemployment proved far more difficult to remedy. This relatively new phenomenon is described as a **jobless recovery**. Surprisingly, one of the reasons for this persistent high unemployment was the effectiveness of labour unions within the collective bargaining process. Although this topic was introduced in Chapter 8, we shall now use supply and demand graphs to explain the effect that unions generally had on the labour market during the 1970s and 1980s.

Most labour unions focused their collective bargaining efforts on securing better wages, working conditions, and benefits (such as cost-of-living allowances as protection against continued inflation) for their members. However, the laws of supply and demand acted to create an additional, unintended effect. In Figure 14.4, as wages improve from $12 to $16 per hour, two changes take place. First, given the nature of the supply curve for labour, there is an increase (E to B along the supply curve) in the number of workers willing and able to supply labour at the higher wage level. At the same time, the quantity of labour being demanded at this higher wage is naturally reduced. As labour becomes more expensive, employers will find methods of production that involve fewer workers. This increase in quantity

supplied, coupled with a simultaneous decrease in quantity demanded (from E to A), produces 7000 unemployed workers in our example.

This example illustrates an interesting paradox for labour unions. As unions collectively negotiate higher wages for members, they may inadvertently negotiate a reduction in their own membership. While wage rates were set at $12 per hour, 11 000 union members were employed. As wages were increased to $16 per hour, only 7000 union members remained employed. In this example, union negotiators

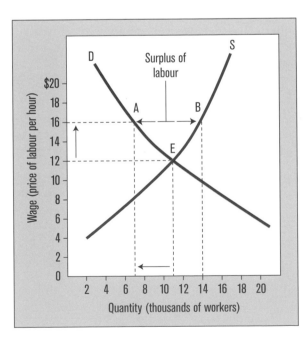

Figure 14.4 The effect of collective bargaining on the labour market during the 1970s and 1980s.

did achieve higher wages but at the cost of lost jobs for their membership. This economic phenomenon happens when workers are being paid more without producing more. When worker productivity increases, the higher cost of labour can be offset by the higher revenues resulting from this increased production. To keep an economy healthy, negotiated wage increases should be proportional to actual or aggregate increases in productivity. When wage increases exceed productivity increases, price inflation can occur.

During the 1990s, as labour costs continued to be quite high, many firms began to **downsize** their workforce. Through incentive packages, veteran workers were encouraged to take early retirement. Retired workers were not replaced, and surplus workers were laid off. Generally speaking, those who remained found that their workload had increased. Another trend involved **rightsizing**, which meant reviewing the size of operations in order to correct the previous overuse of labour. Rightsizing, it was argued, was necessary to keep operations viable in an increasingly competitive global economy. Some unions reluctantly agreed to take wage reductions and to give up negotiated benefits in order to protect jobs. Labour advocates have pointed out that, in some cases, rightsizing produced short-term benefits, such as increased profitability and corporate stock prices, but also produced longer-term costs, such as declines in product quality and customer service.

Automation and Increased Industrial Productivity

During the 1990s, many firms decided to reduce their labour force and trim their payroll in order to protect or improve profit levels. In competitive enterprises, this was accomplished by increasing industrial productivity. Through computer-assisted technological advancements, many low-skill tasks previously performed by workers were assumed by machines. As labour became increasingly more expensive (a result of collectively negotiated wage increases and increases in the minimum wage set by governments), there was added incentive to invest more money in industrial technology.

Furthermore, in an environment where traditional low-technology jobs were becoming more and more difficult to find, it became easier to motivate employees to work harder. Since 1990, the workplace has become a generally "leaner" environment. To organized labour, and many other Canadians, increases in productivity have become synonymous with forcing more work out of fewer employees.

Spurred on by increases in industrial productivity, and using a smaller, better-trained, and better-equipped workforce, firms have been able to maintain and, in some cases, increase production levels. This practice has generally had a positive effect on profit levels. Unfortunately, in the Canadian economy, increases in domestic productivity have not kept pace with increases in the United States and in the economies of other major trading partners. This has prompted many economists to focus attention on comparative productivity levels. Economic prosperity and the recovery of the weak Canadian dollar in foreign money markets, they argue, will require substantial growth in domestic productivity.

Increased productivity of labour can act to increase the demand for labour. If aggregate demand grows with aggregate supply, the demand for labour will increase in order to pursue this growing aggregate demand. If aggregate demand does not increase, as would be the case during a recessionary period, then productivity gains may serve to reduce the number of workers actually needed. This reduction in the demand for labour will be felt most in the low-skill, low-experience (youth) segment of the labour force, where productivity is more difficult to improve.

As aggregate production recovers from a period of economic downturn, employment levels may no longer recover to the same extent that they did in the past because of the effects of technological innovation and increased productivity. Technological innovation replaces low-skill jobs but creates high-skill jobs. Unfortunately, displaced workers may not have the training required to compete for the new technological jobs that have been created. The result is that some new jobs remain unfilled. During the late 1990s, many Canadian employers were concerned about not being able to find the skilled workers that their enterprises required.

Employment Patterns in the Global Economy

Another factor in persistently high unemployment levels during the recovery phase of recent business cycles has been the steady movement toward greater economic globalization. As national borders continue to lose their economic significance, some corporate decisions that are based on profit maximization will have adverse effects on unemployment rates in Canada and other industrialized nations. Generally speaking, some unemployment in industrialized nations can be traced to the loss of manufacturing jobs to less developed nations, where wage levels, working conditions, and environmental protection legislation are conducive to increased profit levels.

As a result of the North American Free Trade Agreement (NAFTA), some US firms have decided to reduce costs by scaling down their Canadian operations and supplying Canadian customers from the closest US plant. Other firms, previously based in Canada, have relocated to Mexico to take advantage of lower wage rates and less stringent environmental regulations. (We shall explore this trend in detail in Unit 5, when we investigate international trade patterns.) Although there have also been some job gains as a result of globalization, for the purposes of this discussion, it will suffice to note that unemployment levels in Canada have remained generally higher, perhaps partially because of the manufacturing jobs lost as a result of globalization.

The Effects of Taxation

High levels of corporate and business taxation can act to discourage investment and corporate expansion. Where consumer and investor confidence is high, lower levels of corporate taxation (relative to the rates paid in nations that are major trading partners) help to create a business climate conducive to expansion and greater employment opportunities.

Levels of personal taxation affect both the disposable income left to consumers and investors and the government's ability to finance the infrastructure improvements necessary to promote increased productivity and economic activity. For example, in Canada, complex and expensive communication and transportation networks have been developed (and are being improved) to link the country together. In addition, government spending on education and health contributes significantly to national productivity.

High taxes can have adverse effects on employment levels. Unless the decreases in disposable income (caused by tax increases) are offset by increases in government spending, taxation can reduce aggregate demand. Decreases in aggregate demand or in consumer confidence prompt firms to cut employment in order to protect profit levels in a declining marketplace.

The Effects of Demographic Changes

The jobless rate may remain high even though jobs are actually being created if the labour force increases faster than the economy's ability to create jobs. For example, as employment prospects increase in an expanding economy, people who had previously given up looking for work may return to the labour force. Some economists have suggested that monitoring the number of employed Canadians is a truer indicator of job creation than monitoring changes in the unemployment rate. Any thorough analysis of whether a recovery period is actually "jobless" should involve the monitoring of both indicators.

Taking Stock

Several reasons have been advanced to explain the recent phenomenon of jobless recovery. The question that remains, however, is an extremely important one for you. Is the incidence of jobless recovery a short-term economic correction or a long-term economic reality? On this issue, the Canadian economic community is clearly divided, and it appears that only time will tell. By the time you write your own economics textbook, you will be able to provide historical documentation to explain the longevity of the jobless recovery phenomenon.

Case Study

The Road to Recovery

Since 1497, when John Cabot found fish that were so plentiful they could be scooped from the water in baskets, cod became the catalyst for the settlement and economic development of Newfoundland and Labrador. By 1992, after years of government reductions in the "Total Allowable Catch," the northern cod was still the biggest single fishery on the east coast, worth $700 million to the Canadian economy. However, by 1994, two years after the federal government closed the northern cod fishery, the cod had been fished to "commercial extinction" according to the United Nations Food and Agriculture Organization. Some of the possible causes of the cod fisheries collapse include the following: overfishing and mismanagement; climatic change that resulted in changes in temperature and aquatic life; an increase in the fish-eating seal population; the use of dragnets, which destroy fish eggs and marine life forms; the use of electronic technology to locate schools of fish; and the use of large automated factory trawlers with built-in filleting and freezing equipment.

Virtually every community in the province depended on the fishery. When the cod fishery collapsed, approximately 31 000 people lost their jobs, most of which were in Newfoundland and Labrador. This represented the largest layoff in Canadian history. The laid-off workers received a $1.9 billion aid package from Ottawa known as **The Atlantic Groundfish Strategy (TAGS)**. This program, which ran from 1994 to 1998, temporarily helped to provide the necessities of life. However, an economic blow such as the collapse of the fisheries— a major employer—had to be met with substantive structural changes to the provincial economy. In the following sections, we shall explore how the provincial economy was diversified.

Aquaculture

Some in the province have turned to **aquaculture**, the breeding and raising of marine life in tanks, ponds, and reservoirs. To date, aquaculture (also known as fish farming) in the province has focused on the production of mussels, steelhead, salmon, and cod. In 2000, the industry produced 2724 tonnes of seafood, generated $13.7 million in exports, and employed 500 people. The federal and provincial governments are promoting this industry aggressively as part of the Canada/ Newfoundland Agreement on Economic Renewal. Research into more ecological methods of aquaculture is being carried out.

Developing the Hibernia Oil Field

Discovered in 1979, the Hibernia oil field is 314 km east-southeast of St. John's, under approximately 80 m of water. The $6 billion drilling-production platform was installed (by a consortium of large oil companies) in 1997 after six years of design, engineering, and construction work. It has been estimated that the site contains 615 million barrels of recoverable oil. The Canadian Association of Petroleum Producers (CAPP) further estimates that there are about 4.6 billion barrels of oil in the Grand Banks. However, the high-risk offshore oil industry requires far too much capital for small enterprises to get into the action.

The estimated direct and indirect employment impact of the Hibernia operation is 3100 new jobs, representing 1.6 per cent of the provincial total. The first full year of production was 1998. The Hibernia operation and its indirect impacts (including suppliers and service providers) produced a GDP increase of $626 million, representing 5.7 per cent of the province's total GDP. Since many

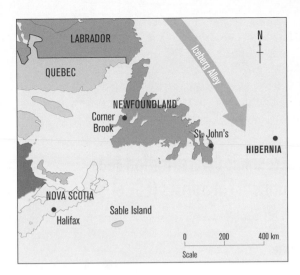

Telecommunications carriers expanded output by 6.1 per cent annually.

The contribution IT makes to the provincial economy is important from two perspectives. First, it generates employment and income for those working in the sector. Second, and perhaps more important, it has an enabling effect on other parts of the economy by enhancing productivity and performance.

Filmmaking

The film industry in Newfoundland and Labrador has produced more than 100 films over the past 30 years. Since the late 1980s, there has been a steady increase in more ambitious projects involving documentaries, feature films, and television programs. Between 1990 and 1996, film production approached $14 million; between 1997 and 2000, it was $38 million. During 2001 alone, projects valued at $14 million were produced in Newfoundland and Labrador.

The very competitive film and video industry offers significant employment possibilities. Film and television productions are labour intensive, with approximately 60 per cent of a film project's budget being spent on salaries and fees for

of the Hibernia jobs pay well, personal income in Newfoundland and Labrador was $168 million higher in 1998. This led to a $124 million increase in consumer spending. The total population was 5000 higher as a result of reduced out-migration and increased in-migration.

Since 1998, oil production has continued to increase. Hibernia produced 54.3 million barrels of oil in 2001, up 2.8 per cent from 2000. The market value of the 2001 production was estimated to be $2.1 billion.

Information Technology

The province's information technology (IT) sector has experienced considerable growth since the collapse of the cod fisheries. Funded by the Canada/Newfoundland Agreement on Economic Renewal in 1996, Operation ONLINE is a non-profit organization created to promote growth in the very competitive IT sector. Of the over 200 high-technology companies (which employ over 8000 workers in the province), 163 are IT companies. Seventy per cent are located in the St. John's Census Metropolitan Area. There are two significant segments of the IT sector: computer and related services and telecommunications carriers. GDP in the computer and related services industry averaged growth of 10.4 per cent annually between 1992 and 1997.

Figure 14.5 The Hibernia oil platform. A 15-m-thick ice belt was designed to protect the platform from icebergs.

creative and technical workers. A typical feature film crew can employ 50 to 60 full-time cast and crew members. The film industry is recognized as a very efficient job creator. Independent production companies create one job for every $36 000 received in gross revenues, compared to one job for every $144 000 for most dominant industrial sectors.

There are also sizable spinoff benefits for communities where productions are actually filmed, in the form of goods and services purchased from local businesses. Statistics Canada estimates that for every dollar spent directly on film and video productions, an additional dollar is generated in spinoff benefits.

In order to attract increased filmmaking activity, the provincial government has instituted a corporate income tax credit administered by the Newfoundland and Labrador Film Development Corporation (NLFDC). The program encourages the development, training, and hiring of local film personnel in all aspects of the production process. It provides incentives to production companies to create economic growth in the province.

Tourism

In recent years, there has been a concerted effort to attract more non-resident tourism to the province in order to create employment in the hospitality and service industries. In 1997, the province celebrated the 500th anniversary of John Cabot's historic voyage from England to Newfoundland. This highly publicized celebration produced a 22 per cent increase in automobile and air visits from the previous year. This increase was maintained in 1998 as well. In 1999, the province celebrated its 50th anniversary of Confederation, which brought an increase of 8 per cent from the previous year in auto, air, and cruise-ship visits.

In 2000, celebrations surrounding the Viking explorers saw a 3 per cent increase in auto, air, and cruise visits over the previous year. The 100th anniversary of Marconi's trans-Atlantic wireless radio transmission from Newfoundland was celebrated in 2001. During the first eight months of the year, tourism grew approxi-

mately 10 per cent, resulting in an increase in hotel occupancy and car rental revenues. Job opportunities and incomes in the hospitality and tourism sector continued to grow. However, after the terrorist attacks of 11 September, airport passenger movements and international arrivals declined sharply.

Economic Diversification and Growth Enterprises (EDGE)

This provincial government initiative is an incentive program intended to attract businesses and promote expansion. It features a ten-year "tax holiday" from provincial corporate income tax and health and payroll taxes. Forty-five municipalities have joined with the province in extending the tax holiday to municipal property and business taxes. With incentives like these, the cost of doing business in Newfoundland and Labrador has been significantly reduced. As part of the EDGE initiative, by 2001, 60 companies had filed business plans projecting the investment of $730 million and the creation of 2437 jobs.

Not only have great strides been made in diversifying the provincial economy, but in 2001, Newfoundland and Labrador also recorded the strongest employment growth of any province. Annual average employment reached a record 211 300, an increase of 6700 (or 3.3 per cent). This was three times the national growth rate.

QUESTIONS

1. What do you think is most responsible for the largest layoff in Canadian history? Explain.
2. How did the government of Newfoundland and Labrador plan to recover from the massive unemployment created by the collapse of the cod fisheries? Make a list of all the strategies used to stimulate job creation in the private sector.
3. Explain the need for economic diversification.
4. To what extent does this Case Study reinforce the thesis presented in Chapter 3 that good economic thinking often comes in times of trouble?

Check Your

Understanding

1. Summarize the main theories used to explain the phenomenon of *jobless recovery*. Which do you consider to be most important?

2. Use the data in Figure 14.1 (page 312) to determine whether the period between 1992 and 2000 should be considered a *jobless recovery*.

3. Consider the impact on the labour market, represented by Figure 14.4 (page 319), of an increase in aggregate demand caused by increased consumer spending and confidence.

Draw a new graph to show the effect on this market of an increase in wages during a period of expanding aggregate demand. Explain the effect on employment.

4. Consider the impact on the labour market, represented by Figure 14.4, of increased globalization. Draw a new graph to show the effect on the market for labour in Canadian manufacturing. Explain the effect on employment.

5. Explain how technological innovation can create both employment and unemployment.

Public Policy Issues and Implications

Defining and Serving the Common Good

Recent, current, and projected unemployment levels are a constant source of concern for many Canadians. Many socio-political implications arise from economic considerations that deal with the employment of the Canadian labour force. Armed with trend graphs and economic theories, first to explain and then to project unemployment levels to the next quarter and beyond, many economists and politicians seek to influence public policy in order to serve the common good. (Others may operate primarily out of self-interest.) This **common good** can be defined as the well-being of Canadian society at large, or as an aggregate.

Some economists have long attempted to isolate themselves from this political decision-making arena, claiming that their role is apolitical and informative rather than partisan and normative (that is, values-based and policy-oriented). There are problems with this notion.

First, in attempting to steer a "values-neutral" course, the science of economics can become relatively academic, dry, and soulless. Second, as we discovered in Chapter 2, the political and economic systems of any nation are usually interconnected. Given the complex multi-interest nature of political decisions, the trade-off realities of the economic world (driven by scarcity and choice), and human nature and its dependency on positive values, very few politico-economic decisions can, in fact, be "values-neutral."

The principal task is not to neutralize values but, rather, to recognize the values inherent in every perspective on a particular social or policy issue. This recognition will, in turn, facilitate the recognition of values that serve and that run counter to the common good. It will allow for the analysis of values-driven benefits and costs to assess policy alternatives. Ultimately, this process will result in better-informed and balanced decisions—decisions that take account of implications and address the repercussions.

Check Your

Understanding

1. Explain what is meant by the *common good*.

2. Why are politico-economic decisions rarely "values-neutral"?

3. How can costs and benefits be used to assess issues related to employment?

A Matter
of Opinion | The Common Good

For each of the following employment-related issues, a brief outline of conflicting perspectives or viewpoints is presented to stimulate personal reflection and class discussion. This is not intended as a complete list. Only three economic reasons are provided to support each perspective. Additional arguments might arise from personal reflection and class discussion.

The task at hand is to apply a decision-making model to establish a *common good* position on each issue. First, identify the value judgement(s) at the heart of each perspective. Then attach an importance factor, or "value," to each reason offered in support. One way to do this is to attach a "high," "mid," or "low" priority to each reason. Some students may prefer to develop a value scale to establish

relative importance. Establish a total value for each viewpoint to determine the perspective or viewpoint most "in sync" with the principle of the common good. It might be useful to review the section in Chapter 2 on establishing economic goals prior to beginning this issues analysis/decision-making activity. Be warned: The common good may prove as elusive as "common sense"!

Conduct an analysis of each issue presented to identify whether the affirmative viewpoint or the adverse viewpoint best represents the common good. Once you have completed your personal reflection, decide (through class discussion) on a collective definition of the common good to illuminate public policy decisions regarding unemployment.

Issue 1: Should governments pursue debt reduction during periods of high unemployment?

Supporting an *Affirmative* Response	Supporting an *Adverse* Response
• Carrying charges on public debt limits government spending on social assistance programs for disadvantaged people. • Government borrowing to carry public debt forces interest rates to climb, affecting both investment and consumer spending adversely. • The present generation does not have a moral right to incur debts that future generations must pay.	• Cutting government spending and raising taxes to reduce the public debt has an adverse effect on aggregate demand and will increase unemployment. • Cutting government spending to balance budgets affects disadvantaged Canadians most. • Debt reduction can be reserved for expansionary phases of the business cycle, where it helps to reduce inflation.

Issue 2: Should corporate taxes be reduced in Canada to stimulate job creation?

Supporting an *Affirmative* Response	Supporting an *Adverse* Response
• Lower taxes make Canadian firms more competitive with their foreign counterparts. • Lower taxes promote increases in consumer spending and aggregate demand. • Lower taxes attract business investment and create new jobs.	• Canadian corporations are not presently paying their fair share of taxes in light of the tax-supported infrastructure on which Canadian firms rely. • Since corporations are afforded the same rights as individuals, corporate income should be treated the same as personal income. • Corporate expansion is driven by confidence and retained profits, not by tax reductions.

Issue 3: Should the powers of large labour unions be reduced?

Supporting an *Affirmative* Response	Supporting an *Adverse* Response
• By negotiating wage increases, labour unions contribute to higher unemployment. • Negotiated wage increases that are not based on productivity increases are inflationary when supply cannot keep pace with demand. • Strikes and other labour disputes affect aggregate production adversely.	• Unions protect the rights and work tions of workers. • Unions are needed to balance the grow powers of large corporations. • Unions help to secure a larger portion of the GDP for the working class, thereby contributing to a more equitable distribution of wealth through income.

Issue 4: Should minimum wage and Employment Insurance benefits be increased?

Supporting an *Affirmative* Response	Supporting an *Adverse* Response
• Disposable income of low-income Canadians is increased, providing a more equitable distribution of wealth. • Increases in consumer spending generate increases in aggregate demand (that is, additional labour is needed to increase production in order to meet demand). • Exploitation of low-skilled labour is reduced (better pay and opportunities to find better jobs).	• There is less incentive for unemployed workers to fill available job vacancies. • There is less incentive for unemployed workers to retrain so that they qualify for better-paying jobs (greater dependency on government assistance). • As wage rates increase, the cost of labour rises and fewer workers are required by employers.

Issue 5: Should robots pay taxes for the workers they displace?

Supporting an *Affirmative* Response	Supporting an *Adverse* Response
• Unemployed workers pay less tax to government but require more assistance from government. • Firms increase profitability by automating production processes and replacing workers. • Firms should assume some responsibility for the unemployment created in pursuit of greater profit.	• Taxing technological innovation and investment would have an adverse effect on productivity and aggregate production. • No other structural economic changes causing the displacement of workers are presently taxed; these changes are inevitable and, in the long run, beneficial. • Taxes would be ultimately passed on to the consumer in the form of higher prices.

QUESTIONS

1. Working in groups, conduct a cost–benefit analysis of one of the five issues outlined above.

2. Compare the cost–benefit analyses conducted by other groups to reach consensus for each issue being discussed.

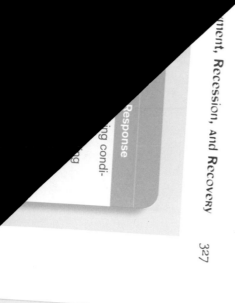

...dy ...ons in ...such as ...the ...on rate.

...sts distin... ...ctural ...ent), and

...the ...red to be between 6 and 7 per cent unemployment.

• Unemployment can create stress, financial hardship, discouragement, and low self-esteem for jobless workers and their families. Chronically high unemployment rates can lead to social unrest and produce negative attitudes toward the government. For the economy as a whole, the costs of unemployment can be determined statistically by using Okun's law to calculate the GDP gap.

• GDP data reveal a continuously alternating pattern of economic slowdown, recovery, and expansion, known as business cycles. If contraction lasts longer than six consecutive months, the economy is said to be in recession.

• Demand-pull price inflation results from excessive increases in consumer demand, relative to available aggregate production. Cost-push inflation results from the passing down of increased operating costs from producer to consumer. Rapid economic expansion often results in inflation. Recession is synonymous with unemployment, and severe recessions (depressions) usually result in deflation.

• The Phillips curve visualizes the inverse relationship between inflation and unemployment rates. Between 1973 and 1982, however, both unemployment and inflation rates increased; this unusual condition became known as stagflation.

• From 1983 to 1992, the economy alternated between recession and recovery. Although inflation was low, unemployment rates remained high, providing a "jobless" recovery. Wage demands from labour unions, corporate downsizing and increased automation, the migration

of manufacturing jobs to less developed nations, the disincentive of high taxes, and a steady increase in the labour force have all been identified as factors sustaining unemployment.

• After the collapse of the cod fishery in 1992, the Newfoundland economy expanded and diversified employment opportunities by investing in aquaculture, developing the Hibernia oil field, creating jobs in the IT sector, promoting tourism, and providing tax breaks to film production companies and tax holidays to industries that created new jobs. In 2001, Newfoundland and Labrador recorded the strongest employment growth of any province.

Key Terms

employment rate
seasonally adjusted rate
participation rate
underemployment
discouraged workers
hidden unemployed
frictional unemployment
seasonal unemployment
structural unemployment
technological unemployment
replacement unemployment
cyclical unemployment
inadequate demand unemployment
natural employment rate
potential output
actual output
business cycle
recession
recovery
demand-pull inflation
cost-push inflation
Phillips curve
stagflation
jobless recovery
downsize
rightsize
The Atlantic Groundfish Strategy (TAGS)
aquaculture
common good

Activities

Thinking/Inquiry

1. Research data in order to compare Canadian unemployment figures with those of other industrialized nations, such as Japan, Germany, the United States, Britain, France, and Italy. How did Canadian unemployment rates compare in the early 1990s? in the late 1990s? in the early 2000s?

2. "Full employment is reached when cyclical unemployment is zero." Do you agree with this statement? Explain.

3. Critics of the way unemployment rates are determined claim that the statistic hides some of the unemployment. What limitations do you see with the way labour force numbers, unemployment rates, and participation rates are determined? Should the participation rate replace the unemployment rate as an indicator of economic health? Explain your position.

4. Referring to the data in Figure 14.1 (page 312), develop a theory to explain the relatively high rate of unemployment among 15- to 24-year-olds.

5. The seesaw was an effective metaphor for the traditional relationship between unemployment and inflation represented by the Phillips curve. Explain this traditional relationship. Research Statistics Canada data to find out what happened to this relationship during the 1980s and the 1990s. In your opinion, is this curve still relevant? Explain.

Communication

6. a) Create an organizer to explain what generally happens to these ten economic variables during each phase of the business cycle:
   - unemployment
   - inflation
   - consumer confidence and spending
   - household savings
   - aggregate demand
   - investor confidence in future profits
   - interest rates
   - stock market prices
   - utilization of factories and production equipment
   - aggregate production (or total national output)

   Use symbols to denote increase (▲), decrease (▼), and no significant change (◆) to each variable.

   b) Explain why the changes in the recession and expansion phases occur.

7. Explain the terms *stagflation* and *jobless recovery* in a way that would make sense to people with no background in economics.

Application

8. Are jobless recoveries short-term adjustments or long-term realities? What economic facts or theories can you use to support your conclusion? Explain.

9. Suppose that full employment in the fictional principality of Burzotta is defined as 7 per cent unemployment. Last year, the actual unemployment rate was 9 per cent and the GDP was US$500 billion. The population of the principality is 25 million. Apply Okun's law to calculate the following:

   a) potential aggregate output

   b) the GDP gap

   c) per capita lost income as a result of the underemployment of labour resources

CHAPTER 15

EQUITY AND INCOME DISTRIBUTION

Canada: A Fair Society?

As we learned in Chapter 13, Canada's social welfare safety net underwent significant "downsizing" during the 1990s as various levels of government attempted to eliminate their deficits. Some critics of Canada's safety net justify this policy change because the Canadian model had clearly become unsustainable. Other Canadians believe these cutbacks were necessary to "harmonize" Canadian practices with those of our dominant economic partner, the United States.

Yet, other Canadians see the deterioration of Canada's social safety net as problematic. The Canadian system has been designed to effect a fairer distribution of incomes and, ultimately, national wealth—a goal many Canadians value. Many believe that the Canadian system for maintaining the well-being of its citizens has been fundamental in establishing Canada's international reputation as one of the best countries in which to live and that the downsizing threatens that hard-earned reputation.

In this political cartoon from October 1998, Prime Minister Jean Chrétien and Finance Minister Paul Martin are shown walking on Parliament Hill. What point is the cartoonist making about the distribution of wealth in Canada? How relevant do you think this cartoon is today?

QUESTIONS

1. What point does the cartoonist make here about the quality of life in Canada at the end of the 20th century?

2. What point does he make about the attitude of the federal government toward individuals pushed to the margins of Canadian society?

3. What point does he make about the public's attitude toward the government that holds this view?

4. Have you noticed a change in the number of poor and homeless people in your community? Explain.

Chapter Goals

By the end of this chapter, you will be able to

- explain how tools such as the Human Development Index, the Lorenz curve, and poverty lines can be used as indicators of socio-economic well-being,
- explain how government is involved in the Canadian economy as a redistributor of income,
- evaluate the effectiveness of government programs designed to ensure greater equity and economic security for Canadians,
- apply economic inquiry skills to analyze public policy issues focused on income inequality and redistribution.

Equity: A Canadian Perspective

Coming to Terms

Equity is often presented as a key economic goal, but what exactly does equity mean? How does equity relate to concepts such as equality, fairness, and distributive justice? The term **equity**, when used in economics, refers specifically to a distribution that is just and fair. Equity as fairness or distributive justice can have different meanings. Sometimes equity is intended to mean equality. Sometimes it is meant to suggest that rewards be proportionate with differences in the effort or workload that is required. Sometimes the term is used to mean that reasonable expectations are not disappointed.

These different interpretations of equity can sometimes conflict. For example, we can apply these concepts of equity to retirement pensions. If equity means equality, it implies that all employees will receive pensions of about equal value. If equity means matching rewards to effort, it implies that hard and responsible work will earn a higher pension than work that is lacking or casual. If equity means conforming to expectations, it implies that workers will not be disappointed relative to the pension they have been led to expect.

You will remember from Chapter 1 that one of the three major choices an economic system must make is how the nation's output should be divided among its citizens. It is undoubtedly the most controversial of the three. Karl Marx attempted to answer this question. Marx believed that all of society's problems are caused by inequality of incomes. He theorized that an economic system that shares goods on a basis of equality would bring out the best in people. This theory contrasted with capitalism, which is built on free enterprise driven by self-interest and the accumulation of personal wealth.

Capitalism appears to have prevailed in almost every nation in the world, and income inequities are now the norm. Although earnings are only part of the picture when we consider income, they do give us some idea of the disparities within our society. Figure 15.1 (page 332) shows the ten highest-paying and ten lowest-paying jobs in Canada.

Despite the vast differences in earnings among various professions, Canada's efforts to redistribute income to make life better for all Canadians has resulted in a society that is recognized around the world as a good place to live. As Canadians, we may not wave our national flag at every opportunity, but most of us consider ourselves fortunate to be living in Canada. Since 1992, this feeling has been confirmed by the United Nations **Human Development Index (HDI)**. This annual index uses education, standard of living, and life expectancy data to rank the world's 175 countries in terms of human development, or "quality of life." Although not first in every category (indicating that there is always room for improvement), Canada placed first overall from 1992 to 2000. Despite this achievement, there is growing evidence that income inequality is increasing within Canada. The issue of equity, or what is a fair distribution of national production, income, and wealth, remains with us still.

Average Incomes in Canada: A Snapshot

Per capita income is one of the factors used to calculate the Human Development Index because the more income people have, the more likely they are to be able to support themselves and their families in a comfortable lifestyle. Canadians earn high incomes, though not the highest among the more developed countries. In the last census of the 20th century, the average income in Canada was reported as $25 196 in constant 1995 dollars. This average, which is calculated by dividing Canada's total income by the total population, is called **mean average income**. Mean averages are useful and easy to calculate, but they tend to be pulled off the centre by either very low figures or very high ones. Another kind of average income is the **median income**, which is the middle income dividing Canada's range of incomes into two equal parts. The number of people earning more than the median

Occupation	Average 1995 earnings ($)		
	Both sexes	Men	Women
Canada: All occupations	**37 556**	**42 488**	**30 130**
Ten Highest-Paying Occupations			
Judges	126 246	128 791	117 707
Specialist physicians	123 976	137 019	86 086
General practitioners and family physicians	107 620	116 750	81 512
Dentists	102 433	109 187	71 587
Senior managers/Goods production, utilities, transportation, and construction	99 360	102 971	58 463
Senior managers/Financial, communications carriers, and other business services	99 117	104 715	71 270
Lawyers and Quebec notaries	81 617	89 353	60 930
Senior managers/Trade broadcasting and other services (not included elsewhere)	79 200	84 237	48 651
Primary production managers (except agriculture)	76 701	78 421	48 479
Securities agents, investment dealers, and traders	75 911	90 391	47 323
Ten Lowest-Paying Occupations			
Sewing machine operators	17 613	20 664	17 340
Cashiers	17 553	20 557	16 977
Ironing, pressing, and finishing occupations	17 322	19 297	16 499
Artisans and craftspersons	16 943	20 555	13 565
Bartenders	16 740	18 899	14 940
Harvesting labourers	16 426	18 683	14 465
Service station attendants	16 203	16 520	14 947
Food service counter attendants and food preparers	15 487	17 912	14 681
Food and beverage servers	14 891	18 192	13 861
Baby-sitters, nannies, and parents' helpers	12 713	15 106	12 662

Source: "Number of Earners Who Worked Full Year, Full Time in 1995 in the 25 Highest Paying and 25 Lowest Paying Occupations and Their Average Earnings by Sex, for Canada, 1995 (20% Sample Data)" from the Statistics Canada publication, *1996 Census Nation Series*, Catalogue 93F0029, May 1998.

Figure 15.1 Highest- and lowest-paying occupations in Canada. The data collected in the last census of the 20th century, in 1996, reveals interesting income patterns. What patterns can you identify in the data listed here?

income is the same as the number of people earning less. Median averages give a good idea of the central tendency in a range of figures, which is what an average is supposed to represent.

In the 1996 census report, Canada's median income was $18 891 in constant 1995 dollars, indicating that substantially fewer Canadians earned more than the mean average income and that the majority of Canadians earned significantly less. The mean average figures were distorted by the extremely high incomes earned by a few Canadians. Mean and median averages are useful for comparing income changes from one year to another and for comparing the present standard of living with that of the past or that of other nations. Generally speaking, when mean and median calculations differ significantly, a disproportionate number of very low or very high figures have pulled the mean average off the centre point. When mean and median calculations are close, the data are said to be more evenly distributed. How would this statistical rule apply to the distribution of marks in an economics class?

Income distribution

To examine income distribution, economists divide Canadian income earners into groups called quintiles. A **quintile** is one-fifth (or 20 per cent) of the total number of earners. Suppose the incomes of all family households in Canada were placed in order from the lowest to the highest. If there were ten million households in Canada, the first quintile would consist of the two million families earning the lowest incomes, the second quintile would be the next two million, and so on until the fifth quintile was grouped together representing the incomes of the two million households earning the highest incomes. The incomes of each of the five quintiles are totalled and represented as a percentage of the total income of all the quintiles. The results for Canada are shown in Figure 15.2.

An examination of Figure 15.2 shows that, in Canada, income is not distributed very equally; the lowest quintile receives only 4.4 per cent of the total national income. In comparison, the highest quintile receives 45.3 per cent of

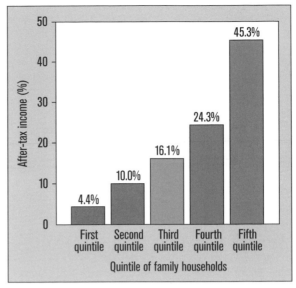

Source: Excerpts from the Statistics Canada publication, *Income in Canada*, Catalogue 75-202, 2000.

Figure 15.2 Shares of Canadians' after-tax income in 1999. How does this distribution pattern help shed light on the issue presented in the editorial cartoon on page 330?

the total income. If the income of the lowest three quintiles is totalled, we can see that 60 per cent of Canadian households receive only 30 per cent of the total income. The top 40 per cent, however, receive the rest (70 per cent) of national after-tax income. This represents a considerable disparity between Canadian households. Economists try to see patterns in quintile data by making use of graphs such as the Lorenz curve described in the Skill Builder feature on page 334.

Reasons for Income Inequalities

Karl Marx grudgingly recognized capitalism's ability to produce goods and services in an efficient manner. However, he was quite correct in his main criticism of capitalism: it does breed inequalities in incomes. Inequality is inevitable in the distribution of wealth, income, and production in a capitalist society because of the very efficiency of the market mechanism in rewarding "winners" and punishing "losers"! Let us explain. People can get their income from many different sources

SKILL BUILDER

Thinking Like an Economist

Reading and Making Lorenz Curves

The distribution of income represented by Figure 15.2 (page 333), can be easily visualized by converting it into a **Lorenz curve**. Unlike the bar graph in the figure, which shows the income for each quintile individually, a Lorenz curve shows cumulative income. That means, for example, that the income shown for the second quintile indicates the income for the second quintile plus the income for the first quintile. To make a Lorenz curve of the data in Figure 15.2, we first make the calculations in Figure 15.3.

On a Lorenz curve, the horizontal axis represents households divided into quintiles, and the vertical axis represents income. To make the curve, we plot the cumulative incomes for the five quintiles on the graph. You can see these as A, B, C, D, and E on the graph in Figure 15.4. To complete the graph, we join these points together in a smooth curve.

You will notice on this graph that a 45-degree line bisects the horizontal and vertical axes. Any point on that line is an equal distance from either axis, representing a perfectly equal distribution of income. In the hypothetical society

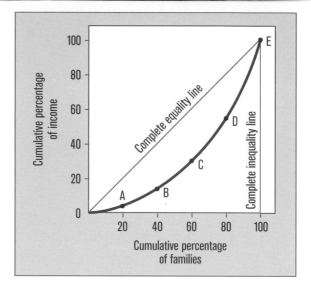

Figure 15.4 Lorenz curve of income distribution in Canada, 1999. Compare this method of presenting data with the bar graph in Figure 15.2 that illustrates the same data.

Cumulative Percentage of Families (lowest- to highest-income earners)	Share of Cumulative After-Tax Income (%)
A. First 20%	4.4
B. First 40%	4.4 + 10.0 = 14.4
C. First 60%	14.4 + 16.1 = 30.5
D. First 80%	30.5 + 24.3 = 54.8
E. 100%	54.8 + 45.3 = 100

Source: Excerpts from the Statistics Canada publication, *Income in Canada*, Catalogue 75-202, 2000.

Figure 15.3 Cumulative shares of Canadians' after-tax income, 1999.

that would match that line of equal distribution, 20 per cent of households would receive exactly 20 per cent of total income, 60 per cent of families would receive exactly 60 per cent of total income, and so on.

The actual distribution of income in virtually all societies, however, creates not a straight line but a curved line that bows out to the right. The greater the distance the line bows out from the line of perfect equality, the greater the degree of inequality. That the Lorenz curve for Canada bows out from the line of perfect equality shows that Canadian incomes are not equally distributed.

What are we to make of the 1999 Lorenz curve? To make it useful, we must compare it to curves showing income distribution in the past or to curves of other countries (to see if Canada has a greater or lesser degree of inequality). Figure 15.5 reveals that income distribution in Canada changed very little in the decades before 1999.

Total Income Received by Each Quintile of the Population (%)					
	1951	**1961**	**1971**	**1981**	**1989**
Lowest income quintile of families	6.1	6.6	5.6	6.4	6.5
Second quintile	12.9	13.4	12.7	12.8	12.6
Third quintile	17.4	18.2	18.0	18.3	17.8
Fourth quintile	22.5	23.4	23.7	24.1	23.8
Highest income quintile	41.1	38.4	40.0	38.4	39.3
All families	100.0	100.0	100.0	100.0	100.0

Source: Statistics Canada, Income Distribution by Size in Canada, as reproduced in David Stager, *Economic Analysis and Canadian Policy* (Toronto: Butterworths, 1992), 618.

Figure 15.5 Distribution of family income in Canada, 1951–1989. How do you think the Lorenz curves for these data would compare with the 1999 curve in Figure 15.4?

QUESTIONS

1. Ten individuals work in a dry-cleaning plant. The total wage bill is $100 000. Some employees work part-time while others work full-time. Here are the ten annual salaries: Individual A = $1000; B = $6000; C = $12 000; D = $8000; E = $10 000; F = $11 000; G = $20 000; H = $14 000; I = $16 000; J = $2000.

   a) What is the average mean salary?

   b) What is the average median salary?

   c) Group the salaries into quintiles, with the first quintile including the two lowest-paid workers, and so on.

   d) Determine the percentage each quintile receives of the total wages paid by the plant.

   e) Construct a Lorenz curve to illustrate the income distribution in the dry-cleaning plant.

2. Reproduce the Lorenz curve shown in Figure 15.4. Using the information provided by Figure 15.5, construct a set of colour-coded Lorenz curves (1951, 1971, 1989) to assess whether or not income distribution in Canada has improved since the middle of the 20th century.

3. Use Figure 15.6 to compare income inequalities in selected countries. How does Canada compare?

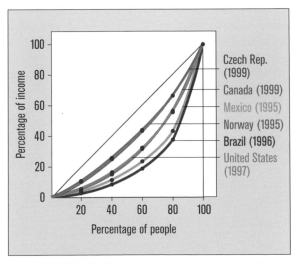

Source: World Bank, World Development Report 2000/2001: Attacking Poverty. Available online at <www.worldbank.org/poverty/wdrpoverty/report/index.htm>.

Figure 15.6 Lorenz curve of income distribution in various countries in the late 1990s.

within the capitalist system, including wages and salaries, rent, capital gains, dividends, interest, profits, and government transfers. Some people may have several sources of income while others have few.

When competition is effectively limited, large producers can influence the marketplace to great advantage. For example, a sole employer in a one-industry town can pay low wages. Should another major employer come to town, wages will rise. Producers of goods and services who are able to meet and satisfy consumer demands are rewarded handsomely by the market. The producer could be a new performer hitting the top of the music charts, an entrepreneur developing a new product, or even a person entering an occupation that is in high demand. Because consumers "vote" with their purchases for the goods and services they want, the singer, the entrepreneur, and the employee have every chance of doing well.

Nonetheless, consumers are equally harsh in punishing those sellers who do not meet their demands. Eventually, the listeners will tire of the performances of the singer, the buyers will switch to a newer product produced by a competitor, and the demand for the occupational field will decline. At one time or another, the singer, the business person, and the employee will find that the flow of income that once gave them a good living will dry up. Our point is this: there is nothing inherent in the market system that guarantees a "fair" or equitable income for anyone, however that is defined. Consumers change their tastes, often very quickly; competitors are free to enter a market; occupational demands change. Let us note, in a little more detail, some of the reasons for inequality in income in a free-market system:

1. *People have different physical and mental abilities.* All of us can learn to throw a ball or shoot a puck, but few of us can do so as well as a professional baseball or hockey player. These elite athletes are rewarded highly for their level of skill. Not all of us are as scientifically minded as doctors or research scientists or have the facility with finance and numerical calculation that accountants must possess. A limited supply of these people combined with a heavy demand for their services means they can demand high incomes.

2. *People differ in the degree of education and training that they receive.* A decision to obtain post-secondary education instead of entering the job market entails a direct cost for tuition, books, and possibly accommodation. Students also pay an opportunity cost in terms of the income they give up while attending the institution. Individuals expect that the future earnings they receive will compensate them for these costs with higher incomes than those who do not assume these costs.

3. *Some individuals are willing to work longer and harder than others are.* Even within the same occupation, some people work more overtime and take on more tasks, clients, patients, or customers to earn higher incomes than their co-workers do. Individuals differ in the value they place on income and leisure, and people are free to substitute one for the other.

4. *The assumption of risk and responsibility is usually rewarded.* The entrepreneur who borrows money and mortgages his or her home to develop a new product or a new service may earn higher than normal profits if successful. This would occur, for example, because the quick infusion of capital might allow the fledgling company to get into a new market before a competing company that chose to take the slow and safe approach. An economist would say that individuals who take these big risks receive a "risk premium" over and above their normal profits. The oil rigger, the high-rise construction worker, and people in other dangerous occupations must also be compensated with a "risk premium." Most often, the assumption of additional responsibilities receives compensation for the extra workload and stress.

5. *Luck and health can always affect income.* A person may inherit money, marry into it, or even win a lottery. On the other side of the coin, a person may be injured unexpectedly, become ill, or suddenly lose a job when a company goes bankrupt or shifts operations. Being at the right place, at the right time, with the right idea may be as much a result of luck as it is of skill.

6. *Family background can affect future earnings.* Children from high-income families certainly benefit from inherited money. Previous capital accumulation and present holdings and investments can provide additional personal income in the forms of interest, profit, dividends, capital gains, and rent. In a market economy, accumulated wealth (if properly managed) serves to create more wealth. Children from high-income families enjoy other benefits as well, such as connections for getting good jobs. Increasing statistical proof suggests that children from better-off families earn more, on average, over a lifetime. The Case Study on page 338 gives reasons and evidence for this theory.

7. *Market power means higher income.* The US billionaire, Bill Gates, dominates the computer software market with his company's Microsoft programs. This high-profile entrepreneur has such tremendous market power that he has been forced to fight a lengthy legal battle to preserve his company from anti-monopoly prosecution in the United States and Europe. Larger companies, like McDonald's Restaurants, for example, often have an advantage over smaller companies in the marketplace owing to their massive advertising campaigns and the public's instant recognition of their brand. Workers, too, may gain some market power as sellers of their labour by belonging to a union or an association that can negotiate collectively for higher wages.

8. *Discrimination has a negative effect on incomes.* Age, gender, visible ethnicity, race, and disability have been widely noted as factors causing differences in average incomes. Figure 15.1 (page 332) clearly shows that women earn lower wages than men in every field listed. With the advent of improved anti-discrimination laws, with numerous successful appeals to the Charter of Rights and Freedoms and the provincial Human Rights Codes, and with shifts in the attitudes of society, discrimination does not affect people's chances at earning a high income as decisively as it once did. Nonetheless, the effects of discrimination are still felt, especially by some cultural groups. Professor James L. Torczyner of McGill University conducted a study about racism in the workplace in 1997. He found that, with comparable levels of education, African-Canadians tend to have a higher rate of unemployment than the average Canadian worker (15 per cent versus 10 per cent). They also tend to earn 15 per cent less. Additionally, more than three out of ten African-Canadians lived below the poverty line in 1991; only 16 per cent of Canadians did so in the same year.

9. *Regional economic disparities contribute to income differences.* Some parts of Canada, depending on the make-up of their regional economy, historically report lower average income levels, as you can see in Figure 15.7. Income levels in these communities may be

Province	Average (After-Tax) Family Income, 1999 ($)	Incidence of Low Income (% of total population)
Newfoundland and Labrador	40 105	14.2
Prince Edward Island	43 282	8.4
Nova Scotia	43 749	12.2
New Brunswick	43 146	10.1
Quebec	44 469	14.7
Ontario	58 517	9.6
Manitoba	45 603	13.8
Saskatchewan	44 755	9.3
Alberta	53 144	11.4
British Columbia	51 773	13.1
CANADA	51 473	11.8

Source: Excerpts from the Statistics Canada publication, *Income in Canada*, Catalogue 75-202, 2000.

Figure 15.7 Average family income and incidence of low income, by region, 1999. According to this table how is income distributed across Canada? Explain. How do average income and incidence of low income relate?

Case Study

How Family Background Can Affect Future Earnings

The following findings are taken from a study, reported by Statistics Canada in 1998, based on income tax information reported by a **cohort** (a group with similar statistical characteristics) of 285 000 young adult Canadians aged 28 to 31. Their total income was compared with the income of their parents 12 years earlier, when the cohort was between the ages of 16 and 19 and still living at home. The study excluded families headed by single mothers and families not residing in urban communities (for the purpose of eliminating some variables). All monetary values are presented in 1986 constant dollars.

Summary of Findings

- The sources of a parent's income (especially the father's income) and the community that the family lives in significantly influence the employment outcomes of their grown-up children.
- A parent's integrity, responsibility, work ethic, and encouragement of the pursuit of higher income tend to have a positive impact on the income levels of their adult children.
- Adult children (especially sons) had substantially higher incomes if their fathers had some **asset income** (income in the form of interest, dividends, or rent). The actual amount of the father's asset income does not matter as much as its presence.
- Adult children (especially sons) had higher incomes if their fathers had self-employed income.
- Adult children (especially sons) were more likely to have low adult incomes if their fathers had received Employment Insurance benefits.
- The affluence of the neighbourhood in which children (especially sons) spend their teens is positively associated with their incomes as adults. These neigbourhoods offer a better-

developed physical infrastructure—higher-quality schools, recreational facilities, and social institutions—as well as social standards that help reinforce parents' goals for their children.
- The adult children of families who moved once during their teen years earned about $550 less than those whose families stayed in the same neighbourhood. Children whose families moved three or more times earned about $2000 less.
- Thirty per cent of the sons and 25 per cent of the daughters of low-income fathers also had low incomes. Only 15 per cent of the sons and 13 per cent of the daughters of high-income fathers had low incomes.
- Thirty-five per cent of the children of high-income fathers also had high incomes. Only 14 per cent of the children of high-income fathers had low incomes.
- Sons and daughters whose very-low-income fathers had self-employed incomes did better than those whose fathers did not. Sons and daughters whose very-low-income fathers had some asset income did much better than those whose fathers had not.

Source: Excerpts from the Statistics Canada publication, *Canadian Social Trends*, Catalogue 11-008, Summer 1998.

Questions

1. State in one or two sentences the most important findings of this study.
2. Note the effect on children's incomes of each of the following, and state a possible reason for each: (a) father had self-employment income, (b) father had asset income, (c) father received employment insurance benefits, (d) child's gender, and (e) type of neighbourhood.
3. What can all parents do to improve the economic prospects of their children?

affected by chronic unemployment and other adverse economic conditions. In communities dependent on few resources and industries, setbacks in these major sources of employment may have severe economic repercussions for many years. For example, the collapse of fisheries in the North Atlantic has had significant impact on the income of many residents of Atlantic Canada, especially in Newfoundland and Labrador. Lumber disputes with the United States have depressed incomes in parts of Canada, like British Columbia, where forestry is a main employer.

Check Your Understanding

1. Assess the three interpretations of equity in reference to the distribution of marks for student achievement in this course at your school. Which interpretations are most appropriate for obtaining distributive justice? Justify your choices.

2. Explain how the Lorenz curve helps economists visualize the distribution of average total income.

3. Group the nine factors affecting income distribution into two groupings as being of high or moderate importance. Further subdivide these groups according to whether or not each factor is justifiable, in your opinion. Explain your reasoning.

4. Refer to Figure 15.1 (page 332).

   a) Use the nine factors affecting income to explain why the occupations in this list command the incomes that they do. Are these differences in income justified?

   b) For all occupations, women earn, on average, 70 per cent of what men earn. Which factors affecting income would help explain this difference? Is a 29 per cent income difference between men and women totally justifiable? What do these data suggest about gender equity in Canada?

Poverty in Canada

What does it mean to be poor in Canada? Most of us would agree that poverty involves substandard housing, poor nutrition, limited social opportunities, difficulties in financing post-secondary schooling, and problems in providing for children. Where we disagree, however, is in how we should determine who is poor, why people become poor, and what measures we should take to reduce poverty.

Measuring Poverty

How many Canadians are poor? We cannot determine the answer to this question until we decide on a poverty level. There are two opposing schools of thought on where to set this "poverty line" depending on whether poverty is considered to be a relative condition or an absolute condition. Television images of poorly clothed children with swollen bellies reflect a desperate condition often referred to as **absolute poverty**—a state of utter destitution. Thanks in part to Canada's complex social welfare safety net, the incidence of this extreme form of poverty is rare in Canada. In comparing the relative abilities of Canadians to command necessary goods and services, however, it quickly becomes evident that the gap between the "haves" and "have nots" in Canadian society is widening.

Proponents of poverty as a relative condition claim that to be poor means to lack the conditions of material life that most other people in Canada have. A poor Canadian, then, does not necessarily lack food, safe water, shelter, and clothing as many millions of people in some other nations so visibly do. Nonetheless, this Canadian feels poor, and we see this person as poor, compared with—or relative to—the rest of us. This form of **relative poverty** is an important policy issue for governments in Canada. Although no Canadians are known to be starving, a growing number are relying on food banks to make ends meet. This relative poverty is disturbing, perhaps because it is found in the midst of affluence.

Since 1968, Statistics Canada has attempted to identify Canadian families that are relatively worse off than other Canadian families by examining income and spending patterns. This statistical measure is based on the establishment of a **low-income cut-off (LICO)** to identify income levels below which a household is statistically classified as being in a relatively limited income situation. Statistically, the average Canadian household spends 35 per cent of its before-tax income (or 44 per cent of its after-tax income) on food, clothing, and shelter. Statistics Canada defines as relatively worse off any household that spends more than 20 percentage points above the national average on the three necessities of food, clothing, and shelter.

Separate low-income cut-off tables are calculated for **before-tax income** and **after-tax income** (total annual income before federal and provincial taxes are deducted and after, respectively). Although before-tax income levels are less complicated and, therefore, easier to calculate, after-tax LICOs have become more common because all purchases of necessities are made with after-tax dollars. Although

Statistics Canada's LICOs are commonly referred to in the media as **poverty lines**, they have no officially recognized status, and Statistics Canada does not promote the use of this term in relation to the LICOs. Nonetheless, they note that many analysts do use the LICO as an indication of poverty in the absence of a more accepted definition of poverty. Figure 15.8 outlines how the low-income cut-offs are influenced by the number of members in the household and the size of the community in which they live. Using this indicator, 12 per cent of Canadians were living in poverty in 1999.

Many analysts consider any household with an after-tax income below the amount stipulated by this table to be poor. For example, a family of four living in a city of 450 000 residents with a combined after-tax income of $23 000 would be considered poor. Note that if that same family had lived on a rural farm their income would have been above the statistical poverty line. Why does Statistics Canada use lower low-income cut-offs for residents of smaller communities? Some critics consider this calculation to be a rather arbitrary measure of poverty. Do you agree? For two points of view on this question, have a look at the Matter of Opinion feature on page 341.

Size of Family Unit	After-tax LICOs Based on Size of Community Where Family Lives				
	Urban Areas				
	500 000 and over	100 000 to 499 999	30 000 to 99 999	Less than 30 000	Rural Areas
1 person	$14 771	$12 442	$12 250	$11 194	$9684
2 persons	$18 024	$15 182	$14 947	$13 659	$11 817
3 persons	$22 796	$19 202	$18 905	$17 276	$14 946
4 persons	$28 392	$23 916	$23 546	$21 517	$18 615
5 persons	$31 733	$26 730	$26 317	$24 048	$20 806
6 persons	$35 075	$29 544	$29 087	$26 580	$22 997
7 or more	$38 416	$32 359	$31 857	$29 111	$25 188

Source: Excerpts from Table 8.4: Low Income After Tax Cut-offs (1992 LICOs Base), 1990–1999 from the Statistics Canada publication, *Income in Canada*, Catalogue 75-202, 2000.

Figure 15.8 After-tax low-income cut-offs (in 1992 dollars) for Canadian households, 1999.

A Matter of Opinion | Relative versus Absolute Poverty

Proponents of defining poverty as an absolute condition claim that to be poor is to lack certain basic necessities. A poor person is homeless, dependent on food banks, or in some other way lacking. This newer, controversial definition is described in the first article below. A contrary view that supports the idea of relative poverty is presented in the second. Which is the better way to measure poverty?

Measuring Poverty in Canada, 2001

❝ A basic-needs standard of living would have all of one's basic necessities covered at a standard of quality considered minimally decent in contemporary society.... The precise nature of this standard will depend on the list of necessities selected. I have put forward a list of physical needs or items closely connected to those physical needs and have deliberately omitted amenities [items that make life pleasant]. My list includes food providing a nutritious diet that satisfies all norms of energy, balance, and palatability and that is purchased at grocery stores using no savings strategies; shelter that consists of apartment accommodation that is not subsidized and is appropriate in size for the family and includes all the usual furnishings and appliances; clothing purchased new at popular department stores; a telephone with local telephone service; all necessary household supplies; household insurance; laundry requirements; public transportation; personal care; any out-of-pocket health-care needs; and a small amount for school supplies and correspondence. The estimated annual cost of this standard of living ... for a single person in 2000 is about $8900....

The basic-needs standard of living is the appropriate level to use as a poverty threshold. It is, I believe, most consistent with commonly held notions of poverty. It is also far more useful in making credible comparisons, both over time and internationally. In that regard, the basic-needs standard will be a far more useful policy tool for evaluating anti-poverty policies than the more purely "relative" counterparts....

The advantages of the basic-needs approach to defining poverty are the following:

• it closely conforms to dictionary definitions of poverty, reflecting common usage;
• it conforms to the understanding that most people living on low incomes have of poverty, as shown in surveys;
• it conforms more closely to journalistic use, as terms like "hunger," "real deprivation," and "hardship" are frequently seen describing the poor;
• it incorporates an aspect of "relativity" by setting the type and quality of necessities at the level that is considered minimally decent in contemporary society.

The debate over absolute and relative approaches has raged over the years. While all poverty lines are relative, "absolute" measures tend to relate to the basic necessities of life and omit, deliberately, items that are widely regarded as non-necessities. [It also measures poverty using a concrete standard, so people know exactly of what the poor are deprived.] The objective for those using a "necessities" approach is clearly to measure the extent of real material deprivation rather than comparative deprivation. ❞

Source: Excerpts from "Measuring Poverty in Canada" by Chris Sarlo from <http://www.fraserinstitute.ca> reprinted by permission of the Fraser Institute.

QUESTIONS

1. What is this writer's central argument against defining poverty in relative terms?
2. How does he define poverty?
3. How would the number of Canadians identified as poor change if statisticians used this writer's basic-needs definition of poverty?
4. Which stakeholders would most likely favour this approach to determining a poverty line?

Defining and Re-Defining Poverty

❝ In Canada, the tradition of defining poverty in terms of very basic needs is most closely associated with the Fraser Institute, which argues that no one is poor if they can meet their "basic needs." This line attempts to calculate the cost of a basket of necessities including food, clothing, shelter, and some limited additional items. Notably absent from the Fraser Institute's basket are items which the great majority of Canadians take for granted, such as coffee, a daily newspaper, and cable TV. There is also no allowance for access to recreation or culture. This definition of poverty has been widely used to discredit the LICOs, which are based, in part, on the incomes of the poor compared to others in society.

So-called "absolute" poverty lines do, in fact, embody community norms and standards, at least to a limited degree. Even the extremely bare-bones poverty line of the Fraser Institute would look "generous" to many citizens of very low-income developing countries, or to average Canadians of a century ago. Indeed, the Fraser Institute itself acknowledges that "the basic-needs poverty line is not absolute ... to be meaningful, a poverty line has to be connected to the society in which people live." (*Measuring Poverty in Canada*, 2001)....

The Organization for Economic Co-operation and Development (OECD) has argued that absolute poverty lines have little meaning in advanced industrialized societies, and that poverty should be seen conceptually not as **deprivation** of very basic needs, but as **exclusion** from the standards of living broadly available to others in the same society. As they note, "in order to participate fully in the social life of a community, individuals may need a level of resources that is not too inferior to the norm of that community." They add that, "from a normative perspective, it may be considered unfair for members of a community to benefit unequally from a general increase in prosperity." ❞

Source: Excerpts from "Defining and Re-Defining Poverty: A CCSD Perspective" reprinted with the permission of the Canadian Council on Social Development.

QUESTIONS (cont.)

5. Explain the significance of this writer's focus on exclusion rather than on deprivation in challenging the Fraser Institute's approach to poverty lines.

6. Which approach, relative or absolute, do you believe defines poverty most accurately? Explain your decision.

Canada's Marginalized

Now that we have looked at the various ways of measuring the level of poverty, we can now look at the situation in Canada today.

According to many analysts, about one in five children in Canada lives in poverty today. In 1980, according to the Canadian Council on Social Development, 14.9 per cent of Canadian children lived in poverty. By 1998, that figure had risen to 18.8 per cent. Clearly, the level of poverty is increasing.

A good indicator of the prevalence of poverty is the number of people who need to use a food bank to supplement their incomes.

Food bank use in Canada is on the increase. In the Greater Toronto Area, for example, over 140 000 people used a food relief agency in 2001 compared with 115 000 in 1995, according to the Daily Bread Food Bank. Although many people using food banks are temporary users experiencing such temporary hardships as being laid off, others have become habitual users because their household income is consistently insufficient to cover the cost of all family necessities.

The poor include people who work for low wages—the **working poor**. The market power of employers, particularly in the absence of organized labour, can force wages down to levels that do not keep workers out of poverty. People in households whose heads are not in the labour force constitute Canada's non-working poor, or **welfare poor**. These are the people left behind by our economic system—individuals who are elderly, have an illness or a disability, or are the head of a single-parent family with young children. "Deadbeat" parents who avoid paying support to their former spouses for the care of their children contribute to the poverty in many single-parent households. Poor physical and mental health contributes to the incidence of poverty, probably because the ability of these people to support themselves is limited. The incidence of poverty among senior citizens who live alone is significantly higher than for those living with families. Differences in wage rates paid to men and women contribute to a higher incidence of poverty among women.

Poverty in rural areas and in some regions results when people depend on seasonal employment in marginally productive primary industries. Examples include farmers operating small farms with inadequate technology and marginally fertile land and fishers forced to suspend operations as a result of depleted fish stocks.

Why do many people find it difficult or impossible to climb out of poverty? Many people live in regions of the country where jobs are scarce. Others lack the marketable skills (education and training) to earn incomes large enough to lift them out of poverty. Children

who are born into poor families are at a distinct disadvantage relative to their counterparts in comfortable families. Children born poor tend to be undernourished and to do less well in school. They are also less likely to move on to post-secondary education. Thus, their chances of experiencing poverty as adults are higher than for the rest of the population. Lack of self-esteem, motivation, hope, and incentive can act to perpetuate poverty, by passing it down from parents to their children.

To examine some of the more interesting facts about poverty in Canada, take a look at Figures 15.9 to 15.12. The data provide

Level of Education	Percentage of Group Living in Poverty
0–8 years of schooling	28.8
Secondary school graduates	22.4
Post-secondary certificate and diploma holders	17.9
University graduates	11.0

Source: Excerpts from the Statistics Canada publication, *Income in Canada*, Catalogue 75-202, 2000.

Figure 15.9 Low income in Canada, by education level, 1999. Explain the statistical pattern that exists between the level of education and the incidence of poverty in Canada. Speculate why so many of Canada's *working poor* are from relatively under-educated groups.

Group	Persons Living in Economic Families with Low Incomes (%)			
	All Persons Living in Canada	Persons < 18 Years of Age	Persons 18–64	Persons > 64 Years of Age
Total population	11.8	13.7	11.8	8.2
Males	10.9	14.0	10.9	4.4
Females	12.6	13.5	12.7	11.1

Source: Excerpts from the Statistics Canada publication, *Income in Canada*, Catalogue 75-202, 2000.

Figure 15.10 Low income in Canada, by gender and age, 1999. According to the data, how does age influence the incidence of poverty in Canada?

Group	Estimated Number Living in Poverty (Percentage)
All children	962 000 (13.7)
Children living in two parent families	481 000 (8.3)
Children living in lone parent families headed by females	422 000 (45.1)
Children in all other economic families	59 000 (18.8)

Source: Excerpts from the Statistics Canada publication, *Income in Canada*, Catalogue 75-202, 2000.

Figure 15.11 Children living in low-income conditions or poverty in Canada, 1999. Under what family circumstances is the incidence of child poverty highest in Canada? Suggest why this is so.

Group	Estimated Number Living in Poverty (Percentage)
For elderly persons living in family households	
All	44 000 (1.8)
Male	17 000 (1.3)
Female	27 000 (2.2)
For individual elderly persons living alone	
All	256 000 (21.7)
Male	53 000 (16.6)
Female	203 000 (23.6)

Source: Excerpts from the Statistics Canada publication, *Income in Canada*, Catalogue 75-202, 2000.

Figure 15.12 Elderly persons living in low-income conditions or poverty in Canada, 1999. According to these data, how does the percentage of elderly Canadians living in poverty differ between those living alone and those living as part of an economic family?

information about the spread and frequency of poverty in Canada based on after-tax low-income cut-offs (LICOs) for 1999. Statistics Canada estimates that, in 1999, there were 3 569 000 Canadians living in low-income conditions—that is, they spent more than 64 per cent of their after-tax incomes on food, clothing, and shelter.

As bad as the level of poverty is for Canadians generally, the situation is worse among Canada's Aboriginal peoples. In 1995,

for example, 43.4 per cent of Aboriginal peoples lived in poverty. This rate is significantly higher than the national average. To read about the damage done to the traditional economy of one group of Aboriginal people, the Innu of Davis Inlet, refer to the Case Study on page 345.

Check Your Understanding

1. Explain the difference between absolute and relative poverty.

2. Is Statistics Canada's low-income cut-off (LICO) a measure of absolute or relative poverty? Explain.

3. According to the LICO, what three factors most determine whether a family is considered to be in a low income bracket? Explain.

4. Distinguish between the working poor and the welfare poor.

5. List at least five factors that contribute to poverty in Canada.

6. What groups are more likely to be poor in Canada and why?

CASE Study

A Traditional Economy Turned Upside Down

In 1993, a video of six Innu children in Davis Inlet, Labrador, sniffing gasoline and screaming that they wanted to die became international news. A study released in November 1999 by Survival for Tribal Peoples International, a charity that works with indigenous peoples around the world, blames Ottawa for the gradual deterioration and high suicide rate of the close to 20 000 Innu in Newfoundland and Quebec. The Survival International report labelled the Innu of Labrador's Davis Inlet "the most suicide-ridden people of the world." The suicide rate in Davis Inlet is 13 times higher than the overall Canadian rate. The report claims that nearly one-third of the entire Innu population of Davis Inlet have attempted suicide. Innu children and teenagers are especially vulnerable. Close to 80 per cent of the adult population suffer from alcoholism. But what does this sad story have to do with economics, and where did things go so terribly wrong?

The Innu began as a nomadic people, travelling through a yearly cycle to follow wild game on the vast barrens of Labrador and Quebec. The economy of the Innu worked well, with smaller groups harvesting the resources of the land over a widely dispersed area.

In 1967, the federal government decided to consolidate the people of Davis Inlet and to move them to their present island location. Government officials viewed centralization as an economically wise form of administration. Bringing small groups of people together and concentrating their populations into permanent communities was the most cost-effective way of providing social services such as education, health care, and emergency relief funds. The underlying assumption was that the traditional subsistence lifestyle of the Innu was impractical in the modern industrialized era. The following words of Walter Rockwood, Director of Northern Affairs for the Government of Newfoundland and Labrador at the time, reflects the misguided outlook of administrators of the era.

Civilization is on the northward march, and for the Eskimo and Indian there is no escape. The last bridges of isolation were destroyed with the coming of the airplane and the radio. The only course now open, for there can be no turning back, is to fit him as soon as may be to take his full place as a citizen in our society. There is no time to lose. No effort must be spared in the fields of health, education, welfare, and economics.

Source: Walter Rockwood, quoted in Carol Brice-Bennett, *Dispossessed: The Eviction of Inuit from Hebron, Labrador*, (1994).

After the move to Davis Inlet, government administration became easier. For the Innu, however, the move had serious repercussions for their community and way of life. The fact that administrators devalued the Innu way of life had particular relevance for the future of the Innu, whose dependence on hunting and fishing had required a highly dispersed and highly mobile population. In Davis Inlet, Innu hunters could no longer freely follow the wild herds because the community is on an island. That means that the Innu could not hunt during the breakup of the ice each spring, prime hunting season. Their traditional economy was severely impaired.

Figure 15.13 A breakfast program at a Davis Inlet school feeds about 150 students each day. For some, it is the only proper meal they receive.

In addition, the transition to a settled industrialized society did not generate sufficient employment opportunities to provide steady income streams for the majority of households in the permanent settlement. As a result, residents became increasingly more dependent on government assistance and increasingly pessimistic about their future. They had no claim on resources, and they lacked the knowledge needed to live off the land in an unfamiliar region. Instead of living a self-sufficient life according to ancient traditions, the Innu were forced to become dependent on government handouts.

Because the Innu identified so closely with the land, relocation affected not only their way of life but also their identity as a people. They were used to living in small family hunting camps. Having to live in a larger community, with people from different tribes and clans, was a difficult social adjustment.

In 2002, the Innu of Davis Inlet live in absolute poverty. Most people share two-room homes with five or six others. The community boasts no roads, no sewers, and no running water. The nearest hospital is a two-hour trip by bush plane. The long-ago promised amenities, such as running water and good schools, did not materialize. The children have to shower in school on Tuesdays and Thursdays. Human waste is often thrown out onto snowbanks.

Living in this environment, many people turn to alcohol. Some of the children turn to glue sniffing. Innu chief Simeon Tshakapesh suggests that anger is at the root of the substance abuse. "They told our people they would have running water, good schools, and everything. They took away our cultural, spiritual values and tried to turn us into modern Canadians. We were told we would be lawyers, doctors, nurses. Instead, our people fell apart."

After the 1993 video, the Canadian government was embarrassed into taking drastic action. It has spent $152 million to relocate the 600 Innu of Davis Inlet to a new 133-home community on the mainland, just 15 km west of Davis Inlet. This site, chosen by the Innu, is in a traditional hunting area known as Natuashish, or "break in the river." Every home will have running water, bedrooms, and windows made of glass. The new community includes a new school, band office, and other public buildings.

QUESTIONS

1. Explain why the consolidation plan for the Innu of Davis Inlet failed both socially and economically.

2. Assume the role of a social activist. Working in groups, prepare a list of recommendations to make the recent relocation more successful than the last one. In your recommendations, consider ways to relieve the immediate problems of poverty and also ways to avoid its development.

Redistribution of National Income

Reflecting on Equality, Equity, and General Welfare

In the first section of this chapter, we saw that income levels vary dramatically among Canadians. Most of us would agree that some of the reasons for higher incomes are justifiable while others are not. Canadian society accepts some unjustifiably higher incomes. This is the trade-off that we must make between equality and efficiency, efficiency being defined as the economy's capacity to get the most out of its productive resources. Entrepreneurs, for example, are allowed to reap the benefits of success because they serve a useful function by making the economy grow.

Let's suppose a nation attempted to bring about complete equality, with all individuals receiving equal incomes. Individuals would be less inclined to work harder, take risks, and study harder and longer if they knew they would end up earning as much as their neighbours, who made less effort. Efficiency would fall, and with it, the economy's ability to increase its production of goods and services. For a capitalist society to work, unequal incomes are essential.

Should we then allow incomes to be determined solely by the market? Perhaps not. Some of the reasons for higher incomes are not justified by efficiency. Income streams that are the direct result of inheritance, for example, may have little to do with efficiency. Further, all societies feel some compulsion to help those whose earning power may be weakened by sickness, accident, age, or other circumstances. This inclination is rooted in fundamental human values with which a majority of people generally agree. (In the feature below, you can read about the universal economic rights that the United Nations enshrined in its Declaration of Human Rights in 1948.)

The quandary faced by all societies is this: how do we ensure people's economic rights and reduce inequality—particularly poverty—without "killing the goose that laid the golden egg"? What good is equity if it leads to a decline in economic efficiency, productivity, and, ultimately, the nation's ability to compete in the global economy?

The welfare state compromise

Is there too much inequality in Canada? Do we need to ensure the economic rights of all citizens? Certainly, governments of all political

P R I M A R Y   S O U R C E

Universal Economic Rights

Since Confederation in 1867, Canadians have enjoyed political, legal, social, and religious rights based on British democratic traditions (and Napoleonic Law, in Quebec). During the 20th century, these human rights were expanded to include voting rights for women, rights for Aboriginal peoples, and basic economic rights. These rights and freedoms, enjoyed by all Canadians, were eventually codified into the Canadian Charter of Rights and Freedoms. Provincial governments passed human rights codes to outline these basic rights further. It is important to understand that these rights and freedoms belong to all Canadians. When a

Canadian is not allowed to enjoy one of these rights, this denial may be contested in a court of law.

An early forerunner of the Canadian Charter of Rights and Freedoms came in the form of the **United Nations Declaration of Human Rights**, which was first proclaimed on 10 December 1948 as an international articulation of the equal and inalienable rights and dignity of all members of the human family. Organized around 30 articles, the Declaration contains several articles that establish what have come to be known as "economic" rights. These are listed in Figure 15.14 (page 348).

Article	Economic Right Established
21(2)	Everyone has the right to equal access to public service in his country.
22	Everyone ... has the right to social security and is entitled to the realization, through national effort and international co-operation and in accordance with the organization and resources of each State, of the economic, social, and cultural rights indispensable for his dignity and the free development of his personality.
23(1)	Everyone has the right to work, to free choice of employment, to just and favourable conditions of work and to protection against unemployment.
23(2)	Everyone, without discrimination, has the right to equal pay for equal work.
23(3)	Everyone who works has the right to just and favourable remuneration ensuring for himself and his family an existence worthy of human dignity, and supplemented, if necessary, by other means of social protection.
23(4)	Everyone has the right to form and to join trade unions for the protection of his interests.
24	Everyone has the right to rest and leisure, including reasonable limitation of working hours and periodic holidays with pay.
25(1)	Everyone has the right to a standard of living adequate for the health and well-being of himself and of his family, including food, clothing, housing and medical care and necessary social services, and the right to security in the event of unemployment, sickness, disability, widowhood, old age or other lack of livelihood in circumstances beyond his control.
25(2)	Motherhood and childhood are entitled to special care and assistance. All children, whether born in or out of wedlock, shall enjoy the same social protection.
26(1)	Everyone has the right to education. Education shall be free, at least in the elementary and fundamental stages. Elementary education shall be compulsory. Technical and professional education shall be made generally available, and higher education shall be equally accessible to all on the basis of merit.
28	Everyone is entitled to a social and international order in which the rights and freedoms set forth in this Declaration can be fully realized.

Source: Excerpts from "Fiftieth Anniversary of the Universal Declaration of Human Rights" from <http://www.un.org/rights/50/decla.htm> reprinted by permission of the United Nations.

Figure 15.14 Economic rights in the UN Declaration of Human Rights.

QUESTIONS

1. How does the language of this document reveal its age?

2. Explain in your own words the important economic rights proclaimed by this international document.

3. Which of these rights do Canadian citizens currently enjoy? Identify at least three ways that Canadian social programs protect these universal rights.

4. How does this document help expand the concepts of economic equality and equity (fairness) beyond income distribution?

persuasions would answer in the affirmative. Early in the 20th century, Canada established a **welfare state** to reduce the inequalities in people's incomes and personal circumstances, differences that became especially evident during the Great Depression of the 1930s. A welfare state reflects a philosophy that governments should use social programs and transfers, financed out of taxation, to help people who are poor, suffer illness, or are otherwise disadvantaged. In addition, the Canadian welfare state attempts to provide universally the social programs and services required for the well-being of all its citizens. All Canadians, both rich and poor, are supposed to have equal, free access to such services as public education, health care, and social services (such as recreational centres and libraries).

The first goal of the welfare state is to allow lower-income earners to keep most of whatever earnings they have. Thus, the Canadian income tax system is a **progressive tax system**, one designed to reduce inequalities in income and to help finance social spending. Such a system taxes higher-income earners at a higher percentage rate than lower-income earners, leaving lower-income earners with a greater percentage of their income. Not only does this allow poorer people to live independently, it also benefits the economy, particularly in the increased ability of lower-income earners to participate as consumers. The welfare state, therefore, attempts to grant people their economic rights without taking away too much of their incomes.

Redistribution for the Common Good

Redistribution of income takes place in many ways in Canada. Our examination of the role of government in Chapter 13 identified the three pillars of Canada's complex social welfare safety net: public education, social services, and health care. This spending, funded principally by tax dollars (collected on an ability-to-pay basis), provides valuable services to all Canadians. Schools, libraries, recreational and cultural centres, transportation networks, hospitals, national security, and law enforcement are just a few examples of how governments

redistribute incomes in ways that benefit all Canadians universally. The government also finances home-ownership programs, student-loan programs, RRSP and RESP programs, as well as business development programs, scientific research and development, environmental initiatives, and the maintenance of our national and provincial parks. This tendency to value the *common good*, or the collective interest over individual interests, is one clear distinction between Canadian and US societies.

Many Canadians see the redistribution of wealth as an opportunity to benefit the whole country. At a high level, we can see this redistribution going on, from region to region, in the federal transfer payments made from regions of generally higher income to regions of generally lower income. Over time, higher incomes usually result in higher accumulation of **wealth**, which can be defined as the accumulated assets of individuals and families less total debts. We can see in Figure 15.15 (page 350) that individual wealth tends to vary from region to region.

Across Canada, significant regional differences appear in wealth accumulation. The average family wealth for the richest 10 per cent of families increases as you travel east to west. In 1999, British Columbia reported the highest average wealth at $251 235. The three provinces of Ontario, British Columbia, and Alberta are considered the "have" provinces. Every year, a portion of the federal taxes collected in these provinces is given to the other provinces to help finance very costly but essential services such as health care.

On further examination of Figure 15.15, you might notice that the average wealth among the poorest 10 per cent of families are negative figures all across Canada, indicating that debts were higher than assets. Collectively, Canada's poorest families wind up more than $1.3 billion in the hole. British Columbia reported the second highest debt among poor families, clearly identifying it as the region with the greatest spread between "have" and "have not" families. The data in this figure add to the long-standing concern of social policy groups, such as the Canadian Centre for Policy Alternatives, about the extent of economic inequality in Canadian society. The tenuous

Region	Average Wealth per Family Unit (total assets less debts)	Average for Richest 10% of Family Units	Average for Poorest 10% of Family Units	Gap Between Richest and Poorest Family Units
British Columbia	$251 235	$1 378 534	–$8126	$1 386 660
Prairies	$213 114	$1 135 499	–$5655	$1 141 154
Ontario	$221 110	$1 088 364	–$7096	$1 095 460
Quebec	$155 189	$868 517	–$7067	$875 584
Atlantic	$122 798	$604 669	–$8227	$612 896
CANADA	$199 664	$1 059 423	–$7110	$1 066 533

Source: Excerpts from Table 2: Regional Differences in Personal Wealth, 1999 from "BC home to greatest wealth gap in Canada" by Steve Kerstetter from *Behind the Numbers*, Canadian Centre for Policy Alternatives, BC Office, 28 November 2001. Reprinted by permission.

Figure 15.15 Regional differences in personal wealth, 1999.

financial position of a significant portion of the population is also revealed.

Attacking Poverty

In addition to Canada's investment in the common good, governments in Canada also redistribute income and share wealth in ways that are intended to address the inequalities and inequities experienced by its poorest citizens.

Programs to combat poverty can be divided into two broad but overlapping categories. Programs that attempt to eliminate the causes of poverty are called **structural strategies**. Structural remedies focus on the long-term economic adjustments needed to reduce income disparities. Programs intended to reduce the incidence of poverty and break its self-perpetuating cycle include educating and retraining workers, helping relocate them to more economically stable regions of Canada, and helping rebuild individual self-esteem and motivation. Structural programs of this nature are extremely important if Canada is to improve its distribution of national wealth, its productivity, and, in turn, its ability to compete in global markets. Structural remedies often involve long-term, gradual systemic changes that combat the root causes of poverty.

Programs that attempt to reduce the symptoms of poverty are called **relief strategies**.

Relief-based remedies focus on the provision of immediate support for needy Canadians. Community food banks and government transfer payments to individual households are two examples of relief-based remedies. Because these remedies do not address the causes of poverty—and, therefore, do not help people to emerge from poverty—critics sometimes refer to them as "band-aid solutions." It must be recognized, however, that these solutions have ensured that few Canadians find themselves in the state of absolute poverty. If Canadians become destitute, they receive help in some form.

Relief programs to combat the symptoms of poverty

1. *Welfare benefits.* Welfare is the social safety net of last resort, administered by the provinces with money both from the federal government under the Canada Assistance Plan and from provincial budgets. The specific amount received is usually set provincially, depending on the circumstances of the individual or family. Figure 15.16 compares the welfare benefits paid out to selected individuals and families by different provinces.

2. *Seniors' benefits.* The old age security plan (OAS) and the Guaranteed Income Supplements (GIS) provide pension benefits to all Canadian senior citizens. GIS

Selected Provinces	Total Welfare Income	Regional Poverty Line	Total Welfare Income (as % of poverty line)
Newfoundland			
Single Employable	$1341	$14 727	9
Single Parent, One Child	$13 924	$19 963	70
Nova Scotia			
Single Employable	$4573	$14 727	31
Single Parent, One Child	$12 558	$19 963	63
Quebec			
Single Employable	$6223	$16 766	37
Single Parent, One Child	$12 957	$22 726	57
Ontario			
Single Employable	$6822	$16 766	41
Single Parent, One Child	$13 704	$22 726	60
Alberta			
Single Employable	$5023	$16 766	30
Single Parent, One Child	$11 375	$22 726	50
British Columbia			
Single Employable	$6330	$16 766	38
Single Parent, One Child	$13 661	$22 726	60

Source: Excerpts from Table 3: Adequacy of 1999 Benefits from *Welfare Incomes 1999*, (Ottawa: National Council of Welfare, Autumn 2000). Reproduced with the permission of the Minister of Public Works and Government Services Canada, 2002.

Figure 15.16 Adequacy of 1999 welfare benefits. Why would no welfare recipients receive 100 per cent of the poverty-line income? Which province had the most generous welfare payments in 1999? Which province had the least generous payments? Speculate on why this was so.

payments are made only when reported incomes do not meet established minimums.

3. *Canada Pension Plan (CPP)*. CPP is a compulsory pension plan for all working Canadians. The amount received on retirement depends on income and contributions made during the individual's working years. It may be received in full at age 65 or partially at age 60. Canadians who are medically identified as no longer able to work as a result of a permanent disability receive a disability pension until they qualify for CPP.

4. *Employment Insurance (EI)*. Formerly called Unemployment Insurance, this plan pays a percentage of the unemployed person's former income level, depending on the number of weeks worked previous to the period of unemployment. All employed Canadians contribute to this compulsory plan.

5. *Child Tax Credit*. Replacing the universal family allowance program, this new approach gives only lower-income families a tax credit for each child.

6. *Compensation for work-related disability*. Workers injured on the job risk falling into the low-income category. Medicare and provincial worker's compensation boards, like Ontario's Workplace Safety and Insurance Board (WSIB), help prevent this.

7. *Charitable and community-based relief*. Many non-profit charitable organizations, such as the St. Vincent de Paul Society and the Salvation Army, seek to provide relief with dignity to needy individuals and families. In addition, by 1999, food banks run by volunteers were active in 488 Canadian communities. It is estimated by the Canadian Association of Food Banks that close to three million Canadians used food

banks in 1999—more than twice the number of people who used the service one decade earlier.

Structural remedies to combat the causes of poverty

1. *Education.* All evidence points to a direct link between educational level and incomes. Governments have provided universal elementary and secondary education for the better part of a century and have expanded access to post-secondary education enormously since the 1960s. Both federal and provincial governments subsidize colleges and universities heavily, with students paying only part of the cost in tuition fees. Some programs are designed to help lower-income students with post-secondary costs, but recent increases in tuition costs have been criticized as discriminating against poorer students. These students often end up with huge student debts that take many years to pay off. Nonetheless, by funding all of the cost of elementary and secondary education and much of the cost of post-secondary education, Canadian governments go a long way to providing students from low-income families with equal opportunities to become educated, productive members of society. Public investment in the development of human capital is one important way to reduce the incidence of poverty in Canada.

2. *Day care.* Because of the high incidence of poverty in single-parent homes, free or subsidized day care is important because it can allow more parents to attend school or work. The programs are provincially run. One model held in high regard is Quebec's plan, which is universal (applying to all citizens regardless of income) and has a $5 per day, per child cost. Anti-poverty activists have lobbied for many years for a universal, national day-care program modelled after the generous European programs. In these days of budgetary restraint, it does not seem likely that a universal program will emerge soon.

3. *Increasing employability and employment.* Workers with limited skills who lose their jobs have every chance of falling below the poverty line. Governments try to increase employment opportunities by funding training intended to teach marketable skills and by sponsoring relocation programs to assist unemployed workers in moving to communities with better job opportunities for their skill set. To date, these programs have helped some Canadians improve their economic conditions, but they don't work in all cases. These programs are more successful when individuals are motivated to seek retraining and relocation. During the 1970s, the federal government (through the former Department of Regional Economic Expansion [DREE]) attempted to create employment by attracting industry to economically depressed areas. This program met with limited success and, in time, the free market was seen as the better source of sustainable job creation. Government efforts focused instead on supporting business expansion.

Check Your Understanding

1. How does the nature of capitalism simultaneously lead to both production efficiency and income inequality?

2. Explain how the UN Declaration of Human Rights has helped expand the concepts of economic equality and equity (or fairness) beyond income distribution.

3. In what two ways does the income tax system used in Canada help address income inequalities?

4. Refer to Figure 15.7 (page 337) and Figure 15.15 (page 350). Explain the difference between income and wealth. How does the distribution of wealth compare to income distribution in Canada?

5. Explain the difference between relief strategies and structural strategies to combat poverty. Provide three important examples of each strategy type.

Case Study

The following letter, to the editor of the student newspaper at Memorial University in Newfoundland, was written by university student Jason White. White presents an assessment of the quality of life of a university student in Newfoundland. Consider whether the situation he describes is representative of that faced by students across Canada.

Before you read, consider that virtually all poorer students must finance their post-secondary education by applying for student loans, which can build to extraordinary amounts, especially for students pursuing postgraduate degrees. After protesting his dire circumstances, White proposes a solution to the poverty he and other students experience during their student years. What do you think about his solution?

How Can We Survive on Less Than the Poverty Line?

This is a question that myself and many others ask everyday. But realistically, is it possible to live comfortably on this petty sum? It is true that we do receive around the poverty line from student loans, but in the calculations of the poverty line there is no addition for tuition, student fees, and books; take these away and you have around half of the poverty line.

I don't know about you, but food and shelter are things that I consider very important, though with this sparse amount of cash I am often reduced to live at the limit of my means. What I mean by limit is having two small meals per day, the bare necessities at that. It is getting to the point where we will be surviving on barley meal, just like the good old days of the middle ages.

What can be done? For starters, we must have a raise in the basic amount of student aid,

with a low cap on the interest to ~~b~~ and it should be handled by the gover~~n~~ which is intended to be non-profit, rathe~~r~~ the banks. The tuition at Memorial must be lowered! Presently it is one of the fastest rising in the country....

What a euphoric dream, to leave university and not have a mortgage greater or equal to that of a midsize house, with often prime plus 5 per cent or more! But it can be done with no additional costs to the government. With the slightest concept of economics, it is easy to see that there is a correlation of the increase in education and the increase in the productivity of labour; with this increased productivity usually comes increased incomes. Thus, the government will have less stress on the social safety net and a greater revenue from taxes. The problem is solved!

Feed us and we will feed you!

Source: Excerpts from "Poverty Line Living" by Jason D. White from *The Muse Online*, Volume 48, Issue 18, 6 March 1998. Reprinted by permission.

QUESTIONS

1. How does the writer describe his quality of life as a university student?

2. Refer to Figure 15.16 (page 351) to determine the poverty line in Newfoundland. Cut this sum in half. Would you be able to pay for a year's housing, food, and clothing with this sum?

3. How does White adapt the poverty line? Is this an example of relative or absolute poverty?

4. Does White's solution represent a relief or a structural remedy to student poverty? Explain.

5. Explain the economic reasoning involved in White's solution. Do you agree with his reasoning?

353

SUMMARY

challenge is to find an acceptable compromise between the two.

• Canada constructed a welfare state after the Second World War in order to reduce income differences; to give citizens equal access to medical care, education, and government services; and to reduce the incidence of poverty.

• The UN Declaration of Human Rights (1948) established the equal and inalienable rights of all persons. Several articles deal with economic rights. Governments in Canada have further expanded these human rights.

• Governments attack both the causes and the symptoms of poverty with various social programs, such as welfare benefits, employment insurance, compensation for injured workers, day care, and adult education and retraining.

... mparing ... rage ... of distribution ... de income receivers ... the percentage of total ... at each group receives in order to ... and income distribution.

• Market economies have an inherent tendency to distribute income unequally to reward effort, education, skills, and risk taking—all of which are essential to economic efficiency and thus to economic growth.

• Other, less defensible, reasons for significant unequal income distribution include discrimination, luck, misfortune, family background, and regional disparity.

• The poverty level has been defined for many years, in relative terms, as a low-income situation in which an individual or family spends more than 44 per cent of after-tax income on basic necessities. Low-income cut-offs are used to determine the statistical incidence of poverty in Canada.

• A contending definition describes poverty as an absolute condition whereby a person or family lacks one or more of the basic necessities. This definition sees poverty in terms of deprivation.

• Some of the causes of poverty are lack of work, age, lack of education, disability, single parenthood, and being a child in a family where these conditions prevail. Canada's working poor are low-income earners while non-working poor are often referred to as the welfare poor.

• The market economy features a trade-off between economic efficiency and equality. The

Key Terms

equity
Human Development Index (HDI)
mean average income
median income
quintile
Lorenz curve
cohort
asset income
absolute poverty
relative poverty
low-income cut-off (LICO)
before-tax income
after-tax income
poverty line
deprivation
exclusion
working poor
welfare poor
United Nations Declaration of Human Rights
welfare state
progressive tax system
wealth
structural strategy
relief strategy

Activities

Thinking/Inquiry

1. Research the Employment Insurance Act of 1996 for the purpose of preparing a brief report on key topics such as eligibility, income benefits, claim period, special benefits, and premiums. Explain how this government program helps redistribute income in Canada. You can find information at the federal government Web site by searching the site using the key words "Employment Insurance."

2. By the end of 1999, one in five children in Canada lived in poverty—an increase of 402 000 children since 1989, when the House of Commons unanimously passed a resolution "to seek to achieve the goal of eliminating poverty among Canadian children by the year 2000." To research child poverty in Canada, visit the Web site of Campaign 2000, a coalition of 85 organizations wanting to end child poverty in Canada. You can locate their site by searching for the key words "campaign 2000 poverty." Use the information you find to produce a newsletter or poster to promote one specific policy initiative to address child poverty.

3. a) Consult the most recent Human Development Index (HDI) data available through an Internet search. Between 1992 and 2000, Canada occupied the top position. What has happened to Canada's ranking since 2000?

   b) Make a list of Canada's ranking for each statistic used in the HDI. For which statistics does Canada receive its highest and lowest rankings? What message does this send to policy makers and others reflecting on normative economics?

Communication

4. Prepare an argument to debate one of the following public policy statements:

   a) "For the sake of distributive justice, wealthy individuals and corporations should be taxed more in order to pay their fair share of taxes."

   b) "For the sake of distributive justice, Canada should introduce an inheritance tax."

   c) "For the sake of distributive justice, Canada would be best served by a public policy focus on income equality as opposed to income equity."

5. Suppose that you are a doctor. How would you argue, using the economic concepts learned in this chapter, that your relatively high income is justified?

6. Write a letter to the editor as an advocate for homeless people. Explain how the factors affecting income distribution help to cause poverty in Canada and suggest what governments, enterprises, social agencies, and concerned citizens can do to address this growing problem.

7. Both the UN Human Development Index and the UN Declaration of Human Rights confirm that there are better indicators of quality of life than per capita income. Defend or refute this claim by making specific reference to the contents of both.

8. "Women are more likely to be poor than men in Canada." Cite four examples of data in tables in this chapter either to support or to refute this claim. Compare your findings with a partner.

Application

9. What is the absolute minimum you would need to live on as a single person? Using flyers from grocery stores, classified sections for rental accommodation from newspapers, and other information, design a budget for yourself. Compare your total with the figures that the relative and absolute poverty measures define as the poverty level for your region, and make comparisons. Compare it with the welfare payments for a single individual living in your region.

10. Refer to Figure 15.7 (page 337), showing the differences in income among the provinces in Canada.

    a) Which parts of Canada reported the highest income levels in 1999? lowest income levels?

b) Compare the incidence of low incomes (or "poverty") in Atlantic Canada, Ontario, the Prairie Provinces, and British Columbia. Which parts of Canada report income levels above and below the national average? Explain the significance of this comparison.

11. In light of what you have learned about the incidence of poverty in Canada, what would you identify as the principal causes? What three specific recommendations would you make to governments regarding effective long-term solutions?

12. Refer to Figure 15.16 (page 351). Calculate each provincial welfare payment for single, employable people as a percentage of that province's poverty-line income for 1999.

Which province had welfare payments closest to its poverty line income? Which province had welfare payments farthest from its poverty-line income? What does this tell you about the priorities of these provincial governments?

13. Right-wing advocates of free-enterprise capitalism are generally less sympathetic to poor people, believing that they should do more to help themselves and that, unless they begin to help themselves, the help that others provide is of limited use. Use economic reasoning to defend or refute this position.

14. Use the contents of this chapter and the additional information that you have researched to support or refute the argument that poverty is passed on from parents to children.

CHAPTER 16
THE ENVIRONMENT AND SUSTAINABLE DEVELOPMENT

QUESTIONS

1. Referring to specific images and symbols used by the cartoonist, explain the message being conveyed.
2. What do you think are the biggest environmental problems today?
3. Why do you think these environmental problems are occurring?

Chapter Goals

By the end of this chapter, you will be able to

• understand the economic pressures on the environment and how they threaten sustainable development,
• identify positive and negative externalities,
• explain why these problems occur through marginal cost and marginal benefit analysis,
• explain a variety of strategies being used to address the impact of negative externalities on the environment.

Impact of Economic Activity on the Environment

In *Inventing the Future*, a book containing a collection of his essays, Canadian scientist David Suzuki calls for ecologists and economists to unite. He begins one of his submissions by comparing the root words of the two disciplines:

> The words ecology and economics *derive from the same Greek word*, oikos, *meaning household or home. So ecology (*logos *meaning* study*) is the study of home, and economics (*nomics *meaning* management*) is home management. These two fields should be companion disciplines, and yet with few exceptions there is little communication between them.*

Suzuki goes on to point out that all the natural resources of our world are really the "fundamental capital that all countries depend on" and that the actions of many of the participants in our economic system do not always take into account our best interests in using these resources. Our natural resources provide benefits that exist beyond the dollar values that they contribute to economic output; yet these benefits—or the destruction thereof—are not factored into the output decisions made in the economy. Suzuki concludes the essay by stating that "Economists cannot afford any longer to ignore their companion discipline of ecology."

This chapter will explore how economists attempt to explain the impact of economic activity on the environment and how this impact should be addressed.

Sustainable Development

Concerns about the relationship between economics and the environment relate to our initial introduction to the study of economics and the underlying economic problem—scarcity. The resources that sustain our world are finite. Some will regenerate given time and effective management, some are used up in the production of goods, and others can be recycled. If our world is to continue and the human race to thrive, all these resources must be managed carefully.

In 1982, sociologist William Catton wrote about the concept of carrying capacity in his book, *Overshoot: The Ecological Basis of Revolutionary Change*. He defined **carrying capacity** as the number of people that the Earth's resources can support indefinitely if managed effectively. In other words, resources must be used such that the environment is not harmed to the extent that it cannot support its human population.

Over the past several decades, concern has grown that economic activity is consuming resources at a pace beyond the Earth's carrying capacity. Catton referred to this as the **drawing down** of resources—the process of using up resources that should be available for future generations. Many people interpret this statement as applying only to the overconsumption of non-renewable resources, such as minerals and fossil fuels, but it goes well beyond this. Poor management of renewable resources (such as forests, fish, fresh water, and even air) must also be included.

In discussions about the balance between economic development and its impact on the environment, the term **sustainable development** is frequently used. The United Nation's World Commission on Environment and Development introduced the concept of sustainable development in its 1987 report titled *Our Common Future*. It stated that "Sustainable development is development that meets the needs of the present without compromising the ability of future generations to meet their own needs." In other words, a sustainable society is one that considers the impact of current production and consumption patterns on the economic viability of future generations. To achieve sustainability, affluent societies must reduce their rate of current consumption and change how they interact with the environment. Paying the full economic and social cost of the resources that they use would be a place to start.

Externalities

The conflict between economic and environmental concerns lies in the existence of a market inefficiency that is known as an externality.

A Matter of Opinion | The Illusory Oil Change

66 The environmental consequences of our technological society with its high consumption and disposable products are forcing us to reassess our lifestyles. Recycling was once the rule, dictated simply by necessity. We have forgotten that our parents conserved routinely and now we are being haunted by the consequences of our profligate ways.

We've all taken our cars in to have the oil changed—perhaps you've even changed the oil yourself. But have you ever wondered what happens to that yucky black stuff that was drained out? That lubricating oil is potentially reusable, but most of it ends up dumped on the ground or in rivers and creeks. It's a classic example of our society's shortsightedness.

We live in a strange world of illusion. The current prices of oil are depressed because of a "glut" on the market, yet every oilperson knows oil is going to run out early in [this] century. We have enormous environmental problems, yet we continue to pay no attention to the destructive effects of many of our products that end up polluting. That brings us back to used oil.

There are two kinds of lubricating oil: the stuff we use in our cars, and industrial oils. Of the 200 million gallons [757 million L] of lubricating oil produced in Canada annually, half is used up in the lubricating process, but the other 100 million gallons are potentially recoverable. In fact, about 37 million gallons are collected, of which about 22 million gallons are re-refined and the remainder is burned or spread on roads. What about the uncollected 63 million gallons? Chances are they go into sewers or onto the ground. Without a doubt we end up drinking it in our water and eating it in our vegetables and meat. So while we waste a precious resource by failing to recycle all this used oil, it is also a major contaminant of the environment.

Used oil is also laced with deleterious chemicals that are removed in the re-refining process but that are liberated when the used oil is burned in low-grade furnaces or dumped. Some of those contaminants include lead, zinc, chromium, arsenic, chlorine, bromine, PCBs, polycyclic aromatics, and volatile and semi-volatile organics—a rather nasty gallery of chemicals.

It costs money to re-refine oil. There has to be a system whereby it can be stored, picked up, and transported to re-refining plants. There is little incentive, especially when "virgin" oil—refined crude oil—is so cheap. Twenty years ago in the US, there were over 200 re-refiners. In 1987, only three remained, and they were struggling to survive. At the same time in Canada, there were six, and they were all barely making it.

Part of the problem is psychological—Canadians believe that re-refined oil is lower quality than virgin oil. Yet a study by the National Research Council of Canada showed that re-refined oil is as good as or even better than the refined. But we are reluctant to purchase the re-refined, especially since it is more expensive.

A major part of the problem for re-refiners is political—all the tax incentives and subsidies go to the discovery and exploitation of crude oil. There are no economic incentives for the re-refiners. There should be every encouragement to conserve through recycling and to protect the environment by removing toxic contaminants and preventing the introduction of the oil into the environment. But therein lies the problem. The producer of a product—any product—usually has no obligation to anticipate its total cost including eventual disposal, yet that should be built into the initial costing.

The best example of our myopia is the nuclear industry, which built plants long before there was any serious consideration of disposal of radioactive wastes or decommissioning aging plants. Economic or legal incentives to recycle in an environmentally responsible way are needed. Re-refining oil ought to be an apple-pie issue, but the industry is on the ropes.

We have to get over the idea that we can dump liquid waste into sewers and forget about it or that we can slop it onto the ground where it will be absorbed. It is ironic that while the PCB spill near Kenora created a public outcry, millions of gallons of used oil—much of it containing PCBs and other toxics—are sprayed onto dirt roads to keep down the dust. More goes into our waters where it is estimated the cost is up to $8 million a year to repair corrosion and replace filtration systems. Millions of gallons of used oil are also burned in furnaces for low-grade heating of greenhouses. The burning temperature is too low to destroy PCBs, which are simply liberated into the air and often end up being absorbed by the plants growing in the greenhouses! Some used oil is actually sprayed on pigs' backs to keep them from getting sunburned in the summer.

Our political and economic systems do not consider the cost of human activity on an ecosystem. Whatever we take from that ecosystem denies it to other life forms, and whatever we dispose into it flows through the various cycles of air, water, and soil. For millennia, our numbers were small and our technology simple, so the environment seemed limitless and end-lessly self-cleansing. Today we are too numerous and our technology is too powerful for nature to be as forgiving. The economic "costs" of new products simply do not include long-term environmental degradation. Governments don't offer enough rewards to those who conserve resources for future generations or adequately punish those who use up or damage the environment. It doesn't make sense to decide on recycling only if it is economically profitable: we live on a finite planet where all life is ultimately interconnected. It's high time we radically changed our system of economics to take into account our impact on the environment.

So the next time you empty your crankcase, think hard before dumping that stuff down the drain. **99**

Source: Excerpt from *Inventing the Future*. Copyright © 1989 by David Suzuki. Reprinted by permission of Stoddart Publishing Co. Limited.

QUESTIONS

1. What is the main argument that David Suzuki is trying to convey in his essay?

2. Identify three examples of negative externalities that are mentioned in this essay.

3. What are the factors that are preventing the more widespread use of re-refined oil?

An **externality** is a side effect of the productive process that is experienced by a third party who does not participate, as either a consumer or a producer, in an actual market transaction related to the good.

For example, a pulp and paper company produces paper that is sold to a printing company. During the manufacturing process, the pulp and paper company dumps liquid waste (known as *effluent*) into a river, which causes fish to be killed. People who catch fish from the river now suffer from the side effect of fewer fish to catch. They are not engaged in the actual transaction yet suffer a cost. This is a **negative externality**, one that imposes some cost (such as pollution or some other annoyance) on a third party. Examples of negative externalities include oil spills, traffic congestion, toxic waste dumping, greenhouse gas emissions, solid waste disposal, and noise generated by a factory near a residential area.

A **positive externality**, on the other hand, results from a transaction that provides benefit to a third party. Examples would include an increase in surrounding property values owing to construction of a new transportation route or the recreational use of an area that is developed for resource extraction.

Externalities are really sources of economic inefficiency because market forces do not always consider all the costs and benefits associated with economic decision making. In fact, for the most part, the only costs and benefits that are considered are the dollars associated with the parties directly involved. The external costs are borne by other parties affected by the transaction. For this reason, they are also called **spillover costs**, or **neighbourhood effects**. They are a problem only if the decision makers are not taking them into account. If the market does not require decision makers to consider these costs, there is no incentive for producers to limit their harmful effects.

In essence, a solution to the problem of externalities would require producers to consider spillover costs as part of their inputs. (Remember that an *input* is any factor used in the production process.) A producer who uses river or coastal waters to discharge effluent, or the air to expel emissions, is really using water and air as inputs. The consumption of these inputs must be considered if the outcome is to be economically efficient.

The problem is that many external costs are associated with natural elements that are used as factors of production and have no clear right of ownership. If someone owns the land that a forestry company uses to harvest trees, it is easy to see who should be reimbursed for the cost of the trees. But no one, for example, owns the air, so how can a cost be determined for the oxygen that the tree no longer produces? If no one owns the river that is polluted by oil leaking from the logging machines, how can a cost be determined for the fish that die as a result? Because no one person owns these elements, it is no one's private business to ensure their well-being.

Check Your Understanding

1. What does David Suzuki mean when he says that the natural resources of the world are really the "fundamental capital that all countries depend on"? How is this statement linked to the concept of sustainable development?

2. Think about the route that you take when travelling from your home to your school. Identify five negative externalities that you have experienced that were likely not factored into the cost of production.

3. Why is it necessary to count the discharge of effluent into a river as an input in the production process?

Marginal Social Costs and Benefits

The inefficiencies that result in pollution occur because of externalities. An economic explanation for these inefficiencies emerges from an analysis of marginal costs and marginal benefits. This approach is very different from the argument that any damage to the existing environment is bad. It suggests that for true efficiency to exist, both dollar costs and external costs must be considered in decisions regarding level of output and price. Only when this equilibrium is achieved will society truly be weighing the impact of human activity on the environment.

In Chapter 7, you learned about marginal cost and benefit analysis. Because it explains the "most profitable" level of output for a firm, such analysis indicates the most efficient allocation of its resources. The firm will achieve a level of output at which the marginal cost is equal to the marginal revenue. In essence, the model states that as long as the added benefits (marginal revenue) exceed the added costs (marginal cost), it makes sense to produce an additional unit of output. This model can also

Economics in the News

My Toxic Playground: The Tar Ponds Were Home for Me, I Always Assumed I Was Safe

Figure 16.1 The water body in the lower part of this aerial photograph is part of the Sydney Tar Ponds. Note how close the residential area is to the Ponds.

When I was young, I thought that I was invincible. Back then, a muddy creek was just a muddy creek. No one ever told us to stay away from it. No one ever told us not to drink the water from the natural spring fountain half a mile away. But now I am 33 years old and I have thyroid cancer. Many of the people I played with as a child have died and many more are very sick. I come from Sydney, NS, but like so many others from Cape Breton, I moved to Alberta for work and what I hoped would be a better life for my kids. I am married to a lovely woman and I have two great children who, for some reason, think

I am the best dad in the world. But my world has changed.

Cape Breton is famous for lots of things and infamous for one—the Sydney tar ponds. The area, home to the Sydney Steel Corp., a century-old dump, and Muggah Creek, is a wasteland of toxic materials. The "ponds" are, in fact, a tidal estuary at the mouth of the creek. It is known that the cancer rate is high in this area, but people haven't looked at the effects that spill past the cancer. How many kids have lost parents at very young ages? How many miscarriages have occurred? How many people have turned to alcohol and drugs to deal with loss and pain? Most of the men in my family died by the age of 45. That gives me 12 years. If God is willing, I'll have more. Every day, I read the *Cape Breton Post* online, and every day I see that someone else I used to know has died. Mothers, fathers, aunts, uncles, sisters, and brothers have all died young from different diseases. But I believe that if you looked closely the causes are all linked to where they lived and played.

It seems as if all of us who spent our younger days on a ball-field in Whitney Pier are now facing down cancer. I can't prove that my childhood haunts are what caused my illness, but many doctors have said that to get my type of thyroid cancer you have to be exposed to extreme amounts of radiation. At first, I thought that meant it was from regular X-rays. I was in a lot of car accidents and had my share of bicycle and skateboard spills growing up. I also injured myself playing football. But after some research, I found out that it's people who had X-ray treatments to their head and necks for things like acne and tonsillitis who are at a greater risk for this type of thyroid cancer, and those treatments stopped about 20 years before I was born.

I was once told that everyone is born with cells within their bodies that can become cancerous— it is simply different things that trigger cancer to grow, be it smoking or whatever else. Yet my doctors in Cape Breton never said that breathing in the fumes from the tar ponds could have done it. I worked at the Sydney steel plant when it was building the "Superburn" project—an incineration system to burn contaminated sediment. About a year after I left, the plant was forced to shut down because of the extremely high levels of PCBs found in the sludge. The toxic levels were too high for the system to burn. And there we were kicking up dust, moving the slime, and had never been told of the danger, of the gases that could be stirred up from our work. We had dust masks and safety glasses, but I was never told to wear a gas mask. And why would I think to do it on my own? The area was home to me, I always assumed it was safe. When I was a kid, I played in the fields next to the plant and in that creek. But now, I have just gone through my first

radioactive iodine treatment and I am wearing rubber gloves to type this out.

I am not a doctor and I can't scientifically prove my theory—but in the middle of this battle with cancer, I had to write it down. Soil tests in my old neighbourhood found arsenic levels up to 67 times the acceptable limit, as well as high levels of lead and benzene. And this summer, Health Canada studied the effects of contamination on the people who still live there, but it hasn't released any results. There are more problems with the tar ponds than just the ugly location, the smell, and how to clean them up. There are families who have been lost, loved ones gone too soon. There are the people who left their homes for something better only to find that long before they were able to start families or earn a living, their lives were irreversibly altered by disease. I am pretty sure it started on those summer days when we were kids, invincible—playing baseball, horsing around in the creek, and drinking water from that fountain.

Source: John MacInnis, "My Toxic Playground: The Tar Ponds Were Home for Me, I Always Assumed I Was Safe," *Maclean's*, 15 October 2001, Volume 114, Number 42, 12.

QUESTIONS

1. What is the anecdotal evidence that there is an environmental problem with the area around the Sydney tar ponds?

2. Testing of soil samples in the area has suggested that while there are higher-than-normal levels of toxic chemicals, the levels are not high enough to prove that there is a health risk. Do you think we should rely on scientific levels of contaminants as the sole determinant of whether there is a health risk? Explain your answer. What other factors do you think should be considered?

3. Many claim that the government should pay to move Sydney residents out of the affected area. What do you think should be done? Who should be held responsible?

be used to determine the most efficient level of output if the environmental costs are included, as shown in the following example.

The production of whizbangs results in the discharge of toxic chemicals into a lake. In Figure 16.2, the **marginal social cost (MSC)** reflects the additional cost to society (from increased levels of pollution) of an increase in the level of production of whizbangs—the more whizbangs the firm produces, the higher the MSC. The **marginal benefit (MB)** reflects the firm's demand for the use of the externality. This marginal benefit is the additional revenue that is generated as additional units are produced. The curve is downward sloping because of the law of diminishing marginal returns. Every additional unit that is produced results in smaller increases in the total benefit to the firm. At some point, the additional benefit falls to zero.

As in marginal cost–revenue analysis for the firm, the most efficient level of output occurs at the point at which the marginal benefit equals the marginal social cost. In our example, this would mean a marginal cost and benefit of $50 per tonne and an amount of discharged waste of 25 tonnes per week. But the firm

actually produces a total of 50 tonnes of waste per week. The reason? Because the firm does not own the lake, it bears none of the burden of the marginal social cost. This cost is borne by the residents around the lake who draw their drinking water from it or the fishers who may no longer catch healthy fish in the lake. The firm, therefore, produces at the level where it receives its greatest benefit (when marginal benefit falls to zero) while the residents pick up the marginal social cost of $100 per tonne. Although the firm's level of output is its most efficient, that same level of output is higher than what is most efficient for society. By this analysis, then, the firm's level of output is inefficient.

What impact does not including the social costs of pollution have on price and output? By not accounting for the externality, the actual cost fails to include the value that members of society place on the damage incurred in the environment. Therefore, the price charged is lower than the actual value of the product. The low price is the result of a failure in the pricing system because the actual costs are not passed on to the consumer.

We will conduct our analysis assuming that the firm is operating in a perfectly competitive market, but the model works equally well for the other three market types. Figure 16.3 displays the marginal cost and revenue curves for a typical, perfectly competitive firm in the whizbangs market. The marginal cost curve has been labelled **MPC (marginal private cost)** instead of MC in order to denote that it includes only the private costs incurred by the firm and ignores the externalities. The firm accepts the current market price for each unit, so the marginal revenue (MR) is equal to the price for each additional unit. Using marginal cost–benefit analysis, we can determine that the firm's most efficient output would be 1000 units (where price = MPC = MR). If, however, marginal cost is to include *all* costs, it must account for external costs as well. For each additional unit added, there is now an increase in the external costs. This shifts the MPC curve to the left. This new curve is now labelled MSC (marginal social cost). Notice that this new curve intersects the marginal

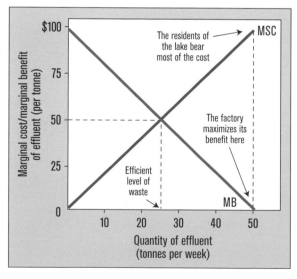

Figure 16.2 Inefficiency due to an externality. An "inefficient" level of waste occurs because the firm bears none of the social costs of pollution. These costs are fully borne by the residents around the polluted lake.

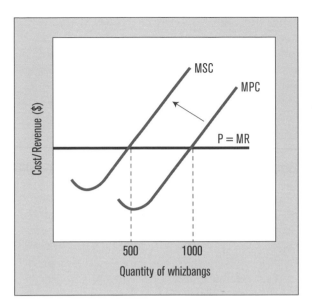

Figure 16.3 Output for a typical whizbang firm considering external costs. When this firm is forced to consider external costs, its most efficient level of output is reduced from 1000 units to 500 units.

revenue curve at a point farther to the left, indicating that a lower output (500 whizbangs) is now the more efficient level of output. Because each typical firm is producing less, the total market supply curve is shifted to the left, as indicated in Figure 16.4. The result is a lower quantity of whizbangs exchanged at a higher price because society is now paying the real cost of the good or service and, therefore, a lower quantity is demanded.

Solving the Dilemma

The entire responsibility for the impact of externalities cannot, however, be placed at the feet of firms and industry. First of all, calculation of the precise financial costs of externalities is inexact and debatable. Second, without some sort of government intervention, a socially conscious firm that seeks to internalize all costs faces a much worse cost structure than its polluting competitors, making competition on the basis of price very difficult. In many cases, the fact that a firm is taking an ethical position is not enough to persuade consumers to pay a higher price for its product. Often, then, the

reward for the pollution-conscious firm is a clear conscience, a declining market for its product, and diminished profits. Therefore, in order to create meaningful change in the reduction of pollution, governments have to take action.

Subsidies

The government might provide a subsidy to firms in order to encourage them to take external costs into account. A **subsidy** is a payment made by the government to a producer on the condition of a desired outcome. For example, if the government wants to reduce the amount of water pollution created in the production of whizbangs, it could ask the company to install technology that removes pollutants from the factory effluent. To achieve this objective, they would offer to subsidize all or part of the cost of the technology necessary to remove the pollutants. A major complaint regarding this strategy is that the producer and consumer of the product are not held accountable for the external cost; rather, the general public pays through the collection of the tax revenue necessary to pay the subsidy.

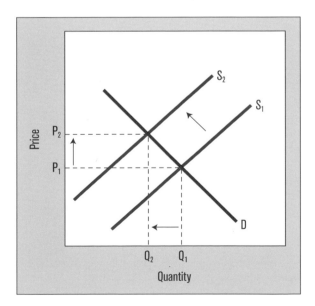

Figure 16.4 Effect on the whizbang market if external costs are included. With each firm producing less at any given market price, the market supply curve is shifted to the left, leading to higher prices and a lower quantity demanded.

Taxes

Another method that governments can use to achieve more acceptable levels of pollution is to tax the polluters. A **Pigouvian tax** (named after Arthur Cecil Pigou, the British founder of welfare economics) is levied on production that causes a negative environmental externality. Its purpose is to force producers and consumers to take into account the external environmental costs. Instead of forcing society as a whole to pay for the pollution costs, the producer is forced to "internalize the externality." The effect of the tax is to shift the supply curve in the market to the left, as shown in Figure 16.5, as producers must now receive a higher price in order to maintain the same level of production. As a result, the equilibrium price in the market rises, and a smaller quantity is bought and sold. This smaller quantity exchanged should also be reflected in a decrease in environmental pollution.

Using taxes to internalize externalities results in a market price that reflects the true social costs of production and forces firms and consumers to bear the full social cost of their economic activities. But these methods have attracted some criticism. First of all, the money raised through the levying of taxes does not actually go toward compensating those who are affected by the externality. For example, the lake that is being polluted in the production of whizbangs is still being polluted—albeit to a lesser degree—but the residents who are not able to draw their drinking water from the lake are not receiving any of the tax revenue to compensate them for their loss. Instead, the compensation goes to the general public at large.

Second, it is difficult for the government to set a tax that makes up for the difference between the marginal cost and the marginal social cost. The best strategy for a government to take is to set a tax rate that slowly creeps upward until the level of pollution is reduced to an acceptable level. This does not mean that the level of pollution will necessarily be what society considers *efficient*. Political concerns may hamper the shift of the marginal cost curve.

Third, pollution is still occurring. The only difference is that the new level of pollution is *efficient* as long as the Pigouvian tax shifts the marginal cost curve so that it is equal to the marginal social cost curve. One advantage of the Pigouvian tax, however, is that it may cause some producers to adopt a technology that reduces external costs. Firms with clean-up costs that fall below the level of the tax will implement the required technology in order to avoid the tax.

Regulation

The federal and provincial governments may use direct regulations that limit externalities. Regulation is usually necessary when the production of a good or service results in a highly toxic or dangerous by-product. For instance, the use of chlorine in bleaching pulp for paper production results in a waste by-product that contains dioxins and furans. These highly toxic compounds have been associated with reduced reproductive capabilities in fish-eating birds that live around the Great Lakes. It is, therefore, necessary for the government to regulate the allowable levels or amounts of these substances permitted to enter the environment. Many environmentalists argue that no dioxins

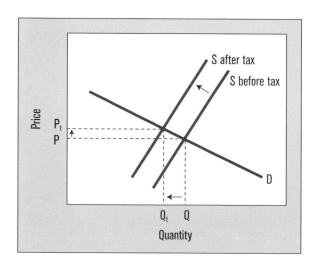

Figure 16.5 Passing on the cost to consumers through a Pigouvian tax. The tax shifts the supply curve to the left, resulting in an increase in price from P to P_t (price with tax) and less pollution, as the quantity exchanged decreases from Q to Q_t (quantity with tax).

or furans should be allowed from industrial sources. On the other hand, industry advocates argue that there are safe levels that the environment can absorb. For extremely dangerous pollutants, the government has little choice but to use regulation in order to protect the public interest. Ontario's "Drive Clean" program, which sets emission standards for automobiles, is an example of direct regulation of harmful externalities.

The government might also use regulations to protect renewable resources such as fish and lumber. Quotas—such as restrictions on the amount of fish that can be caught within territorial waters—are designed to help manage public resources that would otherwise be overused. Critics claim that these regulations are often seen as taxes, in the sense that those who break the law are fined; if offenders feel that paying the fine is cheaper than taking the action necessary to prevent the external cost, they may just pay the fine. Another problem is that such regulations can be costly and difficult to administer. In times of budget cuts, the policing of regulations may be cut back. This complaint was levied against the Ontario government during the Walkerton water inquiry in 2001, held after a number of people died after drinking municipal water that was contaminated with *E. coli* bacteria. It has been suggested that economic tools, such as taxes and subsidies, tend to be more efficient than regulation because compliance is built in through market pricing mechanisms.

Coase Theorem

In 1960, economist Ronald Coase proposed a theorem that suggested externalities do not require government intervention in some circumstances. The **Coase theorem** states that private transactions will be efficient because of bargaining and negotiation under the following conditions:
• The property rights are clearly defined.
• The number of firms, people, or parties involved is limited to only a few.
• The level of cost is low and easily negotiable.
• The issue must be fairly simple and clearly understood.

Coase argued that, when the above criteria are in place, the role of the government is to act as a facilitator, encouraging bargaining between the affected parties or various stakeholders. The idea is to get those who create the pollution together with those who are affected by the externality so that they may find an acceptable solution to the problem. Establishing clearly defined property rights places a price tag on the use of that property. Thus, it is necessary to establish clear property rights and ownership. Because it includes the right to exclude others from using the object, the right to sue for damages to the object caused by others, and the duty of the owner to avoid nuisance and other socially unacceptable consequences, ownership provides incentive for the owner of the externally affected property to act. In some cases, this ownership can extend to common property rights (for example, common-pool resources such as farmer-managed irrigation systems, user-managed groundwater systems, or club-owned recreational facilities).

In a sense, the Coase theorem relates to a complex analysis of opportunity cost into which all costs—both internal and external—are factored. Logging in wilderness areas that also attract tourists provides an example of an instance where the Coase Theorem can be put into effect. If the owner of a large parcel of forest near the area where tour operators conduct their business is considering allowing a large logging company to harvest her forest, the local tour operators face a big problem. The tour operators want to have a pristine wilderness with which to attract tourist dollars. The logging company, on the other hand, wants to log the area using the most cost-effective means possible—clear-cutting. Although fairly cost effective, clear-cutting is environmentally devastating. Furthermore, clear-cutting in a wilderness area that also attracts tourist dollars hurts the tourist industry. In this situation, if the landowner and the tour operators were brought together to establish clear costs and benefits, perhaps a compromise might be reached between the two parties that would consider the external costs.

As long as one of the parties in the dispute has clear property rights to what is at issue, there will be an incentive for both parties to negotiate a mutually acceptable settlement. The owner of the forest holds the property rights to the land to be logged, and the tour operators have an incentive to negotiate with the landowner because excessive logging in the area will seriously affect their operations. The question then arises, what incentive does the owner of the land have to negotiate with the tour operators?

Here we have to look at opportunity cost. In a sense, if the owner of the land allows a logging company to clear-cut her trees, she gives up the payment the tour operators would be willing to make in order to stop the logging. She also gives up the enjoyment derived from pristine wilderness (a non-monetary but relevant cost). The tour operators should be willing to buy the forested land, or at least make user payments at a price that will prevent the logging. These costs can be spread over a number of years since the enjoyment is ongoing. Logging, on the other hand, is a one-time, lump-sum payment. In this case, if the tour operators were willing to negotiate a set of payments that met or exceeded the opportunity cost of not logging the land, the Coase Theorem would predict a negotiated settlement that ends without clear-cutting. Here, private bargaining and negotiation lead to an efficient solution to externalities, even when the government is not involved.

Tort Law

While the Coase theorem suggests that a negotiated settlement may occur under certain circumstances, cases where there are a large number of people affected by the externality, or where property rights are not so clear, may be settled using tort law. **Tort law** is the body of law that allows a person who is injured by the actions of others to seek compensation from the parties who caused the injury by suing them. It also allows a group of people to seek compensation through a **class-action lawsuit**. A class action is a lawsuit in which one or more parties file a complaint on behalf of themselves and all other people who are "similarly situated" or suffering from the same problem. These means are often used when a large number of people have similar claims or individual property rights cannot be determined and, therefore, the Coase theorem does not apply.

Class-action lawsuits in response to the effects of environmental externalities were popularized in the late 1990s through films such as *A Civil Action* and *Erin Brockovich*. While, in general, a class action addresses the externality after it occurs, the possibility of this type of legal action can also serve to prevent the externality in the first place if it raises the fear that compensatory damages may have to be paid to those affected.

Pollution Credits

One solution receiving increasing attention, and stirring up more than a little controversy, is the use of pollution credits. While a form of pollution credits has been in use in the United States since the early 1990s, new focus has been placed on them at an international level because of the Kyoto Protocol of December 1997. Increased emission of *greenhouse gases* (GHGs) is a global problem that affects all countries of the world.

Greenhouse gases occur naturally but are also created through activities that burn fossil fuels, such as the heating and cooling of buildings, the operation of motor vehicles, and electricity production. Without GHGs in the atmosphere, our planet would not be habitable, as these gases trap heat from the Sun's radiation. But in the past two centuries, the levels of certain greenhouse gases, particularly carbon dioxide and methane, have been increasing. There is increasing concern that temperatures are rising. Even small increases in temperature will lead to rising sea levels, changes in vegetation and wildlife habitats, and extreme weather conditions. The *Kyoto Protocol* is an international agreement that is aimed at reducing GHGs through a number of measures. One of the proposals includes the use of pollution credits.

In a **pollution credit** system, an overall reduction target of a particular pollutant is set, and individual firms are required to meet the reduction or face penalties. However, the actual reductions are set in terms of credits. If one firm finds it easy to meet the target reduction, and in fact exceeds its target, it can sell its surplus credits to a firm that is unable to meet the target. The pollution credit system is economically efficient in that the overall goal is met, but in a way that allows businesses to achieve targets through the lowest possible costs. While some firms will continue to pollute, their costs are driven up because they have to buy pollution credits and, therefore, have additional incentive to clean up. Some success with pollution credits seems to be evident through the reduction of sulphur emissions, and the associated problem of acid rain, in the United States after the introduction of the Clean Air Act in 1990.

A Matter of Opinion | Global Warming Spawns a New Breed of Businessman: The Pollution Trader

66 THE HAGUE, Netherlands—In Canada, gas emissions spew from the smokestack of a utilities company. In Finland, a power company switches from coal to biomass, producing fewer greenhouse gases. Thus, the stage is set for a deal—not of power, but of pollution credits.

Efforts to check global warming have created a new commodity: pollution—or the lack of it—that is being traded on the market like sugar or equities. And it is producing a new breed of businessman, the pollution trader.

As negotiators from 175 countries, including Canada, continued talks in The Hague on Tuesday on how to curb greenhouse gases, emissions trading is standing out among the most contentious issues. Some parties denounce it as a huge loophole that will let major polluters go unrestrained.

A small group of professional traders are circulating among the delegates, holding workshops and explaining how trades can be structured, monitored, verified, and regulated. "We are telling them, 'This is how it works, you don't have to be afraid of it,' " said Garth Edward of the New York–based trading company, Natsource.

Natsource put together the deal ... for EPCOR Utilities Inc., of Edmonton, Alberta, to buy about 50 000 tonnes of carbon credits from Fortum, owner of the Finnish power plant that converted to biomass. The price was not disclosed, but credits normally sell for roughly $1 to $3 per tonne, said Edward. EPCOR can bank those 50 000 credits, cashing them in later if it overshoots the emissions allowance set by authorities.

So far, such deals have been small and experimental. But if trading becomes widely accepted, the price of credits could rise phenomenally, developing into a market worth hundreds of billions of dollars. Eventually, they could be traded in an exchange like soya futures.

Emissions trading was enshrined in the agreement concluded in Kyoto, Japan [in 1997], that set reduction targets for the industrial world, but the negotiators could not agree on how much trading should be allowed.

The United States, Japan, Canada, and some other industrialized countries want a free and unlimited market. They argue it will lower the cost of meeting the Kyoto target of trimming emissions globally by 5.2 per cent from 1990 levels by 2012. "We reject quantitative restrictions and artificial limits," said US undersecretary of state David Sandalow, heading the American delegation. Open trading "will promote innovation and reduce cost. We don't have the luxury of wasting dollars, euros, or yen."

Environmentalists and the European Union say trading dilutes the incentive of industrialized countries to curb their own pollution, letting them buy their way out of their commitments rather than take painful steps to reduce pollution.

The United States has been singled out by the Europeans and many environmentalists for trying to evade its commitments to cut pollution by using emissions trading and other methods.

Figure 16.6 In February 2002, demonstrators at the US Embassy in Tokyo protested President Bush's rejection of the Kyoto Protocol. Why might the public also be opposed to the trading of pollution credits?

The most glaring example of a pollution scam, they say, is the "hot air" trade with Russia and Ukraine. After their economies collapsed in the 1990s, the closure of factories led to a drastic drop in carbon emissions—to just 37 per cent of what they were in 1990 in Russia, and 55 per cent in Ukraine. That left both countries with plenty of credits to sell on the open market. Environmentalists call that gap "hot air" because the lower emissions were not achieved through greater efficiency or switching to renewable energy. Some delegates want to review the Russian benchmark, and so far no one has purchased any of the so-called hot air credits.

Emissions trading is not new. American companies have been trading for several years in the industrial pollutants sulphur and nitrogen oxide. The World Wildlife Fund acknowledges the trade has helped meet targets and sharply reduce costs.

But the worldwide trade in carbon equivalents, which is being discussed in The Hague, might be much different, said Mark Kenber of the WWF. The sulphur trade was transparent, tightly regulated, easy to monitor, and subject to severe sanctions. Falsifying emission results could lead to a jail sentence, he said. "These are the lessons we can learn," Kenber said. And the pollution traders will help. "Finding loopholes will only bring down the price of credits—and their commissions," he said. "Traders are an essential part of the system." **99**

Source: Arthur Max, "Global warming spawns a new breed of businessmen: the pollution trader" reprinted with permission of The Associated Press.

QUESTIONS

1. Do you think pollution credits are an effective policy to pursue in reducing levels of pollution? Explain.

2. How could the problem of "hot air" credits be solved?

3. Why were pollution credits successful in reducing sulphur emissions? Do you think that this suggests a problem in using them on a worldwide basis? Explain your answer.

Check Your Understanding

1. An efficient level of output is defined as the point at which marginal cost is equal to marginal benefit. Explain why output is inefficient when external costs are not considered.

2. Create an organizer that compares the advantages and disadvantages of subsidies, taxes, and regulations as means of controlling pollution.

3. Why do you think the Coase theorem has limited influence in controlling major pollution problems such as the greenhouse effect or toxic waste dumps?

CHAPTER SUMMARY

- Concerns about economics and the environment are rooted in the economic concept of scarcity because there are a finite number of resources to meet needs and wants. Exhausting or damaging these resources limits our continued ability to survive.

- Carrying capacity refers to the number of people that the Earth's resources can support indefinitely if the resources are managed effectively.

- The drawing down of resources refers to concerns that we are consuming resources at a pace beyond the Earth's carrying capacity.

- Sustainable development refers to engaging in economic activity in a way that ensures we do not exceed the Earth's carrying capacity.

- Side effects of economic activity that are not considered in actual market activity are considered externalities. Externalities are sources of economic inefficiency and can be either negative (a cost) or positive (a benefit).

- Excessive amounts of pollution, beyond those that occur when resources are allocated efficiently, can be explained through marginal cost and marginal benefit analysis because the costs considered by firms in making output decisions do not include external costs.

- Forcing firms to take external costs into account would result in higher prices as well as lower levels of output and environmental damage.

- Governments may attempt to control the impact of externalities through subsidies, taxes, and regulations.

- The Coase theorem states that in certain limited circumstances, producers and those affected by their externalities may solve the problem without external intervention.

- The judicial process may be used to resolve the impact of externalities through tort law and class-action lawsuits. These means may also act as a deterrent if producers believe that they may be forced to settle costly lawsuits in the future.

- A form of pollution control known as pollution credits has gained prominence because of agreements in the Kyoto Protocol designed to address the problem of greenhouse gas emissions.

Key Terms

carrying capacity
drawing down
sustainable development
externality
negative externality
positive externality
spillover costs
neighbourhood effects
marginal social cost (MSC)
marginal benefit (MB)
marginal private cost
subsidy
Pigouvian tax
Coase theorem
tort law
class-action lawsuit
pollution credit

Activities

Thinking/Inquiry

1. Some say that sustainable development is impossible given advances in technology and the demand that these advances place on the use of more and more resources. Others see technology as the key to finally achieving sustainable development as it allows us to be more efficient and creative in the use of resources such that we do not exhaust them. Identify an example of technology used in each of these roles. To which of these two views do you subscribe? Prepare a list of arguments that you could use to support your point of view.

2. Each of the following quotations can be linked to concepts explored in this chapter. Explain each quotation, referring to at least one key term from the chapter.

   a) We do not inherit the Earth from our ancestors; we borrow it from our children. (Aboriginal Proverb)

   b) We're finally going to get the bill for the Industrial Age. If the projections are right, it's going to be a big one: the ecological collapse of the planet. (Jeremy Rifkin, *World Press Review*, 30 December 1989)

   c) In an underdeveloped country, don't drink the water; in a developed country, don't breathe the air. (Jonathan Raban, 1976)

   d) I am one of the patients of air pollution. When the Japanese economy grew very rapidly, my asthma deteriorated.... For the last ten years I can hardly work. And when the law was enacted, the law concerning the abatement of pollution, it has given me compensation. That is my only income, from the compensation that this law provides. (Yoshi Suzuki, World Commission on Environment and Development hearing, February 1987)

3. Research the rules in your municipality regarding the disposal of household wastes. (Most municipalities send a brochure to households once a year or post this information on a municipal Web site.) How does your municipality attempt to limit the impact of waste disposal on the environment? Is there any attempt to make households accountable for the external costs associated with waste disposal?

Communication

4. Investigate an environmental agreement or program that attempts to address an externality. Briefly outline how it attempts to solve the problem and, if possible, how effective it has been. Some suggestions include:

   a) US–Canada Air Quality Agreement,

   b) Great Lakes Water Quality Agreement,

   c) Canadian Environmental Protection Act, 1999, and

   d) Government of Canada Action Plan 2000 on Climate Change.

5. Write a brief report about a class-action lawsuit related to environmental or economic concerns. Address the following questions:

   a) What was the cause of the problem?

   b) Who was claimed to be responsible?

   c) Who was affected?

   d) What was the outcome?

   e) Are there any laws or programs in effect today to prevent a similar occurrence?

Application

6. Using the theory of the firm studied in Chapter 7, explain why an environmentally conscious firm is at a disadvantage when it considers external costs if other firms in the industry do not.

7. Use the Internet or a newspaper database to research the radiation leak that occurred in the town of Tokaimura, Japan, in September 1999 at JCO Co. How could these events be explained by marginal social cost analysis?

Unit 4 Performance Task: Advocating for the Most Appropriate Role of Government

In this unit of study, we have investigated economic decision making from the perspective of government involvement in the economy, full employment, income distribution, and sustainable growth and development. The following challenge requires you to put your learning to effective use.

Your Task

As a promising economic thinker, you are asked to assume the role of social advocate by your employer, a foundation promoting public policy alternatives. You will produce a five- to ten-minute infomercial advocating the most appropriate role of government in the Canadian economy today. This infomercial must be designed as an "Economics in the News" segment for local news broadcasts. It must deal with issues arising from each of these five topics: *government spending and taxation* (e.g.: Should deficit financing be promoted, discouraged, or made illegal?), *regulating competition* (e.g.: Should mergers, alliances, and business practices be regulated?), *recession, recovery, and full employment* (e.g.: How much responsibility should government assume for job creation?), *income distribution* (e.g.: Should an inheritance tax be introduced to redistribute income?), and *sustainable development* (e.g.: Does the pollution credit program require government support or supervision?).

Task Steps and Requirements

1. Research the topic further (through economic publications, expert opinion, and the Internet). Reflect further on the issues in order to identify policy goals, implications, and economic trade-offs required. Conduct a cost–benefit analysis to determine the most appropriate role of government.
2. Take a definite position, advocating a specific course of action (or public policy) to protect social services, employment levels, citizens with low incomes, and the environment, while promoting such goals as growth and stability, economic freedom, productivity, efficiency, competitiveness, and equity. Prepare a convincing presentation to gain support for your position.
3. Explain how the medium and approach selected provide maximum persuasive impact. Your teacher may provide additional layout and content instructions, models of high-quality work, and a performance assessment rubric. As a final caveat, remember that in the politico-economic arena, it will never suffice to be in the right. To prevail you must be persuasive.

Adapting the Task

Consider creating a Web page that the foundation might add to its Web site to inform public policy. Alternatively, you might produce a position paper or a public information pamphlet to be presented at the foundation's next policy conference. Search Web sites of organizations that influence policy making to find examples of the direction (medium and strategy) that your work might take. Share drafts with your teacher, classmates, and parents or guardians to obtain useful feedback.

Assessment Criteria

The following criteria will be used to assess your work:
- *Knowledge*—accurately using appropriate concepts, principles, and supporting data
- *Thinking and Inquiry*—locating and assessing information from a variety of sources; using sound economic reasoning and thorough analysis
- *Communication*—using language conventions and terminology properly to support medium and presentation strategy; clearly presenting and explaining impact on economic goals
- *Application*—effectively applying cost–benefit inquiry to support the position taken; building and presenting a persuasive argument; making meaningful connections regarding stakeholder interests as presented in this textbook

UNIT 5

THE GLOBAL ECONOMY: INTERNATIONAL TRADE AND DEVELOPMENT

Following the 11 September 2001 terrorist attacks, lengthy delays ensued at the Canada–US border because of tightened security measures. These trucks, which were stopped 27 km from the border crossing at Sarnia, Ontario, contained Canadian goods destined for US markets. What impact do delays in shipments of goods have on Canadian businesses, incomes, and jobs?

Unit Overview

The global economy is vital to our country's economic health. Canada has an *open economy*, which means that a large percentage of our national income and employment depends on international trade. In Unit 5, we'll learn that trade is more than simply importing and exporting goods and services. Indeed, economic theory shows that trade can increase the prosperity of all nations that agree to open their economies to full competition with the rest of the world. A majority of nations today are members of the World Trade Organization, which works to break down barriers to trade. Freer trade, however, is a controversial policy because when new jobs are created in competitive industries, other jobs are inevitably lost in less competitive industries.

Multinational corporations have become the engines of a movement toward a truly worldwide economy, known as globalization. Multinationals have been both praised for the jobs and income they create and censured for questionable working conditions, low wages, and child labour, all of which have occurred in some of these organizations. We'll also examine the financing of international trade, which has been criticized for giving too much financial power to banks and financial institutions and paying less attention to national currencies and investment flows. Finally, we'll explore what many believe to be the most compelling global problem: the great disparity between the rich and poor nations of our world.

Learning Goals

In this unit, you will

- examine the economic theories that are used to support the argument that freer trade benefits all nations,
- identify the value and significance of trade to Canada's economy and the composition of our exports and imports,
- produce an analysis of the costs and benefits to Canadians of freer international trade,
- interpret trade data recorded on a nation's balance of payments accounts and draw conclusions from it about the nature of Canada's trade,
- understand how exchange rates are set internationally and how currencies are converted to facilitate international trade,
- analyze the factors that influence the exchange rate of the Canadian dollar and how changes in the dollar's value affect the economy,
- describe the nature and importance of multinational corporations in international trade,
- explore how economic events in another part of the world can affect the Canadian economy,
- describe international organizations of which Canada is a member, such as NAFTA and the World Trade Organization, and any debate that surrounds them,
- explain what globalization means, and why it is associated with so much controversy.

Skill Builder

Thinking Like an Economist

In this unit, you can develop some of the skills that economists use. These include

- using absolute and comparative advantage theory to determine a nation's best production choices for trade and the best terms of trade between two nations,
- using data tables to assess trade patterns in Canada,
- converting currencies using the current exchange rate,
- interpreting and analyzing data using four sample analytical tools—group sample analysis, internal pattern identification, comparative pattern identification, and the rank correlation coefficient.

Unit Performance Task

The activity at the end of this unit provides a focused opportunity for you to

- assume the role of an economic adviser to a less developed nation,
- apply economic knowledge and skills to an analysis in order to propose the most advantageous plan for this nation,
- prepare a written report or an oral and visual presentation of your recommendations to this less developed nation, and
- use a performance task rubric and feedback to help you prepare high-quality work.

CHAPTER 17
TRADE THEORY, AGREEMENTS, AND PATTERNS

The Quintessential Canadian

In the third millennium, we can imagine the quintessential Canadian as someone who leaves a cinema after seeing an American movie, gets into a German car, and uses a Korean cell phone to make reservations at a favourite French restaurant, where Dutch beer and Danish cheese are served.

On arriving home, the quintessential Canadian takes off a blazer made in Italy, a Taiwanese sweater, Chinese shoes, and slacks made in Hong Kong. The Canadian then puts on a leisure robe made in Portugal from Egyptian cotton, brews a cup of Colombian coffee, turns on a Japanese CD player, sits in a den filled with Scandinavian furniture, switches on an Indonesian computer, and sends an e-mail to the local Member of Parliament to complain about high taxes and unemployment!

Containers full of imports from China arrive in the port of Vancouver. What kinds of products might those containers hold?

QUESTIONS

1. Make a list of all the products that you have used today and determine their place of origin. Are you a "quintessential Canadian"? How important are imports to your present lifestyle?

2. In your opinion, what impact do your buying habits have on the Canadian economy? on Canadian unemployment levels?

3. If you were to decide to buy only Canadian-made products, what impact would your decision have on the Canadian economy?

4. What do you think would happen if everyone in the world decided to buy only domestically made products?

Chapter Goals

By the end of this chapter, you will be able to

- explain the benefits of specialization and international trade, using the concepts of absolute and comparative advantage,
- analyze the costs and benefits to Canadian stakeholders and to the Canadian economy of the global trend toward freer international trade,
- describe the nature and role of the World Trade Organization as an international institution,
- explain the nature of the North American Free Trade Agreement and assess its impact on Canadian stakeholders and the Canadian economy,
- apply economic inquiry to an analysis of public policy issues arising from patterns in trade data.

The Importance of Trade to Canadians

Throughout history, nations have traded with one another, selling some of their surplus products and buying other products that they need. Today, international trade is more important than ever and continues to grow rapidly. Trade is absolutely essential in Canada's economy in order to maintain the lifestyles currently enjoyed by Canadians. Even a quick glance around the parking lot of a shopping mall might reveal Volkswagens and BMWs from Germany; Saabs and Volvos from Sweden; Hondas, Toyotas, Nissans, and Mazdas from Japan; Hyundais and Kias from Korea—all in addition to the cars made by the North American manufacturers General Motors, Ford, and DaimlerChrysler.

If we were to focus only on the foods Canadians like to consume in large quantities, the list would include oranges from California and Florida, pineapples from Hawaii, watermelons from Georgia, grapes from Chile, bananas from Costa Rica, sugar from Jamaica, kiwi and chestnuts from Italy, lamb from New Zealand, coffee from Colombia, tea from India, and so on. Try to imagine how different our lives would be if we no longer had access to the many foreign products presently available.

We are all largely dependent on *imports*, the goods and services bought from other nations. However, the importance of international trade does not stop there. Canadians sell a large amount of goods and services to buyers around the world. These *exports* account for approximately 40 per cent of Canada's GDP, amounting to $423 billion in 2000. Almost one in four jobs in Canada is directly dependent on exports. In comparison, exports account for only about 10 per cent of GDP in the United States, where approximately one in 12 jobs directly depends on exports.

The Case for International Trade

The volume and value of global trade continue to grow each year. Why do nations prefer to trade instead of attempting to become more self-sufficient? Why do they prefer to rely on other nations for certain goods and services instead of developing domestic industries to provide those same goods?

Nations buy goods from other nations for the same reasons that individuals buy from other individuals. No reasonable social being can afford to be totally self-sufficient. The economic costs would be too great. A person cannot independently produce all the food, clothing, construction materials, machines, medicines, entertainment, and information systems that are needed. Your productivity—and, therefore, your standard of living—are much higher if you can specialize in what you do best and buy the rest of what you need from others who are specialists at what they do. Everyone's needs are more efficiently met through this specialized environment.

In this way, trade allows industries (and nations) to specialize, thus achieving greater economic efficiency. This improved productivity, coupled with the benefits of operating at a larger scale, usually improves market prices and living standards for people in both the importing and the exporting nations. The trend toward increased international trade and investment flows, and the resulting spread of large-scale transnational enterprises with international markets for their goods and services, are all part of an economic trend known as **globalization**. Proponents of freer world trade consider peaceful relations among economically interdependent nations to be another important dividend.

Trade benefits all parties

One of the important economic principles of international trade is that both buyer and seller benefit from the transaction. The mutual gains from trade are shown in Figure 17.1 (page 378).

Specialization is often identified as the most important mutual benefit from international trade. There are clear economic advantages in allowing nations to concentrate their industrial activity on the mass production of goods for which they have the necessary resources and the ability to use them most efficiently. However, to understand the economic benefits of international trade, we need to examine absolute and comparative advantage, concepts that were introduced in Chapter 3.

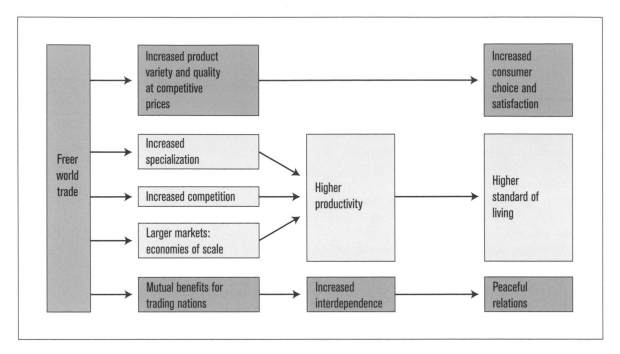

Figure 17.1 Charting the theoretical benefits of freer trade.

Absolute advantage

The concept of absolute advantage can easily be presented through the following hypothetical situation. Suppose your neighbour is a highly trained and naturally skilled automobile mechanic, able to tune up a car engine to factory specifications in 20 minutes. You, on the other hand, are a highly trained and experienced computer technician, able to correct most software and hardware malfunctions in 20 minutes. It takes you an entire Saturday to tune up your own car. It takes your neighbour an entire Saturday, and an assortment of headache remedies, to get a computer to do what is needed.

Since your neighbour can do in 20 minutes what it takes you an entire day to do, the neighbour has a definite advantage over you in automobile mechanics. You, on the other hand, have a definite advantage in the field of computer operation. You can both accomplish more, with greater efficiency, if your neighbour were to specialize in auto mechanics, and you were to pay your neighbour to tune up your car instead of wasting valuable time attempting to do it yourself. Your neighbour would gladly pay you to set up the computer to perform

required tasks. You would both personally benefit from specialization and trade, and your community would become more productive.

If an individual, region, or nation can produce something more efficiently than another (by using up fewer valuable resources), it is said to have an **absolute advantage** in making that product. Saskatchewan has an absolute advantage over British Columbia in the production of wheat. British Columbia has an absolute advantage over Saskatchewan in the manufacture of wood products. Newfoundland and Labrador has an absolute advantage over Ontario in the production of seafood. Ontario has an absolute advantage over Newfoundland and Labrador in the production of automobiles. If each province, in comparison with another, has an absolute advantage producing one item, each province should then specialize in that product and trade with the other province. Interprovincial trade would, therefore, benefit all participants and the Canadian economy as a whole.

In order to see if this idea applies globally, we need to employ the economic concept of *opportunity cost*, as presented in Chapter 1. Let's use a simplified hypothetical case involving the fictional nations of Atlantica and Pacifica to illustrate this application. Assume that these two countries can manufacture only two products, computers and automobiles. Further assume that production costs are constant and that there are no transportation costs and no government restrictions on trade.

According to Figure 17.2, the nation of Atlantica can choose to produce either 200 computers or five automobiles every ten production days. In Pacifica, ten production days can be used to manufacture either 100 computers or 20 automobiles. The table clearly outlines the opportunity costs in each nation.

According to Figure 17.3, in attempting to satisfy the monthly demand for both cars and computers through domestic production, the two nations are able to produce a total of 300 computers and 50 cars when ten production days are used to manufacture computers and 20 days are used to manufacture cars in each country. In the first ten production days, Atlantica manages to produce twice as many computers as Pacifica. In the remaining 20 production days, Pacifica manages to produce four times as many automobiles as Atlantica. Clearly, Atlantica has an absolute advantage over Pacifica in the production of computers while Pacifica has an absolute advantage in automobile production. Atlantica should specialize in the production of computers and trade some to Pacifica for automobiles. In order to understand why, we must reconsider the opportunity costs.

In one month, Pacifica could produce 300 computers or 60 automobiles. To Pacifica, 300 computers are as valuable as 60 automobiles, since both consume 30 days of valuable production time (see Figure 17.3). The opportunity cost of producing 60 automobiles in Pacifica is

Nation	Computer Production (units produced in the first ten days)	Automobile Production (units produced in the remaining 20 days)
Atlantica	200	10
Pacifica	100	40
Total	300	50

Figure 17.3 Output of automobiles and computers per 30-day production cycle, without specialization. Each nation manufactures its own products as needed.

the 300 computers that must be sacrificed in order to produce them. Each car Pacifica produces will cost the nation five computers. To Atlantica, 600 computers are as valuable as 15 automobiles, since either can be achieved in the same production time. The opportunity cost of producing 600 computers is the 15 cars that must be sacrificed in order to produce the computers. Each car Atlantica produces will cost the nation 40 computers. Clearly, given this set of economic realities, Atlantica cannot afford to produce automobiles because it will be forced to sacrifice far too many computers.

As a result of each nation's putting its absolute advantage to use, the total production of both cars and computers has increased through specialization. During the same 30-day production cycle, 300 additional computers and ten additional cars have been produced (see Figure 17.4). However, at the present time, there are no new cars available for purchase in

Nation	Computer Production (units produced in 30 days)	Automobile Production (units produced in 30 days)
Atlantica	600	0
Pacifica	0	60
Total	600	60

Figure 17.4 Output of automobiles and computers per 30-day production cycle, with specialization. Each nation uses its absolute advantage.

Nation	Computer Production (in units)	Automobile Production (in units)
Atlantica	200	5
Pacifica	100	20

Figure 17.2 Production opportunities: quantity of computers or cars that can be made in ten production days.

Nation	Computer Production (units produced in 30 days)	Automobile Production (units produced in 30 days)
Atlantica	600 – 200 = 400	0 + 15 = 15
Pacifica	0 + 200 = 200	60 – 15 = 45
Total	600	60

Figure 17.5 Output of automobiles and computers per 30-day production cycle, after specialization and trade.

Atlantica and no computers available in Pacifica. The two nations can correct this situation by arranging to trade some cars for computers in trade terms that are acceptable to both nations. Generally speaking, acceptable trade terms require the benefits of specialization to be shared by both partners. Let's assume that the two nations agree to trade 200 computers for 15 cars (see Figure 17.5).

Clearly, the productive efficiency of both nations has been improved by specialization and trade. As a result, more computers and more automobiles are available each month to consumers in both trading nations. Over time, it is likely the quality and price of both products will also improve as a result of specialization and trade.

Comparative advantage

Let's now complicate our model to see if specialization and trade continue to provide similar economic benefits when one nation has an absolute advantage in the production of both goods being traded. Surprisingly, the answer is still yes. In order to understand why, we must explore the concept of **comparative advantage**, first outlined by David Ricardo (see Chapter 3) almost 200 years ago. To put it most succinctly, even if one nation has an absolute advantage in every field of production, chances are that it will have a greater advantage in some fields than in others. These differences in relative efficiencies, or comparative advantage, are all that is required to make specialization and trade economically beneficial for individuals, regions, and nations.

Suppose that you are one of the best word processors and lawyers in the community. Since a significantly higher income is earned as a lawyer, you would be wise to concentrate on the practice of law and to hire someone else to do the word processing for the firm. Since an hour spent processing words cannot be spent in the courtroom, the opportunity cost of word processing is too high for you to attempt to be self-sufficient in both areas. You have a comparative advantage (relative to others) in the practice of law. You have a comparative disadvantage (relative to others) in word processing. Let's illustrate this principle with another series of hypothetical production tables.

The nation of Floren has an absolute advantage in the production of both cars and computers. Examine the data in Figure 17.6 to identify differences in relative efficiency, as we did for the lawyer/word processor example. Although Floren has an absolute advantage in both computer and automobile production, Floren's advantage over Guilder in computer production is at the ratio of 2:1 (or 200 computers compared to 100 computers in ten production days). In comparison, Floren's advantage over Guilder in car production is at a ratio of 4:1 (or 40 cars compared to ten cars in 20 production days). Floren, therefore, has a relatively greater absolute advantage (or a comparative advantage) in car production.

In one month, Floren could produce 600 computers or 60 cars. To Floren, 600 computers are as valuable as 60 automobiles, since both consume 30 days of valuable production

Nation	Computer Production (units produced in the first ten days)	Automobile Production (units produced in the remaining 20 days)
Floren	200	40
Guilder	100	10
Total	300	50

Figure 17.6 Output of automobiles and computers per 30-day production cycle, without specialization. Each nation manufactures its own products as needed.

time (see Figure 17.6). The opportunity cost of producing 600 computers in Floren is the 60 automobiles that must be sacrificed in order to produce the computers. Each computer Floren produces will cost the nation 0.1 (or ¹⁄₁₀) of an automobile. To Guilder, 300 computers are as valuable as 15 automobiles, since both consume 30 days of valuable production time. The opportunity cost of producing 300 computers in Guilder is the 15 automobiles that must be sacrificed in order to produce the computers. Each computer Guilder produces will cost the nation 0.05 (or ¹⁄₂₀) of an automobile. Based on comparing opportunity costs, Guilder has a comparative advantage in the production of computers because fewer automobiles are being sacrificed. The two nations should be able to benefit from specialization and trade if each nation uses its comparative advantage.

As a result of specialization, total production in the two nations has improved. Although there are just as many computers as before (300 units produced each month), ten additional automobiles are now produced each month (see Figure 17.7). Using the principle of comparative advantage, the productive capacity of the two nations has been expanded by introducing greater efficiency.

If Guilder were to trade 200 computers for 15 automobiles, it would have an extra five cars available per month—concrete proof that specialization and trade with Floren continue to provide economic benefits. Floren, with 45 cars now available per month, would be able to show an identical benefit of five extra cars. Using the principle of comparative advantage,

Nation	Computer Production (units produced in 30 days)	Automobile Production (units produced in 30 days)
Floren	0 + 200 = 200	60 − 15 = 45
Guilder	300 − 200 = 100	0 + 15 = 15
Total	300	60

Figure 17.8 Output of automobiles and computers per 30-day production cycle, after specialization and trade.

both nations continue to benefit from specialization and trade (see Figure 17.8).

Comparative advantage originates from local, regional, and national variations that exist in the distribution of productive resources. Sometimes referred to as **relative factor endowment**, this distribution represents what a community, province, or nation is naturally given to work with. Comparative advantage also results from the efficiency, effectiveness, and scale of operations. Sometimes referred to as **relative factor intensity**, this efficiency represents how a particular resource endowment is put to use. In conclusion, variations in factor endowment and factor intensity create local, regional, and national conditions of comparative advantage that, in turn, promote co-operation and trade.

Terms of trade

Having recognized that nations benefit from specialization and trade, we can now focus on how trading partners determine a fair exchange of goods. The rate at which a country's exports are exchanged for its imports is known as the **terms of trade**. The terms of trade establish an international price for one product in terms of another product. This international price depends partly on the domestic opportunity costs experienced in both trading nations prior to trade. Traders must, at the very least, recover the opportunity costs that apply in domestic transactions in order to make international trade worthwhile.

Let's return to our hypothetical example. Before trade, the opportunity cost of producing each car in Floren is ten computers. The

Nation	Computer Production (units produced in 30 days)	Automobile Production (units produced in 30 days)
Floren	0	60
Guilder	300	0
Total	300	60

Figure 17.7 Output of automobiles and computers per 30-day production cycle, with specialization. Each nation uses its absolute advantage.

opportunity cost of producing each car in Guilder is 20 computers. If Guilder can acquire a car from Floren for less than 20 computers, it would make economic sense to do so. If Floren can acquire 200 computers from Guilder for less than the 20 cars that it would be forced to sacrifice in order to produce its own computers domestically, it, again, would make economic sense to do so. If Guilder attempts to sell 200 computers to Floren for precisely 20 cars, all the benefits of trade would be assumed by Guilder. These terms of trade would not be acceptable to Floren. Fair negotiations should allow both trading partners to share the economic gains realized through specialization and trade.

Furthermore, over a period of time, market prices in the two nations would also be affected by a trade agreement between Floren and Guilder. In Guilder, given the opportunity cost, the price of a car should be 20 times the cost of a computer. Since cars are available from Floren at the cost of 13.3 computers per unit, the price of cars relative to computers (in Guilder) will be reduced over time. In Floren, given the increase in the monthly supply of cars, the price of cars should also fall over time. Imports should help keep car prices competitive in both nations.

The Case for Trade Restrictions

Even though the gains from trade normally benefit both trading partners, historically, arguments have been made for the restriction of trade. These arguments usually focus on the protection of domestic industries from foreign competition and on the protection of the domestic economy from foreign influence and control.

Economic arguments
The following economic arguments are used, at times, to support national policies that restrict international trade.

Protection of domestic employment
Technically speaking, when a nation imports goods and services, it is simultaneously providing employment opportunities for foreign industry.

Simply put, importing goods, without increasing exports, results in the exporting of jobs.

As imports flow into a nation, money must flow out to pay for them. The demand for domestic products is diminished and production levels are reduced. Lower demand and production can slow down economic growth and create unemployment. On the other hand, a reduction in the level of imports can stimulate economic activity in a nation and provide more jobs for domestic workers, at the expense of foreign workers.

Applying this line of reasoning, imports produced by low-cost labour in less developed economies or by government-subsidized production in other industrialized nations need to be restricted from entering an industrialized nation in order to protect the jobs of domestic workers. In 2001, US President George Bush imposed taxes averaging out to approximately 30 per cent on softwood lumber imports from Canada. These taxes were implemented to protect jobs in the US softwood industry. (The Case Study on page 394 examines this situation.) Critics of such protectionism are quick to point out that jobs in inefficient industries may be protected at the expense of consumer prices, aggregate productivity, and, ultimately, living standards.

Retaliation
When a trading partner adopts a strategy of import reduction to combat domestic unemployment, it is effectively exporting some of its unemployment to the other nation's economy. This other nation may try to recapture some of the lost jobs by imposing new import restrictions of its own. This retaliation generally leaves both partners worse off by reducing the benefits of specialization and trade. However, each nation tries to punish the other more than it will suffer itself. Domestic producers often argue that we should not let foreign goods into our country if our goods are excluded from their markets. This, too, is a retaliatory argument.

Protection against dumping
Sometimes foreign competitors attempt to dump production surpluses abroad to protect

SKILL BUILDER
Thinking Like an Economist

Working with Absolute and Comparative Advantage

Economists use the concept of comparative advantage to determine the benefits of specialization and trade among nations. Calculations involving opportunity costs to determine the most appropriate specializations and the terms of trade can help quantify these mutual benefits.

Figure 17.9 indicates the amounts of coal or steel that can be produced in the nations of Arcticona and Tropicona, using 1000 hours of labour. Refer to the data in this table to answer the questions that follow.

Nation	Steel Production (tonnes)	Coal Production (tonnes)
Arcticona	4	10
Tropicona	3	2

Figure 17.9 Production opportunities with 1000 hours of labour.

QUESTIONS

1. Which nation has an absolute advantage in steel production? in coal production?

2. Calculate the opportunity cost of each product in each nation. Explain your calculations.

3. Which nation has a comparative advantage in the production of steel? Explain.

4. Assume each nation has 4000 labour hours to use each month and, without trade, each nation would use half its labour in the production of each good. Produce a set of tables similar to Figures 17.6, 17.7, and 17.8 to prove that the two nations would benefit from specialization and trade. Support your conclusions by explaining your calculations.

5. Why would trading six tonnes of steel for three tonnes of coal not be acceptable terms of trade for Tropicona? Explain.

6. Explain how the two countries can co-operate to correct a simultaneous shortage of steel and a surplus of coal. Produce a revised total production table to show this correction.

7. Arcticona and Tropicona have an economic incentive to maintain peaceful relations. Explain why.

domestic prices. **Dumping** refers to the deliberate practice of selling a product abroad at a price lower than the domestic price. For example, a shirt that sells for the equivalent of $100 in the country in which it was made might be sold to foreign buyers for $50 in order to unload large quantities of stock without affecting the $100-dollar selling price at home. Dumping makes it very difficult for shirt producers in the second nation to compete. They may not be able to sell their shirts for $50 without incurring heavy losses. Trade restrictions can help reduce the frequency and limit the impact of dumping.

Diversification

Trade restrictions can help to diversify an economy whose prosperity is closely tied to the export of a few products or to a single nation. Extreme reliance on a few export products or on a single trading partner can leave an economy vulnerable to market fluctuations abroad. Trade restrictions allow for the development of new domestic industries and export markets. The more a national economy is diversified, the more self-sufficient it will be in times of conflict or crisis.

Protection of "vital" industries

Trade restrictions can also be used to protect national security and public health. For example, the uncontrolled export of military equipment, biotechnology, and nuclear technology can compromise national and global security if these resources fall into the wrong hands.

Protection of developing industries

Trade restrictions can be used to protect developing, or "infant," industries from foreign competition. Because of their recent origin and small size, newer domestic industries may lack the efficiency and economies of scale needed to compete head to head with established foreign producers. The problem with this argument is the difficulty in determining the point at which a developing industry has had sufficient time to stand on its own against foreign competition. Critics argue that, under protection, there is no incentive to maximize efficiency, and, therefore, protected "infant" industries never mature.

Improvement of terms of trade

When a nation's volume of trade is large enough to affect global markets, it can use trade restrictions to improve its terms of trade. For example, by restricting its exports of petroleum, the world's largest oil-exporting nation could affect the global market price for crude oil by producing a supply shortage. By imposing restrictions on its imports, the world's largest importer of newsprint could decrease the global demand for that product enough to lower the market price. On a smaller scale, trading partners can impose temporary trade restrictions to help negotiate more favourable terms of trade.

Protection of environmental and safety standards

In order to protect workers and the natural environment, many governments impose industrial standards. However, these standards vary greatly. When a nation imposes high standards, this results in increased production costs for domestic industries. These increased costs are generally passed on to the consumer in the form of higher prices. Nations with lower environmental and safety standards effectively reduce the operating expenses and product prices of domestic industries. If trade restrictions are not imposed on products coming from nations with lower standards, increased globalization will be accompanied by more incidents of environmental damage and worker injury. Firms will be able to profit from practices that fall well below the standard of good corporate citizenship. Further, in a global economy, firms may choose to relocate to countries with lower standards in order to gain a competitive advantage and to improve profits.

Protection from foreign influence and control

Trade restrictions can be used to protect key domestic industries from foreign control. Since increased imports result in a net flow of money out of the country, domestic currency in the hands of foreign investors can be used to purchase control of chief domestic industries rather than to purchase consumer goods. Governments may seek to control the flow of currency out of a country by setting restrictions on imports.

Cultural industries can be protected from foreign domination; two such industries are broadcasting (protected by restricting the imported content of radio and television programming) and publishing (protected by restricting the use of foreign textbooks in schools).

There are many arguments in favour of restricting trade, but, generally speaking, at the heart of most arguments is the trade-off between global economic efficiency and the political and economic pursuits of a nation. As the forces of globalization prevail, national agenda will continue to diminish in importance. We shall examine the controversies surrounding the effects of present globalization practices in Chapter 19.

Impediments to trade

At the present time, the volume of international trade is restricted by the seven impediments outlined in Figure 17.10.

Tariffs, or import duties: These are special taxes imposed on certain imported goods. They act to control import levels by making imported goods more expensive to consumers. Generally, as **tariffs** are increased, the quantity of imports decreases. Tariffs are also used by governments to generate revenue, but with the advent of globalization and freer trade, the use of tariffs is presently in decline.

Subsidies: These are government payments made to producers to stimulate economic activity and to protect jobs. In subsidized markets, the price that producers receive is more than the price that consumers actually pay for the product. **Subsidies** for agricultural commodities, softwood lumber, and aircraft construction have been challenged on the grounds of fairness and efficiency.

Transportation costs: Increases in these costs tend to make imports more expensive. Generally, as transportation costs increase, the quantity of imports decreases.

Export taxes: Governments can levy a tax on exports in order to control the goods leaving the country. This tax generally makes exports more expensive and, therefore, less desirable.

Voluntary export restraints: A nation's government may negotiate to persuade an exporter to limit voluntarily the amount of a product being sold in the country. Administrative delays, health and safety standards, and licence requirements can be used to pressure exporters into accepting voluntary export restraints. In 1986, the Canadian government used administrative delays to tie up Japanese cars in the Port of Vancouver to help "persuade" Japanese manufacturers to accept export restraints and to produce more cars in Canada in order to protect Canadian jobs.

Trade sanctions and embargoes: Governments may impose trade **sanctions** on a nation whose political practices are unacceptable. Sanctions effectively stop or severely curtail trade with the offending nation. For example, Canada and many other nations imposed trade sanctions on South Africa until the government renounced its policy of apartheid. (This policy favoured a select cultural group and oppressed the majority of its citizens.) Trade sanctions are intended to apply economic pressure in order to bring about political change. In 1973, many Arab oil-exporting nations decided to impose a trade **embargo** on their oil. This decision meant that the oil was not allowed to leave the home port, thus creating a global shortage. The intent was to secure better prices for exports and to demonstrate the advantages of maintaining good relations with the Arab world.

Quotas: Governments can establish **quotas**, or limits, on the total quantity of imports allowed to enter the country. Quotas control the flow of imports and actually reduce the volume of international trade.

Figure 17.10 Impediments to trade.

Check Your Understanding

1. Explain the importance of exports to Canadian workers and of imports to Canadian consumers.

2. Briefly outline the reasons why global trade has increased significantly since 1980. Explain the single most important benefit of this increased trade.

3. In your own words, explain how the concept of comparative advantage can be used to benefit trading nations. Explain why different nations have different comparative advantages.

4. Outline the main arguments and strategies used to restrict international trade.

Canadian Trade Patterns and Policies

Trade Patterns

In order to understand the magnitude and scope of international transactions, we need to clarify further the terminology of trade. Goods that are grown, extracted, or manufactured in one country and sold to another form part of the global **merchandise trade**. Merchandise trade is also referred to as **visible trade** because of the tangible nature of the goods being transacted. The exchange of services, tourism, investment incomes, and other transfers of funds is known as **non-merchandise (or invisible) trade**. Invisible trade consists of money flows often without tangible products flowing in return. Given its intangible nature, this type of service-based trade is more difficult to document and measure statistically. For example, merchandise imports arriving in Canada from Germany can be easily tracked by government officials. Imports (in the form of both goods and services) bought by Canadian tourists travelling abroad are far more difficult to track.

On a global scale, the volume and value of imports must always equal the volume and value of exports because one country's imports are, automatically, another country's exports. However, for individual nations, the **balance of merchandise trade**—the difference between the value of merchandise exports and merchandise imports—will not necessarily be at equilibrium at any given time. A nation is said to have a favourable balance when the value of exports is greater than the value of imports. A nation is said to have an unfavourable balance when imports exceed exports.

Most years, the Canadian economy generates a favourable balance of merchandise trade. However, Canada's non-merchandise trade typically posts a negative balance. Driven primarily by interest and dividend payments made to foreign investors, this deficit has been increasing steadily in recent years. Obviously, the Canadian economy is extremely dependent on foreign capital to support domestic industrial activity

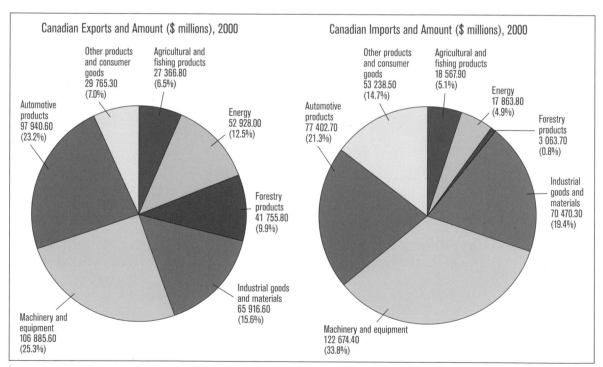

Source: Statistics Canada, "Exports of Goods on a Balance-of-Payments Basis" <http://www.statcan.ca/english/Pgdb/Economy/International/gblec04.htm> and "Imports of Goods on a Balance-of-Payments Basis" <http://www.statcan.ca/english/Pgdb/Economy/International/gblec05.htm>.

Figure 17.11 Canadian merchandise trade estimates (percentages and millions of dollars), 2000.

and to carry the large public/government debt. In the rapidly growing services sector, Statistics Canada estimates that, in 2000, the export of travel, transportation, commercial, government, and financial services totalled $58 billion while imports of these services totalled $64 billion.

If we study the major categories of Canada's merchandise imports and exports for 2000, we can see that almost half of our exports to other countries are natural resource products (see Figure 17.11). Forest products (primarily newsprint, wood pulp, and lumber) and industrial

Assessing Trade Patterns

There has been considerable change in Canadian trade patterns since 1975. Economists use data tables to identify patterns of change and to support their assessment of the long-term implications of recognized patterns. Pie charts and rate-of-change calculations help to illustrate the degree of change. In the following application, Canadian trade data patterns are used to help make decisions regarding economic impact and public policy.

Year	United States $ million	%	Japan $ million	%	European Union $ million	%	Other Countries $ million	%
Exports								
1975	22 059	67.4	2140	6.5	4212	12.9	4321	13.2
1980	48 975	64.2	4275	5.6	9516	12.5	13 554	17.8
1985	93 793	78.8	5597	4.7	6942	5.8	12 730	10.7
1990	110 282	75.5	7638	5.2	11 765	8.1	16 372	11.2
1995	205 631	77.7	13 178	5.0	18 097	6.8	27 846	10.5
2000	359 551	85.1	10 312	2.4	22 109	5.2	30 586	7.2
Imports								
1975	23 058	67.9	1189	3.5	3290	9.7	6446	19.0
1980	47 343	69.7	2810	4.1	5682	8.4	12 068	17.8
1985	73 406	71.5	6063	5.9	10 573	10.3	12 627	12.3
1990	92 892	68.7	8223	6.1	14 866	11.0	19 278	14.3
1995	172 460	75.0	8428	3.7	20 350	8.9	28 702	12.5
2000	267 674	73.7	11 714	3.2	33 428	9.2	50 465	13.9

Source: Compiled from Statistics Canada data from Canadian Economic Observer, Historical Supplement and CANSIM II tables 228-0001, 228-0002, and 228-0003.

Figure 17.12 Canadian merchandise trade, by partner, 1975–2000.

QUESTIONS

1. Construct a pair of pie charts to illustrate the proportion of total trade conducted with each of Canada's major trading partners in 2000. Explain the significance of the trade patterns confirmed by the pie charts.

2. In 2000, Canadian exports to Japan were 3.82 times greater than in 1975:

$$\frac{\text{amount of change}}{\text{initial value of exports}} = \frac{8172}{2140} = 3.82$$

   Using the above formula, calculate the rate of change in the volume of exports for the remaining three partners. Where has the greatest change occurred? Explain the significance of this pattern.

3. In 2000, Canadian imports from Japan were 8.85 times greater than in 1975. Calculate the rate of change in the volume of imports for the four partners. Where has the greatest change occurred? Explain the significance of this pattern.

4. For each trading partner, compare the rate of change in exports and imports over this period. What patterns are evident? Explain the significance of these patterns.

5. Calculate Canada's merchandise balance of trade with the United States for 2000. Is this a favourable balance for Canada? Explain. Is this balance part of a general pattern with the United States, or is it an isolated case?

6. Calculate Canada's merchandise balance of trade with the other trading partners in 2000. How does this compare to its balance with the United States? How does this pattern hold up historically?

7. Canadians trade more with the United States than with the rest of the world combined. Do you see this as an economic problem? Explain.

8. Based on these data, what two important issues should Canadian trade policy seek to address?

9. Research recent Statistics Canada data to assess trade pattern changes since 2000.

materials (including chemicals, fertilizer, iron, steel, aluminum, nickel, copper, and precious metals) account for one-quarter of total exports. Energy materials (primarily natural gas and petroleum) and food products (including wheat and fish) make up the remaining portion of the resource products group. The remaining half of our export business is primarily made up of manufactured goods, such as motor vehicles and parts, aircraft and parts, communications and electronic equipment, and industrial machinery.

The majority of our merchandise imports in 2000 were manufactured goods. In fact, industrial materials, food products, and energy accounted for less than one-third of our merchandise imports. Critics of this trade pattern have argued that, in order to support our lifestyle, Canadians tend to sell the world inexpensive, semi-processed natural resources then buy back these resources once they have been processed into final goods by workers in foreign economies. It is claimed that domestic jobs are lost because of this practice. It is further claimed that we are mortgaging our future by exporting large quantities of finite natural resources each

year. However, this pattern has been improving in recent years: Figure 17.11 shows that, in 2000, almost 50 per cent of Canadian merchandise exports were resource products; a decade earlier that number had been 68 per cent.

Development of Canadian Trade Policy

During the past 150 years, trade restrictions (most often occurring in the form of protective tariffs) have generally decreased globally, with a few notable exceptions. The United States has greatly influenced the evolution of Canada's national trade policy—not surprising given its historic role as our country's major trading partner.

Fluctuations in tariff rates: highlights

Reciprocity Treaty
In 1854, the British and US governments signed the **Reciprocity Treaty**. This established a qualified free trade relationship between what was then called British North America and the United States. By 1866, this reciprocal trade agreement had fallen victim to political and economic pressures. As a result, it was cancelled,

and trade tariffs rose sharply prior to and immediately after Confederation in 1867.

National Policy

In 1879, Canada's first prime minister, Sir John A. Macdonald, succeeded in passing the **National Policy** into law. The main components of this policy were

- the imposition of high tariffs on imported manufactured goods to help develop and protect domestic industries,
- the building of a transcontinental railroad (Canadian Pacific) to open the west for settlement and to promote a strong east–west trading pattern within Canada, and
- the promotion of Prairie settlement through the provision of free land for settlers.

This "tariff wall" persuaded many US manufacturers to open branch plants on the Canadian side of the border so that they could continue selling in Canadian markets without facing tariffs. Tariff rates peaked around 1890, after which the prevailing trend was to slowly reduce trade tariffs. This liberalizing trend was primarily driven by the general economic prosperity of the times and lasted into the 1930s.

Great Depression and Second World War

During the Great Depression of the 1930s, Canada attempted to combat rising domestic unemployment by raising protective tariffs. Governments in most industrialized nations increased tariffs, partially to stimulate domestic employment and partially to retaliate against restrictions imposed on their products in foreign markets. In the end, this general decline in world trade hurt the economies of all industrialized nations.

By 1939, the economic crisis of the Great Depression had been effectively addressed. In most industrialized nations, Canada included, tariff rates had been once again reduced to promote higher levels of world trade. With the outbreak of the Second World War in 1939, world trade was once again adversely affected. Canadian tariff rates were quickly increased during the early 1940s.

General Agreement on Tariffs and Trade

Since the global failure of protectionist trade policies during the 1930s, the prevailing trend has been to liberalize trade through a general reduction in tariffs. In 1947, as the international community attempted to build a lasting peace in the aftermath of a most destructive war, Canada, the United States, and 21 other nations (representing well over 90 per cent of the world's trade) signed the **General Agreement on Tariffs and Trade (GATT)**. This was an international agreement designed to reduce trade barriers among member nations. Through eight successive rounds of multilateral negotiations, tariffs in member nations fell from an average of 40 per cent in 1947 to an average of 5 per cent in 1988 while the volume of international merchandise trade multiplied 20-fold. The 132-member **World Trade Organization (WTO)** institutionalized, strengthened, expanded, and ultimately replaced the GATT in 1995. Since then, 12 more countries have joined, and average tariffs have continued to fall.

Check Your Understanding

1. Describe Canada's merchandise trade pattern in 2000.

2. Classify each of the following transactions as either a visible Canadian export, an invisible Canadian export, a visible Canadian import, or an invisible Canadian import:
   a) the sale of Canadian wheat to China
   b) the sale of the British weekly magazine *The Economist* in Canada
   c) the rental of a hotel room in Vancouver by a Japanese corporate executive
   d) your purchase of postcards while travelling through South Africa
   e) the payment of dividends by a Canadian company to American shareholders

3. Governments are more likely to reduce tariffs during periods of economic growth and to raise tariffs during periods of economic crisis. Explain how Canadian trade policy reflects this principle.

4. Explain the effect of the GATT on international trade.

Major International Trade Agreements

GATT/WTO

Multilateral trade negotiations involve simultaneous agreements among a number of nations. **Bilateral** negotiations produce agreements between two nations. When a nation acts alone, without negotiation, in matters that also involve other nations, the nation is said to be taking a **unilateral** action. The most inclusive, sustained, and successful multilateral negotiations to promote global trade were the eight rounds of GATT meetings that eventually culminated with the establishment of the international institution known as the World Trade Organization (WTO) on 1 January 1995.

Like the GATT of 1947, the WTO Agreement operates according to the following four essential principles:

• Trade must be conducted on the basis of non-discrimination. No member can give special trading advantages or deny equal treatment to another member.

• Once imported products are admitted into a domestic market, they cannot be treated differently than similar domestic products, such as being subjected to more onerous internal taxes.

• Where it is given to domestic industry, protection should be extended through clear and quantifiable customs tariffs instead of through fees and other charges.

• Any country wishing to join the WTO must submit a listing of all presently negotiated tariff levels with member countries and all non-tariff trade restrictions. Thereafter, only reductions can be negotiated.

The WTO's institutional commitment is to liberalize world trade further through multilateral negotiations. Where member nations find themselves in dispute over existing trade practices, the **WTO Dispute Settlement Body** has the sole authority to establish expert panels to consider each argument, render a ruling, review appeals to the ruling, monitor implementation of the ruling, and authorize retaliation when a member nation does not comply. One example of this type of dispute involves the US government's unilateral decision in 2001 to impose a 29 per cent tariff on Canadian softwood lumber imports in retaliation for what it considered unfair government subsidization of the Canadian lumber industry. Canada challenged the United States' action at the WTO (see the Case Study on page 394).

Regional Trade Agreements

Given the increased number of nations participating in recent WTO talks, the negotiation process has become far more complex. Some observers believe that the new trend may be toward more specialized regional trade agreements, such as the Free Trade Agreement between Canada, Mexico, and the United States. These regional agreements, negotiated outside of the WTO, are known as **trading blocs**. The WTO recognizes these regional initiatives as complements (rather than alternatives) in the pursuit of more open trade. There are presently three types of trading blocs: free trade areas, customs unions, and common markets.

Within a **free trade area**, trade between member nations is conducted without tariffs. Members are allowed to impose separate tariffs on imports from non-member nations. The **North American Free Trade Agreement (NAFTA)**, which came into effect in 1994, established a free trade area that includes the nations of Canada, Mexico, and the United States.

A **customs union** represents a stronger degree of regional integration. This type of regional trade agreement includes not only free trade among its members but also a common set of trade restrictions imposed on the rest of the world. However, restrictions on the movement of capital and workers among member nations remain in force. The 12-member Caribbean Community and Common Market (CARICOM) is an example of a customs union.

A **common market** is the strongest form of regional integration. Common market agreements include the free trade of goods and services within the bloc, the free movement of capital and labour within the bloc, and the imposition of a common set of trade restrictions on non-members. The 15-member **European Union (EU)**, formerly called the European Economic Community (EEC), is the largest and most powerful common market. In population

Canada Wins WTO Dairy Row

World Trade Organization (WTO) appeals judges ruled yesterday that Canada was not breaking global trading rules with its latest version of a program managing its dairy products supply system. The ruling overturned an earlier finding by a panel in a four-year-old dispute brought to the WTO by the US and New Zealand.

It also effectively removed a threat by the two countries to impose duties worth US$70 million on Canadian products they import, ranging from dairy produce through cereals and alcoholic drinks to pharmaceuticals.

"It's very good news," International Trade Minister Pierre Pettigrew told journalists in Montreal. "This means that we will be able to continue to export our dairy products," he said.

In 1999 the same panel had found that an earlier version of the program—known as the Special Milk Classes Scheme—provided illegal subsidies for Canadian dairy exports. Canada said it would adjust the program to make it conform to the panel's strictures and announced it had done this in January this year.

But the United States and New Zealand argued that the new version was essentially no different to its predecessor and asked for the original panel to be recalled to study their complaints.

In July, the panel ruled that both milk and cheese were still being exported with government financial support. Canada said it was convinced it was in the right and appealed.

In the ruling yesterday, the three Appellate Body judges said they could not see how the program forced milk producers to export in order to benefit from government subsidies—a key argument by the US and New Zealand.

Source: Reuters, "Canada wins WTO dairy row," *Metro Today*, 4 December 2001, 11.

QUESTIONS

1. How did Canada respond to the original ruling? What was the reaction of the two complainants?

2. On what grounds did Canada finally win its appeal?

3. How long did this dispute take to be resolved? In your opinion, does the WTO Dispute Settlement Body work?

and productive capacity, the European Union rivals the economy of the United States.

On 1 January 1999, the European Union took regional integration a bold step further by introducing a common currency for 11 of its member nations. The currency, the *euro*, has been doing well in foreign money markets since its introduction.

The road to NAFTA

Auto Pact, 1965
Before 1965, a 15 per cent tariff was imposed on American automobiles imported into Canada. To avoid the tariff, US auto makers opened branch plants in Canada. Given the relatively small size of the domestic market, Canadian plants were unable to benefit from economies of scale. As a result, production was less efficient, car prices were significantly higher, and Canadian auto workers earned less than their American counterparts. The **Canada–US Automotive Products Agreement (or Auto Pact)** was signed in 1965 to establish free trade in automotive vehicles and parts between the two nations. This integration and rationalization of the auto

A Matter of Opinion | Protectionism on the Rise in US

❝ Stay tuned for more protectionism south of the border.

Only 15 per cent of Americans work in manufacturing. That is half as many as worked in that sector in 1946, and is back to the same percentage as in 1900 when agriculture dominated the economy. The good news is that manufacturing output has tripled since 1960, thanks to technological productivity gains, and prices have fallen. The bad news is that jobs are disappearing as the smokestack shrinks.

And it's going to get worse. Forecasts are that in rich countries by 2020, manufacturing output, through productivity gains, will double but manufacturing employment will drop to only 10 per cent to 12 per cent of the workforce. The Americans are the most well-advanced toward this productivity bonanza, which is one of the biggest reasons why the US currency is soaring against all others. By comparison, Canada's manufacturing sector has gone from 25 per cent in 1946 to 18.5 per cent of jobs today, but Germany and Japan still employ 30 per cent of their workers in manufacturing.

Not surprisingly, there is fierce resistance to any job losses even in the interests of productivity gains, particularly in those two countries. But their resistance, and that in the United States too, is leading to a "new protectionism" in manufacturing. The problem is already rearing its ugly head—even for Canada within the North American Free Trade Agreement—when it comes to manufactured items such as steel and softwood lumber. The US vested interests in those industries have successfully lobbied for protection against cheaper Canadian exports. Both steel and softwood lumber are perennial trade issues between the two countries because free, unfettered trade is not possible, given the shrinking nature of these industries south of the border. The best we have gotten, or can hope for, is managed trade, or quotas. (Softwood lumber protectionism is more troublesome to combat because it involves a farm lobby as well as an industrial one. Small US farmers provide wood, often as a lucrative sideline.)

Management guru Peter Drucker, who is rarely wrong, speculated that manufacturing protectionism will end up being as serious an issue as agricultural protectionism. As agriculture's importance declined, along with a decline in jobs and prices, farmers everywhere convinced their politicians to help them. Now subsidies by the Europeans are simply breathtaking. Half of the entire European Union's budget is spent propping up French farmers growing wheat on 20 acres [approximately 8 hectares] and other inefficient operations. At the same time as they subsidize, they keep out imports and dump exports all over the world. This drives down prices for everyone, forcing others to subsidize and protect too.

The same problem looms in certain manufacturing sectors. Take steel. The price of hot rolled coil steel for car bodies has dropped from US$460 a ton to US$260 a ton despite boom years as a result of record vehicle sales. Price depression, as a result of productivity gains, benefits both consumers and steel workers, whose real wages go up considerably. But the losers in this are the inefficient steelmakers, who must change, go out of business or obtain subsidies and protection. US steelmakers want protection because they are being damaged by imports from Europe. More than two dozen have closed or applied for bankruptcy protection in recent years. In the case of softwood lumber, US producers are not efficient but they still want protection because they claim they are being damaged by Canadian imports.

The Americans may have a point when it comes to steel subsidies in Europe, but they are totally wrong about subsidies when it comes to lumber. However, it doesn't matter. They're not

CHAPTER 17: Trade Theory, Agreements, and Patterns

always right, but they're never wrong. This is all about politics, not economics.

Protectionism aside, the dramatic productivity gains in manufacturing will also have a dramatic, and negative, effect on the developing world economies because they lose their only competitive advantage—cheap labour. Forty years ago, labour, as a component of manufacturing, was 30 per cent of costs. Now it's 12 per cent to 15 per cent with the auto industry the most labour-intensive at 20 per cent. Technology is making the workforce in Chicago as cheap as the ones in Mexico or China. This means the old "economic miracle" strategy—building economies based on cheap manufactured exports—will no longer work. These countries will have to get rich by developing their own internal markets. Even so, attempts by developing nations to dump cheap exports onto world trade markets will aggravate, and are aggravating, the trading system and help bring about even more protectionism.

As for Canada, we will continue to take some lumps occasionally, even when unfair. That aside, the no-lose strategies are to avoid getting pushed around, when possible; to enhance productivity gains in smokestack industries and to help the workforce make the transition to industries and services that are knowledge-based. In future, an educated and flexible workforce is the only competitive advantage. **99**

Source: Diane Francis, "Protectionism on the rise in US: Canada will keep taking its lumps in trade disputes" from *National Post*, 5 March 2002. Reprinted by permission of National Post.

QUESTIONS

1. What is fuelling this current round of protectionism? Diane Francis claims that "this is all about politics not economics." Do you agree with this viewpoint? Explain.

2. Fair or foul, why must Canadians take some lumps occasionally? What are the alternatives?

3. According to Francis, how can the Canadian economy best position itself in the global economy of tomorrow? Do you agree with this view? Explain.

industry increased efficiency in both nations, protected the jobs and increased the wages of Canadian auto workers, and reduced the relative price of automobiles.

Free Trade Agreement (FTA), 1989

After the recession of 1982, the rising tide of protectionism in the United States threatened to restrict Canadian exports from its major market. In addition, Americans were growing increasingly disenchanted with the Auto Pact, which appeared to have shifted in Canada's favour by the mid-1980s. In order to improve its access to US markets, the Canadian government negotiated a free trade agreement with its biggest trading partner. The **Free Trade Agreement (FTA)**, which came into effect on 1 January 1989, had such provisions as
• phasing out of tariffs and most trade barriers within ten years,

• freer trade in services,
• a binding mechanism to settle trade disputes,
• retention of the Auto Pact provisions,
• elimination of restrictions on the import of used cars into Canada,
• no export subsidies permitted on trade between Canada and the US,
• elimination of restrictions on energy imports and exports,
• easing of restrictions on US investment in Canada (except in cultural industries such as the media) so that takeovers of Canadian firms with assets less than $150 million are no longer subject to Canadian government approval.

As a benefit of this agreement, trade between the partners has increased significantly, but there have also been costs. Workers in some formerly protected industries lost their jobs. Trade theory suggests that, in the long term, jobs lost in declining industries should be replaced by expanded employment opportunities in competitive export industries. However, with the global recession of the early 1990s and the high unemployment rates that persisted during the recovery that followed, the hardships imposed on displaced Canadian workers and their families cannot be taken lightly. Critics argue that an important second cost of free trade is Canada's increased dependence on the US economy and increased US ownership and control of Canadian industry.

North American Free Trade Agreement (NAFTA), 1994

Signed into effect on 1 January 1994, NAFTA established a free trade area with 360 million people and a combined economic output of US$6 trillion. This compares favourably in scale to the 326 million people and US$5 trillion output of the European Union. For all intents and purposes, this agreement extends most of the provisions of the FTA to include Mexico. Although Mexico has never been one of Canada's major trading partners, imports from Mexico doubled from 1990 to 1996. Unfortunately, exports to Mexico remained unchanged in real terms. For the United States, however, NAFTA is a much more significant agreement because, traditionally, Mexico has been its third-largest trading partner, after Canada and Japan.

Advocates of NAFTA are quick to point out that the Canadian economy could ill afford to stay outside a trade area projected to include most of the Americas by the time it is complete. Critics of NAFTA point to the potential loss of jobs that may occur if businesses relocate to Mexico to take advantage of lower wages and of lower worker safety and environmental standards. In both Canada and Mexico, the potential loss of control in cultural industries and the potential for increased US ownership in general continue to raise concern.

Check Your Understanding

1. Explain the difference between multilateral, bilateral, and unilateral actions.

2. Explain four essential principles of WTO membership.

3. Explain why regional trade agreements are not discouraged by the WTO.

4. Create an organizer to compare the three types of trading blocs, based on the following criteria:

   a) free trade among member nations

   b) free movement of capital and labour among member nations

   c) common set of trade restrictions imposed on non-members

5. With a free trade agreement already in place with the United States, why was it important for Canada to enter NAFTA?

Case Study

The Softwood Lumber Dispute

Figure 17.13 What two points is the cartoonist making about the economic impact of taxes imposed on Canadian softwood lumber by the US government in 2001?

Flaring up from time to time, softwood lumber disputes are a standing tradition between Canadians and our American neighbours. Since 1980, on three separate occasions, Canada has challenged the United States' treatment of our lumber products before international trade panels. Each time, the ruling favoured Canada, and each time, the ruling was ignored by the Americans. In August 2001, the US Commerce Department unilaterally imposed a 19.3 per cent tariff on all Canadian softwood lumber that did not come from the Atlantic provinces.

This ruling is expected to cost Canadian exporters in excess of $2 billion per year in tariffs. In British Columbia, which provides about half of the $10 billion annual lumber exports to the US, 15 000 workers were laid off by the end of August 2001 as many sawmills scaled back production or closed down all together.

The Americans claim that the Canadian lumber industry has a price advantage because it is subsidized through low "stumpage" fees charged by most provinces to cut timber on crown lands. The vast majority of Canada's forests (92 per cent) are publicly owned. Provincial and territorial governments give lumber companies the right to log and set the stumpage fee each logging company must pay for the timber it cuts. In the United States, only one-quarter of the forests are publicly owned. American producers must pay market value for the logs they harvest. Between 1990 and 1995, Canada's share of the US softwood market increased from 28 to 36 per cent.

Claiming that the Canadian subsidies were threatening its survival, the US lumber industry continued to lobby for tariffs as high as 50 per cent. American consumer groups reported that the imposed tariff would significantly increase the cost of home construction in the United States (see Figure 17.13). Canadian lobby groups suggested that the Canadian government should expose the American tactics internationally and that, as retaliation, energy shipments to the US should be delayed and charged an identical tariff. Canadian forestry unions believed that the US tariffs were part of a master plan to force an increase in the quantity of raw logs entering the United States in order to protect jobs in American sawmills—at the cost of Canadian jobs. The imposed tariff required a bond or a deposit in the amount of 19.3 per cent of the value of each shipment to the US by Canadian producers. This was particularly difficult for small and medium-sized companies. Many had no choice but to shut down.

The Canadian government preferred a negotiated settlement that would resolve this dispute for an extended period, but it also challenged the tariff at the WTO as a violation of world trade law. The government considered it

	Total Forestry Jobs	Forestry Exports, 1999 ($ millions)	Softwood Exports as % of Total
British Columbia	94 600	$15 300.0	48
Alberta	24 300	$3000.0	27
Saskatchewan	4900	$734.1	29
Manitoba	6500	$607.4	19
Ontario	76 500	$8900.0	11
Quebec	110 300	$11 500.0	19
New Brunswick	18 700	$2600.0	30
Nova Scotia	10 400	$959.9	26
Prince Edward Island	700	$22.6	89
Newfoundland and Labrador	5100	$586.4	4
CANADA*	352 000	$44 210.4	29

*Not including Yukon, Northwest Territories, and Nunavut

Source: Daniel Girard, "At loggerheads" from *The Toronto Star*, 25 August 2001, K3.

Figure 17.14 The Canadian forestry industry. Since forestry is an important industry in many provinces, the impact of the protective tariffs imposed by the US was felt across Canada.

imprudent to start a trade war with its largest trading partner.

In November 2001, ruling that Canadians were dumping their products at below-cost prices, the US Commerce Department slapped an additional duty (averaging 12.6 per cent) on Canadian lumber exports. This second tariff was imposed because, according to US authorities, Canadian exporters were dumping softwood lumber in the United States at prices that were less than the cost of production. It is estimated that an additional 10 000 layoffs were caused by this new tariff. In March 2002, with negotiations stalled, Canada officially launched a second WTO challenge and two additional NAFTA challenges against the crippling US duties. Challenges of this magnitude and complexity generally take years to process.

If they want to have free trade in natural gas and oil, they should have free trade in wood too, because if they were not to have oil and gas from Canada, they would need a lot of wood to heat their homes.

—Prime Minister Jean Chrétien (5 November 2001)

Negotiations between Ottawa and Washington focused on an agreement that would see the United States lift the threat of duties. Canada was required to commit to sweeping reforms of the way timber is sold in Canada. As part of the deal, Ottawa would put in place a temporary export tax of up to 25 per cent on US-bound lumber exports and a floor price for timber sales. This tax, referred to as the "cornerstone of Canadian capitulation" by critics of the deal, would remain in effect until the Canadian industry and provinces changed their pricing regimes for lumber to the satisfaction of the United States. The proposed export tax would be in lieu of duties imposed by the US, and the revenue would at least remain in Canada rather than go to less-competitive US lumber producers.

In order to further satisfy American interests, Canada's major lumber-producing provinces would be required to scrap their present system of "stumpage fees" and adopt a US-like auctioning system where competing lumber companies bid for the different parcels of forest lots available for cutting. Initial Canadian offers to switch to a market-based system of timber distribution were greeted as insufficient. British Columbia offered to auction off 13 per cent of its annual harvest while the US lumber industry demanded something closer to two-thirds. With crippling tariffs already in place, many Canadians believed that the Americans clearly had the upper hand in this dispute.

Canadians were clearly in two opinion camps: those that favoured a lasting negotiated settlement and those that favoured challenging the US action as a heavy-handed violation of international trade laws. This second group opposed concessions from the more efficient Canadian lumber industry unless Canadians received concessions in return. The Canadian lumber industry has long wanted official recognition from US authorities that Canadian softwood exports do not compete directly with domestic softwood lumber; Canadian softwood exports are primarily in the form of specialized woods (for siding, decks, window frames, and doors) while US softwood producers focus primarily on lumber typically used for framing houses. Under the existing pressure tactics, Canada could be easily edged toward further concessions, especially since different provinces have different views on how best to protect their interests. This lack of solidarity among provinces has hurt the Canadian position.

> Timber is our second most lucrative agriculture product, and competition from Canada and its government policies have hurt timber growers in our state.

—Mississippi Senator Thad Cochran (1 March 2002)

The original 19.3 per cent tariff expired in December 2001, but negotiations continued in order to avert a permanent ruling. When US authorities insisted on a 37 per cent export tax, Canadian authorities walked away from the bargaining table. On 22 March 2002, the US Department of Commerce imposed a consolidated 29 per cent duty to replace the two temporary taxes. This was declared "obscene" by Canadian authorities. Toward the end of 2001, one of Canada's largest forest companies, Canfor Corporation, filed notice (under NAFTA) to seek US$250 million in damages from the US government for "arbitrary, discriminatory, and capricious" tariffs. A report by Canada's C.D. Howe Institute applauded the Canfor decision, stating that "independent pursuit of all available legal options, through the US courts, at the World Trade Organization, and in support of Canfor's NAFTA challenge would be the best policy mix for Canada."

For many Canadians, this is a classic case of **extraterritoriality**—an example of how one nation can successfully exercise considerable political influence outside its own borders and on another nation's sovereignty. For others, it is a graphic reminder that Americans make much better friends than adversaries and that, given current economic realities, US interests will always prevail.

QUESTIONS

1. Compare the costs and benefits of a WTO settlement and a negotiated settlement in this trade dispute. Which course of action would you recommend?
2. After three unfavourable earlier rulings, why do you think that the United States has taken this course of action?
3. Update this dispute through an Internet search.

CHAPTER SUMMARY

- Canadians are largely dependent on imports to maintain their present lifestyle. Exports account for approximately 40 per cent of Canada's GDP, amounting to $423 billion in 2000. Almost one in four jobs in Canada is dependent on exports.
- Increased product variety and quality, lower prices, increased specialization, larger markets (providing economies of scale), higher productivity, higher living standards, and peaceful relations through increased interdependence are all dividends of freer global trade.
- When trading partners respect absolute advantages, the productive efficiency of both partners is improved by specialization and trade.
- When a single trading partner has an absolute advantage in production capabilities, it is still economically advantageous to both partners if the nation specializes in the product for which it has the greatest absolute advantage (or comparative advantage).
- A comparative advantage originates from variations in the distribution of different productive resources (factor endowment) and in the efficiency, effectiveness, and scale of operations (factor intensity).
- Arguments favouring trade restrictions focus on protection of domestic employment, on protection against unfair dumping, on protection of "vital" and "infant" industries, on retaliation for the restrictions imposed by others, and on applying pressure to negotiate more favourable terms of trade.
- The major impediments to trade are tariffs (import duties), subsidies, transportation costs, export taxes, voluntary export restraints, sanctions, embargoes, and quotas.
- Generally, the Canadian economy generates a favourable balance of merchandise trade as material exports exceed imports. However, in non-merchandise trade (primarily services), Canada generally imports more than it exports.
- Canadians conduct more trade with the US than with the rest of the world combined.
- Trade tariffs were highest in Canada during the National Policy that followed Confederation, the Great Depression, and the Second World War. Since Canada's participation in the General Agreement on Tariffs and Trade (GATT) in

1947, tariffs have decreased steadily while the volume of trade has increased significantly.
- The World Trade Organization (WTO) institutionalized, strengthened, and ultimately replaced the GATT in 1995. The WTO Dispute Settlement Body has the sole authority to render rulings between disputing member nations.
- Free trade areas, customs unions, and common markets are three examples of trading blocs. The North American Free Trade Agreement (NAFTA) between Canada, the United States, and Mexico is an example of a free trade area. This agreement is projected to include most of the Americas by the time it is complete.

Key Terms

globalization
absolute advantage   comparative advantage
relative factor endowment
relative factor intensity
terms of trade
dumping
tariff
subsidy
sanctions
embargo
quota
merchandise (or visible) trade
non-merchandise (or invisible) trade
balance of merchandise trade
Reciprocity Treaty
National Policy
General Agreement on Tariffs and Trade (GATT)
World Trade Organization (WTO)
multilateral   bilateral   unilateral
WTO Dispute Settlement Body
trading bloc
free trade area
North American Free Trade Agreement (NAFTA)
customs union
common market
European Union (EU)
Canada–US Automotive Products Agreement (or Auto Pact)
Free Trade Agreement (FTA)
extraterritoriality

Activities

Thinking/Inquiry

1. Visit the Web site of the World Trade Organization to find an explanation of how trade disputes are resolved by this international institution. What are the most important elements of this dispute resolution process?

2. Research a current news story that relates to international trade. Explain the economic concepts, principles, and issues involved and the significance of the event to Canadian consumers, producers, and workers. Analyze its treatment in various newspaper and magazine articles. Present your findings in a written report.

3. Many benefits and costs have been identified for the Free Trade Agreement (1989) between Canada and the United States. Some of the most often-cited benefits include

   • removal of Canadian barriers to US imports,
   • removal of US barriers to Canadian exports,
   • more secure access to American markets, and
   • improved productivity and competitiveness.

   Some of the most often-cited costs include

   • loss of jobs in formerly protected industries,
   • threat to sovereignty and independence,
   • loss of control over foreign investment, and
   • loss of control over energy and resources.

   Conduct a cost–benefit analysis to explain and evaluate each argument in order to arrive at a supportable conclusion about the impact of this agreement on the Canadian economy.

Communication

4. Design a flow diagram to explain how decreasing imports constitute the exporting of domestic unemployment. Develop an economic argument to explain the results on the volume of global trade and productivity and on living standards if all nations were to adopt this policy.

5. Compare the cases for and against freer global trade to determine your personal position on this important subject. Write a letter to the editor of your local newspaper to present your position on trade.

Application

6. Use Figure 17.15 to answer the following questions:

Nation	Snowshoe Production	Running Shoe Production
Myopia	8 pairs	5 pairs
Utopia	10 pairs	25 pairs

Figure 17.15 Production opportunities: possible output of either product per worker per day.

a) Which nation has the absolute advantage in producing each product?

b) Which nation has a comparative advantage in producing each product? Prove it!

c) Prove that both these countries can benefit from specialization and trade.

7. Use your knowledge of trade theory to explain the economic reasons why an independent Quebec would require a free trade association with the rest of Canada.

8. During the Uruguay Round of GATT trade negotiations (1980–1994), the United States sought the removal of Canadian agricultural marketing boards. These boards, it was argued, controlled agricultural imports into Canada, unfairly barring entry to less-expensive American products. At the same time, Canada (and other nations) sought to have European farm subsidies reduced by 90 per cent over a ten-year period. The European Union refused, since these subsidies greatly help their farmers sell their products abroad. Agricultural disputes made the Uruguay Round of GATT negotiations the most difficult ever conducted.

a) Explain the effect of a global agreement to reduce farm subsidies to Canadian wheat farmers.

b) Explain the effect of the removal of marketing boards on food prices in Canada.

c) Explain the effect of lower food prices on Canadian hog, poultry, and egg farmers.

Use supply and demand graphs to illustrate and support your explanations of (a) to (c).

CHAPTER 18
FINANCING INTERNATIONAL TRADE

The Import–Export Game

Your goal is to make as much money as possible in the import–export business. Divide the class into competing companies. Each company starts with $1500 in money capital and is allowed seven transactions during the game.

As you start the first round with only dollars, you must buy your first product in Canada. In other rounds, a company can buy something in a country only if it is holding that country's currency. Record your transactions in a chart like the one below, adding rows for rounds two to seven. In order to finish the seventh round with dollars, you must sell your last product in Canada.

Study the market information table in order to determine which products your company should buy and then sell in other markets. Keep decisions confidential. The team with the most money at the end of the game is the winner.

Transactions Record for [Company Name]				
Money Capital	Purchases		Sales	
Round 1:	Product: oranges	Quantity: 300 dozen	Product: oranges	Income: 300 × 10 = 3000 shekels
$1500	Country: Canada	Unit price: 5 dollars	Country: Israel	Unit price: 10 shekels

Product (unit)	Market Information: Current Prices in Each Country				
	Brazil	Canada	Israel	Japan	South Africa
Newsprint (roll)	40 real	50 dollars	150 shekels	9000 yen	500 rand
Wine (litre)	5 real	6 dollars	20 shekels	1000 yen	50 rand
Calculator	10 real	20 dollars	50 shekels	1000 yen	400 rand
Coffee (kg)	3 real	13 dollars	50 shekels	2000 yen	300 rand
Oranges (dozen)	4 real	5 dollars	10 shekels	1000 yen	200 rand

QUESTIONS

1. What strategies did successful companies adopt?
2. How successful was your company? What would you do differently next time?
3. Why is the money that you made not all profit?
4. As trade increases, what will happen to prices in these markets? What will happen to the market value of these foreign currencies?

Chapter Goals

By the end of this chapter, you will be able to

- describe how different currencies complicate trade among countries,
- explain why exchange rates fluctuate and how currencies are converted,
- compare fixed and flexible exchange rates,
- evaluate the arguments for and against *dollarization*,
- demonstrate an understanding of Canada's balance of payments.

Buying and Selling Internationally

We learned in Chapter 17 how important international trade is to the Canadian economy. It accounts for over one-third of the GDP, or the total wealth our economy produces in a given year, as shown in Figure 18.1. More than one-half of all the goods produced by the private sector are exported and sold abroad. These exports provide income for Canadians, produce tax revenues for our federal and provincial governments, and pay for our imports. This chapter will examine how these massive amounts of goods and services flowing in and out of Canada are financed.

The major difference in buying and selling internationally, as opposed to domestically, is the necessity of using different currencies. Exporters demand payment for their goods in their own countries' currencies because they cannot pay for raw materials and employees' wages using foreign currency. Suppose a Canadian manufacturer is selling $10 million worth of industrial machinery to a British company. The British importer would have to exchange pounds for Canadian dollars in order to complete the sale. If the exchange rate is £1 = Can$2.30, the importer would pay a British bank £4 347 826 (10 000 000 ÷ $2.30) to obtain the $10 000 000 necessary to pay the Canadian exporter.

But where would the British bank obtain the Canadian funds? Let's suppose that Canadian importers want to buy $10 000 000 worth of fine china from Britain. They would have to exchange $10 000 000 for £4 347 826 at a Canadian bank in order to pay the British china exporter. The British bank has pounds and needs dollars; the Canadian bank has dollars and needs pounds. Both banks can meet their customers' needs by getting together and completing a transaction.

In the past, currency exchanges were carried out on a bank-to-bank basis. Today, the process of obtaining funds is much more streamlined. Either bank can obtain foreign currency from the foreign exchange market, which is a computerized global network of banks, investment dealers, and financiers. The conversion of currencies is a service provided for a fee, or *commission*. But let us note an important point from the above example: when Britain and Canada buy products from each other, each country supplies the currency—its own—that the other country needs.

In Chapter 17, we learned that there are a number of intangible transactions that are also defined as either exports or imports. Known as invisible, or non-merchandise, trade, these transactions include exchange of services, tourism, and interest and profits earned abroad—all the payments and receipts that

	1989	1990	1991	1992	1993	1994	1995	1996	1997	1998	1999	2000
Total Exports	25.6	25.7	25.0	27.0	30.1	34.0	37.3	38.4	39.1	41.2	43.1	45.6
Goods	22.4	22.4	21.6	23.4	26.2	29.7	32.9	33.6	34.3	35.8	37.6	40.2
Services	3.2	3.3	3.4	3.6	3.9	4.3	4.4	4.8	4.8	5.4	5.4	5.4
Total Imports	25.6	25.7	25.7	27.4	30.2	32.9	34.3	34.4	37.5	39.8	40.2	41.0
Goods	21.2	20.8	20.6	22.1	24.4	27.1	28.5	28.6	31.6	33.6	34.1	35.0
Services	4.4	4.9	5.1	5.3	5.8	5.8	5.7	5.8	5.8	6.2	6.0	6.0

Source: Statistics Canada, *National Income and Expenditure Accounts*, Catalogue no. 13-001-PPB, fourth quarter 2000 and Statistics Canada, *Canada's Balance of International Payments*, Catalogue no. 67-001-XPB, fourth quarter 2000.

Figure 18.1 Trade as a percentage of GDP, 1989–2000. Why is trade growing in importance to Canada?

occur between two countries and that necessitate a conversion of one currency into another. We can best define a Canadian **export (or receipt)** as an international transaction in which a foreign currency must be converted into Canadian dollars. A Canadian **import (or payment)** is an international transaction in which Canadian dollars must be converted into foreign currency.

Using this definition, we can understand why, for example, an American tourist visiting Canada is actually considered a Canadian export. The tourist must convert US dollars into Canadian dollars to pay for hotels, meals, and so on, all of which constitute a Canadian export, or receipt. Alternatively, foreigners who earn interest from deposits in Canadian banks and then convert their Canadian dollars into their respective currencies are creating Canadian imports, or payments.

Exchange Rates

An **exchange rate** is defined as the price at which one currency can be purchased for another. The exchange rate of the Canadian dollar is usually expressed in terms of US dollars. For example, the statement "the Canadian dollar is worth 0.625 US dollars" means that Can$1.00 will obtain US$0.625 in the exchange market.

Another way of looking at the exchange rate of our dollar is to price other currencies in terms of Canadian dollars. For example, the statement "the US dollar is worth 1.60 Canadian dollars" means that US$1.00 will obtain Can$1.60 in the exchange market.

How exchange rates are determined
The value of a currency is measured by its price in terms of other currencies. If that price increases, the currency is said to have appreciated in value. For example, if the Canadian dollar rises from US$0.62 to US$0.64, an **appreciation** of the Canadian dollar, in terms of the US dollar, is said to have occurred. A currency depreciates when its price falls in terms of other currencies. In Figure 18.2, we can see that in terms of the

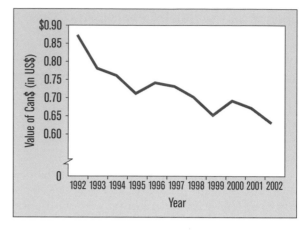

Figure 18.2 The Canadian dollar, 1992–2002. Is this decline in the exchange rate beneficial or harmful to different stakeholders within the Canadian economy? Explain.

US dollar, our dollar has depreciated steadily since 1992.

If the exchange rate is expressed in terms of the amount of Canadian dollars it takes to buy a foreign currency, the dollar appreciates when that amount falls. For example, if the exchange rate for Canadian dollars and British pounds changes from £1 = Can$2.24 to £1 = Can$2.20, the dollar has appreciated against the pound, and the pound has depreciated against the dollar. A dollar **depreciation** occurs when the value of a foreign currency rises in terms of Canadian dollars.

In order to understand how these rates are determined, we apply a familiar economic tool—demand and supply analysis—to Canadian exchange rates. We shall assume that the exchange rates are **flexible**, or **floating**, meaning that they are determined entirely in the market by the forces of demand and supply, with no government intervention.

The demand for Canadian dollars
Remember that when Canadians export goods or services, we want to receive payment in Canadian dollars. A demand for Canadian dollars is thus created in the foreign exchange market by the foreign importers of our good or service. Figure 18.3a shows the demand for Canadian dollars by French importers.

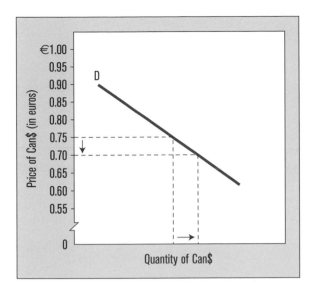

Figure 18.3a Demand for Canadian dollars. Canadian exports create a demand for Canadian dollars by French importers.

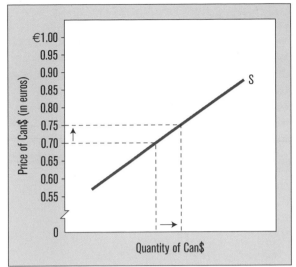

Figure 18.3b Supply of Canadian dollars. French imports purchased by Canadians create a supply of Canadian dollars.

The vertical axis represents the exchange rate between the euro and the Canadian dollar. Note that the dollar appreciates in value as the numbers rise. The horizontal axis represents the quantity of Canadian dollars demanded by French importers. When the exchange rate falls, or depreciates, French importers demand more dollars because our exports become less expensive to them; in other words, the euro "buys" more dollars. For example, at an exchange rate of Can$1.00 = €0.75, a tonne of newsprint worth Can$10 000 costs €7500; the same tonne costs €7000 when the Canadian dollar falls to Can$1.00 = €0.70.

Dollar depreciation (which, as we have learned, causes the euro to appreciate) increases the demand for our exports, thus the quantity of Canadian dollars demanded will rise as well. If the dollar appreciates, our exports become more expensive to French importers, so they demand fewer Canadian dollars. Therefore, the demand curve has the familiar inverse, or negative, relationship between the vertical axis (representing the exchange rate) and the horizontal axis (representing the number of dollars demanded). As the dollar appreciates, fewer dollars are demanded; as it depreciates, more dollars are demanded.

The supply of Canadian dollars
When Canadians import goods and services, we must pay foreign exporters in their own currency. We supply Canadian dollars in the exchange market and demand foreign currency in exchange. The supply curve in Figure 18.3b illustrates that when the dollar appreciates in terms of the euro (one dollar now buys more euros), Canadians find that French goods and services are less expensive. By demanding more euros in order to buy these goods and services, Canadians supply more dollars. Imported French perfume priced at €60 costs Can$85.71 when the exchange rate is Can$1.00 = €0.70. When the dollar appreciates to Can$1.00 = €0.75, the price of the perfume falls to $80.00, and imports rise.

Alternatively, dollar depreciation makes foreign imports more expensive for Canadians, thus, fewer euros are demanded and fewer Canadian dollars are supplied. Therefore, the supply curve has the familiar direct, or positive, relationship between the vertical and horizontal axes. As the dollar appreciates, more dollars are supplied; as it depreciates, fewer dollars are supplied.

The exchange rate at equilibrium
The actual exchange rate will be set at the point where the quantity of euros demanded

Converting Currencies

Canadians are very conscious of exchange rates, particularly between our country and the US because we trade with and travel to the US extensively. In order to understand how the prices for goods and services in the US compare to Canadian prices, we need to know how to calculate the value of our dollar in terms of the US dollar.

1. *The exchange rate is quoted in terms of US dollars, for example, Can$1.00 = US$0.62:*

    a) To convert Canadian dollars into US dollars, multiply the original amount of money by the exchange rate.

    Example:
    Suppose you are planning a short vacation in the US. You have budgeted $700 for your expenses. How much American money does this equal?

    $$\$700 \times \$0.62 = US\$434$$

    b) To convert US dollars into Canadian dollars, divide the original amount by the exchange rate.

    Example:
    You have US$150 left over from your trip. How much will you receive in Canadian dollars when you exchange this money?

    $$\$150 \div \$0.62 = Can\$241.93$$

2. *The exchange rate is quoted in terms of Canadian dollars, for example, US$1.00 = Can$1.60:*

    a) To convert Canadian dollars into US dollars, divide the original amount by the exchange rate. Using the example from 1(a):

    $$\$700 \div \$1.60 = US\$437.50$$

    b) To convert US dollars into Canadian dollars, multiply the original amount by the exchange rate. Using the example from 1(b):

    $$\$150 \times \$1.60 = Can\$240$$

QUESTIONS

1. You have $1200 to spend during a beach vacation in Florida. How much in US dollars will you have to spend if the exchange rate is (a) US$1.00 = Can$1.61, and (b) Can$1.00 = US$0.64?

2. a) A British company wants to invest £5 million in Canadian government bonds. The exchange rate is £1 = Can$2.24. How many dollars worth of Canadian bonds can the company buy?

    b) The bonds pay the company Can$600 000 in interest. How much will that convert to in pounds?

3. A Canadian tourist in Britain converts Can$2000 to British pounds at a rate of Can$1.00 = £0.445. At the end of her vacation, she has £150 remaining. When she converts her pounds to dollars, she finds that the exchange rate has changed to Can$1.00 = £0.48. Has she lost or gained money when she reconverts to Canadian dollars? By how much?

4. A tourist travelling in France converts Can$2000 into euros. How many euros will he be able to spend if the exchange rate is Can$1.00 = €0.73?

equals the quantity of Canadian dollars supplied, that is, where demand and supply are at equilibrium. As shown in Figures 18.4a and 18.4b, demand and supply intersect at Can$1.00, or €0.75. Figure 18.4a illustrates that if the exchange rate were set at Can$1.00 = €0.80, the supply of Canadian dollars would exceed the demand for them, causing the rate to fall to Can$1.00 = €0.75. If the exchange rate were set too low, at Can$1.00 = €0.65, the demand for Canadian dollars would exceed the supply of them, causing the exchange rate to rise to Can$1.00 = €0.75, as shown in Figure 18.4b. Assuming no other forces are operating

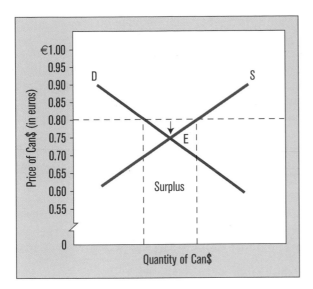

Figure 18.4a The exchange rate above market equilibrium. If the exchange rate is set too high, the surplus created will cause the exchange rate to fall.

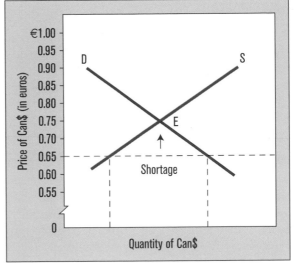

Figure 18.4b The exchange rate below market equilibrium. If the exchange rate is set too low, it will rise in order to correct the shortage created.

in this market, the exchange rate moves toward equilibrium at Can$1.00 = €0.75. However, we know that other forces are always present, and the exchange rate does change.

Causes of fluctuations in the exchange rate

Up to this point, we have learned how changes in the exchange rate of the Canadian dollar affect our exports and imports. But what causes the exchange rate itself to change? This is a particularly important question for Canadians because our dollar has fallen approximately 30 per cent against the US dollar since 1990. Although economists do not agree on the exact causes of this decline, let's consider some of the reasons that *usually* explain fluctuations in the exchange rate.

A change in demand for Canadian goods

Figure 18.5 illustrates a rise in Canadian exports as the demand curve moves to the right from D_1 to D_2. Such an increase creates an increased demand for Canadian dollars because Canadian exporters want to be paid in their own currency. The exchange rate rises, or appreciates, from $0.75 to $0.80, where the demand for dollars equals the supply of them. Conversely, a decrease in exports would move the demand curve to the

left, causing the exchange rate to fall, or depreciate, as a result of the new equilibrium point. In order to find out what causes these changes in demand, let's explore two factors:

• *Canadian exports tend to increase when the economies of our trading partners, particularly the*

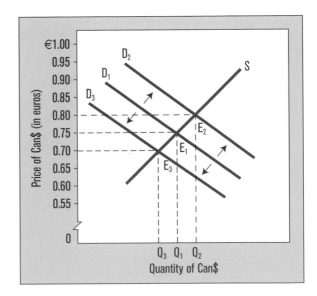

Figure 18.5 An increase in demand, from D_1 to D_2, will cause the Canadian dollar to appreciate; a decrease in demand, from D_1 to D_3, will cause it to depreciate.

US, are growing. During the 1990s, the US economy was prospering, which increased the demand for Canadian products. However, the demand for our products was partially offset by a slowdown in the economy of another significant trading partner, Asia, during the late 1990s. As a result, the demand in the Asian market for Canada's natural resource products, such as lumber, decreased. The key point here is that the demand for exports depends, to a large extent, on the economic health of our trading partners.

• *Canadian interest rates affect the demand for Canadian dollars*. If interest rates in Canada rise, Canadian bonds and bank deposits become more attractive to foreign financiers and traders, increasing the demand for Canadian dollars. If Canadian rates fall, the inflow of foreign capital seeking interest rate profits declines, and the demand for the dollar falls. From 1989 to 1991, high interest rates in Canada drove up the value of our dollar to US$0.89. Since then, interest rates have fallen, and the Canadian dollar has fallen along with it to its present value in the low US$0.60s.

A change in the supply of Canadian dollars
Figure 18.6 illustrates a rise in Canada's imports as the supply curve moves to the right

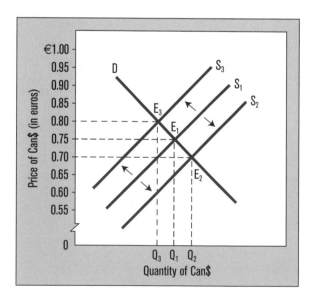

Figure 18.6 An increase in supply, from S_1 to S_2, will cause the Canadian dollar to depreciate; a decrease in supply, from S_1 to S_3, will cause it to appreciate.

from S_1 to S_2. Such an increase creates an increased supply of Canadian dollars and causes the equilibrium point to shift to E_2, where the supply of Canadian dollars equals the demand for them. The value of the dollar has depreciated from $0.75 to $0.70. A decrease in imports would move the supply curve to the left, causing the equilibrium rate (E_3) to rise to $0.80, or to appreciate to the point where supply equals demand. These different equilibrium rates also cause changes in the quantity of dollars (Q_1, Q_2, Q_3) actually transacted. Imports tend to increase when the Canadian economy is growing and to decrease when it is in recession, similar to the demand for domestic goods.

Exchange rate systems

Fixed exchange rates

Until the 1970s, most nations had **fixed exchange rates**, meaning that they fixed, or pegged, their exchange rate in terms of the US dollar. In order to maintain the pegged rate, governments bought or sold their own currencies in the foreign exchange market and kept foreign currencies in special reserve funds.

Suppose the Canadian dollar was pegged at US$0.75 and, because of a fast-growing US economy, demand for Canadian exports was rising. The demand for Canadian dollars would move upward, pressuring the Canadian dollar upward. To prevent the dollar from appreciating beyond its pegged rate of US$0.75, the Bank of Canada would intervene in the exchange market by purchasing US dollars and supplying Canadian dollars. Figure 18.7a illustrates the result, showing the supply curve moving to the right, which causes the exchange rate to move down to its pegged rate.

Conversely, the Canadian dollar could be pressured downward by a fall in exports or by a rise in Canadian imports. Suppose Canadian imports were rising from S_1 to S_2, as shown in Figure 18.7b. To prevent the Canadian dollar from depreciating, the Bank of Canada would have to use the US dollars in its reserve fund to buy Canadian dollars on the foreign exchange market. This purchase would increase the demand for Canadian dollars from D_1 to D_2, restoring the exchange rate to its pegged value of US$0.75. However, if increases in the

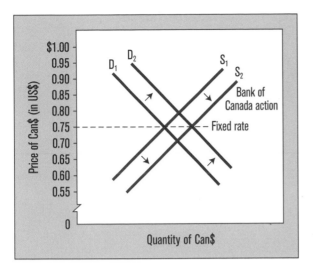

Figure 18.7a To prevent the dollar from appreciating beyond a fixed rate of US$0.75, prior to 1973, the Bank of Canada would buy US dollars.

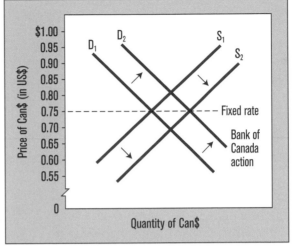

Figure 18.7b To prevent the dollar from depreciating beyond a fixed rate of US$0.75, prior to 1973, the Bank of Canada would buy Canadian dollars.

market demand for dollars were met with equal increases in market supply, the government would not have to intervene in order to support the pegged value.

Although central banks tried to prevent the **devaluation** or depreciation of their nation's currency by using foreign reserves to purchase it, the actions of corporations and individual speculators often nullified the central banks' efforts. For example, if these groups believed that the Canadian dollar was pegged too high, they would cash in their Canadian investments and invest the money in other countries. They were counting on the fact that the amount of money they were moving out would be so large that the Bank of Canada could not possibly buy back Canadian dollars with the limited foreign exchange reserves on hand. If they were proved correct, and the dollar could not be defended at the official rate, the Bank of Canada would be forced to devalue the dollar—in other words, reduce its value in relation to other currencies. The businesses and speculators would then reconvert their investments into Canadian funds at a profit. For this and other reasons, fixed exchange rates were abandoned in 1973.

Under the market value system that replaced it, the value of the Canadian dollar continues to be greatly influenced by international confi-

dence in the Canadian economy. For example, as Quebec approached each referendum on sovereignty-association (an arrangement that would grant the province political independence), the Canadian dollar took a direct hit on money markets. As the size of Canada's public debt continued to grow during the 1980s, the dollar lost value in international money markets.

At this point, it is important to clarify our terms. If a currency loses value in money markets as a result of some government or central bank intervention, this is described as *currency devaluation*. If a currency loses value as a result of the transactions of businesses and speculators, this is described as *currency depreciation*. *Revaluation* and *appreciation* both refer to currency value gains, but they result from different actions.

Flexible rates
As explained earlier, a flexible, or floating, exchange rate is set solely by demand and supply, without government intervention. Few nations are willing to allow their exchange rate to float without some intervention from time to time. Since the 1970s, most nations have used a system call a **managed float**, a compromise between flexible and fixed rates.

Under this system, the government allows the international market to set the exchange

A Matter of Opinion | Common Currency No Panacea

" If 12 countries can share a single currency, why shouldn't Canada share one with the US? That's bound to be the question that many corporate executives will be putting to Ottawa, now that Austria, Belgium, Finland, France, Germany, Greece, Ireland, Italy, Luxembourg, the Netherlands, Portugal, and Spain have abandoned their own currencies in favour of the new euro.

But there's a big difference between the 15 European countries (Britain, Denmark, and Sweden are still slated to join) sharing a common currency, and Canada adopting the US dollar [dollarization], which is all that is being proposed here.

The countries in the European Union [EU] are much more uniform in terms of size and clout than are Canada and the United States. They have their own supranational parliament and a common central bank. Interest rates and the exchange rate with other currencies thus must be set in the interest of all members, not just one. European social policies are based on shared philosophy, unlike Canada and its giant neighbour to the south.

Europeans can work anywhere in the union. If jobs are plentiful in Germany, and there is high unemployment in Italy, Italians are free to move. By contrast, Canadians cannot drive across the border at will in search of a job.

Now compare the European situation to what is being proposed here. If Canada were to adopt the US dollar, our monetary policy would be made in Washington in the interests of Americans alone. We would have no meaningful representation in the decisions on interest rates or the currency. If American monetary policy caused Canadian unemployment to rise, Canadians without work would simply have to tough it out, because they wouldn't have access to jobs in the States. And even if we did create a common market that allowed people to move freely across the border, it would probably mean the end of programs like medicare because its eligibility would not at all be clear.

The European example would only make sense for Canada if the US consisted of ten separate countries, all on a par with us. "

Source: Editorial, "Common currency no panacea" from *The Toronto Star*, 3 January 2002. Reprinted with permission—The Toronto Star Syndicate.

Figure 18.8 What message is the cartoonist relaying about the current health and future prospects of the Canadian loonie?

QUESTIONS

1. What important differences does the editorialist point out between the EU, and Canada and the US? How do they complicate the issue of currency union?

2. Suppose that Canadians could easily work in the US, as Europeans can within the EU. Explain if this would change our need for a separate Canadian currency.

3. What view might the Bank of Canada have on dollarization and the future of Canadian monetary policy?

4. Explain your viewpoint on dollarization.

rate in the long run, as it would under a flexible exchange rate system, but intervenes from time to time to smooth out short-term fluctuations. In Canada, the Bank of Canada mainly uses interest rates to control short-term fluctuations in the exchange rate. If the dollar is depreciating, the Bank can raise rates to increase the demand for the dollar; if the dollar is appreciating, it can lower rates.

The Bank of Canada can also use foreign exchange reserves to buy or sell Canadian dollars in the international market, in the same way it would under a fixed exchange system. In 2002, the Bank had approximately $34 billion in foreign exchange reserves, which could be used to prevent the dollar from falling. However, the

Bank appeared to be reluctant to use the reserves to stop the decline in the dollar. That same year, the governor of the Bank of Canada stated that the reserves were being saved for an emergency. As we saw in Figure 18.2 (page 402), the overall trend of the Canadian dollar in terms of the US dollar has been downward. It appears that the Bank's policies alone cannot prevent the long-term slippage of the Canadian dollar. Given this steady slippage, some Canadians have started to advocate the rethinking of what was unthinkable a mere decade earlier—*dollarization*, or the possible adoption of the US dollar as the official Canadian currency. This debate promises to intensify, as the Matter of Opinion feature on page 408 illustrates.

Check Your Understanding

1. Explain whether each of the following is a Canadian export (receipt) or a Canadian import (payment).

   a) A Canadian family takes a vacation in Florida.

   b) A Canadian investor receives dividends from shares held on the New York Stock Exchange.

   c) A German investment firm buys an issue of Canadian government bonds.

   d) A Canadian lumber company hires a foreign vessel to ship lumber to Asia.

2. a) Suppose the exchange rate of the British pound in terms of our dollar changes from £1 = Can$2.25 to £1 = Can$2.30. Would Canadian exporters to Britain gain or lose by this fluctuation? How would British exporters to Canada be affected?

   b) What would be the effect of the change in the rate for both British visitors to Canada and Canadian visitors to Britain?

3. From 1986 to 1989, the Canadian dollar rose from US$0.69 to US$0.89.

   a) How do you think Canadian exporters and importers were affected?

   b) In 1989, a delegation of Ontario retail merchants from border towns protested that the current exchange rate was driving them into bankruptcy. Explain the reasons for this protest.

4. Since 1989, the Canadian dollar has fluctuated between US$0.60 and US$0.64. What do you

think is the effect on Canadian exporters and importers? Would the Ontario retail merchants protest or support the lower exchange rate? Explain.

5. Indicate whether each of the following would increase the demand for, or the supply of, the Canadian dollar.

   a) The US experiences a building boom and needs increased supplies of foreign lumber.

   b) The Canadian economy enters a recession, causing a downturn in consumer purchases of imports.

   c) Canadian interest rates rise, attracting foreign purchases of Canadian bonds.

   d) Canadian pension funds are allowed to invest increased amounts in foreign bonds and shares.

6. Suppose Canada fixed its exchange rate at Can$1.00 = US$0.70. What pressure would the following have on the exchange rate? What action would the Bank of Canada have to take to maintain the fixed rate?

   a) The Canadian economy improves, increasing the volume of imports.

   b) Foreign investment in Canada increases.

   c) Higher interest rates in the US attract Canadian investors.

7. If Canada had a system of completely flexible exchange rates, what effect would each of the situations in question 1 have on the value of the dollar?

The Balance of Payments

Nations keep track of their international payments and receipts in their **balance of payments account**. This account is divided into two main parts: the current account, and the capital and financial account.

The Current Account

The **current account** includes three components: goods (or visibles), services (or invisibles), and investment income. Goods include raw materials and processed or manufactured goods. Services include tourism; transportation charges for shipping goods by rail, sea, and air; commercial services such as management and consulting; and government assistance to other nations, the UN, and other international organizations. Investment income is composed of dividends and interest earned from investments in Canada and abroad.

Figure 18.9 illustrates the structure of Canada's current account from 1989 to 2000. It indicates whether Canada has a surplus or deficit balance on each of the three components, and whether the three add up to an overall surplus or deficit balance on the entire account. The goods trade balance shows that between 1989 to 2000 Canada always exported more visible, or merchandise, goods than it imported, producing a surplus balance. Services, or invisibles, tended to record a slight deficit balance. While not indicated in Figure 18.9, goods and services are often combined to arrive at the balance of trade. This balance almost always records a surplus, reflecting Canada's traditional role as an exporting nation.

Investment income shows a deficit balance in Figure 18.9. This means that foreign investors are collecting more interest and dividends from their investments in Canada than Canadian investors are collecting from their investments abroad. This investment income deficit is large enough that, when combined with the other two balances on goods and services, Canada usually records a current account deficit. How can a country pay out more than it receives? The answer is found in the capital and financial account, which must record a surplus.

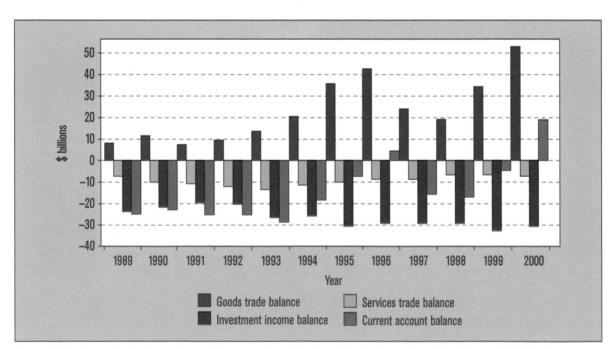

Source: *Trade Update 2001: Second Annual Report on Canada's State of Trade*, Economic and Trade Analysis Division of the Department of Foreign Affairs and International Trade.

Figure 18.9 The structure of Canada's current account, 1989–2000.

Alternatively, if the current account records a surplus, then the capital and financial account must record a deficit.

The Capital and Financial Account

The **capital and financial account** is subdivided into two accounts.

Capital account

The **capital account** includes migrants' funds, inheritances, and government pension payments to Canadians living abroad. These items are further divided into **inflows** and **outflows**. For example, when Canadians receive an inheritance from a relative in another country, it is considered an inflow. When immigrants to Canada send money to their home country, it is an outflow. A government pension paid to a "snowbird" in Florida is also considered an outflow.

Financial account

The **financial account** includes two types of investment. The first is **direct investment**, either by Canadians abroad (abbreviated as **CDI**) or by foreigners in Canada (**FDI**). This type of investment involves investors who either establish a new plant or business or take over an existing one by purchasing controlling shares. When foreigners invest in our country, it is an inflow, or receipt, for Canada; when Canadians invest abroad, it is an outflow, or payment.

The second type is **portfolio investment**. This type of investment involves investors who receive dividends or interest on stocks or bonds, but who do not control a company, as is the case with direct investment. Purchases of Canadian stocks or bonds by foreigners represent an inflow, or receipt, for Canada, while similar purchases of foreign stocks or bonds by Canadians represent an outflow, or payment. In Figure 18.10, we see a pattern of more foreign portfolio investment than Canadian, except for the periods 1996 and 1999–2000.

Official international reserves

The **official international reserves** are another important component of the financial account. Managed by the Bank of Canada, the official reserves are composed of foreign currencies, mostly US dollars, and gold. In 2002, they totalled $34 billion. The reserves are similar to a bank account held by an individual. When income exceeds expenditures for a period of time, the individual's bank account increases. However, when expenditures exceed income, the individual must use the savings in the account to make up the difference. The official reserves can be used by the Bank of Canada in the same way. If Canada's current account and capital account are in surplus, then the official reserves increase. If the current account and the capital account are in deficit then the official reserves can be drawn down to pay for the shortfall.

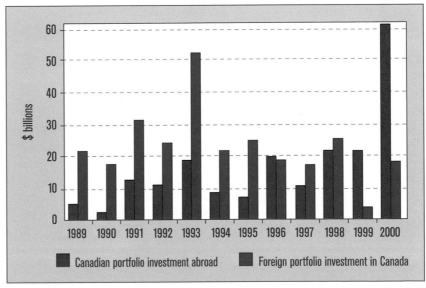

Source: *Trade Update 2001: Second Annual Report on Canada's State of Trade*, Economic and Trade Analysis Division of the Department of Foreign Affairs and International Trade.

Figure 18.10 Foreign portfolio investment in Canada and Canadian portfolio investment abroad, 1989–2000.

Balancing the Account

When the accounts are totalled, the current account and capital and financial account should balance, as indicated in Figure 18.11. In order to understand this concept, let's start with the current account, which measures exports and imports of goods and services. We know that foreigners need Canadian dollars in order to buy Canadian exports. Canada supplies these dollars by importing foreign goods. (Remember that when we import goods and services, we convert Canadian dollars into foreign currency.) If Canada is exporting more goods and services than it is importing, the supply of Canadian dollars will be insufficient for foreigners to buy our exports. This is where the financial and capital account comes into play. It must finance foreign demand for our dollars by recording more outflows of Canadian money than inflows of foreign money. It runs a deficit to pay for the surplus on Canada's current account.

The opposite occurs if the current account runs a deficit. If Canadians are importing more than they are exporting, they are demanding more foreign money than foreign buyers are supplying. The financial and capital account of Canada records more inflows of foreign money than outflows. It runs a surplus to pay for the deficit on the current account.

Current Account	
Total receipts	526 226
Total payments	499 334
Balance	26 894
Capital and Financial Account	
Capital account balance	5261
Financial account balance	−20 426
Balance	−15 164
Current minus Capital/Financial	11 730
Statistical Discrepancy	−11 730
Balance of Payments	0

Source: Excerpts from Statistics Canada, *Canada's Balance of International Payments*, <http://www.statcan.ca/english/Pgdb/Economy/Economic/econ01a.htm> and <http://www.statcan.ca/english/Pgdb/Economy/Economic/econ01b.htm>.

Figure 18.11 Canada's balance of international payments (in millions of dollars), 2000. This table shows a simplified balance of payments for Canada in 2000. The minus signs indicate an outflow of Canadian money.

Since it is impossible to track all transactions, the current account does not balance exactly with the capital and financial account. An adjustment called the **statistical discrepancy** is calculated to bring the two main divisions of the account into balance.

Check Your Understanding

1. For each of the following, determine whether it represents a payment or a receipt and whether it is part of the current or capital and financial account.

   a) A company in New Brunswick sells lumber to the US.

   b) A business in Ontario buys industrial machinery from Germany.

   c) A Canadian consulting firm wins a contract to advise a Mexican firm.

   d) A Canadian software firm buys controlling shares in a US firm.

   e) A Canadian mutual fund purchases shares on the New York Stock Exchange.

   f) A Japanese bank purchases an issue of Canadian government bonds.

2. How does a flexible exchange rate adjust automatically to avoid a deficit in the balance of trade?

CHAPTER SUMMARY

- International sales of goods and services are more complicated than domestic sales because the seller, or exporter, has to be paid in the currency of the exporting country.

- An export, or receipt, is defined as an international transaction in which foreign currency is converted into domestic currency.

- An import, or payment, is defined as an international transaction in which domestic currency is converted into foreign currency.

- An exchange rate is the price at which one currency can be purchased in terms of another currency.

- A currency appreciates when its value, in terms of another currency, rises; it depreciates when its value, in terms of another currency, falls.

- Demand for a currency such as the Canadian dollar comes about when foreigners want to import Canadian goods.

- If the Canadian dollar appreciates in value, foreign importers demand fewer dollars because our exports become more expensive for them. If our dollar depreciates, foreign importers demand more dollars because our exports become less expensive for them.

- The supply of a currency such as the Canadian dollar comes about when Canadians buy foreign goods and demand foreign currency in exchange for our dollars.

- When our dollar appreciates, foreign goods become less expensive for Canadians to buy, so we buy more, thus supplying more dollars. When our dollar depreciates, foreign goods become more expensive for Canadians, so we buy less, thus supplying fewer dollars.

- A nation may have flexible or fixed exchange rates or a managed system of exchange rates (managed floats). Today, most nations have managed floats.

- With flexible rates, the exchange rate is set by the forces of demand and supply, with no government intervention.

- Fixed rates are pegged in relation to a major currency such as the US dollar.

- Managed floats are a compromise between fixed and flexible rates, whereby the central bank intervenes to change short-term fluctuations in the exchange rate but allows the long-term trend to be decided by the market.

- Nations keep track of their international transactions on their balance of payments accounts, which, in theory, must always balance.

Key Terms

export (or receipt)
import (or payment)
exchange rate
appreciation
depreciation
flexible (or floating) exchange rate
fixed exchange rate
devaluation
managed float
balance of payments account
current account
capital and financial account
capital account
inflow
outflow
financial account
direct investment
CDI
FDI
portfolio investment
official international reserves
statistical discrepancy

Activities

Thinking/Inquiry

1. What would each of the following likely prefer—a higher or a lower exchange rate for the Canadian dollar: (a) a Canadian sports team owner with American players who want to be paid in US dollars; (b) a Canadian forestry company selling on world markets; (c) a Canadian company that must import equipment from abroad; (d) a Canadian retiree who spends the winter in Florida; (e) Canadian hotels, resorts, and restaurants catering to foreign tourists. Explain why in each case.

2. a) Suppose the inflation rate is rising in Canada. Would a lower or higher exchange rate for our dollar be more beneficial in addressing this problem? Explain.

   b) What action could the Bank of Canada take to achieve the solution you chose in (a)?

3. a) Suppose the unemployment rate is rising in Canada. Would a lower or a higher exchange rate for our dollar be more beneficial in addressing this problem? Explain.

   b) What action could the Bank of Canada take to achieve the solution you chose in (a)?

4. A country that is on a fixed exchange rate has been running a deficit on its balance of trade.

   a) Has it overvalued or undervalued its exchange rate? Explain.

   b) What action must it take regarding its exchange rate: devaluation or revaluation?

   c) What action could it take with its reserves to carry out either revaluation or devaluation?

   d) Explain how speculators might profit by correctly anticipating the Bank of Canada's actions.

5. Find out more about "money laundering" and the use of offshore accounts as challenges to national monetary systems.

6. At present, the US has a large trade deficit, partly because of the strength of its dollar. Some economists argue that the US can deal with this situation; others predict major problems in the future if the deficit keeps growing. Find out more about this situation and its possible impact on Canada if the US dollar is devalued.

Communication

7. Set up a round-table discussion and debate the future of the dollar. Different students will role-play the following individuals: a representative from the Canadian exporter's association, a representative from the tourism industry, an owner of the Blue Jays baseball team, and an economist.

Application

8. For the following, draw small free-hand graphs to illustrate the change in the demand for, or the supply of, the dollar. Indicate whether the dollar would appreciate or depreciate.

   a) Bombardier of Montreal lands a big contract to build aircraft to be sold in Europe.

   b) A Canadian mining company invests in developing a new mine and smelter in Indonesia.

   c) A Hollywood movie company decides to make its next two movies in St. John's and Toronto.

   d) A Canadian auto manufacturer buys parts from a manufacturer in Mexico.

   e) A provincial government borrows money from financial institutions in the US.

9. a) Determine the balance on the current account below. Explain whether the account has a deficit or surplus.

Investment income payments:	$100
Merchandise exports:	$300
Non-merchandise payments:	$100
Investment income receipts:	$40
Merchandise imports:	$300
Non-merchandise receipts:	$150

   b) Determine the balance on the capital and financial account below. Explain whether it has a deficit or surplus.

Direct investment abroad:	$200
Foreign direct investment in Canada:	$275
Portfolio investment abroad:	$250
Portfolio investment in Canada:	$200
Capital account balance:	−$15

   Explain whether this account balances with the current account.

CHAPTER 19
INTERNATIONAL ECONOMIC ISSUES

The Anti-Globalization Movement

Over the years, Canadians have taken to the streets to voice their opinions on many social movements, including those of civil rights, women's right to vote, nuclear disarmament, opposition to the war in Vietnam, and protection of the environment. In recent years, as global organizations have met behind closed doors, activist groups from around the world have reacted with persistent, sometimes violent, protests. Many use the Internet to monitor new developments and solidify the anti-globalization movement. Globalization, in its present form, is perceived by many to promote the exploitation of the poor by the rich, through the spread of capitalism. In this chapter, we shall investigate many issues arising from the globalization movement.

Anti-globalization protesters demonstrate in front of riot police outside the Summit of the Americas site in Quebec City on Saturday, 21 April 2001. Inside, leaders of 34 countries in the Western Hemisphere approved the establishment of a Free Trade Area of the Americas by 2005. Why might protesters resort to protest action?

QUESTIONS

1. What are the people in the above photograph protesting against?
2. What do you understand about the meaning of the word *globalization*?
3. American psychologist and philosopher Rollo May once wrote that "powerlessness breeds mad violence." How does his vision of powerlessness apply to some of the more violent anti-globalization protests?
4. What seem to be the main problems with the globalization movement in its present form?

Chapter Goals

By the end of this chapter, you will be able to

• define the term *globalization* and assess issues related to current trends in globalization,
• understand why Canada, along with most other nations, is becoming more globally interdependent,
• describe how multinational corporations and international financial markets operate in a global economy,
• understand the debt and trade problems facing less developed nations,
• identify the factors affecting global poverty and economic development,
• analyze statistical data dealing with development indicators.

What Is Globalization?

Globalization is the process of creating a global economy, a process driven by three forces. First, aided by improvements in telecommunications, computer technology, and transportation infrastructure, large companies can now produce goods and services on a global basis, and market them around the world. Second, many nations have removed, or are now removing, various barriers to cross-border trade, resulting in a huge increase in the volume of international trade. Third, a vast international financial system is facilitating trade and financing international business activity. Each of these three forces has been stoutly promoted by globalization's defenders as beneficial for national economies and their citizens and just as strongly attacked by globalization's detractors as damaging to people. Let's examine each factor in turn.

The Multinational Corporation

As introduced in Chapter 6, the **multinational corporation (MNC)**—a firm that operates in several countries—is fundamental to globalization. Also called **transnational corporations**, these large businesses can now set up production in any number of countries, communicate orders and production plans by computer and satellite links, and then sell their products and services wherever they can find buyers.

Consider the example of Caterpillar, a Canadian tractor manufacturer located near Toronto. The various parts for the tractor are manufactured in several countries: engines in Japan, the transmission in the United States, the winches in Brazil, and the axles in Belgium. The parts are all shipped to an Ontario plant, where they are assembled into tractors. Finally, the completed tractors are sold to Japan, the United States, Brazil, Belgium, and other countries. Computer and satellite links enable companies such as Caterpillar to send their specifications for parts from the home office to their foreign parts manufacturers quickly and to test a finished part while it is still on the factory floor on another continent.

The business arrangement of hiring outside contractors to produce either parts or finished products is called **outsourcing**. Using this strategy, multinationals can "shop around" in many countries for the subcontractor that will produce the good for the least amount of money. The business arrangement of setting up a **subsidiary**, or branch plant, in another country, is another way of conducting an international operation.

In the case of multinationals that sell services, arrangements usually depend on the transfer of data via computers and satellite links. For example, Ireland has become a major centre for the processing of US insurance claims. A US insurance company, New York Life, sends the day's claims to an Irish branch office at the end of the business day in the United States. Because of the five- to six-hour time difference, Irish employees can spend their workday processing the claims before their US counterparts even wake up. They then relay the processed claims back to the United States, where the American employees can begin their day by sending out the processed claims to the company's insurance claimants. With this international arrangement, the US company takes advantage of lower labour costs in Ireland, favourable tax levels offered to foreign companies by the Irish government, the fact that the Irish employees speak English, and the time difference between the two countries to create a competitive advantage for itself.

Caterpillar and New York Life give us what appear to be positive examples of the global economy. If the manufacturer or service company opens a branch plant, it builds, buys, or leases a plant for its operations in the host country. It hires and trains local people, sometimes introducing them to advanced technology, pays wages to these employees, and pays taxes to the host government. The host country may be able to negotiate with the company to use local suppliers for component parts needed in its production process. If the transnational company contracts for the services of a subcontractor, the subcontractor pays both the employees and the taxes.

Figure 19.1 Many multinationals hire subcontractors to produce their products, which they then sell using their brand name and marketing expertise to guarantee wide sales. Because subcontractors don't make much money, however, they may not pay their employees fair wages or guarantee safe working conditions. (Factories with such conditions are sometimes called **sweatshops**.)

Foreign multinationals in Canada

The debate today over foreign multinationals in Canada has shifted from concern over their presence to concern when they shift their operations to other countries and eliminate jobs for Canadians. On the one hand, many foreign multinationals moved operations from Canada while they continued to sell products here. On the other hand, many Canadian firms have expanded their operations to export products and services to markets in other countries. Over the last 30 years, larger and larger companies have been expanding their operations to larger and larger markets in their quest for profit. According to *Fortune* magazine, by 2000, the list of the world's top 30 economies included five multinationals: General Motors, Wal-Mart, Exxon Mobil, Ford, and DaimlerChrysler. The multinationals, therefore, are a fundamental force driving globalization.

Removing the Barriers to International Trade

The second major force that is driving globalization is the removal of numerous barriers to international trade. As a consequence of this process, trade among countries is now much more important than it was in the past. Figure 19.2 illustrates that international trade has been increasing far more quickly than world output since the 1970s, increasing at a rate of about 7 per cent per year. Trade now constitutes about 21 per cent of total world income and is likely to keep increasing.

The major reason for the dramatic increase in the volume of world trade over the last 30 years or so stems directly from the theories of trade you learned about in Chapter 17: absolute and comparative advantage. Those theories promise great gains from trade if it is open and free from trade barriers such as tariffs. Industrialized countries made a determined effort among themselves to lower barriers to trade that prevented the gains that freer trade would provide. A series of international agreements, first negotiated under the General Agreement on Tariffs and Trade (GATT) and later under the World Trade Organization (WTO), steadily lowered tariff barriers from as high as 40 per cent to an average of only about 5 per cent today.

Other international changes contributed to a worldwide trade expansion. The Cold War,

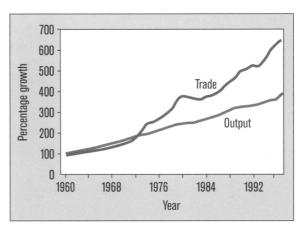

Source: US Council of Economic Advisors, cited in R. Gilpin, *The Challenge of Global Capitalism* (Princeton, NJ: Princeton University Press, 2000), 21.

Figure 19.2 Growth in world output and trade, 1960–1997. Note that world output, even in 1960, is actually greater than trade. This line graph shows how each of output and trade has grown in relation to its 1960 value (set at 100 per cent for both). Trade has expanded much faster than output, especially since the 1970s.

which had divided much of the world into the "East" led by the former USSR and the "West" led by the United States, ended in the late 1980s when communism fell in Russia and Eastern Europe. Russia, East Germany, Poland, and other Eastern European countries replaced their command economies with capitalist economies. Central to this process, they opened up their economies to trade and investment.

In another major shift in East Asia, the "Asian tigers" of South Korea, Singapore, Taiwan, and Hong Kong flourished under capitalism, becoming industrial powers and major trading nations. China, although still technically a communist nation, opened its doors to welcome international investment. Many subsidiaries of foreign multinationals are now located in China, which has recently joined the World Trade Organization. Figure 19.3 shows the top 10 exporters and importers of goods among the top 50 trading nations.

The World Trade Organization

The one organization most responsible for removing trade barriers is the World Trade Organization. The WTO is the focus of much of the debate and protest surrounding globalization. It is probably fair to say that most governments, economists, and businesspeople support the organization, while most labour organizations, environmentalists, and social activists oppose it. The general population holds mixed opinions. (The genesis of this international institution was covered in Chapters 17 and 18.)

As of 2002, WTO had 144 members with China's entry in December 2001. More than 30 other nations have applied for membership. The large numbers of members makes governing the organization somewhat unwieldy. Trade rules are set by a simple majority vote of the members. Trade disputes that arise between WTO members are brought before special tribunals of trade experts and lawyers. The tribunals decide who is at fault, and the country found at fault might be asked to change its law to conform to the WTO rule, face economic sanctions, or pay compensation to the wronged country.

The WTO has had to deal with newer kinds of international trade items and issues than the GATT, which dealt mostly with trade in goods. At present, trade in services—telecom-

Exporters	Value	Share	Importers	Value	Share
1. United States	695.2	12.4	1. United States	1059.1	18.0
2. Germany	541.5	9.6	2. Germany	472.5	8.0
3. Japan	419.4	7.5	3. UK	320.3	5.4
4. France	300.4	5.3	4. Japan	311.3	5.3
5. UK	269.0	4.8	5. France	290.1	4.9
6. Canada	238.4	4.2	6. Canada	220.2	3.7
7. Italy	230.6	4.1	7. Italy	216.9	3.7
8. Netherlands	200.4	3.6	8. Netherlands	187.6	3.2
9. China	195.2	3.5	9. Hong Kong	180.7	3.1
10. Belgium	176.3	3.1	10. China	165.8	2.8

Source: Excerpts from "World Trade in 1999—Overview" from International Trade Statistics 2000, <http://www.wto.org/english/res_e/statis_e/wt_overview_e.htm>.

Figure 19.3 Leading exporters and importers in world merchandise trade, in billions of dollars, and as a percentage, 2000. (Note that these figures account for only merchandise trade, not trade in services.) Compare Canadian and American exports and imports. Which country has a trade deficit in goods?

munications, insurance, finances, health, education—now accounts for over 60 per cent of world Gross Domestic Product. Another area prominent on the WTO's agenda is the issue of **intellectual property rights**—patents for such products as technology, recorded music, and pharmaceutical drugs. Rules regarding foreign investment by multinationals are another area in which the WTO tries to achieve consensus among its members.

Proponents of the WTO claim that these negotiations lead to a "level playing field" for all nations that want to participate. Opponents claim that only the most powerful nations can finance the permanent lobbyists who can sway WTO rulings to their benefit. In any case, the WTO's ongoing attempts to establish rules that apply to all nations have provoked controversy, as the Economics in the News feature on page 419 indicates.

Economics in the News

World Trade or World Domination?

Is the WTO a Democratic Institution?

The [WTO] has always emphasized that its decisions are "democratic," insofar as they are made by the entire membership of nation-states, and usually by consensus. Some developing nations have a seat at the table alongside world powers.

But to a great extent, the wealthier countries dominate decision making. The US, for instance, maintains a small army of permanent negotiators in Geneva—something most WTO member nations can't afford. WTO agreements ... are often decided upon by a small group.... Smaller nations are growing increasingly frustrated at being left out of important negotiation processes altogether. [It is argued] that developing nations have been strong-armed into ratifying agreements by way of direct or indirect threats regarding IMF loans upon which many of them depend. [The **International Monetary Fund (IMF)** is an organization designed to address international monetary issues, including the provision of financial assistance.]

Everyday citizens, in turn, theoretically have a voice through their governments. All of the WTO's discussions and records of trade disputes, however, are closed to the public.

"In reality," says Steven Shrybman, executive director of West Coast Environmental Law in Vancouver, BC, and author of "The Citizen's Guide to the WTO," the organization "is not accountable to [most] people whose lives are affected by it. Most of them live in developing countries. While they have a seat at the table, they don't even have a tiny scintilla of the resources they need to engage effectively in the complex and myriad functions, disputes, and negotiations under the auspices of the WTO."

Enforcement of WTO trade-dispute resolutions similarly favors the major powers. In theory, the WTO serves as the mechanism through which trade disputes are impartially resolved. When one country challenges another for not complying with WTO regulations, the matter is taken before an appointed, secret panel of "trade experts."

If the trade experts find that a WTO trade agreement has indeed been violated, the WTO has the power to insist that the offending country change its practices or face fines and/or trade sanctions from the injured nation. That, however, hardly makes for a level playing field. If Panama, say, were to impose sanctions on the US, hardly anyone would notice; but US sanctions could cripple Panama's economy.

WTO supporters respond that the organization's consensus-based system prevents this sort of thing from happening. And in fact, the WTO has on occasion ruled in favor of smaller nations in trade disputes with major powers.

But such rulings are hardly the norm. In one highly publicized case, the WTO ruled in January 1999 that the EU could no longer give preferential treatment to banana imports from former colonies in the Caribbean, a decision which is likely to hurt the region's already-impoverished, primarily small-scale banana farmers. Who brought up the complaint? The US—home base to banana giants Chiquita, Dole, and Del Monte, which control an estimated two-thirds of world banana exports....

But What's So Terrible About Global Free Trade?

Trade is one thing, but unrestricted, worldwide, corporate-dominated trade runs roughshod over the environment, workers' rights, small nations, and local self-determination, critics say.

Lori Wallach and Michelle Sforza, co-authors of Public Citizen/Global Trade Watch's *Whose Trade Organization?*, have made a study of the 167 contested trade issues brought to the WTO as of last March. Their conclusion: In every case in which an environmental, health, or food safety law was chal-lenged at the WTO, such laws have been declared illegal barriers to trade. WTO rulings have forced South Korea to lower meat safety rules and the US to weaken its Clean Air Act, to cite just two.

Source: Excerpts from "World Trade or World Domination" originally published on 24 November 1999, by the Mojo Wire, *Mother Jones* magazine's online sister. Copyright © 1999, Foundation for National Progress. Reprinted by permision.

QUESTIONS

1. a) According to the definition on page xxx, what is the purpose of the WTO?

   b) How are small and large nations supposed to be on an equal basis within it?

   c) According to this article, what do the critics say about this "equal treatment"?

2. Critics argue that the WTO overrides the powers of national governments. Give an example from the article.

3. If the WTO is so bad, why are so many nations lined up to join?

4. Proponents of the WTO claim that this organization cannot be held accountable for the enormous sway the United States enjoys by virtue of the massive size of its economy, and the huge amount of inter-national trade in which it participates. They claim that the WTO at least goes some way in limiting US power to govern world trade. What is your opinion on this issue?

Globalized Financial Markets

The third force driving the creation of a global economy is the **global financial market**, a network of 100 or so of the world's banks and large brokerages linked by computers. This net-work enables *traders* to buy or sell foreign cur-rencies, along with government and corporate bonds or stocks, exceedingly quickly, using specialized computer technology. The amounts traded in these markets are vast; it is estimated that $2.5 trillion is traded daily on these global money markets. To visualize this amount, one writer estimated that a year's trading would be equal to a stack of $100 bills reaching from the Earth to the Moon!

The traders who work for major financial institutions specialize in performing one of sev-eral functions. First, they may carry out currency conversions for individuals or businesses buying or selling with foreign countries. The buyer (importer) contacts a bank trader, who purchases the exporter's currency in the world money market and arranges payment to the seller.

Second, another group of traders specializes in bonds sold worldwide by corporations and businesses. To finance deficits, governments sell these bonds to investors abroad through the

global market. The bond market alone trades over $300 billion per day.

Finally, a third group of traders buys and sells shares for multinationals. This global stock exchange buys and sells about $40 billion per day, but this figure is likely to increase quickly.

The traders in these global markets make money by charging their clients for the service of buying or selling currencies, bonds, or stocks. They also profit by taking advantage of small differences in prices of currencies or assets between different countries. If a currency, bond, or share sells for a lower price in one country, the trader will buy it there and then sell it in another country where the price is slightly higher. A trader can make these transactions from a computer terminal using computer tech-nology that acts at lightning speed. Here is one commentator's impression of these traders:

Who are these new masters of the universe, the traders whose instant decisions and lightning investments can drive markets, cut federal budgets, export jobs, transform companies, and override governments? By and large they are very young, very quick, with the reflexes of a good third base-man.... [These] practitioners are extraordinarily well paid, with annual salaries and bonuses in

*the millions of dollars.... Most are in their twen-
ties and thirties; it's a high burn-out business.*

Source: From Richard C. Longworth, *Global Squeeze*
(Lincolnwood, IL: Contemporary Books, 1999), 57.

Concerns about global finance

The very speed and efficiency of the global markets that allow sellers and buyers of shares, bonds, and currencies to transact business have become an issue of concern. In 1997, the countries of East Asia suffered a devastating financial crisis that spread to many countries around the world. The exact causes are still disputed—some analysts say that the governments and banking systems in these countries were inefficient—but most experts agree that the responses of global markets intensified and spread the financial malady.

Thailand, South Korea, Malaysia, and Indonesia had been economic success stories before 1997. Their economies boomed, and the markets pumped in billions of dollars into real estate, new factories, and financial assets. Then, in 1997, the markets grew pessimistic about these countries. Their currencies appeared to be overvalued; their exports had fallen; it seemed that their comparative advantage in production was slipping away to China with its lower wages. Investors pulled out of these countries, businesses closed, and the currencies were devalued.

The crisis spread to Hong Kong, where the stock market fell 25 per cent in four days; then on to South Korea, the world's 11th largest economy, where the currency collapsed. The International Monetary Fund (IMF) engineered a $94 billion loan to South Korea, the largest ever, but the financial markets were not appeased. They turned against economies with no connection to East Asia: Brazil's currency was sold, driving its value down by 33 per cent in spite of a loan of $53 billion; tiny Estonia's currency came under attack, then Russia's, where the ruble collapsed and the government defaulted on its debt. The US stock market's Dow Jones index registered the panic when it slid 2000 points, ending the long boom of the 1990s. The Canadian dollar fell from US$0.73 in 1997 to US$0.63 in 1998 because of the fall in demand in Asian markets for commodities such as lumber, grains, and minerals exported by the western Canadian economy.

In human terms, this financial crisis, according to the **World Bank**, plunged 10 million people into "extreme poverty" (income of $1 a day or less), threw 24 million into "poverty" ($2 a day), and left an estimated 27 million workers without jobs in the five countries most severely hit. What lessons can be drawn from this tragedy?

At present, the global financial system has no mechanism to regulate international flows of capital. Regulations to prevent sudden withdrawals of capital have been proposed to reform the global financial system.

Check Your Understanding

1. Identify and describe the three forces responsible for the global economy.

2. Explain the difference between outsourcing and creating a subsidiary.

3. Why is Canada, along with other nations, striving to become more globally interdependent? How have attitudes toward multinational presence in Canada changed?

4. Refer to Figure 19.3 (page 418).

   a) The Canadian GDP is about $750 billion. Approximately what percentage do exports in goods contribute to it?

   b) The GDP of the United States is about ten times the size of Canada's. Compare the export figure (for goods) to the GDP of the United States. Are exports of goods as important to the US economy as they are to the Canadian economy?

   c) Considering your answers to the above, why did Canada negotiate a free trade agreement with the US?

5. Explain how computer technology worsened the financial crisis in East Asia in the 1990s.

Underdevelopment: The Status Quo?

Although the proportion of poor Canadians continues to increase statistically, most Canadians live a relatively comfortable lifestyle in contrast to the majority of Earth's people. To help recognize the disparities that exist between rich and poor nations, the World Bank classifies national economies into three groups based on annual per capita GDP data: high-income, middle-income, and low-income economies.

High-income economies (also known as **industrially advanced countries** or IACs) are nations with per capita GDPs high enough to provide a substantial majority of citizens with prosperity. In its 2000/2001 report, the World Bank set US$9266 (about Can$15 000) as the minimum GNP per capita for this group. In this report, 52 nations qualified for this distinction, representing 903 million people.

Middle-income economies are those in which a sizable minority of the population avoids living in acute poverty. In the 2000/2001 report, 92 nations, representing 2.7 billion people, were classified as middle-income economies. Included in this group are China, Russia, the Eastern European countries formerly under Soviet domination, several Central and South American nations, the Middle East, the extreme northern and southern regions of Africa, and the newly industrializing countries of Southeast Asia.

Low-income economies (also known as **less developed countries** or LDCs) include the poorest nations of the world. In the 2000/2001 report, the maximum GNP per capita was set at $755. Sixty-three nations were placed in this category, representing 2.5 billion people. Many of these nations share a common history as former colonies, at one time under the control of other nations. In many cases, the economies developed under **colonialism** were designed to benefit the home country and exploit the colonies for their natural resources. Consequently, colonialism retarded healthy economic development in these nations.

Many contemporary economists have concluded that the gap between high- and low-income nations continues to widen. It has been stated by various economists, relief workers, and religious leaders that in order for the world to experience lasting peace, it must first do away with existing injustices that serve to keep low-income nations from achieving sustained economic progress.

Yet the reality of the **80/20 rule** appears to be a permanent economic fixture in the world economy. At present, more than 80 per cent of the world's productive resources are effectively controlled by some 20 per cent of the world's people. Conversely, the remaining 80 per cent of the world's people control only 20 per cent of the resources. Under these circumstances, some economists argue, a more equitable distribution of global wealth is virtually impossible. Some of the more radical voices suggest that, in fact, the rich are rich precisely because of their advantageous position over the poor and vulnerable. Famines, as the argument goes, are not as much a case of insufficient food production to meet global needs as they are of distribution breakdowns between the "have" and "have-not" nations.

Barriers to Economic Development

Economists judge the economic success of a country by noting whether living standards are growing. An economy shows **economic development** when a nation's living standards have increased, something we can easily see when there is a measurable increase in per capita GDP that is shared by the bulk of its population. To achieve economic development, a country requires both economic growth and a widespread distribution of the benefits of this economic growth. In attempting to facilitate economic growth, low-income nations generally face a series of obstacles.

Lack of economic freedom and stability
Many low-income countries have politico-economic systems in place that limit economic freedom and the individual pursuit of self-interest. Some of these nations, such as Afghanistan, Angola, Cambodia, and Somalia, have experienced long civil wars that have further devastated their already fragile economies.

In some low-income countries, military and other forms of dictatorship control the governments. The stability present in a strong dictatorship comes at the price of lost personal and economic freedom. In these "controlled" economies, national wealth rarely manages to trickle down to the majority of citizens.

Malnutrition

Nations with a low GDP per capita usually have insufficient food supplies to distribute, resulting in a malnourished population. Other goods and services that contribute to improved health standards are also in short supply. To complicate matters, available food and productive resources may be controlled by a small minority of the population and used only for their benefit. For example, many low-income countries grow cash crops intended for export. These cash crops are usually grown on huge plantations owned by a small minority. The majority may be powerless to do anything about this imbalance.

Low levels of investment

Because individuals, households, and firms must use most of their income to purchase essential goods and services, only a minor portion of income can be saved. Without substantial savings in banks, the financing of investment projects and the development of a capital-goods infrastructure are very difficult to achieve. Further, when foreign interests supply money or real capital, their interests (profit maximization) may not always be in the best interests of the host nation, so they may be unwelcome. Finally, traditions that discourage self-interest, competition, and profit may inhibit local entrepreneurship.

Without high levels of investment capital, production tends to rely on labour because labour is relatively cheap and offers the only means of achieving profitability. Labour-intensive industries provide many people with jobs. As long as people receive a wage they can live on, often referred to as a **living wage**, this situation is not problematic. However, in many low-income nations, the earnings of the majority of workers are not sufficient to provide the necessities of a healthy life.

Population growth

Population growth in most low-income economies tends to be too high to be sustained by the existing levels of production growth. Consequently, living standards decline steadily over time. Rapid population growth and low incomes are linked. Large families are seen as an economic necessity in low-GDP nations, especially in areas where the child mortality rate is high. In economies with limited social security programs in place (such as retirement pensions), children provide labour to help the family survive. Later, they provide security for aging parents.

Dependence on child labour

According to the International Labour Organization, by the end of the 20th century, the number of working children had climbed to more than 250 million. In many low-income countries, children are required to work in factories or at home sewing garments, stitching baseballs, weaving rugs, making bricks, treating leather, hawking wares in markets, and serving as domestics for wealthy families. One of the most dangerous activities involves scavenging through refuse dumps in order to find materials that can be sold.

Many families run home businesses in which all family members must work in order to put food on the table. In other cases, businesses hire children because they can be paid very low wages and are easier to control than adults. In the case of rug weaving, the agility of tiny fingers is

Figure 19.4 A boy at work in a garment factory in Dhaka, Bangladesh. Why is child labour such an emotionally charged issue?

an asset. Often, the parents must stay at home unemployed because the local factory will not hire them, preferring to employ children.

As a direct result of child labour, millions of children miss the chance to go to school, and most never learn to read or write. High levels of illiteracy are always associated with high levels of poverty.

Child labour cannot be solved easily. It is a complex issue, as the following excerpt demonstrates:

> *Delwar is 12 years old. Pressed by overseas groups to stop employing children, Delwar's factory in the Bangladeshi capital fired him last September, along with his young co-workers. But it didn't do Delwar much good. He now ekes out a living selling waste paper that he picks up along the roadside.*
>
> *Delwar and his mother, a mentally ill beggar, sorely miss his $20-a-month factory salary. They live with his half-brother's family, eight people jammed into a one-room, dirt-floored hovel. Lately they have been skipping meals. For two months, they haven't been able to pay the rent.*

Source: Gordon Fairclough, "It Isn't Black and White," *Far Eastern Economic Review*, 7 March 1996, 54-57.

Natural-resource-intensive production

For many of the world's less developed countries, economic enterprise is limited largely to primary industrial activity. Their economic revenue is based on the exportation of limited natural resources such as bauxite, latex rubber, coffee, bananas, and sugar cane. Exporting relatively inexpensive natural resources, while importing expensive manufactured goods, usually results in a steady drain of money out of an economy. This imbalance serves to limit the economy's ability to grow. If discounted prices (whether as a result of market forces or exploitation) are being paid for the resources purchased from less developed countries,

then economic growth potential can be even more adversely affected.

In Figure 19.5, you can see that banana growers receive very little for their product. This situation is made worse if foreign interests control the natural resources, taking potential profits out of the country. An example would be a foreign company that owns agricultural land in a less developed nation, where it grows flowers for export to developed nations.

Debt burden

Many less developed nations have borrowed money from foreign banks, governments, and international institutions such as the World Bank and the International Monetary Fund. Monies were borrowed to finance infrastructure projects (to build roads, schools, and water works), to feed hungry citizens, to prevent the collapse of the domestic currency and banking system, and to pay for imports. Debt repayment can happen only when the nation that owes the debt has a surplus of exports over imports, resulting in a positive flow of money into the country and, ultimately, in economic growth. In order to achieve this, industrialized nations must open their markets to exports from less developed nations. Few low-income economies have ever managed to achieve this situation, particularly as many more developed countries

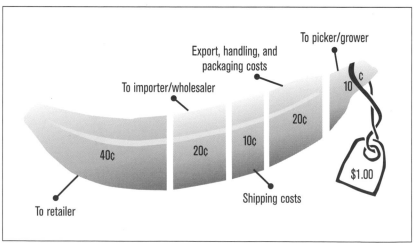

Source: Adapted from *Ten Days for Global Justice*, Education and Action Guide, 1998, p. 20, by permission of KAIROS: Canadian Economical Justice Initiatives.

Figure 19.5 How the banana splits. For bananas grown for consumption in the North American market, what percentage of the sales price do growers and pickers receive? Why? Who has the most power to set prices?

maintain trade barriers to protect their own industries. As a result, many less developed countries fall deeper and deeper into debt, and the interest payments get larger. Having to pay the interest on the incurred debt becomes a further burden for debtor economies and serves to limit their ability to invest and grow.

Check Your Understanding

1. What are the three classifications of economies? Why does a country fall into one category or another? How many countries are in each category?

2. Compare the 80/20 rule to the situation represented by the Lorenz curve for Canada, shown on page 334.

3. What are the causes of low levels of development? Rank-order the causes of low levels of development, giving a justification for your choices.

4. If you had to pick one root cause of poverty in low-income countries, what would it be? Explain.

5. Why is child labour a complex economic issue?

Development Strategies: Breaking the Cycles of Poverty

While it would be a difficult task, it is not impossible to break the cumulative downward cycles presented in the previous section, and shown below in Figure 19.6. Breaking the cycle involves the efforts of many individuals and organizations, working on many different fronts.

Political and Economic Stability

A stable politico-economic system is a prerequisite for lasting development. Political and

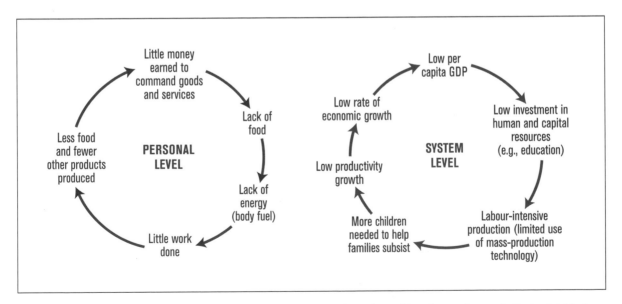

Figure 19.6 The vicious circles of poverty. At what point in each cycle could a change be made that might help people trapped in poverty break out of the cycle? Who would be capable of making this change?

SKILL BUILDER
Thinking Like an Economist

Developing Data Interpretation and Analysis Skills

The table in Figure 19.7 (below) presents selected development indicators for a sample of countries. Economists study tables like this one to determine the significance of patterns in the data. In this feature you will apply four sample analytical tools that economists employ.

Country (1999 population in millions)	Per Capita GNP (in US$)	Public Spending on Health (% of GDP)	Annual GNP Growth Rate 1998–99 (%)	Average Annual Population Growth 1990–99 (%)	Life Expectancy at Birth, Males (years)	Life Expectancy at Birth, Females (years)	Infant Mortality Rate (per 1000 births)	Children Age 10–14 in Labour Force (%)	Adult Male Illiteracy Rate (%)	Adult Female Illiteracy Rate (%)	Personal Computers (per 1000 people)	Per Capita Energy Consumption (kg of oil equivalent)
High-Income Countries (HICs) (891)												
Australia (19)	20 050	5.5	3.8	1.2	76	82	5	0	—	—	412	5484
Canada (31)	19 320	6.4	3.8	1.1	76	82	5	0	—	—	330	7930
Germany (82)	25 350	8.3	1.2	0.4	74	80	5	0	—	—	305	4231
Japan (127)	32 230	5.9	1.0	0.3	77	84	4	0	—	—	237	4084
Sweden (9)	25 040	7.2	3.9	0.4	77	82	4	0	—	—	361	5869
USA (273)	30 600	6.5	4.1	1.0	74	80	7	0	—	—	459	8076
All HICs	*25 730*	*6.2*	*2.6*	*0.6*	*75*	*81*	*6*	*0*	*—*	*—*	*311*	*5369*
Middle-Income Countries (MICs) (2667)												
Brazil (168)	4 420	3.4	–2.0	1.4	63	71	33	15	16	16	30	1051
China (1250)	780	2.0	7.2	1.1	68	72	31	9	9	25	9	907
Egypt (62)	1 400	1.8	5.7	1.9	65	68	49	10	35	58	9	656
Mexico (97)	4400	2.8	4.1	1.8	69	75	30	6	7	11	47	1501
Russia (147)	2270	4.5	1.3	–0.1	61	73	17	0	0	1	41	4019
Thailand (62)	1960	1.7	4.9	1.2	70	75	29	14	3	7	22	1319
All MICs	*2000*	*3.1*	*2.6*	*1.2*	*67*	*72*	*31*	*7*	*10*	*20*	*23*	*1368*

Continued

Country (1999 population in millions)	Per Capita GNP (in US$)	Public Spending on Health (% of GDP)	Annual GNP Growth Rate 1998-99 (%)	Average Annual Population Growth 1990-99 (%)	Life Expectancy at Birth, Males (years)	Life Expectancy at Birth, Females (years)	Infant Mortality Rate (per 1000 births)	Children Age 10-14 in Labour Force (%)	Adult Male Illiteracy Rate (%)	Adult Female Illiteracy Rate (%)	Personal Computers (per 1000 people)	Per Capita Energy Consumption (kg of oil equivalent)
Low-Income Countries (LICs) (2417)												
Ethiopia (63)	100	1.7	7.4	2.8	42	44	107	42	58	70	—	287
Haiti (8)	460	1.3	3.1	2.1	51	56	71	24	50	54	—	237
India (998)	450	0.6	6.9	1.8	62	64	70	13	33	57	3	479
Tanzania (33)	240	1.3	5.6	2.9	46	48	85	38	17	36	2	455
Pakistan (135)	470	0.9	3.6	2.5	61	63	91	16	42	71	4	442
Vietnam (78)	370	0.4	4.2	1.8	66	71	34	7	5	9	6	521
All LICs	*410*	*1.3*	*4.4*	*2.0*	*59*	*61*	*68*	*19*	*30*	*49*	*3*	*563*
World (5975)	4890	2.5	2.7	1.0	65	69	54	12	18	32	71	1692

Source: Excerpts from Tables 1, 2, 3, 7, 10, and 19 from *World Development Report 2000–2001: Attacking Poverty* (New York: Oxford University Press, 2001). Reprinted by permission of Oxford University Press, Inc.

Figure 19.7 Selected world development indicators for randomly selected countries.

Analytical Tools

Group Sample Analysis

An economist's question: For each grouping of countries, how representative is the sample? Does the sample do a good job of representing the whole group?

Sample strategy: We can tackle this question by examining the country selection. For example, for the data in Figure 19.7, we can compare the GNP for each high-income country with the average for that grouping, examine whether the sample represents the various areas of the world in which high-income countries (HICs) exist, and determine how much of the population in HICs is represented by the selection.

Analysis: The average per capita GNP for HICs is reported as $25 730. The average of the six sample countries is only $22 090. Clearly, this is not a list of the six highest-income countries. The sample does, however, include representation from the different parts of the world where HICs are found. In addition, the six countries in the sample represent 61 per cent of the population living in HICs. This selection does therefore represent a reasonable sample of the whole group. Because the six countries were selected randomly, as indicated in the figure caption, these six nations adequately represent the whole group of 52 nations. Generally, the larger the sample size, the better the representation. Random selection helps eliminate bias in the data.

Continued

Pattern Identification: Internal

An economist's question: When considering only one development indicator, how do the data compare for each grouping of countries?

Sample strategy: We can examine the GNP per capita for each of the high-, middle-, and low-income countries in Figure 19.7.

Analysis: Although a great range in values exists within each grouping, a substantial difference in per capita GNP (income) does exist among the three groups, especially when the three averages are compared.

Pattern Identification: Comparative

An economist's question: For two development indicators, how do the data compare for the same set of sample countries? Do they indicate a direct (positive) or inverse (negative) relationship?

Sample strategy: We can determine whether there is a direct or indirect relationship between per capita GNP and public spending on health care for the three groupings of countries in Figure 19.7.

Analysis: There is a direct relationship between per capita GNP and public spending on health care. The data confirm the general pattern that average public health spending is highest in high-income countries at 6.2 per cent and lowest in low-income countries at 1.3 per cent. Note, however, that we cannot conclude that the highest-income country is automatically the highest spender on public health.

Rank Correlation Coefficient

An economist's question: How significant is the relationship between two sets of data?

Sample strategy: We can tackle this question by using a calculation known as the **rank correlation coefficient** to help determine the statistical significance of any pattern found in two sets of data. The formula for this coefficient is

$$R = 1 - \frac{6 \, \Sigma d^2}{n \, (n^2 - 1)}$$

where n represents the number of samples in the data set and d represents the difference in rank order for each indicator. Using this formula, the perfect direct correlation is represented by the value 1. The perfect inverse relationship is –1. Generally, the higher the R value, the more statistically significant the relationship is between the two sets of variables being compared.

In order to use this formula you must first determine the rank order of the two data sets being compared. When two countries are tied in the ranking, award each the same rank and then skip the next rank number in order to preserve the overall count. For example, if three countries were tied for 13th place, all would be assigned a ranking of 13. The next in line, however, would be ranked 16th in order to maintain the arithmetic progression.

For the data in Figure 19.7, we can compare the GNP per capita and public health spending to determine the significance of the positive or negative correlation.

Analysis: The table on page 429 measures the correlation between GNP per capita and public health spending. As this table shows, the sum total of all squared differences (Σd^2) is 106. We then work this into the rank correlation formula as follows:

$$R = 1 - \frac{6 \, \Sigma d^2}{n \, (n^2 - 1)} = 1 - \frac{6 \, (106)}{18 \, (324 - 1)}$$

$$= 1 - \frac{636}{5814} = 1 - 0.11 = 0.89$$

The rank correlation coefficient is 0.89, which indicates a direct relationship between per capita GNP and public spending on health. More importantly, the coefficient indicates that this relationship is extremely significant. For data sets based on 18 samples, a relationship is statistically significant if the R value is greater than 0.60. The smaller the sample size, the higher the minimum R value required to establish significance. Luckily, these calculations are all computer assisted.

Country	GNP/Capita Rank	Public Health Spending Rank	Difference in Rank (d)	Rank Difference Squared (d²)
Australia	5	6	1	1
Canada	6	4	2	4
Germany	3	1	2	4
Japan	1	5	4	16
Sweden	4	2	2	4
USA	2	3	1	1
Brazil	7	8	1	1
China	12	10	2	4
Egypt	11	11	0	0
Mexico	8	9	1	1
Russia	9	7	2	4
Thailand	10	12	2	4
Ethiopia	18	12	6	36
Haiti	14	14	0	0
India	15	17	2	4
Tanzania	17	14	3	9
Pakistan	13	16	3	9
Vietnam	16	18	2	4
Sum total of all squared differences (Σd^2)				106

QUESTIONS

1. Complete a comparative pattern identification analysis of the data in Figure 19.7 to prepare a summary profile of high-, middle-, and low-income countries.

2. Assess how well the sample middle-income and low-income countries represent their groups.

3. Explain the significance of comparing GNP change to population change for these sample countries.

4. Use these data to explain why couples in low-income countries tend to have large families.

5. According to Figure 19.7, where will the most population growth occur during the first 20 years of the 21st century? Explain the global implications.

6. Working in groups to divide up the work, use the rank correlation coefficient to determine whether data patterns between any two variables (besides the pairing examined above) are statistically significant. Use this new information to revisit the three profiles prepared in question 1.

economic stability discourages the flight of investment funds and profits out of a less developed economy to safer markets. Political stability permits long-term planning and promotes capital investment. If investors are confident that their investments will not be seized by government, they are more likely to invest. Political stability is usually not assured until a country experiences a substantial period of rule by a democratically elected government.

Population Control

In many nations experiencing rapid population growth (relative to GDP), great effort is expended on state-sponsored birth-control programs. In India, for example, birth-control programs have been in place for decades. Nonetheless, the national birth rate remains relatively high. In another prominent example, China's more severe "one-child" policy has reduced that country's birth rate substantially. The success of the program depends on the state-imposed limits on the number of children allowed to each couple. There are certainly drawbacks to China's approach. For example, because many families prefer male children, some will go to extreme measures to ensure that they get one.

In another approach, population-control programs focusing on raising income and education levels have proven to be both effective and respectful of human dignity and life. Government programs that improve basic social services (health care, nutrition, and education) and provide programs that improve income distribution and employment opportunities also tend to encourage people to have fewer children. Evidence of this result appears in almost all industrialized nations, where birth rates are extremely low.

Investing in Productive Resources

For many low-income economies, natural resource endowment is limited. In the absence of these resources, governments can instead work toward the development of human resources by focusing on education, health care, and nutrition. Education and training increase the supply of skilled labour, which in turn increases productivity and living standards. Government programs can also work toward the development of capital resources by encouraging savings. Financial institutions then have capital that they can use to lend to entrepreneurs. Developing "intermediate technology" that makes good use of plentiful, low-cost labour is an effective strategy for less developed countries.

Freer Trade

Lasting and healthy development for many low-income economies requires the efficient use of whatever productive resources the economy has, especially labour. By offering efficiency, for example, in the form of low production costs, the economy has something to trade internationally. When industrially advanced countries open their markets to the goods (especially labour-intensive manufactured goods) produced by low-income economies, in the long run and in a fair trade arrangement, both parties share the benefits of the law of comparative advantage as presented in Chapter 17.

In the last two decades, a considerable number of manufacturing jobs have shifted from industrially developed countries to less developed nations. Many people in low-income nations have gained employment. Consider the various points of view about freer international trade presented in the Matter of Opinion feature on page 431.

Foreign Aid

Direct aid from developed nations is needed to help break the vicious circles of poverty at work in less developed nations. Relief programs are needed to deal immediately with crises resulting from drought, famine, civil war, earthquakes, and other natural disasters. Structural programs are necessary to help build the infrastructure, education systems, and capital resources necessary to provide a foundation for lasting economic development. In Canada, government aid is administered by the **Canadian International Development Agency (CIDA).**

A Matter of Opinion | Views of a Globalized World

Institutions from the WTO to the Canadian government have advocated increased international trade as the route to decreasing poverty levels in developing nations around the world. Think about the following opinions on free trade, and then consider your opinion on this issue.

Trade and the Canadian Economy

❝ (Canada)—Trade enhances the quality of Canadian life. Success in the international marketplace helps gives Canadians the economic energy we need to create the nation we want....

Canada's increasingly complex economy—bursting with potential—can't keep growing unless we continue to develop markets outside our borders. Only one out of every 200 people in the world is Canadian. If we ignore what the other 199 have to buy and sell, Canada's cash registers will soon turn quiet and increasing numbers of Canadians will find themselves out of work. Every $1 billion increase in Canada's exports sustains 10 000 Canadian jobs. One out of three Canadian jobs depends on exports....

Trade brings in technology and materials needed to create exports and offers Canadians a wider range of personal choice in purchasing everything from oranges, to cars, to medication. It encourages competitive pricing, creates jobs, stimulates technological advances and promotes more educated societies....

Canadians know who they are. Canada needs to grow economically to sustain the kinds of unique social and cultural programs that have made our country special. We can't stand still—we need to win globally to grow domestically. Trade puts money in the pockets of Canadians who work in our hospitals, teach in our schools and run our social programs. The last thing Canadians need to do is to hide from the rest of the world. ❞

Source: Excerpts from "Trade and the Canadian Economy" from <http://www.dfait-maeci.gc.ca/tna-nac/text-e.asp>, Department of Foreign Affairs and International Trade, 10 October 2001.

Fair Wages for Good Work

❝ (Indonesia)—[In the factory, 70 per cent were women.] We worked from 7:00 a.m. until 6:00 p.m. If they wanted us to work overtime, they would tell us to continue until 9:00. We worked a 14-hour day as often as three times a week.

By 1992, I was making US$1.45 [about Can$2.50] a day. On this salary I had to pay US$0.50 a day for rent and US$0.75 for food. If I missed the factory bus, I would have to use the remaining US$0.20 for transportation ... if you made a mistake on only one pair of shoes, you would be fined US$0.50.

Workers want a living wage. Right now we are not making enough to survive. We are unable to save even a little bit for our families or for our dreams for the future. The current minimum wage is US$2.33 a day, but we require US$4.00 a day to adequately meet our basic needs. That is why we have to work so much overtime, even when we are not being forced to do so. The choice is work overtime or not eat. ❞

Source: Excerpts from interview with Cicih Sukaesih in "Fashion Freedom" from *Ten Days for Global Justice*, 1999, 19.

QUESTIONS

1. What is the point of view and frame of reference for each speaker?

2. Cicih Sukaesih worked in a factory in Indonesia making running shoes. She was fired after attempting to organize a union. Working conditions have not changed significantly since her dismissal. Wages remain well below the cost of living, while the multinational corporation contracting this work continues to report profits in excess of $1 billion each year. Should workers in less developed countries earn wages that cover the cost of living? Explain your viewpoint.

3. Does your opinion on globalization shift if you think of yourself as an economic citizen of the world as opposed to an economic citizen of Canada?

4. If we assume that globalization is not going to go away, as many experts contend, how might we go about making sure that all people who participate may enjoy the economic benefits to be had from freer trade?

Debt Reduction

During the 1990s, actions were taken to help debtor nations. Negotiations with bankers helped reduce some debts. The World Bank provided low-interest loans and technical assistance for large-scale development projects. The International Monetary Fund provided loans to governments in return for specific corrections to the economy, such as reductions in government spending. These tactics did little to help. Money infusions do not address the cycle of exploitation. In time, the money flows back to wealthy nations.

By 1998, Brazil, the most indebted less developed nation, owed $374 billion to other nations; Mexico owed $258 billion; China owed $250 billion; Argentina owed $232 billion; and India owed $158 billion. By 2000, it had become clear that the debt crisis continued to be an insupportable burden for many debtor nations. Led by Pope John Paul II, many concerned world leaders began to advocate an international debt forgiveness plan to free less developed countries from the burden of paralyzing debt.

In 2001, Argentina defaulted on its loan payments because it was unable to pay. This plunged the bankrupt nation into a political, economic, and financial crisis. When Argentine banks closed their doors, people were unable to get their money out. Street riots led to several changes of government.

Check Your Understanding

1. What economic adjustments can be made to promote growth and development?

2. Which adjustments can be made only by less developed nations? Which adjustments could be encouraged by actions from developed nations?

3. List the benefits and costs of plans to forgive the debts of less developed countries.

4. One of the slogans used by anti-globalization protesters is "Globalization must work for people, not just for profits." Explain this viewpoint by listing the positive and negative features of globalization to date.

Economics in the News

Globalization Can't Ignore Social Justice

Despite protesters, globalization is not the issue....

According to World Bank president James Wolfensohn, "in the next 30 years, the population of the world will increase from 6 to 8 billion, and virtually all of those 2 billion additional people will live in the developing world. The sooner we are able to grasp the implications of this, the better."

One of those implications is that "poverty and frustration in Central Asia can create havens for terrorists whose acts are felt across the planet."

Another is that AIDS originating in Africa is now part of an epidemic that affects all countries. "If the argument of a common humanity did not convince us of the importance of acting together before September 11, then an expanded understanding of our self-interest will surely do so now," Wolfensohn said.

The challenges are enormous—to reduce the number of people living in absolute poverty by half, to achieve primary education for all children and to reduce child mortality rates by two-thirds, all by 2015 [the target date set by the nations that participated in the November 2001 meetings in Ottawa].

As Finance Minister Paul Martin put it, "no country can develop its economic potential without meeting the basic needs of its people."

To help the great majority of people on our planet, we need to give these countries better access to our markets for the things they make, such as clothing, shoes, and agricultural products.

Another big need is to raise foreign aid. Brown called on the rich countries to double their annual foreign aid budgets to US$100 billion a year so that the 2015 target can be met....

Figure 19.8 Thousands of people march behind a banner that translates as "Assassins" to protest the death of an anti-globalization activist who was shot by police during street riots that broke out during the G-8 summit in Italy on 20 July 2001.

Martin has promised that Canada will increase its aid. But there's strong opposition from the United States, which provides [proportionally] less assistance to the world's poor than any other advanced economy. This past weekend, US Treasury Secretary Paul O'Neill insisted foreign aid did little good.

There's another issue as well, one which touches on Canada's innovation agenda. Advanced economies are dragging their heels on needed reforms, said Horst Kohler, the IMF's managing director. Indeed, advanced economies are resisting change by blocking steel imports from the developing world, maintaining high tariffs and quotas on clothing, footwear, and other labour-intensive products and defending high barriers to many agricultural products.

"To fight poverty successfully means we need to be serious that growth is based on structural reform in two ways: the poor countries have to adapt to a modern economy, but also the advanced countries have to adapt and have to restructure their economies. Labour markets and subsidies which are based on the 20th-century economy in principle are outdated and have to be updated," he said. Advanced economies, including Canada, should hasten their transition to the knowledge-based economy, which is what Ottawa's innovation agenda should be about, so developing countries can move into mature industries where lower costs matter.

"Some form of globalization is with us to stay," Wolfensohn said. "But the kind of globalization is not yet certain: it can be either a globalization of development and poverty reduction—such as we have begun to see in recent decades, although this trend still cannot be taken for granted—or globalization of conflict, poverty, disease, and inequality."

Our huge task is to tip the scales toward good globalization.

Source: Excerpts from "Globalization can't ignore social justice" by David Crane from *The Toronto Star*, 20 November 2001. Reprinted with permission— The Toronto Star Syndicate.

QUESTIONS

1. During the meetings of the World Bank, the International Monetary Fund, and the G-20 Nations (held in Ottawa, 16–18 November 2001) what challenges or targets were set to fight global poverty?

2. According to the writer, what is "good" globalization? What changes must industrially developed countries adopt to promote this kind of globalization effectively?

3. The article suggests that Canadians can help eliminate social injustice globally by opening our borders to products from less developed nations. What further role might be played by effective governments (both national and international) to redistribute wealth more equitably?

4. In this article, social injustice is linked to terrorism and violence. Do you agree with this theory? Keep in mind that the 11 September terrorists chose as their target the World Trade Center, a symbol of US corporate power. Explain your opinion.

CHAPTER SUMMARY

- The process of creating a global economy is driven by multinational corporations, the removal of trade barriers worldwide, and the existence of a massive international financial system.

- Multinational corporations either use foreign subcontractors to provide goods or services or set up subsidiaries in other countries for production. Computers and satellite communication allow the multinational to co-ordinate production.

- The multinational search for low-cost production locations throughout the world has caused controversy. Although jobs, incomes, and tax revenues are created in host countries, wages can be low and working conditions questionable.

- Globalization has benefited from the dismantling of trade barriers, first by GATT and today by the World Trade Organization (WTO), along with the conversion of former communist nations to capitalism and the development of dynamic economies in East Asia.

- The WTO's achievements in lowering trade barriers and settling trade disputes has been criticized as often favouring the large economies at the expense of the smaller, less developed ones.

- The global financial system formed by a network of banks and brokerages allows currencies, corporation shares, and bonds to be bought and sold quickly. However, its speed in buying and selling currencies, shares, and bonds has been criticized as destabilizing to the world economy.

- An ongoing concern of globalization is the disparity between rich and poor nations, a gap that many economists believe is becoming worse.

- National economies are placed in one of three categories—high, middle and low—with approximately 80 per cent of people living in middle- and low-income economies.

- Barriers to development of low-income countries include lack of economic freedom and stability, malnutrition, low levels of investment, high population growth, reliance on primary industrial activity, and high debt burdens.

- Child labour, prevalent in low-income countries, is a complex issue because it combines both exploitation of the weak and economic necessity for the children and their families.

- Breaking the cycle of poverty in low-income countries is difficult. If political stability is lacking in the country, investors and businesspeople are discouraged and will move to safer markets.

- Population control can be achieved either by state-imposed limits on family size or by raising income and education levels, developments that encourage families to have fewer children.

- High-income countries can help by opening up their markets to goods produced by low-income countries, by increasing foreign aid, and by reducing or cancelling the debts owed to them.

Key Terms

globalization
multinational corporation (MNC)
transnational corporation
outsourcing
subsidiary
sweatshop
intellectual property rights
International Monetary Fund (IMF)
global financial market
World Bank
high-income economy (or industrially advanced country)
middle-income economy
low-income economy (or less developed country)
colonialism
80/20 rule
economic development
living wage
rank correlation coefficient
Canadian International Development Agency (CIDA)

Activities

Thinking/Inquiry

1. Which of the three factors that helped create the global economy is most important in your opinion? Give reasons to support your answer.

2. On the Internet, search for information about the initiative to establish an international excise tax called the Tobin Tax. Find out who thought of it, what it would tax, and what the revenues could buy. How much money could this tax potentially bring in? Give your opinion on this initiative.

3. Conduct an Internet search to find out more about sweatshops that anti-globalization forces have targeted. What kinds of products have been connected with these places of production? How have the manufacturers answered their critics? Do you think that major sports figures who advertise these products have a responsibility to speak out on this issue?

4. A multinational corporation decides to move a plant from Canada to another country. What responsibility do you think each of the following have to the employees who lose their jobs: (a) the government; (b) the multinational; (c) the employees themselves.

5. Conduct an Internet search to help prepare a list of the benefits and costs of child labour in less developed countries. Should child labour be abolished or regulated? Justify your position. Identify organizations that are fighting child labour, and highlight some of their initiatives.

6. The developed nations have always maintained a pledge to increase the size of their foreign-aid budgets to 0.7 per cent of their GDP. Do some research to determine Canada's current contribution. In your opinion, is Canada doing enough? Explain.

7. Do free enterprise and free trade contribute to global injustice? Do you think that this is a permanent condition, or are the current problems just "economic growing pains"? Prepare an argument to support your point of view.

Communication

8. Each of the three factors responsible for the global economy—which you learned about in the first section of this chapter—reinforces the others. Draw a triangle with a factor at each corner, and show, using arrows and phrases, how each factor reinforces the others. Explain which is most important, in your opinion.

9. Make a summary list of the causes and remedies for low levels of economic development.

10. You are a representative of a less developed country. Research your nation's economic profile, and make a case before the World Trade Organization for fairer treatment of exports and for the establishment of rules regarding multinational activities in your country.

11. Does freer trade bring people closer together, or do trade disputes and import competition force them apart? Organize a debate on this issue, or prepare a short position paper.

12. a) Imagine you are attending a demonstration in the streets outside a meeting of the World Trade Organization. Design a logo and create a slogan, either supporting or opposing globalization.

    b) Form a small group of pro- or anti-globalization supporters. Prepare a reasoned argument for your point of view. Deliver it to the opposing group, either informally or in a formal debate.

13. Write a letter to the editor of your local newspaper, presenting your viewpoint on current trends in global development. Provide economic evidence to support your opinion.

Application

14. Draw a supply and demand graph to help explain why the price of labour in less developed countries tends to be low. What other factors contribute to low wages?

15. How do the economic theories of Karl Marx (Chapter 3) help explain wage rates in less developed countries where foreign investors have provided employment opportunities in manufacturing? How might Milton Friedman view this same phenomenon?

16. Explain the reasoning behind the argument that foreign aid does little good. What is your position on this issue?

Unit 5 Performance Task: Advising a Less Developed Nation

This unit of study has introduced us to the fundamentals of international economics. Chapters 17 and 19, in particular, have focused attention on the great debate surrounding globalization, with its emphasis on freer trade, open markets, international competition, global financing, and multinational investment and activity. You are now in a position to apply what you have learned in this unit to the immense problems faced by less developed nations that are trying to improve the lives of their citizens.

Your Task

You are an economic adviser to a less developed nation. This nation's government would like to improve the per capita GDP and bring it in line with that of middle-income economies. However, the government is divided on the merits of two competing economic strategies: (i) heavy government involvement in the economy, including the nationalization of key industries, the imposition of tariffs on imports in order to protect industry and agriculture, and the establishment of controls over multinational investment; or (ii) limited government involvement in the economy, including the advancement of privately owned industry, the reduction or elimination of tariffs on imports, and the implementation of an open-door policy on multinational investment. Your challenge is to assess each strategy and decide which one would allow the nation to improve its standard of living, taking into consideration its economic potential and current problems.

Task Steps and Requirements

1. Review all the work you have done in this unit to refresh your understanding of related concepts and skills.
2. Using resources on the Internet and in the library, draw up a one-page economic profile of a less developed nation of your choice. Your profile should include information regarding (i) population size, per capita income, average educational level, life expectancy, and child mortality rate; (ii) major industries, agricultural activity, and other natural resources both presently exploited or potentially available for development; (iii) major exports and imports, balance of payments, and the state of the national currency; (iv) the nation's external debt level.
3. Determine the major problems and needs of the country and compare them with the barriers to economic development described in Chapter 19.
4. Select a decision-making process or a model that includes the analysis of costs and benefits in order to make a decision.
5. In preparing your report, be sure to include the economic concepts, principles, and theories you studied that are most appropriate to your analysis and most useful in supporting your recommendation.
6. Decide on your method of presentation: a written report, or an oral presentation using visual aids.

Adapting the Task

Discuss the selection of a format (oral, written, or perhaps recorded) for your report with your teacher. Keep the language appropriate for the intended audience. Share drafts with your teacher, classmates, and parents or guardians in order to obtain useful feedback.

Assessment Criteria

The following criteria will be used to assess your work:
- *Knowledge*—accurately using economic concepts, principles, and supporting data
- *Thinking and Inquiry*—researching and assessing information from a variety of sources; using sound economic reasoning and thorough analysis; effectively using a decision-making model
- *Communication*—presenting economic information and analysis clearly and accurately, in an appropriate format and style
- *Application*—presenting a persuasive argument to inform decision making

CHAPTER 20

THE ECONOMICS OF TOMORROW

Trends, Forecasts, and Futures

In this final chapter, we shall review some of the trends and issues identified in earlier chapters in order to forecast the most likely changes in the Canadian economy over the next few decades. Before we embark on this task, we should recall that given the existence of many interdependent variables, economic forecasting is far from an exact science. Training in economics will help you to think more analytically about complex issues and to be better informed and deliberate in your decision making. However, it cannot, in and of itself, guarantee success in business endeavours and stock market investments. Economics does not provide a high-definition crystal ball to view the future. As the dramatist Eugène Ionesco once wrote, "You can only predict things after they have happened."

"Regular or high-definition?"

QUESTIONS

1. What is the cartoonist suggesting in the above cartoon about the forecasting of future events?

2. Why do you think that many people have the image shown in the cartoon of individuals who claim to be able to forecast future events?

3. What factor do you think creates the most difficulty in forecasting economic change?

4. What changes do you forecast for the Canadian economy? On what assumption are these forecasts based?

Chapter Goals

By the end of this chapter, you will be able to

- synthesize economic trends identified in this text to determine future prospects for the Canadian economy within a global context,

- bring together the economic concepts, principles, and theories learned in order to explain important economic realities, relationships, and interactions,

- explore possible future scenarios and discuss their implications for different stakeholders,

- demonstrate the full extent of your learning by applying your knowledge and skills to a culminating performance task.

The Dynamics of Change

The future is not something imposed on us by external and mysterious forces. Human behaviour creates social, economic, technological, and political change. In the collective sense, for the most part, we create our own future.

Technological innovation advances human knowledge and ability. Human activity causes environmental pollution; human knowledge can provide the technology and the inclination to clean it up. Producers create a new product; consumers determine whether producers will be rewarded for their investment. Some people create bureaucratic "red tape"; others learn to break through it to get things done. People vote for a politician in an election; in the next election, they vote to replace this same politician. It appears that the only real constant is change!

SKILL BUILDER
Thinking Like an Economist

Trends and Forecasts

Like weather forecasting, economic forecasts are based on
- recognizing a behavioural pattern,
- observing this pattern over time to establish a trend,
- hypothesizing the forces of change at work in creating a new trend, and
- forecasting an occurrence based on the continuation of an identified trend.

Economic forecasts can miss the mark when trends fail to continue as expected as a result of unforeseen circumstances, such as the rapid meltdown of information technology stocks and the terrorist attacks of 2001. As a result, forecasts are generally more accurate for the short term than they are for the long term (for example, a forecast for the next business quarter would likely be more reliable than a five-year business forecast).

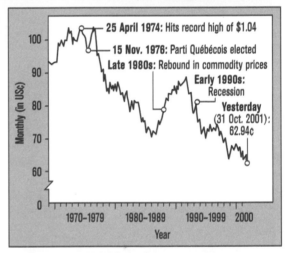

Source: Canadian dollar graph by Danielle Delaurier from *The Globe and Mail*, 1 November 2001. Reprinted with permission from The Globe and Mail.

Figure 20.1 The changing value of the Canadian dollar relative to the US dollar. This graph appeared on the front page of *The Globe and Mail* on 1 November 2001, as the Canadian dollar fell to a record low in international money markets.

QUESTIONS

1. What is the general trend of the graph in Figure 20.1?
2. What economic factors have most contributed to this pattern?
3. What changes do you expect in these factors? Research statistical indicators to support your projections.
4. Do you expect this graph to show decline, recovery, or stabilization if you were to extend it to the year 2010? Justify your decision and revisit it once you have completed this chapter.

Scenarios of Change: Implications for our Economy

Demographic trends

Thanks to medical advances and healthier lifestyles, Canadians are living longer. As the baby boom generation (those Canadians born between 1946 and 1966) continues to age, the average age of Canadians continues to increase. In an aging society, the demand for health-care services will grow substantially. During the early 21st century, the number of Canadians aged 65 and older will surpass the number of Canadians aged 18 or younger. The largest segment of the population, the baby boomers, will be between 40 and 60 years old. Elder care may eventually replace child care as a socio-economic concern. Furthermore, a labour shortage may arise if large numbers of immigrants do not continue to join the Canadian workforce each year.

As more Canadians retire relative to the active workforce, there will be increased pressure on government pension and health-care plans. Many critics have suggested that these plans will not be able to meet future obligations without substantial infusions of cash. In response, many Canadians have put their savings into registered pension plans in order to provide for their own needs after retirement. Unfortunately, a large number of Canadians have not planned well for retirement, expecting the same level of government benefits that the previous generation has received.

If a majority of Canadians retire with large amounts of disposable income, the demand for leisure services (including recreation, entertainment, and culture industries) and health-care services will increase substantially, creating many new jobs in this sector of the economy. If Canadians retire with smaller amounts of disposable income, the demand for health-care services may increase more than the demand for leisure services as available funds are channelled into necessary services. Either way, there is no doubt that changes in population patterns will cause significant adjustments in the Canadian economy. Socialized health care and the escalating costs associated with current approaches to medicare will continue to be a source of public debate for years to come.

Job markets

During the period of economic growth from 1995 to 2000, many Canadian employers experienced difficulties in finding and keeping skilled workers. People looking for work did not always have the skills that employers needed. Some economists have started to question whether Canadians are adequately prepared for full participation in the new knowledge/information economy. In light of recent global trends, more employment opportunities are forecast to occur in the service and technology sectors of industrially developed economies rather than in the primary or manufacturing sectors, which, in Canada, have traditionally employed large numbers of workers. Some experts have stated that technology can create as many jobs as it replaces. This may be true, but, from an economic perspective, the fact remains that high-skill jobs are created while low-skill jobs are replaced.

Other changes forecast in the job market deal with the length of employment. First, according to recent trends, Canadians are going to have to make more frequent career changes than did earlier generations. Second, part-time and contract work appear to be increasing relative to rates of full-time and permanent employment. Needless to say, your generation of Canadians will have to be more flexible and globally competitive than earlier generations have had to be. Employment training will remain an ongoing priority. The focus of government employment insurance programs must be placed on worker retraining.

Unemployment rates in Canada are expected to remain higher than those in the United States. If the productivity of Canadian labour increases through training and technological advances then wage rates and working conditions could improve without any negative impact on business profits. If productivity does not increase then wage rates and working conditions (such as working hours, scheduled breaks, and workload) might have to be adjusted to keep Canadian labour globally

SKILL BUILDER

Thinking Like an Economist

Making, Assessing, and Verifying Forecasts

Economic forecasts are often presented for public consumption. This type of presentation can lead to oversimplifications and omissions. An economic thinker must be a critical thinker, able to read between the lines in order to assess and verify forecasts. This is accomplished by separating fact from opinion in order to find a basis in reality for the forecast, and by testing the assumptions being made and the economic reasoning being applied. To develop your critical thinking skills, read the news story below, then answer the questions that follow.

Stunning job leap biggest since 1976

Gum maker Wrigley Canada finds itself in a rather sticky situation. The Chicago-based parent company chose its Canadian unit to make a new product destined exclusively for the United States. But Canada's booming job market has Wrigley hoping it hasn't bitten off more that it can chew. The gum, Orbit, is now so successful the company needs to add 100 people to its Don Mills factory. Wrigley hired 22 people last month [March 2002] but it's desperately trying to fill another 76 positions, mostly skilled and semi-skilled workers for plant operations. "We are very much searching high and low, all over the world actually, for folks right now," said Dave McGregor, vice-president of human resources, in an interview yesterday. "These are well-paying jobs."

Statistics Canada shed some light on McGregor's dilemma. In March [2002], the Canadian economy added a stunning 88 000 jobs.... That's the largest jump since January 1976, when the statistical agency changed the way it collects employment data. The March number surpassed the equally astounding 75 900 jobs created in January. In total, 170 000 net new positions were created in the first three months of the year, the biggest quarterly increase since

1987. The 88 000 new jobs in March—40 000 full-time and 48 000 part-time—stunned forecasters. They had expected a modest gain of 10 000....

The report garnered so much attention because it was released 90 minutes before the US employment numbers for March.... Turned out the US employment numbers were weaker than expected. A gain of 58 000 positions wasn't enough to keep the US unemployment rate from rising to 5.7 per cent in March, from 5.5 per cent the previous month.

Canada's unemployment rate edged down to 7.7 per cent, from 7.9 per cent in February. The fall in the jobless rate was tempered by a 68 000 increase in the number of people seeking work. If the labour force participation rate, now at an 11-year high, had remained unchanged, Canada's unemployment rate would have sunk to 7.3 per cent.

Economists, still dizzy from the massive job creation figures in January, ran out of unused superlatives to describe the March report.... Strength was virtually across the board, with all major provinces and industries posting employment gains.... [Marc Lévesque, senior economist at the Toronto Dominion Bank,] says two main factors can take credit for Canada's incredible recovery from last year's slump. First, the impact from the September 11 terrorist attacks never really materialized in Canada beyond the month.... Second, the Bank of Canada and the US Federal Reserve aggressively slashed their trend-setting interest rates, keeping consumer confidence, and the economy, afloat. Interest-rate-sensitive items such as housing and vehicles set and continue to set sales records. The bad news is that those low borrowing costs are going up sooner rather than later.

Yesterday's [5 April 2002] job report will prompt the Bank of Canada to start cranking up its trend-setting interest rates starting next month, said Ted Carmichael, chief economist at J.P. Morgan Securities Canada Inc. Last year, the bank cut its overnight rate by 3.75 percentage points, including 2 percentage points following September 11, to spur the then-sputtering economy.... Carmichael believes the bank will raise rates by 1.5 percentage points by year's end, in slow but steady quarter-point increments.

The stream of good economic news, underscored by yesterday's job report, will hopefully prompt businesses to start investing again, the missing ingredient to a sustained rebound, said Jay Myers, chief economist at Canadian Manufacturers & Exporters. "If these indicators continue, we can move up the recovery in capital spending from early next year to the fourth quarter of this year or perhaps late into the third."

Source: Excerpts from "Stunning jobs leap biggest since 1976" by Steven Theobald from *The Toronto Star*, 6 April 2002. Reprinted with permission—The Toronto Star Syndicate.

QUESTIONS

1. How accurate were March 2002 employment forecasts for Canada?

2. Create a chart to compare March unemployment figures and job creation in Canada and the US. Which economy performed better?

3. How did economists explain Canada's apparent recovery? Research subsequent monthly employment figures to determine whether the recovery forecast was accurate. What happened to the Canadian economy after this report was published that made the recovery forecast accurate or inaccurate?

4. Explain the economic reasoning behind the forecast increase in interest rates. Research subsequent interest rate adjustments by the Bank of Canada to determine whether the forecast was accurate. What happened to the Canadian economy after this report was published that made the interest rate forecast accurate or inaccurate?

5. Compare the rate of full-time job creation to that of part-time job creation rate for March 2002. Research employment data to confirm whether this pattern is part of a general trend. What are the economic implications of this trend? What forecast can be made using these data? How can your forecast be tested for accuracy?

6. What do you anticipate will happen to employment rates in Canada over the next quarter? Explain your decision.

---

competitive. If Canadian workers are paid more without proportionate gains in productivity, then price inflation could increase, exports could decrease, employment levels could fall as employers shed surplus workers, and, ultimately, the international value of the Canadian dollar might continue to decline.

Clean energy and economic activity

Given our country's cold climate, great distances between communities, and highly industrialized economy, Canadians will most likely continue to be high per capita consumers of energy reserves. The search for alternative forms of energy, if successful, will reduce both our reliance on imported fossil fuels and the harmful emission of greenhouse gases.

Canadians have been interested in the development of solar energy since the global fuel crisis of the mid-1970s. From an economic perspective, capital investment in solar energy technology and wind power technology should increase proportionately as pioneer utilities demonstrate the profitability of these ventures. Recent experiments with giant wind turbines, such as the one built at the Pickering nuclear power plant in south-central Ontario (see Figure 20.2), have demonstrated encouraging results. The power utility has committed to invest $50 million over a five-year period to produce 500 MW of clean energy. Each megawatt is considered sufficient energy to power 300 homes.

Newfoundland experimented with wind generation in the 1960s. Advances in turbine technology have convinced the provincial government to reconsider harnessing the average wind speeds of up to 30 km/h that swirl around the island. Successful applications in Alberta, Quebec, and Ontario indicate that new efforts might succeed where earlier experiments failed. However, icy winters and salty air could still prove to be hurdles in the operation of turbines.

The challenge of meeting Canada's energy needs while reducing harmful emissions will continue to require sizable capital investment. With the potential for great profits, renewable energy initiatives should continue to attract investor interest and create employment opportunities. For example, Ballard Power Systems in Vancouver is recognized as the world leader in developing, manufacturing, and marketing zero-emission fuel cells to power automobiles and electrical equipment.

Economic freedom and corporate power

If current patterns (that is, smaller governments and greater concentration of corporate power) continue, Canadians can reasonably expect that the first decade of the new millennium will most probably be a "golden age" for corporations and big business, both in Canada and in the global economy. In a free-enterprise market, successful businesses will continue to expand their capital assets, their scale of operations, and their ability to acquire smaller rivals. As a result, the concentration of corporate power in Canada is expected to grow. In addition, successful businesses will continue to enter into more alliances with other large enterprises in order to share technology, reduce operating expenses, and gain additional market share. If these changes improve their ability to operate efficiently and on a global scale then three important outcomes could follow:

- As long as there is enough competition to ensure that the benefits of improved efficiency will be shared with consumers, prices could remain competitive, with no adverse effect on corporate profits.
- The productivity gap between Canada and our biggest trading partner, the United States, could be narrowed significantly. As long as interest rates remain competitive, this productivity gain could have a favourable effect on profitability and exports, ultimately increasing foreign demand for Canadian dollars.

Figure 20.2 In November 2001, after months of technical problems, the giant white windmill at the Pickering, Ontario, nuclear station began to produce enough electrical energy to power up to 600 homes. Built by Vestas Wind Systems of Denmark, this is the first model of its size to be put into operation.

- More attention might be focused on environmental stewardship (for example, compliance with the 1997 Kyoto Protocol to reduce greenhouse gas emissions such as carbon dioxide from cars and factories).

Such change would reflect good corporate citizenship. If these socio-economic benefits are not achieved through market forces (such as trading in pollution credits, a solution examined in Chapter 16), public attention might focus on a political remedy to modify the power and social conscience of big business. This political remedy could take the form of protective legislation (such as emission controls and taxes) or consumer action (such as public protests, boycotts, and stock acquisition) to effect change.

Sharing growth and prosperity

In recent years, the vision of limitless growth under free enterprise has come under closer scrutiny. The focus has shifted more toward the concept of sustainable growth, based on managing resources responsibly and reducing the environmental impact of economic activities. Aside from temporary and cyclical setbacks, business profits continue to grow and stock market indicators continue to inch upward. Some firms have improved worker productivity by instituting profit-sharing programs and allowing workers to become shareholders. These strategies give workers an added interest in the firm's success and an additional income stream.

Canada's focus on the common good requires reflection, not just on the achievement of prosperity but also on the equitable distribution of the wealth generated. At present, with the government spending cuts of the 1990s, an increasingly larger portion of the Canadian population is living in circumstances of poverty and food insecurity. In addition, household spending on necessities has increased to the point where families have had to deplete their savings in order to make ends meet. This leaves an increasing number of households and individuals vulnerable in the event of economic and personal crisis.

The number of homeless people in Canada and the number of Canadians forced to use food banks continue to increase. At the same time, corporate profit levels continue to grow and provide additional income for investors. At what point do profit levels become excessive? At what point do they suggest that resources, workers, or consumers may have been exploited? Many Canadians still believe that one important role of government is to ensure a more equitable distribution of income by providing direct assistance to those most in need. Others maintain that dependence on government assistance discourages self-reliance. Whatever the case, Canadians will most probably need to continue the fight against poverty and to rebuild the self-esteem of those pushed to the margins of society. Education and employment training are essential in reversing the vicious cycle of poverty.

Canadians need to investigate how other nations have chosen to deal with poverty. Ironically, even though Canada ranked first in the United Nations Human Development Index from 1992 to 2000, its lowest comparative rankings were often for the way that it addressed the issue of poverty. In the future, this situation will have to change, otherwise Canadians will face both social and economic consequences.

Globalization

Canada is not a closed economy. In the new global economy, no nation can isolate itself from economic events abroad. The terrorist attacks of 11 September 2001 on the United States served as a potent reminder that no nation (not even the most powerful) can insulate itself from political happenings in other parts of the world. Today each nation-state or economy is a "province" of the world. Canadian workers are now part of the global labour pool, and jobs will be created where market forces dictate.

As we saw in the previous chapter, present levels of globalization demonstrate both good and bad effects. It is hoped that Canadian business and government leaders will have a positive impact on the future direction of globalization. In order for globalization to succeed, it must be seen to work for people and not just for profits. If we are able to promote this cause successfully, the biggest dividends will be sustainable development and peace. If we are not able to promote this cause, political unrest in less developed nations may escalate and may have an adverse impact on the Canadian economy. Some critics suggest that a return to a renewed form of communism or socialism is one likely political reaction to capitalist exploitation in some less developed nations.

Globalization requires freer trade. As Canada commits to freer trade, markets will open up for Canadian resources, manufactured goods, and technology. As manufacturing continues to shift to less developed nations, Canada's economic future does not rest in the manufacturing sector, but rather on the natural resources sector and the post-industrial services and technology sectors. According to World Bank data, high- and medium-technology goods are the fastest-growing components of international trade while resources and other primary products are in decline. This pattern is expected to continue for some time, further highlighting the importance of the services and technology sectors in Canada's future.

Economic and political sovereignty

Since we conduct more business with the United States than with the rest of the world combined, Canada's economic fortunes are closely tied to the fortunes of our biggest trading partner. The success of the Free Trade Agreement between Canada, the US, and Mexico will promote intensive negotiations for a Free Trade Area of the Americas (FTAA). This will be an important undertaking for Canada since it will open up markets in Central and South America for Canadian goods and services. Developing trade with other nations will lessen Canada's current dependence on the US economy.

Under the present arrangement, Canadian sovereignty is often challenged by economic decisions made in the US to address American issues and to serve US policy needs. One recent example is Canada's reluctant compliance with American requests for improved border and airport security as a result of the terrorist attacks on the US. Since our economy could not withstand any impediment to the steady flow of goods and people to and from the US, Canadian political leaders felt compelled to make these expenditures and to cut spending in other areas. Another recent example, the imposition of 29 per cent import duties on Canadian softwood lumber entering the US, was examined in Chapter 17.

Given the current plight of the Canadian dollar, some economists have started to advocate economic and even currency union with the US, as we saw in Chapter 18. This action would further limit Canada's ability to make economic decisions in Canada and in the best interests of the Canadian people. Others suggest that economic union would simply remove the veneer of independence that presently exists, considering the US's domination of the Canadian economy. Opinion polls suggest that Canadians are warming up to the idea of currency union, but they are not yet ready for economic or political union with the US. Over the next few years, Canadians will have to deal with these issues.

Consumer confidence

As we have learned throughout this course, one of the most important indicators of the health of any economy is consumer confidence. If Canadian consumers remain optimistic about our income prospects, economic and political security, and ability to achieve greater prosperity (as individuals, households, and firms), consumer spending levels should continue to trigger cumulative rounds of increased product demand, capital investment, employment, production, and efficiency. When Canadian consumers lose this sense of confidence, as a result of deteriorating economic or political conditions, consumer spending may decrease. This reduction in the demand for goods and services, especially those considered to be luxuries, can result in a downward economic spiral.

Productivity and innovation

In order for Canadians to sustain and improve the standard of living we have come to enjoy, we must work hard to create efficiencies in every field of economic endeavour. Productivity growth is also important because it determines how fast an economy can grow and create jobs without triggering rounds of price inflation.

Recent studies by Industry Canada economists indicate that Canada faces a formidable challenge in narrowing the productivity gap with the US. Some economists expect this gap to widen between 2001 and 2006. In 1973, Canadian labour productivity in manufacturing was about 85 per cent of the US level. By 2001, it had declined to about 65 per cent. By comparison, in 1973, the Canadian dollar was valued at par with the US dollar. At the end of 2001, the Canadian dollar was trading for US$0.63. A strong productivity revival in all sectors of the economy is required to help offset this imbalance.

Many factors influence productivity growth, including the amount and quality of technology available per worker, the quality of the workforce and the pace of innovation, and investment in new technology.

The quality of the workforces in Canada and the United States is comparable in terms of education and skill. US businesses, however, tend to invest in more technology per worker and tend to adopt the latest technologies faster than their Canadian counterparts. In recent years, there has been a significant boost to productivity from the efficiency gains that have occurred in the information and communications technology industries. One advantage that the US presently enjoys is a much larger information and communications technology industry. In order to reduce this productivity gap, Canadian businesses must increase their investment levels in innovation.

The Canadian government can support this approach by introducing a comprehensive long-term innovation strategy for the Canadian economy, providing investment incentives (such as tax breaks) to Canadian businesses, and promoting increased research and development (R&D) facilities in Canada. At present, Canadians tend to import much of their R&D from facilities in the US. Toward the end of the last century, the ratio of R&D scientists and engineers in Canada was 2719 per 1 million people. In the US, this ratio was 3676 per 1 million people, reflecting a significantly higher concentration of R&D expertise. If we do not close this productivity gap, the long-term economic outlook for the Canadian economy, for Canadian living standards, and for the foreign value of the Canadian dollar is not as healthy.

In 2001, the Canadian government announced the economic goal of transforming Canada into the fifth most research-intensive economy by 2010. Although no specific plans were announced before this text was printed, this ambitious goal would involve
• doubling federal spending on R&D,
• adding approximately 100 000 R&D scientists, researchers, and engineers,
• bringing venture capital funding to US levels on a per capita basis,
• tripling new-product and new-service sales by Canadian companies, and

• connecting all parts of Canada through a high-speed broadband communications network.

Several public and private challenges remain if this economic goal is to become a reality. What specific measures and funding (both private and public) will be required to achieve this goal? Will Canadians be adequately prepared and positioned to participate effectively in the knowledge/information economy? Will Canadian entrepreneurs be able to turn new ideas into job-creating, profitable businesses? Will Canadian universities be able to train a large number of high-calibre scientists, researchers, and engineers without substantial financial assistance from government? Will quality researchers opt to stay in Canada or accept lucrative offers abroad? Will talent and expertise be drained out of Canada, or will the Canadian economy attract knowledge and expertise from abroad? Will the private sector generate sufficient investment funds for the large-scale innovation ventures and infrastructure improvements required, or will the government have to participate? The answers to these questions will help to determine how successful Canadians will be in achieving this important goal.

Role of government

What do Canadians expect from our government? How much are we willing to pay in taxes in order to receive the social programs that we expect? How can we ensure that government dollars are spent efficiently? Ultimately, how much of our economic freedom are we prepared to trade for increased government involvement and regulation in the economy?

At present, Canadian public opinion is divided. Some people favour the continued downsizing of government. Some people want public health care and the other pillars of Canada's social safety net protected. Those who want less government are often the same people who want public health care safeguarded. There is no shortage of opinion on what the government's role should be. The principal task of this course has been to help you recognize opinion for what it is; decide if it is based on fact, logic, and acceptable assumptions; and, ultimately, evaluate the impact that suggested initiatives will have on economic goals.

During the second half of the 1990s, all levels of government attempted to balance their operating budgets in order to reduce deficit spending. One approach was to cut spending on social programs. Another was to reduce governments' direct role in the Canadian economy. Publicly owned corporations like PetroCanada and Air Canada were privatized. Having observed Air Canada's monopoly-like power in the marketplace, some Canadians strongly advocate re-regulation. If the processes of deregulation and privatization continue, Canada will slowly be transformed into more of a free-market economy and less of a mixed-market economy.

In Ontario, this process has involved the privatization and deregulation of hydro-electric utilities, despite the warnings of critics who observed the power shortages and price spikes resulting from deregulation in Alberta and California. Most Canadians expect government to remain closely involved in protecting competition and ensuring fair business practices, especially as businesses continue to grow and become more powerful.

From time to time, there will be calls from the corporate sector for greater "harmonization," that is, the adoption of more "American-like" practices that will allow Canadian firms to compete on a level playing field. The US model calls for less government involvement in the economy and emphasizes individual freedom and self-reliance. The traditional Canadian model reflects a more collectivist, or *common good*, approach, similar to the economies of Sweden and France, for example. Public debate on the most appropriate role for government in Canada will likely continue for many years.

Hope for the Future

How Canadians collectively rise to the challenges ahead and respond to the changing job market will significantly affect living standards. In 2001, Canada finally lost its first-place ranking in the United Nations Human Development Index. Will we reclaim this distinction as the "best country in which to live," or will we continue to move down the list of industrially developed nations? How we respond to the many challenges posed in this final chapter will determine our fate among nations. During the 20th century, Canada made great strides forward as an industrialized nation, eventually joining the prestigious circle of the G-7/G-8 nations.

It remains to be seen whether the 21st century will be as kind to Canada's dreams of continued economic growth and prosperity. In the final analysis, much will depend on the decisions you and your classmates make in balancing self-interest with the common good as voters, consumers, producers, investors, workers, and leaders. Balancing self-interest with the common good has historically been the Canadian way. Welcome to the set of challenges and promises we affectionately refer to as "the Canadian economy." We certainly hope that you are up to this challenge. Our collective future depends on it!

ISSUES AND IMPLICATIONS

While previous chapters have explained and analyzed contemporary economic issues, this chapter has attempted to synthesize them. Now the time has come for you to consider the issues as a whole and to assess their impact on future prospects for the Canadian and global economies. As you reflect on these public policy issues, the questions below will help to clarify the alternatives and focus your thinking:

- To what extent will demographic trends influence changes in public health-care spending, retirement pension planning, and immigration policy?
- In what ways will the job market be different for your generation of Canadians? How can you best prepare for these changes? To what extent should higher education or skills training be considered a public or private good, and what policies should be adopted to support this position?
- How effectively can trading in pollution credits support sustained economic growth and prosperity while protecting the environment? Will consumers be willing to pay more for environmentally friendly products and production processes?
- Should we be selling resources such as water in bulk to foreign buyers? Should we be exporting privatized hydro-electric power to the US even if it means higher rates for Canadian consumers?
- What effect will increased corporate power have on markets and consumers? To what extent can public policies help achieve market balance? Do government-supported, but privately owned, monopolies like Air Canada represent appropriate policy decisions?
- What level of production growth is most sustainable and appropriate? At what point do profit levels become excessive? At what point do they suggest exploitation?
- How does our society strike a balance between individual freedom to pursue self-interests and social responsibility? What strategies should be used by government to redistribute income? Should unpaid housework be recognized for pension purposes? Should day care be publicly subsidized to allow more Canadians to enter the labour force? How will this spending be funded?

- Does public policy help or limit the ability of Canadian industries to compete effectively in the global economy?
- What can be done to promote consumer and investor confidence?
- Will Canadians be prepared and positioned to participate effectively in the knowledge/information economy? Will entrepreneurs be able to turn new ideas into job-creating, profitable businesses? Will our universities be able to train high-calibre scientists, researchers, and engineers without financial assistance from government?
- Will the private sector generate sufficient investment funds for the large-scale innovation ventures and infrastructure improvements required to boost productivity and make enterprises more efficient? To what degree will the government have to participate in order to close the productivity gap?
- How much are we willing to pay in taxes in order to safeguard our social programs? How can we ensure that government dollars are spent efficiently? Finally, how much of our economic freedom are we prepared to trade-off for increased government involvement and regulation in the economy?

Activities

Thinking/Inquiry

1. Among the scenarios of change presented for the Canadian economy, identify the three most important and explain your reasoning.

Communication

2. Review and revise the forecasts you made earlier in this chapter. Prepare an economic rationale to support your conclusions. Identify your key assumptions and key facts.

Application

3. Develop an additional economic scenario for the Canadian economy based on the work you have done during this course. To support your forecast, identify the key assumptions you have made and the key facts you have used.

Culminating Performance Task: Tying It All Together

For centuries, economists have worked to clarify complex realities, to explain human behaviour, and to illuminate responsible decision making. Now that you have participated in the learning activities presented throughout this course, the time has come to weave your learning together in a meaningful way and into a comprehensive whole.

As we have discovered during this course, the whole is often worth more than merely the sum of its parts. In any profound treatment of economic realities, the following components must be considered: stakeholder groups and interests, institutions, relationships, interactions, change indicators, and measurements.

Your Task

You are an economics major in university. You have been hired by the Canadian Foundation for Economic Education (CFEE) to design a poster-size flow chart to help educate the general public about the interconnectedness of a chosen economic element. This flow chart must illustrate the element's impact on the economy and identify the economic factors affecting it. For maximum effect, the flow chart should illustrate the impact on the personal lives of readers.

Economic Elements

- productivity • stock market • organized labour
- interest rates • foreign investment • free trade
- innovation • fiscal policy and public debt
- regional disparity • information technology
- money supply • balance of payments • globalization

Task Steps and Requirements

1. Select one of the economic elements from the list above, or negotiate an alternative selection with your teacher.
2. Review all units of study to refresh your understanding of this element and its related concepts, principles, and theories. Then prepare a summary chart or mind map.
3. In your preparation notes, link your chosen element to all components (institutions, stakeholder groups, etc.), activities (transactions and exchanges), and relationships (interdependence, cause and effect, etc.) that it influences in the Canadian economy. Also identify the economic elements and factors that, in turn, exercise considerable influence on it.
4. Map out a poster-size flow chart to represent all links and relationships identified.
5. For each link that you make (each arrow on your flow chart), provide a concise explanation on the chart.
6. Strive for high-quality content, thoroughness of detail, and visual impact.

Adapting the Task

Consider creating a board game that integrates the links, relationships, and patterns identified in your flow chart. Discuss topic selection and approach with your teacher. Keep the language appropriate for the intended audience. Share drafts with your teacher, classmates, and parents or guardians in order to obtain useful feedback.

Assessment Criteria

The following criteria will be used to assess your work:

- *Knowledge*—presenting accurate and complete content
- *Thinking and Inquiry*—using sound economic reasoning and thorough analysis
- *Communication*—presenting economic information and analysis clearly and accurately, in an appropriate style
- *Application*—creating a visual impact; making meaningful connections

Glossary

Absolute advantage The capacity of one economy to produce a good or service with fewer resources than another.

Absolute poverty Poverty defined as lacking the basic essentials for survival such as food, shelter, or clothing.

Accounting profit The excess of a firm's revenues over its costs.

Actual output The GDP that the economy actually produces, which may be lower than its potential GDP.

After-tax income Total annual income after federal and provincial taxes are deducted.

Aggregate demand The total demand for all goods and services produced in the economy.

Aggregate supply The total supply of all goods and services produced in the economy.

Analytical economics The branch of economics that deals with facts and direct observation of the world; also called positive economics.

Appreciation An increase in a domestic currency's value in terms of another currency.

Aquaculture The breeding and raising of marine life in tanks, ponds, and reservoirs; also known as fish farming.

Arithmetical progression A number sequence (such as 1, 3, 5, 7, 9, 11, 13…) that has the *same difference* (in this case, 2) between each number in the sequence; associated with food production in the pessimistic theories of Thomas Malthus.

Articles of incorporation A legal document, filed with the government, that incorporates a business.

Asset Anything that is owned by a business, company, or government.

Asset income Income received by an individual in the form of interest, dividends, or rent.

Asset value A corporate share's portion of the corporation's net worth, represented by its assets minus its liabilities.

Atlantic Groundfish Strategy, The (TAGS) A $1.9 billion federal aid program from 1994 to 1998 for the 31 000 people who lost their livelihood with the collapse of the Atlantic cod fishery.

Automatic stabilizers Mechanisms built into the economy that help to stabilize it by automatically increasing or decreasing aggregate demand, such as Employment Insurance, welfare programs, and progressive taxes; often contrasted with discretionary fiscal policy.

Balance of merchandise trade The difference between a nation's merchandise exports and imports.

Balance of payments account National account of international payments and receipts, divided into current account, and capital and financial account.

Balance sheet A snapshot of the financial health of a business such as a bank, recording its assets and liabilities.

Balanced budget The situation that occurs when a government spends an equal amount to what it has collected in tax revenue.

Bank deposit money Money composed of people's deposits and loans granted by the banks, exchangeable by cheque or electronic transfer.

Bank note Paper currency issued by a country's central bank.

Bank rate The rate of interest charged by the Bank of Canada to the chartered banks, which serves as a benchmark for the interest rates charged by financial institutions to their customers.

Barter The trading of goods and services without the use of a monetary system; such transactions are common in traditional economies.

Bear market A stock market under the influence of traders expecting prices to fall, an expectation that is usually self-fulfilling.

Before-tax income Total annual income before federal and provincial taxes are deducted.

Bilateral Involving two nations, as in an agreement reached between two nations.

Black market The illegal exchange of goods in short supply, as when some people buy up as much of a good as possible, stockpile it, and sell it at a higher price.

Blue-chip stock Shares of large corporations that are commonly regarded as safe and stable investments.

Bond A financial asset that represents a debt owed by a corporation to the holder, on which interest is paid by the corporation.

Book value The value of a share when it was first issued; also known as face value.

Bourgeoisie Term used by Karl Marx for industrial capitalists who, he theorized, would be overthrown by the working class.

Boycott A union tactic of bringing pressure upon an employer by encouraging the public not to purchase the employer's product.

Brain drain Emigration of Canadians talented in research and management to the US and other countries.

Branch banking A banking system, such as Canada's, that restricts the number of banks that can operate, but allows them to have as many branches as they want.

Branch-plant economy A somewhat censorious term applied to Canada in the past, referring to the numerous branch plants of foreign multinationals operating here, particularly US ones.

Bull market A market influenced by investors expecting prices to rise, an expectation that is usually self-fulfilling.

Bureau of Competition Policy Government agency that administers the Competition Act.

Bureaucracy The administrative structure of government responsible for delivering programs such as Employment Insurance and Medicare.

Business cycles Swings in national economic performance characterized by four phases: peak, contraction, trough, and expansion.

Canada Assistance Plan (CAP) A federal transfer of money to the provinces to help fund welfare programs for Canadians.

Canada Pension Plan (CPP) A pension paid to all retired workers who have made compulsory payments to the plan during their working years.

Canada–US Automotive Products Agreement (Auto Pact) A 1965 agreement between Canada and the USA to eliminate tariffs on auto parts and automobiles.

Canadian International Development Agency (CIDA) The Canadian government agency responsible for administering foreign aid.

Canadian Labour Congress A federation of Canadian unions, which lobbies the federal government on labour legislation and other social and economic policies affecting workers.

Capital A factor of production that refers to machinery, factories, warehouses, and equipment used to produce goods and services.

Capital account Part of a balance of payments account that records totals for migrant's funds, inheritances, and government pension payments.

Capital and financial account Part of an economy's balance of payments account that measures flows of capital and investment.

Capital goods Goods such as tools or machinery used to produce consumer goods.

Capital-intensive (production) Production in which machinery rather than labour dominates the process, characteristic of the factory system.

Capitalism An economy characterized by private ownership of business and industry, the profit motive, and free markets.

Carrying capacity Environmental term referring to the number of people that the Earth's resources can support indefinitely if those resources are managed effectively.

Cash drain The proportion of a bank deposit that a person chooses to hold in cash outside the bank, reducing the bank's excess reserves and thus the its ability to lend.

Cause-and-effect fallacy See Post hoc fallacy.

CDI Canadian direct investment abroad, in the form of building a new plant, establishing a new business, or taking over an existing one.

Ceiling price A restriction imposed by a government in order to prevent the price of a product from rising above a certain level.

Ceteris paribus Latin for "other things being equal" or "as long as other things do not change"; an assumption made when economists want to understand the cause-and-effect relationship between any two factors and want other factors affecting that relationship to be held constant.

Chain Fisher volume index A newer method of determining the GDP deflator that uses a formula to "rebase" the GDP each quarter instead of comparing it to a base year.

Chartered bank A bank established by a charter passed by the Canadian federal government.

Chequing account An account that serves primarily as a medium of exchange, paying little or no interest.

Child Tax Credit A federal payment to low-income households with children under 18 years; replaced the Family Allowance in 1978.

Circular flow of income A model of the economy that sees the GDP as a total of all the money payments made to businesses and individuals.

Class-action lawsuit A lawsuit brought by one or more persons who file a complaint on behalf of themselves and others affected by a problem, such as pollution caused by a firm's activities.

Closed shop A clause in the collective agreement between a union and an employer that stipulates that the employer may hire only union members.

Coase theorem Theory of economist Robert Coase, which states that in some circumstances private negotiations are more efficient than government intervention in dealing with negative externalities such as pollution.

Cohort A group with similar statistical characteristics, such as all Canadians between 18 and 25 years of age.

Collective agreement A contract lasting a specific period of time, negotiated by a union with the employer through the process of collective bargaining.

Collective bargaining A process whereby a union negotiates wages and working conditions with the employer on behalf of all members of the union.

Collusion An illegal agreement among competing firms to set prices, limit output, divide the market, or exclude other competitors.

Colonialism A policy of bringing foreign peoples under the control of one country for its economic benefit; pursued in the 19th and 20th centuries by European nations over sizable areas of Asia, Africa, and South America.

Combines Investigation Act (1889) Canada's first act to prevent firms from fixing prices or lessening competition to the detriment of consumers; replaced in 1986 by the Competition Act.

Command economy An economic system in which production decisions are made by central planners.

Commodity A raw or semi-processed good such as minerals, lumber, or grain.

Commodity money Money that has value in itself such as cattle, wheat, or salt.

Common good The well-being of Canadian society at large.

Common market The strongest form of free trade agreement, which includes free movement of labour and capital among members, tariff-free movement of goods, and a common policy on trade restrictions against non-members.

Communism A political system on the extreme left, based upon the theories of Karl Marx, that calls for government or community ownership of the means of production.

Comparative advantage The capacity of one economy to produce a good or service with comparatively fewer resources than another (e.g., having a lower opportunity cost).

Competition Act (1986) The act that replaced the old Combines Investigation Act to address problems caused by business mergers, acquisitions, and price fixing.

Competition Tribunal The board empowered to make decisions on disputes between corporations and the Bureau of Competition Policy that cannot be decided through negotiation.

Complement goods Goods that are sold together along with other goods, e.g., gasoline and automobiles.

Compulsory arbitration A process in which a government forces both sides in a labour dispute to accept the decision of a third party.

Conciliation A process in which a third party helps a union and an employer reach an agreement; also called mediation.

Conglomerate A group of companies involved in different industries, but controlled by a central management group.

Constant-dollars GDP See Real GDP.

Consumer equilibrium The state of satisfaction a consumer reaches when the marginal utility divided by price is equal for two or more products bought by that consumer.

Consumer expectations What consumers believe will happen to the price of a product in the future; such beliefs have the effect of changing consumer demand for the product in the present.

Consumer goods Those goods or services that an economy produces to satisfy human needs.

Consumer Price Index (CPI) A price index that measures changes in the prices of consumer goods.

Consumer sovereignty A principle of market economies that the production choices of the economy are ultimately made by the buying decisions of consumers.

Consumer surplus The difference between what consumers are willing to pay for an item and what they actually pay.

Consumption Household spending on goods and services.

Contractionary fiscal policy Government policies to decrease aggregate demand through tax increases and/or decreased spending.

Co-operative A business owned equally by its members who have a common relationship, goal, or economic purpose.

Corn Laws Early 19th-century taxes on grains imported into Britain that drove up the market price of domestic grain in order to benefit the landed classes. These taxes became a focus of opposition for David Ricardo's wage and free trade theories.

Corporate alliance A group of companies that agree to operate as a single company while retaining separate ownership.

Corporate income taxes Taxes paid to the federal and provincial governments by corporations as a percentage of their profits.

Corporation A business firm recognized legally as a separate entity in its own right.

Cost-of-living allowance (COLA) A wage agreement that allows for wages to rise at the same rate as the general price level.

Cost per unit A measure of a firm's efficiency, obtained by dividing total costs by the number of units produced.

Cost-push inflation Inflation caused by the passing down of increased production costs to consumer goods and services.

Cottage system Production carried out in the homes of workers, characteristic of medieval times.

Craft unions See Trade unions.

Crowding out The theory that government borrowing drives up interest rates and reduces the amount of loanable funds, thereby making it more difficult for businesses to borrow.

Crown corporation A business owned by the federal government.

Crown land A Canadian term for government-owned land.

Currency Coins and notes that compose the money supply of an economy.

Current account A bank account for a business that operates like a chequing account, paying little or no interest and serving as a medium of exchange; also, part of a balance of payments account that records totals for three components: goods, services, and investment income.

Custom duty A tax charged on foreign goods entering the country; also called tariff.

Customs union Extension of a free trade agreement among members to include a common policy on trade restrictions on non-members.

Cyclical deficit The part of a deficit that is incurred when the government is trying to pull an economy out of a recession.

Cyclical unemployment Unemployment caused by a downturn in the business cycle.

Debt The total amount that a government owes on money it has borrowed to fund deficit budgets in the past.

Decision lag The time required for a government to decide on an appropriate fiscal policy after recognizing that an economic problem exists.

Deficit budget The situation that occurs when the government spends more than it collects in taxes, causing a shortfall or deficit, which it must cover through borrowing.

Deflation A general fall in the price levels of an economy.

Demand The quantity of a good or service that buyers will purchase at various prices during a given period of time.

Demand curve A straight line or curve on a graph illustrating the demand schedule for a product.

Demand deposit Bank deposits (such as chequing accounts) that can be used to make immediate payment.

Demand–pull inflation Inflation caused by excessive increases in consumer demand relative to available production.

Demand schedule A table showing the quantities demanded of a product at particular prices.

Democracy A political system characterized by a freely elected government that represents the majority of its citizens.

Demographics Population statistics that show changes in age, income, and overall numbers, often used by businesses in their planning.

Deposit multiplier The amount by which a change in the monetary base is multiplied to determine the resulting change in the money supply; also called money multiplier.

Depreciation A decrease in a domestic currency's value in terms of a foreign currency.

Depression A prolonged recession characterized by falling GDP, very high unemployment, and price deflation.

Deprivation A term associated with the idea of absolute poverty; that is, income so low that an individual cannot afford the basic necessities of life.

Deregulation The opening of a market to more competition by eliminating government regulations originally put in place to limit competition.

Derived demand Demand for resources (such as labour) that is dependent on, or derived from, the direct demand of consumers for the goods and services being produced.

Devaluation A depreciation or fall in the exchange value of a currency resulting from intervention on the part of a government or its central bank.

Dictatorship A political system in which a single person exercises absolute authority over an entire nation.

Direct demand Consumer demand for goods and services that directly determines the kind and quantity produced; see derived demand for contrast.

Direct investment Investment in the form of building a new plant, establishing a new business, or taking over an existing one, carried out by Canadians abroad or by foreigners here.

Direct tax A tax (such as income tax) whose burden cannot be passed on to others by the taxpayer.

Discouraged workers Those who would like to work but have stopped looking because they believe nothing is available for them.

Discretionary fiscal policy Deliberate government action taken to stabilize the economy in the form of taxation or spending policies; often contrasted with automatic stabilizers.

Dividend Corporation profits distributed to shareholders on a per-share basis.

Division of labour The specialization of workers in a complex production process, leading to greater efficiency.

Double coincidence of wants The problem of barter: for a trade to occur, both parties must want what the other is willing to trade.

Dow Jones Industrial Average The most widely known indicator of stock market activity based upon the daily closing prices of 30 blue-chip US corporations.

Downsize Reduce the number of employees in a company to lower production costs.

Drawing down Environmental term referring to the process of using up resources (such as minerals or forests) or abusing ones (such as fresh water or air) that should be available for future generations.

Dumping The deliberate practice of selling a product internationally at a price lower than its domestic price.

Easy money A monetary policy of low interest rates, easy availability of credit, and growth of the money supply.

Economic development A rise in a country's standard of living as measured by a rise in per capita GDP.

Economic growth An increase in an economy's total production of goods and services.

Economic system The laws, institutions, and common practices that help a nation determine how to use its resources to satisfy as many of its people's needs and wants as possible.

Economics The study of the way society makes decisions about the use of scarce resources.

Economies of scale The greater efficiency a firm can achieve when it produces very large amounts of output.

Economize To use limited resources efficiently in production.

Economy A self-sustaining system in which many independent transactions in a society create distinct flows of money and products.

Effective (use of resources) A particular use of resources that achieves a desired end, such as consumption.

Efficiency A firm's ability to produce at the lowest possible cost, measured by either its cost per unit or its unit labour cost.

Efficient (use of resources) The use of a bare minimum of resources to achieve a desired end, such as consumption.

80/20 rule An expression of the observation that 80 per cent of the world's productive resources are controlled by 20 per cent of its people.

Elastic coefficient A coefficient for a product of more than one, indicating that a given percentage change in price causes a greater percentage change in quantity demanded.

Elasticity The responsiveness of quantities demanded and supplied to a change in price.

Elasticity of supply The responsiveness of the quantity supplied by a seller to a rise or fall in its price.

Electronic money Money in electronic networks, or cash cards that can be used by consumers.

Embargo An action taken by one nation against another for some political purpose to prevent import or export of goods.

Employment Insurance (EI) A federal program to assist those temporarily out of work due to job loss, illness, or birth or adoption of a child; called Unemployment Insurance (UI) until 1996.

Employment rate The total number of Canadians employed divided by the total labour force.

Entrepreneurship The contribution made by an owner, manager, or innovator who organizes land, labour, and capital to produce goods and services.

Environment for enterprise A society's social values and institutions, such as stable government, that are favourable to businesses attempting to produce and sell goods and services.

Equilibrium price A price set by the interaction of demand and supply in which the absence of surpluses or shortages in the market means there is no tendency for the price to change.

Equity Fair and just distribution of income within an economy.

European Union (EU) The 15-member European common market, the largest in the world, which introduced its own currency, the euro, in 1999.

Excess reserves The amount of cash over and above what is needed to meet demand from depositors and so can be lent.

Exchange rate The price at which one currency can be purchased with another.

Excise tax A tax paid to the federal and provincial governments, as a set dollar amount per unit, on items such as liquor, gasoline, and tobacco.

Exclusion A term associated with the idea of relative poverty; that is, income so low that an individual cannot enjoy the standard of living of the majority of society.

Expansion An extended period of increasing national production, or real output.

Expansionary fiscal policy Government policies to increase aggregate demand through tax cuts, increased spending, or both.

Expenditure approach A calculation of the GDP that totals all that the economy spends on final goods and services in one year.

Export An international transaction in which a foreign currency is converted into a domestic one in order to purchase a domestic good; also called receipt.

Externality A side effect of production, either positive or negative, experienced by a third party who is neither a producer nor a consumer of the product.

Extraterritoriality The imposition of political, economic, or legal influence by one nation over another that is seen to infringe upon its sovereignty; charged by Canadians against the US from time to time.

Factors of production Resources (such as land, labour, and capital) that are used to produce goods and services.

Fallacy A hypothesis that has been proven false but is still accepted by many people because it appears to be true.

Fallacy of composition A mistaken belief that what is good for an individual is automatically good for everyone, or what is good for everyone is good for the individual.

Fallacy of single causation A mistaken belief, based on oversimplification, that a particular event has one cause rather than several.

Family Allowance A program of monetary support, started in 1942, for all Canadian households with children under 18; replaced by Child Tax Credit in 1978.

Fascism A political system on the extreme right, combining a free-market economy with a non-democratic form of government.

FDI Foreign direct investment in Canada in the form of building a new plant, establishing a new business, or taking over an existing one.

Fiat money Money that represents value because governments have declared it to be legal tender, not because it is valuable in itself or exchangeable for gold.

Financial account The part of the balance of payments that records totals for direct investment and portfolio investment.

Firm Units of ownership engaged in business activities.

Fiscal policy Government taxation, spending, and borrowing policies used to try to stabilize the economy.

Fixed costs Costs (such as rent and property taxes) that remains the same at all levels of output and must be paid whether the firm produces or not.

Fixed exchange rate An exchange rate for a currency that is fixed in relation to another currency, such as the US dollar.

Flexible exchange rate An exchange rate for a currency that is determined entirely in the international market by demand and supply, with no government intervention; also called floating exchange rate.

Floating exchange rate See Flexible exchange rate.

Floor price A restriction that prevents a price from falling below a certain level.

Foreign exchange reserve The store of foreign currencies and gold held by the central bank, used at times to intervene in the foreign exchange market.

Fractional reserve banking The discovery made by goldsmiths that they could lend much of the gold deposited with them for safe keeping because only a fraction of it was usually withdrawn by the depositors.

Free Trade Agreement (FTA) The 1989 agreement reached between Canada and the USA to phase out trade restrictions, establish mechanisms to settle trade disputes, relax investment rules, and settle other trade issues; it became part of NAFTA in 1994.

Free trade area An agreement between two or more nations to eliminate tariffs between them while retaining the right to impose tariffs upon non-members.

Frictional unemployment Unemployment caused by workers who are between jobs or who are entering or re-entering the labour force.

Frontier The curve on a production possibilities graph representing the maximum numbers of two items that can be produced with a given amount of resources.

Full employment The lowest possible rate of unemployment, seasonally adjusted, after allowing for frictional and structural unemployment.

Full-employment equilibrium The intersection of aggregate demand and aggregate supply, at which full employment is reached and prices have just started to rise.

Futures market A market for commodities that are bought and sold for future delivery.

GDP deflator A broad price index to measure price changes on all goods and services in the GDP, not just consumer goods and services.

GDP gap The cost of unemployment to the economy, measured by the amount of potential output that exceeds actual output.

General Agreement on Tariffs and Trade (GATT) The 1947 agreement reached by major trading nations for the gradual reduction of tariffs over time; replaced in 1995 by the World Trade Organization (WTO).

Geometrical progression A number sequence (such as 2, 4, 8, 16, 32, 64…) that has the *same ratio* (in this case, 2) between each number in the sequence; associated with population growth in the pessimistic theories of Thomas Malthus.

Global financial market A computerized network of 100 or so of the world's banks and large brokerages that buy and sell currencies, bonds, and stocks.

Globalization The creation of a world economy caused by increased international trade, investment flows, and the spread of multinational corporations.

Gold standard A promise by a government that it will exchange gold for the national currency on demand.

Goods and Services Tax (GST) A Canadian federal government sales tax levied on a range of goods and services.

Government enterprise A business that provides services owned by the federal, provincial, or municipal government.

Gross Domestic Product (GDP) The total value of all final goods and services produced by an economy in a given year.

Gross Domestic Product (GDP) per capita The total value of a nation's goods and services divided by its population; also called per capita GDP.

Gross National Product (GNP) An older measure of national output; the total of all Canadian-owned factors of production in Canada, or located anywhere in the world. The GNP was replaced as an economic indicator by the GDP in 1986.

Guaranteed Income Supplement (GIS) A program of extra support for older Canadians whose primary income source is Old Age Security (OAS).

Hidden economy The growing practice in Canada and other mixed economies of citizens trading one service for another to avoid taxation or to ensure a more personal level of services; illegal transactions occurring in the economy that are not recorded in GDP calculations (such as payment of employees "off the books"); and non-market production.

Hidden unemployed The total of all underemployed workers plus all discouraged workers, a number not included in calculating the official unemployment rate.

High-income economy A nation with high enough GDP per capita (set at about Can$15 000) to provide the majority of its citizens with prosperity; also called industrially advanced country.

High-tech (industries) Industries that develop, provide, or use highly complex technology.

Holding company An enterprise that holds shares in other producing companies.

Horizontal integration The merging of two firms that produce the same product or service.

Horizontal merger A consolidation of two firms producing the same product or service.

Human capital The knowledge, skills, and talents possessed by workers.

Human Development Index (HDI) A United Nations measurement of a country's achievements in three aspects of human development: life expectancy, literacy and education levels, and GDP per capita. In 2001, Canada ranked third among 162 nations.

Hypothesis A speculative theory requiring proof or verification.

Impact lag The time required for a fiscal policy to bring about a change in the economy.

Implementation lag The time required to implement an appropriate fiscal policy after making the decision to carry it out.

Import An international transaction in which a domestic currency is converted into a foreign one in order to purchase a foreign good; also called payment.

Inadequate demand unemployment Unemployment caused by declining aggregate demand; another term for cyclical unemployment.

Income approach A calculation of the GDP that totals all the incomes earned by the different factors of production in producing all final goods and services.

Indexing An adjustment made to some wages and pension payments to offset year-to-year price increases, using the CPI as a guide.

Indirect tax A tax (such as sales taxes) whose burden is passed on by the seller to the buyer of the good.

Industrial Revolution The period of technological innovation and factory production, beginning in Britain in the late 18th century, that eventually changed the economy from one that was largely agricultural and rural to one that was industrial and urban.

Industrial unions Unions that represent all workers in a given industry, regardless of the type of job they do.

Industrially advanced country (IAC) See High-income economy; also referred to as developed country.

Inelastic coefficient A coefficient for a product of less than one, indicating that a given percentage change in price causes a smaller percentage change in quantity demanded.

Inflation A general rise in the price levels of an economy.

Inflation premium An allowance for inflation that is built into all interest rates.

Inflation rate The annual percentage by which the Consumer Price Index (CPI) has risen.

Inflationary gap The gap between aggregate demand and full employment equilibrium; characterized by high inflation, low unemployment, and high GDP growth.

Inflow A receipt that flows into Canada and is recorded on the capital account, such as an inheritance received by a Canadian from another country.

Infrastructure The foundation of goods and services (such as roads, power grids, communications systems, schools, and hospitals) that allows an economy to operate efficiently.

Injection Any expenditure (such as investment, government spending, and exports) that causes money to be put into the income–expenditure stream of the economy.

Input A productive resource such as land, labour, or capital used to produce an output.

Intangible resources Resources that are necessary for production, such as entrepreneurship, knowledge, and an environment for enterprise. Intangibles are not as visible as tangible resources, but they are no less important.

Intellectual property rights Patents for technology, recorded music, and pharmaceutical drugs.

Interest rate The price charged for borrowing money.

International Monetary Fund (IMF) An organization of 183 nations that lends money to help members facing balance of payments and exchange rate problems.

Investment A business's purchase of capital goods, construction of new buildings, or changes to inventories, with a view to increasing production and profit.

Invisible hand Adam Smith's notion that the unintended result of an individual producer's desire for profit is the supply of the whole society with the goods and services it needs, together with reasonable price levels ensured by competition.

Invisible trade See Non-merchandise trade.

Jobless recovery A phenomenon, not fully understood, of a rise in GDP unaccompanied by a fall in unemployment.

Joint liability A legal requirement that all partners in a partnership are together liable for the debts of the partnership.

Labour A factor of production comprising the physical and mental effort contributed by people to producing goods and services.

Labour force The total of all Canadians holding jobs plus all those actively seeking work.

Labour-intensive (production) Industry in which labour, rather than machinery, dominates the production process.

Labour union A workers' organization that negotiates with employers and promotes the interests of its members.

Labour value Karl Marx's notion that the value of any item is equal to the value of the labour used to produce it.

Laissez-faire A French term meaning "leave to do" or "let alone," which became associated with the idea that an economy operates best if individuals are allowed to pursue their own self-interest without government interference.

Land A factor of production that includes all natural resources used to produce goods.

Law of accumulation Adam Smith's theory that businesspeople who invest a percentage of their profits in new capital equipment increase the economy's stock of capital goods, thus ensuring economic growth and future prosperity.

Law of demand A law stating that the quantity demanded of a product varies inversely with it price, as long as other things do not change.

Law of diminishing returns The eventual decline in the rate of extra outputs produced that occurs when one input used in production of the output is held constant and the others are increased.

Law of increasing relative cost The increase in the relative cost of producing more of item A, measured by the numbers of another item, B, that could be produced with the same resources.

Law of increasing returns to scale The increase in the rate of extra outputs produced when all inputs used in production are increased and no inputs are held constant.

Law of population Adam Smith's theory that the accumulation of capital by businesspeople requires more workers to operate the equipment, leading to higher wages, which in turn lead to better living conditions, lower mortality rates, and an increase in population.

Law of supply A law stating that the quantity supplied of a product will increase if price increases and fall if price falls, as long as other things do not change.

Leakage Any use of income (such as saving, paying taxes, and spending on imports) that causes money to be taken out of the income–expenditure stream of the economy.

Legal tender Money that a government has declared must be accepted within the national economy as payment for goods and services.

Less developed country (LDC) See Low-income economy; also referred to as developing country.

Liability Anything owed by an individual, a business, or a government.

Liquidity The relative ease with which an asset can be used to make a payment. Money is the most liquid asset.

Living wage A wage high enough to enable the earner to live on it.

Lockout The shutting down of the workplace by an employer to force the union to accept the employer's contract offer.

Long run A time period in which the firm can adjust both its fixed and variable costs to increase its maximum capacity.

Lorenz curve A graph used to show the degree of inequality that exists among groups of income receivers of the same size.

Low-income cut-off (LICO) A Statistics Canada measurement of low income, defined as any household spending more than 55 per cent of its before-tax income on food, shelter, and clothing.

Low-income economy A nation in which a majority of citizens live in poverty, with incomes below $755 per capita (2001); also called less developed country.

M1 The narrowest measurement of the money supply, comprising cash in circulation along with chequing and current accounts.

M2 A larger measurement of the money supply than M1, comprising M1 plus all types of personal savings accounts, term deposits, and non-personal notice deposits.

M2++ A larger measurement of the money supply than M2, comprising M2 plus deposits at non-bank deposit-taking institutions, money market mutual funds, and annuities.

M3 A larger measurement of the money supply than M2++, comprising M2++ plus foreign currencies held by Canadians and large term deposits held by businesses.

Macroeconomics The study of the economy as a whole in contrast to microeconomics, which studies its parts.

Managed float A policy of allowing a currency's exchange value to be set by the international market, with intervention by the country's central bank from time to time to smooth out fluctuations.

Marginal benefit (MB) A firm's demand for the use of an externality, such as a lake for dumping waste.

Marginal cost The additional cost for a firm of producing one more unit of its product.

Marginal private cost Additional production costs incurred by a firm that do not include external costs, such as treating waste before disposal.

Marginal propensity to consume (MPC) A measurement of the change in consumption divided by a change in income.

Marginal propensity to withdraw (MPW) A measurement of the change in withdrawals from national income due to savings, taxes, and buying of imports divided by a change in income.

Marginal revenue The additional revenue gained by a firm from producing one more unit of its product.

Marginal revenue product of labour (MRPL) The amount of additional, or marginal, revenue that is generated for a firm as a result of adding one more worker to the production process.

Marginal social cost (MSC) The additional cost to society in terms of an increase in pollution caused by an increase in production.

Marginal tax rate The tax rate paid on an increase in an individual's income.

Marginal utility A measure of the extra satisfaction that a consumer achieves from consuming one more unit of a product.

Marginal utility theory of consumer choice A theory stating that the extra satisfaction that a consumer achieves from consuming successive units of a good diminishes. With two or more items, consumers maximize their satisfaction when they receive the same amount of satisfaction per dollar for each item, a condition called consumer equilibrium; also called utility theory.

Market A place for commerce; a network of buyers or sellers. Also, the demand for a product; a price-determination process.

Market demand schedule The sum total of all the consumer demands for a good or service.

Market economy An economic system in which production decisions are made by the actions of buyers and sellers in the marketplace.

Market labour demand curve A graphical representation of the quantity of labour demanded by all firms in an industry at each of the possible wage rates.

Market labour supply curve A graphical representation of the number of people willing to offer their services to firms at each of the possible wage rates.

Market maker A Nasdaq broker who concentrate on trading specific stocks.

Market value The actual price at which a share will sell on the stock market.

Marketing board An agricultural organization established to administer quotas and market the products of its producers.

Mean average income An average income figure that is calculated by dividing the total income by the total population.

Means testing An income test applied to an individual as a prerequisite to receiving social welfare programs such as the Child Tax Credit or Guaranteed Income Supplement.

Measure of value A function of money that allows comparisons of the value of various goods and services; also called standard unit of account.

Median income An average income figure that represents the middle income, dividing an economy's range of incomes into two equal parts.

Mediation See Conciliation.

Medicare A program whereby the medical and hospital expenses of all Canadian citizens are paid from federal and provincial funds.

Medium of exchange The main function of money, allowing the exchange of goods and services.

Mercantilism An economic system that emphasized state control of trade, with the goal of exporting as many goods as possible and importing as few foreign goods as possible.

Merchandise trade Tangible goods that are grown, extracted, or manufactured; also called visible trade.

Middle-income economy A nation in which a sizable minority of citizens avoids living in acute poverty.

Mill rate The property tax rate; a percentage of the value of a property as assessed by the local tax authorities.

Minimum wage A government-established wage, higher than one set by the demand for, and supply of, workers.

Mixed economy An economic system, such as Canada's, that contains elements of market, command, and traditional systems.

Monetarist A belief that the most effective way for government to affect the economy is by regulating the money supply.

Monetary policy A process by which the government affects the economy by influencing the expansion of money and credit.

Money Anything generally acceptable in an economy to purchase goods and services.

Money capital The funds used to acquire real capital.

Money GDP See Nominal GDP.

Money market mutual fund Mutual funds specializing in short-term governmental and corporate securities.

Money multiplier See Deposit multiplier.

Money supply The total amount of cash in circulation plus bank deposits.

Monopolistic competition A market structure in which many small to medium-sized firms sell a differentiated product, each having some control over price.

Monopoly A market structure in which one firm has complete control over supply, allowing it to set a profit-maximizing price.

Monopoly bank A hypothetical example of a single bank with no competitors.

Multilateral Pertaining to many nations, as an agreement reached among many countries.

Multinational corporation (MNC) A firm that operates in more than one country; a corporation with a global production and selling strategy, having headquarters in one country and branch plants in several other countries.

Multiple-counting Inflating the size of the GDP by including the value of the components of the final goods in the total.

Multiplier effect The multiplied effect upon GDP that results from a change in people's income.

Mutual fund A fund comprising the investments of many clients; it is invested in the shares of other companies and managed by professional managers.

Nasdaq Commonly used acronym for the National Association of Securities Dealers Automated Quotation.

Nasdaq Composite Index An electronic network that functions as a stock market for over 4100 companies, with many technology companies listed. Its index is an indicator of its daily activity.

National Policy A policy of tariff protection for Canadian industry, linked to railroad building and western settlement, that was launched by the Conservative government of Sir John A. Macdonald in 1879.

Nationalization Another term for state ownership of business enterprise.

Natural monopoly A field with high fixed costs (such as public utilities) in which greater efficiencies result when one firm supplies the product or provides the service.

Natural unemployment rate Another term for full employment, seasonally adjusted, which includes frictional and structural unemployment but excludes cyclical unemployment.

Near money Deposits or assets that can act as a store of value and can be converted into a medium of exchange but are not themselves a medium of exchange.

Negative externality A side effect of production (such as pollution) that imposes a cost upon a third party.

Neighbourhood effects See Spillover costs.

Newfoundland and Labrador Federation of Labour A federation of provincial unions that lobbies the provincial government on labour legislation and other social and economic policies affecting workers.

Nominal GDP The total value of the GDP before it is adjusted for price increases; also called money GDP.

Nominal interest rate An interest rate that includes an inflation premium, an allowance for risk, and credit worthiness.

Non-merchandise trade Services, tourism, investment income, and other transfers; also called invisible trade.

Non-price competition Competition among firms in areas other than price (e.g., quality of product).

Non-price factor A factor held constant in the relationship between price and quantity demanded and supplied. Non-price factors include, on the demand side, income, population, tastes and preferences, expectations, and prices of substitute goods; and on the supply side, costs, number of sellers, technology, nature and the environment, and prices of related items.

Normative economics The branch of economics that deals with value judgements about economic subjects rather than facts and observations; also called policy economics.

North American Free Trade Agreement (NAFTA) The 1994 free trade agreement among Canada, the United States, and Mexico.

Notice account A deposit that requires the depositor to give some notice to the bank before withdrawal of funds.

Official international reserves The foreign currencies and gold held by the Bank of Canada.

Okun's law A formula that states that for every percentage point that the actual unemployment rate exceeds the natural rate, a GDP gap of two percent occurs.

Oikos A Greek word meaning "household" or "estate," which historically was the first subject of economics analysis.

Old Age Security (OAS) A program whereby all Canadians are paid a monthly benefit after the age of 65.

Oligopoly A market structure characterized by a few large firms, selling an identical or differentiated product, each with some to substantial control over price.

Open shop A clause in the collective agreement between a union and an employer that allows union membership to be voluntary.

Operating band The range of 0.5 per cent between the bank rate charged by the Bank of Canada and the interest it pays on deposits; the overnight rate target is set at its midpoint.

Opportunity cost The sum of all that is lost from taking one course of action over another or of producing one item measured in terms of another that could have been produced with the same resources.

Origin As used in graphs, the point at which the vertical and horizontal axes meet.

Outflow A payment that flows out of Canada, recorded on the capital account, such as a pension paid to a Canadian living outside of the country.

Output The products produced by using resources or inputs such as land, labour, or capital.

Outsourcing The practice (common to multinational corporations) to save on costs by contracting out work to be done to outside companies that are often located in less developed countries.

Overnight rate The rate of interest, controlled by the Bank of Canada, that is charged by financial institutions on short-term loans made between them; it is set within the operating band.

Overnight rate target A monetary tool used by the Bank of Canada to control the overnight rate; it is set by the Bank of Canada at the midpoint of the operating band.

Paradox of value A seeming contradiction in the economy in which the demand for necessities needed for survival is not high enough to ensure that their prices at least match the prices of luxury items, which are unnecessary for survival.

Participation rate The labour force expressed as a percentage of the total employable population.

Partnership A firm owned by two or more people.

Partnership agreement The legal agreement between individuals in a partnership.

Patronage Profits made by a co-operative enterprise that are paid out to co-operative members.

Payment See Import.

Per capita GDP See Gross Domestic Product (GDP) per capita.

Perfect competition A rare market structure characterized by many sellers (selling exactly the same product) and many buyers, no barriers to entry into the market for new firms, and perfect knowledge of prices (so there are no price differences and no individual can influence them); also called pure competition.

Personal income tax A tax paid to the federal and provincial governments by individuals on their income.

Phillips curve A diagram demonstrating an inverse relationship between inflation and unemployment rates.

Physiocrat A believer in the 18th-century philosophy that argued that laws created by humans are artificial and unnecessary because they interfere with natural laws, such as an individual's pursuit of self-interest, which would ultimately benefit all of society.

Pigouvian tax A tax levied on producers and consumers of any good that causes a negative externality such as pollution; named after economist Arthur Pigou.

Policy economics See Normative economics.

Pollution credit Pollution reduction requirements for firms that earn credits for reducing pollution; credits can be sold to other firms.

Portfolio investment Investment in the form of purchases of stocks or bonds.

Positive check Thomas Malthus's theory that war, famine, and disease would check population increases to some extent, but not enough to prevent the geometric progression of the world's population to unsustainable levels.

Positive economics See Analytical economics.

Positive externality A side effect of production that provides a benefit to a third party (such as construction of a new subway that raises property values of homes nearby).

Post hoc fallacy A mistaken belief that what occurs before some event is logically the cause of it; also called cause-and-effect fallacy.

Potential GDP The output that the economy can produce if the unemployment rate is not higher than the natural unemployment rate.

Potential output The GDP that the economy could produce with full employment.

Poverty line The unofficial term used for the Statistics Canada low-income cut-off.

Preventive check Thomas Malthus's theory that restraints such as late marriage and sexual abstinence would help reduce the birth rate to some extent, but not enough to prevent the geometric progression of the world's population to unsustainable levels.

Price elasticity of demand An expression of how much more or less consumers will buy of a product if its price changes.

Prime rate The lowest rate of interest a financial institution offers to its best customers, such as large corporations.

Principal The original amount a corporation borrows with a bond, repayable to the bondholder, and on which interest is paid.

Private enterprise A term applied to the private ownership of productive resources, a characteristic of market economies.

Privatization The sale of public assets in a government enterprise to private firms.

Privatize To turn over the ownership and operation of a government enterprise to the private sector.

Product differentiation The attempt by competing firms to distinguish their product in some desirable way from that of their competitors in order to gain greater control over price.

Production possibilities curve A graphical representation of the production choices facing an economy.

Productive resources Anything that can be used to manufacture goods or services.

Productivity A firm's ability to maximize output from the resources available, usually measured as the firm's output per worker.

Progressive tax A tax (such as income tax) that rises in percentage terms as an individual's income rises.

Progressive tax system A taxation system that taxes higher incomes at a higher percentage rate than lower incomes; it is designed to reduce income inequalities and finance social spending.

Proletariat Term used by Karl Marx to describe the working class who, he theorized, would rise up and overthrow the bourgeoisie, or industrial capitalists.

Property tax A tax paid to local governments (such as cities and towns) by holders of houses and commercial properties.

Proportional tax A tax that takes a constant percentage for all income earners.

Prosperity cycle An increase in aggregate demand leading to a cycle of higher production, more jobs, increased income, and greater consumption, resulting in even higher aggregate demand.

Protectionist A policy of limiting imports through tariffs.

Provincial Sales Tax (PST) A Canadian provincial government sales tax levied on a range of goods and services.

Proxy A document signed by a shareholder appointing another person to vote on behalf of that shareholder.

Public debt The total debt held by federal and provincial governments accumulated from their past borrowings, on which interest must be paid.

Public sector unions Unions representing workers employed by governments.

Pure competition See Perfect competition.

Quebec Pension Plan (QPP) The pension plan similar to the Canada Pension Plan (CPP) but administered by the Quebec government.

Quintile One-fifth (or 20 per cent) of the total number of income earners in an economy; used to examine income distribution.

Quota A restriction placed on the amount of product that domestic producers are allowed to produce; also, a limit on the total quantity of goods imported into a country.

Rand Formula A 1945 ruling stating that all workers in a workplace in which a union exists and bargains for all workers must pay union dues, even if they are not union members.

Rank correlation coefficient A calculation to determine the statistical significance of any pattern found in two sets of data, such as a nation's per capita income and its spending on health care.

Rate of return The amount of extra revenue an investment by a business in new machinery, new technology, or a new plant will bring in.

Raw materials All natural resources used in production.

Real capital A more precise term than capital for the machinery, factories, warehouses, and equipment used to produce goods and services, as distinct from financial capital.

Real Gross Domestic Product (GDP) The total value of all goods and services produced in Canada in a given year, adjusted for price changes; also called constant-dollars GDP.

Real rate of interest The nominal rate of interest minus the expected rate of inflation.

Receipt See Export.

Recession A contraction of the economy lasting longer than two business quarters (six months).

Recessionary gap The gap between aggregate demand and full employment equilibrium, characterized by high unemployment, low inflation, and low GDP growth.

Reciprocity Treaty A free trade agreement between British North America and the US, lasting from 1854 to 1866.

Recognition lag The time it takes a government to recognize a problem in the economy that requires an appropriate fiscal policy to correct.

Recovery The first part of an expansionary period following a downturn in the economy.

Regressive tax A tax rate that takes a proportionally lower percentage from higher-income earners.

Relative cost The cost of producing one item, A, expressed in terms of the numbers of another item, B, which must be given up in order to produce A (i.e., A's opportunity cost).

Relative factor endowment The natural advantages, in terms of resources, that one nation or area has compared to another.

Relative factor intensity The advantage that one nation or area has over another in the way it uses its resources.

Relative poverty Poverty defined as lacking the conditions of life enjoyed by most people in the same economy.

Relief strategy An anti-poverty program that provides immediate relief for poor Canadians, such as government transfer payments and community food banks.

Rent The price people pay for accommodation, determined by demand and supply for rental accommodation.

Replacement unemployment Unemployment caused by the movement of firms with labour-intensive production to foreign countries in which labour rates are lower.

Research and development (R&D) A process of investigating, experimenting, and developing new products, technology, and production methods carried out by universities, governments, and businesses.

Reserve ratio The ratio between the reserves a bank keeps on hand and the amount it has on deposit.

Rightsize Review the size of a company's workforce to correct the previous overuse of labour.

Rotating strike A union strategy, used when an employer has several workplaces, of withdrawing services for a short time from each workplace on a rotating basis.

S&P/TSX Composite Index The indicator of stock market activity used in Canada.

Sales tax A tax (such as the Goods and Services Tax or the Provincial Sales Tax) paid to the federal and provincial governments on the purchase and consumption of goods and services by the end user.

Sanctions Restrictions on trade with one country levied by another for some political purpose.

Savings account A bank account that allows holders to earn interest on saved money.

Scientific method A method of study used to make discoveries in natural science and social sciences (such as economics) that has four steps: observation, data collection, explanation, and verification.

Seasonal unemployment Unemployment caused by recurring climatic factors, such as the impact of winter on construction, tourism, farming, and so on.

Seasonally adjusted rate An unemployment rate adjusted to eliminate recurring and unavoidable unemployment due to seasonal factors.

Self-interest An idea, central to the philosophy of Adam Smith, that each individual's strongest drive is to better his or her own condition.

Several liability A legal requirement that if one or more partners do not pay their share of a partnership's debts, the other partners are required to do so.

Shareholders The owners of the shares of a corporation, entitling them to voting rights and a share of the profits.

Shares Corporate assets divided into equal parts which are sold to buyers, giving them ownership and a share of the corporation's profits.

Short run A time period in which the firm's maximum capacity is fixed by the shortage of at least one resource.

Social costs The transfer of part of a firm's production costs (such as cleaning up pollution caused by the release of wastes into the air, soil, or water supply) to the public (the third party); also called third-party costs.

Social science Sciences, such as economics, history, and sociology, that study some aspect of human behaviour.

Social welfare safety net Government programs, such as Employment Insurance and the Child Tax Credit, established to help vulnerable Canadians.

Socialism A political system of the moderate left that calls for public ownership of the principal means of production, to be achieved in a democratic and peaceful manner.

Sole proprietorship A business owned and operated by one person.

Spillover costs Costs (such as those associated with cleaning up pollution) that are borne by a third party instead of the producers and consumers of the product; also called neighbourhood effects.

Spot market A market (such as the Ontario Food Terminal) for commodities that are bought and sold for immediate delivery.

Stabilization policies Government intervention in the economy to try to stabilize it, using fiscal and monetary policies.

Stagflation A period of slow growth when both unemployment and inflation increase, as seen in the mid-1970s.

Standard of living The quantity and quality of goods and services that people are able to obtain to accommodate their needs and wants.

Standard unit of account See Measure of value.

Staple Products requiring little processing such as fish, fur, and lumber; Canada's main exports from the 16th to the 18th centuries.

Statistical discrepancy An adjustment made to bring the current account into balance with the capital and financial account on a country's international balance of payments.

Stock exchange The actual building in which shares are traded.

Stock market Either a physical place or an electronic network through which shares can be bought or sold.

Stockbroker An agent who buys and sells shares on the stock market for individuals and companies.

Store of value A function of money that allows value to be stored for the future, allowing it to be used in the purchase of goods and services.

Strike A temporary work stoppage by employees to force their employer to accept the union's contract demands.

Structural deficit The amount above the cyclical deficit that would exist even if the economy were operating at full employment.

Structural strategy A long-term program to reduce poverty, such as retraining and relocating workers.

Structural unemployment Unemployment caused by long-term changes in the economy, such as shifts from goods production to services, or the introduction of technology that replaces labour.

Subsidiary A branch plant of a multinational corporation.

Subsidy A payment made by a government to a producer to achieve some desired outcome, such as installing pollution control equipment.

Substitute goods Goods that are similar to other goods and serve as an alternative if the price of the latter goods rises.

Supply The quantities that sellers will offer for sale at various prices during a given period of time.

Supply schedule A table showing the quantities of a product supplied at particular prices.

Surplus budget The situation that occurs when a government spends less than it collects in taxes, causing it to have money left over (a surplus).

Surplus value The difference between the value of a good measured in terms of the labour used to produce it, and its higher selling price, a surplus that Karl Marx believed was stolen from labour by capitalists.

Sustainable development Economic development that considers how current production and consumption patterns affect the ability of future generations to meet their needs.

Sweatshop A factory characterized by low wages and poor working conditions, often seen in less developed countries selling their goods to multinationals.

Tangible resources Physical resources (such as land and labour) that are necessary for production and are visible.

Tariff A tax on an import levied by a nation; also called custom duty.

Technological unemployment Unemployment caused by replacement of workers with more capital-intensive production methods; a type of structural unemployment.

Term deposit Bank accounts in which the holder agrees to deposit a fixed amount of money for a fixed period of time for a fixed interest rate.

Terms of trade The rate at which a country's exports are exchanged for its imports.

Theory of the Firm The relationships that exist between a firm's revenues, costs, and profits.

Third-party costs See Social costs.

Tight money A monetary policy of high interest rates, more difficult availability of credit, and a decrease in the money supply.

Tort law The body of law that allows a person injured by another to seek compensation by suing; used as a basis for class-action lawsuits against companies causing environmental externalities.

Total cost The total of a firm's fixed and variable costs, which includes all the purchases made by a firm for productive resources to produce a good or service.

Total revenue The price of a product multiplied by the quantity demanded of the product.

Trade unions Unions that represent workers in a single occupation; also called craft unions.

Trade-off The sacrifice of one resource or production choice for another.

Trading bloc Regional trade agreements, such as NAFTA and those of the European Union, negotiated outside the World Trade Organization.

Traditional economy An economic system in which production decisions are determined by the practices of the past.

Transfer payments Direct payments from governments to other governments or to individuals; a mechanism for providing social security, income support, and alleviation of regional disparities.

Transnational corporation A firm that operates in more than one country; also called multinational corporation.

Underemployment A situation in which workers hold jobs that do not fully utilize their skills or that employ them only part time when they wish to work full time.

Unemployment Insurance (UI) A federal program started in 1942 to assist those temporarily out of work due to job loss, illness, or birth or adoption of a child; renamed Employment Insurance (EI) in 1996.

Unemployment rate The percentage of the labour force that is not working at any given time; the total number of Canadians unemployed divided by the total labour force.

Unilateral Action taken by one nation without regard for its effects on other nations.

Union dues The amount of money that each member of a union pays to support it.

Union shop A workplace where all employees must be members of the union that bargains collectively for a contract.

Unit labour cost A measure of a firm's efficiency, obtained by dividing its total labour costs by the number of units it produces.

Unitary coefficient A coefficient for a product equal to one, indicating that a given change in price causes an equal percentage change in quantity demanded.

United Nations Declaration of Human Rights A declaration of equal rights for all people, proclaimed in 1948 by the UN, that contains several economic rights such as the right to work.

Universality A principle of the Canadian welfare state specifying that some benefits, such as health care, should be available to all citizens regardless of income.

Util A theoretical unit of satisfaction that a person gains from consuming an item.

Utility theory See Marginal utility theory of consumer choice.

Value added The increase in market value of a product resulting from additional processing or refinement of that product.

Variable costs Costs that change or vary with the level of output, such as labour and raw materials.

Vertical integration The merging of two firms involved in different stages of the production process of a good or service.

Visible trade See Merchandise trade.

Voluntary arbitration A process during a labour dispute in which a third party is given the power to decide which proposal, the union's or the employer's, is fairer.

Wage The price a worker receives for supplying labour to a business with a demand for it.

Wage differentials Differences in wage rates among different labour markets.

Wealth Accumulated assets of individuals and families less their total debts.

Welfare poor Non-working people who are poor because they are ill, disabled, elderly, or single parents, or for other reasons.

Welfare state A philosophy that government should intervene to help people who are poor, sick, or unemployed as well as provide equal access to education, health care, and social services.

Work-to-rule A union tactic of performing only the duties required in the contract, and not extra work carried out voluntarily or after hours.

Working poor People who work for low wages and are defined as poor.

World Bank An international agency financed by the richer nations that attempts to help less developed nations by providing direct grants and programs.

World Trade Organization (WTO) The successor (as of 1995) to the General Agreement on Tariffs and Trade (GATT); the WTO has expanded and strengthened the procedures for reducing trade barriers.

WTO Dispute Settlement Body A mechanism for settling a trade dispute between two or more nations; it involves setting up expert panels to arrive at a decision.

Index

Photo Credits

Every effort has been made to trace the original source of material and photographs contained in this book. Where the attempt has been unsuccessful, the publisher would be pleased to hear from copyright holders to rectify any omissions.

2 CP PHOTO/Maclean's (Phil Snel); 4 © Spencer Platt/ Getty Images (with graph adapted from *The Globe and Mail*, 9 October 2001); 7 By permission of Johnny Hart and Creators Syndicate, Inc.; 15 Toronto Star/National Archives of Canada/C-029397; 21 CP PHOTO/AP Photo (Ed Bailey); 27 © Tim Pannell/CORBIS/MAGMA; 30 CP PHOTO/AP Photo/Ford Motor Company, W.A. Harewood. Reproduced by permission of The Ford Motor Company; 36 © PhotoSphere Images/PictureQuest; 46 Reprinted with permission—The Toronto Star Syndicate; 47 Copyright © Tribune Media Service, Inc. All Rights Reserved. Reprinted with Permission; 54 © Bettmann/ CORBIS/MAGMA; 56 Mary Evans Picture Library; 57 © Bettmann/CORBIS/MAGMA; 61 © Bettmann/ CORBIS/MAGMA; 62 Dick Hemingway; 64 © Roger Ressmeyer/CORBIS/MAGMA; 70 Dick Hemingway; 83 © Reuters NewMedia Inc./CORBIS/MAGMA; 85 CP PHOTO/Andrew Vaughan; 94 Peter Bregg/Maclean's; 110 CP PHOTO/Toronto Sun (Alex Urosevic); 113 CP PHOTO/AP Photo/Jakub Mosur; 119 © Tribune Media Services, Inc. All Rights Reserved. Reprinted with permission; 132 CP PHOTO/AP PHOTO (Matthias Rietschel); 136 Reprinted by permission—The Toronto Star Syndicate; 140 By permission of Johnny Hart and Creators Syndicate, Inc.; 149 Courtesy of Garrison Guitars; 156 CP PHOTO/AP Photo (Sarah Martone); 174 CP PHOTO/ AP Photo/Odessa American (Larry Beckner); 175 © Comstock Images/KS14156; 185 CP PHOTO/Montreal Gazette (Pierre Obendrauf); 194 CP PHOTO/Ottawa Citizen (John Major); 216 R. Ordonez/First Light.ca; 229 CP PHOTO/Toronto Star; 244 CP PHOTO; 255 Reproduced by permission of the First Nations Bank of Canada; 264 © Tony Freeman/PhotoEdit/PictureQuest; 276 CP PHOTO/AP Photo (Walter Astrada); 279 © Tom Bean/CORBIS/MAGMA; 284 CP PHOTO/Chuck Stoody; 286 © Peter Zazulak; 293 Reproduced by permission of the Prairie Farm Rehabilitation Administration (PFRA), Department of Regional and Economic Expansion (DREE)/22150; 304 CP PHOTO/The Telegram (Joe Gibbons); 309 John Collins/Montreal Gazette. Reproduced with permission; 323 Reprinted by permission of Hibernia; 330 © Steve Nease; 346 © Scott Dunlop; 357 © Dusan Petricic; 362 CP PHOTO/Len Wagg; 370 CP PHOTO/AP Photo/David Guttenfelder; 374 CP PHOTO/The London Free Press (Morris Lamont); 376 CP PHOTO/Chuck Stoody; 395 Copyright © 2001 Tim Dolighan. All right reserved; 408 Reprinted with permission—The Toronto Star Syndicate; 415 CP PHOTO/Kevin Frayer; 417 CP PHOTO/Charles Dharapak; 423 © Trygve Bolstad/Panos; 434 CP PHOTO/AP PHOTO (Pier Paolo Cito); 438 © Bernard Schoenbaum from cartoonbank.com. All Rights Reserved; 443 Ken Faught/The Toronto Star.